The Fiscal Theory of the Price Level

JOHN H. COCHRANE

PRINCETON UNIVERSITY PRESS

PRINCETON AND OXFORD

Published by Princeton University Press
41 William Street, Princeton, New Jersey 08540
99 Banbury Road, Oxford OX2 6JX

press.princeton.edu

Library of Congress Cataloging-in-Publication Data

Names: Cochrane, John H. (John Howland), 1957– author.
Title: The fiscal theory of the price level / John H. Cochrane, Hoover
    Institution, Stanford University.
Description: Princeton : Princeton University Press, [2023] | Includes
    bibliographical references and index.
Identifiers: LCCN 2022006785 (print) | LCCN 2022006786 (ebook) |
    ISBN 9780691242248 (hardback) | ISBN 9780691243245 (epub)
Subjects: LCSH: Inflation (Finance) | Monetary policy. | Prices.
Classification: LCC HG229 .C553 2023 (print) | LCC HG229 (ebook) |
    DDC 339.5/3—dc23/eng/20220214
LC record available at https://lccn.loc.gov/2022006785
LC ebook record available at https://lccn.loc.gov/2022006786

British Library Cataloging-in-Publication Data is available

Editorial: Joe Jackson, Josh Drake
Jacket Design: Heather Hansen
Production: Erin Suydam
Publicity: Kate Hensley, Charlotte Coyne
Copyeditor: Alison S. Britton

Jacket Credit: © Godlikeart / Shutterstock

This book has been composed in Arno Pro.

Printed on acid-free paper. ∞

Printed in Canada

10 9 8 7 6 5 4 3

To Eric W. Cochrane and Lydia G. Cochrane.
Their memory and example are with me always.

A prince, who should enact that a certain proportion of his taxes be paid in a paper money of a certain kind, might thereby give a certain value to this paper money.

—ADAM SMITH, *WEALTH OF NATIONS*, VOL. I, BOOK II, CHAPTER II.

CONTENTS

     25.1   *Episodes*   523
     25.2   *Theory and Models*   525

                    Bibliography   527
                       Index   541

PREFACE

THIS BOOK IS a midpoint, I hope, of a long intellectual journey. It started in the fall of 1980, drinking a beer and eating nachos on a sunlit afternoon in Berkeley, with my good friends and graduate school study group partners, Jim Stock, Eric Fisher, Deborah Haas-Wilson, and Steve Jones. We had been studying monetary economics, and thinking about what happens as electronic transactions reduce the demand for money. When money demand and money supply converge on fast-moving electronic claims to a single dollar bill, framed at the Federal Reserve, will supply and demand for that last dollar really determine the price level? If the Fed puts another dollar bill up on the wall, does the price level double? Jim and I, fallen physicists, joked about a relativistic limit. Signals are limited by the speed of light, so maybe that puts a floor to money demand.

The conversation was playful. Clearly, long before the economy is down to the last dollar bill, each of us holding it for a microsecond at a nanodollar interest cost, the price level becomes unhinged from money supply. Such a "cashless limit" is a good example of a result in economics that one should not take seriously. But is there a theory of the price level that continues to work as we move to electronic transactions and a money-less economy, or equivalently as money pays interest? Why is inflation apparently so stable as our economy moves in that direction? Or must economic and financial progress be hobbled to maintain money demand and thereby control inflation? Having no ready answers, the conversation moved on, but the seed was planted.

Berkeley was, it turns out, a great place to be asking such questions. Our teachers, and especially George Akerlof, Roger Craine, and Jim Pierce, mounted a sustained and detailed critique of monetarism. They had their own purposes, but the critique stuck and my search continued for an alternative theory of the price level. Berkeley also gave us an excellent grounding in microeconomics and general equilibrium, for which I thank in particular Rich Gilbert, Steve Goldman, and Gerard Debreu, together with unmatched training in empirical economics and econometrics, for which I thank especially Tom Rothenberg.

I spent a year as a research assistant at the Council of Economic Advisers, working under Bill Poole on many policy-oriented monetary economics issues. This was a formative experience, and one of those projects turned into my Ph.D. dissertation. I owe Bill many thanks for his gracious guidance.

I was then supremely lucky to land a job at the University of Chicago. Chicago was a natural fit for my intellectual inclinations. I like the way standard economics works. You start with supply, demand, and frictionless markets. You add frictions and complications carefully, as needed. It also often turns out that if you work a little harder, a simple supply and demand story explains many puzzles, and you don't need the frictions and complications.

For my tastes, economists too often give a clever name to a puzzle, proclaim that no standard economic model can explain it, and invent a new theory. Ninety-nine revolutions are pronounced for each one that succeeds.

This statement may sound contradictory. In this book I argue that the fiscal theory is a genuinely new theory that unseats its predecessors at the foundation of monetary economics. Yet fiscal theory is, at least as I present it, much in the Chicago tradition. It allows a less-is-more approach, in which with a little bit of hard supply and demand work takes you further than you might have thought.

These were, in hindsight, glorious years for macroeconomics at Chicago. Efficient markets, Ricardian equivalence, and rational expectations were just in the past. Dynamic programming and time-series tools were cutting through long-standing technical limitations. Kydland and Prescott (1982) had just started real business cycle theory, showing that you can make remarkable progress understanding business cycles in a neoclassical framework, if you just try hard enough and don't proclaim it impossible before you start. For me, it was a time of great intellectual growth, learning intertemporal macroeconomics and asset pricing, privileged to hang out with Lars Hansen, Gene Fama, Bob Lucas, and many others, and to try out my ideas with a few generations of amazing students.

But monetarism still hung thick in the air at Chicago, and monetary doubts nagged me. I wrote some papers in monetary economics, skeptical of the standard stories and the VAR literature that dominated empirical work. Still, I didn't find an answer to the big price-level question.

A watershed moment came late in my time at the Chicago economics department. I frequently mentioned my skepticism of standard monetary stories. The conversations usually didn't get far. Then one day, Mike Woodford responded that I really should read his papers on fiscal foundations of monetary regimes, which became Woodford (1995) and Woodford (2001). I did. There it was at last: a model able to determine the price level in a completely cashless economy. I knew in that instant this was going to be a central idea that I would work on for the foreseeable future. I was vaguely aware of Eric Leeper's (1991) original paper, but I didn't understand it or appreciate it until I went back to it much later. Papers are hard to read, and I was not well-read in the new-Keynesian tradition to which Leeper rightly addressed his paper. Social networks are important to point us in the right direction.

It is taking a lot longer than I thought it would! I signed up to write a *Macroeconomics Annual* paper (Cochrane (1998a)), confident that I could churn out the fiscal theory analogue of the Friedman and Schwartz (1963) *Monetary History* in a few months. Few forecasts have been more wrong. That paper solved a few puzzles, and paved the way for many more, but I'm still at the larger question more than two decades later.

I thought then, and still do, that the success of fiscal theory will depend on its ability to organize history, to explain events, and to coherently analyze policy; on its usefulness; not by theoretical disputation or formal time-series tests, just as Friedman's monetarism and Keynes' Keynesianism had done. Nonetheless, my first years with the fiscal theory were dragged into theoretical controversies. One has to get a theory out of the woods where people think it's logically wrong or easily dismissed by armchair observations before one can get to the business of matching experience.

"Money as Stock" (Cochrane (2005b)) addressed many controversies. I wrote it in the same year as "Stocks as Money" (Cochrane (2003)), an attempt at CV humor as well as to point toward a theory that integrates fundamental value with value deriving from transactions frictions, which applies to stocks as well as to government debt. I owe a debt of gratitude to critics who wrote scathing attacks on the fiscal theory, for otherwise I would not have had a chance to rebut the similar but more polite dismissals that came up at every seminar.

I then spent quite some time understanding and then documenting the troubles of the reigning new-Keynesian paradigm, including "Determinacy and Identification with Taylor Rules" (Cochrane (2011a)), "The New-Keynesian Liquidity Trap" (Cochrane (2017c)), and "Michelson-Morley, Occam, and Fisher" (Cochrane (2018)). The first paper emphasized flaws in the theory, while the second two pointed to its failures to confront the long zero interest rate episode. To change paradigms, people need the carrot of a new theory that plausibly accounts for the data, but also a stick, to see the flaws of the existing paradigm and how the new theory mends those flaws.

Matching the fiscal theory with experience turns out to be more subtle than noticing correlations between money and nominal income. The present value of surpluses is hard to measure independently. In the wake of the decades-long discussion following Friedman and Schwartz (1963), we approach causality and equilibrium-formation discussions in a sophisticated way. Easy predictions based on natural simplifying assumptions quickly go wrong in the data. For example, deficits in recessions correlate with less, not more, inflation. I spent a lot of time working through these puzzles. "A Frictionless View of U.S. Inflation" (Cochrane (1998a)) already suggests that a surplus process with an s-shaped moving average representation and discount rate variation in the present value formula are crucial to understanding that pattern. "Long-Term Debt and Optimal Policy" (Cochrane (2001)) took on the surplus process more formally, but with a cumbersome argument using spectral densities. Only in "Fiscal Roots" (Cochrane (2021a)) did I really express how discount rate variation rather than expected surplus variation drives inflation in postwar U.S. recessions. Only while dealing with some contemporary "puzzles" have I realized just how bad a mistake it is to write a positively autocorrelated process for government surpluses. Though "A Frictionless View" pronounced observational equivalence, only now have I come to my current understanding of its implications, and that it is a feature, not a bug.

It turned out to be useful that I spent most of my other research time on asset pricing. Indeed, I sometimes refer to fiscal theory as "asset pricing imperialism." I recognized the central equation of the fiscal theory as a valuation equation, like price = present value of dividends, not an "intertemporal budget constraint," a point that forms the central insight of "Money as Stock" (Cochrane (2005b)) and surmounts a first round of objections to fiscal theory. Intellectual arbitrage is a classic source of progress in economic research. I also learned in finance that asset price-dividend ratios move largely on discount rate news rather than expected cash flow news (see "Discount Rates" Cochrane (2011c) for a review). More generally, all the natural "tests of the fiscal theory" you might want to try have counterparts in the long difficult history of "tests of the present value relation" in asset pricing. Dividend forecasts, discounted at a constant rate, look nothing like stock prices. So don't expect surplus forecasts, discounted at a constant rate, to look like the value of debt, and their differences to quickly match inflation. The resolution in both cases is that discount rates vary. This analogy let me cut through a lot of knots and avoid repeating two decades of false starts. Again, it took me an embarrassingly long time to recognize such simple analogies sitting right in front of me. I wrote about time-varying discount rates in asset prices in Cochrane (1991b) and Cochrane (1992). I was working on volatility tests in 1984. Why did it take nearly 30 years to apply the same lesson to the government debt valuation equation?

"Interest on Reserves" (Cochrane (2014b)) was another important stepping stone. The Fed had just started trying to run monetary policy with abundant reserves, and controlling market interest rates by changing the interest rate the Fed pays on reserves. But the Fed also controls the size of reserves. Can the Fed control the interest rate on reserves, and simultaneously the quantity? Will doing so transmit to other interest rates? It took some puzzling, but in a fiscal theory framework, I came to an affirmative conclusion. This paper introduced the expected-unexpected inflation framework, and much of the merging of fiscal theory with new-Keynesian models that occupy the first part of this book. It only happened as John Taylor and Mike Bordo invited me to present a paper at a Hoover conference to mark the 100th birthday of the Federal Reserve. The opportunity, and obligation, to write a paper that connects with practical policy considerations, and to present it to a high-powered group of economists and Fed officials, brought me back to thinking in terms of interest rate targets. I should have been doing so all along—Eric Leeper's papers have for decades—but such is life.

Another little interaction that led to a major step for me occurred at the Becker-Friedman Institute conference on fiscal theory in 2016. I had spent most of a year struggling to produce any simple sensible economic model in which higher interest rates lower inflation, without success. Presenting this work at a previous conference, Chris Sims mentioned that I really ought to read a paper of his, "Stepping on a Rake" (Sims (2011)). Again, I was aware of Chris's paper, but had found it hard. After Chris nagged me about it a second time, I sat down to work through the paper. It took me six full weeks to read and understand it, to the point that I wrote down how to solve Chris's model, in what became Cochrane (2017e). He had the result, and it became important to the unified picture of monetary policy I present here. Interestingly, Chris's result is a natural consequence of the analysis in my own "Long-Term Debt" paper, Cochrane (2001). We really can miss things that are right in front of our noses. The simple exposition of the result in this book is a nice case of how economic ideas get simpler over time and with rumination.

Marty Eichenbaum and Jonathan Parker then kindly agreed to my proposal for a *Macroeconomics Annual* essay, "Michelson-Morley, Fisher, and Occam" (Cochrane (2018)), putting together these thoughts along with an overview of how the zero bound era provides a decisive test of theories. The result is rather sprawling, but the chance to put it together and to get the incisive feedback of the top economists at that event was important to producing the (I hope) cleaner vision you see here.

These events allowed me to complete a view that has only firmed up in my mind in the last year or so, which I call the "fiscal theory of monetary policy," expressed most recently in Cochrane (2021b) and in this book. Monetary policy implemented by interest rate targets remains crucially important. The fiscal theory neatly solves the determinacy and equilibrium selection problems of standard new-Keynesian models. You can approach the data armed with interest rate rules and familiar models. You really only change a few lines of computer code. The results may change a lot, especially by emphasizing fiscal–monetary interactions. Without the conferences, and Chris's and others' sharp insights, none of it would have happened.

My fiscal theory odyssey has also included essays, papers, talks, op-eds, and blog posts trying to understand experience and policy with the fiscal theory, and much back and forth with colleagues. This story-telling is an important prelude to formal work, and helps to focus and distill formal work. Story-telling is hard too. Is there at least a possible, and then a plausible story to interpret events via the fiscal theory, on which we can build formal model descriptions? That's what "Unpleasant Fiscal Arithmetic" (Cochrane (2011e)), "Inflation and Debt" (Cochrane (2011d)), "Michelson-Morley, Fisher, and Occam" (Cochrane (2018)), and "The Fiscal Roots of Inflation" (Cochrane (2021a)) attempt, building on "Frictionless View" (Cochrane (1998a)), among others. This book contains many more stories and speculations about historical episodes, which I hope inspire you to do more serious theoretical and empirical work.

I owe a lot to work as referee and journal editor, especially for the *Journal of Political Economy*. Editing and refereeing forced me to understand many important papers that I might otherwise have put aside or read superficially in the usual daily crush. Discussing papers at conferences had a similar salutary effect. "Determinacy and Identification" is one example that can stand for hundreds. I grasped a central point late one night while working on Benhabib, Schmitt-Grohé, and Uribe (2002). Their simple, elegant paper finally made clear to me that in new-Keynesian models, the central bank deliberately destabilizes an otherwise stable economy. I immediately thought, "That's crazy." And then, "This is an important paper. The JPE has to publish it." Several of my papers were born that moment. Research is all a conversation.

I also owe a deep debt to generations of students. I taught a Ph.D. class in monetary economics for many years. Discussions with really smart students helped me to understand the standard models and key parts of fiscal theory alternative. Working through Mike Woodford's book (Woodford (2003)), and working through papers such as Werning (2012), to the point of understanding their limitations is hard work, and only the pressure of facing great students forced the effort. There are important externalities between teaching, service, and research.

More recently, writing a blog has allowed me to try out ideas and have a discussion with a new electronic community. My understanding of the Fisherian question – does raising interest rates maybe raise inflation? – developed in that forum.

Over the years, I benefited from the efforts of many colleagues who took the time to engage in discussions, write me comments, discuss my and other papers at conferences, write referee and editor reports, and listen to and contribute to many seminars where I presented half-baked versions of these ideas. Research *is* a conversation.

I owe debts of gratitude to institutions as well as to people. Without the Berkeley economics department, I would not have become a monetary skeptic, or, probably, an economist at all. Without Chicago's economics department and Booth school of business, I would not have learned the dynamic general equilibrium tradition in macroeconomics, or asset pricing. Without the Hoover Institution, I would not have finished this project, or connected it to policy.

I am also grateful to many people who have sent comments on this manuscript and the recent work it incorporates, including Jean Barthélemy, Christopher Ball, Marco

Bassetto, Michael Ben-Gad, Tom Coleman, François Gourio, Jon Hartley, Zhengyang Jiang, Greg Kaplan, Marek Kapička, Bob King, Mariano Kulish, Eduardo Leitner, Fulin Li, Gideon Magnus, Livio Cuzzi Maya, Simon Mongey, Edward Nelson, Jón Steinsson, George Tavalas, Harald Uhlig, anonymous reviewers, and the members of Kaplan's reading group at the University of Chicago, especially Chase Abram, Arisha Hashemi, Leo Aparisi de Lannoy, Santiago Franco, Zhiyu Fu, Agustín Gutiérrez, Sangmin S. Oh, Aleksei Oskolkov, Josh Morris-Levenson, Hyejin Park, and Marcos Sora. Ross Starr pointed me to the lovely Adam Smith quotation. I am especially grateful to Eric Leeper, who capped off decades of correspondence and friendship with extensive comments on this manuscript, some of which substantially changed my thinking on basic issues.

Why tell you these stories? At least I must express gratitude for those sparks, for the effort behind them, and for the institutions that support them. By mentioning a few, I regret that I will seem ungrateful for hundreds of others. Still, in my academic middle age, I think it's useful to let younger readers know how one piece of work came about. Teaching, editorial and referee service, conference attendance and discussions, seminar participation, working with students, writing reference letters, and reading and commenting on colleague's papers all are vital parts of the collective research enterprise, as is the institutional support that lets all this happen. I hope to have returned some of these favors in my own correspondence on others' work. I hope also to give some comfort to younger scholars who are frustrated with their own progress. It does take a long time to figure things out.

My journey includes esthetic considerations as well. I pursued fiscal theory in part because it's simple and beautiful, characteristics which I hope to share in this book. That's not a scientific argument. Theories should be evaluated on logic and their ability to match experience, elegance be darned. But it is also true that the most powerful and successful theories of the past have been simple and elegant, even if they initially had a harder time fitting facts. I hope that clarity and beauty attracts you and inspires you, as it does me, to the hard work of seeing how this theory might fit facts and analyze policy.

I was attracted to monetary economics for many reasons. Monetary economics is (even) more mysterious at first glance than many other parts of economics, and thus beautiful in its insights. If a war breaks out in the Middle East and the price of oil goes up, the mechanism is no great mystery. Inflation, in which all prices and wages rise together, is more mysterious. If you ask the grocer why the price of bread is higher, the grocer will blame the wholesaler. The wholesaler will blame the baker, who will blame the wheat seller, who will blame the farmer, who will blame the seed supplier and workers' demands for higher wages, and the workers will blame the grocer for the price of food. If the ultimate cause is a government printing up money to pay its bills, there is really no way to know this fact but to sit down in an office with statistics, armed with economic theory. Investigative journalism will fail. The answer is not in people's minds, but in their collective actions. It is no wonder that inflation has led to so many witch hunts for "hoarders," "speculators," "greed," "middlemen," "profiteers," and other phantasms.

This Book

I am reluctant to write this book, as there is so much to be done. Perhaps I should title it *Fiscal Theory of the Price Level: A Beginning*. I think the basic theory is now settled, and theoretical controversies over. We know how to include fiscal theory in standard macroe-conomic models including sticky prices and monetary and financial frictions. But just how to use it most productively, which frictions and specifications to include, and then how to understand episodes, data, institutions, and guide policy, has just started.

We have only started to fit the theory to experience. This is as much a job of historical and institutional inquiry and story-telling as it is of model specification, formal estima-tion, and econometric testing. Friedman and Schwartz did not offer a test of monetarism. Keynes did not offer a statistical test of the General Theory. They were pretty influential, because they were useful.

Our task is likewise to make fiscal theory useful: to understand its message, to construct plausible stories, then to construct formal models that embody the stories, to quantita-tively account for data and episodes, and to analyze policy. This book offers a beginning, and some effort to light the way. It is full of suggestions, but these are suggestions of paths to follow and episodes to analyze, not reports of concluded voyages.

I argue that an integration of fiscal theory with new-Keynesian and DSGE models is a promising path forward, and I provide a recipe for such integration. But just how do such merged models work exactly? Which model ingredients will fit the data and best guide policy decisions? How will their operation differ with fiscal foundations? The project is conceptually simple, but the execution has only just begun. In particular, the mechanism by which higher interest rates may temporarily lower inflation, and the Fisherian implica-tions of rational expectations, are deeply troublesome questions. These are central parts of the rest of the model, not really part of the fiscal theory contribution. It is unsettling that such basic ingredients are still so uncertain. But that is an invitation as well. The international version, extending the theory to exchange rate determination, has barely begun.

We have also only started to apply fiscal theory to think about how monetary institu-tions could be better constructed. How should the euro be set up? What kinds of policy rules should central banks follow? What kind of fiscal commitments are important for sta-ble inflation? Can we set up a better fiscal and monetary system that produces stable prices and without requiring clairvoyant central bankers to divine the correct interest rate? I offer some ideas, but we have a long way to go.

I also pursue a different direction than much current fiscal theory literature. In an effort to identify fiscal versus monetary regimes, that literature ties monetary and fiscal policy, which we see, to equilibrium selection policies, which we do not see. It assumes that in a fiscal regime, the government cannot commit to raise future surpluses when it runs a current deficit, so all deficits are inflated away. "Fiscal dominance" is a bad state, in which intractable deficits force large and volatile inflation.

This book emphasizes a few innovations that together fundamentally alter this approach. The observational equivalence theorem, the s-shaped surplus process, writ-ing models in a way that separates observed fiscal and monetary policy from equilibrium selection policy, along with attention to discount rates and long-term debt, open the door to understanding the whole sample with fiscal theory, to regard the fiscal theory as the only theory of the price level, and to consider fiscal–monetary institutions that can produce low and quiet inflation.

You may find this book chatty, speculative, and constantly peering forward murkily. Some sections will surely turn out to be wrong. I prefer to read short, clear, definitive books. But this is the fiscal theory book I know how to write. I hope you will find it at least interesting, and the speculative parts worth your time to work out more thoroughly, if only to disprove them or heavily modify them.

The point of this book is to spur us to *use* fiscal theory. There are many articles and books with lots of equations, but it's not clear how to apply the equations to issues of practice. As a result, many theories have had more limited impact than they should. Many other books and popular articles have lots of beautiful prose, but one is often left wondering just how it all fits together, and whether contrary ideas could be just as persuasive. This book spends hundreds of pages trying to understand deeply very simple models, and to draw their lessons for history and policy. The models are there, with equations. But the models are simplified down to their minimal essence, to understand what they are trying to tell us. I hope that this middle ground is at least rewarding to the reader. This simplicity is not the end goal, though. Having really understood simple foundations, one should build up again more complex and realistic models.

For years I put off writing this book because I always wanted to finish the next step in the research program first. But life is short, and for each step taken I can see three others that need taking. It's time to encourage others to take those steps. It is also time to put down here what I understand so far so we can all build on it.

On the other hand, every time I give a fiscal theory talk, we go back to basics, and answer questions from 25 years ago: "Aren't you assuming the government can threaten to violate its intertemporal budget constraint?" (No.) "Doesn't Japan violate the fiscal theory?" (No.) That's understandable. The basic ideas are spread out in three decades' worth of papers, written by a few dozen authors. Simple ideas are often hidden in the less-than-perfect clarity of first papers on any subject, and in the extensive defenses against criticisms and what-ifs that first papers must include. Responses to such questions are buried in the back ends of papers that rightly focus on positive contributions. By putting what we know and have digested in one place, in simple frameworks, I hope to move the conversation to the things we genuinely don't know, and broaden the conversation beyond the few dozen of us who have worked intensely in this field.

The fiscal theory has been until recently a niche pursuit, an alternative to standard theory. Real progress comes when a group of critical mass works on an issue. I hope in writing this book to help get that snowball rolling, to the point that fiscal theory becomes the standard way to think about monetary economics. This book is littered with suggestions for papers to write and puzzles to solve, which I hope will offer some of that inspiration.

Where's the fire? Economic theories often emerge from historical upheavals. Keynes wrote the *General Theory* in the Great Depression. Friedman and Schwartz offered an alternative explanation of that searing episode, and Friedman saw the great inflation in advance. Yet inflation was remarkably quiet in the developed world, for the 30 years from 1990 to 2020 when the fiscal theory I describe was developed. Fiscal theory is in some ways a slow rumination over 1980, started by a sequence of Tom Sargent and Neil Wallace articles studying that era. But its development was not propelled by a continuing policy problem.

I finish this book in the late 2021 inflation surge, which may make fiscal theory more immediately relevant to policy. This inflation spurt seems clearly related to the massive fiscal expansion of the COVID-19 recession. If inflation continues, it is likely to have fiscal roots. In the shadow of large debt and deficits, taming inflation will require stronger fiscal–monetarys coordination. So fiscal theory may soon have important policy application, either to forestall or to remedy inflation.

We are, however, at a less public and well-recognized crisis in monetary economics. Inflation was *too* quiet in the 2010s. Current economic theory doesn't understand that quiet. Nobody expected that if interest rates hit zero and stayed there for a decade or more, *nothing* would happen, and central banks would agonize that 1.7% inflation is below a 2% target. Clearly predicting big events that did not happen is just as much a failure as not predicting the inflation that did break out in the 1970s, or its end in the 1980s. (Chapter 20.)

More deeply, it's increasingly obvious that current theory doesn't hold together logically, or provide much guidance for how central banks should behave if inflation or deflation do break out. Central bankers rely on late 1970s IS-LM intuition, expanded with some talk about expectations as an independent force. They ignore the actual operation of new-Keynesian models that have ruled the academic roost for 30 years. They tell stories of great power and minute technocratic control that are far ahead of economists' models or solid empirical understanding.

If you think critically as you study contemporary monetary economics, you find a trove of economic theories that are broken, failed, internally inconsistent, or describe economies far removed from ours. Going to the bank once a week to get cash to make transactions? Who does that anymore? IS-LM-based policy models with "consumption," "investment," etc., as basic building blocks, not people making consistent, intertemporal, cross-equation, and budget-constrained decisions? The Fed threatening hyperinflation to make people jump to the preferred equilibrium?

So the intellectual fire is there. And, given government finances around the world, the painful lessons of a thousand years of history, and the simple logic of fiscal theory, a real fire may come sooner than is commonly expected.

As it evolved, this book took on a peculiar organization. I write for a reader who does not already know fiscal theory, has only a superficial knowledge of contemporary macroeconomics and monetary theory, in particular new-Keynesian DSGE style modeling, and is not deeply aware of historical developments and controversies. Thus, I develop fiscal theory first, standing on its own. I make some comparisons with monetarist and new-Keynesian thought, but a superficial familiarity should be enough to follow that, or the reader may just ignore that discussion. Only toward the end of the book do I develop the standard new-Keynesian model, monetary models, and theoretical controversies, discussions of active versus passive policies, on versus off equilibrium, and so forth. The controversies are really all what-ifs, responses to criticisms, what about other theories, and so on. If the fiscal theory takes off as I hope it will, alternative theories and controversies will fade in the rear-view mirror. The front of the book – what is the fiscal theory, how does it work, how does it explain facts and policy – will take precedence. But if you're hungry to know just how other theories work, how fiscal theory compares to other theories, or answers to quibbles, just keep going.

I also develop ideas early on using very simple models, and then return to them in somewhat more general settings, rather than fully treat an idea in generality before moving on. If on reading you wish a more general treatment of an issue, it's probably coming in a hundred pages or so. The benefit of this strategy is that you will see hard issues show up first in simple clear contexts. The cost is a bit of repetition as you see the same idea gain nuance in more general contexts.

Economists who think rigorously in the general equilibrium tradition may find the presentation frustratingly informal. The point of this book is to make fiscal theory accessible, to develop stories and intuition for how it can help us to understand the world. For this reason, I focus on bits and pieces of fully fleshed-out models, only occasionally spelling out the full details. For example, we spend a lot of time looking at the government debt valuation equation, which states that the real value of government debt equals the present value of primary surpluses. That equation by itself is not a model. It is one equilibrium condition of a model. The surpluses and discount rate are endogenous variables. Though it is easy to slip into saying that changing expected surpluses or discount rates "cause" changes in inflation, that is sloppy thinking. We are really evaluating equilibrium inflation given equilibrium surpluses and discount rates. Likewise, price equals expected discounted dividends does not mean that expected dividends "cause" price changes. That too is one equilibrium condition of a full model, relating endogenous variables. Yet looking at this equilibrium condition in isolation has been enormously productive for asset pricing.

I write this disclaimer because many economists (including some who generously sent comments on this book) are so well-trained in general equilibrium that they find it hard and frustrating to look at bits and pieces of models that are not fully fleshed out. Start with preferences, technology, market structure, fundamental shocks, and write the whole bloody model already, they advise. Being of the Chicago/Minnesota school that believes this is the "right" way to do economics, at least eventually, I am sympathetic. But I have found that at this stage, full models hide much intuition. Moreover, while in this framework one should never think of x causing y unless x is a truly exogenous structural shock, the actual exogenous structural shocks to the economy are awfully hard to pin down. So, brace yourself. We will largely look at a few equilibrium conditions and see how they work and organize the world. By and large, though, the models in this book are so simple that if you know enough to ask these questions, you know enough to fill in the details on your own—a representative agent, constant endowment, complete markets, and so on.

Relative to most of the literature in macroeconomics and monetary economics that appears in academic journals, the models in this book are simple and stripped down. I think a good deal of macro theory has built complicated elaborations and frictions while we still are not completely sure of basic stability and determinacy questions. Shouldn't we first settle whether an interest rate peg is stable and determinate?

General readers may be put off that this book has a lot of equations. Fear not. One really doesn't need any more economics or math than is covered in a good undergraduate economics course to understand them all. One can get by with a good deal less. The hard equations are mostly general cases, building blocks for future research but not necessary to understand most of the book. You don't have to actually *do* much math at all, or derive any equations. We mostly just stare at equations and untangle their meaning. But equations and the models they embody are central to the enterprise. Without the equations, you can't check that the story is internally consistent. Mathematical models do not prove economics is right, but economic theories that cannot be written in models are almost certainly wrong. Popular writing in monetary economics is particularly full of beautiful prose that falls apart when looked at analytically. Time and again, in writing this book, I wrote a section of beautiful prose, convinced of one or another effect. I then went back to flesh out some equations, only to discover that most of my beautiful intuition was wrong. The remaining verbal sections may suffer a similar fate. They are written to encourage others to do some of that difficult fleshing out.

So while a reader can understand most of what I have to say simply glossing over the math, the core point of this book is a set of simple models, whose operation is not obvious at a verbal level, but that help us to understand the world. Economic theory consists of quantitative parables, and examples in which one applies those parables to illuminate a complex world. While this book has a lot of equations, it could have a lot more. An Online Appendix is available on my website, https://www.johnhcochrane.com/. This appendix contains detailed algebra for many of the more complex expressions that I present here. It also contains a number of extensions and additional topics. There is a chapter, "How Not to Test the Fiscal Theory," devoted to some common mistakes. Another chapter gives detailed treatment of multiple equilibria in models with money. The "Fiscal Theory of the Price Level" tab of my website also includes additional material, including related essays, updates, and typos or other corrections.

Monetary economics, and this book, offer a surprisingly high ratio of talk to equations. We fancy ourselves a science in which equations speak for themselves. They do not. They often do not speak directly in physical sciences either. You will see that circumstance throughout this book. The equations are quite simple, but there is lots of debate about what they mean and how to read them, interpret them, or apply them. Seeing the world through the lens of the model, finding what specifications might match an episode or policy question, is harder than solving equations. This comment should be encouraging if you don't view yourself as a top-notch mathematician. The math is simple. Seeing how the math describes the world is hard.

John H. Cochrane
December 2021

NOTATION

I TRY TO USE capital letters for nominal variables and levels, and lowercase letters for real variables, logs, and rates of return. Variables without subscripts are steady-state values, though sometimes I use them to refer to the variable in general rather than at a specific date, or to indicate that a variable is constant over time. I use the same symbol for variables and for their deviations from steady-state, so you have to look in context. If it's a deviation from steady-state, then there are no constants and $0 = 0$ is a solution. I use a comma to separate an identifying subscript from a time subscript, e.g. $\varepsilon_{i,t}$ is an interest rate i shock at time t. I do not use a comma when an identifying subscript uses two letters, e.g. $i_t = \theta_{i\pi}\pi_t$. I follow the usual convention of dating variables when they are known. Thus the nominal interest rate i_t and a real risk-free rate r_t are returns for an investment from t to $t+1$, as are risky returns r_{t+1} or R_{t+1}. I only define widely used symbols here. When symbols are defined and only used within a section, I omit them here.

Roman Letters

A.	Transition matrix, $z_{t+1} = Az_t + B\varepsilon_{t+1} + C\delta_{t+1}$ or $dz_t = Az_t dt + Bd\varepsilon_t + Cd\delta_t$.
$a(L)$.	Lag polynomial, e.g., $s_t = a(L)\varepsilon_t$.
a_x.	Vector that selects a variable from a vector, e.g., $x_t = a_x' z_t$.
B_t.	Face value of nominal debt. $B_{t-1}^{(t)}$ is one-period debt issued at $t-1$ due at time t. B_t used with no superscript can mean one-period debt when there is no long-term debt in the model, or an aggregate quantity of debt.
B.	Part of the matrix representation of a model, e.g. $z_{t+1} = Az_t + B\varepsilon_{t+1} + C\delta_{t+1}$.
b_t.	Real (indexed) debt.
$b_{y,x}$.	Regression coefficient, e.g., $y_t = a + b_{y,x}x_t + u_t$.
C_0.	An arbitrary constant in the solution to a differential equation.
C.	Part of the matrix representation of a model, $z_{t+1} = Az_t + B\varepsilon_{t+1} + C\delta_{t+1}$.
c_t.	Real consumption, e.g., $u(c_t)$. Where necessary for clarity, I use capital letters for the level and lowercase letters for the log, $c_t = \log(C_t)$.
D.	Differential operator, $D = d/dt$.
D_t.	Fraction of debt coming due at time t that is repaid in a partial default.
d.	Differential operator, e.g., dx_t. Also dividends, e.g. $R_{t+1} = (p_{t+1} + d_{t+1})/p_t$.
dz_t.	Compensated jump or diffusion, e.g., $dx_t = \mu_t dt + \sigma_t dz_t$; $E_t dz_t = 0$.
E.	Expectation. $E_t(x_{t+1})$ conditional expectation at time t.
$f'(k)$.	Marginal product of capital.

g_t.   Real GDP growth rate. Also used as a government spending or other Phillips-curve disturbance.

i_t.   Net or log nominal interest rate.

i_t^m.   Interest rate on money, e.g., interest on excess reserves.

i_t^*.   Interest rate target, equilibrium interest rate, e.g., $i_t = i_t^* + \phi(\pi_t - \pi_t^*)$.

I.   Identity matrix.

I_t.   Investor information set, e.g., $E(x_{t+1}|I_t)$.

j.   Used as index for sums, e.g., $\sum_{j=1}^{\infty} \beta^j s_{t+j}$.

L.   Lag operator, e.g., $x_{t-1} = Lx_t$. Also used to express money demand, e.g., $M_t/P_t = L(y, i_t)$.

$\mathcal{L}$.   Continuous time-lag operator, $\mathcal{L}(D)$, corresponding to $a(L)$. For example, if $ds_t = -\eta s_t dt + d\varepsilon_t$, then $(\eta + D)s_t = D\varepsilon_t$. The moving average representation is $s_t = \int_{\tau=0}^{\infty} e^{-\eta\tau} d\varepsilon_{t-\tau} = 1/(\eta + D)D\varepsilon_t$.

M_t.   Money. Usually only money issued by the government, i.e., cash and reserves. M_t is held from time t to time $t + 1$. M^d, M^s money demand and supply. Mb, Mi monetary base and inside money.

m_t. $\log(M_t)$.

n.   Population growth rate, e.g., $r = \delta + \gamma(g - n)$.

P_t.   Price level, dollars per goods.

P_t^*.   Price level target.

p_t.   Log price level, $p_t = \log(P_t)$, or proportional deviation from steady-state. Also stock price.

Q_t.   Nominal bond price. $Q_t^{(t+j)}$ price at time t of a zero coupon bond that comes due (pays \$1) at time $t + j$. Q_t is also the price of a bond with geometrically declining coupon.

q_t.   Log bond price, or proportional deviation of bond price from steady-state, $q_t = \log(Q_t)$, or $q_t = Q_t/Q$.

R_{t+1}.   Real gross rate of return. Ten percent is 1.10, not 0.10 or 10.

R_{t+1}^n.   Nominal gross rate of return.

r_{t+1}.   Real net or log rate of return. Ten percent is 0.10. When riskfree, r_t.

r_{t+1}^n.   Nominal net or log return.

r.   A constant or steady-state real rate of return.

s_t.   Real primary surplus or surplus to GDP ratio.

$\tilde{s}_t$.   Real primary surplus expressed in units of a fraction of the real value of debt, e.g., $\tilde{s}_t = s_t/V$.

T.   Upper time limit for sums, integrals, transversality conditions.

$u(c)$.   Utility.

u_t.   Serially correlated disturbances. Additional subscripts distinguish variables when needed, e.g., $i_t = \theta\pi_t + u_{i,t}$, $u_{i,t+1} = \eta_i u_{i,t} + \varepsilon_{i,t+1}$. Also used to denote an arbitrary regression disturbance, e.g., $y_t = a + b_{y,x}x_t + u_t$.

V, v.   Velocity, $MV = Py$. When a function of other variables $V(i, \cdot)$. $v = \log(V)$. Also steady-states of the value of government debt V_t, v_t.

V_t, v_t.   Real value of government debt, e.g., $V_t = B_t/P_t$. May have units of debt to GDP, $V_t = B_t/(P_t y)$.

Introduction

WHAT DETERMINES the overall level of prices? What causes inflation, deflation, or currency appreciation and devaluation? Why do we work so hard for pieces of paper? A $20 bill costs 10 cents to produce, yet you can trade it for $20 worth of goods or services. And now, $20 is really just a few bits in a computer, for which we work just as hard. What determines the value of a dollar? What is a dollar, really?

As one simple story, the fiscal theory of the price level answers: Money is valued because the government accepts money for tax payments. If on April 15 you have to come up with these specific pieces of paper, or these specific bits in a computer, and no others, then you will work hard through the year to get them. You will sell things to others in return for these pieces of paper. If you have more of these pieces of paper than you need, others will give you valuable things in return. Money gains value in exchange because it is valuable on tax day. This idea seems pretty simple and obvious, but as you will see it leads to surprising conclusions.

The fiscal theory is additionally interesting by contrast with more common current theories of inflation, and how its simple insight solves the problems of those theories. Briefly, there are three main alternative theories of the price level. First, money may be valued because it is explicitly backed: The government promises 1/32 of an ounce of gold in return for each dollar. This theory no longer applies to our economies. We will also see that it is really an interesting instance of the fiscal theory, as the government must have or obtain gold to back dollars.

Second, intrinsically worthless money may be valued if people need to hold some money to make transactions and if the supply of that money is restricted. This is the most classic view of fiat money. ("Fiat" means money with no intrinsic value, redemption promise, or other backing.) But current facts challenge it: Transactions require people and business to hold less and less money. More importantly, our governments and central banks do not control internal or external money supplies. Governments allow all sorts of financial and payments innovation, money multipliers do not bind, and central banks follow interest rate targets, not money supply targets.

Third, starting in the late 1970s a novel theory emerged to describe that reality, and in response to the experience of the 1970s and 1980s. In this theory, inflation is controlled when the central bank follows an interest rate target, so long as the target varies more than one for one with inflation, following what became known as the Taylor principle. We will analyze the theoretical problems with this view in detail below. Empirically, the fact that inflation remained stable and quiet even though interest rates did not move in long-lasting zero bound episodes contravenes this theory.

The fiscal theory is an alternative to these three great classic theories of inflation. The first two do not apply, and the third is falling apart. Other than the fiscal theory, then, I argue that there is no simple, coherent economic theory of inflation that is vaguely compatible with current institutions.

Macroeconomic models are built on these basic theories of the price level, plus descriptions of people's saving, consumption, production, and investment behavior, and potential frictions in product, labor, or financial markets. Such models are easily adapted to the fiscal theory instead of alternative theories of inflation, leaving the rest of the structure intact. Procedurally, changing this one ingredient is easy. But the results of economic models often change a lot if you change just one ingredient.

Let's jump in to see what the fiscal theory *is*, how it works, and then compare it to other theories.

1

A Two-Period Model

THIS CHAPTER introduces the fiscal theory and previews many following issues, with a simple two-period model. The model has perfectly flexible prices, constant interest rates, short-term debt, and no risk premiums. I add these elements later, as they add important realism. But by starting without them we see that they are not necessary in order to determine the price level, nor do they change the basic logic of price level and inflation determination.

1.1   The Last Day

We look at a simple one-period frictionless fiscal theory of the price level

$$\frac{B_0}{P_1} = s_1.$$

In the morning of day 1, bondholders wake up owning B_0 one-period, zero-coupon government bonds coming due on day 1. Each bond promises to pay \$1. The government pays bondholders by printing up new cash. People may use this cash to buy and sell things, but that is not important to the theory.

At the end of the day, the government requires people to pay taxes $P_1 s_1$ where P_1 denotes the price level (dollars needed to buy a basket of goods) and s_1 denotes real tax payments. For example, the government may levy a proportional tax τ on income, in which case $P_1 s_1 = \tau P_1 y_1$ where y_1 is real income and $P_1 y_1$ is nominal income. Taxes are paid in cash, and soak up money.

The world ends on day 2, so nobody wants to hold cash or bonds after the end of day 1. Figure 1.1 illustrates the timing of events in this little story.

In equilibrium, then, cash printed up in the morning must all be soaked up by taxes at the end of the day,

$$B_0 = P_1 s_1$$

or

$$\frac{B_0}{P_1} = s_1. \tag{1.1}$$

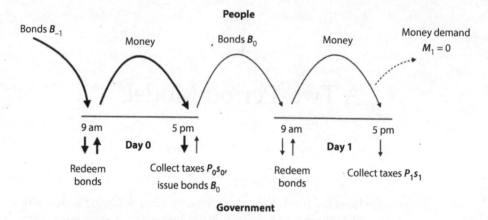

FIGURE 1.1. Timing of the Two-Period Model

Debt B_0 is predetermined. The price level P_1 adjusts to satisfy (1.1). *We just determined the price level.* This is the fiscal theory.

1.2 Intuition of the One-Period Model

The mechanism for determining the price level can be interpreted as too much money chasing too few goods, as aggregate demand, or as a wealth effect of government bonds. The fiscal theory does not feel unusual to people, even economists, who live in it. The fiscal theory differs on the measure of how much money is too much, and the source of aggregate demand. Fiscal theory builds on a completely frictionless foundation.

If the price level P_1 is too low, more money was printed up in the morning than will be soaked up by taxes in the evening. People have, on average, more money in their pockets than they need to pay taxes, so they try to buy goods and services. There is "too much money chasing too few goods and services." "Aggregate demand" for goods and services is greater than "aggregate supply." Economists trained in either the Chicago or Cambridge traditions living in this economy would not, superficially, notice anything unusual.

The difference from the standard (Cambridge) aggregate-demand view lies in the source and nature of aggregate demand. Here, aggregate demand results directly and only as the counterpart of the demand for government debt. We can think of the fiscal theory mechanism as a "wealth effect of government bonds," again tying the fiscal theory to classical ideas. Too much government debt relative to fiscal surpluses acts like net wealth, which induces people to try to spend, raising aggregate demand.

The difference from the standard (Chicago) monetary view lies in just what is money, what is the source of money demand, and therefore how much money is too much. Here, inflation results from more money in the economy than is soaked up by net tax payments, not by more money than is needed to mediate transactions or to satisfy asset, liquidity, precautionary, etc. sources of demand for money. Here, only outside money, government liabilities, drives inflation, along with government bonds that promise such money. If in this economy someone were to set up a bank, issuing notes and making loans, to a monetarist those notes would count as money that causes inflation. They are irrelevant to the price level in the fiscal theory.

We may view the fiscal theory as a backing theory of money. Dollars are valuable because they are backed by the government's fiscal surpluses. Many financial liabilities are valuable because they are a claim to some assets. Many currencies have been explicitly backed by assets such as gold. Dollars say "This note is legal tender for all debts, public and private," so you have the right to pay your taxes with dollars. That right constitutes a backing. Dollars backed by gold can be soaked up by giving people the gold in return for dollars. Our dollars can be soaked up by taxes.

My story that money is valued because the government accepts its money in payment of taxes goes back to Adam Smith himself:

> A prince, who should enact that a certain proportion of his taxes be paid in a paper money of a certain kind, might thereby give a certain value to this paper money. (*Wealth of Nations*, Vol. I, Book II, Chapter II.)

My story about money printed up in the morning and soaked up in the afternoon helps to fix intuition, but it is not essential. People could redeem debt for money five minutes before using the money to pay taxes. Or, people could just pay taxes directly with maturing government bonds. "Cash" can be reserves, electronic accounts at the Fed. A "morning" versus "afternoon" is not a necessary part of the model. It can all happen continuously, or in an instant.

How people make transactions is irrelevant to the price level in this model. People could make transactions with maturing bonds, foreign currency, or Bitcoin. People could make transactions with debit cards or credit cards linked to bank accounts, netted at the end of the day with no money changing hands, which is roughly how we do things today. People could wire claims to funds that hold government bonds, private bonds, mortgages, or stocks. The dollar can be a pure unit of account, with nobody ever holding actual dollars.

The simple model shows that the fiscal theory can determine the price level in a completely frictionless economy. In this model, money has no extra value from its use in transactions or other special features. Money does not pay a lower return than other assets, people do not carry around an inventory of money, and the government does not limit the supply of inside liquid assets. This model has perfectly flexible prices, and markets clear instantly. Backing theories naturally continue to determine the price level in a frictionless context: If money is valued because it is a claim to something else that has value in a frictionless model, then money has value absent any transactions, liquidity, pricing, or other frictions.

By contrast, the monetarist story of money supply and demand and the Keynesian story of interest rate targets and Phillips curves, which are the two standard theories of the price level, require monetary or pricing frictions to determine the price level at all. This is a beautiful aspect of fiscal theory and makes it an attractive starting point for monetary economics today. Electronic transactions and financial innovation undermine money demand. Our central banks do not limit money supply. The internet might undermine sticky prices and wages.

One can add monetary, financial, and pricing frictions to fiscal theory, and I will do so presently in order to create a more realistic model. But the fiscal theory allows us to *start* to analyze the price level with a simple frictionless, flexible price, backing model, and to add frictions as needed for realism; or not to add them when not needed. One can often understand basic mechanisms of more complex models with the simple supply and demand logic of the frictionless underpinning.

In this simple model *all* the government does is collect taxes, requiring that people surrender money or maturing government bonds. The government can use some of that money to make cash transfers, with $P_t s_t$ denoting primary surpluses, the difference between taxes and transfers.

That we pay taxes in dollars is not essential. The government could accept goods or foreign currency for tax payments and then sell those to soak up dollars. What matters to price level determination is that the government uses tax revenues in excess of spending to soak up any excess dollars at the end of the day, and thereby maintain their value. While not necessary, offering the right to pay taxes with money, or requiring such payment, is a useful way of communicating and pre-committing to fiscal backing.

Equation (1.1) is one equilibrium condition of a model, not a full model on its own, just as price = present value of dividends is one equilibrium condition of a full model. Both are useful if one remembers that limitation. I return below to describe a complete economic model, though most readers who know enough to ask the question can fill in the details quickly on their own (representative agent, constant endowment, flexible prices, etc.). The "government" here unites Treasury and central bank balance sheets. All debt B is debt in private hands, canceling out central bank holdings of Treasury debt.

1.3   A Two-Period Model and Present Value

We add an initial period time 0, and bond sales B_0. The price level in each period is determined by

$$\frac{B_0}{P_1} = s_1$$

$$\frac{B_{-1}}{P_0} = s_0 + \beta E_0(s_1).$$

The price level P_0 adjusts so that the real value of nominal debt equals the *present value* of real primary surpluses. The theory need not predict a strong relation between inflation and contemporaneous debt and deficits. A higher discount rate, lower β, can lead to inflation even with no change in surpluses.

Next, let us add the previous day, time 0. This addition allows us to think about where the debt B_0 came from, and what the effects are of changing this second policy lever.

The time 0 flow equilibrium condition is

$$B_{-1} = P_0 s_0 + Q_0 B_0. \tag{1.2}$$

Money printed up in the morning of day 0 to pay maturing nominal bonds B_{-1} is soaked up by surpluses $P_0 s_0$, and now also by nominal bond sales B_0 at the end of time 0, at nominal bond price Q_0. In this flexible price, constant interest rate world, that bond price is

$$Q_0 = \frac{1}{1 + i_0} = \beta E_0\left(\frac{P_0}{P_1}\right) = \frac{1}{R} E_0\left(\frac{P_0}{P_1}\right). \tag{1.3}$$

The first equality defines the notation i_0 for the nominal interest rate. The second and third equalities are the bond pricing equation, with subjective discount factor β or real gross interest rate R. It is a nonlinear version of the statement that the nominal interest rate equals the real interest rate plus expected inflation.

Substituting (1.3) in (1.2), we have

$$\frac{B_{-1}}{P_0} = s_0 + \beta E_0\left(\frac{1}{P_1}\right) B_0,$$

and using time 1 equilibrium,

$$\frac{B_0}{P_1} = s_1, \tag{1.4}$$

we have

$$\frac{B_{-1}}{P_0} = s_0 + \beta E_0(s_1). \tag{1.5}$$

- *The price level P_0 adjusts so that the real value of nominal debt equals the present value of real primary surpluses.*

I refer to (1.5) as the "government debt valuation equation." It works like stock, in which the stock price adjusts so that the value of a given number of shares equals the present value of dividends.

The present value on the right-hand side of (1.5) has immediate, fortunate, and important consequences: The theory does not necessarily predict a strong contemporaneous relationship between inflation, debt, and deficits. Governments can run large deficits $s_0 < 0$ or have large debts B_{-1} with no inflation, if people believe that the governments will pay back new B_0 and old B_{-1} debt with subsequent surpluses, s_1. Conversely, inflation can break out today (0) if people see intractable future fiscal problems (s_1) despite healthy debt and deficits today. Higher discount rates—higher real interest rates, a lower β—can also induce inflation, with no change in surpluses.

1.4 Monetary Policy, Fiscal Policy, and Inflation

If the government sells additional debt B_0 without changing surpluses, it lowers the bond price, raises the nominal interest rate, raises no additional revenue, and raises the expected price level and future inflation. The government may follow a nominal interest rate target, by offering to sell debt B_0 at a fixed interest rate i_0, with no change in surpluses. I call these operations "monetary policy." Monetary policy can set a nominal interest rate target and thereby determine expected inflation. Fiscal policy sets unexpected inflation. An interest rate rise with no change in fiscal policy raises inflation one period later, with no contemporaneous change in inflation in this model, a natural neutrality benchmark. This combination is the simplest example of what I shall call the "fiscal theory of monetary policy." Inflation is stable and determinate under an interest target, even an interest rate peg.

The government has two policy levers, debt B_0 and surpluses s_0, s_1. The two-period model lets us think about the effect of selling debt B_0.

The price levels at the two dates are given by

$$\frac{B_0}{P_1} = s_1 \tag{1.6}$$

$$\frac{B_{-1}}{P_0} = s_0 + \beta E_0(s_1). \tag{1.7}$$

Suppose the government sells more debt B_0 at time 0, without changing surpluses s_0 and s_1. The price level P_0 does not change, and P_1 rises.

To understand the result, write

$$\frac{B_{-1}}{P_0} = s_0 + \frac{1}{1+i_0}\frac{B_0}{P_0} = s_0 + \beta E_0\left(\frac{P_0}{P_1}\right)\frac{B_0}{P_0} = s_0 + \beta E_0(s_1). \tag{1.8}$$

Money printed up to redeem debt B_{-1} is soaked up by surpluses s_0 or by new bond sales B_0. In turn, bond sales B_0 raise real revenue equal to $\beta E_0(s_1)$. With P_0 determined and no change in s_0 or s_1, greater bond sales B_0 just lower the bond price $Q_0 = 1/(1+i_0)$, raise the nominal interest rate, and raise the price level P_1, but generate no extra time-0 revenue.

Selling more debt B_0 without changing surpluses s_1 is like a share split. When a company does a 2-for-1 share split, each owner of one old share receives two new shares. People understand that this change does not imply any change in expected dividends. The price per share drops by half and the total value of the company is unchanged. Here a doubling of B_0 with no change in surpluses halves the bond price $Q_0 = 1/(1+i_0)$. In the morning of time 1, additional bonds B_0 with no more surplus s_1 are like a currency reform. They imply an instant and proportionate change in price level. Doubling debt B_0 doubles the price level P_1.

Rather than auction a fixed quantity of nominal debt B_0, the government can announce an interest rate target i_0, and allow people to buy all the bonds B_0 they want at that price. It can offer a flat supply curve rather than a vertical supply curve of nominal debt. Now the B_0 terms of (1.8) describe the number of bonds that people will choose to buy at the fixed price.

Buying and selling government bonds in return for cash, or offering a fixed nominal interest rate, without changing fiscal policy, is a reasonable abstraction of a central bank. Thus, I will call this interest rate target "monetary policy." We learn that a central bank can set the nominal interest rate even in this frictionless and cashless world. The interest rate target sets the expected rate of inflation, by

$$\frac{1}{1+i_0} = \beta E_0\left(\frac{P_0}{P_1}\right). \tag{1.9}$$

Thus the central bank can determine *expected* inflation via its interest rate target. The "fiscal" theory of the price level does not mean that central banks are powerless!

An increase in the interest rate target i_0 has no effect on the price level P_0 and no effect on contemporaneous inflation P_0/P_{-1}. It raises expected inflation entirely by raising the expected future price level P_1 (really, by lowering $E(1/P_1)$). This "Fisherian" response contrasts with the usual presumption that raising nominal interest rates lowers inflation, at least for a while. We will study many mechanisms that produce a negative response. However, first recognize how natural a positive response is: This is a frictionless model, with flexible prices and without monetary distortions. Monetary policy ought to be "neutral" in this model. It is. Higher nominal interest rates coincide with higher inflation in the long run of almost all models, once real interest rates settle down, prices adjust, and output returns to normal. With no frictions, this model's immediate positive reaction of expected inflation to an interest rate rise embodies a natural neutrality proposition.

Monetary policy sets expected inflation, so fiscal policy sets unexpected inflation. We can see this result easily by multiplying (1.6) by P_0 and taking innovations,

$$\frac{B_0}{P_0}(E_1 - E_0)\left(\frac{P_0}{P_1}\right) = (E_1 - E_0)(s_1). \tag{1.10}$$

The combination (1.9)–(1.10) completely determines expected and unexpected inflation. It is the simplest example of what I shall call the "fiscal theory of monetary policy." The government, and its idealized central bank, can follow an interest rate target. The interest rate target determines expected inflation. Fiscal policy determines unexpected inflation. The interest rate target may, but need not, vary with inflation. Inflation is stable and determinate even with an interest rate peg.

1.5   Fiscal Policy Debt Sales

If the government sells more debt B_0 and at the same time promises proportionally greater surpluses s_1, the policy has no effect on the price level P_1, and raises revenue at time 0. That revenue can fund a deficit, less s_0, or lower the price level P_0. A bond sale *with* more surplus is like an equity issue, not a share split.

A government that runs a deficit, lower s_0, can fund that deficit by such borrowing with greater s_1, leaving constant P_0 and P_1, and raising the real value of debt $Q_0 B_0/P_0$. If the government does not change s_1, then it funds the deficit s_0 by inflating away outstanding debt. If the government lowers s_1 as well as s_0, then it produces a large inflation P_0 and the value of debt declines following the deficit s_0. Since we see larger values of debt following deficits in most time-series data, the former reaction dominates, which requires an "s-shaped" surplus process. Fiscal theory can produce a completely steady price level despite wide variation in deficits and debt.

Now, let us think about debt sales B_0 that *are* accompanied by changes in surpluses and deficits s_0 and s_1. Suppose that at time 0, the government sells more debt B_0, but this time it promises additional surpluses s_1. Look again at (1.6) and (1.8),

$$\frac{B_0}{P_1} = s_1 \tag{1.11}$$

$$\frac{B_{-1}}{P_0} = s_0 + \frac{1}{1+i_0}\frac{B_0}{P_0} = s_0 + \beta E_0\left(\frac{P_0}{P_1}\right)\frac{B_0}{P_0} = s_0 + \beta E_0(s_1). \tag{1.12}$$

TABLE 1.1. Strategies for Financing a Deficit at Time 0

Strategy	Time 0 surplus s_0	Time 1 surplus s_1	Value of debt Q_0B_0/P_0; B_0/P_1
Borrow	lower	rise by $-R\Delta s_0$	rise
Inflate	lower	no change	no change
AR(1)	lower	lower	lower

In (1.11), if the government raises B_0 and s_1 proportionally, there is no effect on the price level at time 1, P_1. Looking from right to left in (1.12), this action raises the real value of debt at the end of period 0, and raises the real revenue the government obtains by selling that debt. The additional revenue can fund a deficit, a decline in s_0, with no change in P_0 or P_1. Or additional revenue can be used to lower the price level P_0.

The debt sale B_0 with corresponding rise in surplus s_1 is like an equity issue, in contrast to a share split. In an equity issue, a firm also increases shares outstanding, but it promises to increase future dividends. By doing so, the firm raises revenue and does not change the stock price. The value of the company increases. The revenue can be used to fund investments—a negative s_0—that generate the larger dividends.

Turning it around, let us think about the government's options for financing a deficit. Suppose that the government at day 0 runs a deficit $s_0 < 0$, or reduces the surplus s_0 from what was previously expected. How does the government finance this deficit? Examine three options, also summarized in Table 1.1.

First, as in the last scenario, the government can borrow, and thereby have no effect on either price level, P_0 or P_1. In order to raise real revenue from borrowing, the government must promise larger future surpluses to repay additional debt. The government lowers s_0 by $\Delta s_0 < 0$ but raises s_1 by $-R\Delta s_0$. The price level P_0 at time 0 does not change, since the present value of surpluses $s_0 + \beta E_0 s_1$ does not change. The dollars printed to redeem debt B_{-1} that are not soaked up by the lower surplus s_0 are now soaked up by the larger real value of bond sales Q_0B_0/P_0, which is also the real value of nominal debt at the end of the period. If the government sells extra nominal debt B_0, so that $(B_0 + \Delta B_0)/P_1 = s_1 + R\Delta s_0$, then the price level P_1 does not change either, as in the previous scenario.

Second, the government can inflate away outstanding debt. If s_0 declines and there is no change in s_1, then the price level P_0 rises. The real value of debt at the end of period 0, $Q_0B_0/P_0 = \beta E_0(s_1)$, a claim to unchanged surpluses at time 1, does not change. As the price level P_0 rises, the value of the dollars that redeem bonds B_{-1} falls by exactly the fall in the surplus s_0.

Third, suppose the government lowers s_1 along with the lower s_0. A typical AR(1) model of serially correlated deficits produces this result. We might imagine that the initial deficit comes with persistent bad fiscal news. Now the present value $s_0 + \beta E_0(s_1)$ drops even more than the initial deficit s_0. The time 0 inflation is even larger, inflating away the larger present value of both deficits s_0 and s_1. The deficit in time 0 is accompanied by a *decline* in the end-of-period value of debt.

In typical advanced countries and episodes, including postwar U.S. time series, larger deficits lead to a rise in the value of debt, not equality, and not a decline. Deficits are not strongly correlated with inflation. Inflation shocks are much smaller than deficit shocks. These observations, and especially the first, tell us that fiscal policy largely consists of borrowing, credibly promising future surpluses to repay debt, and therefore on average doing so. They tell us that fiscal policy does not routinely inflate away debt. I call the result an "s-shaped" surplus process: If today's surplus s_0 declines, the surplus must turn around and rise later on. A government that wants steady inflation, and can do so, will arrange its fiscal affairs in this way. There is some unexpected inflation, but we will have to see its fiscal roots on top of this dominant pattern.

The fiscal theory *can* describe an economy with widely varying debt and deficits, yet little or no inflation at all. The fiscal theory does *not* imply that large variation in debt and deficits must result in inflation.

Other countries and time periods are different. On occasion we see deficits associated with inflation. On occasion we see large inflation or currency devaluation associated with deficit shocks that seem too small to provoke them. The persistent deficit model can capture these episodes.

Discussion of debts, deficits, inflation, stimulus, and fiscal theory often refers to "Ricardian" and "non-Ricardian" policies. Briefly, and acknowledging different uses of the term, a "Ricardian" debt issue includes a full expectation of repayment by future surpluses. It therefore has no "wealth effect" on aggregate demand, and thereby no stimulus or inflation. Keynesian analysis of fiscal stimulus by borrowed money typically asserts that people don't pay attention to the future taxes that retire debt, so debt has a wealth effect on consumption. The consequent negative wealth effect of those taxes when they arrive is not commonly analyzed. Moreover, if the debt sale raises revenue, bondholders must fully expect future surpluses or they must be somehow symmetrically irrational in the other direction, buying debt despite no expectation that it will be repaid.

By analyzing explicitly nominal debt, fiscal theory allows such "non-Ricardian" debt sales, without a rise in expected future surpluses, like share splits. Yet there need be no irrationality or asymmetry in people's expectations. Fiscal theory allows "Ricardian" debt sales as well, and everything in between. How much a debt sale inflates, raises revenue, and is or is not expected to be paid off is not a constant, but varies with many circumstances. Fiscal theory is sometimes called "non-Ricardian," but I find this name confusing. Fiscal theory allows the possibility of selling debt without changes in future surpluses, but does not require it. And the value of debt is always equal to the present value of future surpluses. The price level adjusts.

1.6   Debt Reactions and a Price Level Target

I introduce a price level target P_1^* and a fiscal rule $s_1 = B_0/P_1^*$. This rule produces $P_1 = P_1^*$ in equilibrium. Additional nominal debt sales B_0 now generate surpluses to pay them off at the price level P_1^*. The decision to borrow or inflate away a deficit is implemented by borrowing or not borrowing rather than by changing a promised stream of surpluses.

I introduced these fiscal exercises by thinking about changes in the sequence of surpluses $\{s_0, s_1\}$. But that's not the way economists or policy people usually think of fiscal affairs. It is more common to think in terms of a surplus or deficit today, s_0, borrowing or inflation today, and to characterize the future by fiscal reactions to outstanding debt, the price level, and other state variables, endogenous variables, or shocks. More generally, macroeconomics and finance are often expressed in terms of state variables and actions that are functions of state variables rather than sequences of actions. This dynamic programming approach is often useful conceptually and not just (very) useful for solving models. If you're like me, you think of the cost of buying something in terms of the value of wealth, not a specific alternative future purchase.

Think then of surplus at time 1 that responds to the quantity of debt B_0, according to a rule

$$s_1 = \frac{B_0}{P_1^*}. \tag{1.13}$$

I will call the variable P_1^* a price level target. With this rule, equilibrium inflation is given uniquely from $B_0/P_1 = s_1$ by $P_1 = P_1^*$. Parameterizing the surplus decision this way, we think of the government as committing to respond to an increase in the quantity of debt B_0 by raising real surpluses to repay that debt, rather than think of the larger surplus s_1 with a direct connection to the previous deficit s_0. This fiscal rule does not respond to the future price level itself P_1, or to deviations of that level from the target, $P_1 - P_1^*$.

The price level target may represent an inflation target, a gold price target, or an exchange rate target. It may represent less formal rules and traditions, expectations, or it may simply model fiscal behavior and therefore expectations of fiscal behavior, as the Taylor rule $i_t = \theta_\pi \pi_t$ started as a description of Fed behavior. It can capture the idea that governments often respond to inflation with "austerity" and to deflation with "stimulus." If inflation breaks out, $P_1 > P_1^*$, for example, the government deliberately runs a larger real surplus to fight inflation and bring the price level down to P_1^*, even though the government can avoid formal default by running a smaller surplus $s_1 = B_0/P_1$. If deflation breaks out, $P_1 < P_1^*$, this government refuses to raise surpluses to pay an unexpected windfall to bondholders. It runs deliberate "helicopter money" unbacked fiscal stimulus instead. I use a subscript P_1^* to allow the price level target to vary over time and according to information or, later, other variables at time 1, perhaps as a transitory deviation from stated long-run price level or inflation targets. Many more interpretations of the price level target specification follow. For now, let's just follow (1.13) as a potentially interesting possibility for fiscal policy.

Consider again the government's options to finance a deficit s_0. We rephrase the previous three options. In addition to (1.13) and consequent $P_1 = P_1^*$, we have at time 0,

$$\frac{B_{-1}}{P_0} = s_0 + \beta E_0 s_1 = s_0 + \beta E_0 \left(\frac{B_0}{P_1^*} \right).$$

To finance a deficit s_0 by borrowing, without affecting the price level at either date, the government issues more nominal debt B_0, without changing the price level target P_1^*. The greater borrowing produces larger surpluses s_1. But now rather than try to communicate promises about a specific stream of surpluses, the government communicates a commitment to raising whatever surpluses are needed to repay debt at the price level target P_1^*. In an intertemporal model, the government does not need to be specific about just when the surpluses will arrive.

To finance the deficit by inflating away outstanding debt, the government simply does not sell more debt B_0. With lower surpluses s_0, the money printed up to redeem bonds B_{-1} is left outstanding. People try to spend that money, driving up the price level P_0. Again, rather than make promises about future surpluses, the government acts by not selling more debt. To super-inflate, as in the AR(1) surplus model, the government sells even less debt B_0, which lowers surpluses s_1.

1.7   Fiscal Policy Changes Monetary Policy

The fiscal policy rule with a price level target $s_1 = B_0/P_1^*$ dramatically changes the effects of monetary policy. A rise in debt B_0, or a rise in nominal interest rate i_0, with no change in this fiscal policy *rule*, lowers P_0 with no effect on P_1 rather than raise P_1 with no effect on P_0. Higher interest rates lower inflation, immediately.

The effects of monetary policy depend crucially on the fiscal policy rule. We will see this lesson repeatedly. The price level target rule offers a simple and important example.

Suppose that the central bank sells more debt B_0 without directly changing fiscal policy. Specifying fiscal policy as an unchanged s_0 and s_1, this action had no effect on P_0 and raised P_1. But suppose fiscal policy is specified by s_0 and the rule $s_1 = B_0/P_1^*$, and let us think of "unchanged fiscal policy" as not making changes to this rule. This question gives exactly the opposite result: Larger debt B_0 has no effect on $P_1 = P_1^*$, and it lowers the price level P_0 immediately. The larger debt B_0 generates more surplus s_1. It therefore generates more revenue from bond sales at time 0, and more revenue soaks up dollars, lowering P_0.

Fixing surpluses $\{s_0, s_1\}$, the demand curve for nominal debt was unit elastic, giving the same total real revenue $\beta E_0(s_1)$ for any amount of bonds B_0 that the government sells. Now, the debt demand curve is flat, giving the same real price Q_0/P_0 for any amount sold B_0. The more bonds B_0 sold, then, the more total real revenue such sales produce. If the bonds are sold as "fiscal policy," to finance a larger deficit s_0, they allow the government to run such a deficit without inflation. If the bonds are sold as "monetary policy," with no change in s_0, and no change in the *fiscal rule*, bond sales soak up more cash at time 0 and lower the price level P_0.

Likewise, fixing surpluses $\{s_0, s_1\}$, a higher interest rate target i_0 raised expected inflation, via $1/(1 + i_0) = \beta E_0(P_0/P_1)$, having no effect on the price level P_0 and raising the expected price level P_1. Now a higher interest rate still raises expected inflation. But with $P_1 = P_1^*$ unchanged, the rise in interest rate i_0 raises expected inflation by lowering the price level P_0, and thus lowers current inflation P_0/P_{-1}. We have a model that overturns the Fisherian prediction, a model in which higher interest rates lower inflation!

Monetary policy drives down inflation because of a different *fiscal* policy rule. Monetary policy does not change the fiscal rule, but monetary policy can change a variable that fiscal policy responds to, and thereby indirectly change fiscal policy. We see a simultaneous fiscal tightening along with the interest rate rise. That fiscal tightening produces the lower time 0 inflation. But it is only an expected future fiscal tightening. We do not see a deficit in the period 0 when the interest rate rises. Looking at data, it could be hard to see what's going on.

This is an important story, by highlighting the importance of the fiscal policy rule for the effects of monetary policy. It also highlights one of the central mechanisms in many models for producing a negative inflation response to interest rates: Higher interest rates induce a future fiscal contraction.

1.8 Budget Constraints and Active versus Passive Policies

I preview two theoretical controversies.

$B_0/P_1 = s_1$ is an equilibrium condition, not a government budget constraint. The government could leave cash M_1 outstanding overnight. People who don't want to hold cash overnight drive the equilibrium condition.

The government may choose to set surpluses s_1 so that $B_0/P_1 = s_1$ for any P_1. In this case the fiscal theory does not determine the price level. This is called a "passive" fiscal policy. Such a policy is a choice, however, not a budget constraint. It is also not a natural outcome of a proportional tax system.

This simple model helps us to preview a few common theoretical concerns.

First, isn't the fiscal theory equation $B_0/P_1 = s_1$ or $B_{-1}/P_0 = s_0 + \beta E_0(s_1)$ the government's budget constraint? Shouldn't we solve it for the surplus that the government must raise to pay off its debts, given the price level P_1? Economic agents must obey budget constraints, for any price. Budget constraints limit quantities given prices, they don't determine prices given quantities. You and I can't fix the real amount we want to repay for a mortgage and demand that the price level adjust so we can afford a mansion. Are we specifying, weirdly or perhaps incorrectly, that the government is some special agent that can threaten to violate its budget constraint at off-equilibrium prices?

No. Equation (1.1),

$$\frac{B_0}{P_1} = s_1 \tag{1.14}$$

is not a budget constraint. The condition that holds at any price level is

$$B_0 = P_1 s_1 + M_1 \tag{1.15}$$

where M_1 is money left over at the end of the day after paying taxes, plus any of the debt B_0 that people may have chosen not to redeem. (I assume no default here. We'll add that later.) For any given B_0 and P_1, government choices of $\{s_1, M_1\}$ must satisfy (1.15). If the government specifies s_1, then M_1 follows from (1.15). No budget constraint says that the government may not leave money M_1 outstanding at the end of the day. If people decide to line their caskets with money or un-redeemed debt, if we add $u(M_1)$ to the consumer's utility, no budget constraint forces the government to soak up that money with taxes.

Consumer demand is why $M_1 = 0$, and hence why $B_0 = P_1 s_1$. People don't *want* to hold any money at the end of the day, because they get no utility, purchasing power, tax-paying ability, or pleasure from doing so. Equation (1.14) results from the budget constraint (1.15) *plus* that consumer demand. Equation (1.14) is thus an equilibrium condition, a market-clearing condition, a supply = demand condition, deriving from consumer optimization together with consumer and government budget constraints. Equation (1.14) is not a "government budget constraint."

Budget constraints hold at off-equilibrium prices. Equilibrium conditions need not hold at off-equilibrium prices. Prices adjust to make equilibrium conditions hold. There is no reason that equation (1.14) should hold at a non-equilibrium price, any more than the supply of potatoes should equal their demand at $10 per potato. When we substitute private sector demands, optimality conditions, or market-clearing conditions into government budget constraints, on our way to finding an equilibrium, we must avoid the temptation to continue to refer to the resulting object as a "budget constraint" for the government.

Why can't you and I demand that the "price level adjust to make our budget constraints hold?" Because we do not issue the currency and nominal debt that define the price level. You and I are like a government that uses another country's currency. We pay debts at the given price level, or we default. Nominal government debt is like corporate equity, whose price adjusts to make a valuation equation hold. Real or foreign currency government debt is like personal or corporate debt, which we must repay or default.

Suppose that the government *chooses* to adjust surpluses s_1 so as to make the equilibrium condition (1.14) $B_0/P_1 = s_1$ hold for any price level P_1. Suppose the government follows a fiscal rule, setting the surplus at time 1 by

$$s_1 = \tau_1 y_1 = \frac{B_0}{P_1}, \qquad (1.16)$$

as if it were a budget constraint, lowering the tax rate as the price level rises and raising the tax rate as the price level falls. This is a possible *choice*. This choice is known as a "passive" fiscal policy. If the government follows such a policy, P_1 cancels from left and right, and (1.14) no longer determines the price level. In essence, the government's supply curve lies directly on top of the private sector's demand curve. A government that wishes to let the price level be set by other means, such as a foreign exchange peg, a gold standard, a currency board, use of another government's currency, the equilibrium-selection policies of new-Keynesian models, or $MV = Py$ once we add money demand, follows a passive fiscal policy.

The converse of "passive" is "active." The fiscal theory requires an "active" fiscal policy. Active fiscal policy does not require that surpluses s_T are fixed or exogenous. The surplus may respond to the price level P_1, $s_1(P_1)$ or to other variables including output and employment. The surplus may respond to the quantity of debt, as in $s_1 = B_0/P_1^*$. We just have to exclude the one-for-one case $s_1 = s_1(P_1) = B_0/P_1$, or multiple crossings, so that there is only one solution to (1.14), one P_1 such that $B_0/P_1 = s_1(P_1)$.

Standard theories of inflation include the government debt valuation equation (1.14), but they add this passive fiscal policy assumption so that other forces may determine the price level. Specifying the mechanics of fiscal policy that achieves that passive response is an important and neglected part of such models. "Passive" does not mean easy. Coming up with the surpluses to defend the price level involves painful and distorting taxes or unpopular limitations on government spending. Many papers add a footnote in which they assume the government charges lump-sum taxes to satisfy (1.14), but do not examine or test the resulting fiscal side of their models.

You may now want to follow decades of literature and try to test for active versus passive policy. Such tests are difficult. Both active and passive fiscal regimes include the valuation equation (1.14) as an equilibrium condition. They differ on the direction of its causality, the mechanism by which it comes to hold, and how governments behave for a price level away from the equilibrium which we observe. When the same equation holds in two models, arguing about how it comes to hold brings up subtle identification and observational equivalence issues. Is the price level set somewhere else, and $B_0/P_1 = s_1$ describes how the government sets surpluses? Or does $B_0/P_1 = s_1$ determine the price level given surpluses? All we see in the data is $B_0/P_1 = s_1$. The two views are *observationally equivalent*, at least before we add identification or other restrictions.

We will consider these issues at some length. The important point for now is that the government does not *have to* follow a passive fiscal policy, in the same way that we, and the government, have to follow budget constraints. An active fiscal policy is a logical and economic possibility, one that does not violate any of the rules of Walrasian equilibrium.

A passive fiscal policy is not a natural description of tax and spending policies. With a proportional tax on income, the nominal surplus is $P_1 s_1 = \tau P_1 y_1$. The real surplus $s_1 = \tau y_1$ is then independent of the price level, so fiscal policy is active. Transfer payments and social programs are either explicitly indexed or rise with market prices, so a primary surplus fixed in real terms $s_1 = \tau y_1 - g_1$ is again a natural specification. To engineer a passive policy, the government must change the tax *rate* and real spending in response to the price level, and in the opposite of a natural direction. To achieve $s_1 = B_0/P_1 = \tau_1 y_1$, passive policy requires $\tau_1 = B_0/(P_1 y_1)$. The government must systematically lower the tax rate, or increase real transfers, as the price level rises, and raise the tax rate or cut real transfers as the price level declines. If anything, the tax code generates the opposite sign: Inflation pushes people to higher tax brackets, inflation generates taxable capital gains, and inflation devalues depreciation allowances and past nominal losses carried forward. Inflation reduces the real value of sticky wage payments to government workers, and price-sticky health care payments. Governments facing inflation typically raise taxes and cut spending to fight inflation, while governments facing deflation typically lower taxes and spend more. A passive policy is a deliberate choice, requiring unusual and deliberate action by fiscal authorities.

1.9   Active versus Passive with a Debt Rule

The policy rule $s_1 = B_0/P_1^*$ clarifies active versus passive policy. It seems that governments which respond to debt by raising surpluses therefore have passive policies. Active policy allows the government to respond to changes in the value of debt that come from changes in nominal debt B_0 or from changes in the price level target P_1^*. Active policy only requires that governments ignore changes in the value of debt that come from unexpected, undesired, multiple-equilibrium inflation.

The active versus passive question is often framed in terms of responses to debt. Interpret the passive surplus policy (1.16) $s_1 = B_0/P_1$ as a fiscal policy rule, in which governments raise surpluses in response to increases in the value of debt. Stated that way, passive policy sounds reasonable, the sort of thing that responsible governments do. (Or at least that they used to do!) One is tempted to run a regression, say $s_1 = a + \gamma(B_0/P_1) + u_1$, and to interpret γ as a test of active versus passive policy.

The active policy example (1.13) $s_1 = B_0/P_1^*$ and equilibrium $P_1 = P_1^*$ clarifies how this idea is mistaken, and how little is actually required of active fiscal policy. This active fiscal government responds one-for-one to changes in its nominal debt B_0. We observe it to respond one-for-one to changes in the equilibrium value of its debt, $s_1 = B_0/P_1 = B_0/P_1^*$. The regression would estimate $\gamma = 1$.

There are three sources of variation in the real value of debt: nominal debt B_0 built up from financing previous deficits, unexpected changes in the price level target $(E_1 - E_0)(1/P_1^*)$, and unexpected inflation different from the target $(E_1 - E_0)(1/P_1 - 1/P_1^*)$. Active fiscal policy only requires that the government respond less than one-for-one to the last component.

It is possible and natural that fiscal policy should respond differently to these three sources of variation in the value of debt. Responding to variation in the nominal value of debt B_0, accumulated by financing past deficits s_0, allows the government to borrow in the first place, to meet a deficit by borrowing rather than time 0 inflation. Responding to changes in an inflation target allows the government to have some inflation or deflation, for example as state-contingent defaults or stimulus in response to wars, pandemics, or crises. Committing not to respond to arbitrary unexpected inflation-induced variation in the value of debt allows the government to produce a stable and determinate price level, avoiding the indeterminacy that (here) would accompany passive policy. And governments do behave this way. They try to pay off debts, conscious of the reputation doing so engenders for future borrowing; they try to coordinate fiscal and monetary policies; yet they respond to undesired inflation with austerity and to undesired deflation with stimulus, not the opposite reactions that passive policy requires.

Thinking in terms of a reaction to debt, we begin to see identification and observational equivalence more clearly. In equilibrium, we see $s_1 = B_0/P_1^* = B_0/P_1$. The regression that attempts to test active versus passive policy is $s_1 = \alpha(B_0/P_1^*) + \gamma(B_0/P_1 - B_0/P_1^*) + u_1$. The coefficient $\gamma = 1$ ($\gamma > 0$ in the later intertemporal model) indicates passive policy. But we never see $P_1 \neq P_1^*$ in equilibrium. The parameter γ that measures active versus passive fiscal policy is not identified. We cannot easily look at time series and distinguish whether price level is set elsewhere and fiscal policy follows passive $\alpha = \gamma = 1$, or whether fiscal policy is active with $\alpha = 1$ and $\gamma = 0$. Testing for active versus passive regimes at least requires identifying assumptions.

Observational equivalence and parameter nonidentification do not mean the enterprise is pointless. It is a crucial guiding theorem, like other observational equivalence theorems throughout economics and finance.

As we look deeper, I will argue that the active versus passive debate has been a dead end. It is a historical theoretical controversy that a fiscal theorist must understand, for now. The active-fiscal passive-money and active-money passive fiscal extremes are useful thought experiments. However, especially as they are observationally equivalent, they are not useful concepts for additional investigation, to understand data, to productively test for one or the other regime, or to analyze policy. In the end, fiscal and monetary policy must be coordinated. The extreme game-of-chicken view that coordination comes about because one is "active" and the other "passive" is not necessary, realistic, or productive.

The "active" and "passive" labels are due to Leeper (1991). The labels are not perfect, as "active" fiscal policy here includes leaving surpluses alone, and "passive" policy means adjusting tax rates and spending according to the price level, which takes a lot of activity. The same possibilities are sometimes called "money-dominant" versus "fiscal-dominant," which has a lot of other meanings, and "non-Ricardian" versus "Ricardian," which I find terribly confusing. It is not true that active-fiscal regimes fail to display Ricardian equivalence, or that in them government debt is a free lunch. Recognizing the deficiency of good labels, some authors offer symbols such as "Regime F" and "Regime M." Words are better. For this book, I use "active" and "passive" as defined here, and elaborated in context later.

2

An Intertemporal Model

THIS CHAPTER introduces a simple intertemporal model. The basic fiscal theory equation quickly generalizes to say that the real value of nominal debt equals an infinite present value of surpluses,

$$\frac{B_{t-1}}{P_t} = E_t \sum_{j=0}^{\infty} \beta^j s_{t+j}.$$

I start by developing this model fully, writing out the economic environment. The ideas sketched in the two-period model of the last chapter gain detail and nuance. We take an important step towards model useful for empirical application.

I then consider again "monetary policy," changes in debt B_t with no change in surpluses, as opposed to "fiscal policy," which changes surpluses, in the context of the intertemporal model. "Monetary" and "fiscal" debt issues are again analogues to share splits versus equity offerings. This insight suggests a reason for the institutional separation between treasury and central bank. We will see that a form of "fiscal stimulus" can cause inflation.

Monetary policy can target the nominal interest rate. Linearizing, a fiscal theory of monetary policy emerges that looks much like standard new-Keynesian models, and resembles current institutions. Therefore, the "fiscal" theory of the price level does not require us to throw out everything we know and our accumulated modeling skills, to ignore central banks, and to think about inflation in terms of debts and surpluses. We can approach data and institutions much as standard monetary modelers do, specifying interest rate targets, and making minor changes in the ingredients and solution methods of standard models.

Distinguishing fiscal theory of monetary policy from new-Keynesian and monetarist alternatives introduces observational equivalence theorems, elaborated in this intertemporal context.

This chapter maintains the other simplifications used so far: one-period debt, flexible prices, an endowment economy with a constant real interest rate and no risk premiums. Later chapters add price stickiness, discount rate variation, risk premiums and other realistic complications.

2.1   The Intertemporal Model

I derive the simplest intertemporal version of the fiscal theory. The government debt valuation equation is

$$\frac{B_{t-1}}{P_t} = E_t \sum_{j=0}^{\infty} \beta^j s_{t+j}.$$

The price level adjusts so that the real value of nominal debt equals the present value of future surpluses.

The two-period model is conceptually useful, but we need a model that describes economies over time. It is also useful to fill out economic foundations to see a complete model. This section describes a full, if still simple, intertemporal model.

The economy starts with bonds B_{-1} outstanding. At the end of each time period $t-1$ the government issues nominal one-period debt B_{t-1}. Each nominal bond promises to pay one dollar at time t. At the beginning of period t, the government prints up new money to pay off the maturing debt. At the end of period t, the government collects taxes net of transfers s_t, and sells new debt B_t at a price Q_t. Both actions soak up money.

Following the money, the government budget constraint is

$$M_{t-1} + B_{t-1} = P_t s_t + M_t + Q_t B_t \tag{2.1}$$

where M_{t-1} denotes non-interest-paying money held overnight from the evening of $t-1$ to the morning of time t, P_t is the price level, $Q_t = 1/(1+i_t)$ is the one-period nominal bond price, and i_t is the nominal interest rate. Interest is paid overnight only, from the end of date t to the beginning of $t+1$, and not during the day.

A representative household maximizes

$$\max E \sum_{t=0}^{\infty} \beta^t u(c_t)$$

in a complete asset market. The household has a constant endowment $y_t = y$.

The household's period budget constraint is almost the mirror of (2.1). The household enters the period with money M_{t-1} and nominal bonds B_{t-1}, receives income $P_t y$, purchases consumption $P_t c_t$, pays net taxes net of transfers $P_t s_t$, buys bonds B_t, and potentially holds money M_t,

$$M_{t-1} + B_{t-1} + P_t y = P_t c_t + P_t s_t + M_t + Q_t B_t. \tag{2.2}$$

Household money and bond holdings must be nonnegative, $B_t \geq 0, M_t \geq 0$.

The consumer's first-order conditions and equilibrium $c_t = y$ then imply that the gross real interest rate is $R = 1/\beta$, and the nominal interest rate i_t and bond price Q_t are

$$Q_t = \frac{1}{1+i_t} = \frac{1}{R} E_t \left(\frac{P_t}{P_{t+1}}\right) = \beta E_t \left(\frac{P_t}{P_{t+1}}\right). \tag{2.3}$$

When $i_t > 0$ the household demands no money, $M_t = 0$. When $i_t = 0$ money and bonds are perfect substitutes, so the symbol B_t can stand for their sum. The interest rate cannot be less than zero in this model. Thus, we can eliminate money from (2.1), leading to the flow equilibrium condition

$$B_{t-1} = P_t s_t + Q_t B_t. \tag{2.4}$$

Substituting the bond price (2.3) into (2.4), dividing by P_t, we have

$$\frac{B_{t-1}}{P_t} = s_t + \beta B_t E_t \left(\frac{1}{P_{t+1}} \right). \tag{2.5}$$

Household maximization, budget constraint, and equilibrium $c_t = y$ also imply the household transversality condition

$$\lim_{T \to \infty} E_t \left(\beta^T \frac{B_{T-1}}{P_T} \right) = 0. \tag{2.6}$$

If the term on the left is positive, then the consumer can raise consumption at time t, lower this terminal value, and raise utility. A no-Ponzi condition rules out a negative value.

The transversality condition takes the place of the second day in my two-day model. Transversality conditions lead to many confusing debates, which is why I stopped to show how fiscal theory works in a two-period model, at the cost of some repetition. Online Appendix Section A1.1 covers the transversality condition in more detail.

As a result, we can then iterate (2.5) to

$$\frac{B_{t-1}}{P_t} = E_t \sum_{j=0}^{\infty} \beta^j s_{t+j}. \tag{2.7}$$

The government sets debt and surpluses $\{B_t\}$ and $\{s_t\}$. Debt B_{t-1} is predetermined at time t. The right-hand side of (2.7) does not depend on the price level in this simple model. Therefore, the price level must adjust so that (2.7) holds. The right-hand side of (2.7) is the present value of future primary surpluses. The left-hand side is the real value of nominal debt. So, the fiscal theory says that *the price level adjusts so that the real value of nominal debt is equal to the present value of primary surpluses.*

We have determined the price level, in a completely frictionless intertemporal model.

Another useful approach is to add the transversality condition to the household flow budget constraint (2.2), iterate forward, and express the household present value budget constraint in real terms

$$\frac{B_{t-1}}{P_t} = \sum_{j=0}^{\infty} \beta^j (c_{t+j} - y + s_{t+j}). \tag{2.8}$$

If the value of debt is greater than the present value of surpluses, then the household has extra wealth, which they try to spend on consumption greater than endowment.

Some details and clarifications: The surplus concept denoted by s_t is the real *primary* surplus in government accounting. The usual deficit or surplus includes interest payments on government debt. The surplus in this simple model includes only cash tax receipts less cash transfers. I do not include government purchases of goods and services (roads, tanks), which subtract from produced output to lower private consumption, and may provide benefits in utility. Thus, equilibrium in the goods market is $c_t = y$, not $y = c_t + g_t$, and marginal utility depends on private consumption only. We can easily add those realistic complications.

Rather than a real lump sum, we can also specify that surpluses are a proportional income (endowment) tax less a lump-sum indexed transfer,

$$P_t s_t = \tau_t \left(P_t y \right) - P_t x_t,$$

and that the tax rate τ_t and real transfer payments x_t are independent of the price level. This specification ensures that the price level is absent from the right-hand side of (2.7), and taxes do not distort asset or goods prices.

I do not, here or later in this book, write down an objective for the government. That extension is important, and integrates fiscal theory with dynamic public finance. I do not take the next step, and describe government policy as the outcome of a game between players with different objectives. That extension is important too. I simply study the mapping between policy levers and outcomes, with a verbal understanding that governments like low inflation and greater output.

2.2   Dynamic Intuition

The government debt valuation equation in fiscal theory is an instance of the basic asset pricing valuation equation. Nominal government debt acts as a residual claim to primary surpluses. The price level is like a stock price, and adjusts to bring the real value of nominal debt in line with the present value of primary surpluses, just as the stock price adjusts to bring the value of shares in line with the present value of dividends.

The government debt valuation equation (2.7) is an instance of the basic asset pricing equation: price per share $1/P_t$ times number of shares B_{t-1} equals present value of dividends $\{s_{t+j}\}$. We quote the price level as the price of goods in terms of money, not the price of money in terms of goods, so the price level goes in the denominator not the numerator. Primary surpluses *are* the "dividends" that retire nominal government debt. In an accounting sense, nominal government debt *is* a residual claim to real primary surpluses.

The fact that the price level can vary means that nominal government debt is an equity-like, floating-value claim. If the present value of surpluses falls, the price level can rise to bring the real value of debt in line, just as a stock price falls to bring market value of equity in line with the expected present value of dividends. Nominal government debt *is* "stock in the government."

Continuing the analogy, suppose that we decided to use Apple stock as numeraire and medium of exchange. When you buy a cup of coffee, Starbucks quotes the price of a venti latte as 1/10 of an Apple share, and to pay you tap your iPhone, which transfers 1/10 of a Apple share in return for your coffee. If that were the case, and we were asked to come up with a theory of the price level, our first stop would be that the value of Apple shares equals the present value of its dividends. Then we would add liquidity and other effects on top of that basic idea. That is exactly what we do with the fiscal theory.

This perspective also makes sense of a lot of financial commentary. Exchange rates go up and inflation goes down when an economy does better, when productivity increases, and when governments get their budgets under control. Well, money is stock in the government.

Backing government debt by the present value of surpluses allows for a more stable price level than the one- or two-period models suggest. In the one-period model any unexpected variation in surplus s_1 translates immediately to inflation. In the dynamic model, examine (2.4):

$$B_{t-1} = P_t s_t + Q_t B_t. \tag{2.9}$$

If the government needs to finance a war or counter a recession or financial crisis, it will want to run a deficit, a lower or negative s_t. In the dynamic model, the government can soak up those dollars by debt sales $Q_t B_t = \beta E_t s_{t+1}$ rather than a current surplus s_t. For that strategy to work, however, the government must persuade investors that more debt today will be matched by higher surpluses in the future.

Surpluses are not "exogenous" in the fiscal theory! Surpluses are a *choice* of the government, via its tax and spending policies and via the fiscal consequences of all its policies. The government debt valuation equation is an equilibrium condition among endogenous variables. Surpluses may react to events. For example, surpluses may rise as tax revenues rise in a boom. Surpluses may also respond to the price level, by choice or by non-neutralities in the tax code and expenditure formulas. We only have to rule out or treat separately the special case of "passive" policy, that the present value of surpluses reacts exactly one-for-one to changes in the value of nominal debt brought about by changes in the price level, so that equation (2.7) holds for any price level P_t.

It is initially puzzling that this model with one-period debt relates the price level to an infinite present value of future surpluses. One expects one-period assets to lead to a one-period present value, and long-term assets to be valued with a long-term present value. Equation (2.9) tells us why: The government plans to roll over the debt. Most of the payments to today's one-period debtholders, B_{t-1}/P_t, come from new debtholders willing to pay $Q_t B_t / P_t$. If the rollover fails, or if the government retires the debt, not selling new debt, we have $B_{t-1}/P_t = s_t$ only as in the one-period model.

As a result, inflation in the fiscal theory with short-term debt has the feel of a run. If we look at the present value equation (2.7), it seems today's investors dump debt because of bad news about deficits in 30 years. But today's investors really dump debt because they fear tomorrow's investors won't be there to roll over the debt. Directly, consider the flow equation written as

$$\frac{B_{t-1}}{P_t} = s_t + \frac{Q_t B_t}{P_t}.$$

The price level P_t rises because the revenue that debt sales $Q_t B_t / P_t$ generate won't be enough to pay off today's debt B_{t-1} at the originally expected price level. Why are people unwilling to buy bonds? Well, they look at the same situation a period ahead, and worry that investors will not buy bonds B_{t+1}, to pay them off in real terms, and so on. Yes, the indirect cause of inflation can be a worry about surpluses in the far future. But the direct mechanism is a loss of faith that debt will be rolled over. Short-term debt, constantly rolled over, to be retired slowly by a very long-lasting and illiquid asset stream, is the classic ingredient of a bank run or sovereign debt crisis. The main difference is the fiscal theory government in a rollover crisis can devalue via inflation rather than default explicitly.

The fact that inflation can break out based on fear of fiscal events in the far future tells you that inflation can break out with little current news, seemingly out of nowhere, or as an unpredictable apparent overreaction to seemingly small events. This is a helpful analysis because inflation and currency devaluation do often break out with little current news, seemingly out of nowhere. Central bank and private inflation forecasts miss almost as much as stock market forecasts miss. Run mechanics increase this rootless sense. I emphasize rational expectations for simplicity, but one can quickly spy multiple equilibrium variants, a sensitivity to exactly rational expectations, or fear of fear of such events. You may well dump Treasury securities just because you fear others will do so next year, and you want to get out before the flood. Section 7.2.2 investigates these run mechanics in more detail, and analyzes how long-term debt offers governments protection against inflation.

Since the government debt valuation (2.7) looks a lot like a stock valuation equation, we might expect inflation to be as variable as stock prices, and real returns on government bonds as risky as stock returns. However, as we saw briefly in Section 1.5, and will see in more detail later, surpluses typically follow a process with an s-shaped moving average. A deficit, negative s_t in the short run, corresponds to surpluses, positive s_t later on, which at least partially repay the debt issued to finance deficits. As a result, large shocks to near-term deficits may have little impact on the present value of surpluses, and therefore little impact on inflation or the real returns of government bonds. For stocks, we usually think that cash flow shocks are more persistent, and do not substantially reverse. Thus, changes in stocks' cash flows have larger effects on prices. Bonds have s-shaped cash flows: Borrowing is followed by repayment, all or in part. Bonds and stocks are valued by the present value formula. Bond prices also decline when expected future cash flows decline, due to default fears. But bond prices are much less volatile than stock prices. A similar valuation formula with a different cash flow process produces a different result. Government debt has a bond-like surplus process.

What about the first period? If we start with $B_{-1} = 0$, then the price level P_0 must be determined by other means. To tell a story, perhaps the economy uses gold coins, or foreign currency on the day the government first issues nominal bonds. Then, at date 0, the government issues nominal bonds B_0. It could sell these bonds in return for gold coins to finance a deficit, or in exchange for its outstanding real or foreign currency debt. Then the economy starts in period 1 with maturing government debt B_0, or money printed up to redeem that debt, and a determined price level. The government could also just give people an initial stock of money at the beginning of period zero, which counts as a transfer or negative surplus.

I start here with the simplest possible economic environment, abstracting from monetary frictions, financial frictions, pricing frictions, growth, default, risk and risk aversion, output fluctuations, limited government precommitment, distorting taxes, and so forth. We can add all these ingredients and more. But starting the analysis this way emphasizes that no additional complications are *necessary* to determine the price level.

The fiscal theory does rely on specific institutions. The government in this model has its own currency and issues nominal government debt. We use maturing debt, or the currency it promises, as numeraire and unit of account. This is not a theory of clamshell money, or of Bitcoins. It is a theory adapted to our current institutions: government-provided fiat money, rampant financial innovation, interest rate targets, governments that generally inflate rather than explicitly default.

More generally, our monetary and financial system is built around the consensus that short-term government debt is an abundant safe asset, and thus a natural numeraire. This faith may be a weak point in our institutions going forward. If we experience a serious sovereign debt crisis, not only will the result be inflation, it will be an unraveling of our payments, monetary, and financial institutions. Then we shall have to write an entirely new book, of monetary arrangements that are insulated from sovereign debt. We shall have to construct a numeraire that is backed by something other than the present value of government surpluses. This is a fun bit of free-market financial engineering. I pursue the issue briefly in Section 10.6. But it is so far from current institutions that I do not pursue it at great length. Given the financial and economic calamity that a U.S. or European sovereign debt crisis would be, let us hope that day does not come to pass anytime soon.

2.3 Equilibrium Formation

What force pushes the price level to its equilibrium value? I tell three stories, corresponding to three consumer optimization conditions. If the price level is too low, money may be left overnight. Consumers try to spend this money, raising aggregate demand. Alternatively, a too-low price level may come because the government soaks up too much money from bond sales. Consumers either consume too little today relative to the future or too little overall, violating intertemporal optimization or the transversality condition. Fixing these, consumers again raise aggregate demand, raising the price level.

What force pushes the price level to its equilibrium value?

The basic intuition is "aggregate demand," just as in the one-period model. If government bonds are worth more than the present value of surpluses, people try to get rid of government bonds. The only way to do so, in the end, is to try to buy more goods and services, thereby bidding up their prices. Aggregate demand is, by budget constraint, always the mirror image of demand for government debt. Equation 2.8 expresses aggregate demand as extra wealth.

People trying to get rid of government bonds might initially try to buy assets. This step would raise the value of assets, and higher asset values induce them to buy more goods and services, the "wealth effect" of consumption.

Technically, if the price level is not at its equilibrium value, the economy is off a supply curve or a demand curve. To tell a story, let us suppose the latter: One of the consumers' optimality conditions is violated. I'll suppose the price level is wrong in the first place because money demand (zero), intertemporal optimization, or the transversality condition are violated. We then ask what actions the consumer takes to improve matters, and how that action brings the price level into equilibrium.

One good story is that if the price level is too low, the government will leave more money outstanding at the end of period t than people want to hold, just as in the one-period model. That money chases goods, driving up the price level, and vice versa. Specifically, the flow budget constraint says that money printed up in the morning to retire debt is soaked up by bond sales or money left outstanding,

$$B_{t-1} = P_t s_t + Q_t B_t + M_t. \tag{2.10}$$

We reasoned from a constant endowment, intertemporal optimization, and the transversality condition, that debt sales generate real revenue equal to the present value of following surpluses, that $Q_t B_t$ in (2.10) comes from

$$\frac{Q_t B_t}{P_t} = E_t \sum_{j=1}^{\infty} \beta^j s_{t+j}. \tag{2.11}$$

Thus, if the price level P_t is too low, the current surplus and the revenue from bond sales in (2.10) do not soak up all the money printed to redeem bonds. Money M_t is left overnight, violating the consumer's money demand $M_t = 0$. As people try to spend the extra money, the price level rises. If you're bothered by negative money in the opposite direction, add a money demand $M_t = M$, which we do explicitly later, so money is insufficient rather than negative.

Alternatively, the price level may be too low because debt sales are soaking up too much money. Debt sales generate more revenue than the present value of surpluses on the right-hand side of (2.11). Consumers try to buy too many bonds, either violating their intertemporal first-order conditions or their transversality condition.

In the first case, consumers save too much now, to dis-save later. That extra saving drives consumption demand below endowment (goods market supply) now, and higher later. When consumers restore a smooth intertemporal allocation of consumption, they provide aggregate demand, raising the price level today. Such intertemporal optimization is the main source of aggregate demand in standard new-Keynesian models.

In the second case, consumers buy too many bonds and hold them forever, letting bond wealth grow at the rate of interest. In this case, via

$$\frac{B_{t-1}}{P_t} = s_t + \frac{Q_t B_t}{P_t} = s_t + E_t \sum_{j=1}^{\infty} \beta^j s_{t+j} + \lim_{T \to \infty} E_t \beta^T \frac{B_{t+T}}{P_{t+T+1}},$$

bonds soak up too much money because consumers are violating the transversality condition. Debt grows at the real interest rate. People could hold less debt, and increase consumption at all dates. When they do so, this wealth effect, as opposed to the previous intertemporal substitution effect, is the source of aggregate demand, pushing up the price level. Contrariwise, a too-high price level pushes debt to negative values, which is ruled out by budget constraint.

Much fiscal theory analysis focuses on the latter possibility. Fiscal price determination is said to rely on a "threat by the government to violate the transversality condition at off-equilibrium prices." But the transversality condition is only one of three sets of consumer optimization conditions: zero money demand, intertemporal optimization, and transversality condition. And there are lots of additional equilibrium formation stories that we can tell in which the transversality condition holds. Violation of the transversality condition is *an* equilibrium formation story, but not the only or most interesting one.

Moreover, the government doesn't *do* anything. It does not take any action that the word "threat" implies. It simply ignores the bubble in government debt and waits for consumers to come to their senses and drive the price level back up. Likewise, if a bubble appears in share prices, a corporation takes no action, it just waits for the bubble to disappear. We do not critique asset pricing as relying on a threat by firms to violate the transversality condition at off-equilibrium prices. Finally, the transversality condition in this model is a combination of consumer optimization and consumer budget constraint, and does not apply to government or firms.

An alternative, and better, perspective on these sorts of exercises starts by recognizing that the equilibrium object is not just today's price level P_t, but the whole sequence of price levels $\{P_t\}$. Rather than say consumers are off an optimality condition, we should say that they optimize, but given a sequence of price levels at which markets do not clear. For example, if the price level is too low today, but will rise later, then the bond price $Q_t = \beta E_t(P_t/P_{t+1})$ is too low. Consumers correctly optimize, but the resulting consumption demand today is below endowment while demand in the future is above the endowment. Likewise, we generate the transversality condition or wealth effect story with a price level that is too low forever.

I don't pursue this inquiry too deeply. As in all supply-demand economics, one can tell many stories about out-of-equilibrium behavior. Whether out-of-equilibrium allocations follow a demand curve or a supply curve makes a big difference to the equilibrium formation story. Out of equilibrium, market-clearing conditions do not hold, so don't expect out-of-equilibrium economies to make much sense. As in classic microeconomics, Walrasian equilibrium describes equilibrium conditions compactly with a simple, though unrealistic, description of off-equilibrium behavior, the Walrasian auctioneer. Walrasian equilibrium does not describe well a dynamic equilibrium formation process. Game-theoretic treatments of off-equilibrium behavior are more satisfactory though much more complicated. They are also a bit arbitrary, as many dynamic games lead to the same equilibrium conditions. Bassetto (2002) and Atkeson, Chari, and Kehoe (2010) are good examples of game-theoretic foundations in this sphere.

Still, it is useful to tell at least one or two equilibrium formation stories behind any model, as part of ensuring the model makes intuitive sense, and in order to use the model as a quantitative parable for describing the world. If you can't tell at least one plausible equilibrium formation story, you don't really understand a model, or the model may be more fragile than you think. Models with multiple equilibria and equilibrium selection criteria are vulnerable to this critique.

Equilibrium formation stories are not common in economics, but reappear throughout this book. I think we should take them more seriously, at least at the verbal level I pursue them. I hope you find that reading them or thinking about them makes the models more believable as quantitative parables. The related concern about supply and demand for the last dollar bill crops up repeatedly as well. It's easy to write down models in which the supply and demand for the last dollar bill uniquely determine the price level. But a quick examination of the utility or financial costs of deviating even slightly from supply and demand curves, or an attempt to write just what would people do out of equilibrium, gives us a sense that the force of this equilibrium condition is slight. Cochrane (1989) argues more generally to think of robust predictions that include a range of behaviors with small utility or financial costs.

2.4   Fiscal and Monetary Policy

I break the basic present value relation into expected and unexpected components:

$$\frac{B_t}{P_t}\Delta E_{t+1}\left(\frac{P_t}{P_{t+1}}\right) = \Delta E_{t+1}\sum_{j=0}^{\infty}\beta^j s_{t+1+j},$$

$$\frac{B_t}{P_t}\frac{1}{1+i_t} = \frac{B_t}{P_t}\frac{1}{R}E_t\left(\frac{P_t}{P_{t+1}}\right) = E_t\sum_{j=1}^{\infty}\beta^j s_{t+j},$$

$$\frac{B_{t-1}}{P_t} = s_t + \frac{B_t}{P_t}\frac{1}{1+i_t} = E_t\sum_{j=0}^{\infty}\beta^j s_{t+j}.$$

In this model, unexpected inflation results entirely from innovations to fiscal policy $\{s_t\}$. A change in debt B_t with no change in surpluses $\{s_t\}$ can determine the nominal interest rate and *expected* inflation. The government can also target nominal interest rates, and thereby expected inflation, by offering to sell any amount of bonds at the fixed interest rate. I call the latter two operations "monetary policy."

Government policy is so far described by two settings, nominal debt $\{B_t\}$ and surpluses $\{s_t\}$. We will spend some time thinking about their separate effects: What if the government changes nominal debt without changing surpluses, or vice versa? Almost all actual policy actions consist of simultaneous changes of both instruments, so beware jumping too quickly from these exercises to the analysis of episodes or policy. But answering these conceptual questions lets us understand the mechanics of the theory more clearly.

We will learn a lot by breaking the basic government debt valuation equation into expected and unexpected components. It will be clearer to move the time index forward and to start with

$$\frac{B_t}{P_{t+1}} = E_{t+1}\sum_{j=0}^{\infty}\beta^j s_{t+1+j}. \tag{2.12}$$

I mostly follow a convention of describing expectations at time t, and news or shocks at time $t+1$.

2.4.1   Fiscal Policy and Unexpected Inflation

Multiply and divide (2.12) by P_t, and take innovations

$$\Delta E_{t+1} \equiv E_{t+1} - E_t$$

of both sides, giving

$$\frac{B_t}{P_t}\Delta E_{t+1}\left(\frac{P_t}{P_{t+1}}\right) = \Delta E_{t+1}\sum_{j=0}^{\infty}\beta^j s_{t+1+j}. \qquad (2.13)$$

As of time $t+1$, B_t and P_t are predetermined. Therefore, in this simple model,

- *Unexpected inflation is determined entirely by changing expectations of the present value of fiscal surpluses.*

If people expect lower future surpluses, the value of the debt must fall. In this model, unexpected inflation is the only way for that to happen.

In this simple model, bad fiscal news affects inflation for one period only, giving a price level jump. Higher expected inflation cannot devalue short-term debt that has not been sold yet, and you can't expect future unexpected shocks. In reality, we see protracted inflations around fiscal shocks. Long-term debt, varying discount rates, and sticky prices will give us a more drawn-out response.

2.4.2 *Monetary Policy and Expected Inflation*

Next, multiply and divide (2.12) by P_t, and take the expected value E_t of both sides, giving

$$\frac{B_t}{P_t}E_t\left(\frac{P_t}{P_{t+1}}\right) = E_t\sum_{j=0}^{\infty}\beta^j s_{t+1+j}.$$

Multiplying by β, and recognizing the one-period bond price and interest rate in

$$Q_t = \frac{1}{1+i_t} = \beta E_t\left(\frac{P_t}{P_{t+1}}\right), \qquad (2.14)$$

we can then write

$$\frac{B_t}{P_t}\frac{1}{1+i_t} = \frac{B_t}{P_t}\frac{1}{R}E_t\left(\frac{P_t}{P_{t+1}}\right) = E_t\sum_{j=1}^{\infty}\beta^j s_{t+j}. \qquad (2.15)$$

The first term in (2.15) is the real revenue the government raises from selling bonds at the end of period t. The last term expresses the fact that this revenue equals the present value of surpluses from time $t+1$ on. The outer terms thus express the idea that the real value of debt equals the present value of surpluses, evaluated at the *end* of period t. The inner equality tells us about *expected* inflation, the counterpart of the unexpected-inflation relation (2.13).

Now, examine equation (2.15), and consider what happens if the government sells more debt B_t at the end of period t, without changing surpluses $\{s_{t+j}\}$. The price level P_t is already determined by the version of (2.12) that holds at time t. In particular from (2.13) at time t, bond sales B_t, though they may change unexpectedly at time t, do not change the price level at time t. If surpluses do not change in (2.15), then the bond price, interest rate, and expected future inflation must move one-for-one with the debt sale B_t.

- *The government can control interest rates i_t, bond prices Q_t and expected inflation $E_t(P_t/P_{t+1})$, by changing the amount of debt sold, B_t, with no change in current or future surpluses.*

If the government does not change surpluses as it changes debt sales B_t, then it always raises the same revenue $Q_t B_t/P_t$ by bond sales. Equation (2.15) with unchanged surpluses describes a unit elastic demand curve for nominal debt: Each 1% rise in quantity gives a 1% decline in bond price, since the real resources that pay off the debt are constant. The analysis is just like that of the two-period model with the present value of surpluses in place of the time 1 surplus s_1. Selling bonds without changing surpluses is again like a share split.

This fact explains why only surplus innovations $\Delta E_{t+1} s_{t+j}$ change unexpected inflation in (2.13), and why changing expectations of future bond sales $\Delta E_{t+1} B_{t+j}$, $j \geq 1$ make no difference at all to either formula. Given the surplus path, selling more bonds, $\Delta E_{t+1} B_{t+1}$ in particular, raises no additional revenue.

2.4.3   Interest Rate Targets

Rather than announce an amount of debt B_t to be sold, the government can also announce the bond price or interest rate i_t and then offer people all the debt B_t they want to buy at that price, with no change in surpluses. A horizontal rather than vertical supply curve of debt can intersect the unit elastic demand for government debt. In that case, equation (2.15) describes how many bonds the government will sell at the fixed price or interest rate.

- *The government can target nominal interest rates by offering debt for sale with no change in surpluses.*

This is an initially surprising conclusion. You may be used to stories in which targeting the nominal rate requires a money demand curve, and reducing money supply raises the interest rate. That story needs a friction: a demand for money, which pays less than bonds. We have no frictions.

You might have thought that trying to peg the interest rate in a frictionless economy would lead to infinite, zero, negative, or otherwise pathological demands; or other problems. Equation (2.15) denies these worries. The debt quantities are not unreasonably large either. If the government raises the interest rate target by one percentage point, it will sell one percent more nominal debt.

Contrary intuition comes from different implicit assumptions. The proposition only states that the government can fix the *nominal* interest rate. An attempt to fix the real rate in this model would lead to infinite demands.

From (2.14), $1/(1 + i_t) = \beta E_t(P_t/P_{t+1})$,

- *The nominal interest rate target determines expected inflation.*

I use the word "monetary policy" to describe setting a nominal interest rate target or changing the quantity of debt without directly changing fiscal policy. Central banks buy and sell government debt in return for money. Central banks cannot, at least directly, change fiscal policy. They must always trade one asset for another. They may not write checks to voters. They may not drop money from helicopters. Those are fiscal policies. I will spend some time later mapping these ideas to current institutions.

The definition of "monetary policy" will generalize in other contexts and require some thought. For example, rather than specify surpluses directly, I will later characterize fiscal policy by a rule, in which surpluses respond systematically to inflation, output, debt, interest costs, or other variables. In the two-period model, we already saw how a fiscal rule that targets the price level alters the effects of monetary policy. With such rules in place, it can be interesting to define "monetary policy" as a change in interest rates that does not change the fiscal policy *rule*, though surpluses themselves may change. We will also add non-interest-paying money, in which case central bank actions can directly produce one source of surplus: seigniorage. In the end, no single clean definition of "monetary policy" independent of fiscal policy emerges. The most general direction is to be aware of monetary–fiscal interactions and to make sure you ask an interesting question. Still, it is useful first to explore this simple conceptual experiment of interest rate targets with no change in surpluses, and to add various mechanisms for fiscal–monetary interactions later.

Terminology: "Monetary policy" is a somewhat antiquated term. Central banks now set interest rate targets directly, by simply offering to borrow (pay interest on reserves) and lend at specified rates. "Monetary policy" in this model has nothing to do with the quantity of money, an interest spread for liquid assets, and so forth. However, I follow convention and continue to call setting an interest rate target "monetary policy" with this disclaimer.

An interest rate *peg* means an interest rate that is constant over time and does not respond to other variables. A peg can also mean a commitment to buy and sell freely at a fixed price, as in a gold standard or foreign exchange rate peg. A *time-varying peg* moves the interest rate over time but does not respond systematically to other endogenous variables like inflation and unemployment. An interest rate *target* means that the government sets the nominal interest rate, but may change that rate over time and also in response to endogenous variables such as inflation and unemployment, as in a Taylor rule. A "target" can also mean an aspiration, a goal that a central bank tries to move toward slowly while controlling another variable. A 2% "inflation target" works this way. I do not distinguish between "target" and "instrument" as Poole (1970) suggests. A more precise language would say that the central bank uses an interest rate instrument to achieve an inflation target.

I refer to "the government" uniting treasury and central bank balance sheets, and treating government decisions as those of a unitary actor. In this model, the separation between treasury and central bank balance sheets is irrelevant, and will remain so until we start to think about considerations that revive its relevance.

2.4.4   Fiscal Theory with an Interest Rate Target

In sum,

- *Monetary policy can target the nominal interest rate, and determine expected inflation, even in a completely frictionless model. Fiscal policy determines unexpected inflation.*

You might have thought "fiscal theory" would lead us to think about inflation entirely in terms of debt and deficits. We learn that this is not the case. "Monetary policy," choosing interest rates $\{i_t\}$ without changing fiscal policy, can fully control expected inflation in this simple model. Fiscal policy fills in the gap, determining unexpected inflation and thus fully determining inflation.

It is a classic doctrine that the government cannot peg the nominal interest rate. An attempt to do so leads to inflation that is unstable (Friedman (1968)) or indeterminate (Sargent and Wallace (1975)). The fiscal theory overturns these classic doctrines.

- *Inflation can be stable and determinate under an interest rate target, or even an interest rate peg.*

The classic propositions are not wrong, they just assume passive fiscal policy. Details follow.

In a perfect foresight version of this economy, monetary policy generates a family of price level paths, while fiscal policy only determines the first "shock," the time-zero price level given preexisting debt B_{-1}, thereby choosing which of the many price level paths is unique. With that sort of model in mind, one might complain that we have a theory of the price level, not a theory of inflation; a theory of equilibrium selection, not of inflation dynamics. However, in a stochastic economy there is a new shock every period, so fiscal policy matters continually. Inflation is the change in the price level, so if fiscal concerns determine the price level each period they are a necessary part of a theory of inflation. More deeply, when we add sticky prices in continuous time, we will see the price level jump disappear entirely. Fiscal policy chooses one of many inflation paths, each of which starts from the same price level. And "equilibrium selection" is a central part of any theory, indispensable to generating its predictions. If we remove any one of the equilibrium conditions, the others generate multiple equilibria and the removed condition is reduced to "equilibrium selection," so the disparaging view really does not make sense.

The neat separation that "monetary policy" determines expected inflation and "fiscal policy" determines unexpected inflation does not generalize directly. Typically, we can read the equilibrium conditions that monetary policy along with the rest of the model generates a family of equilibria and the government debt valuation equation selects among them, choosing the innovation in one combination of state variables. That combination of state variables may not even include an unexpected change in inflation. In some examples, only expected future inflation changes.

2.5 The Fiscal Theory of Monetary Policy

We linearize the model with an interest rate target, to

$$i_t = r + E_t \pi_{t+1}$$

$$\Delta E_{t+1} \pi_{t+1} = -\Delta E_{t+1} \sum_{j=0}^{\infty} \beta^j \tilde{s}_{t+1+j} \equiv -\varepsilon_{\Sigma s, t+1}.$$

This is the simplest example of a fiscal theory of monetary policy. The interest rate target sets expected inflation, and fiscal news sets unexpected inflation.

Figure 2.1 presents the response of this model to an interest rate shock with no fiscal change, and a fiscal shock with no interest rate change. The interest rate shock is Fisherian—inflation rises one period later—as it should be in this completely frictionless model.

By "fiscal theory of monetary policy," I mean models that incorporate fiscal theory, yet in their other ingredients incorporate standard DSGE (dynamic stochastic general equilibrium) models, including price stickiness or other non-neutralities of new-Keynesian models that are most commonly used to analyze monetary policy. In particular, a central bank follows an interest rate target, and we want to understand how movements of that target spread to the larger economy, or offset other shocks to the economy.

I start here with an interest rate target in the simple model we are studying so far, with one-period debt and no monetary or pricing frictions. I do so in a conscious parallel to the similar and beautifully clarifying development of new-Keynesian models in Woodford (2003, Chapter 2). Later, I add long-term debt, pricing frictions, and the other elements of contemporary models. We obtain more realistic responses.

Here and later, I stay within a textbook new-Keynesian framework, with simple forward-looking IS and Phillips curves. Like everyone else, I recognize the limitations of those ingredients. But it's best to modify one ingredient at a time, to understand the effect of changing fiscal assumptions in well-known standard models before innovating other ingredients. And in this case, there is not yet a better, simple, well-accepted alternative.

The connection to standard models is clearer by linearizing the equations of the last section, as standard models do. Monetary policy sets an interest rate target i_t, and expected inflation follows from

$$\frac{1}{1+i_t} = E_t\left(\frac{1}{R}\frac{P_t}{P_{t+1}}\right)$$

$$i_t \approx r + E_t\pi_{t+1}. \tag{2.16}$$

When we think of variables as deviations from steady-state, we drop r. Fiscal policy determines unexpected inflation via (2.13). Linearizing, denoting the real value of nominal debt by

$$V_t \equiv B_t/P_t,$$

and denoting the surplus scaled by steady-state debt with a tilde,

$$\tilde{s}_t = s_t/V,$$

we can write (2.13) at time $t+1$ as

$$\Delta E_{t+1}\pi_{t+1} = -\Delta E_{t+1}\sum_{j=0}^{\infty}\beta^j\tilde{s}_{t+1+j} \equiv -\varepsilon_{\Sigma s,t+1} \tag{2.17}$$

The final equality of equation (2.17) defines the notation $\varepsilon_{\Sigma s,t+1}$ for the shock to the present value of surpluses, scaled by the value of debt. I add the Σ to distinguish this shock from the shock to the period $t+1$ surplus itself, $\varepsilon_{s,t+1} = \Delta E_{t+1}\tilde{s}_{t+1}$.

Debt B_t now follows from the interest rate target and other variables. We can recover the quantity of debt from the expected valuation equation (2.15),

$$\frac{B_t}{P_t}\frac{1}{1+i_t} = \frac{B_t}{P_t}\beta E_t\left(\frac{P_t}{P_{t+1}}\right) = E_t\sum_{j=1}^{\infty}\beta^j s_{t+j}. \tag{2.18}$$

It has no further implications for inflation or anything else. I linearize this equation later. The value of debt will be useful as it directly measures the present value of surpluses. We also typically express models in VAR(1) form, and the value of debt is an important state variable. Including debt is useful to solve the model numerically. But for solving the model analytically, we can pretend we see the surplus shock $\varepsilon_{\Sigma s,t+1}$ and ignore the value of debt.

The combination (2.16) and (2.17),

$$i_t = E_t\pi_{t+1}$$

$$\Delta E_{t+1}\pi_{t+1} = -\varepsilon_{\Sigma s,t+1}$$

now form the simplest example of a fiscal theory of monetary policy. Here I drop r and interpret variables as deviations from steady-state.

Using

$$\pi_{t+1} = E_t\pi_{t+1} + \Delta E_{t+1}\pi_{t+1},$$

then, the full solution of the model—the path of inflation as a function of monetary and fiscal shocks—is

$$\pi_{t+1} = i_t - \varepsilon_{\Sigma s,t+1}. \tag{2.19}$$

Using (2.19), Figure 2.1 plots the response of this model to a permanent interest rate shock at time 1 with no fiscal shock $\varepsilon_{\Sigma s,1} = 0$, and the response to a fiscal shock $\varepsilon_{\Sigma s,1} = -1$ at time 1 with no interest rate movement.

In response to the interest rate shock, inflation moves up one period later. The Fisher relation says $i_t = E_t\pi_{t+1}$ and there is no unexpected time-t inflation without a fiscal shock.

The response is the same if the interest rate movement is announced ahead of time, so I don't draw a second line for that case. If $E_{t-k}i_t$ rises, then $E_{t-k}\pi_{t+1}$ rises. Many models offer different predictions for expected versus unexpected policy, and in many models announcements of future policy can affect the economy on the date of the announcement. Not in this case. An announcement only affects long-term nominal bond prices. Since so many interest rate changes are announced long ahead of time, we should spend more effort evaluating the response to expected policy changes.

In response to the negative fiscal shock $\varepsilon_{\Sigma s,1} = -1$ with no change in interest rates, there is a one-time price level jump, corresponding to a one-period inflation. The fiscal shock is a shock to the present value of surpluses, so when surpluses actually change does not matter. The "expected fiscal shock" line makes this point. This is the same change in surpluses, but the shock is the announcement that occurs at time -2. Actual surpluses do not change until after time 1. Inflation happens when the shock is announced, not when surpluses appear.

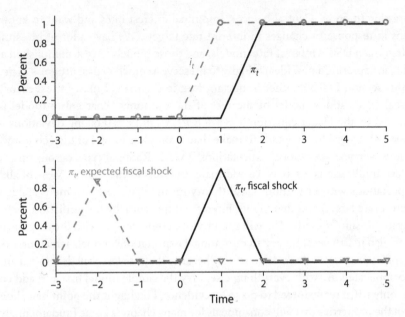

FIGURE 2.1. Impulse Response Functions, Simple Model. Top: Responses to a permanent interest rate shock, with no fiscal response, both expected and unexpected. Bottom: Responses to a fiscal shock, with no interest rate response. The "expected" fiscal shock is a decline in surpluses that starts at time 1, but is announced at time -2. The model solutions are (2.19), $\pi_{t+1} = i_t - \varepsilon_{\Sigma s, t+1}$.

These are unrealistic responses. They are, on reflection, exactly what one expects of a completely frictionless model. That's good news. A model with no pricing, monetary, or expectational frictions *should* be neutral. The model shows us that we *can* rather easily construct a fiscal theory of monetary policy, even in a completely frictionless model. It verifies that in a frictionless model, monetary policy is neutral, and makes specific just what "neutral" means. To get realistic and interesting dynamics, we should expect that we have to add monetary–fiscal interactions, sticky prices, long-term debt, cross-correlated and persistent policy responses, or dynamic economic mechanisms in preferences, production, and capital accumulation, or other ingredients.

In particular, these graphs give a perfectly "Fisherian" monetary policy response. An interest rate rise leads to *higher* inflation, one period later. Since in the long run higher nominal interest rates must come with higher inflation, an immediate jump to this long-run equilibrium is again natural behavior of a frictionless, neutral model.

These simple plots are best, then, for showing exactly how a neutral and frictionless fiscal theory of monetary policy model with one-period debt works. It's not realistic, but it's *possible*. It also shows us how simple and transparent the basic theory is, before we add elaborations. Yes, there is something as simple as money demand and supply, epitomized by $MV = Py$, and flexible prices, on which to build realistic dynamics.

You don't *have to* apply fiscal theory via a fiscal theory of monetary policy. In later chapters I step away from interest rate targets. We analyze quantitative easing, fiscal stimulus, and money supply rules. But you *can* apply fiscal theory by making technically small modifications to standard new-Keynesian models based on interest rate targets. And it is interesting to do so. Central banks set nominal interest rates and want to know what happens in response to changes in interest rate targets. We have a lot of investment in new-Keynesian DSGE interest rate models, and those models have accomplished a lot. It is useful, in exploring a new idea, initially to preserve as much of past progress as possible.

In this section I take another important fork in the road: I marry fiscal theory with a rational expectations model of the rest of the economy. That entire model is here represented by the Fisher equation $i_t = r + E_t \pi_{t+1}$ (and $r = 0$ taking deviations from a steady-state). Later I fill in details to make that a complete model of the economy. Right there, however, you see rational expectations at work. Rational expectations turns out to have deep implications, even as we add many frictions to the model. Most of all, rational expectations with or without fiscal theory means that the economy is stable under an interest rate target, and that higher interest rates eventually *raise* inflation, as they do quickly in this simple model. We will spend a lot of time dealing with those implications. One can also marry fiscal theory to nonrational expectations models which do not have that stability property. I don't do so largely because they are less well developed and a lot more complicated. As with everything else, I try the simple model first and add complications only when really forced to do so by evidence. I highlight the point here, however: Many of the properties that will consume us for many chapters come fundamentally from marrying fiscal theory with rational expectations models of the rest of the economy. If the total edifice proves wanting, fiscal theory itself may well survive, but married to different models of the rest of the economy.

2.5.1   Monetary–Fiscal Interactions

A fiscal policy rule that sets surpluses to attain a price level target produces a response to monetary policy in which higher interest rates lower inflation.

We can produce an inflation decline even in this frictionless model by combining the interest rate rise with an unexpected fiscal contraction. In that case, the joint monetary–fiscal shock produces one period of lower inflation $\Delta E_{t+1} \pi_{t+1} = -\varepsilon_{\Sigma s,t+1}$. Sticky prices will smear out this negative response, producing more realistic dynamics. But is such a pairing of monetary and fiscal shocks interesting, or realistic as a description of policy or events? Why might monetary and fiscal shocks come together?

The two-period model of Section 1.3 presents one such specification, which will reappear in several guises. The surplus at time 1 responds to nominal debt at time 0, whether issued by treasury or central bank, via $s_1 = B_0/P_1^*$. The equilibrium price level at time 1 is $P_1 = P_1^*$. We saw that with this fiscal policy specification, a rise in the interest rate target i_0 lowers the price level P_0, leaving P_1 alone, rather than raising P_1 leaving P_0 alone, as was the case with a fixed s_1.

The same idea works in our linearized intertemporal model,

$$i_t = E_t \pi_{t+1}$$
$$\Delta E_{t+1} \pi_{t+1} = -\varepsilon_{\Sigma s,t+1}.$$

Suppose that the fiscal authority again will raise or lower surpluses as necessary to attain price level targets $\{p^*_{t+1}, p^*_{t+2}, \ldots\}$. The central bank raises the interest rate i_t at time t. Then the price level at time t, p_t, must decline so that $i_t = E_t(p^*_{t+1} - p_t)$. A higher interest rate now immediately lowers inflation. The higher interest rate spurs greater bond sales. To defend the price level targets $\{p^*_{t+1}, p^*_{t+2}, \ldots\}$, the fiscal authority will be induced to raise future surpluses, producing the fiscal contraction that lowers inflation $\Delta E_t \pi_t = \Delta E_t p_t - p_{t-1} = -\varepsilon_{\Sigma s,t}$.

This dynamic extension emphasizes the perpetual need for fiscal–monetary coordination. If the fiscal authority is also committed at date t to do what it takes to set $p_t = p^*_t$, then we are at a loggerhead. To describe this regime in a symmetric way for all time periods, we need to specify that fiscal policy allows p^*_t to decline when monetary policy wishes it to do so, but not otherwise. I take up this fuller description below.

This is not a realistic example, just as fixed surpluses are not realistic. I present it to show how a different fiscal policy rule can result in dramatically different conclusions about the effects of monetary policy, and how fiscal–monetary interactions offer one route to understanding lower inflation with higher interest rates.

Other mechanisms can also provoke a fiscal contraction coincident with a monetary policy shock, without imagining that the central bank directly controls fiscal policy.

Higher interest rates that provoke higher long-term inflation can raise long-term surpluses through a variety of mechanisms, including imperfect indexing, sticky prices and wages for the things government buys, seigniorage revenue, imperfect tax indexation, and fiscal rules or habits by which fiscal authorities fight inflation with austerity. With any of these mechanisms, a higher nominal interest rate can produce a rise in the present value of surpluses, and thus lower inflation immediately.

A correlation between fiscal and monetary shocks may also describe historical episodes. Monetary and fiscal authorities respond to the same underlying shocks, so we see a decline in inflation coincident with an interest rate rise just because of that correlation of actions. Monetary stabilizations frequently involve coincident monetary tightening and fiscal reforms. VARs to measure the effects of monetary policy shocks do not (yet) try to find interest rate shocks uncorrelated with changes to the present value of fiscal surpluses. These thoughts offer a contrary warning that history may include correlated shocks that would not be present should the central bank use that historical evidence and move interest rates without the typical coincident fiscal shock.

The new-Keynesian approach to this simple economic model, as in Woodford (2003), produces a negative inflation response to an interest rate shock by creating a contemporaneous fiscal tightening. In that model, the central bank has an "equilibrium selection" policy on top of an interest rate policy. The bank threatens hyperinflation for any but one value of unexpected inflation. That threat gets the private sector to jump to the bank's desired value of unexpected inflation. Fiscal policy is "passive," setting $\varepsilon_{\Sigma s,t+1} = -\Delta E_{t+1} \pi_{t+1}$ in response to whatever inflation happens. This passive fiscal policy produces the necessary coincident fiscal shock. In Section 16.1, I judge this not to be a compelling story, but you can see it here as a possibility in which a joint monetary–fiscal regime produces a negative response of inflation to an interest rate shock.

2.6   Interest Rate Rules

I add a Taylor-type rule

$$i_t = \theta \pi_t + u_t$$

$$u_t = \eta u_{t-1} + \varepsilon_{i,t}$$

to find the equilibrium inflation process

$$\pi_{t+1} = \theta \pi_t + u_t - \varepsilon_{\Sigma s,t+1}.$$

Figure 2.2 plots responses to monetary and fiscal policy shocks in this model. The persistence of the monetary policy disturbance and the endogenous response of the interest rate rule introduce interesting dynamics, and show how monetary policy affects the dynamic response to the fiscal shock.

The standard analysis of monetary policy specifies a Taylor-type interest rate rule rather than directly specifying the equilibrium interest rate process, as I did in the last section. The model becomes

$$i_t = E_t \pi_{t+1} \tag{2.20}$$

$$\Delta E_{t+1} \pi_{t+1} = -\varepsilon_{\Sigma s,t+1} \tag{2.21}$$

$$i_t = \theta \pi_t + u_t \tag{2.22}$$

$$u_t = \eta u_{t-1} + \varepsilon_{i,t}. \tag{2.23}$$

The variable u_t is a serially correlated monetary policy disturbance: If the Fed deviates from a rule this period, it is likely to continue deviating in the future as well. Rules are often written with a lagged interest rate,

$$i_t = \eta_i i_{t-1} + \theta \pi_t + \varepsilon_{i,t},$$

which has much the same effect. The variables are deviations from steady-state, or $r = 0$ in (2.20).

Terminology: I use the word "disturbance" and the symbol u for deviations from structural equations. Disturbances may be serially correlated or predictable from other variables. I reserve the word "shock" and the letter ε for variables that only move unexpectedly, like $\varepsilon_{i,t+1}$ with $E_t \varepsilon_{i,t+1} = 0$. I use "shock" and "structural" somewhat loosely, to refer to forces external to the simplified model at hand. For example, the fiscal policy "shock" $\varepsilon_{\Sigma s,1}$ reflects news about future surpluses, which in turn has truly structural roots in productivity, tax law, politics, and so forth. A full general equilibrium model would reserve the "structural" word for the latter.

Eliminating the interest rate i_t, the equilibria of this model are now inflation paths that satisfy

$$E_t \pi_{t+1} = \theta \pi_t + u_t \tag{2.24}$$

$$\Delta E_{t+1} \pi_{t+1} = -\varepsilon_{\Sigma s,t+1}$$

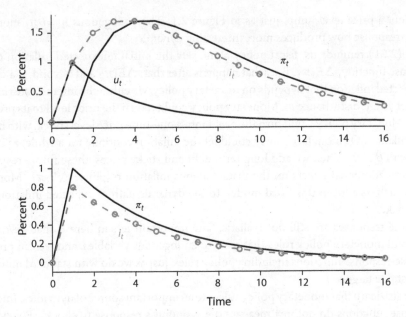

FIGURE 2.2. Responses to Monetary and Fiscal Shocks. The top panel graphs the response of inflation π_t and interest rate i_t to a unit monetary policy shock $\varepsilon_{i,1} = 1$. The monetary policy disturbance is u_t. The parameters are $\eta = 0.7$, $\theta = 0.8$. The bottom panel plots the response of inflation and interest rate to a unit fiscal shock $\varepsilon_{\Sigma s,1} = -1$.

and thus

$$\pi_{t+1} = \theta\pi_t + u_t - \varepsilon_{\Sigma s,t+1}. \tag{2.25}$$

The top panel of Figure 2.2 plots the response of inflation and interest rates to a unit monetary policy shock $\varepsilon_{i,1}$ in this model, and the line labeled u_t plots the associated monetary policy disturbance in (2.22).

The combination of two AR(1)s—the shock persistence η and the interest rate rule θ—generates a pretty hump-shaped inflation response. Inflation still follows the interest rate with a one-period lag, following $i_t = E_t\pi_{t+1}$, and with no time 1 fiscal shock, π_1 cannot jump either way.

Comparing the top panels of Figure 2.1 and Figure 2.2, you can see the same economic model at work. Since $i_t = E_t\pi_{t+1}$, if we had fed the equilibrium $\{i_t\}$ response of Figure 2.2 into the calculation (2.19) behind Figure 2.1, as if that path were an exogenous time-varying peg, we would have obtained the same result as in Figure 2.2. The monetary policy rule is a mechanism to endogenously produce an interest rate path with interesting dynamics, and for us to ask questions of the economy in which we envision monetary policy reacting systematically to inflation. But inflation follows the interest rate in the same way, whether we model the interest rate as following a rule or whether we specify the resulting equilibrium interest rate directly.

The lower panel of Figure 2.2 plots the response to a unit fiscal shock $\varepsilon_{\Sigma s,1} = -1$. By definition, this disturbance is not persistent. The fiscal loosening produces an instant inflation, a price level jump, just as in Figure 2.1. The endogenous $i_t = \theta \pi_t$ monetary policy response now produces more interesting dynamics.

As (2.21) reminds us, fiscal policy alone sets the initial unexpected inflation of this response function, $\Delta E_1 \pi_1$. But what happens after that, $\Delta E_1 \pi_2$ and beyond, is a change in expected inflation that depends on monetary policy, via either the interest rate rule $\theta \pi_t$ or a persistent disturbance u_t. Monetary policy could return the price level to its previous value. Monetary policy could turn the event into a one-time price level shock, with no further inflation. Or monetary policy could let the inflation continue for a while, as it does here with $\theta > 0$. When we add long-term debt and sticky prices, these future responses will have additional effects on the instantaneous inflation response $\Delta E_1 \pi_1$. Monetary policy matters a lot in this fiscal model, to the dynamic path of expected inflation after the shock.

These responses are still not realistic. The important lesson here is that we *can* use fiscal and monetary policy rules that react to endogenous variables, and we can produce impulse-response functions including policy rules, just as we do with standard models of interest rate targets.

We also learn that monetary policy rules are an important source of dynamics. Impulse-response functions do not just measure the economy's response to shocks. Policy rules are particularly useful for defining interesting conceptual experiments: What if there is a fiscal shock, and the Fed responds by raising interest rates in response to any subsequent inflation? A drawn-out inflation results.

2.7   Fiscal Policy and Debt

A rise in debt that is accompanied by larger future surpluses raises revenue that can fund a deficit or lower inflation. Normal fiscal policy consists of deficits, funded by increased debt that corresponds to higher subsequent surpluses. The value of debt measures how much expected surpluses have risen.

Monetary policy as I have defined it here consists of changing debt B_t, without changing surpluses. Fiscal policy may change debt B_t while also changing surpluses.

To gain a picture of fiscal policy operations in this intertemporal context, write the debt valuation equation (2.15)

$$\frac{B_{t-1}}{P_t} = s_t + \frac{1}{1+i_t}\frac{B_t}{P_t} = s_t + E_t \sum_{j=1}^{\infty} \beta^j s_{t+j}. \tag{2.26}$$

and take innovations,

$$\frac{B_{t-1}}{P_{t-1}}\Delta E_t\left(\frac{P_{t-1}}{P_t}\right) = \Delta E_t\left(s_t + \frac{1}{1+i_t}\frac{B_t}{P_t}\right) = \Delta E_t\left(s_t + E_t\sum_{j=1}^{\infty}\beta^j s_{t+j}\right). \tag{2.27}$$

Suppose that the government raises debt B_t and raises expected subsequent surpluses. The real value of debt $1/(1+i_t)B_t/P_t = E_t\sum_{j=1}^{\infty}\beta^j s_{t+j}$ rises. The bond sale soaks up extra money. This extra money can finance a deficit, a lower s_t, with no unexpected inflation.

As in the two-period model, this "fiscal policy" increase in debt B_t *with* higher expected subsequent surpluses is like an equity issue, as contrasted with the "monetary policy" increase in debt without higher expected surpluses, which acts like a share split. In the intertemporal context, the analogy to stock pricing is clearer, and we see that the corresponding surpluses can be long delayed.

This bond sale can generate a disinflation, $\Delta E_t(P_{t-1}/P_t) > 0$ rather than fund a deficit. Inflations are often successfully fought by getting the fiscal house in order. But it does not matter whether the government produces a *current* surplus s_t, or even an immediate future surplus s_{t+1}. What matters is generating a long-lasting credible stream of surpluses $\{s_{t+j}\}$. Doing so often requires an institutional reform; solving the underlying structural problem causing deficits, rather than just acts of today's politicians. Such a credible fiscal reform can coexist with ongoing or even larger short-term deficits, yet produce a disinflation.

The case that future surpluses just balance the current deficit, so there is no unexpected inflation, $\Delta E_t(P_{t-1}/P_t) = 0$, is particularly important. To generate this case, the change in future surpluses balances the near-term deficits, so there is no innovation to the present value $\Delta E_t \sum_{j=0}^{\infty} \beta^j s_{t+j} = 0$. To generate such a pattern, the surplus process must have an s-shaped moving average; that is, one which changes sign.

If we think of responsible governments in "normal times" adapting to fiscal needs without state-contingent devaluations via inflation, and instead maintaining a steady price level, this is "normal" fiscal policy.

- *Normal fiscal policy consists of debt sales that finance current deficits. Such sales promise higher future surpluses, and do not change interest rates or the price level.*

In our intertemporal context, the higher surpluses may be delayed, and may last decades, rather than showing up immediately in s_1.

Equation (2.27) offers a breakdown of how a deficit $\Delta E_t s_t < 0$ may be financed in this intertemporal context. The government may borrow, promising future surpluses, with no inflation. The government may inflate, with no change in future surpluses, in which case the value of debt does not rise despite the deficit. And if the surplus follows an AR(1) $s_t = \eta s_{t-1} + \varepsilon_{s,t}$ or similar process, in which the deficit is followed by additional deficits, then unexpected inflation is larger than the deficit shock, $\Delta E_t (P_{t-1}/P_t) = \Delta E_t \sum_{j=0}^{\infty} \beta^j s_{t+j} = 1/(1 - \beta\eta)\varepsilon_{s,t}$. The AR(1) generates a value of debt $\Delta E_t \sum_{j=1}^{\infty} \beta^j s_{t+j} = \beta\eta/(1 - \beta\eta)\varepsilon_{s,t}$ that goes *down* when there is a deficit $\varepsilon_{s,t} < 0$.

In the postwar data for the United States and other advanced countries, the value of debt increases with deficits and falls with surpluses, debt sales raise revenue, and surprise inflation is small relative to surplus and deficit shocks. The borrowing mechanism predominates, and the AR(1) is particularly bad model.

The second terms of (2.26) and (2.27), $1/(1 + i_t)B_t/P_t = E_t \sum_{j=1}^{\infty} \beta^j s_{t+j}$ make an important point: The revenue raised from bond sales is a direct measure of how much bond investors believe future surpluses will rise to pay off the debt. Survey expectations, CBO projections, regression forecasts, and economists' intuitions about future surpluses, including my own, may doubt that surpluses are coming. The investors who are buying bonds have more faith, and measurably believe that each increase in debt corresponds to an increase in eventual surpluses.

The fact that we can *observe* market expectations of future surpluses by observing changes in the value of debt is often overlooked. In the discussion of fiscal stimulus, one faces the baseline prediction of Ricardian equivalence: When the government runs deficits, people anticipate future taxes to pay back the debt, and so fiscal stimulus has no effect (Barro (1974)). The counterargument is that people ignore future taxes. The value of debt allows us to *measure* changes in expectations of future surpluses and resolve this controversy. If a deficit raises the value of debt, then at least the people who hold the debt expect higher taxes or lower spending. If the value of debt does not rise, the deficit stimulates. With no price stickiness, here, the deficit results instantly in inflation. In fact, deficits clearly raise the value of debt, and surpluses lower the value of debt in U.S. time series. Now, the Ricardian case is not completely closed: One could argue that households ignore the surpluses that bond markets foresee. And discount rates may also change, affecting the value of debt. But measurement of the amount by which the value of debt rises as a result of a deficit is a powerful tool for addressing the Ricardian debate.

2.8   The Central Bank and the Treasury

The institutional division that the treasury conducts fiscal policy and the central bank conducts monetary policy works like the institutional division between share splits and secondary offerings. Treasury issues come with promises of subsequent surpluses. Central bank open-market operations do not.

To create a fiscal inflation, the treasury must persuade people that increased debt will not be paid back by higher future surpluses. That has proved difficult to accomplish. It is more difficult still to accomplish while preserving a reputation that allows later borrowing.

The "monetary policy" debt sale and the "fiscal policy" debt sale of the last section look disturbingly similar. The visible government action in each case is identical: The government as a whole sells more debt. One debt sale engenders expectations that future surpluses will not change. That sale changes interest rates and expected inflation, and raises no revenue. The other debt sale engenders expectations that future surpluses will rise to pay off the larger debt. That sale raises revenue with no change in interest rates or prices. How does the government achieve these miracles of expectations management?

Answering this question is important to solidify our understanding of the simple frictionless model as a sensible abstraction of current institutions. It also stresses the importance of monetary *institutions*. A government, like any asset issuer, must form people's expectations about how it will behave in distant, state-contingent, and infrequently or even never-observed circumstances. Monetary and fiscal institutions serve the role of communicating plans and committing government to those plans.

Stock splits and equity issues also look disturbingly similar. The visible corporate action in each case is identical: More shares are outstanding. A split engenders expectations that overall dividends will not change, so a 2:1 split cuts the stock price per share in half. A share issue engenders expectations that total dividends will rise, so the price per share is unaffected and the company gets new funds for investment. (Yes, a long litera-ture in finance studies small price effects of splits and offerings, as these corporate actions may reveal information about the company. Such wrinkles operate on top of the clear first-order effect.)

Companies achieve this miracle of expectations management by issuing shares in care-fully differentiated institutional settings, along with specific announcements, disclosures, and legal environments that commit them to different paths. Companies do not just increase shares and let investors puzzle out their own expectations.

This parallel helps us to understand the institutional separation between central banks and treasuries. The Treasury conducts "fiscal policy" debt sales. Before the 1940s, many U.S. federal debt issues were passed by Congress for specific and transitory purposes, and backed by specific tax streams (see Hall and Sargent (2018)). That legal structure is an obvious aid to assuring repayment; that is, to promising higher future surpluses. Many state and municipal bonds continue these practices: They issue bonds to finance a toll bridge, say, and promise that the tolls will repay the bonds. The gold standard also gave a promise to repay rather than inflate. That commitment was not ironclad as govern-ments could and did suspend convertibility or devalue, but it was helpful. U.S. federal debt now has no explicit promises, but the Treasury and Congress have earned a repu-tation for largely paying back debts incurred by Treasury issues, going back to Alexander Hamilton's famous assumption of Revolutionary War debt, and lasting at least through the surpluses of the late 1990s. Large debts, produced by borrowing, produce political pres-sure to raise taxes or cut spending to pay off the debts, part of Hamilton's point, rather than default explicitly or routinely devalue via inflation. The implicit promise to repay debt has not always been ironclad, and one can read it to include escape clauses, state-contingent defaults in certain emergencies. But it has helped.

Hall and Sargent (2014) note a less celebrated fact: Following Hamilton's plan, the U.S. government did not repay colonial *currency*, which largely inflated away. The experi-ence emphasizes different promises implicit in currency versus debt, which we may trace to central banks versus Treasuries today. Devaluation of paper currency by inflation did not have the same reputational cost as default on the debt would have had. The U.S. gov-ernment did default on a large part of its Revolutionary War debt, via inflation, but still acquired a reputation that allowed it to borrow when it later needed to do so.

The idea that Treasury debt sales raise revenue rather than just raise nominal interest rates and expected inflation is now so ingrained, that the possibility of a share-split-like outcome may seem weird. Outside of a currency reform, who even imagines an increase in Treasury debt that does not raise revenue, and instead just pushes up nominal inter-est rates? The requirement that the debt sale engender expectations of higher subsequent surpluses is less well recognized, but the outcome requires that expectation (absent con-current changes in real interest rates). Other governments are not so lucky, and they have lost investors' confidence and a reputation for repayment. Their debt issues fail or just push up interest rates. You can only signal so much, and reputations are finite.

"Monetary policy" is conducted by a different *institution*. Central banks are, to a first approximation, legally *forbidden* from fiscal policies. They cannot alter tax rates or expen-ditures directly. At most, central bankers can give speeches advocating fiscal stimulus or fiscal responsibility, though even these are often seen as exceeding their mandates.

Though central banks are mandated to control inflation, central banks are legally forbidden from "helicopter drops," perhaps the most effective means of inflating. Central banks cannot send cash or write checks to people or businesses. They must always buy something in return for issuing cash or reserves; or lend, counting the promise to repay as an asset. Central banks doubly cannot conduct a helicopter vacuuming, confiscating money from people and businesses without issuing a corresponding asset, though that would surely be an effective way to stop inflation! Only the Treasury may write checks to voters or confiscate their money, and for many good political as well as economic reasons. Independence, in a democracy, must come with limited authority. Central banks are limited in the securities they may buy, typically government securities, high-quality fixed income securities, or securities with government guarantees, to avoid central banks holding risk that eventually floats back to the Treasury. Federal Reserve asset purchases and lending in the financial and COVID-19 crises were largely conducted by lending to special purpose vehicles, in which the Treasury took an equity and risk-absorbing share.

The separation between fiscal and monetary policy is not perfect. In the presence of non-interest-paying currency, inflation produces seigniorage revenue, which the central bank remits to the Treasury. We will model this interaction. Liquidity spreads on government debt offer similar opportunities. Some central bank profits from crisis lending likewise flowed to the Treasury, as the losses would have done had asset prices not recovered.

Central bank actions have many *indirect* fiscal implications, which will be a central modeling concern. Inflation raises surpluses through an imperfectly indexed tax code. Monetary policy affects output and employment, with large budgetary consequences. With sticky prices and short-term debt, interest rate rises also raise the Treasury's real interest expense. Many central banks are charged to keep government interest expense low, as was the U.S. Fed through WWII and into the 1950s. With debt-to-GDP ratios now over 100%, interest expense will certainly weigh on the Fed should it need to raise rates in the future. We can and will model many of these indirect fiscal effects.

Still, a central bank open-market operation is a clearly distinct action from a Treasury issue, though in both cases the government as a whole exchanges money (reserves) for government debt. Treasury issues typically fund deficits, raise revenue, and are therefore expected to be repaid from subsequent surpluses. Open-market operations do not fund deficits or raise revenue. The restriction against central bank fiscal policy is closer to holding than not.

Our legal and institutional structures have many additional provisions against inflationary finance, adding to the separation between treasuries and central banks, and helping to guide expectations. The Treasury cannot sell bonds directly to the Fed. The Fed must buy any Treasury bonds on the open market, ensuring some price transparency and reducing the temptation to inflationary finance. The legal separation and tradition of central bank independence adds precommitments against inflationary finance. These limitations make sense if people regard central bank debt sales as inflationary.

In sum, the separation between Treasury and central bank is useful. One institution sells debt that raises revenue, implicitly promising future surpluses, and does not affect interest rates and inflation. A distinct institution sells debt without raising revenue, without changing expected surpluses, and in order to affect interest rates and inflation. This separation mirrors the different institutional structures for equity offerings versus share splits.

There are many additional reasons for the institutional separation of the Treasury and Congress from a central bank, and strong limitations on central bank actions, including a force against loose monetary policy around every election, and a force to limit central banks from subsidizing credit or directing bank credit to businesses or constituencies that central bankers or politicians may favor.

However, these observations should not stop us from institutional innovation. A government under fiscal theory that wishes to stabilize the price level faces a central problem: If we just think of surpluses as an exogenous stochastic process, as we often model corporate dividends, then the price level as present value of those surpluses is likely to be quite volatile, like that of stocks. The government would like to offer some commitments: that the present value of surpluses will not change much, that deficits will be repaid by surpluses rather than cause inflation, and that surpluses will just pay down debt rather than cause deflation. The separation between Treasury and central bank helps to make and communicate such a commitment. But the current structure evolved by trial and error, and it certainly was not designed with this understanding in mind.

To stabilize the price level, how can the government minimize variation in the present value of surpluses, and commit to those surpluses? When the government wishes to inflate or to stop deflation, how can it better commit *not* to repay debts, but in a defined amount, and preserving its reputation for future borrowing?

Our institutions evolved in response to centuries of experience with the need to fight inflation, to commit *to* back debt issues with surpluses. Fighting deflation or persistent below-target inflation became a central policy concern in the 2010s. Fighting deflation, modifying institutions to commit *not to* back some debt issues, but in a limited and defined amount, is new territory.

Our institutional structures also did not evolve to mitigate a potential sovereign debt crisis, which large short-maturity debts and unfunded promises leave as an enduring possibility. The Euro debt crisis could be the first example of others to come.

Can we construct something better than implicit, reputation-based Treasury commitments, along with implicit, state-contingent defaults, devaluation via inflation? Can we construct something better than nominal interest rate targets following something like a Taylor rule? We'll come back to think about these issues. For now, the point is merely to make my parable about debts with and without future surplus expectations come alive.

2.9   The Flat Supply Curve

In our simple model, the government fixes interest rates and offers nominal debt in a flat supply curve. In reality, the Treasury auctions a fixed quantity of debt, which seems to contradict this assumption. But the Treasury sets the quantity of debt *after* seeing the interest rate, raising the quantity of debt if the bond price is lower. The Treasury and central bank acting together generate a flat supply curve.

The above description of monetary policy, in which a government sets interest rates by offering any amount of debt B_t at a fixed interest rate i_t, while holding surpluses constant,

seems unrealistic. The U.S. Treasury and most other Treasuries auction a fixed quantity of debt. However, on closer look, the horizontal supply mechanism can be read as
a model of our central banks and Treasuries operating together, taken to the frictionless
limit.

The Fed currently sets the short-term rate by setting the interest rate it pays to banks on
reserves. It also sets the discount rate at which banks may borrow reserves, and the rates it
offers on repo and reverse repo transactions for non-bank financial institutions. Reserves
are just overnight, floating-rate government debt. Central banks allow free conversion of
cash to interest-paying reserves. Thus, paying interest on reserves and allowing free conversion to cash really is already a fixed interest rate and a horizontal supply of overnight
debt. In reality, people still also hold cash overnight, but that makes little difference to the
model, as we will shortly see by adding such cash.

Historically, the Federal Reserve controlled interest rates by open-market operations
rather than by paying interest on reserves. The Fed rationed non-interest-bearing reserves,
affecting i via M in $MV(i) = Py$. But the Fed reset the quantity limit daily, forecasting daily
demand for reserves that would result in the interest rate hitting the target. So on a horizon
longer than a day, reserve supply was flat at the interest rate target.

One could stop here, and declare that Treasury auctions involve longer maturity debt,
which we have not yet included. But there is another answer, which remains valid with
longer maturities: If the central bank sets the interest rate, and the Treasury then auctions
a fixed quantity of debt, the central bank and Treasury together produce a flat supply curve
for that debt.

The central bank sets the interest rate, by setting interest on reserves. The Treasury
decides how many bonds B_t to sell *after* it observes the interest rate and bond price. Given
the bond price Q_t, the flow condition (2.15),

$$\frac{B_{t-1}}{P_t} = s_t + Q_t\frac{B_t}{P_t},$$

(2.28)

then describes how much nominal debt B_t the Treasury must sell to roll over debt and to
finance the surplus or deficit s_t. It describes the process that the Treasury accountants go
through to figure out how much face value of debt B_t to auction. If the central bank raises
interest rates one percentage point, the Treasury sees 1% lower bond prices. The Treasury
then raises the face value of debt it sells by 1% to obtain the same revenue. In this two-step
process, the central bank plus Treasury thus really do sell any quantity of debt at the fixed
interest rate, though neither Treasury nor central bank may be aware of that fact.

Treasury auctions do change interest rates by a few basis points, because the Treasury
auctions longer-term bonds and there are small financial frictions separating reserves from
Treasury bonds. But if the resulting bond price is unexpectedly low, and revenue unexpectedly low, the Treasury must still fund the deficit s_t. The Treasury goes back to the
market and sells some more debt. In the end only the small spread between short-term
Treasury and bank rates can change as the result of Treasury auctions, and that spread
disappears in our model with no financial frictions.

It is a bit of a puzzle that the central bank can set market interest rates by setting interest
on reserves, while also limiting the supply of reserves. It can. If the central bank offers

more interest on reserves, competitive banks will offer more interest on deposits to try to attract depositors from each other, and they will require higher interest rates on loans to try to divert investments to reserves. That they cannot do so in aggregate does not mean that they do not try individually, so the higher interest on reserves leaks out to market prices. Banks aren't that competitive, so in reality the process may be slow. Offering an unlimited supply curve, open to nonbank financial institutions, may be more effective. But the theoretical possibility is valid. Cochrane (2014b) offers a more extended analysis on these points.

When the Fed wishes to lower interest rates, it may have to spruce up the discount window, to allow freer borrowing at a lower rate than the market wishes. Just why the Fed keeps a relatively large band between its borrowing and lending rates, discourages borrowing, and pays different rates to different borrowers—a lower rate on repos from money market funds than it pays to banks on reserves—is all a bit of a puzzle from a monetary policy point of view.

Just *how* the central bank sets the short-term interest rate is important, and usually swept under the rug. Most papers do not mention the question. Woodford (2003) invokes a cashless limit: The Fed manipulates a vanishingly small quantity of money, which via $MV(i) = Py$ sets the nominal interest rate. This proposal undercuts the idea that the interest rate target alone is a full theory of the price level, though Woodford is not as concerned with that purity as I am here.

Woodford wrote before 2008, when the U.S. Fed began paying interest on reserves. The New York Fed did actually each morning try to guess the quantity of reserves for that day that would lead to an equilibrium federal funds rate equal to the Fed's target. Reserves were small, on the order of $10 billion. (Hamilton (1996) is an excellent description of the procedure and its flaws.) The financial and banking system did plausibly approximate Woodford's cashless limit. However, most other countries had already moved to a corridor system, lending freely at the interest rate target plus a small spread, and borrowing freely at that target minus a small spread. After 2008, the United States moved to immense reserves, in the trillions of dollars, which are only adjusted slowly, and pay essentially the same interest rates as those on other short-term government debt. So the standard new-Keynesian tradition is missing a story roughly conformable to current institutions on just how the central bank sets the nominal interest rate. The analysis of this section might be adapted to new-Keynesian models, if anybody cares to do so.

2.10   Fiscal Stimulus

A deliberate fiscal loosening creates inflation in the fiscal theory. However, to create inflation one must convince people that future surpluses will be lower. Current deficits per se matter little. The U.S. and Japanese fiscal stimulus programs contained if anything the opposite promises, and did not overcome their long traditions of debt repayment.

In the great recession following 2008, many countries turned to fiscal stimulus, in part as a deliberate attempt to create inflation. Japan tried these policies earlier. This simple fiscal theory can offer perspectives on this attempt.

There are two ways to think of fiscal inflation, or "unbacked fiscal expansion," in our framework. First, equation (2.13),

$$\frac{B_{t-1}}{P_{t-1}} \Delta E_t \left(\frac{P_{t-1}}{P_t} \right) = \Delta E_t \sum_{j=0}^{\infty} \beta^j s_{t+j},$$

describes how lower surpluses can create immediate unexpected inflation. Second, we might think of fiscal stimulus as an increase in nominal debt B_t that does not correspond to future surpluses, designed to raise nominal interest rates and, in equilibrium, to raise expected future inflation,

$$\beta \frac{B_t}{P_t} E_t \left(\frac{P_t}{P_{t+1}} \right) = \frac{1}{1+i_t} \frac{B_t}{P_t} = E_t \sum_{j=1}^{\infty} \beta^j s_{t+j}.$$

Now, the point of stimulus is to raise output. To see that, we need a model in which inflation raises output. Such models distinguish expected and unexpected inflation, and the time path of expected inflation. For now let's just ask how the government might create inflation, either expected or unexpected.

Both equations point to the vital importance of *future* deficits in creating inflation via fiscal stimulus. Current debt and deficits matched by future surpluses won't create any inflation.

The U.S. fiscal stimulus of the 2008 recession and following years of deficits, and the long-standing Japanese fiscal stimulus programs that added more than 100% of GDP to its debt, failed at the goal of increasing inflation. This observation suggests an explanation. The U.S. administration promised debt reduction to follow once the recession was over; that is, that the new debt would be paid back. That is what a Treasury does that wants to finance current expenditure *without* creating current or expected future inflation. To create inflation, the key is to promise that future surpluses will *not* follow current debts. Even in a traditional Keynesian multiplier framework, which is how the U.S. administration analyzed its stimulus, one wishes people to ignore future surpluses in order to break Ricardian equivalence. One wishes that people do not see future taxes to pay off the debt and do not save more to pay those taxes. Calling attention to the future surpluses is counterproductive. Japan was similarly criticized for never being clear that it would not repay debt, instead raising taxes on several occasions to signal the opposite.

The debt issues of fiscal stimulus did not raise interest rates, did raise revenue, and did raise the total market value of debt. These facts speak directly to investors' expectations that subsequent surpluses would rise, or at least that real discount rates fell. From the perspective of this simple model, such conventional fiscal stimulus—borrow money, don't drive up interest rates, spend the money, repay the debt—has no effect at all on current, unexpected, or expected future inflation. It is simply a rearrangement of the path of surpluses: less now and more later.

Even if the U.S. administration had tried to say that the debt would not be paid back, reputations and institutional constraints on inflationary finance are often hard to break. Once people are accustomed to the reputation that Treasury issues, used to finance current deficits, will be paid back in the future by higher surpluses, and the idea that the central bank is fully in charge of inflation, it is hard to break that expectation. Institutions, especially regarding debt repayment, long outlast politicians and their promises. That is the point of institutions.

The expectations involved in a small inflation are harder yet to create. A government might be able to persuade bondholders that a fiscal collapse is on its way, debt will not be repaid, and create a hyperinflation. But how do you persuade bondholders that the government will devalue debt by 2%, and only by 2%? If you can do that, how do you later convince them that new debts, when the government wishes to raise revenue, will be fully repaid? A partial and temporary unbacked fiscal expansion is tricky to communicate on the fly. It needs institutional commitment, not ephemeral promises by the political leaders of a moment. We will see some ideas later.

The $5 trillion fiscal expansion in 2020–2021 did result in substantial inflation. Chapter 21 covers this episode and explores how it is different from the 2008–2020 efforts at fiscal stimulus.

3

A Bit of Generality

THE THEORY developed so far is simple, and I hope clear, but it is unrealistic in many ways. By generalizing the environment in natural directions, this chapter brings in interesting effects that pave the road to a realistic theory. There can be long drawn-out inflation responses to fiscal shock, not just price level jumps. Inflation may initially decline after an unexpected interest rate increase. A rise in the discount rate can lower the present value of debt and thereby induce inflation.

To see these effects, I add natural generalizations of the fiscal theory valuation formula: I add risk and risk aversion in place of the constant discount rate, I add long-term debt, and I express the model in continuous time. I also express the model in terms of debt-to-GDP and surplus-to-GDP ratios, which is useful for analyzing time series data. I extend the theory to include non-interest-bearing money and seigniorage, vital for many theoretical and empirical questions. I pursue a linearization, parallel to present value linearizations in asset pricing, which allows us to use VAR tools for empirical analysis and linearized solution methods for more complex models, including models with price stickiness.

These are useful formulas for applications, they highlight important and novel mechanisms, and show that the simplifications of the model so far are in fact just simplifications and not necessary assumptions.

3.1   Long-Term Debt

With long-term debt, the basic flow and present value relations become

$$B_{t-1}^{(t)} = P_t s_t + \sum_{j=1}^{\infty} Q_t^{(t+j)} \left(B_t^{(t+j)} - B_{t-1}^{(t+j)} \right)$$

and

$$\frac{\sum_{j=0}^{\infty} Q_t^{(t+j)} B_{t-1}^{(t+j)}}{P_t} = E_t \sum_{j=0}^{\infty} \beta^j s_{t+j}.$$

A fiscal shock may be met by lower bond prices instead of a higher price level, which implies future rather than current inflation. A rise in nominal interest rates with no change in surpluses, which lowers bond prices, can result in a lower price level.

Long-term debt adds much to the fiscal theory. As we move to higher-frequency observations and continuous time, more debt is effectively long-term debt, so its analytics become more important.

Denote by $B_{t-1}^{(t+j)}$ the quantity of nominal zero coupon bonds, outstanding at the end of period $t-1$, that come due at time $t+j$. $B_{t-1}^{(t)}$ are the one-period bonds coming due at t that we have studied so far. Denote by $Q_t^{(t+j)}$ the price at time t of bonds coming due at time $t+j$. Continuing the constant real interest rate frictionless case with $R = \beta^{-1}$, bond prices are

$$Q_t^{(t+j)} = E_t \left(\beta^j \frac{P_t}{P_{t+j}} \right). \tag{3.1}$$

The flow condition now includes sales or repurchases of longer-maturity bonds,

$$B_{t-1}^{(t)} = P_t s_t + \sum_{j=1}^{\infty} Q_t^{(t+j)} \left(B_t^{(t+j)} - B_{t-1}^{(t+j)} \right). \tag{3.2}$$

Money created to redeem maturing bonds is soaked up by primary surpluses, or by debt sales, including sales of long-term debt, which may be incremental sales.

The present value condition now reads

$$\frac{\sum_{j=0}^{\infty} Q_t^{(t+j)} B_{t-1}^{(t+j)}}{P_t} = E_t \sum_{j=0}^{\infty} \beta^j s_{t+j}. \tag{3.3}$$

The real *market value* of nominal debt equals the present value of real primary surpluses.

We can derive (3.3) from (3.2) by iterating forward and applying the condition that the real value of debt not grow faster than the interest rate, as before. We can derive (3.2) from (3.3) by considering its value at two adjacent dates.

The present value condition (3.3) now allows a fiscal shock to be met by a decline in nominal bond prices $Q_t^{(t+j)}$ rather than a rise in the price level P_t. However, the bond pricing formula (3.1) tells us that this event means future inflation rather than current inflation. With one-period debt, expected future inflation did nothing in the valuation equation. Now, expected future inflation devalues long-term bonds as they come due. A fiscal shock may be met by such expected future inflation, and thus by a drawn-out inflation. Equation (3.3) essentially marks that future inflation to market via bond prices.

Long-term debt allows an unexpectedly higher interest rate with no change in surpluses to temporarily lower inflation: A shock that persistently raises nominal interest rates lowers bond prices $Q_t^{(t+j)}$ and thus the numerator on the left-hand side of (3.3). If surpluses do not change, the price level must also fall.

3.2   Ratios to GDP and a Focus on Inflation

In terms of ratios to GDP, the basic valuation equation reads

$$\frac{B_{t-1}}{P_t y_t} = E_t \sum_{j=0}^{\infty} \beta^j \frac{y_{t+j}}{y_t} \frac{s_{t+j}}{y_{t+j}}.$$

We can focus on inflation, rather than the value of all government debt, with

$$\frac{1}{P_t} = E_t \sum_{j=0}^{\infty} \beta^j \frac{s_{t+j}}{B_{t-1}}$$

or

$$\frac{1}{P_t} = E_t \sum_{j=0}^{\infty} \beta^j \left(\frac{y_{t+j}}{y_t}\right) \left(\frac{s_{t+j}}{y_{t+j}}\right) / \left(\frac{B_{t-1}}{y_t}\right).$$

Debt, spending, and taxes scale with GDP over time and across countries, so ratios to GDP, consumption, or some other common trend are useful ways to try to produce stationary variables for statistical analysis. We can easily express the basic present value and flow equations in terms of ratios to GDP by multiplying and dividing by real GDP y_t. Then we can write the government debt valuation equation to state that the debt-to-GDP ratio is equal to the present value of surplus-to-GDP ratios, with an adjustment for GDP growth:

$$\frac{B_{t-1}}{P_t y_t} = E_t \sum_{j=0}^{\infty} \beta^j \left(\frac{y_{t+j}}{y_t}\right) \left(\frac{s_{t+j}}{y_{t+j}}\right).$$

More growth means greater surpluses, with the same surplus-to-GDP ratio.

This expression, like the basic valuation equation, expresses the value of all government debt. In the end, we are really interested in the price level, or the value of a single dollar. We can focus on that issue with

$$\frac{1}{P_t} = E_t \sum_{j=0}^{\infty} \beta^j \frac{s_{t+j}}{B_{t-1}}. \tag{3.4}$$

Here, the value of a dollar today depends on future surpluses divided by *today's* debt. Initially, one expects future surpluses to be divided by future debts. However, in valuing today's debt, people must expect that any additional unexpected future deficits will be met by additional unexpected surpluses in the further future. There can be no expected shocks to the present value of surpluses, $E_t (E_{t+1} - E_t) \sum_{j=0}^{\infty} \beta^j s_{t+j} = 0$. So, today's expected surpluses are, on net, only those that pay off today's debts, though there will be additional future deficits and surpluses.

Merging the two ideas, we can write an equation for the price level that recognizes stationary ratios to GDP as

$$\frac{1}{P_t} = E_t \sum_{j=0}^{\infty} \beta^j \left(\frac{y_{t+j}}{y_t}\right) \left(\frac{s_{t+j}}{y_{t+j}}\right) / \left(\frac{B_{t-1}}{y_t}\right).$$

3.3   Risk and Discounting

With a general stochastic discount factor Λ_t, e.g. $\Lambda_t = \beta^t u'(c_t)$, we have

$$\frac{B_{t-1}}{P_t} = E_t \sum_{j=0}^{\infty} \frac{\Lambda_{t+j}}{\Lambda_t} s_{t+j}.$$

We can also discount using the ex post real return to holding government bonds,

$$\frac{B_{t-1}}{P_t} = \sum_{j=0}^{\infty} \left(\prod_{k=1}^{j} \frac{1}{R_{t+k}} \right) s_{t+j}$$

where

$$R_{t+1} = \frac{1}{Q_t} \frac{P_t}{P_{t+1}} = (1 + i_t) \frac{P_t}{P_{t+1}}$$

in this case of one-period debt.

To introduce risk, let the endowment y_t vary, and let

$$\frac{\Lambda_{t+1}}{\Lambda_t} = \beta \frac{u'(c_{t+1})}{u'(c_t)}$$

denote the stochastic discount factor. Then the bond price is

$$Q_t = E_t \left(\frac{\Lambda_{t+1}}{\Lambda_t} \frac{P_t}{P_{t+1}} \right)$$

and the flow condition (2.5) becomes

$$\frac{B_{t-1}}{P_t} = s_t + E_t \left(\frac{\Lambda_{t+1}}{\Lambda_t} \frac{P_t}{P_{t+1}} \right) \frac{B_t}{P_t}.$$

Iterating forward, and applying the transversality condition, which now reads

$$\lim_{T \to \infty} E_t \left(\frac{\Lambda_T}{\Lambda_t} \frac{B_{T-1}}{P_T} \right) = 0,$$

we obtain the standard stochastically-discounted valuation formula:

$$\frac{B_{t-1}}{P_t} = E_t \sum_{j=0}^{\infty} \frac{\Lambda_{t+j}}{\Lambda_t} s_{t+j}. \tag{3.5}$$

It is often useful to discount using the ex post return on government debt, to use a stochastic discount factor $\Lambda_{t+1}/\Lambda_t = 1/R_{t+1}$. Since $1 = R_{t+1}^{-1} R_{t+1} = E_t(R_{t+1}^{-1} R_{t+1})$, the inverse return is a one-period ex post and ex ante discount factor, using any set of probabilities. This fact is useful empirically when one does not wish to specify a model such as a utility function connecting the discount factor to other economic quantities, but instead one wishes to think about present values in terms of empirical models of expected returns.

To express the fiscal theory with the inverse government bond portfolio return as discount factor, write the one-period flow relation as

$$\frac{B_{t-1}}{P_t} = s_t + \frac{Q_t B_t}{P_t} = s_t + \frac{Q_t P_{t+1}}{P_t} \frac{B_t}{P_{t+1}}.$$

Now,

$$R_{t+1} = \frac{1}{Q_t} \frac{P_t}{P_{t+1}} = (1 + i_t) \frac{P_t}{P_{t+1}}$$

is the ex post real return on debt. Thus, we can write the flow condition

$$\frac{B_{t-1}}{P_t} = s_t + \frac{1}{R_{t+1}} \frac{B_t}{P_{t+1}}$$

and iterate forward,

$$\frac{B_{t-1}}{P_t} = \sum_{j=0}^{\infty} \left(\prod_{k=1}^{j} \frac{1}{R_{t+k}} \right) s_{t+j} + \lim_{T \to \infty} \left(\prod_{k=1}^{T} \frac{1}{R_{t+k}} \right) \frac{B_{t+T-1}}{P_{t+T}}. \tag{3.6}$$

This equation holds ex post, so it also holds ex ante. We can take expectations of both sides. If the expected value of the final term goes to zero and the sum converges, we then have a convenient present value relation using ex post returns,

$$\frac{B_{t-1}}{P_t} = E_t \sum_{j=0}^{\infty} \left(\prod_{k=1}^{j} \frac{1}{R_{t+k}} \right) s_{t+j}.$$

The expectation can refer to any set of probabilities, including sample frequencies. The formula is really just a rearrangement of the definition of return.

That the terms of (3.6) converge is a separate condition. It is possible that the present value is well defined using marginal utility or the discount factor as in (3.5), but the present value and terminal condition using ex post returns (3.6) explode.

The same principles hold with long-term debt. We just get bigger formulas. We discount using the ex post return on the entire portfolio of debt,

$$R_{t+1} = \frac{\sum_{j=0}^{\infty} Q_{t+1}^{(t+1+j)} B_t^{(t+1+j)}}{\sum_{j=0}^{\infty} Q_t^{(t+1+j)} B_t^{(t+1+j)}} \frac{P_t}{P_{t+1}}. \tag{3.7}$$

This return reflects how the change in bond prices from Q_t to Q_{t+1} affects the market value of debt outstanding at the end of time t. Then the flow identity is

$$\frac{\sum_{j=0}^{\infty} Q_t^{(t+j)} B_{t-1}^{(t+j)}}{P_t} = s_t + \frac{1}{R_{t+1}} \frac{\sum_{j=0}^{\infty} Q_{t+1}^{(t+1+j)} B_t^{(t+1+j)}}{P_{t+1}}. \tag{3.8}$$

We iterate again to

$$\frac{\sum_{j=0}^{\infty} Q_t^{(t+j)} B_{t-1}^{(t+j)}}{P_t} = \sum_{j=0}^{\infty} \left(\prod_{k=1}^{j} \frac{1}{R_{t+k}} \right) s_{t+j}$$

using now the definition (3.7) for the real bond portfolio return R_{t+1}.

3.4 Money

When people hold non-interest-bearing money, the government debt valuation equation generalizes to

$$\frac{B_{t-1} + M_{t-1}}{P_t} = E_t \sum_{j=0}^{\infty} \beta^j \left(s_{t+j} + \frac{i_{t+j}}{1 + i_{t+j}} \frac{M_{t+j}}{P_{t+j}} \right)$$

or

$$\frac{B_{t-1}}{P_t} = E_t \sum_{j=0}^{\infty} \beta^j \left(s_{t+j} + \frac{\Delta M_{t+j}}{P_{t+j}} \right).$$

These equivalent expressions account for seigniorage revenue in two ways.

At the zero bound, $i = 0$ or when money pays full interest $i = i^m$, money and bonds become perfect substitutes.

Seigniorage is small in most advanced economies. Seigniorage and interest costs invite us to think more seriously about what fiscal reactions occur in response to a monetary policy change.

With money demand, the central bank must passively accommodate the desired split of overall debt $B + M$ between B and M. Monetary policy consisting of the choice of $B + M$ or interest rate targets, remains and still controls expected inflation.

We can easily add cash or interest rate spreads between government bonds of varying liquidity. We no longer *have to* do so in order to determine the price level, but we can do so to recognize the presence of such assets and to investigate their impact.

Suppose that people hold cash overnight. The flow equilibrium condition becomes

$$B_{t-1} + M_{t-1} = P_t s_t + \frac{1}{1 + i_t} B_t + M_t. \tag{3.9}$$

M_t stands here for non-interest-bearing government money; that is, cash and reserves. Only direct government liabilities count in this M_t, not checking accounts or other inside money. M_t is held overnight from period t to period $t + 1$.

I iterate forward in two ways, yielding[1]

$$\frac{B_{t-1} + M_{t-1}}{P_t} = E_t \sum_{j=0}^{\infty} \frac{\Lambda_{t+j}}{\Lambda_t} \left(s_{t+j} + \frac{i_{t+j}}{1 + i_{t+j}} \frac{M_{t+j}}{P_{t+j}} \right) \tag{3.10}$$

and

$$\frac{B_{t-1}}{P_t} = E_t \sum_{j=0}^{\infty} \frac{\Lambda_{t+j}}{\Lambda_t} \left(s_{t+j} + \frac{\Delta M_{t+j}}{P_{t+j}} \right) \tag{3.11}$$

where $\Delta M_t \equiv M_t - M_{t-1}$. In the second term on the right-hand side of (3.10), we count seigniorage as an interest saving. Money is a form of government debt that pays a lower interest rate. That form also expresses the idea that money is valued as an asset that provides an unmeasured dividend of liquidity services, a "convenience yield." In (3.11), the government prints money to spend or transfer.

It is interesting to track the case that money pays interest, potentially lower than that of government bonds. Reserves currently pay interest, and some kinds of government debt are more liquid and pay lower interest than others. When money pays interest i^m, the flow condition becomes

$$B_{t-1} + M_{t-1} = P_t s_t + \frac{1}{1 + i_t} B_t + \frac{1}{1 + i_t^m} M_t.$$

Here I quote the interest on money M on a discount basis, paralleling bonds. It's more conventional to quote the interest the next day; that is, to write

$$B_{t-1}(1 + i_{t-1}) + M_{t-1}(1 + i_{t-1}^m) = P_t s_t + B_t + M_t,$$

but discount notation is easier for bonds, especially long-term bonds, and keeping the same notation for bonds and money is useful. Proceeding the same way, the present value

---

1. To derive (3.10), write the flow equation (3.9) as

$$\frac{B_{t-1} + M_{t-1}}{P_t} = s_t + \frac{1}{1 + i_t} \frac{B_t + M_t}{P_t} + \frac{i_t}{1 + i_t} \frac{M_t}{P_t}$$

$$\frac{B_{t-1} + M_{t-1}}{P_t} = s_t + E_t \left(\frac{\Lambda_{t+1}}{\Lambda_t} \frac{P_t}{P_{t+1}} \right) \frac{B_t + M_t}{P_t} + \frac{i_t}{1 + i_t} \frac{M_t}{P_t}$$

$$\frac{B_{t-1} + M_{t-1}}{P_t} = s_t + E_t \left(\frac{\Lambda_{t+1}}{\Lambda_t} \right) \frac{B_t + M_t}{P_{t+1}} + \frac{i_t}{1 + i_t} \frac{M_t}{P_t}$$

and iterate. To derive (3.11), write (3.9) as

$$\frac{B_{t-1}}{P_t} = s_t + E_t \left(\frac{\Lambda_{t+1}}{\Lambda_t} \frac{P_t}{P_{t+1}} \right) \frac{B_t}{P_t} + \frac{M_t - M_{t-1}}{P_t}$$

and iterate.

relation becomes[2]

$$\frac{B_{t-1} + M_{t-1}}{P_t} = E_t \sum_{j=0}^{\infty} \frac{\Lambda_{t+j}}{\Lambda_t} \left[s_{t+j} + \frac{i_{t+j} - i_{t+j}^m}{(1 + i_{t+j})(1 + i_{t+j}^m)} \frac{M_{t+j}}{P_{t+j}} \right] \qquad (3.12)$$

or[3]

$$\frac{B_{t-1}}{P_t} = E_t \sum_{j=0}^{\infty} \frac{\Lambda_{t+j}}{\Lambda_t} \left(s_{t+j} + \frac{\frac{1}{1 + i_{t+j}^m} M_{t+j} - M_{t+j-1}}{P_{t+j}} \right).$$

The formulas are prettier in continuous time, below.

We can discount at the ex post rate of return on government debt. Now that return is distorted downward by people's willingness to hold money at a low rate of return,

$$R_{t+1} = \frac{B_t + M_t}{Q_t B_t + M_t} \frac{P_t}{P_{t+1}}. \qquad (3.13)$$

Then,

$$\frac{B_{t-1} + M_{t-1}}{P_t} = s_t + \frac{Q_t B_t + M_t}{P_t} = s_t + \frac{1}{R_{t+1}} \frac{B_t + M_t}{P_{t+1}}. \qquad (3.14)$$

Iterating forward, we obtain the obvious formula, with this rate of return,

$$\frac{B_{t-1} + M_{t-1}}{P_t} = \sum_{j=0}^{\infty} \left(\prod_{k=1}^{j} \frac{1}{R_{t+k}} \right) s_{t+j}. \qquad (3.15)$$

---

2. The intermediate steps:

$$\frac{B_{t-1} + M_{t-1}}{P_t} = s_t + \frac{1}{1 + i_t} \frac{(B_t + M_t)}{P_t} + \left(\frac{1}{1 + i_t^m} - \frac{1}{1 + i_t} \right) \frac{M_t}{P_t}$$

$$\frac{B_{t-1} + M_{t-1}}{P_t} = s_t + E_t \left(\frac{\Lambda_{t+1}}{\Lambda_t} \frac{(B_t + M_t)}{P_{t+1}} \right) + \left(\frac{1}{1 + i_t^m} - \frac{1}{1 + i_t} \right) \frac{M_t}{P_t}.$$

3. The intermediate steps:

$$B_{t-1} = P_t s_t + \frac{1}{1 + i_t} B_t + \frac{1}{1 + i_t^m} M_t - M_{t-1}.$$

$$\frac{B_{t-1}}{P_t} = s_t + E_t \left(\frac{\Lambda_{t+1}}{\Lambda_t} \frac{B_t}{P_{t+1}} \right) + \frac{\frac{1}{1 + i_t^m} M_t - M_{t-1}}{P_t}.$$

3.4.1   The Zero Bound

If $Q_t = 1/(1 + i_t) = 1$ and the interest rate is zero, then money and bonds are perfect substitutes. Following (3.10), we still have

$$\frac{B_{t-1} + M_{t-1}}{P_t} = E_t \sum_{j=0}^{\infty} \beta^j s_{t+j} \tag{3.16}$$

so the price level is determined at the zero bound. Since the United States, Europe, and Japan spent so many years at the zero bound with little apparent unhinging of the price level, and since many alternative monetary theories predict instability or indeterminacy at the zero bound, this feature is a little feather in the fiscal cap.

The same result (3.16) holds when money pays full interest $i = i^m$. Again, money and bonds are perfect substitutes, and fiscal theory nonetheless delivers a determinate price level. The fiscal theory is in fact simplest and most transparent at the zero bound, or with full interest on money.

At the zero bound, or with money that pays the same interest as bonds, the story (Section 2.3) that the government will leave unwanted money outstanding, $M_t > 0$, if the price level is below equilibrium, no longer works. People are indifferent between money and bonds. The mechanism for equilibrium formation then relies only on a restoration of the intertemporal allocation of consumption or its overall level, the wealth effect of government bonds and money together, or other stories.

3.4.2   Money, Seigniorage, and Fiscal Theory

The valuation equations with money, equations (3.10) and (3.11), seem to offer an interesting opportunity for fiscal–monetary interactions. By exchanging bonds for money in open-market operations, the central bank affects seigniorage and thereby fiscal surpluses and the price level. Likewise, higher nominal interest rates can provoke seigniorage revenue, which can drive down the price level when the higher interest rates are announced. As always, however, the effect of monetary policy depends on fiscal policy. If the rest of the government spends seigniorage, or raises surpluses to offset lost seigniorage, adjusting surpluses s_t, any seigniorage effect of monetary policy vanishes.

However, for most advanced economies, seigniorage is a small part of government finances so this is not an important channel to analyze. The government-provided non-interest-bearing money stock, primarily physical cash, is typically less than a tenth of the stock of outstanding government debt. Demand for the monetary base declines further when the interest rate rises.

For example, in the United States in 2019 the currency stock was about $1.5 trillion, federal debt and GDP about $20 trillion, federal spending about $5 trillion and the deficit about $1 trillion. The interest rate was about 2%, so seigniorage revenue counted as interest savings was about $30 billion, or 3% of the deficit, less than 1% of federal spending and 0.15% of GDP. At a constant currency/GDP ratio, even 5% growth of nominal GDP

(2% inflation, 3% real) implies 5% growth of the monetary base and thus 5%×$1.5 trillion = $75 billion of free spending. The amount by which these numbers *change* upon monetary policy actions is an order of magnitude smaller. If the Fed raises interest rates by one percentage point, and ignoring the consequent decline in money holdings, that move would only imply $15 billion of additional seigniorage revenue.

Even in times of high inflation in the United States, direct seigniorage was a small part of the fiscal story. In the early 1980s, currency was only about $100 billion, GDP about $3 trillion, so currency/GDP about 3%. Higher nominal interest rates induced lower real money demand. Even at 10% interest rates, seigniorage was $10 billion or 0.3% of GDP. Currency was growing about 10% per year, giving the same answer. Federal debt was about $1 trillion, 33% of GDP, with deficits bottoming out at $200 billion or 5% of GDP, and roughly 3% of GDP throughout the 1980s. Seigniorage represented less than a tenth of the deficit throughout the great inflation and its aftermath. Whatever caused that inflation, direct monetization of deficits wasn't it.

Seigniorage does matter for many episodes and other countries, including many wars and currency collapses. Marginal seigniorage may matter even when average seigniorage is small, if a country embarks on a large money-financed spending spree. Most large inflations and hyperinflations result clearly from issuing large amounts of non-interest-bearing money to cover fiscal deficits.

A persistent fiscal deficit may result in devaluation of outstanding nominal debt through inflation. This is the central message of the fiscal theory. But this effect is not seigniorage. It occurs in models with no money at all. Don't confuse devaluation with seigniorage.

In the shadow of large debts, if monetary policy induces unexpected inflation or deflation, it changes the real value of nominal bonds, requiring a change in surpluses. (The causality may go the other way too, that monetary policy causes the unexpected inflation or deflation by provoking the change in surpluses.) If prices are sticky so that a nominal interest rate increase implies a real interest rate increase, then raising the interest rate raises the government's real cost of borrowing, which must be met by surpluses if it is not to cause inflation. Equivalently, the discount rate rises, which is an inflationary force. These mechanisms of monetary–fiscal interaction are not seigniorage. They exist in economies without money, or when money pays full interest. They are much larger for advanced economies, and less studied. I focus on them for this reason.

Suppose there is a money demand function $MV = Py$. If the government or central bank fixes money supply M_t, then money supply equals money demand can, potentially, determine the price level. Then fiscal policy must "passively" adjust surpluses to the monetary-determined price level so that the government debt valuation equation holds. (I write "potentially," because interest elastic demand $V(i)$ or inside moneys muddy that claim, issues I return to in Chapter 19. We usually write money demand as $M_t^d = L(P_t y_t, i_t)$, but the forms are equivalent, especially if we write explicitly $V(P_t, y_t, i_t)$. I stick with $MV = Py$ for simplicity and as a reminder of the central monetarist idea.)

For now, our job is to generalize fiscal theory, so I assume the opposite: The valuation equation (3.10) or (3.11) determines the price level. The government must then "passively" provide the amount of money people demand by $MV = Py$. The central bank must adjust the *composition* of government debt, the split of debt $B_t + M_t$ overall between B_t and M_t to satisfy money demand. For example, the central bank could allow banks to freely exchange interest-paying reserves B_t for cash M_t, which is precisely what the Fed does.

The decision of the overall level of $B_t + M_t$ with fixed surpluses that I have called "monetary policy" remains, or an interest rate target that is implemented by a flat supply curve for debt remains. So, to be clear, we could call the needed policy a "passive money supply" policy.

With this passive money supply assumption, the presence of non-interest-bearing cash is a straightforward extension of, and often a minor footnote to, fiscal theory. Cash is just one of many flavors of government debt that bear small interest rate spreads, including off-the-run and agency securities. These yield differences are important for precise accounting, and for measurement of the discount rate for government debt. But those features do not disturb the basic picture of price level determination.

This question poses a modeling fork in the road. The vast majority of work on fiscal–monetary interactions, on the function of central banks, on the importance of their operations and balance sheets, rests fundamentally on the modeling choice that central banks issue non-interest-bearing currency and hold interest-bearing government debt, that they control that split directly or via interest rate targets, and that the seigniorage profits are important to overall government finance. These may be relevant modeling assumptions for economic history. But not now. Everything is simpler, but fundamentally different, if we start the analysis with a central bank that pays full interest on its money, and an economy in which seigniorage is absent. That's the modeling choice I emphasize here, and it is more appropriate to our current monetary and financial systems. We can add a bit of liquidity spread and seigniorage revenues on such a view, but its basic propositions are not much altered.

3.5   Linearizations

I develop convenient linearized flow and present value relations,

$$\rho v_{t+1} = v_t + r^n_{t+1} - \pi_{t+1} - g_{t+1} - \tilde{s}_{t+1}$$

$$v_t = \sum_{j=1}^{\infty} \rho^{j-1} \tilde{s}_{t+j} + \sum_{j=1}^{\infty} \rho^{j-1} g_{t+j} - \sum_{j=1}^{\infty} \rho^{j-1} r_{t+j}.$$

Taking an innovation, we have an unexpected inflation identity,

$$\Delta E_{t+1} \pi_{t+1} - \Delta E_{t+1} r^n_{t+1} = - \sum_{j=0}^{\infty} \rho^j \Delta E_{t+1} \tilde{s}_{t+1+j}$$

$$- \sum_{j=0}^{\infty} \rho^j \Delta E_{t+1} g_{t+1+j} + \sum_{j=1}^{\infty} \rho^j \Delta E_{t+1} r_{t+1+j}.$$

Linearizing the maturity structure around a geometric steady-state, we can write a linearized identity for the bond return,

$$\Delta E_{t+1} r_{t+1}^n = -\sum_{j=1}^{\infty} \omega^j \Delta E_{t+1} r_{t+1+j}^n = -\sum_{j=1}^{\infty} \omega^j \Delta E_{t+1} \left(r_{t+1+j} + \pi_{t+1+j} \right).$$

Using this equation in the unexpected inflation identity, we have

$$\sum_{j=0}^{\infty} \omega^j \Delta E_{t+1} \pi_{t+1+j} = -\sum_{j=0}^{\infty} \rho^j \Delta E_{t+1} \tilde{s}_{t+1+j} - \sum_{j=0}^{\infty} \rho^j \Delta E_{t+1} g_{t+1+j}$$

$$+ \sum_{j=1}^{\infty} (\rho^j - \omega^j) \Delta E_{t+1} r_{t+1+j}.$$

These linearizations allow us to transparently see many interesting effects. A rise in expected return lowers the present value of surpluses and causes inflation. With long-term debt $\omega > 0$, a rise in expected future inflation lowers current inflation. By this mechanism, monetary policy can temporarily lower inflation. A fiscal shock may be met by a decline in bond return, which corresponds to a rise in expected future inflation. By this means, monetary policy can smooth forward the inflationary consequences of a fiscal shock, reducing or even eliminating the contemporaneous inflation response.

With time-varying discount rates and long-term debt it is convenient to linearize the flow and valuation equations. The linearizations allow us to apply standard VAR time series techniques. They also let us analyze long-term debt and discount rate variation with a simple apparatus, and easily understand important mechanisms.

I follow a procedure adapted from the ideas in Campbell and Shiller (1988). I start with a linearized version of the debt evolution identity, derived from a Taylor expansion of the exact nonlinear version,

$$\rho v_{t+1} = v_t + r_{t+1} - g_{t+1} - \tilde{s}_{t+1}. \tag{3.17}$$

The log debt-to-GDP ratio at the end of period $t + 1$, v_{t+1}, is equal to its value at the end of period t, v_t, increased by the log real return return on the portfolio of government bonds, less log GDP growth g_{t+1}, and less the scaled surplus $\tilde{s}_{t+1}$. The log real return equals the log nominal return less inflation,

$$r_{t+1} \equiv r_{t+1}^n - \pi_{t+1}.$$

The parameter ρ is a constant of linearization, $\rho = e^{r-g}$. One can take $\rho = 1$, which is simpler, but everyone is so used to $\rho < 1$ that it often takes less explaining to leave it in. Deriving (3.17) takes some algebra, in Online Appendix Section A1.2.

The symbol $\tilde{s}_{t+1}$ here represents the surplus-to-GDP ratio, scaled by the steady-state value of the debt-to-GDP ratio,

$$\tilde{s}_{t+1} = \frac{\rho}{V/(Py)} \frac{s_{t+1}}{y_{t+1}},$$

where V/Py is the steady-state debt to GDP ratio, and y_t denotes GDP or similar divisor. I often refer to $\tilde{s}_{t+1}$ as simply the "surplus" for brevity.

Iterating (3.17) forward, we have a present value identity,

$$v_t = \sum_{j=1}^{T} \rho^{j-1} \tilde{s}_{t+j} + \sum_{j=1}^{T} \rho^{j-1} g_{t+j} - \sum_{j=1}^{T} \rho^{j-1} r_{t+j} + \rho^T v_{t+T}. \qquad (3.18)$$

Equation (3.18) holds ex post, so it holds ex ante. We can take E_t of both sides. Taking the limit as $T \to \infty$, and assuming that the sums converge and the limiting term is zero, we have

$$v_t = E_t \sum_{j=1}^{\infty} \rho^{j-1} \tilde{s}_{t+j} + E_t \sum_{j=1}^{\infty} \rho^{j-1} g_{t+j} - E_t \sum_{j=1}^{\infty} \rho^{j-1} r_{t+j}. \qquad (3.19)$$

The log value of debt as a ratio to GDP, equals the present value of future surplus-to-GDP ratios, plus GDP growth, discounted at the real return on government debt.

In this equation we see how linearization simplifies analysis. Normally, discount rates multiply surpluses. Linearizing, we add rather than multiply, so we can easily measure and talk about separate surplus and discount rate effects. The approximation leaves out the interaction between surpluses and discount rates.

The use of expected real returns to discount in (3.19) is a useful technique from asset pricing. A discount factor is any random variable Λ_t such that $1 = E_t(\Lambda_{t+1}/\Lambda_t R_{t+1})$. Marginal utility of consumption $\Lambda_{t+1} = \beta u'(c_{t+1})/u'(c_t)$ is one particularly important discount factor. But there are many others. In particular, the inverse ex post real return is also a discount factor, since $1 = E_t(R_{t+1}^{-1} R_{t+1})$. We can say from the identity $p_t = E_t(d_{t+1} + p_{t+1})/E_t(R_{t+1})$ that prices are low when expected returns are high. It is a useful identity, as we summarize a lot of thought and experience about asset prices in observations about expected returns. That statement leaves aside just why expected returns are high. A complete general equilibrium model needs to say why expected returns are high or low, adding utility, production, financial structure, and shocks. But, for example, it will be useful to us to see that times of high government debt valuation and low inflation correspond to times of low expected returns, and we can leave for another day the general equilibrium foundations of those low expected returns. It will be useful to discuss how expected returns respond to a policy intervention, without specifying a particular general equilibrium foundation for expected returns.

That the terminal condition in (3.19) vanishes, $E_t \rho^T v_{t+T} \to 0$ means that the debt-to-GDP ratio is expected to grow no faster than ρ^{-T}. The assumption or observation that debt/GDP is a stationary process is enough. If we use $\rho = 1$, then $E_t v_{t+T} \to E(v)$, and equation (3.19) continues to hold, describing deviations from this mean. One may take these statistical assumptions as justification for using the infinite horizon formulas without getting too deep into transversality conditions.

Equation (3.19) is a forward-iterated decomposition of the debt flow condition, as the analogous asset-price decomposition iterates forward the definition of return. It expresses the value of debt in terms of bondholders' expectations of future repayment, and the rate of return they will accept given alternatives. It is more common to iterate (3.17) *backwards*, even if backwards sums do not converge. In doing so, we answer the question, where did today's debt come from? Did it come from initial debt rolled over, past surpluses and deficits that pay down or increase debt, or changes in the ex post return of past debt issues—that is, higher and lower real interest rates and devaluation due to inflation? Hall and Sargent (2011) use an identity much like (3.17) in this way for U.S. data, and Cochrane (2019) contrasts the forward and backward approaches. We iterate forward here because that is the interesting question for us.

Taking time $t+1$ innovations of (3.19) and rearranging, we have an unexpected inflation identity,

$$\Delta E_{t+1}\pi_{t+1} - \Delta E_{t+1}r^n_{t+1} = -\sum_{j=0}^{\infty} \rho^j \Delta E_{t+1}\tilde{s}_{t+1+j}$$

$$-\sum_{j=0}^{\infty} \rho^j \Delta E_{t+1}g_{t+1+j} + \sum_{j=1}^{\infty} \rho^j \Delta E_{t+1}r_{t+1+j}. \qquad (3.20)$$

A decline in the present value of surpluses, coming either from a decline in surplus-to-GDP ratios, a decline in GDP growth, or a rise in discount rates, must correspond to a lower real value of the debt. This reduction can come about by unexpected inflation that devalues outstanding one-period debt, or by an unexpected decline in nominal long-term bond prices, which gives rise to a negative return $\Delta E_{t+1}r^n_{t+1}$. Since v_t is known at time t, it usefully disappears from this innovation accounting.

What determines the long-term bond return r^n_{t+1}, and whether bond prices or inflation soak up a fiscal shock? Linearizing around a geometric maturity structure, in which the face value of maturity j debt declines at rate ω^j,

$$B_t^{(t+j)} = \omega^j B_t.$$

Online Appendix Section A1.3 develops a second approximate identity,

$$\Delta E_{t+1}r^n_{t+1} = -\sum_{j=1}^{\infty} \omega^j \Delta E_{t+1}r^n_{t+1+j} = -\sum_{j=1}^{\infty} \omega^j \Delta E_{t+1}\left(r_{t+1+j} + \pi_{t+1+j}\right). \quad (3.21)$$

A lower ex post bond return on the left-hand side mechanically corresponds to higher expected nominal returns, which in turn are composed of real returns and inflation, on the right-hand side.

We can then eliminate the bond return in (3.20)–(3.21) to focus on inflation and fiscal affairs alone,

$$\sum_{j=0}^{\infty} \omega^j \Delta E_{t+1}\pi_{t+1+j} = -\sum_{j=0}^{\infty} \rho^j \Delta E_{t+1}\tilde{s}_{t+1+j} - \sum_{j=0}^{\infty} \rho^j \Delta E_{t+1}g_{t+1+j} \qquad (3.22)$$

$$+ \sum_{j=1}^{\infty} (\rho^j - \omega^j)\Delta E_{t+1}r_{t+1+j}.$$

A *sum* of current and expected future inflation, weighted by the maturity structure of government debt, responds to the present value of surpluses.

3.5.1   Identity Intuition

The linearized identities allow us to see and calculate many fiscal theory effects more transparently than we can do by using the equivalent nonlinear formulas.

Equations (3.20) and (3.22) capture the entire effect of long-term bonds on inflation by the nominal return r_{t+1}^n. With one-period debt $\omega = 0$, $r_{t+1}^n = i_t$ and is known ahead of time. Thus, the possibility that long-term bond prices lower the numerator on the left-hand side of the valuation equation is captured in a negative r_{t+1}^n.

The bond return r_{t+1}^n captures many interesting mechanisms. Money that pays no interest or reduced interest, liquidity premiums or inflation hedge premiums in government securities, and other interesting questions about returns and discount rates for government debt are all captured by r_{t+1}^n. That doesn't make these issues easy, if one wishes to model them rather than simply use empirical estimates of the nominal bond return. But it allows an easy way to incorporate many ideas about government bond returns into fiscal theory formulas.

The identities easily connect mechanisms we could see in special cases to more general cases. A constant expected return occurs with $E_t r_{t+1} = 0$, $E_t r_{t+1}^n = E_t \pi_{t+1}$. Conversely, we see the effects of time-varying real rates and time-varying risk premiums by allowing expected real bond returns $E_t r_{t+1}$ to vary. One-period debt occurs with $\omega = 0$. Conversely, we see the effects of long-term debt by raising ω. For the rest of this section, I simplify by ignoring the growth term $g_t = 0$ as well.

3.5.2   Responses to Fiscal Shocks

To start on familiar territory, consider constant expected real returns, $E_t r_{t+1} = 0$, and one-period debt, $\omega = 0$. The identities (3.20) and (3.22) reduce to

$$\Delta E_{t+1} \pi_{t+1} = - \sum_{j=0}^{\infty} \rho^j \Delta E_{t+1} \tilde{s}_{t+1+j}.$$

A negative shock to the present value of surpluses results in a positive shock to inflation. We saw this result in the nonlinear model; for example, in (2.13), which I write as

$$\Delta E_{t+1} \left(\frac{P_t}{P_{t+1}} \right) = \Delta E_{t+1} \sum_{j=0}^{\infty} \beta^j s_{t+1+j} / \left(\frac{B_t}{P_t} \right).$$

Also, (3.4) suggested that it is useful to divide the surplus by the value of debt to focus on the price level or inflation.

Recall in the linearization the symbol $\tilde{s}_t$ is scaled by the value of debt, which accounts for the B_t/P_t term here. In our first-order linearization, we look at variation in the surplus divided by the steady-state value of debt. Variation in value of debt leads to a nonlinear interaction term. Debt-to-GDP ratios vary a great deal, so such terms are not necessarily small. When debt is 100% of GDP, as in 2021, it takes four times as much actual surplus-to-GDP to produce the same effect as when debt is 25% of GDP, as in 1980. One can ameliorate this issue by linearizing in terms of the surplus-to-value ratio, as outlined in the Online Appendix. In empirical work, I create the scaled surplus $\tilde{s}_t$ from the linearized identity (3.17). This procedure creates data series that obey the identity, which is useful, and implicitly takes care of the issue by scaling up the surplus when the debt is small and vice versa. One can use a different scaling for calculations that apply to different eras. Use 100% debt to GDP for current calculations, 25% to simulate the 1980s. When possible, of course, use exact nonlinear calculations.

Adding time-varying expected returns on government bonds, we now have

$$\Delta E_{t+1}\pi_{t+1} = -\sum_{j=0}^{\infty} \rho^j \Delta E_{t+1}\tilde{s}_{t+1+j} + \sum_{j=1}^{\infty} \rho^j \Delta E_{t+1} r_{t+1+j}.$$

A shock to the present value of surpluses and hence to inflation can come from the discount rate rather than, or as well as, from surpluses themselves. Suppose the expected or required return rises. At the initial price level, government bonds are worth less. People try to get rid of them, first buying real assets and then buying goods and services. This rise in aggregate demand pushes the price level up. Again, the linearization allows us to see the separate effect cleanly.

Now, add long-term debt $\omega > 0$. Start with constant expected returns. In this case, the inflation identity (3.22) reads

$$\sum_{j=0}^{\infty} \omega^j \Delta E_{t+1}\pi_{t+1+j} = -\sum_{j=0}^{\infty} \rho^j \Delta E_{t+1}\tilde{s}_{t+1+j}. \tag{3.23}$$

An unexpected rise in expected future inflation $\Delta E_{t+1}\pi_{t+1+j}$ can now help to soak up a fiscal shock, not just current $\Delta E_{t+1}\pi_{t+1}$ inflation. If there is future inflation, then long-term bonds are paid back in less valuable dollars when they come due.

This result offers a major change in our view of fiscal shocks. With short-term debt, $\omega = 0$, fiscal shocks give rise to one period of inflation, a one-time price level jump that devalues maturing bonds. There may be continued inflation—we may see $\Delta E_{t+1}\pi_{t+j}$ following such a shock—but that is entirely incidental and does nothing to absorb the fiscal shock. With flexible prices, short-term bondholders can escape expected future inflation by demanding higher nominal interest rates. But holders of long-term bonds, outstanding on the day of the shock, cannot escape the devaluation of their holdings that comes from future inflation.

Future inflation is less effective than current inflation at absorbing a fiscal shock, since $\omega < 1$. A shock to expected future inflation can only devalue debt that is already outstanding today. However, if a fiscal shock is met by a long drawn-out inflation, $\Delta E_{t+1}\pi_{t+1+j}$ that lasts for many j, the size of each period's inflation can be much smaller than a one-period price level jump, even though the cumulative price level rise is larger. For example, with $\omega = 0.7$, a permanent 1% rise in inflation soaks up the same surplus as a $1/(1 - 0.7) = 3.3\%$ price level jump. In many models, a drawn-out small inflation is less economically disruptive than a one-period price level jump. It is even possible that the fiscal shock comes with no contemporaneous inflation at all, $\Delta E_{t+1}\pi_{t+1} = 0$, and inflation rises slowly over time in response to the fiscal shock.

Which is it? The central bank controls the path of expected inflation, through the interest rate target. If the central bank raises interest rates in response to a fiscal shock, raising expected inflation, then there will be a long period of small inflation. If the central bank leaves interest rates alone, then we get a one-period price level jump. By raising interest rates sufficiently, the central bank can cancel completely the immediate inflationary impact of the fiscal shock, though by allowing a slow larger inflation to appear later. Thus, with long-term debt the central bank controls the *timing* of fiscal inflation, with (3.23) as a sort of budget constraint for inflation at different dates.

This simple model offers an important change in perspective, and greater realism. We do not see sudden price level jumps in the U.S. economy. We see drawn-out inflation accompanying fiscal problems, for example in the 1970s. A common view is that the fiscal theory is unrealistic, as it only predicts one-time price level jumps. That prediction is a feature of simplified models with short-term debt, or ignoring monetary policy—the choice of $\{B_t\}$ or $\{i_t\}$—not of the fiscal theory per se.

All of these possibilities require outstanding long-term debt here. The longer the maturity structure, the greater ω, the greater the government's ability to meet a fiscal shock by a period of small drawn-out inflation rather than a price level jump. *Long-term debt is a valuable buffer for government finance*, in this and other respects.

In this context of constant expected returns and no growth, the inflation identity with bond return (3.20) simplifies to

$$\Delta E_{t+1}\pi_{t+1} - \Delta E_{t+1}r_{t+1}^n = - \sum_{j=0}^{\infty} \rho^j \Delta E_{t+1}\tilde{s}_{t+1+j} \qquad (3.24)$$

and the bond return identity (3.21) simplifies to

$$\Delta E_{t+1}r_{t+1}^n = - \sum_{j=1}^{\infty} \omega^j \Delta E_{t+1}\pi_{t+1+j}. \qquad (3.25)$$

If the government (central bank) chooses a drawn-out inflation response to a fiscal shock, that action lowers bond prices, and thus produces a negative ex post return $\Delta E_{t+1}r_{t+1}^n$ in (3.25) and (3.24). In the nonlinear version,

$$\frac{\sum_{j=0}^{\infty} B_{t-1}^{(t+j)} Q_t^{(t+j)}}{P_t} = E_t \sum_{j=0}^{\infty} \beta^j \tilde{s}_{t+j}, \qquad (3.26)$$

we saw that a decline in long-term bond prices $Q_t^{(t+j)}$ in the numerator could bring the valuation equation into balance following a fiscal shock. The r_{t+1}^n terms capture this mechanism.

Our present value equations such as (3.26) use mark-to-market accounting, as the left-hand side is the market value of debt. In essence, the $\Delta E_{t+1}r_{t+1}^n$ term of (3.24) marks to market the expected future inflation $\sum_{j=1}^{\infty} \omega^j \Delta E_{t+1}\pi_{t+1+j}$ (note $j = 1$ here) of the ω-weighted inflation identity (3.23). I find it more insightful to use the version (3.23) that substitutes out the bond return r_{t+1}^n and looks directly at the path of inflation. However, thinking of long-term bonds as absorbing fiscal pressure by being devalued when they come due, or thinking in mark-to-market terms by lower bond prices on the date of the shock, are two sides of the same coin.

3.5.3 Monetary Policy Responses

In Section 2.5, I considered a fiscal theory of monetary policy, using flexible prices and a constant real interest rate, $i_t = E_t\pi_{t+1}$, together with what we recognize now as the unexpected inflation identities with a constant discount rate and one-period debt,

$$\Delta E_{t+1}\pi_{t+1} = -\sum_{j=0}^{\infty} \rho^j \Delta E_{t+1}\tilde{s}_{t+1+j}. \qquad (3.27)$$

I defined "monetary policy" as a rise in the interest rate with no change in surpluses. This investigation left us with a "Fisherian" response to monetary policy, as captured by Figure 2.1. A higher interest rate provokes higher inflation, after a one-period lag. I promised that long-term debt offered one way to overcome this prediction. The linearized identities show that possibility quickly. With long-term debt, we have ω-weighted future inflation terms on the left-hand side of (3.27). We use the more general equation (3.23). A monetary policy change, as we have defined it so far, then specializes (3.23) to

$$\sum_{j=0}^{\infty} \omega^j \Delta E_{t+1}\pi_{t+1+j} = -\sum_{j=0}^{\infty} \rho^j \Delta E_{t+1}\tilde{s}_{t+1+j} = 0,$$

which we can solve for

$$\Delta E_{t+1}\pi_{t+1} = -\sum_{j=1}^{\infty} \omega^j \Delta E_{t+1}\pi_{t+1+j}. \qquad (3.28)$$

Note the minus sign and that the index starts at $j = 1$. The central bank can only change the timing of inflation. Now, if the central bank raises interest rates unexpectedly and persistently, it raises expected future inflation on the right-hand side. This change lowers current inflation on the left-hand side. With long-term debt, an unexpected persistent rise in interest rates lowers today's inflation, even though we still have completely flexible prices, and with no concurrent change to fiscal policy.

The mechanism continues to feel like aggregate demand. When the nominal interest rate rises persistently, bond prices fall. But surpluses have not changed. The value of government debt to investors is greater than its real market value. People try to buy more government debt, and thus fewer goods and services.

In this analysis, the expected path of interest rates matters more than the immediate rate in determining a deflationary force. A credible, persistent interest rate rise—more terms $\Delta E_{t+1}\pi_{t+1+j}$—that lowers long-term bond prices a lot has a stronger disinflationary effect than a large but tentative or transitory rate rise that induces smaller changes to

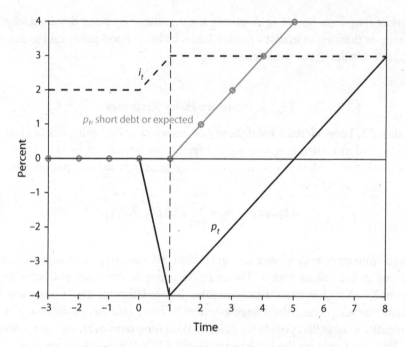

FIGURE 3.1. Response to an Interest-Rate Shock with Long-Term Debt

long-term bond prices. The deflationary effect is larger if there is more long-term debt outstanding, if ω is larger. This state-dependence of the deflationary effect of monetary policy is a potentially testable implication. In this simple model the deflationary force is measured by the decline in bond prices. That prediction is muddied up by expected return variation, but also is potentially useful for measurement.

Figure 3.1 plots an example. I use $\omega = 0.8$, which roughly approximates the U.S. maturity structure. I suppose that interest rates rise unexpectedly and permanently at time 1. I plot the path of the log price level rather than the inflation rate for clarity. Expected inflation π_2, π_3, etc., rise by 1%. The price level rises 1% per year. But the price level first declines, by $\pi_1 = -\omega/(1 - \omega)$ times 1%.

The gray line marked "short debt or expected" in Figure 3.1 plots the price level in the $\omega = 0$ case of only one-period debt. In this case, inflation also starts one period after the interest rate rise, but with no downward jump, as in Figure 2.1.

The disinflation only happens if the interest rate rise is *unexpected*. If the interest rate rise is completely expected, it is already priced into long-term bonds. The long-term bond case follows exactly the same path as the short-term bond case. An announcement of a future interest rate rise has a disinflationary effect on announcement, but no effect when interest rates actually rise.

This is a second important question one should ask models of monetary policy experiments: Do *expected* interest rate rises affect inflation in the same way as *unexpected* interest rate rises do? The answer here is no.

Equation (3.28) opens quite a door for monetary policy, even in this frictionless fiscal theory. Monetary policy can now shift inflation over time as it pleases, including the present moment, with the maturity structure of outstanding debt giving a sort of budget constraint to its possibilities.

3.5.4   Time-Varying Expected Returns

With time-varying expected returns, additional interesting dynamics emerge. With sticky prices, a higher nominal interest rate can raise the real interest rate and discount rate. This is an inflationary force in equations (3.20) and (3.22), which offsets the direct initial deflationary force. In debt service terms, stickier prices mean that higher nominal rates translate to higher real rates and higher interest costs of the debt. Higher interest costs act just like lower surpluses to create additional inflation.

The difference in discount rate terms in (3.20) and (3.22), weighted by ρ^j versus weighted by $\rho^j - \omega^j$, is minor in practice. The United States and most other countries maintain a relatively short maturity structure, $\omega \approx 0.8$ or less. With $\rho \approx 0.99$, the difference between ρ^j and $(\rho^j - \omega^j)$ only affects the first few terms, usually with little consequence.

The presence of $(\rho^j - \omega^j)$ in (3.22) points to an interesting possibility, however. If governments dramatically lengthened the maturity structure of their debt, adopting perpetuities or near-perpetuities with $\rho = \omega$, then discount rate terms would drop from long-run unexpected inflation in (3.22). Roughly speaking, a government that finances itself with perpetuities is insulated from interest rate risk in how it repays outstanding government debt, and its monetary policy is not constrained by interest costs on the debt.

3.6   Continuous Time

Continuous time formulas are straightforward and often prettier analogues to the discrete time versions. With a stochastic discount factor Λ_t, the present value formulas are, with short-term debt

$$V_t = \frac{B_t}{P_t} = E_t \int_{\tau=t}^{\infty} \frac{\Lambda_\tau}{\Lambda_t} s_\tau \, d\tau;$$

with long-term debt

$$V_t = \frac{\int_{j=0}^{\infty} Q_t^{(t+j)} B_t^{(t+j)} \, dj}{P_t} = E_t \int_{\tau=t}^{\infty} \frac{\Lambda_\tau}{\Lambda_t} s_\tau \, d\tau;$$

with money, either

$$\frac{M_t + B_t}{P_t} = E_t \int_{\tau=t}^{\infty} \frac{\Lambda_\tau}{\Lambda_t} \left[s_\tau + \left(i_\tau - i_\tau^{m} \right) \frac{M_\tau}{P_\tau} \right] d\tau;$$

or, in the case $i_t^m = 0$,

$$\frac{B_t}{P_t} = E_t \int_{\tau=t}^{\infty} \frac{\Lambda_\tau}{\Lambda_t} \left(s_\tau \, d\tau + \frac{dM_\tau}{P_\tau} \right).$$

We can also discount using the cumulative return on government debt including money,

$$\frac{B_t + M_t}{P_t} = \int_{\tau=t}^{\infty} \frac{W_t^m}{W_\tau^m} s_\tau \, d\tau.$$

The flow conditions express the idea that money printed up to redeem debt must be soaked up by surpluses or by new debt sales. For one-period debt,

$$\frac{B_t}{P_t} i_t dt = s_t dt + \frac{dB_t}{P_t};$$

for long-term debt,

$$\frac{B_t^{(t)}}{P_t} dt = s_t dt + \frac{\int_{j=0}^{\infty} Q_t^{(t+j)} dB_t^{(t+j)} dj}{P_t};$$

and with money,

$$\frac{B_t}{P_t} i_t dt + \frac{M_t}{P_t} i_t^m dt = s_t dt + \frac{dB_t}{P_t} + \frac{dM_t}{P_t}.$$

The linearized flow and present value identities are

$$dv_t = -\tilde{s}_t dt + dR_t^n - (r + \pi_t)\, dt + rv_t dt$$

$$v_t = \frac{V_t}{V} = \int_{\tau=0}^{\infty} e^{-r\tau} \tilde{s}_{t+\tau}\, d\tau - \int_{\tau=0}^{\infty} e^{-r\tau}\, (dR_{t+\tau} - rd\tau),$$

with

$$dR_t = dR_t^n - \pi_t dt.$$

Taking innovations, we have the unexpected inflation identity,

$$\Delta_t dR_t^n = \int_{\tau=0}^{\infty} e^{-r\tau} \Delta_t \tilde{s}_{t+\tau}\, d\tau - \int_{\tau=0}^{\infty} e^{-r\tau} \Delta_t dR_{t+\tau}.$$

The linearized bond return identity with a geometric maturity structure is

$$\Delta_t dR_t^n = -\int_{\tau=0}^{\infty} e^{-(r+\omega)\tau} \Delta_t dR_{t+\tau}^n = -\int_{\tau=0}^{\infty} e^{-(r+\omega)\tau} \left(\Delta_t dR_{t+\tau} + \Delta_t \pi_{t+\tau}\, d\tau\right).$$

Equating the latter two, we have the weighted inflation identity,

$$\int_{\tau=0}^{\infty} e^{-(r+\omega)\tau} \Delta_t \pi_{t+\tau}\, d\tau = -\int_{\tau=0}^{\infty} e^{-r\tau} \Delta_t \tilde{s}_{t+\tau}\, d\tau$$

$$+ \int_{\tau=0}^{\infty} \left(e^{-r\tau} - e^{-(r+\omega)\tau}\right) \Delta_t dR_{t+\tau}.$$

Continuous time formulas are prettier, but they take care to set up correctly. Continuous time formulas avoid many of the timing conventions that are a distraction to discrete time formulations. They also force one to think through which variables are differentiable, and which may jump discontinuously or move with a diffusion component. I use discrete time in this book largely to keep the derivations transparent, but it is really more elegant and simple to use continuous-time formulas once the logic is clear. The bottom lines are transparent analogues of the discrete time formulas.

Continuous time makes a big difference to intuition, shifting our focus away from instantaneous inflation to drawn-out periods of inflation.

Cochrane (2015a) offers an accessible short summary of the continuous time mathematics I use here.

3.6.1 Short-Term Debt

In continuous time, it is easier to think of instantaneous debt as a floating rate perpetuity than as an infinitesimal maturity discount bond. The quantity is B_t, the price is $Q_t = 1$ always, and it pays a flow of interest $i_t dt$. Let $s_t dt$ denote the flow of primary surpluses. The symbol d represents the forward differential operator, loosely the limit as $\Delta \to 0$ of $dP_t = P_{t+\Delta} - P_t$. In general, continuous time ideas are expressed more rigorously in integral rather than differential form.

The nominal flow condition is

$$B_t i_t dt = P_t s_t dt + dB_t \tag{3.29}$$

and in real terms,

$$\frac{B_t}{P_t} i_t dt = s_t dt + \frac{dB_t}{P_t}.$$

Interest on the debt must be financed by surpluses or by selling more debt. Since the first two quantities sport dt terms, debt B_t is also differentiable, with neither jump nor diffusion components. For now, the price level may have jumps or diffusions. However, we will soon write sticky price models that rule out price level jumps, even in their flexible-price limit, which is a useful case to keep in mind.

It's useful to describe the evolution of the real value of government debt

$$d\left(\frac{B_t}{P_t}\right) = \frac{dB_t}{P_t} + B_t d\left(\frac{1}{P_t}\right) = \frac{B_t}{P_t} i_t dt - s_t dt + B_t d\left(\frac{1}{P_t}\right) = \left(\frac{B_t}{P_t}\right) dR_t - s_t dt$$

or

$$dV_t = V_t dR_t - s_t dt, \tag{3.30}$$

where

$$dR_t \equiv i_t dt + \frac{d\left(1/P_t\right)}{1/P_t}$$

is the real ex post return on government debt, and

$$V_t \equiv B_t/P_t$$

is the real market value of debt. Equation (3.30) states that the real value of debt grows at the ex post real return, less primary surpluses.

Let Λ_t denote a generic continuous time discount factor

$$\Lambda_t = e^{-\delta t} u'(c_t).$$

The valuation equation with this discount factor and short-term debt is

$$\frac{B_t}{P_t} = E_t \int_{\tau=t}^{\infty} \frac{\Lambda_\tau}{\Lambda_t} s_\tau d\tau. \tag{3.31}$$

The distinction between $t-1$ and t vanishes. Instead, you have to remember that B_t is predetermined at time t, meaning it cannot have a diffusion or jump. A diffusion or jump on the right-hand side, which is how we model uncertainty, shows up in a diffusion or jump in the price level.

The risk-neutral case and constant real interest rate case specialize quickly to

$$\frac{\Lambda_\tau}{\Lambda_t} = e^{-\int_{j=t}^{\tau} r_j dj}; \quad \frac{B_t}{P_t} = E_t \int_{\tau=t}^{\infty} e^{-\int_{j=t}^{\tau} r_j dj} s_\tau d\tau$$

$$\frac{\Lambda_\tau}{\Lambda_t} = e^{-r(\tau-t)}; \quad \frac{B_t}{P_t} = E_t \int_{\tau=t}^{\infty} e^{-r(\tau-t)} s_\tau d\tau.$$

We can also discount at the ex post real return on nominal government debt, yielding

$$\frac{B_t}{P_t} = \int_{\tau=t}^{\infty} \frac{W_t}{W_\tau} s_\tau d\tau, \tag{3.32}$$

where W_t is the ex post real cumulative return from investment in nominal government debt. It satisfies

$$\frac{dW_t}{W_t} = dR_t = i_t dt + \frac{d(1/P_t)}{1/P_t}. \tag{3.33}$$

Integrating, we can define the cumulative return explicitly as

$$\frac{W_t}{W_0} = e^{\int_{\tau=0}^{t} i_\tau d\tau} \frac{P_0}{P_t}.$$

As in discrete time, equation (3.32) holds ex post, and therefore it also holds ex ante with any set of probabilities.

The Online Appendix includes the algebra to connect the flow (3.29) and present value relations (3.31) and (3.32).

3.6.2   Long-Term Debt

The flow relation is

$$B_t^{(t)} dt = P_t s_t dt + \int_{j=0}^{\infty} Q_t^{(t+j)} dB_t^{(t+j)} dj, \tag{3.34}$$

or in real terms,

$$\frac{B_t^{(t)}}{P_t} dt = s_t dt + \frac{\int_{j=0}^{\infty} Q_t^{(t+j)} dB_t^{(t+j)} dj}{P_t}.$$

Here, $B_t^{(t+j)}$ is the quantity of debt due at time $t+j$, or more precisely between $t+j$ and $t+j+dj$, and $Q_t^{(t+j)}$ is its nominal price. Debt $B_t^{(t)}$ coming due between t and $t+dt$ must be paid by primary surpluses or net sales of additional long-term debt. (If not, a dM_t would emerge but people don't want to hold money.) The quantity $dB_t^{(t+j)}$ represents the amount of debt of maturity j sold between time t and $t+dt$. I simplify by writing debt that is paid continuously. One can straightforwardly add lumps of debt to be paid at specific instants.

The nominal market value of government debt is

$$\int_{j=0}^{\infty} Q_t^{(t+j)} B_t^{(t+j)} \, dj,$$

so the present value relations are

$$V_t = \frac{\int_{j=0}^{\infty} Q_t^{(t+j)} B_t^{(t+j)} \, dj}{P_t} = E_t \int_{\tau=t}^{\infty} \frac{\Lambda_\tau}{\Lambda_t} s_\tau \, d\tau \qquad (3.35)$$

and

$$V_t = \frac{\int_{j=0}^{\infty} Q_t^{(t+j)} B_t^{(t+j)} \, dj}{P_t} = \int_{\tau=t}^{\infty} \frac{W_t}{W_\tau} s_\tau \, d\tau, \qquad (3.36)$$

where W_t denotes the cumulated real return on the value-weighted portfolio of all government bonds. The nominal return on a single bond is

$$dR_t^{(n,j)} \equiv \frac{dQ_t^{(t+j)}}{Q_t^{(t+j)}}$$

and the real return is

$$dR_t^{(j)} \equiv \frac{d\left(Q_t^{(t+j)}/P_t\right)}{\left(Q_t^{(t+j)}/P_t\right)},$$

so the cumulated real return W_t obeys

$$\frac{dW_t}{W_t} = dR_t \equiv \frac{\int_{j=0}^{\infty} \left[\frac{d\left(Q_t^{(t+j)}/P_t\right)}{Q_t^{(t+j)}/P_t}\right] \frac{Q_t^{(t+j)}}{P_t} B_t^{(t+j)} \, dj}{\int_{k=0}^{\infty} \left(Q_t^{(t+k)}/P_t\right) B_t^{(t+k)} \, dk} = \frac{\int_{j=0}^{\infty} d\left(\frac{Q_t^{(t+j)}}{P_t}\right) B_t^{(t+j)} \, dj}{\int_{k=0}^{\infty} \frac{Q_t^{(t+k)} B_t^{(t+k)}}{P_t} \, dk}. \qquad (3.37)$$

To express the evolution of the market value of debt, take the differential.

$$dV_t = d\left[\frac{\int_{j=0}^{\infty} Q_t^{(t+j)} B_t^{(t+j)} \, dj}{P_t}\right] =$$

$$= \frac{\int_{j=0}^{\infty} Q_t^{(t+j)} dB_t^{(t+j)} \, dj}{P_t} + \int_{j=0}^{\infty} d\left(\frac{Q_t^{(t+j)}}{P_t}\right) B_t^{(t+j)} \, dj - \frac{B_t^{(t)}}{P_t} \, dt.$$

Using the flow relation (3.34),

$$dV_t = -s_t \, dt + \int_{j=0}^{\infty} d\left(\frac{Q_t^{(t+j)}}{P_t}\right) B_t^{(t+j)} \, dj \qquad (3.38)$$

and the definition of portfolio return (3.37),

$$dV_t = -s_t dt + V_t dR_t. \tag{3.39}$$

The total real market value of government debt grows at its ex post real rate of return, less repayment via primary surpluses.

3.6.3   Linearized Identities

We can derive the continuous time versions of the linearized identities following the same logic as in discrete time. Use a steady-state of (3.39) with $dV = 0$, $dR_t = rdt$ and hence $s = rV$. Linearizing (3.39), we have a flow identity,

$$dV_t = -s_t dt + V(dR_t - rdt) + rV_t dt. \tag{3.40}$$

If we wish variables that are deviations from steady-states, the rdt term vanishes here and later. We write

$$dV_t = -(s_t - s)dt + V(dR_t - rdt) + r(V_t - V)dt$$

and each term in parentheses is a deviation from steady-state.

Integrating (3.40) forward, we have a linearized value identity,

$$\frac{V_t}{V} = \int_{\tau=0}^{\infty} e^{-r\tau} \frac{s_{t+\tau}}{V} d\tau - \int_{\tau=0}^{\infty} e^{-r\tau} (dR_{t+\tau} - rdt). \tag{3.41}$$

The nominal and real returns are related by

$$dR_t^n = dR_t - \frac{d(1/P_t)}{1/P_t} = dR_t + \frac{dP_t}{P_t} = dR_t + \pi_t dt.$$

I apply these formulas in the model of Section 5.7, in which the price level does not have jumps or diffusions, though the inflation rate may have them. The latter two equalities reflect this restriction, which I maintain for the rest of this section. I use the previous notation for surplus divided by steady-state value of debt, now

$$\tilde{s}_t = s_t/V,$$

and I define

$$v_t \equiv V_t/V.$$

Note v_t here denotes the proportional deviation from steady-state, not the log, as value can have an Ito or jump term.

With this notation, we can write the linearized flow and value identities (3.40) and (3.41) as

$$dv_t = rv_t dt + dR_t - rdt - \tilde{s}_t dt \tag{3.42}$$

and

$$v_t = \int_{\tau=0}^{\infty} e^{-r\tau} \tilde{s}_{t+\tau} d\tau - \int_{\tau=0}^{\infty} e^{-r\tau} (dR_{t+\tau} - rd\tau). \tag{3.43}$$

These are straightforward cousins of the discrete time versions (3.17)–(3.18).

As in discrete time, I take innovations. I use the notation Δ_t to denote innovations in continuous time; loosely, $\Delta_t(x) = E_{t+\Delta}(x) - E_t(x)$. In continuous time we usually write a process explicitly; for example, $dx_t = \mu_t dt + \sigma_t dz_t$ where dz_t can be a compensated jump or a diffusion. Since $E_t dz_t = 0$, and $E_t(dx_t) = \mu_t dt$, the innovation is then

$$\Delta_t(dx_t) = dx_t - E_t(dx_t) = \sigma_t dz_t.$$

Similarly, conditional expectations follow a stochastic process, $y_t dt \equiv E_t(dx_{t+\tau})$ or $y_t dt \equiv E_t(x_{t+\tau} d\tau)$. If we write that process

$$dy_t = \mu_t dt + \sigma_t dz_t, \tag{3.44}$$

then the innovation is

$$\Delta_t(dx_{t+\tau}) \text{ or } \Delta_t(x_{t+\tau} d\tau) = dy_t - E_t(dy_t) = \sigma_t dz_t. \tag{3.45}$$

For example, if s_t follows an AR(1),

$$ds_t = -\eta s_t + \sigma d\varepsilon_t,$$

Then

$$E_t s_{t+\tau} = e^{-\eta\tau} s_t$$

$$E_t \int_0^\infty e^{-r\tau} s_{t+\tau} d\tau = \int_0^\infty e^{-(r+\eta)\tau} s_t d\tau = \frac{s_t}{r+\eta}.$$

The innovation in the present value is then

$$\Delta_t\left(\int_0^\infty e^{-r\tau} s_{t+\tau} d\tau\right) = \frac{\Delta_t s_t}{r+\eta} = \frac{\sigma}{r+\eta} d\varepsilon_t.$$

From the linearized flow identity (3.42), with no price level jumps or diffusions, the innovation to the value of debt equals the bond return innovation,

$$\Delta_t dv_t = \Delta_t dR_t^n.$$

Then, the innovation to the value identity (3.43) gives

$$\Delta_t dR_t^n = \int_{\tau=0}^\infty e^{-r\tau} \Delta_t \tilde{s}_{t+\tau} d\tau - \int_{\tau=0}^\infty e^{-r\tau} \Delta_t dR_{t+\tau}. \tag{3.46}$$

This is the continuous time cousin to the identity (3.20). In this case, there is no unexpected inflation on the left-hand side.

As in discrete time, I substitute out $\Delta_t dR_t^n$ in terms of future expected bond returns and expected future inflation using a linearized bond pricing identity with a geometric maturity structure.

To model a geometric maturity structure, let government bonds pay a geometrically declining coupon. A bond at time t pays coupon $e^{-\omega\tau} d\tau$ at time $t + \tau$. The price of this bond is Q_t. The bond yield y_t is defined as the constant discount rate that generates the bond price. By definition, the yield satisfies

$$Q_t = \int_{\tau=0}^{\infty} e^{-\tau y_t} e^{-\omega\tau} d\tau = \frac{1}{\omega + y_t}.$$

There are B_t such bonds. Between time t and $t + \Delta$, each bond pays a coupon 1Δ. Since its coupons at time $t + \Delta + \tau$ are now $e^{-\omega(t+\Delta+\tau)}$, the time-$t$ bond turns into $e^{-\omega\Delta}$ time $t + \Delta$ bonds. The nominal return on government bonds is thus

$$dR_t^n = \frac{\Delta + e^{-\omega\Delta}Q_{t+\Delta} - Q_t}{Q_t} = \frac{\Delta + e^{-\omega\Delta}(Q_{t+\Delta} - Q_t) - (1 - e^{-\omega\Delta})Q_t}{Q_t}$$

$$dR_t^n = \frac{1dt + dQ_t}{Q_t} - \omega dt = y_t dt + \frac{dQ_t}{Q_t}. \tag{3.47}$$

(The 1 in $1dt$ is a bit pedantic mathematically, but I remind you here that the bond pays a $1 coupon.)

Linearize the first definition of return in (3.47) around a steady-state with $dR^n = rdt$, $\pi = 0, dQ = 0$ and hence $r + \omega = 1/Q$,

$$Q_t dR_t^n = 1dt + dQ_t - \omega Q_t dt$$

$$Qrdt + Q(dR_t^n - rdt) + (Q_t - Q)rdt = 1dt + dQ_t - \omega Q_t dt$$

$$Q(dR_t^n - rdt) + Q_t rdt = 1dt + dQ_t - \omega Q_t dt$$

$$(dR_t^n - rdt) = dq_t - (r + \omega)(1 - q_t)dt,$$

where

$$q_t \equiv Q_t/Q$$

is the proportional deviation of the bond price from steady-state. Solve for the bond price change

$$dq_t = (dR_t^n - rdt) + (\omega + r)(q_t - 1)dt. \tag{3.48}$$

Integrate forward to express the bond price in terms of future returns,

$$q_t = 1 - \int_{\tau=0}^{\infty} e^{-(r+\omega)\tau}(dR_{t+\tau}^n - rd\tau). \tag{3.49}$$

We have from (3.48) that the unexpected proportional bond price movement is the unexpected return,

$$\Delta_t dq_t = \Delta_t dR_t^n.$$

So, taking innovations of (3.49), the unexpected bond return is

$$\Delta_t dR_t^n = -\int_{\tau=0}^{\infty} e^{-(r+\omega)\tau} \Delta_t dR_{t+\tau}^n = -\int_{\tau=0}^{\infty} e^{-(r+\omega)\tau} \Delta_t (dR_{t+\tau} + \pi_{t+\tau} d\tau). \tag{3.50}$$

This is the continuous time counterpart to the bond return identity (3.21).

Now substituting (3.50) into (3.46), we have the weighted inflation identity

$$\int_{\tau=0}^{\infty} e^{-(r+\omega)\tau} \Delta_t \pi_{t+\tau} d\tau = -\int_{\tau=0}^{\infty} e^{-r\tau} \Delta_t \tilde{s}_{t+\tau} d\tau + \int_{\tau=0}^{\infty} \left(e^{-r\tau} - e^{-(r+\omega)\tau} \right) \Delta_t dR_{t+\tau}.$$
(3.51)

Equation (3.51) differs from its discrete time counterpart (3.22) in that unexpected inflation at time t alone contributes an infinitesimal amount to the integral on the left-hand side. In present value terms, the entire fiscal shock is absorbed by a persistent fall in expected inflation, which devalues long-term bonds. In the case of short-term debt $\omega = 0$, the left-hand side is zero and any fiscal shock is exactly matched by the discount rate term; that is, a slow decline in the real value of short-term debt. Again, this linearization specifies no price level jumps or diffusions.

3.6.4   Money in Continuous Time

The nominal flow condition in continuous time, corresponding to the discrete time version (2.1), is

$$dM_t = i_t B_t dt + i_t^m M_t dt - P_t s_t dt - dB_t.$$
(3.52)

The government prints money to pay interest on nominal debt, to pay interest on money, and the government soaks up money with primary surpluses and new debt issues. We can write this flow condition in real terms as

$$\frac{B_t}{P_t} i_t dt + \frac{M_t}{P_t} i_t^m dt = s_t dt + \frac{dB_t}{P_t} + \frac{dM_t}{P_t}.$$

The sum $dB_t + dM_t$ is of order dt. To keep the analysis simple I also specify that each of dB_t and dM_t is of order dt rather than allow offsetting diffusion terms or jumps.

To express seigniorage as money creation, specialize to $i_t^m = 0$, rearrange (3.52), and substitute the definition of the nominal interest rate and integrate forward with the transversality condition to obtain

$$\frac{B_t}{P_t} = E_t \int_{\tau=t}^{\infty} \frac{\Lambda_\tau}{\Lambda_t} \left(s_\tau d\tau + \frac{dM_\tau}{P_\tau} \right).$$
(3.53)

The algebra for this and other results of this section is a bit tedious, so I relegate it to Online Appendix Section A1.4.

To express seigniorage in terms of interest cost, including the case that money pays interest $0 < i_t^m < i_t$, start again from (3.52), and integrate forward differently, obtaining

$$\frac{M_t + B_t}{P_t} = E_t \int_{\tau=t}^{\infty} \frac{\Lambda_\tau}{\Lambda_t} \left[s_\tau + \left(i_\tau - i_\tau^m \right) \frac{M_\tau}{P_\tau} \right] d\tau.$$
(3.54)

To discount with the ex post return, define W_t as the cumulative real value of investment in government bonds, all short-term here, so dW_t/W_t is the ex post real return. After some more pleasant algebra in Online Appendix Section A1.4, we obtain

$$\frac{B_t}{P_t} = \int_{\tau=t}^{\infty} \frac{W_t}{W_\tau}\left(s_\tau d\tau + \frac{dM_\tau}{P_\tau}\right)$$

and

$$\frac{B_t + M_t}{P_t} = \int_{\tau=t}^{\infty} \frac{W_t}{W_\tau}\left[s_\tau + \left(i_\tau - i_\tau^m\right)\frac{M_\tau}{P_\tau}\right]d\tau.$$

Perhaps a more revealing way to express this condition, looking ahead to a model with long-term debt and debt with various liquidity distortions, is to write the discount factor as a rate of return that mixes the bond rate of return and the lower (zero) money rate of return. The demand for money allows the government to borrow at lower rates.

To pursue this idea, define W^{nm} and W^m as the cumulative nominal and real value of an investment in the overall government bond portfolio, now including money,

$$\frac{dW_t^{nm}}{W_t^{nm}} = \frac{B_t}{B_t + M_t}i_t dt + \frac{M_t}{B_t + M_t}i_t^m dt.$$

More algebra leads to the natural result

$$\frac{B_t + M_t}{P_t} = \int_{\tau=t}^{\infty} \frac{W_t^m}{W_\tau^m}s_\tau d\tau. \tag{3.55}$$

Here we fold seigniorage and money distortions into the discount rate for all government debt.

4

Debt, Deficits, Discount Rates, and Inflation

THIS CHAPTER begins to tie fiscal theory to data. Two crucial ingredients take center stage.

First, to account for time series data such as those of the postwar United States, we must specify a surplus process with an s-shaped moving average representation. A period of deficits, negative s_t, is expected to be, and on average is, followed by a period of surpluses, positive s_t. With such a process, deficits are mostly financed by issuing debt, and surpluses pay down that debt.

Most of the fiscal theory literature assumes that an active fiscal policy must have a positively autocorrelated surplus process, or at least rules out a process in which deficits are financed by debt and the debt is completely repaid. This is the central identification restriction for the common desire to estimate regimes or test fiscal theory. But when we look at it more closely, it makes no sense. Fiscal theory governments do not *have to* follow such a process, and sensible governments will not choose to follow such a process.

Opening up fiscal theory to allow surplus processes in which deficits can be at least partially repaid opens the door to understanding all data with fiscal theory, rather than reserving fiscal theory for particularly pathological moments of fiscally driven inflation. That opening revises the results of essentially all current fiscal theory models, as well as all current estimates and tests of regimes.

Second, discount rate variation matters. Most clearly, inflation falls in recessions not because expected surpluses rise, but because the expected return on government bonds falls. This is a second key innovation that likewise opens many doors. On a technical level, these two innovations are the central pillars driving how this book's approach differs from the current literature.

We start with some facts, and then move on to specifications of the theory that accommodate the facts.

4.1   U.S. Surpluses and Debt

Most variation in U.S. primary surpluses is related to output variation, with deficits in recessions and surpluses in expansions. There is little visible correlation between debt, deficits, and inflation. The business cycle correlation often consists of higher deficits with less inflation during recessions, and vice versa in expansions. Surpluses clearly pay down debt.

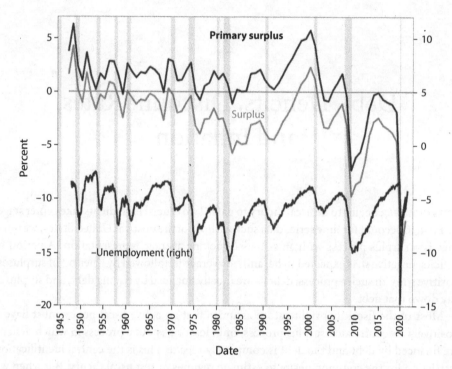

FIGURE 4.1. Surplus and Unemployment. "Surplus" is the U.S. federal surplus/deficit as a percentage of GDP as reported by BEA. "Primary surplus" is the BEA surplus plus BEA interest costs. Both are a percentage of GDP. The graph plots the negative of the unemployment rate using the right-hand scale. Vertical bands are NBER recessions.

One's first reaction to the fiscal theory may be, "Surpluses, what surpluses? We seem to have only perpetual deficits. The right-hand side of the valuation equation is negative!" Figure 4.1 plots the U.S. federal surplus-to-GDP ratio in the postwar period. Indeed, except for a few brief years in the late 1990s, the federal government has run steadily increasing deficits since 1960, even as a percentage of GDP.

However, the valuation equation wants *primary* surpluses, not counting interest costs. This figure plots conventional NIPA data. In empirical work, I use a more accurate but broadly similar measure based on what the Treasury actually borrows each month.

The difference between the usual surplus/deficit and the primary surplus is important to understanding the history of fiscal policy. The U.S. government historically did run small primary surpluses on a regular basis. Much of the "Reagan deficits" of the early 1980s represent interest payments on existing debt as interest rates rose sharply; not unusually large tax and spending decisions in the primary surplus, especially when we account for the severe recession of that period as captured by the unemployment rate.

The primary surplus-to-GDP ratios in Figure 4.1 follow a clear cyclical pattern, shown by their close correlation with the negative of the unemployment rate, and by the NBER recession bands. Surpluses fall—deficits rise—in recessions. Surpluses rise in good economic times. Surpluses, like unemployment, are related to the *level* of economic activity, where recessions are defined by *growth rates*. The GDP gap, (GDP - potential GDP)/

potential GDP, not shown, looks about the same as the negative of unemployment in the plot.

This surplus movement has three primary sources. When income (GDP) falls, tax revenue = tax rate × income falls. Automatic stabilizers such as unemployment insurance increase spending, and the government predictably embarks on discretionary counter-cyclical spending. We see correlation of primary surpluses with GDP and unemployment at decade frequencies as well.

The actual surplus matters in our theory, not the surplus-to-GDP ratio. Variation in GDP growth amplifies these patterns. Higher surplus-to-GDP ratios at times of higher GDP are doubly higher actual surpluses.

The fact that so much primary surplus-to-GDP ratio variation is regularly and reliably related to the business cycle means that much of a current deficit or surplus is transitory, and does not tell us much about the present value of all future surpluses that appears in the fiscal theory. That fact also suggests an s-shaped surplus process, that much of a deficit in a recession is repaid by surplus in the following expansion. And it tells us that surplus policy rules such as $s_t = \theta_{sx} x_t + \theta_{s\pi} \pi_t \ldots$ will be key parts of a reasonable model.

First in the 1970s, and then dramatically since 2000, the trend has shifted toward large primary deficits even when unemployment is low, a development of obvious concern to a fiscal theorist. Reasons for this trend need research, but three obvious possibilities suggest themselves. First, both 1970 and 2000 showed a break in productivity and GDP growth. The former reversed in 1980 but the latter is ongoing. To some extent we are seeing the usual forces of lower surplus to GDP when GDP is lower, just in response to decades-long, growth-driven rather than business cycle fluctuations. That observation does not make the additional debt sustainable, however. Second, since the 1980s real interest rates have come down steadily. Though debt is large, 100% of GDP in 2021, the combination of low real interest rates and short-term financing mean that real interest costs on the debt are low. Governments may respond to low real interest costs as households and businesses do, by piling on debt, rather than respond to the value of the debt itself. Most models, including mine, specify the latter. We might need a different specification. The habit of gearing fiscal policy to interest costs rather than the amount of debt may prove unwise if interest costs rise. Third, one may ascribe exploding debt and deficits to political dysfunction. However, the pattern appears also in many countries in Europe; Japan is famous for large debts, and corporate and household debt have also bloomed.

Figure 4.2 presents the primary surplus along with debt, both as percentages of GDP, and CPI inflation. The U.S. debt-to-GDP ratio started at 90% at the end of World War II. It declined slowly to 1975, due to a combination of surpluses, inflation (especially in the late 1940s and early 1950s), GDP growth, and relatively low real interest rates. There *were* steady primary surpluses from the end of WWII all the way to 1975. The narrative that we entirely grew out of WWII debt is false. (Hall and Sargent (2011) and Cochrane (2019) offer quantitative decompositions.) The downward trend ended with the large (at the time) deficits of the 1970s and 1980s. The surpluses of the 1990s drove debt down again, but then debt rocketed up starting in the 2008 great recession, with another immense surge starting with the COVID-19 recession.

Comparing surplus and debt lines, you can see clearly at both cyclical and lower frequencies that surpluses pay down the value of debt, and deficits drive up the value of

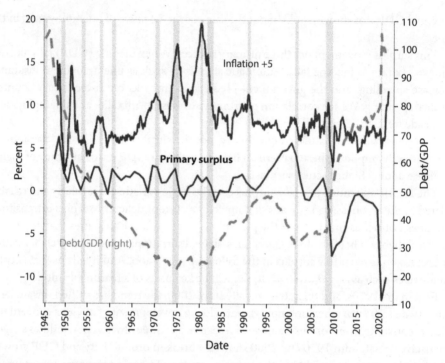

FIGURE 4.2. Primary Surplus-to-GDP Ratio, Debt-to-GDP Ratio, and Inflation. Debt is federal debt held by the public, as a percentage of GDP (right scale), as reported by the BEA. Inflation is the percent change of the CPI from the previous year. Vertical bands are NBER recessions.

debt. This fact may seem totally obvious, but it is an important piece of evidence for an s-shaped rather than AR(1) or positively correlated surplus processes, which make the opposite prediction. Fiscal roots of inflation will have to be seen on top of this dominant pattern.

Looking at inflation in Figure 4.2, fiscal correlations do not jump out of the graph. They are not absent. One can eyeball a correlation between the structural shift in surplus/GDP ratios in the 1970s and the emergence of inflation, and lower GDP itself compounded fiscal problems. Historical accounts stress that fiscal challenges in the late 1960s and early 1970s had a lot to do with the emergence of inflation, dollar devaluation, and the end of Bretton Woods. Contrariwise, the economic boom that started in 1982 resulted by the 1990s in large primary surplus/GDP ratios, large surpluses, and the sudden end of inflation. The end of inflation made fiscal sense, at least ex post. Most successful inflation stabilization plans involve monetary, fiscal, and microeconomic policy. Typically, fiscal policy involves reforms, not just raising distorting tax rates, and microeconomic reform contributes to larger GDP growth, producing greater tax revenue at lower marginal rates, but with a reformed base.

But that's it for obvious correlations of debt or deficits with inflation in the postwar United States. The inflation of the 1970s had deficits, but historically low debt-to-GDP ratios, relative to WWII or the 2000s. Primary surpluses turned into primary deficits after 2000, and especially after 2008, driven by another two-decade growth slowdown, the great recession, the COVID-19 recession, and the inexorable expansion of entitlement programs. Long-term fiscal forecasts, such as the Congressional Budget Office's long-term outlook, describe ever-rising deficits and warn darkly of debt unsustainability if policy does not change. Yet inflation continued its slow decline through 2020. Even if the 2021 surge underway as I complete this book continues, one will wonder what took so long. Low real interest rates will likely be part of the story, but the story needs telling.

There is a *positive* correlation between surpluses and inflation in many business cycles. In most recessions, budget deficits increase, and inflation falls. In most recoveries, the budget turns toward surplus and inflation rises. We basically see here the Phillips curve, since deficits are so well correlated with unemployment. This pattern is not ironclad. The year 1975 is a notable exception, emblematic of 1970s stagflation.

Clearly, if fiscal theory is to hope to explain the data, it will have to find more sophisticated predictions than strong correlations between debt or deficits and inflation. Fortunately, that answer is not far off.

One cannot close a look at the data without some worry about our current (as I write in 2021) situation. The U.S. debt/GDP ratio has surpassed its peak at the end of WWII. The United States now runs primary deficits close to 5% of GDP in expansions, and immense deficits in the once-per-century crises that now seem to happen once a decade. Many debt-funded transfer payments of the COVID recession seem, as I write, headed for permanence. Entitlement promises are about to kick in. Should a fiscal theorist worry? One school of thought says no. After all, the United States paid off the WWII debt. However, the United States did that by a combination of several factors absent now. The war, and its deficit spending, was over. The United States entered a period of unprecedented real growth, driven by the supply side of increasing productivity in a lightly regulated economy with modest social spending and social program disincentives. The United States also had substantial financial repression holding down interest rates: financial regulation, capital controls, and so forth. Our economy has none of these features today. And even so, the 1971 end of Bretton Woods was essentially a U.S. debt crisis, and we did have two bouts of debt-reducing inflation. The late 1940s raised the price level about 40%, cutting the real value of mostly long-term war debt by that much.

Yet for most of the 2000s, inflation remained surprisingly low. As I write in 2021, bond investors remain willing to lend the U.S. government astonishing amounts of money at surprisingly low real interest rates. Why? Perhaps people recognize that the U.S. fiscal problems are not insoluble. Sensible fiscal and entitlement reforms could easily solve the U.S. structural fiscal problems. European benefits require European tax revenues, either from European tax rates or from unleashed free-market growth. The uniquely expensive American health-care system could be reformed. The United States does not face external fiscal problems. A fiscal crisis, leading either to inflation or partial default, will be a self-inflicted wound of a once grand political system turned inward to self-destruction. Investors, price setters, and shoppers may expect that the United States will once again, as the aphorism goes, do the right thing after it has tried everything else. But both fiscal theory and conventional fiscal sustainability analyses point out just how dangerous the situation is. If bond investors change their minds, and decide that the debt will be defaulted on or inflated away, then a classic crisis breaks out. The combination of unsustainable fiscal plans, short-term debt, and political chaos preventing sensible reforms leave the United States in danger of a debt crisis, which likely will involve substantial inflation or default.

Figure 4.1 creates a NIPA primary surplus series by removing the NIPA measure of interest expense from the NIPA surplus/deficit. This interest expense only tracks coupon payments. Figure 4.2 shows the standard NIPA value of debt. This measure gives the face value of debt, not market value. The face value is typically somewhat larger than market value. This relationship changes over time as interest rates change and as the composition of debt varies.

As a result, the NIPA surplus and debt series do not accurately measure the quantities we want, nor do they satisfy identities. In empirical work I use market value of debt data from[1] Hall, Payne, and Sargent (2018). I derive the primary surplus from the market value of government debt and its rate of return, i.e., using the flow identity: Treasury borrowing or repayment equals growth in market value of debt less than the rate of return applied to the initial value of debt. This procedure measures how much the government actually borrows. It gives us data series of the surplus and value of debt that satisfy the flow identity, which helps a lot in empirical work. When running VARs or evaluating terms of the linearized identities, I infer the surplus from the linearized flow identity (3.17) so that linearized identities hold exactly. The Appendix to Cochrane (2021a) details data construction and includes a plot, which shows that the surplus series are broadly similar.

4.2   The Surplus Process—Stylized Facts

An array of stylized facts points to a surplus process with an s-shaped moving average representation, in which deficits this year correspond to subsequent surpluses, rather than an AR(1) or similar positively autocorrelated process.

With a positively correlated surplus process, inflation and deficits are strongly correlated, there is a lot of inflation, deficits lower the value of debt, deficits are financed by inflating away outstanding debt, bond returns are highly volatile, countercyclical, and give a high risk premium. With a surplus process that has an s-shaped moving average, all of these predictions are reversed, consistent with the facts. None of the counterfactual predictions are rejections of the fiscal theory. They are rejections of the auxiliary assumption that the surplus follows a positively correlated process. The risk premium on government debt is likely negative, so government bonds pay less than the risk-free rate, because inflation and interest rates decline in recessions.

The s-shaped process is reasonable, not a technical trick. Any entity borrowing follows an s-shaped cash flow process, and any government desiring to borrow, to raise revenue by borrowing, and not to cause volatile inflation chooses an s-shaped surplus process.

What ingredients do we need to put in a model for it to be consistent with the facts? You know where we're going: We need a surplus with an s-shaped moving average representation and we need discount rate variation. But many facts come together in this characterization, and some classic puzzles get solved along the way.

---

1. Data are available at https://people.brandeis.edu/~ghall/. The Dallas Fed now also has market value of debt data, https://www.dallasfed.org/research/econdata/govdebt/.

In this section, I focus on the surplus process. We can write any stationary surplus process in moving average form as

$$s_t = \sum_{j=0}^{\infty} a_j \varepsilon_{t-j} = a(L)\varepsilon_t. \tag{4.1}$$

In general, $a(L)$ and ε_t can both be vectors. Think of the following scalar calculations as the response to one element of ε_t at a time.

By writing this moving average, we do not assume that surpluses are exogenous. The surplus may respond to endogenous variables, it may be generated by tax rates times endogenous income, and so forth. In the resulting general equilibrium, a moving average of the form (4.1) results. That's the object we are looking at.

Consider this surplus process in the simplest model, with one-period debt, a constant real rate, and flexible prices. The linearized identity (3.22) then says that unexpected inflation is the negative of the revision of the discounted value of surpluses,

$$\Delta E_{t+1} \pi_{t+1} = -\Delta E_{t+1} \sum_{j=0}^{\infty} \rho^j \tilde{s}_{t+1+j} = -\sum_{j=0}^{\infty} a_j \rho^j \varepsilon_{t+1} = -a(\rho)\varepsilon_{t+1}. \tag{4.2}$$

Thus, the weighted sum of moving average coefficients $a(\rho)$ is a crucial discriminating feature of the surplus process. (The beautiful final formula in (4.2) comes from Hansen, Roberds, and Sargent (1992).)

The exact present value model gives similarly

$$\frac{B_t}{P_t} \Delta E_{t+1} \left(\frac{P_t}{P_{t+1}} \right) = \Delta E_{t+1} \sum_{j=0}^{\infty} \beta^j s_{t+1+j} = a(\beta)\varepsilon_{t+1}.$$

The points of this section can be made in either framework. I largely use the linearized identities, which give slightly prettier algebra.

Keep in mind a few simple examples. First, the AR(1),

$$\tilde{s}_{t+1} = \eta \tilde{s}_t + \varepsilon_{t+1}; \ a(L) = \frac{1}{1 - \eta L} \tag{4.3}$$

is common, simple, and as we shall see, utterly wrong. In this case

$$a(\rho) = \frac{1}{1 - \rho \eta}$$

is a number greater than one. Its lesson extends to any moving average with positive coefficients, or loosely a process dominated by positive serial correlation.

Second, keep in mind $a(\rho) = 0$. In this case, shocks to current surpluses have no information at all about the discounted sum of surpluses, and there is no unexpected inflation at all. In the end, I conclude that a small, less than one, positive value for $a(\rho)$ is a good choice, and thinking of these extremes will lead us there.

Since by normalization $a_0 = 1$, $a(\rho) < 1$ means that some of the higher moving average terms a_j must be negative. If smooth with one zero crossing, the plot of the moving average or impulse-response coefficients a_j must move from positive to negative, in an s-shape.

An MA(1) is the simplest example that captures the range of options for $a(\rho)$,

$$\tilde{s}_{t+1} = \varepsilon_{t+1} - \theta\varepsilon_t = (1 - \theta L)\varepsilon_{t+1}.$$

If this government has a deficit shock $\Delta E_{t+1}\tilde{s}_{t+1} = \varepsilon_{t+1} = -1$, then that shock changes the expected value of the next surplus to $\Delta E_{t+1}(\tilde{s}_{t+2}) = \theta$. A deficit today is partially repaid by a surplus θ next period. This process has

$$a(\rho) = (1 - \theta\rho).$$

For $\theta = \rho^{-1}$, we have $a(\rho) = 0$. In this case, a shock $\tilde{s}_1 = -\varepsilon_1$ sets off an expectation $\tilde{s}_2 = \rho^{-1}\varepsilon_1$ that the borrowing will be paid off completely with interest. Smaller values of θ accommodate $0 < a(\rho) \ll 1$ with partial repayment and some inflation. The value $\theta = 0$ gives an i.i.d. surplus process with $a(\rho) = 1$, and a negative θ generates positive serial correlation and $a(\rho) > 1$ as in the AR(1) case.

Now, consider a range of model predictions and facts.

4.2.1   Inflation Volatility and Correlation with Deficits

Equation (4.2)

$$\Delta E_{t+1}\pi_{t+1} = -a(\rho)\Delta E_{t+1}\tilde{s}_{t+1} \tag{4.4}$$

gives directly our first puzzle. A large $a(\rho)$ produces highly volatile inflation for a given surplus process. Annual regressions in Section 4.3 give a standard deviation of surplus shocks equal to roughly 5 percentage points. If the surplus follows an AR(1) with coefficient 0.55, as suggested by those regressions, then we predict that unexpected inflation has $5/(1 - 0.55) = 11\%$ annual volatility, an absurdly large value. On its own, the relative volatility of surpluses versus inflation suggest $a(\rho)$ well below 1.

Moreover, if $a(\rho)$ is a large number, as in the AR(1), then the model predicts a strong correlation between shocks to inflation and shocks to deficits. The deficits of recessions would correspond to inflation, and the surpluses of booms would correspond to deflation. There is typically little correlation between inflation and current deficits across time and countries, and if anything, the opposite pattern.

By contrast, consider the case $a(\rho) = 0$, an s-shaped moving average in which debts are fully repaid. Now the model predicts no correlation between deficits and inflation. When we add other shocks, a value $0 < a(\rho) \ll 1$ can still remove the prediction of a strong correlation between deficits and inflation, since other shocks to inflation will swamp the small effect of surplus shocks.

One could go the opposite direction with $a(\rho) < 0$ to generate a negative correlation of inflation with surpluses, but this specification violates empirical results to follow and common sense. Discount rates will account for the negative correlation of surpluses with inflation.

A correlation of inflation with current debt and current deficits is *possible*. Large inflations typically correlate with deficits, and some cross-country experience lines up inflation and devaluation with deficits. Some large inflations have followed unsustainable large debts. The surplus process does not *have* to be s-shaped as a matter of theory. The point here is that the surplus process *can* be s-shaped. A correlation of current debt or deficits with inflation is not a *necessary* prediction of the fiscal theory. Their absence is not a rejection of fiscal theory. When specifying or estimating models we should *allow* for an s-shaped process, not rule it out a priori.

4.2.2 *Surpluses and Debt*

With an AR(1) surplus (4.3) and constant expected return, the value of debt is

$$v_t = E_t \sum_{j=0}^{\infty} \rho^j \tilde{s}_{t+1+j} = \frac{\eta}{1 - \rho \eta} s_t. \tag{4.5}$$

The AR(1) model makes a stark prediction: The value of debt and surplus are perfectly positively correlated. Figure 4.2 shows how horribly wrong that prediction is. Surpluses are roughly the *negative* of the *growth* in value of debt, not proportional to the level of the value of debt.

Break formula (4.5) down to

$$v_t = E_t \left(\tilde{s}_{t+1} + \sum_{j=1}^{\infty} \rho^j \tilde{s}_{t+1+j} \right) = E_t \left(\tilde{s}_{t+1} + \rho v_{t+1} \right). \tag{4.6}$$

With a positively correlated surplus, a higher surplus $\tilde{s}_{t+1}$ *raises* the value of debt, since it raises subsequent surpluses. Conversely, deficits lower the value of debt. This is a disastrously wrong prediction for U.S. government debt. Higher surpluses lead to lower debts and deficits are financed by borrowing, which leads to larger debts, as you can see in Figure 4.2.

To state the point more precisely, take innovations of the flow identity (3.17) to write

$$\rho \Delta E_{t+1} v_{t+1} = -\Delta E_{t+1} \pi_{t+1} - \Delta E_{t+1} \tilde{s}_{t+1} = [a(\rho) - 1] \varepsilon_{t+1}. \tag{4.7}$$

If $a(\rho) > 1$, as with an AR(1), then a surprise surplus implies higher subsequent surpluses, and raises the value of debt. We see nothing like this in the data, an apparent puzzle. If $a(\rho) < 1$, however, then a higher surplus lowers subsequent surpluses and lowers the value of debt. In the case of full repayment $a(\rho) = 0$, then a higher surplus lowers the value of debt one for one. The s-shaped surplus moving average solves the value-of-debt puzzle. (This puzzle is due to Canzoneri, Cumby, and Diba (2001). They acknowledge that an s-shaped surplus process solves the puzzle, but regard it as implausible.)

The debt accumulation equation

$$\rho v_{t+1} = v_t + i_t - \pi_{t+1} - \tilde{s}_{t+1}$$

seems to state already that a higher surplus $\tilde{s}_{t+1}$ lowers the value v_{t+1}. How does the AR(1) example reverse that prediction? Because with $a(\rho) > 1$, the AR(1) example states that inflation π_{t+1} moves at the same time, in the opposite direction (more surplus, less inflation) and by a greater quantity than the surplus. A deficit tries to raise the value of debt, but it comes with a large inflation, which wipes out even more debt than the deficit implies. In the case $a(\rho) = 0$, inflation is unaffected by the surplus shock and the conventional reading of the equation applies.

4.2.3   Financing Deficits—Revenue or Inflation?

How does the government finance a deficit? As before, it can borrow, inflate, or super-inflate. Equation (4.7) expresses the possibilities with our moving average representation and usefully ties our observations together.

We usually think that the government borrows to finance a deficit. Such borrowing naturally increases the debt. But to borrow and raise the value of debt, the government must promise to repay, to run an s-shaped surplus. Equation (4.7) captures this intuition with $a(\rho) = 0$.

Suppose instead that $a(\rho) = 1$ and the government runs an unexpected deficit at time $t + 1$. Now, looking at equation (4.7), inflation π_{t+1} devalues the outstanding real debt, by just the amount of the unexpected deficit. The value of debt at the end of the period is then the same as it was at the beginning. In this sense we can say that the government finances the deficit entirely by inflating away outstanding debt. The burden falls on existing bondholders, not future taxpayers.

If $0 < a(\rho) < 1$, then the deficit is partially financed by unexpected inflation, and partially financed by borrowing. For $a(\rho) > 1$, the inflation-induced devaluation is even larger than the current deficit, and the government then sells even *less* debt than previously planned. The government finances the current and higher expected future deficits by inflating away outstanding debt.

Most deficits in postwar advanced-country time series data are clearly financed by borrowing. The government raises additional revenue from debt sales. The value of debt rises after periods of deficit, and falls after periods of surplus. This is more evidence that $a(\rho)$ is a small number.

The fact that debt sales raise revenue to finance deficits is perhaps the clearest indication of an s-shaped surplus process in investors' expectations. Since the value of debt is set by *investors'* expectations of future surpluses, the rise in value of debt after a period of deficits tells us that *investors* expect higher surpluses, no matter what economists may think.

This analysis may be clearer in the exact model from Section 2.7. From the flow identity

$$\frac{B_t}{P_{t+1}} = s_{t+1} + Q_{t+1}\frac{B_{t+1}}{P_{t+1}}$$

we can write

$$\frac{B_t}{P_t}\Delta E_{t+1}\left(\frac{P_t}{P_{t+1}}\right) = \Delta E_{t+1}s_{t+1} + \beta \Delta E_{t+1}\left(\frac{B_{t+1}}{P_{t+2}}\right) \tag{4.8}$$

$$= \Delta E_{t+1} s_{t+1} + \beta \Delta E_{t+1} \left(\sum_{j=0}^{\infty} \beta^j s_{t+2+j} \right) \qquad (4.9)$$

$$= \varepsilon_{t+1} + [a(\beta) - 1] \varepsilon_{t+1}. \qquad (4.10)$$

The second term on the right-hand side of (4.9)–(4.10) is the revenue that the government gets from bond sales at the end of period $t+1$. Equation (4.9) says that the real revenue from bond sales equals the discounted value of subsequent surpluses. Relative to the earlier (2.27), we link the present values to the moving average representation via $a(\beta)$.

If a deficit $\Delta E_{t+1} s_{t+1} < 0$ corresponds to a positive innovation in subsequent surpluses, s_{t+2+j}, then the revenue from selling debt at the end of the period rises, the value of debt rises, and that revenue finances the deficit. If $a(\beta) = 0$, that extra revenue completely finances the deficit.

If, however, the negative surplus $\Delta E_{t+1} s_{t+1}$ is not followed by any net news about subsequent surpluses, if $a(\beta) = a_0 = 1$, then the government gets no additional revenue from bond sales. The extra deficit is entirely financed by inflating away outstanding debt, an inflation innovation $\Delta E_{t+1}(P_t/P_{t+1})$. If the negative surplus $\Delta E_{t+1} s_{t+1}$ is followed by additional negative surpluses, as modeled by an AR(1), if $a(\beta) > 1$, then the government raises *less* revenue from selling bonds at the end of the period, and the deficit is followed by *lower* values of debt, as we have seen.

In terms of the linearized identity, (4.8)–(4.10) are the same as a rearrangement of the linearized flow identity (4.7),

$$v_t - \pi_{t+1} = \tilde{s}_{t+1} - i_t + \rho v_{t+1}$$

$$-\Delta E_{t+1} \pi_{t+1} = \Delta E_{t+1} \tilde{s}_{t+1} + \rho \Delta E_{t+1} v_{t+1}$$

$$= \Delta E_{t+1} \tilde{s}_{t+1} + \rho \Delta E_{t+1} \left(\sum_{j=0}^{\infty} \rho^j \tilde{s}_{t+2+j} \right)$$

$$= \varepsilon_{t+1} + [a(\rho) - 1] \varepsilon_{t+1}.$$

Though this formulation is algebraically simpler, the meaning of the terms of the formula may be clearer in the exact case.

4.2.4   The Mean and Risk of Government Bond Returns

The ex post real return on government debt in this simple example (constant expected return, one-period debt) is

$$\Delta E_{t+1} r_{t+1} = \Delta E_{t+1} (i_t - \pi_{t+1}) = -\Delta E_{t+1} \pi_{t+1} = a(\rho) \varepsilon_{t+1}.$$

As an AR(1) or other large $a(\rho)$ process predicts a large standard deviation of inflation, they predict a large standard deviation of ex post real bond returns, on the order

$5/(1 - 0.55) = 11\%$. As unexpected inflation actually has about a 1% per year standard deviation, the actual real one-year Treasury bill return has about a 1% per year standard deviation. The AR(1) model predicts volatility of real bond returns that is off by a factor of 10.

A smaller $a(\rho)$ solves this puzzle. With $a(\rho) = 0$, unexpected inflation in this simple model is zero, and nominal government bonds are risk free in real terms, for any volatility of surpluses.

Surpluses are procyclical, falling in recessions at the same time as consumption falls, dividends fall, and the stock market falls. (See Figure 4.1.) A volatile, procyclical, positively autocorrelated surplus would generate a large procyclical risk, and therefore a high risk premium, similar to the equity premium. But government bonds have a low average return, low volatility, and if anything a negative stock market and consumption beta. Inflation is low and interest rates drop in recessions, so bonds have good returns in those events.

The s-shaped surplus process solves the expected return and positive beta puzzles as well. In turn, the low average return of government bonds and their acyclical or countercyclical returns are additional evidence for the s-shaped surplus process.

With an s-shaped surplus response, government debt becomes like a security whose price rises as its dividend falls, so even a volatile dividend stream has a steady return, and hence a low average return. Each deficit, each decline in s_t, corresponds to a rise in subsequent surpluses, $E_t \sum_{j=1}^{\infty} \beta^j s_{t+j}$, and hence a rise in value or "price."

This point is easiest to see algebraically with the linearized identities and still specializing to one-period debt. From the debt accumulation equation (3.17) we can write the one-period real return

$$r_{t+1} = i_t - \pi_{t+1} = \rho v_{t+1} - v_t + \tilde{s}_{t+1}$$

$$\Delta E_{t+1} r_{t+1} = \rho \Delta E_{t+1} v_{t+1} + \Delta E_{t+1} \tilde{s}_{t+1}$$

$$\Delta E_{t+1} r_{t+1} = [a(\rho) - 1] \varepsilon_{t+1} + \varepsilon_{t+1}.$$

Here I split the return into a "price change" and a "dividend."

With $a(\rho) \geq 1$, the innovation in value v_{t+1} reinforces the surplus innovation, since higher surpluses at $t + 1$ portend higher surpluses to follow. The rate of return is more volatile than surpluses. With $a(\rho) = 0$, a surprise surplus s_{t+1} is met by a decline in the value of debt v_{t+1}, driven by a decline in subsequent surpluses, so the overall return is risk free.

Again, perhaps it is clearer to see the point in the nonlinear exact version of the model, at the cost of a few more symbols. The end-of-period value of debt is given by

$$\frac{Q_t B_t}{P_t} = E_t \left[\beta \frac{u'(c_{t+1})}{u'(c_t)} s_{t+1} \right] + E_t \left[\sum_{j=2}^{\infty} \beta^j \frac{u'(c_{t+j})}{u'(c_t)} s_{t+j} \right]$$

$$= E_t \left[\beta \frac{u'(c_{t+1})}{u'(c_t)} s_{t+1} \right] + E_t \left[\beta \frac{u'(c_{t+1})}{u'(c_t)} \frac{Q_{t+1} B_{t+1}}{P_{t+1}} \right].$$

The first term, and more generally the first few such terms, generates the apparent paradox. Shocks to the surplus s_{t+1} are positively correlated with shocks to consumption c_{t+1}, and thus negatively correlated with marginal utility growth. That negative correlation lowers the value on the left-hand side and thus raises the required return. But with an s-shaped moving average, when consumption c_{t+1} and surpluses s_{t+1} decline, subsequent surpluses rise, and the value $Q_{t+1}B_{t+1}/P_{t+1}$ rises. The overall risk is reduced, absent, or even negative, so the mean return need not be large.

By contrast, a higher dividend typically raises the value of a stock because the higher dividend forecasts uniformly higher subsequent dividends. But bonds are not stocks. Though the valuation formula looks the same and follows similar logic, the cash flow process for government debt is dramatically different from the process for stock dividends, and similar to that of corporate debt, in this crucial respect. What matters to one-period return risk is the covariance of surpluses *and the value of debt* with consumption. The value of debt behaves oppositely to surpluses and to stock prices, though immediate shocks to surpluses behave similarly to dividend or earnings shocks.

Another difference causes confusion: The government debt valuation formula applies to the total market value of government debt, where the usual asset pricing formula applies to a specific security. The individual bond investor does not receive a cash flow s_{t+1}. That investor receives the promised \$1. There may be a surplus or deficit, and a corresponding decrease or increase in the value of debt, but that comes from selling fewer or more new bonds. One can look at total market value or return to an individual asset holder, but do not confuse the two. One can also synthesize a security whose payoffs are the surplus and whose value is the total value of debt, by buying additional debt when the government sells it.

Consider the $a(\rho) = 0$ case. Individual bonds are risk free because they give a risk-free \$1 payout with no inflation risk. The total value of debt and its synthetic portfolio are also risk free, but now because the cash flow risk of one-period surplus is exactly matched by the "price" risk of the next period's value of debt. These are two different but congruent views.

If the government follows an $a(\rho) > 1$ surplus process, then inflation is large in recessions when marginal utility is high. Individual bond real returns are then low in recessions. The total value or its portfolio strategy is risky because both cash flow and price—value of debt—decline in recessions. None of this happens.

In sum, that in the United States as in other advanced economies in the postwar period we do not see volatile government bond returns, that their returns are if anything countercyclical, that the value of debt rises when there are deficits, and that mean bond returns are low, are all signs that the surplus process for normal advanced economies is negatively autocorrelated, closer to $a(\rho) = 0$ than to $a(\rho) = 1$.

Jiang et al. (2019) proclaim a puzzle of low mean bond returns. Their paper is not directly aimed at fiscal theory, but proclaims a puzzle of the government debt valuation equation, which would undermine fiscal theory as well if true. They omit the value of debt from their VAR forecast, which leads to a false estimate of a large $a(\rho)$. (In an appendix, they chop the data into subsamples in which debt appears nonstationary, or surpluses appear not to respond to debt.) They use a complex discount factor model, though the discount factor existence theorems tell that absent arbitrage, a discount factor always exists to rationalize observed prices. When their model produces stock-like average returns for government bonds, they proclaim a puzzle. It took asset pricing 20 painful years to figure out that you cannot fit models of dividends and discount rates, and try to test the present value relation. Those lessons have been slow to soak into government debt analysis. (Online Appendix Chapter 2.)

Jiang et al. (2019) suggest large bond liquidity premiums as an explanation. They do not address their model's (large $a(\rho)$) prediction that current deficits lower the value of debt, along with all of the other above puzzles. Tacking on a large liquidity premium to change the low mean return does not explain any of these other counterfactual predictions. They claim that the government of an economy whose GDP is nonstationary *cannot* issue riskless debt—it cannot promise $a(\rho) = 0$. But the mean surplus does not have to scale with GDP. And if their claim were true it would apply to all governments. A government with a unit root in GDP that does not borrow in its own currency—the members of the euro, gold standard governments, any government financed by foreign borrowing—would eventually have to default.

4.2.5   *Stylized Fact Summary*

These phenomena are tied together. With an AR(1) or $a(\rho) > 1$ surplus process, inflation and deficits are strongly correlated; there is a lot of inflation; deficits are followed by lower values of debt; deficits are financed by inflating away outstanding debt; and bond returns are highly volatile, countercyclical, and give a high risk premium. With a surplus process that has an s-shape moving average with small $a(\rho)$, all of these predictions are reversed. And therefore all of these observations scream for a small value of $a(\rho)$, at least for postwar U.S. time series data and that of similar countries. None of the counterfactual predictions is a rejection of the fiscal theory. They are rejections of the auxiliary assumption that the surplus follows an AR(1) or similar process with $a(\rho) \geq 1$, or econometric restrictions that force such estimates. The phenomena are tied together so you can't fix one alone.

We move on in the next section to estimates of the surplus process. But I emphasize this set of stylized facts above particular estimates. Estimates vary based on regression specification and sample period, and honest standard errors are always regrettably large in U.S. time series applications. Multiple shocks raise thorny orthogonalization issues.

By contrast, the combined weight of the stylized facts in the context of the model is more powerful evidence. The logic and cross-equation restrictions of the model tie facts together. A direct estimate of $a(\rho)$ may be uncertain, but the indirect estimate of $a(\rho)$ coming from the relative volatility of inflation and surpluses, the correlation between surpluses and debt, and the other puzzles, as filtered through the model, is more powerful evidence for the kind of surplus process that we will need for that model to make sense. Of course, a formalization of this estimate should include time-varying expected returns, and a model with sticky prices and other ingredients that produce realistic results. But the signs and magnitudes are strong stylized facts that will clearly be hard to turn around. We must at least allow that a surplus process describing U.S. postwar time series has a substantial component in which deficits today are financed by expectations of surpluses to follow.

4.2.6 An S-Shaped Surplus Process is Reasonable

Perhaps an s-shaped surplus process with $a(\rho) < 1$ seems like an artificial device or a technical trick?

Governments under the gold standard, members of the euro, those using foreign currency, and state and local governments *must* follow a surplus process with $a(\rho) = 0$ if they wish to avoid default. If they wish to borrow, they must repay in expectation. People and businesses who wish to borrow must commit to an s-shaped cash flow process and follow through in expectation. If you take out a mortgage, or a business borrows, there is a big positive cash inflow today, mirrored by a long string of negative cash outflows in the future. Weighted by interest rates, the inflows must be expected to match the outflows: $a(\rho) = 0$. (By referring to $a(\rho)$, I refer to the model with constant expected return. More generally, they must promise to repay their debts, also adapting to potentially higher interest rates.)

Governments with their own floating currencies, facing temporary deficits, that do not want lots of unexpected inflation, will *choose* a surplus process with a small if not zero $a(\rho)$. Such governments wish to finance deficits by borrowing rather than inflating away outstanding debt and wish to raise revenue from bond sales rather than just drive down bond prices. To do so, they must credibly promise to raise subsequent surpluses.

When transitioning from the gold standard or an exchange rate peg to fiat money, surely governments *could* and mostly did maintain the same general set of fiscal affairs and traditions that they followed to maintain the gold standard or peg; as a matter of prudence, deliberate inflation control, and desire to borrow in bad times. An s-shaped surplus process is what one expects from the classic theory of public finance, such as Barro (1979): Governments adapt to temporary spending such as a war or recession by borrowing, and promise a long string of higher surpluses later to pay off the debt, in order to keep a smooth path of distorting taxes.

Monetarist, new-Keynesian and much fiscal theory literature specifies an s-shaped surplus policy when fiscal policy is "passive," reacting to price level changes determined elsewhere. Then it is logically *possible* for the same policy to be followed "actively."

In short, choosing and committing to a surplus process with $a(\rho)$ small or zero is not strange or unnatural. It is normal responsible debt management for a government that wishes to control inflation and maintain its ability to borrow real resources in times of need.

We do not have or need $a(\rho) = 0$ always. Governments inflate away some debt in some circumstances. The government may choose to meet bad news with an effective (Lucas and Stokey (1983)) partial "state-contingent default," engineered by devaluation via inflation. The economic damage of inflation, which one may formalize with sticky prices, versus the damage due to distorting taxation or explicit default, poses an interesting question in dynamic public finance and often leads to an interior solution with a bit of both taxation and inflation. People sometimes distrust that the persistent component of surpluses will rise quite as much as needed to fully pay off the debt, and some inflation will arise. Or, the required surpluses may run into long-run Laffer limits: Permanent taxes reduce the long-run level of economic activity enough that the present value of revenues does not increase. In all these cases, some or all of a deficit shock is met by an unexpected inflation, and we see $a(\rho) > 0$. But fiscal theory governments do not *have to* fund every deficit with inflation. They do not need to follow $a(\rho) \geq 1$.

Canzoneri, Cumby, and Diba (2001) articulate the puzzle captured by (4.7): A positively correlated surplus process means that surpluses should paradoxically raise, rather than reduce, debt. They interpret their natural opposite empirical finding as a rejection of the fiscal theory. But it is a rejection of a positively correlated surplus process, not of fiscal theory per se. Puzzles are useful. Thinking about this paper made me first realize the importance of an s-shaped surplus process. But puzzles cease to be tests when they are solved.

In retrospect, this all may seem obvious. *Of course* governments promise higher surpluses when they sell debt. Governments want to raise revenue when they borrow, and not just inflate away debt. Of course the surplus process is s-shaped, just like your cash flow process when you buy a house and then pay down the mortgage. Why has this point taken decades to sort out? Well, everything in economics is only clear in retrospect.

Part of the confusion has stemmed from a misunderstanding that fiscal theory assumes surpluses are "exogenous," like an endowment, and that "exogenous" means a fixed stochastic process beyond the government's control. While acknowledging that $a(\rho) < 1$ is possible, Canzoneri, Cumby, and Diba (2001) write "We will argue that this correlation structure seems rather implausible in the context of an NR [active-fiscal] regime, where surpluses are governed by an exogenous political process." No, *the surplus process is a choice.* Governments, even "political" governments, choose tax policies, choose spending policies, and invest in a range of institutional commitments and reputations to ensure bondholders that the governments will usually repay rather than inflate away debts. Fiscal theory is completely compatible with such a view, and does not require either "exogenous" or positively autocorrelated surpluses. An exogenous surplus, like an endowment economy, is an easy modeling simplification. But sometimes modeling simplifications take on a life of their own. And even exogenous surpluses need not be positively autocorrelated.

Some of the confusion results from failing to distinguish fiscal shocks or disturbances from surpluses themselves. A useful model of many governments is $\tilde{s}_{t+1} = \alpha v_t + u_{s,t+1}$, where v_t is the value of debt following $\rho v_{t+1} = v_t + r_{t+1} - \tilde{s}_{t+1}$, and $u_{s,t}$ is a positively autocorrelated disturbance. Wars last a while, and do not automatically generate fiscal surpluses when they are over. The $u_{s,t}$ term may have $a_u(\rho) > 1$. But governments finance wars by issuing debt and promising to raise taxes to repay that debt. In this structure, which is compatible with active fiscal policy, surpluses themselves s_t may be fully repaid with $a_s(\rho) = 0$, even if $a_u(\rho) > 1$.

Finally, this is a good example of how the observational equivalence theorem guides one productively. If you know about observational equivalence, you are prodded to write down just what the identifying assumptions are that make fiscal theory testable. You realize that the content of the test is the assumption $a(\rho) > 1$. You look hard at the assumption. You may then realize it doesn't make much sense. But if you don't know or think about observational equivalence, a positively autocorrelated surplus just looks like one of hundreds of harmless modeling assumptions, and there is no reason to suspect that it so centrally drives the model or test.

None of this was obvious at the time. Indeed, other than a too-complex appearance in the back pages of too-long articles Cochrane (1998a) and Cochrane (2001), most fiscal theory papers including my own until Cochrane (2021b) use AR(1) or similar surplus processes, with large $a(\rho)$. The damage caused by this apparent simplifying assumption was also not clear.

Leeper, Traum, and Walker (2017) specify fiscal rules in which tax *rates* follow an AR(1) but endogenous movements in output generate primary surpluses with an s-shaped pattern. See for example their Figure 4. The same may be true of other papers. But the tax rate AR(1) is restrictive too, and this specification is not necessarily flexible enough to capture the facts; it does not obviously allow $a(\rho) = 0$.

Perhaps Cochrane (2005b) "Money as Stock" is also a bit to blame. That paper emphasizes the analogy with stocks, to counter critiques that the government debt is a "budget constraint" rather a valuation equation. For example, Jiang et al. (2019) are clearly influenced in their insistence that the surplus is positively autocorrelated and procyclical by the analogy with stock dividends. Stocks plausibly have persistent dividend processes. But government debt, like corporate debt, plausibly has an s-shaped, debt-like payoff process. Perhaps I should have titled the paper "Money as Bonds." The s-shaped surplus is clear in Cochrane (1998a), but I didn't emphasize it in "Money as Stock." Simplicity is not always an unalloyed virtue.

So, yes, these apparently simple realizations took time. They were not obvious in the thick of things. But with the benefit of hindsight, we can recognize that imposing a positively correlated surplus process, a priori restricting fiscal theory away from low $a(\rho)$, thereby inducing a range of grossly counterfactual behavior, is a conceptual mistake that we should not continue to make.

4.2.7   *A Generalization*

This discussion has all taken place in the context of the constant discount rate model. It, and the Hansen, Roberds, and Sargent (1992) formula, can be generalized to time-varying expected returns.

In our context, the linearizations of Section 3.5 invite a natural generalization. Write each series as an element of a vector-valued moving average representation,

$$\pi_t = a_\pi(L)' \varepsilon_t$$
$$\tilde{s}_t = a_s(L)' \varepsilon_t,$$

and so forth. The unexpected inflation identity (3.20) leads to

$$\Delta E_{t+1} \pi_{t+1} = \left[-a_s(\rho) - a_g(\rho) + a_r(\rho) \right]' \varepsilon_{t+1},$$

which generalizes the expression

$$\Delta E_{t+1} \pi_{t+1} = -a_s(\rho)' \varepsilon_{t+1}.$$

The equivalent of $a(\rho) = 0$ to characterize debt repayment is now

$$a_s(\rho) + a_g(\rho) = a_r(\rho). \tag{4.11}$$

The $a_g(\rho)$ term transforms between surpluses and surplus-to-GDP ratios. The $a_r(\rho)$ term expresses the important idea that a government that repays its debts must also raise surpluses when there is a rise in the interest costs of its debt. The condition $a_s(\rho) = 0$ is the special case of no growth, or a stationary surplus, and of constant expected returns.

The weighted inflation identity (3.22) gives

$$a_\pi(\omega)'\varepsilon_{t+1} = \left[-a_s(\rho) - a_g(\rho) + a_r(\rho) - a_r(\omega)\right]'\varepsilon_{t+1}. \tag{4.12}$$

A similar generalization of Hansen, Roberds, and Sargent (1992) may be useful in finance. From the Campbell and Shiller (1988) linearization,

$$p_t - d_t = \sum_{j=1}^{\infty} \rho^{j-1}\left(\Delta d_{t+j} - r_{t+j}\right)$$

we have the Campbell and Ammer (1993) decomposition,

$$\Delta E_{t+1} r_{t+1} = \Delta E_{t+1} \sum_{j=1}^{\infty} \rho^{j-1}\Delta d_{t+1} - \Delta E_{t+1} \sum_{j=2}^{\infty} \rho^{j-1}\Delta r_{t+j}$$

or

$$\Delta E_{t+1} r_{t+1} = \{a_d(\rho) - [a_r(\rho) - a_r(0)]\}'\varepsilon_{t+1}.$$

It follows that

$$0 = a_d(\rho) - a_r(\rho), \tag{4.13}$$

generalizing the Hansen, Roberds, and Sargent (1992) test of a present value relation, $a_d(\rho) = 0$, to time-varying expected returns.

However, relations (4.11), (4.12) and (4.13) are no longer *tests* of the present value relation. They are based on identities, so they hold as identities. Looking at identities is useful. It helps us to characterize what sorts of processes $a_d(L)$, $a_r(L)$, and so forth account for the data. The whole discovery that price-dividend ratios move on news of expected returns rather than dividend growth comes from looking at terms of this identity. The original $a(\rho) = 0$ is, in retrospect, a test. But it is only a test of the hypothesis that expected returns are constant over time. Section 4.4 calculates the terms of (4.11) and (4.12).

4.3   Surplus Process Estimates

I estimate the surplus process with a VAR, a small VAR, and an AR(1). The VAR estimates show an s-shaped response. The AR(1), though barely distinguishable in its initial responses and forecasting ability, gives a dramatically higher estimate of the sum of responses. It is a mistake to leave the value of debt out of a VAR.

Table 4.1 presents three vector autoregressions involving surpluses and debt. Here, v_t is the log market value of U.S. federal debt divided by consumption, scaled by the

TABLE 4.1. Surplus and Debt Forecasting Regressions. Variables are $\tilde{s}=$ surplus, $v=$ debt/GDP, $\pi =$ inflation, $g =$ growth, $i =$ 3-month rate, $y =$ 10-year yield. Sample 1947–2018.

	$\tilde{s}_t$	v_t	π_t	g_t	r_t^n	i_t	y_t	$\sigma(\varepsilon)$	$\sigma(s)$
$\tilde{s}_{t+1}=$	0.35	0.043	−0.25	1.37	−0.32	0.50	−0.04	4.75	6.60
std. err.	(0.09)	(0.022)	(0.31)	(0.45)	(0.16)	(0.46)	(0.58)		
$v_{t+1}=$	−0.24	0.98	−0.29	−2.00	0.28	−0.72	1.60		
std. err.	(0.12)	(0.03)	(0.43)	(0.61)	(0.27)	(0.85)	(1.04)		
$\tilde{s}_{t+1}=$	0.55	0.027						5.46	6.60
std. err.	(0.07)	(0.016)							
$v_{t+1}=$	−0.54	0.96							
std. err.	(0.11)	(0.02)							
$\tilde{s}_{t+1}=$	0.55							5.55	6.60
std. err.	(0.07)								

consumption/GDP ratio. I divide by consumption to focus on variation in the debt rather than cyclical variation in GDP. Consumption is a good stochastic trend for GDP, without the look-ahead bias of potential GDP. π_t is the log GDP deflator, g_t is log consumption growth, r_t^n is the nominal return on the government bond portfolio, i_t is the three-month Treasury bill rate and y_t is the 10-year government bond yield. I infer the surplus $\tilde{s}_t$ from the linearized identity (3.17), allowing growth,

$$\rho v_{t+1} = v_t + r_{t+1}^n - \pi_{t+1} - g_{t+1} - \tilde{s}_{t+1}.$$

Conceptually, $\tilde{s}_t$ is the ratio of real primary surplus to consumption, scaled by the steady-state consumption/GDP ratio, and scaled by the steady-state debt-to-GDP ratio. I include the short-term interest rate i_t in the VAR, which represents monetary policy in our models, and the 10-year interest rate y_t, which is an important forecasting variable for interest rates. Cochrane (2021a) describes the data and VAR in detail.

The first two regressions in Table 4.1 present the surplus and value regressions in a larger VAR. I omit the other equations of the VAR in the table, but they are there in the following impulse response functions. The surplus is moderately persistent (0.35). Most importantly, the surplus responds to the value of the debt (0.043). This coefficient is measured with a t-statistic of barely 2, with simple OLS standard errors. However, this point estimate confirms estimates such as Bohn (1998a). Bohn includes additional contemporaneous variables in the regression, which soak up a good deal of residual variance. For this reason, and by using longer samples, Bohn finds greater statistical significance despite similar point estimates. Debt is very persistent (0.98), and higher surpluses pay down debt (−0.24).

The second two estimates present a smaller VAR consisting of only surplus and debt. The coefficients are similar to those of surplus and debt in the larger VAR, and we will see that this smaller VAR contains most of the message of the larger VAR for the surplus process. The third estimate is a simple AR(1). Though the small VAR and AR(1) have the same coefficient of surplus on lagged surplus, 0.55, we will see how they differ crucially on long-run properties.

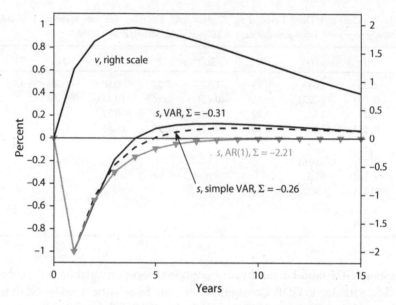

FIGURE 4.3. Responses to a 1% Deficit Shock. "$\Sigma =$" gives the sum of the indicated responses.

Figure 4.3 presents responses of these VARs to a 1% deficit shock at time 0. *The VAR shows an s-shaped surplus response.* The initial 1.0% deficit is followed by two more periods of deficit, for a cumulative 1.75% deficit. But then the surplus response turns positive. The many small positive surpluses chip away at the debt. The sum of surpluses in response to the shock is only $\sum_{j=0}^{\infty} \tilde{s}_{1+j} = -0.31$, so $a(1) = 0.31$.

Mechanically, the value of debt jumps up when surplus jumps down due to contemporaneous correlation of surplus with debt shocks. This is already evidence for an s-shaped response, as in our AR(1) examples a lower surplus meant lower debt. The negative surpluses continue to push up the value of debt via the coefficients of debt on lagged surplus (-0.24). But surpluses also respond to the greater value of debt. After the autoregressive (0.35) dynamics of the surplus shock have died out, the surplus response to the more persistent debt (0.043) brings positive surpluses, which in turn help to slowly bring down the value of debt.

Thus, the s-shaped surplus response is robust and intuitive. It comes from the negative sign of the regression of surplus on debt, the persistent debt response, and the pattern that higher surpluses bring down the value of debt. The s-shape estimate here does not come from direct estimates of very long-run surplus autocorrelations.

The simple VAR shows almost exactly the same surplus response as the full VAR, emphasizing how the response comes from the intuitive features of that VAR. The point estimate of the sum of coefficients in the simple VAR is smaller, $a(1) = 0.26$. The simple VAR surplus response crosses that of the full VAR and continues to be larger past the right end of the graph, accounting for the smaller value of $a(1)$.

The simple AR(1) surplus response looks almost the same, but it does not rise above zero. It would be very hard to tell the AR(1) and VAR surplus responses apart based on autocorrelations or short-run forecasting ability emphasized in standard statistical tests. The coefficient of surplus on debt (0.027) is less than two standard errors from zero

(0.016). But selecting variables based on t-statistics is a bad econometric habit. Zero is also less than two standard errors away from 0.027, and there is no reason one should be the null and the other the alternative. Adding debt to the surplus regression only lowers the standard error of the residual from 5.55% to 5.46%. But the long-run implications of the AR(1) are dramatically different. For the AR(1), we have $a(1) = 2.21$, a factor of 10 larger! In the context of our simple model with constant discount rates, short-term debt, and flexible prices, the VAR-implied surplus process predicts 0.26%-0.31% inflation in response to a 1% fiscal shock. The same model fed the AR(1) surplus model predicts 2.28% inflation—a factor of 10 larger—and the same increase in bond return volatility. Leaving the value of debt out of the VAR makes an enormous difference to the results.

The AR(1) estimate is not just different, it is *wrong*. We start with a present value relation based on people's information, in the constant interest rate case

$$v_t = E\left(\sum_{j=0}^{\infty} \rho^j \tilde{s}_{t+1+j} | \Omega_t\right)$$

where Ω_t is the set of all information used by people to form expectations at time t. When we apply this formula, we must condition down to a smaller information set, such as that generated by the variables in the VAR. We take $E(\cdot|I_t)$ of both sides, where $I_t \subset \Omega_t$, to obtain

$$v_t = E\left(\sum_{j=0}^{\infty} \rho^j \tilde{s}_{t+1+j} | I_t\right).$$

This conditioning down is valid, so long as $v_t \in I_t$, so long as we include v_t in the VAR. If not, the left-hand side should be $E(v_t|I_t)$, not v_t.

It is a natural project to forecast the surplus using a set of variables not including the value of debt; use a discount factor model to construct the present value of surpluses; see if the calculation spits out the value of debt; and proclaim a puzzle or rejection of the present value model if it does not do so. Empirical asset pricing wasted a lot of time on such exercises. But it is *wrong* to do so.

The only way to rescue such a calculation is to assume that people use exactly the same information to forecast that we include in the VAR, $I_t = \Omega_t$. Any (many) papers that make such calculations using present value formulas in consumption (permanent income), investment, asset pricing, and fiscal affairs make this assumption, usually implicitly. But in that case, v_t would be an exact function of the observed information, with 100% R^2. The value v_t would be redundant in the VAR. It is a testable implicit assumption, and it fails.

Noninvertibility is the second problem in this effort. If $\tilde{s}_t = a(L)\varepsilon_t$ with $a(\rho) = 0$, the moving average representation we are looking for has a root inside the unit circle, and therefore cannot be recovered from a VAR that excludes the value of debt.

Consider the MA(1) example again, and let $\theta = \rho^{-1}$. Now $\tilde{s}_t = \varepsilon_t - \rho^{-1}\varepsilon_{t-1}$, which has $a(\rho) = 0$. But $\rho^{-1} > 1$, a noninvertible root. (More precisely, the shock ε_t is a function of current and *future* surpluses, not current and past surpluses.) An autoregression will estimate $\tilde{s}_t = u_t - \theta u_{t-1}$ with $\theta = \rho$ and $u_t = \tilde{s}_t - E(\tilde{s}_t|\tilde{s}_{t-1}, \tilde{s}_{t-2} \ldots)$. You will falsely estimate $a(\rho) = 1 - \rho^2 \neq 0$. The structural representation we are interested in is a noninvertible moving average. There is nothing wrong with noninvertible structural moving averages, but you cannot recover them from any statistical procedure based on the history of surpluses alone.

In this example, we have $v_t = -\theta \varepsilon_t = -\rho^{-1} \varepsilon_t$. The value of debt reveals the true shock. Then a VAR including surplus and value of debt can recover the true process.

In this case, with only $\theta < 1$, and thus $a(\rho) > 1 - \rho$, the moving average is technically invertible. However, close-to-unit roots in moving averages are hard to estimate, so the noninvertibility problem bleeds over the boundary. Including the value of the debt makes for a more precise estimate, through the mechanism visible in the VAR.

If you do include the value of debt, and discount with expected returns, however, the present value relation is an identity. Even if you do not discount with returns, a discount rate always exists by which the present value relation holds. The present value relation per se is not testable. We should no longer try to forecast surpluses and discount rates without using the value of debt to make those forecasts; then calculate what the value of debt should be, and call the result a test or proclaim puzzles. Doing so is simply wrong. This lesson took decades of hard work in macroeconomics and finance to learn. Let us not repeat the wasted effort. (More in Online Appendix Chapter 2.)

Finally, and perhaps most importantly, a second error tempts. The standard errors on the coefficient linking surplus to lagged debt are large. One might fail to reject zero, and impose that view or use successive t-tests to eliminate variables. One might even accept (fail to reject) a view that the debt-to-GDP ratio has a root greater than one. One might use the resulting estimate of the surplus process, plug it in the model, and conclude there is a puzzle in that the model then predicts wildly counterfactual results for the joint process of surplus, debt, inflation, and bond returns. But all of the model predictions bear on the surplus process. The fact that surpluses lower, not raise, the value of debt is a central piece of evidence for an s-shaped process. Full-model estimates would reveal that fact. One should use all of a model's important moments to estimate parameters, and then test overidentifying restrictions.

This little exercise is oversimplified in one crucial respect. The response of actual surpluses matters, which sums the response of the surplus-to-consumption ratio and the response of consumption. We should sum the two responses. The point, however, is an illustration of an econometric pitfall, not a good estimate. The next section presents that estimate also including discount rate variation.

4.4   The Roots of Inflation

I calculate impulse-response functions and I estimate the terms of the inflation decompositions. A shock to inflation comes about 2/3 from higher discount rates and 1/3 from lower growth. An "aggregate demand" shock that lowers inflation and output by 1% produces deficits and lower growth. The latter would produce higher inflation, but a large discount rate decline overwhelms them to produce lower inflation. A 1% shock to the sum of future surpluses and a 1% shock to the discount rate produce essentially no inflation. Each comes with an offsetting movement in the other.

Understanding the time series of inflation in the postwar United States requires us to include time-varying discount rates, rather than just focus on changes in expected surpluses.

Now, I use the full VAR from the top panel of Table 4.1 to answer the fundamental question, where does inflation come from? I estimate the terms of the linearized identity (3.22) (also (4.12))

$$\sum_{j=0}^{\infty} \omega^j \Delta E_1 \pi_{1+j} = -\sum_{j=0}^{\infty} \Delta E_1 \tilde{s}_{1+j} - \sum_{j=0}^{\infty} \Delta E_1 g_{1+j} + \sum_{j=1}^{\infty} (1 - \omega^j) \Delta E_1 r_{1+j}. \quad (4.14)$$

Unexpected inflation, weighted by the maturity structure of government debt, corresponds to the revision in forecast future surpluses, growth, and discount rates. The surplus $\tilde{s}_t$ is surplus-to-GDP ratio, so lower growth lowers actual surpluses. Thus we have two cash flow terms and a discount rate term. Relative to (3.22), here I use a weighting factor and point of linearization $\rho = 1$. All the variables are stationary, impulse-responses die out, so we do not need an additional weighting factor for convergence. Results using a ρ slightly less than 1 are nearly identical.

I also tabulate the mark-to-market constituents of this identity, (3.20) and (3.21)

$$\Delta E_1 \pi_1 - \Delta E_1 r_1^n = -\sum_{j=0}^{\infty} \Delta E_1 \tilde{s}_{1+j} - \sum_{j=0}^{\infty} \Delta E_1 g_{1+j} + \sum_{j=1}^{\infty} \Delta E_1 r_{1+j} \quad (4.15)$$

$$\Delta E_1 r_1^n = -\sum_{j=1}^{\infty} \omega^j \Delta E_1 r_{1+j}^n = -\sum_{j=1}^{\infty} \omega^j \Delta E_1 \left(r_{1+j} + \pi_{1+j} \right). \quad (4.16)$$

Changes in the present value of surpluses coming from surpluses, growth, or discount rates are absorbed by inflation or by a decline in long-term bond prices. In turn, long-term bond prices reflect future expected real returns or inflation.

The terms of these identities are sums of the VAR impulse-response functions. Though they are identities, they can tell us whether inflation corresponds to changes in surpluses, in growth, or in discount rates, and by plotting the response functions we can see the pattern of those changes. The terms of the impulse-response function can also be interpreted as decompositions of the variance of unexpected inflation. They answer the question, "What fraction of the variance of unexpected inflation is due to each component?"

This section summarizes Cochrane (2021a). This approach to evaluating present value relations follows Campbell and Shiller (1988), Campbell and Ammer (1993), and Cochrane (1992). Cochrane (2011c) summarizes this literature in asset pricing. Asset pricing finds that discount rate variation accounts for a great deal of asset price variation, across many asset classes, and variation in expected cash flows accounts for much less asset price variation. From that perspective, finding the same result for government bonds is not terribly surprising.

The VAR has many shocks, so one has to choose interesting shocks. I start by examining an unexpected inflation movement, $\Delta E_1 \pi_1 = \varepsilon_{\pi,1} = 1$. I allow all other variables to move contemporaneously with the inflation shock. We would not want, for example, to keep surpluses, the value of debt, or bond returns constant. A surplus or discount rate shock may have caused the inflation shock.

To allow all other shocks to move by their customary amount when there is an inflation shock, I fill in shocks to the other variables by running regressions of their shocks on the inflation shock. Denote the VAR

$$x_{t+1} = A x_t + \varepsilon_{t+1}. \tag{4.17}$$

For each variable $z_t \in x_t$, then, I run

$$\varepsilon_{z,t+1} = b_{z,\pi} \varepsilon_{\pi,t+1} + u_{z,t+1},$$

where $u_{z,t+1}$ denotes the regression error. Then I start the VAR at

$$\varepsilon_1 = \begin{bmatrix} b_{r^n,\pi} & b_{g,\pi} & \varepsilon_{\pi,1} = 1 & b_{s,\pi} & \cdots \end{bmatrix}'.$$

This procedure is equivalent to the usual orthogonalization of the shock covariance matrix, but it is more transparent and it generalizes more easily later.

Figure 4.4 plots responses to this inflation shock. Table 4.2 collects the terms of the decomposition identities (4.14), (4.15), (4.16). Figure 4.4 also presents some of the main terms in the identities.

In Figure 4.4, the inflation shock is moderately persistent. Inflation initially follows AR(1) dynamics induced by its coefficient on its own lag, and then turns slightly negative. As a result, the weighted sum $\sum_{j=0}^{\infty} \omega^j \Delta E_1 \pi_{1+j} = 1.59\%$ is greater than the 1% initial shock. The subsequent inflation devalues long-term bonds, so we look for a 1.59% total fiscal shock.

In the top panel of Figure 4.4, the inflation shock coincides with deficits $\tilde{s}_1$, which build with a hump shape. One might think that these persistent deficits account for inflation. But surpluses eventually rise to pay back almost all of the incurred debt with an s-shape. The sum of all surplus responses is -0.06%, essentially zero. In response to this shock—an inflation shock, not directly a surplus shock—the government borrows, but then repays essentially all of its deficits as a ratio to GDP.

The inflation shock also coincides with a persistent decline in economic growth g. Lower growth lowers surpluses, for a given surplus-to-GDP ratio. The growth decline contributes 0.49% to the inflation decompositions, accounting for about a third of the total inflation.

The line marked $r^n - \pi$ plots the response of the real discount rate, $\Delta E_1 r_{1+j}$. These points are plotted at the time of the ex post return, $1+j$, so they are the expected return one period earlier, at time j. The line starts at time 2, where the terms of the discount rate sums in the inflation decompositions start, and representing the time 1 expected return. After two periods, this discount rate rises and stays persistently positive. The weighted sum of discount rate terms is 1.04%, while the unweighted sum is 1.00% (really 1.004%). The weight ω is 0.69, chosen to make the identity (3.21) hold exactly for this response function. Therefore, weighting by 1 versus $1 - \omega^j$ makes little difference in the face of such a persistent response. Weighted or unweighted, the discount rate terms account for 1% inflation. A higher discount rate lowers the value of government debt, an inflationary force.

Overall, then, as also summarized in the first row of Table 4.2,

- *A 1% shock to inflation corresponds to a roughly 1.5% decline in the present value of surpluses and 1.5% overall inflationary devaluation of government debt. A rise in*

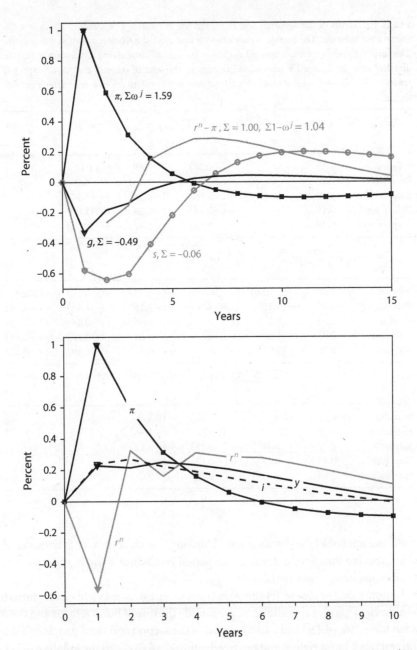

FIGURE 4.4. Responses to a 1% Inflation Shock. Σ gives the sum of the responses and $\Sigma\omega^j$ gives the ω-weighted sum of responses, which are terms of the inflation-decomposition identities.

discount rate contributes about 1% and a decline in growth accounts for about 0.5% of that decline. Changes in the surplus-to-GDP ratio account for nearly nothing.

This is an important finding for matching the fiscal theory to data, or for understanding the fiscal side of passive-fiscal models. Thinking in both contexts has focused on the presence or absence of surpluses, via taxing and spending policies, not surpluses induced

TABLE 4.2. Terms of the Inflation and Bond Return Identities. The inflation shock is a 1% unexpected inflation. The recession shock is a 1% unexpected decline in inflation and growth. The surplus shock is a 1% unexpected decline in the sum of current and future surpluses. The discount rate shock is a 1% unexpected decline in the sum of current and future expected returns. The "surplus, no i" shock holds the interest rate constant for two years after a surplus shock.

$$\sum_{j=0}^{\infty} \omega^j \pi_{1+j} = -\sum_{j=0}^{\infty} \tilde{s}_{1+j} - \sum_{j=0}^{\infty} g_{1+j} + \sum_{j=1}^{\infty} (1-\omega^j) r_{1+j}$$

	π	=	$\tilde{s}$	g	r
Inflation	1.59	=	$-(-0.06)$	$-(-0.49)$	$+(1.04)$
Recession	−2.36	=	$-(-1.15)$	$-(-1.46)$	$+(-4.96)$
Surplus	−0.10	=	$-(-0.66)$	$-(-0.34)$	$+(-1.10)$
Disc. Rate	−0.18	=	$-(-0.54)$	$-(-0.28)$	$+(-1.00)$
Surplus, no i	0.38	=	$-(-0.52)$	$-(-0.48)$	$+(-0.62)$

$$\pi_1 - r_1^n = -\sum_{j=0}^{\infty} \tilde{s}_{1+j} - \sum_{j=0}^{\infty} g_{1+j} + \sum_{j=1}^{\infty} r_{1+j}$$

	π	r^n	=	$\tilde{s}$	g	r
Inflation	1.00	$-(-0.56)$	=	$-(-0.06)$	$-(-0.49)$	$+(1.00)$
Recession	−1.00	$-(1.19)$	=	$-(-1.15)$	$-(-1.46)$	$+(-4.79)$
Surplus	0.02	$-(0.27)$	=	$-(-0.66)$	$-(-0.34)$	$+(-1.25)$
Disc. Rate	−0.03	$-(0.28)$	=	$-(-0.54)$	$-(-0.28)$	$+(-1.13)$
Surplus, no i	0.36	$-(0.03)$	=	$-(-0.52)$	$-(-0.48)$	$+(-0.67)$

$$r_1^n = -\sum_{j=1}^{\infty} \omega^j r_{1+j} - \sum_{j=1}^{\infty} \omega^j \pi_{1+j}$$

	r^n	=	r	π
Inflation	−0.56	=	$-(-0.03)$	$-(0.59)$
Recession	1.19	=	$-(0.17)$	$-(-1.36)$
Surplus	0.27	=	$-(-0.15)$	$-(-0.12)$
Disc. Rate	0.28	=	$-(-0.13)$	$-(-0.15)$
Surplus, no i	0.03	=	$-(-0.05)$	$-(0.02)$

by growth and least of all the discount rate. Thinking in both contexts has considered one-period unexpected inflation to devalue one-period bonds, not a rise in expected inflation that can devalue long-term bonds.

The bottom panel of Figure 4.4 shows us the response of bond yields and returns to the inflation shock. This plot also allows us to examine the role of bond returns and the mark-to-market identities (4.15) and (4.16) shown in the second and third panels of Table 4.2. The interest rate i, bond yield y, and expected return r^n all rise with the inflation shock, and thereafter move together and persistently. The expected return moves a bit more than the interest rate, indicating a rise in risk premium. The slight sawtooth in r^n is not significant. The immediate return shock r_1^n moves in the opposite direction as the expected returns, as bond prices decline when yields rise unexpectedly.

The rise in real discount rates stems from the more persistent movement in nominal rates than that of inflation on the right-hand side of this graph. That nominal rates and inflation move in such disconnected ways is a bit disconcerting. An s-shaped real interest rate movement is hard to digest economically. But this calculation is pure data characterization and does not impose any economic structure. If inflation and nominal rates go their own way, we measure a movement in the real rate.

In terms of the decompositions (4.15) and (4.16), we now have a 1% inflation, which is soaked up in part by the 0.56% decline in bond return r_1^n. The bottom panel of Table 4.2 shows that the decline in bond return corresponds almost exactly to the 0.56% rise in subsequent expected inflation, with no contribution from discount rates. Discount rates matter in the inflation decompositions but not in this bond return decomposition because the former have weights that emphasize long-term movements (1 and $1 - \omega^j$), while the ω^j weights of the bond return decomposition (4.16) emphasize short-run movements in discount rate.

Comparing the two analyses, you see how the government bond return essentially marks to market the expected future inflation.

In sum, viewed through the lens of (4.15) and (4.16),

- *The 1.5% fiscal shock that comes with 1% unexpected inflation is buffered by an 0.5% decline in bond prices, which corresponds to 0.5% additional expected future inflation.*

These calculations are terms of identities, and can be interpreted with either active-fiscal or passive-fiscal points of view. In a fiscal-theoretic interpretation, they answer, "What changes in expectations caused the 1% inflation?" In a passive-fiscal interpretation, they answer, "What changes in expected surpluses and other variables follow a 1% inflation?" I emphasize the former because that's what this book is about.

I use the words "shock" and "response," which have become conventional in the VAR literature, and compactly describe the calculations. The calculations do not imply or require a causal structure or a structural interpretation of "shocks." Responses answer the question, "If we see an unexpected 1% inflation, how should we revise our forecasts of other variables?" Indeed, I offer a reverse causal story: News about future surpluses and discount rates causes inflation to move. That news in turn reflects news about future productivity, fiscal and monetary policy, and other truly exogenous or structural disturbances. Dividends likewise "respond" to stock price "shocks," but we usually read causality in the other direction and we regard dividends as the result of deeper underlying economic shocks. A "shock" here is only an "innovation," a movement that the VAR does not forecast. A "response" is a change in VAR expectations of a current or future variable coincident with such a movement. Many VAR exercises do attempt to find an "exogenous" movement in a variable by careful construction of shocks, and "structural" VAR exercises aim to measure causal responses of such shocks. Not here.

We do not implicitly assume that agents use only the information in the VAR in order to make these calculations. $v_t = E(\cdot | \Omega_t)$ implies $v_t = E(\cdot | x_t \subset \Omega_t)$ since $v_t \in x_t$. But "unexpected" here means relative to the VAR information set. The VAR forecasts are only the average of people's forecasts on all dates that have the same VAR state variables, but that have other realizations of the variables that people see. The VAR forecasts are not full-information forecasts. A decomposition using larger information sets, survey forecasts, or people's full information sets, may be different. These calculations just capture history. They say, if we saw inflation unexpected by the VAR, what happened on average after that event?

The impulse-responses characterize average events in the postwar United States, the time period over which the VAR was estimated. They provide no guarantee that today's immense debts and deficits, and the surpluses and discount rates to come, conform to similar patterns.

4.4.1   Aggregate Demand Shocks

We can use the same procedure to understand the fiscal underpinnings of other shocks. For any interesting ε_1, any linear combination of the seven VAR shocks, we can compute impulse-response functions, and thereby the terms of the inflation decompositions.

I start with a recession shock, which we might also call an aggregate demand shock. The response to the inflation shock in Figure 4.4 is stagflationary, in that growth falls when inflation rises. Unexpected inflation is, in this sample, negatively correlated with unexpected consumption (and also GDP) growth. The stagflationary episodes in the 1970s drive this result.

However, it is interesting to examine the response to disinflations that come in recessions, and inflations that come in expansions, following a conventional non-shifting Phillips curve. Such events are common, as in the recession following the 2008 financial crisis. But such events pose a fiscal puzzle: In such a recession, deficits soar, yet inflation declines. How is this possible? Well, as (4.14) reminds us, larger subsequent surpluses or lower discount rates could give that deflationary force. Can we see these effects in the data, and which one is it?

To answer this question, we want to study a shock in which inflation and output go in the same direction. I simply specify that inflation and consumption each drop 1% at the same time, $\varepsilon_{\pi,1} = -1$, $\varepsilon_{g,1} = -1$. The model is linear, so the sign doesn't matter, but the story is clearer for a recession. Yes, we may combine and orthogonalize shocks as we please. These responses answer the question, "If we see a negative 1% inflation shock coincident with a negative 1% growth shock, how does that observation change our forecasts of other variables?"

The response function is the average over all similar events, not the history of a particular event such as 2008. We cannot know for one event how much of the following path was expected or not. By looking at the average over all similar events, we can hope to estimate what people expect.

Again, we want shocks to other variables to have whatever value they have, on average, conditional on the inflation and output shock. To initialize the other shocks of the VAR, then, I run a multiple regression

$$\varepsilon_{z,t+1} = b_{z,\pi}\varepsilon_{\pi,t+1} + b_{z,g}\varepsilon_{g,t+1} + u_{z,t+1}$$

for each variable z. I fill in the other shocks at time 1 from their predicted variables given $\varepsilon_{\pi,1} = -1$ and $\varepsilon_{g,1} = -1$, i.e., I start the VAR at

$$\varepsilon_1 = -\left[\begin{array}{ccccc} b_{r^n,\pi} + b_{r^n,g} & \varepsilon_{g,1}=1 & \varepsilon_{\pi,1}=1 & b_{s,\pi} + b_{s,g} & \cdots \end{array}\right]'.$$

Figure 4.5 presents responses to this recession shock, and the "recession" rows of Table 4.2 tabulate terms of the decompositions. Inflation π and growth g responses start

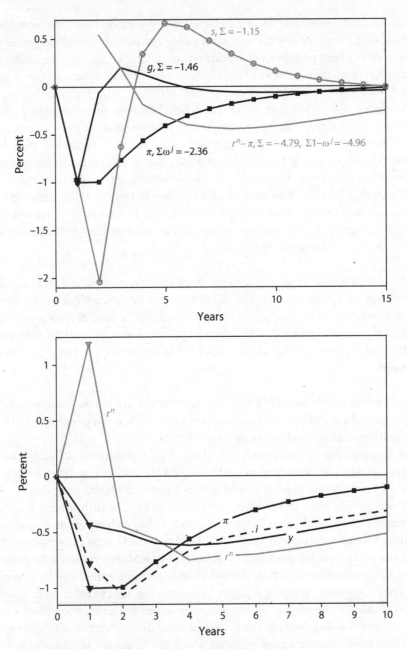

FIGURE 4.5. Responses to a Recession or Aggregate Demand Shock, $\varepsilon_{\pi,1} = \varepsilon_{g,1} = -1$

at −1%, by construction. Inflation is again persistent, with a ω-weighted sum of current and expected future inflation equal to −2.36%. Consumption growth g returns rapidly, but does not much overshoot zero, so the level of consumption does not recover much at all. Consumption is roughly a random walk in response to this shock. The nominal interest rate i falls in the recession, and recovers more slowly than inflation. Long-term bond yields y also fall, but not as much as the short-term rate, for about four years. We see here the standard interest rate decline and upward-sloping yield curve of a recession. The expected bond return follows the long-term yield. The persistent fall in expected return corresponds to a large positive ex post bond return $\Delta E_1 r_1^n$. The recession includes a large deficit that continues for three years. In short, we see a standard picture of an "aggregate demand" recession similar to the history of 2008–2009.

Why do we not see inflation with these deficits? Perhaps future surpluses offset the current deficits? Surpluses do subsequently turn positive with the usual s shape, paying down some of the debt. But the total surplus is still −1.15%. Left to their own devices, surpluses would produce a 1.15% *inflation* during the recession. Declining growth also adds an inflationary force. The decline in consumption is essentially permanent, so the sum of growth is −1.46%. This would lead on its own to another 1.46% inflation.

Discount rates are the central story for disinflation in recessions. After one period, expected real returns $r^n - \pi$ decline persistently, accounting for 4.96% cumulative disinflation. In sum, rounding the numbers,

- *Disinflation with an "aggregate demand" shock that lowers output and prices together is driven by a lower discount rate, reflected in lower interest rates and bond yields. For each 1% disinflation shock, the expected return on bonds falls so much that the present value of surpluses rises by nearly 5%. This discount rate shock overcomes a 1.1% inflationary shock coming from persistent deficits, and 1.5% inflationary shock coming from lower growth.*

The opposite conclusions hold of inflationary shocks in a boom. Discount rate variation gives us a fiscal Phillips curve, accounting for the otherwise puzzling correlation of deficits with disinflation and surpluses with inflation.

This decomposition puts a present value face on the obvious events. In 2008 there was a "flight to quality." People wanted to hold more government debt, and people tried to sell private debt and equities to get it, as well as to buy fewer goods and services.

Just *why* people want to hold more government debt in such events, despite low prospective returns, and are reluctant to spend or buy private assets is not our job right now, though an economic model will need to include such a mechanism. Part of the answer is the liquidity premium for government debt. For example, Berentsen and Waller (2018) offer a theoretical model with changing liquidity premiums for government debt. They show such changing liquidity premiums can lead to inflation and deflation with no changes in surpluses, by discount rate movement and a fiscal theory mechanism. The time-varying discount rate for government debt surely reflects also a pervasive rise in risk aversion, precautionary saving and flight to quality in recessions, and the potentially negative-beta character of government debt. (Cochrane (2017a) is a recent survey.)

Likewise, the secular decline in real interest rates, and cross-country variation—very low interest rates in Japan and Europe—can *account* for low inflation but raises the economic question just why real interest rates are so low.

In the mark-to-market decompositions of the second and third panels of Table 4.2, we see too that the bond price rise accompanying initial inflation comes almost entirely from future disinflation, not discount rate changes.

4.4.2   Surplus and Discount-Rate Shocks

We have studied what happens to surpluses and to discount rates given that we see unexpected inflation. What happens to inflation if we see changes in surpluses or discount rates? These are not the same questions. An inflation shock may come on average with a discount rate shock, but a discount rate shock may not come on average with inflation. If inflation moves less often than discount rates and surpluses, this outcome is likely.

I calculate here how the variables in the VAR react to an unexpected change in current and expected future primary surpluses including growth,

$$\Delta E_1 \sum_{j=0}^{\infty} (\tilde{s}_{1+j} + g_{1+j}) = -1,$$

and all shocks to the VAR take their average values given this innovation. I call this event a "surplus shock." A decline in growth with constant surplus-to-GDP ratio is also a shock to surpluses. The results are almost the same with or without the growth term in the shock definition, as growth declines in response to a pure surplus shock. A shock to s_1 alone turns out to provoke about the same responses as well.

Here I *force* a surplus response $a(\rho) = 1$. I find whatever linear combination of VAR shocks produces that result, and we see what inflation results. Since now we have other terms in the identity, the answer is not necessarily 1%.

Then I calculate responses to an unexpected fall in discount rates,

$$\Delta E_1 \sum_{j=1}^{\infty} (1 - \omega^j) r_{1+j} = -1,$$

again letting all other variables take their average values given this innovation. I call this event a "discount rate shock." I do not orthogonalize the fiscal and discount rate shocks, and in fact we will see they are highly correlated.

Rather than move inflation on the left-hand side of the identities to see which terms on the right-hand sides move, I move each of the two terms on the right-hand side of the identities to see how inflation moves, or how the other term on the right-hand side moves.

The response of the sum of future surpluses and growth to a shock ε_1 is

$$\Delta E_1 \sum_{j=0}^{\infty} (\tilde{s}_{1+j} + g_{1+j}) = (a_s + a_g)' (I - A)^{-1} \varepsilon_1,$$

in the notation of (4.17), where and a_s, a_g pick s and g out of the VAR, $s_t = a_s' x_t$. To specify a surplus shock, then, I run for each variable z a regression

$$\varepsilon_{z,t+1} = b_z \times (a_s + a_g)' (I - A)^{-1} \varepsilon_{t+1} + u_{z,t+1}. \tag{4.18}$$

Then, I start the surplus-shock response function at

$$\varepsilon_1 = - \begin{bmatrix} b_{r^n} & b_g & b_\pi & \cdots \end{bmatrix}'.$$

Similarly, to calculate responses to a discount rate shock, I run

$$\varepsilon_{z,t+1} = b_z \times (a_{r^n} - a_\pi)' \left[A(I - A)^{-1} - \omega A(I - \omega A)^{-1} \right] \varepsilon_{t+1} + u_{z,t+1}.$$

I start the discount rate response function with the negative of these regression coefficients as well, capturing the response to a discount rate decline.

Figure 4.6 presents the responses to the surplus shock, and the "surplus" rows of Table 4.2 tabulate the decompositions. The sum of surplus and growth responses to the surplus shock is $-0.66 - 0.34 = -1.00$ by construction. Surpluses follow an s-shaped response, but the initial deficits are not fully matched by subsequent surpluses.

This decline in surpluses and growth has essentially no effect on inflation. Starting in year 2, inflation declines—the "wrong" direction—by less than a tenth of a percent, and the overall weighted sum of inflation declines by a tenth of a percent.

Why is there no inflation? Because discount rates also decline, with a weighted sum of 1.10%, almost exactly matching the surplus decline. The lower panel of Figure 4.6 adds insight. We see a sharp and persistent decline in the interest rate, long-term bond yield, and expected bond return.

This figure captures the event of a widening deficit, accompanied by a decline in growth and interest rates (i.e., a recession). The deficits are not completely repaid by subsequent surpluses or growth. That fact occurs by construction, as we are selecting such events by forcing a 1% decline in the discounted sums. We find however, that real interest rates decline persistently in this recession and its aftermath. This decline in real returns essentially pays for the deficits. Viewed in ex post terms, the government runs a deficit, builds up the debt and then a low real return brings the value of debt back rather than larger taxes or lower spending. There is, on average, very little inflation or deflation.

The response to the discount rate shock in Figure 4.7 is almost exactly the same. The weighted discount rate response is -1.00 here by construction. This discount rate decline should be deflationary, and it is, a bit. But the disinflation peaks at -0.1% and the weighted sum is only -0.18%. Why is there no deflation? Because a sharp growth and surplus decline accompanies this discount rate decline, with a pattern almost exactly the same as we found from the growth and surplus shock. In the bottom panel, the expected return decline comes with a decline in interest rates and bond yields, as we would expect.

Clearly, the surplus + growth shock and the discount-rate shock have isolated essentially the same events: recessions in which growth falls, deficits rise persistently, interest rates fall, and, on average in this sample, inflation *doesn't* move much, with the converse pattern for expansions. The fiscal roots of the *absence* of inflation, in the end, characterize these movements in the data.

One can read the responses as Fed reactions. In response to an adverse economic shock, which lowers surpluses and would cause fiscal inflation, the Fed persistently lowers interest rates. With sticky prices this move lowers real interest rates and the discount rate for government debt, which is a counteracting deflationary force. Or one can read them as straightforward economic reactions, that the same economic shocks lower real interest rates directly.

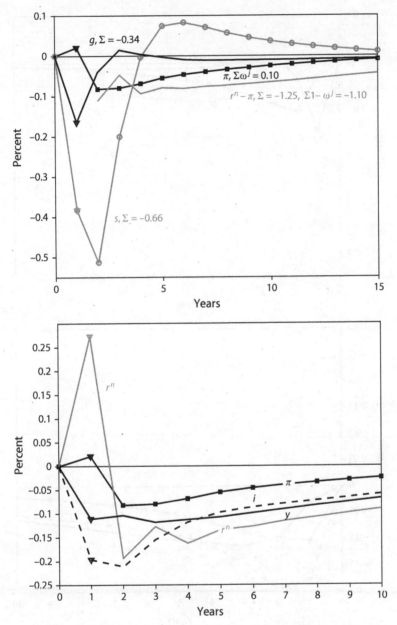

FIGURE 4.6. Responses to a Surplus and Growth Shock, $\Delta E_1 \sum_{j=0}^{\infty} \left(\tilde{s}_{1+j} + g_{1+j} \right) = -1$

In sum,

- *Surplus and discount rate shocks paint the same picture: Large deficits are not completely repaid by subsequent growth or surpluses. Instead, they correspond to extended periods of low returns. The deficit and discount rate effects largely offset, leaving little inflation on average. Discount rate variation explains why deficits, not repaid by future surpluses, do not result in inflation.*

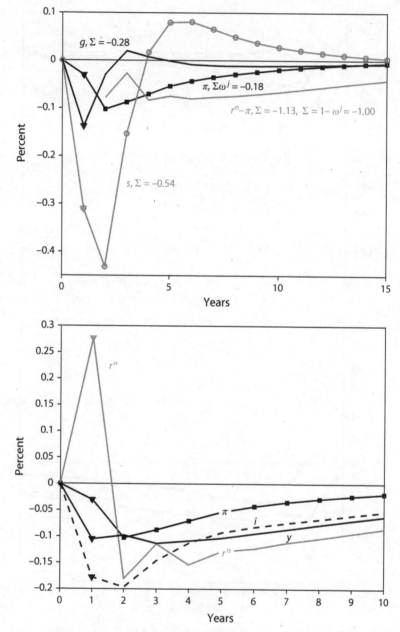

FIGURE 4.7. Responses to a Discount Rate Shock $\Delta E_1 \sum_{j=1}^{\infty} (1 - \omega^j) \left(r_{1+j}^n - \pi_{1+j} \right) = -1$

These fiscal roots of the *lack* of inflation, a dog that did not bark, are just as important as the fiscal roots of inflation. Except for the 1970s, the postwar United States saw quiet inflation, relative to the size of its recurring deficits and surpluses. Some recessions, like 2008, have disinflation, yet others have no change, and others stagflation. In any case, the inflation is small relative to the deficit shocks. Yet we have a completely fiat currency, with no redemption promise.

The postwar period in the United States, Europe, and Japan is unusual relative to the long history of fiat currency that swiftly inflates at the first sign of trouble. Yes, we experienced steady inflation unknown in the previous gold standard era, but we did not see the sudden devaluation so common in earlier history. What are the implicit fiscal and monetary commitments that allowed this miracle? We are looking at them. The U.S. Treasury has gained a sufficient reputation for repaying its debts, either directly or by low real interest rates that bring the debt-to-GDP ratio back again, but not via large inflation or default. Studying and understanding these commitments is an essential precondition to speculating how long they will endure or whether and how they will fall apart.

4.4.3   Results Vary with Shock Definitions

Since there are multiple shocks in the VAR, the results depend on which combination of shocks one looks at. One wishes for a one-dimensional story, that all recessions are in some sense alike. But the data are not one-dimensional. Some recessions come with disinflation, some come with more inflation. An inflation shock that ends up being negatively correlated with output, and an aggregate demand shock that drives a positive correlation of output and inflation, come to different results. Conditioning on seeing inflation, there is no change in the discounted sum of surpluses. Conditioning on a change in the discounted sum of surpluses, there is no inflation. The last two exercises suggest that deficit shocks in a recession are not repaid with subsequent surpluses. Yet Cochrane (2019) finds that deficit shocks in recessions are largely repaid by surpluses in the following expansion. Well, here we define the shock by a permanent reduction in surpluses, so of course there is a permanent reduction in surpluses. There I looked only at the event of a recession.

Beyond this VAR, one would like to identify monetary and fiscal policy shocks. For example, one might want to identify a movement in interest rates unconnected to changing fiscal policy as well as the traditional goal that the shock is unconnected with changing forecasts of the economy. One would like to identify the true structural shocks of explicit models. This is a characterization of the relatively benign 1948–2018 U.S. economy. Our past, our future, and other countries may be different.

The multiple ways to define shocks should not surprise or discourage us. There *are* many shocks to the economy. The economy responds differently as different shocks are turned on and off. Defining and orthogonalizing interesting shocks is hard, and remains fertile ground for both theory and empirical investigation. Once again, there is much low-hanging fiscal theory fruit.

5

Fiscal Theory in Sticky Price Models

NOW, WE BUILD toward a fiscal theory of monetary policy model that is consistent with data. To do that, we add three essential ingredients: sticky prices, long-term debt, and a surplus process with an s-shaped moving average representation.

The models so far have been completely frictionless, representatives of the "classical dichotomy" that changes in the price level have no effect on real quantities. Inflation is like measuring distances in feet rather than in meters. In reality, changes in the price level are often connected to changes in real quantities. Monetary economics is centrally about studying ways that inflations and deflations can *cause* temporary booms and recessions.

Many mechanisms have been considered to describe nominal-real interactions. I work here with the standard and simple model that prices are a bit sticky. I'm no happier about the assumption of sticky prices than anyone else who works in this area, or with the specification of common sticky price models. We certainly need a deeper understanding of just why monetary shocks often seem to have real effects, yet sometimes none whatsoever as in currency reforms. But one should not innovate in two directions at once. Therefore, in this book I explore how the fiscal theory of the price level behaves if we combine it with utterly standard, though unrealistic, models of sticky prices. Equivalently, I explore how standard sticky price models behave if we give them fiscal underpinnings rather than the conventional "active" monetary policy assumption. Let us first see *how* to mix price stickiness with fiscal theory, how fiscal theory alters this most familiar model, and then add or alter ingredients.

Adding sticky prices we also see how close the statement and techniques of fiscal theory of monetary policy can be to standard new-Keynesian DSGE models. The results, however, can be quite different. By using the same specification as in standard new-Keynesian models, we see clearly how the fiscal theory assumption alone changes the results.

I proceed by building models of increasing complexity, adding one ingredient at a time. Though it takes a bit more space, I find this approach helps to understand the intuition, mechanisms, and practical application of a model, which are obscured if we start with the most general case.

5.1   The Simple New-Keynesian Model

We meet the standard new-Keynesian sticky price model

$$x_t = E_t x_{t+1} - \sigma (i_t - E_t \pi_{t+1})$$

$$\pi_t = \beta E_t \pi_{t+1} + \kappa x_t.$$

The standard new-Keynesian sticky price model is

$$x_t = E_t x_{t+1} - \sigma (i_t - E_t \pi_{t+1}) \tag{5.1}$$

$$\pi_t = \beta E_t \pi_{t+1} + \kappa x_t. \tag{5.2}$$

These two equations generalize the simple model $i_t = E_t \pi_{t+1}$ of Section 2.5 to include sticky prices, which affect output x_t. Equation (5.1) is the "IS" equation, which I like to call the Intertemporal Substitution equation. Higher real interest rates induce the consumer to save more, and to consume less today than tomorrow. With no capital and no government purchases, consumption equals output. Equation (5.2) is the new-Keynesian Phillips curve. Output is high when inflation π is high relative to expected *future* inflation.

To derive (5.1), start from consumer first-order conditions,

$$1 = E_t \left[\beta \left(\frac{C_{t+1}}{C_t} \right)^{-\gamma} (1 + i_t) \frac{P_t}{P_{t+1}} \right].$$

Linearize and approximate to

$$E_t(c_{t+1} - c_t) = -\sigma \delta + \sigma (i_t - E_t \pi_{t+1}),$$

where $c_t = \log C_t$, $\sigma = 1/\gamma$ and $\delta = - \log \beta$. Suppressing constants and with consumption equal to output $c_t = x_t$, we get (5.1).

The Phillips curve (5.2) comes from the first-order condition for monopolistically competitive price setters, facing costs of changing prices or a random probability of being allowed to change price. Firms set prices today knowing that prices will be stuck for a while, so they set prices with expected future prices in mind. While prices are stuck, they meet extra demand by selling more. Both equations are deviations from steady-states, so x represents the output gap.

I jump to these linearized equilibrium conditions, but a big point of the new-Keynesian enterprise is that this structure has detailed microfoundations, and can thus hope to survive the Lucas (1976) critique. King (2000), Woodford (2003), and Galí (2015) are good expositions.

We can integrate the equations separately to express some of their intuition:

$$x_t = -\sigma E_t \sum_{j=0}^{\infty} \left(i_{t+j} - \pi_{t+j+1} \right) \tag{5.3}$$

$$\pi_t = \kappa E_t \sum_{j=0}^{\infty} \beta^j x_{t+j}. \tag{5.4}$$

Output is low when current and expected future real interest rates are high. Inflation is high when current and expected future output gaps are high. Equation (5.4) helps us to see that $\kappa \to \infty$ is the flexible price limit. In that limit, output is the same for any value of inflation.

Most models add disturbances to equations (5.1) and (5.2), and study the economy's responses to shocks to these disturbances, in addition to the responses to fiscal and monetary policy shocks that I study here. IS shocks to (5.1) can be formalized as discount rate shocks, and are often viewed as a stand-in for financial shocks such as 2008. Phillips curve shocks, often called "marginal cost" shocks, are also important in the data.

I leave out such disturbances for now. My purpose is pedagogical: Once you see *how* to adapt this model to fiscal theory, adding other disturbances is technically easy. We are often most interested in analyzing the effects of policy, so that is a good place to start. However, analyzing the effects of other shocks and how fiscal theory affects those responses is likely to be revealing. Such questions need us to move quickly to more realistic models, not just this textbook playground.

5.1.1   An Analytical Solution

Inflation is a two-sided moving average of interest rates, plus a moving average of past fiscal shocks. We see the same concepts of the flexible price model with smoothed dynamics.

We can eliminate output x_t, from (5.1)–(5.2), leaving a relation between interest rates i_t and leads and lags of inflation π_t. First difference (5.2), substitute in (5.1), invert the lag polynomial and expand by partial fractions to obtain

$$\pi_{t+1} = \frac{\sigma \kappa}{\lambda_1 - \lambda_2} \left[i_t + \sum_{j=1}^{\infty} \lambda_1^{-j} i_{t-j} + \sum_{j=1}^{\infty} \lambda_2^{j} E_{t+1} i_{t+j} \right] + \sum_{j=0}^{\infty} \lambda_1^{-j} \delta_{t+1-j}. \tag{5.5}$$

(Algebra in Section A1.5 of the Online Appendix.) Here,

$$\lambda_{1,2} = \frac{(1+\beta+\sigma\kappa) \pm \sqrt{(1+\beta+\sigma\kappa)^2 - 4\beta}}{2}, \tag{5.6}$$

and δ_{t+1} is an expectational shock, corresponding to an undetermined initial condition in a nonstochastic difference equation, with $E_t \delta_{t+1} = 0$. I use the letter δ to indicate expectational shocks as distinct from structural ε shocks. In words, inflation is a two-sided moving average of past and expected future interest rates. We have $\lambda_1 > 1$ and $\lambda_2 < 1$, so the moving averages as expressed converge.

Taking innovations of (5.5), we now have

$$\Delta E_{t+1}\pi_{t+1} = \frac{\sigma\kappa}{\lambda_1 - \lambda_2}\left[\sum_{j=1}^{\infty}\lambda_2^j \Delta E_{t+1}i_{t+j}\right] + \delta_{t+1}. \quad (5.7)$$

We have

$$\frac{\sigma\kappa}{\lambda_1 - \lambda_2} = \left(1 + \frac{\lambda_1^{-1}}{1 - \lambda_1^{-1}} + \frac{\lambda_2}{1 - \lambda_2}\right)^{-1}. \quad (5.8)$$

This expression shows that the sum of the coefficients in (5.5) is one. A 1% permanent interest rate rise leads eventually to a 1% rise in inflation.

Recognize in (5.5) a generalization of the simple model

$$\pi_{t+1} = i_t + \delta_{t+1}, \quad (5.9)$$

deriving from its flexible-price "IS" equation,

$$i_t = E_t\pi_{t+1}. \quad (5.10)$$

Equation (5.5) is the same equation, with moving averages on the right-hand side as a result of sticky prices. We can anticipate that sticky prices will give us smoother and thus more realistic dynamics by putting a two-sided moving average in place of sharp movements. In (5.5), past expectational shocks also affect inflation today, again leaving more realistic delayed effects in place of the sudden jumps of the frictionless model. Similarly, (5.7) naturally generalizes $\Delta E_{t+1}\pi_{t+1} = \delta_{t+1}$.

Equation (5.5) looks like the response of inflation to a time-varying peg, but it is more general than that. It describes the relationship between equilibrium interest rates and inflation, no matter how one arrives at those quantities. It tells you what inflation is given the interest rate path. For example, if one writes a monetary policy rule $i_t = \theta\pi_t + u_t$, (5.5) still holds of the equilibrium i_t and π_t.

We have multiple equilibria and an expectational shock δ_t because we haven't completed the model. Our next job is to complete the model by adding the government debt valuation equation. Our task, conceptually, is to proceed exactly as in Section 2.5. There, we united $i_t = E_t\pi_{t+1}$ with

$$\Delta E_{t+1}\pi_{t+1} = -\varepsilon_{\Sigma s,t+1}, \quad (5.11)$$

where

$$\varepsilon_{\Sigma s,t+1} \equiv \Delta E_{t+1}\sum_{j=0}^{\infty}\rho^j \tilde{s}_{t+1+j},$$

to conclude

$$\pi_{t+1} = i_t - \varepsilon_{\Sigma s,t+1}. \quad (5.12)$$

I plotted responses to monetary and fiscal shocks. We take the same steps here.

To compute the simplest example, start with short-term debt $\omega = 0$. With short-term debt, the nominal bond return equals the nominal interest rate $i_t = r^n_{t+1}$. Then, the linearized unexpected inflation identity (3.22) adds a discount rate term to (5.11), because real interest rates may vary,

$$\Delta E_{t+1}\pi_{t+1} = \Delta E_{t+1}\sum_{j=1}^{\infty} \rho^j\left(i_{t+j} - \pi_{t+1+j}\right) - \varepsilon_{\Sigma s,t+1}. \tag{5.13}$$

The model thus consists of (5.5) and (5.13) in place of (5.11).

In addition to the smoothing effects of sticky prices, monetary policy now has a fiscal effect, by changing the real discount rate for government debt. Higher interest rates can provoke an unexpected inflation without any direct change in surpluses.

Output now varies as well. We can find output from inflation via the Phillips curve, or directly,

$$\kappa x_{t+1} = \frac{\sigma\kappa}{\lambda_1 - \lambda_2}\left[\left(1 - \beta\lambda_1^{-1}\right)\sum_{j=0}^{\infty}\lambda_1^{-j}i_{t-j} + \left(1 - \beta\lambda_2^{-1}\right)\sum_{j=1}^{\infty}\lambda_2^j E_{t+1}i_{t+j}\right]$$
$$+ \left(1 - \beta\lambda_1^{-1}\right)\sum_{j=0}^{\infty}\lambda_1^{-j}\delta_{t+1-j}. \tag{5.14}$$

5.1.2 Responses to Monetary and Fiscal Shocks

We add fiscal theory of the price level to the basic new-Keynesian model by adding the linearized flow equation for the real value of government debt, $\rho v_{t+1} = v_t + i_t - \pi_{t+1} - \tilde{s}_{t+1}$. I calculate the response to monetary and fiscal policy shocks. The responses resemble those of the frictionless model, but with dynamics drawn out by sticky prices.

While the present value expressions of individual equations or pairs of equations such as (5.13) or (5.5) provide a lot of intuition, they are not a practical route to solving more complex models. Instead, it is easier to write the model in first-order form and then solve the whole system, usually numerically, by matrix methods.

To specify and compute solutions to this model, then, I add the linearization (3.17) of the fiscal flow condition to the new-Keynesian model (5.1)–(5.2). Retaining one-period debt and hence $i_t = r^n_{t+1}$, the resulting model is

$$x_t = E_t x_{t+1} - \sigma\left(i_t - E_t\pi_{t+1}\right) \tag{5.15}$$
$$\pi_t = \beta E_t\pi_{t+1} + \kappa x_t$$
$$\rho v_{t+1} = v_t + i_t - \pi_{t+1} - \tilde{s}_{t+1}. \tag{5.16}$$

We write this set of equations in matrix form, and then solve unstable eigenvalues of the system forward and stable eigenvalues backward, rather than solve forward or backward

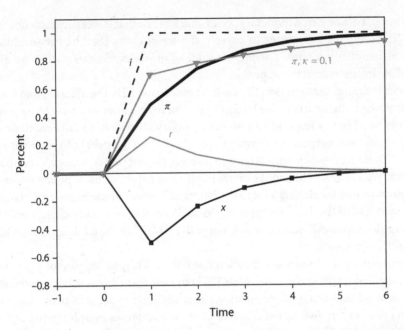

FIGURE 5.1. Response to an Unexpected Permanent Interest Rate Shock. No fiscal shock, simple sticky-price model. Parameters $r = 0.01$, $\sigma = 1$, $\kappa = 0.5$.

individual equations and then attempt to solve for individual endogenous variables. I defer the algebra to Online Appendix Section A1.5. Since $\rho \leq 1$, equation (5.16) provides the additional forward-looking root needed to determine the expectational error δ_{t+1} and give a unique solution. The previous identities came from solving (5.16) forward on its own, so they are incorporated by this method. They remain useful guides to the intuition of model solutions.

Figure 5.1 presents responses to an unexpected permanent interest rate rise, with no change in surpluses. Compare this figure to the responses of the flexible price model in Figure 2.1. There are two big differences and one disappointment. First, sticky prices are, well, sticky. The inflation response is drawn out.

Second, there is an immediate positive inflation response, $\pi_1 > 0$, on the same date as the interest rate shock, while previously inflation did not move until the next period. How can inflation move instantly without a shock to surpluses? Inflation moves because of the discount rate effect, seen in equation (5.13). Expected interest rates rise, expected inflation does not rise by the same amount, so the real interest rate rises. A higher real interest rate raises the discount rate for unchanged future surpluses. The *present value* of unchanged surpluses falls, pushing up inflation π_1. Equivalently, the higher debt service costs resulting from higher real interest rates and rolling over one-period debt add to the fiscal burden, and provoke the same response that a decline in surpluses would provoke.

This is an important mechanism. Monetary policy can have indirect fiscal effects on inflation, because monetary policy can change the discount rate for surpluses or, using flow budget intuition, the real interest costs of the debt.

However, I define here a monetary policy shock as one that leaves surpluses unchanged. If the Treasury raises surpluses to cover real interest costs, then higher surpluses just match higher discount rates. The present value of surpluses remains unchanged and this immediate inflation does not appear.

Which is the right assumption? There is no easy answer. Do the Treasury and Congress routinely adapt other parts of the budget to pay for higher interest costs? More generally, how does fiscal policy respond to a monetary policy change, or to the economic consequences (inflation, output, employment, interest costs of the debt) of a monetary policy change? There are lots of possibilities, and no hard and fast rule covering all countries and all times. We see again the more general point: The nature of fiscal policy responses to endogenous variables matters a lot to the effects of changes in the interest rate target.

No matter what the Treasury typically does, "What if interest rates change and there is no change to surpluses?" remains valid, as a policy what-if, as are its alternatives. One may ask multiple questions.

One might say the immediate inflation rise is more likely to happen for a government in fiscal difficulty, whose Treasury is less likely to raise taxes to cover larger interest costs on the debt, while the immediate inflation rise is less likely to occur in an economy whose Treasury aims to zero overall deficits; that is, to raise surpluses in order to pay higher real interest costs of the debt, and that has the fiscal space to do it. One might say that the rise in inflation is more likely for a government or a time with larger outstanding debt, which raises interest costs proportionally.

The disappointment is that sticky prices alone do not lead to a negative response of inflation to interest rates. You might have thought higher nominal interest rates would mean higher real rates, which depress aggregate demand, and via the Phillips curve lead to less inflation. That IS-LM thinking does not apply in this model.

In fact, *stickier* prices lead to larger time 1 inflation in this model, as shown by the gray line in Figure 5.1. As inflation becomes infinitely sticky, as $\kappa \to 0$, this model approaches an inflation jump at time 1. That response is not just "Fisherian"—inflation starts at time 2, one period after the interest rate rise—but "super-Fisherian"—inflation starts immediately at time 1, and rises exactly by the amount of the nominal interest rate. With very sticky prices, a nominal interest rate permanently above inflation has a large discount rate effect.

Higher interest rates do lead to lower output. With this forward-looking Phillips curve, output is low when inflation is low relative to future inflation. Equivalently, output is low when current and future real interest rates are high, as in (5.3). So, this model generates the conventional wisdom that higher interest rates with sticky prices lower output.

Output does not return exactly to zero, as this model features a small permanent inflation-output tradeoff. From (5.2), permanent movements in x and π follow

$$x = \frac{1 - \beta}{\kappa} \pi.$$

One way to eliminate the long-run tradeoff is to set $\beta = 1$, so that expected future inflation shifts the Phillips curve one for one. Another solution, which also helps to fit the data, is to include a lag of inflation,

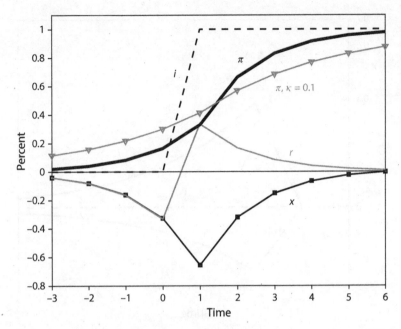

FIGURE 5.2. Response to a Fully Expected Rise in Interest Rates. Fiscal theory model with price stickiness. Parameters $r = 0.01, \kappa = 0.5, \sigma = 1$.

$$\pi_t = (1 - \theta)\,\pi_{t-1} + \theta E_t \pi_{t+1} + \kappa x_t.$$

Now there is no long-run output-inflation tradeoff, and this modification improves the empirical fit. This change can be rationalized as the effects of indexation (Cogley and Sbordone (2008)).

Figure 5.2 presents the response to a fully *expected* rise in interest rates. In the simple model of Figure 2.1, we found that expected and unexpected interest rates had exactly the same effect on inflation. That is no longer true. Inflation now moves *ahead* of the expected interest rate rise, reflecting the two-sided moving average in (5.5). The expected interest rate rise also lowers output, but now output goes down in advance of the interest rate rise that causes it. We see a form of "forward guidance." Announcements of future interest rate changes, if believed, affect inflation and output today.

Figure 5.3 presents the model's response to a time 1 fiscal shock, with no change in nominal interest rates. Compare this response to the response to the same shock without price stickiness in Figure 2.1.

First, a deficit shock still raises inflation. But with price stickiness we now have a drawn-out response, rather than a one-period price level jump. We are on our way to describing drawn-out inflation in response to fiscal shocks.

Second, the 1% fiscal shock now only produces a 0.4% immediate rise in inflation, not 1% as before. In the first period we see the lower real return, a lower discount rate, which is a deflationary force.

The deficit still must all come eventually out of the pockets of period 0 bondholders. One-period bondholders receive a lower real return on their bonds. With flexible prices and constant real rates, expected future inflation cannot devalue one-period bonds. But

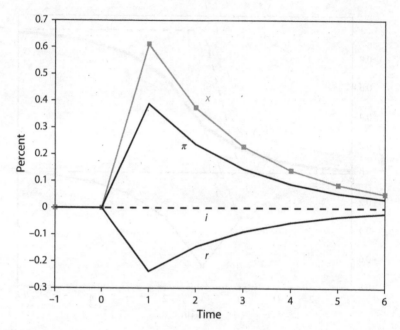

FIGURE 5.3. Response to a Deficit Shock $\varepsilon_{\Sigma s, 1} = -1$, with No Interest Rate Movement. Sticky price fiscal theory model. Parameters $r = 0.01$, $\sigma = 1$, $\kappa = 0.25$, $\eta_s = 0$.

with sticky prices, higher expected inflation can produce lower real returns, so even one-period debt can be slowly devalued. This mechanism helps to overcome the unrealistic instantaneous price level jumps of the flexible price model. In continuous time, below, it becomes the entire mechanism, with no price level jumps.

Third, high inflation relative to future inflation means an output expansion in response to the deficit shock. This inflationary fiscal expansion thus looks a bit like "fiscal stimulus." Again, however, the present value of future surpluses matters, not the current deficit. The usual promises of deficit today, returning to budget balance and debt repayment tomorrow, if believed, have no effect in this model.

I have not specified here when the deficits come, as it does not matter given their present value in this simple model. If the shock is to expectations of future deficits, this graph or its opposite offers an interesting picture of a boom and inflation, or recession and disinflation, that seems to come from nowhere, from animal spirits or sunspots, without any visible fundamental shocks to the economy or to policy.

5.1.3   A Comment on Responses to Expected Movements

I highlight responses to expected as well as unexpected policy movements. The response to expected policy variables is not often calculated, but it should be.

The habit of plotting responses to unexpected disturbances derives from comparing the results to vector autoregressions (VARs). VARs want to answer the causal question, what if the central bank deviates from the policy rule or raises interest rates? But we cannot answer this question by simply regressing inflation on interest rates. If, say, higher interest rates are followed by higher inflation, it might be the case that the Fed raises interest rates when it sees higher inflation ahead, not that higher interest rates cause higher inflation. To estimate the answer to the causal question, VARs try to find a movement in interest rates that is not taken in response to changing expectations of future inflation or output growth. It helps in this quest to find interest rate disturbances that are unanticipated. I write "helps," as being unexpected is neither necessary nor sufficient for the causal question. An interest rate movement known ahead of time may still be orthogonal to inflation or output forecasts, and an unexpected movement can respond to contemporaneous inflation news. The latter possibility is the subject of a huge orthogonalization search. Variables left out of the VAR still undermine causal interpretation.

The habit of looking at responses to unexpected shocks also derives from experience with information-based rational expectations models such as Lucas (1972), in which only unexpected monetary policy shocks have any real output effect. To characterize the economics of such a model, it makes sense to calculate the response to unexpected movements.

But those habits are not relevant to our purposes here. Many of our central banks' policy interventions are announced months or years ahead, with no contemporaneous change in interest rates. Such "forward guidance" has become an explicit part of the Federal Reserve's "toolkit." The response of the economy to the announcement of future interest rate changes is a more relevant exercise to this policy question than "What if we surprise people with an out-of-the-blue 1% interest rise, followed by AR(1) decay?"

Unexpected and identified monetary policy shocks are also overemphasized in seeing how a model matches data. Truly exogenous and unexpected monetary policy shocks are small and rare, if they exist at all. Our central banks explain every action as a response to events, not as deliberate random experiments. Monetary policy shocks account for small fractions of the variation of interest rates, inflation, and output in most VAR estimates and model-based variance accounting.

We often make response plots to understand the workings of a model. Sticky-price models give output responses to expected monetary policy disturbances, unlike the early rational expectations models, so responses to expected policy are interesting characterizations of the models. And even in the information-based rational expectations models, expected monetary policy moves *inflation*.

For understanding the logic of a model, conventional impulse-response functions mix several ingredients. The policy variable also responds to the shock. An interest rate surprise raises our forecast of subsequent interest rates. Is the response of endogenous variables such as inflation and output a structural, economic, lagged response to the original shock? Or is it a structural, contemporaneous response to the future disturbance? Does the *model* have interesting dynamics, or are the dynamics all coming from dynamics of the forcing variables?

The flexible-price model offers an example. We have $i_t = E_t \pi_{t+1}$ and thus $E_t i_{t+j} = E_t \pi_{t+j+1}$. A drawn-out response of inflation π_{t+j} to an interest rate shock $\varepsilon_{i,t+1}$ is *entirely* the result of a drawn-out interest rate response to the same shock and a one-period response of inflation to those future interest rates. The model has no dynamics, no matter how pretty the dynamics of the plot. Figure 2.2 is a good example.

The effects of expected policy changes are also rarely calculated, because the solution method leads naturally to VAR(1) representations. It's not hard to shoehorn an expected movement into an VAR(1), but people tend not to do it.

For all these reasons, it's interesting to know how the economy reacts to anticipated policy movements, or more generally it's interesting to separate announcement effects from effects of the later expected policy variable movement.

(In Cochrane (1998b) I reinterpreted monetary VAR estimates through the lens that anticipated money might matter, unwinding thereby the response function to the structural effect and the effect of expected future policy. Since policy shocks are persistent, that exercise led to a much less persistent estimate of the dynamic structure in the economy than if we regard the response function as a delayed economic response to the initial shock.)

5.2   Long-Term Debt

I introduce long-term debt into the discrete time, sticky price model. The model modifies the debt accumulation equation, and adds an expectations hypothesis model of bond prices:

$$\rho v_{t+1} = v_t + r_{t+1}^n - \pi_{t+1} - \tilde{s}_{t+1}$$

$$E_t r_{t+1}^n = i_t$$

$$r_{t+1}^n = \omega q_{t+1} - q_t.$$

This modification gives a temporary inflation decline after an interest rate rise.

Next, I add long-term debt. As a reminder, in Section 3.1 with flexible prices we found that with long-term debt, an interest rate rise leads to a one-period inflation decline as shown in see Figure 3.1. We have just seen how sticky prices give rise to smooth dynamics. Putting the two ingredients together, we produce smooth dynamics and negative output and inflation responses to higher interest rates.

The model consists of the usual IS and Phillips curves, (5.1)–(5.2), the linearized flow condition now with long-term debt (3.17), and two bond-pricing equations to determine the government bond portfolio rate of return r_{t+1}^n:

$$x_t = E_t x_{t+1} - \sigma (i_t - E_t \pi_{t+1}) \tag{5.17}$$

$$\pi_t = \beta E_t \pi_{t+1} + \kappa x_t \tag{5.18}$$

$$\rho v_{t+1} = v_t + r_{t+1}^n - \pi_{t+1} - \tilde{s}_{t+1} \tag{5.19}$$

$$E_t r_{t+1}^n = i_t \tag{5.20}$$

$$r_{t+1}^n = \omega q_{t+1} - q_t. \tag{5.21}$$

Just adding (5.19) with $r_{t+1}^n \neq i_t$ would not be enough, as we need to determine the ex post nominal bond return r_{t+1}^n. To this end, I assume the expectations hypothesis that the expected return on bonds of all maturities is the same in equation (5.20), and I add the

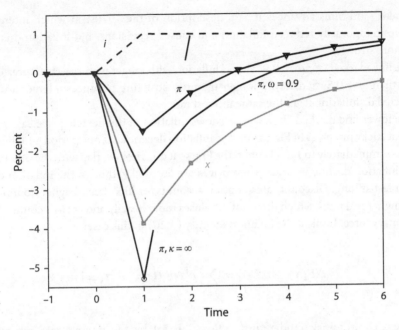

FIGURE 5.4. Response to an Unanticipated Permanent Interest Rate rise. Sticky prices, no change in surpluses, and long-term debt. Parameters $r = 0.01$, $\sigma = 1$, $\kappa = 0.25$, $\omega = 0.85$.

linearized pricing equation for bonds with geometric maturity structure $B_{t-1}^{(t+j)} = \omega^j B_{t-1}$ in (5.21). The variable q_t in equation (5.21) is the log bond price. This equation is derived as equation (A1.25) in the Online Appendix. Generalization to time-varying bond risk and liquidity premiums and the actual maturity structure beckons.

Again, we solve all the flow relations together by the matrix method outlined in Online Appendix Section A1.5. I write (5.20) as $r_{t+1}^n = i_t + \delta_{r,t+1}$. I then substitute out r_{t+1}^n. Equations (5.19)–(5.21) become

$$\rho v_{t+1} = v_t + i_t - \pi_{t+1} - \tilde{s}_{t+1} + \delta_{r,t+1}$$

$$\omega q_{t+1} = q_t + i_t + \delta_{r,t+1}.$$

The latter, solved forward, gives one more explosive root to determine the additional expectational error $\delta_{r,t+1}$.

Figure 5.4 presents the response to an unexpected permanent interest rate rise in this model using $\omega = 0.8$. Where with short-term debt and sticky prices in Figure 5.1 inflation started rising immediately, now we have a disinflation. Relative to the flexible price, long-term debt case in Figure 3.1, we have a drawn-out disinflation, rather than a one-time downward price level jump. The temporary disinflation coincides with an output decline as well, capturing standard intuition.

Higher inflation eventually reemerges. This model does not produce the view, common in the policy world, that higher interest rates permanently reduce inflation. That result occurs in an old-Keynesian, irrational expectations model, but not in rational expectations models. Sims (2011) calls the pattern of lower and then higher inflation "stepping on a rake," and Sims advances it as a description of the 1970s, in which interest rate increases temporarily reduced inflation and caused recessions, but inflation then came back more strongly.

The line marked "π, $\omega = 0.9$" shows inflation with longer maturity structure, $\omega = 0.9$ rather than $\omega = 0.8$. Sensibly, a longer maturity structure produces a larger and more protracted disinflation from the same interest rate path.

The lower line marked "π, $\kappa = \infty$" shows inflation in the flexible price case $\kappa = \infty$. Without sticky prices, as in Figure 3.1, the inflation decline lasts one period and then inflation rises immediately to 1%. (I cut off the line so it does not overlap with the others.) The initial inflation decline is *larger* when prices are *less* sticky, though the inflation decline doesn't last as long. Discount rate variation accounts for this effect. Higher nominal rates mean higher real rates, which discount surpluses more heavily and act as a countervailing inflationary force. Look at the inflation identity (3.20) in this case:

$$\Delta E_1 \pi_1 - \Delta E_1 r_1^n = \sum_{j=1}^{\infty} \rho^j \Delta E_1 \left(r_{1+j}^n - \pi_{1+j} \right).$$

The negative nominal bond return $\Delta E_1 r_{t+1}^n$ is set by the interest rate rise and the expectations hypothesis, independent of the debt maturity structure. Without the right-hand term, inflation has to decline by the same amount as the bond return. But with sticky prices, the right-hand term kicks in. The higher discount rate in that last term is an inflationary force, which partially offsets the deflation induced by higher interest rates.

That stickier prices imply less disinflation reminds us that even though the *response* functions capture common IS-LM or monetarist intuition, the *mechanism* is entirely different. The usual intuition would not work at all with flexible prices. Yet flexible prices produce a *greater* disinflation in this model.

Long-term debt has no effect on the responses to a fully anticipated interest rate rise, so Figure 5.2 with sticky prices and short-term debt also applies to long-term debt. Inflation rises one period after the interest rate rise. Like a fiscal shock, only an unanticipated shock to bond prices can lower their value. More generally, an announcement of higher future interest rates lowers long-term bond prices and inflation on the day of the announcement, not when the interest rates actually rise.

Long-term debt has no effect at all on the response to a fiscal shock when interest rates do not change in this model. Figure 5.3 is also completely unaltered. If current and expected future nominal rates do not respond to the fiscal shock, then long-term nominal bond prices do not respond to the fiscal shock, and the only reason in this model for a difference between long- and short-term debt disappears.

We can mix fiscal and monetary shocks. For example, monetary policy may offset the inflationary effect of a fiscal shock by raising interest rates. By doing so, the central bank can substitute a long, slow, later inflation for current inflation in response to the fiscal shock. A policy rule can achieve the same thing, as we will see shortly: If the central bank systematically raises interest rates in response to inflation, then it will raise interest rates in response to a fiscal shock, and automatically perform this inflation-smoothing function.

5.3 Neutrality, and Higher or Lower Inflation?

Do higher interest rates raise or lower inflation? That higher nominal interest rates raise inflation is a natural neutrality result. But there may be a negative relationship in the short run, prodded by frictions and other complications.

I summarize the lessons of the simple sticky-price model for this question with a list of considerations: Is the interest rate rise permanent, or temporary? Is the policy likely to be reversed, if inflation goes temporarily the other way? Is there a lot of long-term domestic-currency debt outstanding? Is the interest rate rise a surprise or widely anticipated? Are prices sticky? Is fiscal policy likely to react either to the same events or to the monetary policy intervention? How will fiscal policy react to larger interest costs? Each of these considerations is important to the sign of the effect of interest rates on inflation.

So far, our economic models are Fisherian: Higher nominal interest rates eventually produce higher, not lower, inflation. Long-term debt can briefly overturn that result in some circumstances. In the verbal intuition that pervades analysis of monetary policy, it is natural and unquestioned that higher interest rates lower inflation. Relative to that tradition, the difficulty we have to produce that result in a model is striking. Can we really believe the Fisherian result? When do higher interest rates raise versus lower inflation, really? I start by discussing how higher interest rates eventually raising inflation is a natural expression of long-run neutrality for interest rate targets. Then I analyze how that long-run result may or may not matter for interest rate policy using the specific case that long-term debt gives a temporary negative result. The case allows me to speculate a bit how other ingredients that deliver temporary short-run nonneutrality might behave.

5.3.1 Neutrality

That higher nominal interest rates eventually produce higher, not lower, inflation is a natural neutrality proposition for models with interest rate targets. It is analogous to the monetarist proposition that doubling the money supply must eventually double the price level and change nothing else. Real quantities and relative prices, including the real interest rate, are eventually independent of the units of measurement. Given the immense variation in the price level over long spans of time, the experience of hyperinflations, currency reforms (when a country changes to a new currency, cutting a few zeros off all prices instantly), and currency changes such as adopting the euro, and given that prices include more zeros in Japan than the U.S. with little apparent consequence, some form of underlying neutrality is a natural feature one desires of any good model of the price level. The monetary neutrality proposition was once also not so obvious, as evidenced by the immense influence of Milton Friedman's (1968) presidential address.

But monetary economics is centrally concerned with "short-run" or otherwise qualified nonneutrality. Inflation may have temporary real effects. Higher interest rates may temporarily lower inflation. However, that short-run nonneutrality must come from some friction or other model complication. And short-run nonneutrality is always qualified, not an always-and-everywhere phenomenon, as the potent example of currency reforms reminds us.

Neutrality is such a natural force that standard models also struggle to produce a negative sign. The standard new-Keynesian model is also Fisherian in the long run— permanently higher interest rates lead to permanently higher inflation. When it achieves a negative short-run response, it does so by constructing a positive fiscal shock, a rise in expected primary surpluses, coincident with the rise in interest rates (as Chapter 16 demonstrates). That sort of joint fiscal–monetary policy can produce the desired result, but it is clearly an important qualification to a pure interest rate movement.

The standard old-Keynesian model achieves a negative sign by adaptive expectations. The condition $i = r + \pi$ is a steady-state, but sufficiently adaptive expectations reverse the basic stability and determinacy properties of the model, turning $i = r + \pi$ into an unstable steady-state. The central bank first lowers interest rates to get inflation going, then like a seal balancing a ball on its nose, quickly raises rates to follow inflation and keep it from exploding. Thus, the positive long-run correlation goes with a negative causal relation. But expectations that are always adaptive, people that never learn, no matter how large the inflation, is a difficult foundation for an economic theory. One obviously needs a hyperinflation and currency-reform patch. In any case, disallowing even partly rational expectations qualifies as a major friction used to overturn the natural neutrality result.

In the standard monetarist story, if the central bank raises money growth, which uniformly raises inflation, interest rates temporarily go the other way as we work down the money demand curve, $MV(i) = Py$. That negative sign needs a money demand curve and adaptive expectations.

A misinterpretation of the discount rate effect provides a seductive and common story for a negative response of inflation to interest rates. The central bank raises nominal rates; prices are somewhat sticky so real rates rise. That makes government debt more attractive, lowering inflation. Similarly, higher real interest rates attract investors to dollar-denominated assets including government debt, raising the exchange rate.

What's wrong with this sensible-sounding story? Apply it to bonds: If bond yields rise, bonds are more attractive, so the bond price should rise. That's obviously wrong: Higher bond yields mechanically mean lower prices. The same thought applies to the less obvious case of stocks. Higher expected returns are a higher discount rate, which other things constant should lower stock prices. But wouldn't higher expected returns attract investors, driving prices up? Here you can see the subtle trap. If expected dividends rise, stocks are indeed more attractive. People buy and drive the price up until the expected return is unchanged. This story is the adjustment mechanism to a dividend shock, not the effect on prices of a higher equilibrium and observed rise in expected return with no change in dividends.

The same logic applies to government debt. If expected surpluses rise, and the price level does not move, government debt has a larger expected return. People buy, driving down the price level until the expected return has returned to normal. This is the mechanism for equilibrium formation in response to a fiscal shock, a process that we do not observe. In this case, we observe constant expected returns. A higher expected return with no change in surplus makes government debt less valuable.

Thus, higher real interest rates with no change in surpluses are inflationary, not deflationary. Higher real rates, which may come from higher nominal rates and sticky prices, lower the value of debt. Equivalently, they add to the interest costs of government debt, which has the same effect as lower surpluses.

Two questions remain: Do we trust the model's guidance that the economy displays long-run interest rate neutrality? If we do, is it relevant for most policy discussions, or is the "short-run" or otherwise qualified force for a negative sign overwhelming for practical policy advice outside currency reforms and hyperinflations? What are the preconditions for each case? The next subsection analyzes these questions using the simple sticky price model, in which long-term debt is the ingredient giving a temporary negative response.

5.3.2 *Higher or Lower Inflation?*

So, does raising interest rates raise or lower inflation, and conversely? These models offer a loud "it depends." There is no mechanistic answer. Sometimes you will see a positive sign and sometimes a negative sign. That is a useful observation, as we see conflicting evidence. If the theory is right, and if we interpret it correctly, the theory will help us to avoid exporting experience from one event to another where the preconditions have changed. The theory will help us to design policies with either sign: It will tell us *how* to raise inflation by raising interest rates, or *how* to lower inflation by raising interest rates. The point of an economic model is to spell out the "it depends" clauses. Historical correlations are always contingent, but without theory we know not on what.

The issue was in the air throughout the 2010s. The United States, Japan, and Europe, despite long periods of near-zero or even negative interest rates, and forward guidance of more to come, still had inflation below their targets. Most policy discussion remained anchored on how to raise inflation by applying more "stimulus" and "accommodation," lowering long-term rates through quantitative-easing bond purchases, or by banning cash to allow negative interest rates. But a few academics and commentators started to question that perhaps the steering wheel is attached backwards. Perhaps a steady and widely preannounced interest rate rise might *raise* inflation, at least eventually. For examples, see Schmitt-Grohé and Uribe (2014), Uribe (2018), and Kocherlakota (2010). A Fisherian response is a robust prediction of standard new-Keynesian models, as these authors, Garín, Lester, and Sims (2018), and Chapter 17 below point out, only made stronger when one rules out or limits a fiscal contraction contemporaneous with an interest rate rise. Could these countries, if they wished to do so, raise inflation by raising interest rates? If so, how? What combination of announcement, commitment, persistence, debt, and fiscal support is necessary?

A range of opinion in Brazil and Turkey, each dealing with persistent inflation, started to think that perhaps lowering interest rates is the secret to lowering inflation. But do these economies have the preconditions for that strategy to work? As I write in 2021, the answer seems to be no.

Contrariwise, the memory of 1980 is strong, in which a sharp and persistent interest rate rise is thought to have been the key for lowering inflation. The memory of the 1970s is likewise strong, in which too-low interest rates are thought to have raised inflation. Are these memories of a contingent event, or do they establish truths that hold always and everywhere?

Since the nominal interest rate equals the real rate plus expected inflation, $i_t = r_t + E_t \pi_{t+1}$, for a nominal interest rate rise to lower expected inflation, it must raise the real interest rate by more than one for one. That requires a substantial nonneutrality. With long-term debt or a contemporaneous fiscal shock, a higher nominal rate can lower *unexpected* inflation, which is easier, but not guaranteed.

For an interest rate rise to lower inflation in this simple model, exploiting the long-term debt channel without contemporary fiscal tightening, the interest rate rise must be *persistent* and *unexpected*. It must lower long-term bond prices, and only a credible and persistent interest rate rise will do that. It's easy to write down a persistent process, but harder for the central bank to communicate that expectation and commit to its communications. If people think this is a trial or experimental effort, or if they worry that the bank will quickly back down if events don't conform to the banks' forecasts—for example, if shocks or short-run responses move inflation the opposite from the desired direction and cause the bank to change course—then people will not perceive the move as persistent. If the rate rise is expected, bond prices will have already declined and the deflationary effect will have passed. A sudden shock that is believed to be long-lasting, a belief reflected in bond prices, is most likely to be disinflationary. The 1980–1982 shock, for example, is widely thought to have had more commitment behind it than earlier attempts to lower inflation by raising interest rates, and it had a greater impact on long-term rates.

For an interest rate rise to lower inflation in this model, there must be *long-term debt outstanding*. Many countries in fiscal stress have moved to short-term financing, so there just isn't that much long-term debt left. They are more likely to see higher interest rates raise inflation and vice versa.

The interest rate rise only affects *domestic-currency* debt. A government that has largely borrowed in foreign-currency debt cannot change the value of that debt by interest rate rises. Thus, a country that borrows more abroad is likelier to see inflation rise rather than decline when it raises interest rates.

Conversely, in this model, if the government wants to raise inflation by raising interest rates, the rise should be preannounced far ahead of time, and also persistent. If the move is preannounced before a lot of debt is sold, the inflation decline induced by the long-term debt mechanism is reduced. It helps if there is not much long-term debt outstanding so the initial negative effect can be smaller. The United States' slow, widely preannounced, and credible interest rate rises of the 2015–2019 period, which featured more inflation than in Europe which did not follow that policy, is a suggestive example, or at least a contrast with 1980–1982.

The *discount rate* or *interest cost* effect adds an inflationary force of interest rate rises. With sticky prices, a nominal rate rise raises real rates, which lowers the present value of surpluses. Equivalently, higher real rates raise interest costs on the debt. Loyo (1999) finds higher interest rates raised inflation in Brazil by this mechanism. Under fiscal stress, the central bank tried to defend the currency and to lower inflation by repeated interest rate rises. Each one seemed to quickly and perversely lower the exchange rate and result in more inflation.

The discount rate or interest cost effect is more important for highly indebted countries. At 100% debt-to-GDP ratio, each one percentage point rise in real interest rates adds 1% of GDP to interest costs. At 10% of GDP, the same rate rise only adds 0.1% of GDP to interest costs. So highly indebted countries, with much short-term debt and sticky prices, are more likely to see higher interest rates translate into higher, not lower inflation, and vice versa, as they are less likely to take fiscal actions that offset interest costs. The *stickier* prices are, then, the more likely it is that higher interest rates *raise* inflation.

Concurrent fiscal events and monetary–fiscal interactions matter for the effects of interest rate policies. If fiscal authorities react to higher real interest costs by reducing primary deficits, that adds a deflationary effect of an interest rate rise. If fiscal authorities react to a reduction in real interest costs by abandoning fiscal reforms, a reduction in rates that monetary authorities hope to create disinflation will fail to do so. In analyzing episodes, we are likely to see a contemporaneous fiscal shock, or a fiscal response to monetary policy. If fiscal authorities see a rate rise and say, "Whew, the central bank is going to solve inflation for us, we can relax," or if the monetary authorities tighten in response to what they see as too much fiscal stimulus, then we may see fiscal inflation, not temporary monetary disinflation, when the central bank raises rates. If the fiscal authorities cooperate with a joint monetary–fiscal contraction, then the inflation decline can be larger.

5.3.3 Implications

If the short-run opposite dynamics are strong enough, and if central banks understand them, central banks can exploit them to push inflation where the banks desire more quickly, at least away from the effective lower bound. Whether inflation would converge to interest rates or diverge in the long run then makes essentially no difference to central bank policy or what we observe. The pattern of lowering rates to get inflation going, and then raising interest to contain the inflation, and vice versa, is consistent with the long-run Fisherian prediction that *if* the central bank were to raise rates, wait out a negative response and sit there, inflation would eventually rise. In this view, the opportunity to raise interest rates, wait out transitory dynamics, and wait for inflation to slowly catch up, is only an expedient the bank would try at the zero bound, or when for some other reason it cannot follow the conventional policy.

This model captures only one simple mechanism, long-term debt, by which higher interest rates may lead temporarily to lower inflation. The large literature on channels of monetary policy suggests many other mechanisms that might work, and continue to work in a fiscal theory model. More elaborate Phillips curves, credit constraints, balance sheet channels and more financial frictions offer potential mechanisms. Higher real interest rates mean that households with short-term mortgages have to pay higher rates, and if the corresponding receipt of more interest revenue by lenders does not offset, inflation may decline. Integrating such models with fiscal theory is more low-hanging fruit. The results may deliver interesting additional preconditions for the sign of interest rates on inflation.

Empirical work is surprisingly unclear, given the strong and widespread belief that higher interest rates lower inflation and vice versa. Monetary policy shocks give rise to transitory interest rate movements, so we don't see a measurement of long-term neutrality. And even the short-run negative sign is hard to see. Starting with Sims (1980), VAR estimates routinely find a "price puzzle" that tighter monetary policy raises inflation.

The opposite prior being so strong, the result was chalked up to reverse causality, the Fed tightening in response to information about future inflation. It took a lot of delicate shock-identification carpentry to see the hoped-for result, prominently in Christiano, Eichenbaum, and Evans (1999), and even then a monetary tightening only slowly sets off a small downward drift in the price level. (Most of the literature also identifies tightening with a change in monetary aggregates.) In a survey and replication of this vast literature, Ramey (2016) finds that the "price puzzle" that higher interest rates result in higher inflation remains the central finding of VARs. Rusnak, Havranek, and Horvath (2013) conduct a meta-analysis of monetary VARs, using a variety of statistical techniques to correct for the selection and publication biases that want to produce a negative effect of interest rates on inflation, with the same result. Uribe (2018), looking with a different prior in mind, presents VAR evidence that permanent interest rate rises increase inflation in the United States. Cochrane (1994a) discusses a key problem why this seemingly simple response is hard to measure: Central banks always react to events, and never randomly change interest rates. One must look for interest rate changes that do not respond to the specific variable one wishes to examine, a so-far unused suggestion.

You can see by the length of this discussion that I struggle with the clear Fisherian predictions of theory, that the economy is stable at a peg and thus once short-run dynamics work themselves out, higher nominal interest rates result in higher inflation. The prediction is clear, and has been part of rational expectations model predictions for at least 30 years. The prediction is a natural expression of neutrality, that real quantities eventually do not depend on units of measurement. But it is so counter to conventional doctrine that it was first ignored for decades, and when recognized, it stands out like a sore thumb. This is a great story of how difficult it is to translate equations of simple models to intuition and policy. The most sensible reconciliation of theory and doctrine, alluded to above, is that central banks regularly exploit a short-run negative reaction, so we never see the positive long-run relation in the data. That reconciliation suggests, however, that a widely preannounced interest rate rise and patience would be useful for governments that wish more inflation at the zero bound, or when otherwise the negative short-run relationship cannot be exploited.

The Fisherian prediction centrally comes from rational expectations, not fiscal theory per se. It is equally true of rational-expectations new-Keynesian models. If it is wrong, it is rational expectations and the rest of the economic model that needs fixing. The conventional policy view of instability, so higher interest rates produce only lower inflation, comes from adaptive expectations. One could merge fiscal theory with adaptive expectations. But expectations aren't always irrational either, and the resulting model is likely to be a muddle.

In sum, nothing is easy in economics. The answer to "What happens if the central bank raises rates and leaves them there forever?" is not easily answered by historical experience of transitory and reversible rate changes, and monetary and fiscal policy that continuously reacts to events. Models robustly point to a long-run positive relationship, counter to policy world intuition. This section summarizes my struggles to see if the prediction is believable, by recognizing the long list of its preconditions that may make it true but not visible or frequently exploitable. The predictions are not as simple as just raise or lower rates and inflation will painlessly follow, and the facts are not nearly as contradictory as conventional wisdom would have one believe. But the point of economics is not to judge "beliefs" but to look at the world through the eyes of models.

5.4   A Surplus Process

I introduce a simple parametric surplus process that allows an s-shaped response, allows some unexpected inflation, and retains active fiscal policy. The surplus responds to a latent variable:

$$\tilde{s}_{t+1} = \alpha v_t^* + u_{s,t+1}$$

$$\rho v_{t+1}^* = v_t^* + \beta_s \varepsilon_{s,t+1} - \tilde{s}_{t+1}$$

$$u_{s,t+1} = \eta_s u_{s,t} + \varepsilon_{s,t+1}.$$

We may interpret the latent variable v_t^* as the value of debt if the surplus responds to changes in the value of debt that come from past deficits but does not respond to changes in the value of debt brought about by arbitrary unexpected inflation or deflation. In equilibrium, debt v_t is equal to v_t^*.

Our next step is to write a reasonable, flexible, realistic, and tractable surplus process. Building to larger models, we want a process written in first-order, VAR(1) form, describing variables at time $t + 1$ in terms of variables at time t and shocks at time $t + 1$, as most recently the standard new-Keynesian IS and Phillips equations (5.17)-(5.21). We want a process that allows an s-shaped moving average, one in which today's deficits ($s < 0$) are followed by future surpluses ($s > 0$) that can at least partially pay off the debt.

The natural way to induce an s-shaped moving average in a VAR(1) structure is to add a latent state variable, which I denote v_t^*. I write

$$\tilde{s}_{t+1} = \alpha v_t^* + u_{s,t+1} \tag{5.22}$$

$$\rho v_{t+1}^* = v_t^* + \beta_s \varepsilon_{s,t+1} - \tilde{s}_{t+1} \tag{5.23}$$

$$u_{s,t+1} = \eta_s u_{s,t} + \varepsilon_{s,t+1}. \tag{5.24}$$

A positive shock $\varepsilon_{s,t+1}$ raises $\tilde{s}_{t+1}$ and following $\tilde{s}_{t+j}$ persistently. But higher $\tilde{s}_{t+j}$ mean lower v_{t+j}^* in (5.23), and lower v_{t+j}^* gradually bring $\tilde{s}_{t+j}$ back down again via (5.22).

To see this behavior explicitly, we can find the moving average representation for $\tilde{s}_t$ implied by the system (5.22)-(5.24). Substituting (5.22) in (5.23),

$$\rho v_{t+1}^* = (1 - \alpha)v_t^* + \beta_s \varepsilon_{s,t+1} - u_{s,t+1}$$

$$v_{t+1}^* = \frac{\rho^{-1}}{1 - (1 - \alpha)\rho^{-1}L}\left(\beta_s \varepsilon_{s,t+1} - u_{s,t+1}\right).$$

(I specify $\alpha > (1 - \rho)$.) Substituting back to (5.22),

$$\tilde{s}_{t+1} = \alpha \frac{\rho^{-1}L}{1 - (1 - \alpha)\rho^{-1}L}\left(\beta_s \varepsilon_{s,t+1} - u_{s,t+1}\right) + u_{s,t+1}$$

$$\tilde{s}_{t+1} = \left[1 - \frac{\alpha\rho^{-1}L}{1 - (1 - \alpha)\rho^{-1}L}\right]u_{s,t+1} + \beta_s \frac{\alpha\rho^{-1}L}{1 - (1 - \alpha)\rho^{-1}L}\varepsilon_{s,t+1}. \tag{5.25}$$

This representation is convenient for some intuition below. We can go further, writing

$$\tilde{s}_{t+1} = a(L)\varepsilon_{s,t+1} = \frac{\left(1 - \rho^{-1}L\right) a_u(L) + \beta_s \alpha \rho^{-1}L}{1 - (1-\alpha)\,\rho^{-1}L}\varepsilon_{s,t+1}, \qquad (5.26)$$

where, reflecting (5.24),

$$a_u(L) \equiv \frac{1}{1 - \eta_s L}.$$

The point so far: The structure (5.22)–(5.24) can be seen as a way to encode the moving average (5.25) or (5.26) in standard VAR(1) form.

This initially intimidating surplus process is actually pretty and intuitive. Let us see how it works in a simple frictionless model with one-period debt,

$$i_t = E_t \pi_{t+1}$$
$$\tilde{s}_{t+1} = a(L)\varepsilon_{s,t+1}$$
$$\Delta E_{t+1}\pi_{t+1} = -a(\rho)\varepsilon_{s,t+1}. \qquad (5.27)$$

In (5.25) and (5.26) we have quickly

$$a(\rho) = \beta_s. \qquad (5.28)$$

Now you know what the β_s is doing in (5.23)! With $\beta_s = 0$, the latent variable setup (5.22)–(5.24) embodies a completely s-shaped surplus process. All deficits are paid, inflation is always zero, yet surpluses vary, and the model is completely fiscal theory. Fiscal theory of the price level does not require that the government refuses to pay its debts, or always inflates away all or even any debt, or that there is any correlation at all between debt, deficits, and inflation.

The first term in (5.25) shows more clearly how debt is repaid. We can write it

$$1 - \frac{\alpha\rho^{-1}L}{1 - (1-\alpha)\,\rho^{-1}L} = 1 - \frac{\alpha}{\rho}\left[L + \frac{1-\alpha}{\rho}L^2 + \left(\frac{1-\alpha}{\rho}\right)^2 L^3 + \cdots \right].$$

This term has a movement in one direction, 1, followed by a string of small negative movements in the opposite direction. They are small, since α is a small number. And they decay over time slowly, with a $(1-\alpha)/\rho$ autocorrelation coefficient. Adding dynamics $u_{s,t+1}$ smears out this pattern, giving a persistent stream of deficits that are slowly followed by a longer-lasting persistent stream of surpluses.

However, we want the model to allow some unexpected inflation. The $\beta_s \neq 0$ parameter introduces unexpected inflation in a convenient way. The second term of (5.25) adds a small, AR(1)-shaped decay in the same direction as the original shock.

Now, what happens to debt? Debt follows the identity

$$\rho v_{t+1} = v_t + i_t - \pi_{t+1} - \tilde{s}_{t+1}$$

or, with $i_t = E_t \pi_{t+1}$,

$$\rho v_{t+1} = v_t - \Delta E_{t+1}\pi_{t+1} - \tilde{s}_{t+1}.$$

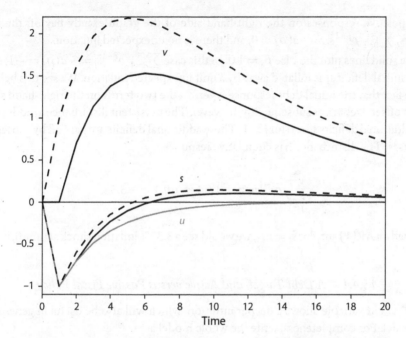

FIGURE 5.5. Response of the Simple Example Surplus Process to a Unit Deficit Shock. The solid lines present the case $\beta_s = 1.0$. The dashed lines present the case $\beta_s = 0$. Other parameters $\rho = 0.99$, $\eta_s = 0.7$, $\alpha = 0.1$.

Comparing this identity with the latent variable definition (5.23),

$$\rho v_{t+1}^* = v_t^* + \beta_s \varepsilon_{s,t+1} - \tilde{s}_{t+1},$$

and the outcome for unexpected inflation (5.27)–(5.28) $\Delta E_{t+1} \pi_{t+1} = -\beta_s \varepsilon_{s,t+1}$, we see that in this simple model, in equilibrium, debt v_t turns out to be equal to the latent variable v_t^*. (Some reverse-engineering went into this model!) You can also derive $v_t = v_t^*$ by taking the present value $v_t = E_t \sum_{j=0}^{\infty} \rho^j \tilde{s}_{t+1+j}$ using the surplus moving average, and either some algebra or the Hansen-Sargent prediction formulas. Or, you can difference the last two equations to note

$$\rho\left(v_{t+1} - v_{t+1}^*\right) = \left(v_t - v_t^*\right) - \left(\Delta E_{t+1} \pi_{t+1} + \beta_s \varepsilon_{s,t+1}\right),$$

and the condition that debt cannot explode means $v_t = v_t^*$, $\Delta E_{t+1} \pi_{t+1} = -\beta_s \varepsilon_{s,t+1}$.

The latent variable v^* is not automatically equal to debt, and v^* is not equal to debt away from equilibrium. It is, so far, just a latent state variable that helps us to create an s-shaped and (here) exogenous surplus process. Debt v_t turns out, in equilibrium, to equal v_t^*, but that is a result not an assumption.

Figure 5.5 presents two cases of the surplus and debt process (5.22)–(5.24), equivalently the surplus moving average (5.26). The dashed lines present $\eta_s = 0.7$, $\alpha = 0.1$, $\beta_s = 0$. I plot the response to a deficit shock, $\varepsilon_{s,1} = -1$, which tells a cleaner story. The surplus starts by following the AR(1) pattern of the surplus disturbance $u_{s,t}$. These deficits increase debt v_t. In turn, increased debt slowly pushes up surpluses. Eventually deficits cross the zero line to surpluses, and positive surpluses start to pay down debt. The many small positive responses on the right-hand side of the graph exactly pay off the initial deficits, $\sum_{j=1}^{\infty} \rho^{j-1}\tilde{s}_j = -a(\rho) = 0$, and there is no unexpected inflation.

The solid lines plot the case $\beta_s = 1.0$. In this case $\sum_{j=1}^{\infty} \rho^{j-1}\tilde{s}_j = -a(\rho) = -1$, so the entire initial deficit s_1 is inflated away by a unit unexpected inflation. We see this behavior by the fact that the initial debt response is zero—the two terms on the right-hand side of (5.23) offset. Debt rises subsequently, however. The persistent disturbance u_s adds persistent additional deficits $s_j < 0$ for $j > 1$. These additional deficits are paid off by subsequent surpluses. The disturbance has cumulative response

$$\sum_{j=1}^{\infty} \rho^{j-1}u_j = -1/(1 - \rho\eta_s) = -3.33.$$

If we had an AR(1) surplus $\tilde{s}_t = u_{s,t}$, we would see a 3.33% inflation shock at time 0, not 1%.

5.4.1   A Debt Target, and Active versus Passive Fiscal Policy

The v^* latent variable allows a deeper intuition, which will also be useful in generalizing the model. For completeness, write the whole model as

$$i_t = E_t\pi_{t+1} \tag{5.29}$$

$$\tilde{s}_{t+1} = \alpha v_t^* + u_{s,t+1} \tag{5.30}$$

$$\rho v_{t+1}^* = v_t^* - \Delta E_{t+1}\pi_{t+1}^* - \tilde{s}_{t+1} \tag{5.31}$$

$$\rho v_{t+1} = v_t - \Delta E_{t+1}\pi_{t+1} - \tilde{s}_{t+1} \tag{5.32}$$

$$\Delta E_{t+1}\pi_{t+1}^* = -\beta_s\varepsilon_{s,t+1} \tag{5.33}$$

$$u_{s,t+1} = \eta_s u_{s,t} + \varepsilon_{s,t+1}. \tag{5.34}$$

Equation (5.29) repeats the flexible price model with an interest rate target. Equations (5.30), (5.31), (5.33), and (5.34) jointly describe the evolution of primary surpluses $\tilde{s}_t$. Equation (5.32) is the debt evolution equation (3.17), with one-period debt so $i_t = r_{t+1}^n$, using the Fisher equation (5.29).

As a first step toward solving the model, difference (5.31) and (5.32) to give

$$(v_{t+1} - v_{t+1}^*) = \rho^{-1}(v_t - v_t^*) - \rho^{-1}(\Delta E_{t+1}\pi_{t+1} - \Delta E_{t+1}\pi_{t+1}^*). \tag{5.35}$$

As in the last section, the condition that debt v_t does not explode tells us that $v_t = v_t^*$ and $\Delta E_{t+1}\pi_{t+1} = \Delta E_{t+1}\pi_{t+1}^*$.

(The variable v_t^* does not explode either, so $v_t - v_t^*$ not exploding is the same as v_t not exploding. Substitute (5.30) into (5.31) to obtain

$$\rho v_{t+1}^* = (1 - \alpha)v_t^* - \Delta E_{t+1}\pi_{t+1}^* - u_{s,t+1}.$$

Thus, adding the natural assumption that $\Delta E_{t+1}\pi_{t+1}^*$ is stationary, v_t^* grows at less than the steady-state interest rate for $\alpha > 0$, and it is stationary for $\alpha > 1 - \rho$. Choosing $\rho = 1$ conveniently unites the two cases.)

Now, you may ask, why do I go through all the trouble of specifying a latent state variable v_t^* that turns out to be equal to debt, in equilibrium, rather than just let the surplus respond to debt itself? It would seem simpler to write

$$\tilde{s}_{t+1} = \gamma v_t + u_{s,t+1} \tag{5.36}$$

$$\rho v_{t+1} = v_t - \Delta E_{t+1}\pi_{t+1} - \tilde{s}_{t+1} \tag{5.37}$$

$$u_{s,t+1} = \eta_s u_{s,t} + \varepsilon_{s,t+1}.$$

A deficit, negative $\tilde{s}_{t+1}$, that comes with no inflation in (5.37) raises the value of debt v_{t+1}. In turn, the higher debt gives rise to larger subsequent surpluses, which can pay off the debt: an s-shaped surplus process. If the deficit in (5.37) is matched by inflation then there is no change in value of debt and no subsequent surpluses. So, the structure can also accommodate both cases. These simpler equations seem to flexibly capture a general surplus process in a first-order system.

The trouble with this idea is that fiscal policy becomes passive. Substituting the surplus equation (5.36) into the value equation (5.37), we have

$$\rho v_{t+1} = (1 - \gamma)v_t - \Delta E_{t+1}\pi_{t+1} - u_{s,t+1}.$$

For $\gamma > 1 - \rho$, debt converges going forward for any value of unexpected inflation. Any unexpected inflation leads to a change in debt, which leads to changes in surpluses that validate that unexpected inflation. We lose the central idea of the whole project, that fiscal policy can determine unexpected inflation. Indeed, this is a standard specification of passive fiscal policy, which we shall return to.

(For $\gamma > 0$, debt grows at less than the interest rate, so the transversality condition holds. Any unexpected inflation is an equilibrium. It is convenient for empirical work to deal in stationary quantities. If one wishes to allow debt, or a debt-to-GDP ratio that grows over time, one can deflate everything by a geometric factor smaller than the discount rate before starting. However, we often think of constraints beyond the transversality condition, that the debt-to-GDP ratio must be bounded, for example. I generally work with that case, and require a stationary debt-to-GDP ratio, so I do not spell out the case that debt grows but slowly enough that the transversality condition applies.)

Comparing the v^* equation (5.31) to the debt v equation (5.32), then, we can give a deeper interpretation. The surplus responds to a version of debt v_t^* that accumulates past deficits in the same way as does the actual value of debt v_t, but v_t^* ignores changes in the value of debt that come from unexpected inflation different from one specific value $\Delta E_{t+1}\pi_{t+1} \neq \Delta E_{t+1}\pi_{t+1}^*$. This specification gives us a fiscal policy that remains active, picks one specific value for unexpected inflation, but nonetheless pays off debts accumulated from past deficits in a way that $\tilde{s}_t = u_{s,t}$ plus an AR(1) for $u_{s,t}$ would not do.

By contrast, when the surplus responds to debt itself in (5.36)–(5.37), the surplus responds to *all* variation in the value of debt, not only that induced by past deficits but also variation in the value of debt induced by arbitrary unexpected inflation or deflation.

It is common to specify, measure, and test active versus passive fiscal policy by the regression coefficient of surplus on debt, $\gamma > 0$ versus $\gamma = 0$ in (5.37). The v versus v^* formulation shows us how overly restrictive this approach is. Indeed, since we have

$v_t = v_t^*$ in equilibrium, we have in hand a counterexample: In equilibrium, we see $\tilde{s}_{t+1} = \alpha v_t + u_{s,t+1}$ with $\alpha > 0$, even though this is an active fiscal regime, and the surplus actually responds to v^* not to v. We could write

$$\tilde{s}_{t+1} = \alpha v_t^* + \gamma (v_t - v_t^*) + u_{s,t+1}. \tag{5.38}$$

The condition for active fiscal policy is $\gamma = 0$, not $\alpha = 0$.

I introduce notation $\Delta E_{t+1} \pi_{t+1}^*$ in (5.31) and (5.33) for additional intuition. We can regard $\Delta E_{t+1} \pi_{t+1}^*$ as a stochastic inflation target. The target is stochastic, as it may vary over time and in response to shocks to other variables. Equation (5.33), $\Delta E_{t+1} \pi_{t+1}^* = -\beta_s \varepsilon_{s,t+1}$, relates this inflation target to the surplus shock. I use the notation β_s, as when there are multiple shocks, this setup generalizes to a regression coefficient of the stochastic inflation target on the multiple underlying shocks.

We can view the government in this model as having an interest rate target i_t and an unexpected inflation target $\Delta E_t \pi_{t+1}^*$. Expected inflation follows from the interest rate target via $i_t = E_t \pi_{t+1}$. We can also think that the government starts with a stochastic inflation target, $\{\pi_t^*\}$. The government implements the inflation target by setting the interest rate target to $i_t = E_t \pi_{t+1}^*$ and by using the unexpected value of the inflation target in the fiscal rule (5.31).

The star variables disappear in equilibrium, and the fiscal and monetary parts of the model separate. With $v_t = v_t^*$ and $\pi_t = \pi_t^*$ in equilibrium, inflation determination now reduces to the pair

$$i_t = E_t \pi_{t+1} \tag{5.39}$$

$$\Delta E_t \pi_{t+1} = -\beta_s \varepsilon_{s,t+1}. \tag{5.40}$$

We can then find the surplus and value of debt from the equilibrium versions of (5.30), (5.31) and (5.34),

$$\tilde{s}_{t+1} = \alpha v_t + u_{s,t+1}$$

$$\rho v_{t+1} = v_t - \beta_s \varepsilon_{s,t+1} - \tilde{s}_{t+1}$$

$$u_{s,t+1} = \eta_s u_{s,t} + \varepsilon_{s,t+1}. \tag{5.41}$$

Equations (5.39)–(5.41) are the system we see, estimate, and simulate. The v and v^* business serves one purpose: to understand why unexpected inflation is given by $\Delta E_{t+1} \pi_{t+1}^* = -\beta_s \varepsilon_{s,t+1}$, not some other value. Empirically, one could just estimate β_s and ignore the theory, or relegate the theory to a footnote about equilibrium uniqueness. We do not see $v_t \neq v_t^*$ or $\pi_t \neq \pi_t^*$ in equilibrium.

One could also choose unexpected inflation and justify (5.40) by an analogous "active-money" specification,

$$i_t = i_t^* + \phi (\pi_t - \pi_t^*), \quad \phi > 1, \tag{5.42}$$

standard in the new-Keynesian literature, in which $\pi_t \neq \pi_t^*$ generates an explosion. I explore this alternative model below.

Writing active fiscal policy as in equation (5.38) makes the analogy clear and expresses observational equivalence. In equilibrium, when the starred variables equal their unstarred counterparts, the observables (5.39)–(5.41) do not distinguish active money, passive fiscal $\phi > 1$, $\gamma > 0$, from active fiscal, passive money $\phi < 1$, $\gamma = 0$ theories of why π_t^* or β_s in (5.40) are unique.

I argue below that we should embrace observational equivalence, rather than spend a lot more time on identifying assumptions to try to test for regimes. Observational equivalence just means that we have to look at the plausibility and consonance with institutional and historical facts of the equilibrium selection underpinnings, my v versus v^* story, and the corresponding new-Keynesian $\phi > 1$ story, rather than hope some fancy time-series test will settle the issue.

5.4.2 Active and Passive Policy in a Nonlinear Model

The active versus passive policy, α versus γ issues are important and confusing enough that they bear expression in a simple exact nonlinear context. Start by remembering how real debt works. If the government issues real debt b_t at constant rate r, then the flow condition is

$$\frac{db_t}{dt} = r b_t - \tilde{s}_t. \tag{5.43}$$

Integrating forwards, and assuming perfect foresight for simplicity,

$$b_t = \int_{\tau=0}^{T} e^{-r\tau} s_{t+\tau} d\tau + e^{-rT} b_{t+T}. \tag{5.44}$$

The present value formula results when the transversality condition

$$\lim_{T \to \infty} e^{-rT} b_{t+T} = 0$$

holds. Equivalently, turning (5.44) around,

$$b_{t+T} = e^{rT} \left[b_t - \int_{\tau=0}^{T} e^{-r\tau} s_{t+\tau} d\tau \right].$$

Debt grows at the interest rate. The transversality condition is violated unless the valuation equation holds.

For real debt, we interpret this condition as a constraint on surplus processes: To avoid default, or to raise debt in the first place, the government must arrange surpluses to satisfy the right-hand side of the valuation equation.

One, but not the only way to generate such a policy is for the primary surplus to respond to the value of debt,

$$\tilde{s}_t = s_{0,t} + \gamma b_t, \tag{5.45}$$

where $\{s_{0,t}\}$ does not grow over time. If $\gamma > 0$—if the primary surplus responds to debt at all—then debt grows more slowly than the interest rate, and the present value condition and transversality conditions hold. If $0 < \gamma < r$, debt grows, but more slowly than the interest rate. If $\gamma \geq r$—if the primary surplus at least pays interest on outstanding debt—then the value of debt remains finite. Stated in terms of the more conventional total surplus

$\tilde{s}_t - rb_t$, a positive total surplus, a surplus that at least pays interest on outstanding debt, keeps debt bounded.

To see these results, substitute (5.45) into the flow condition (5.43), yielding

$$\frac{db_t}{dt} = (r - \gamma) b_t - s_{0,t}.$$

Integrating forward,

$$b_{t+T} = e^{(r-\gamma)T} \left[b_t - \int_{\tau=0}^{T} e^{-(r-\gamma)\tau} s_{0,t+\tau} d\tau \right].$$

Then, so long as $\gamma > 0$ and $s_{0,t}$ is bounded, real debt grows more slowly than the interest rate and the transversality condition and present value relation (5.44) hold. (The integral in brackets is not the present value, and discounting $s_{0,t}$ at rate $r - \gamma$ doesn't have a particular interpretation that I see. The point of this equation is only to find the growth rate of b_{t+T}, and thereby to verify the present value relation (5.44). The surpluses in the present value formula include the γb_t term, per (5.45).)

The response γb_t generates endogenously an s-shaped surplus response function, that deficits today are matched by future surpluses. The condition $\gamma > 0$ is sufficient, but not necessary for debt repayment, however. The process $s_{0,t}$ could have the negative autocorrelation property $a(\rho) = 0$ all on its own. That point is one of many important qualifiers for attempted tests based on γ.

With nominal debt, the flow condition is

$$\frac{d}{dt} \left(\frac{B_t}{P_t} \right) = r \left(\frac{B_t}{P_t} \right) - \tilde{s}_t.$$

Integrating forwards,

$$\frac{B_t}{P_t} = \int_{\tau=0}^{T} e^{-r\tau} s_{t+\tau} d\tau + e^{-rT} \left(\frac{B_{t+T}}{P_{t+T}} \right). \tag{5.46}$$

The present value formula results with the transversality condition

$$\lim_{T \to \infty} e^{-rT} \left(\frac{B_{t+T}}{P_{t+T}} \right) = 0.$$

Equivalently, writing (5.46) as

$$\left(\frac{B_{t+T}}{P_{t+T}} \right) = e^{rT} \left[\left(\frac{B_t}{P_t} \right) - \int_{\tau=0}^{T} e^{-r\tau} s_{t+\tau} d\tau \right],$$

we see that for a given surplus process $\{\tilde{s}_t\}$, real debt grows at the interest rate, so the transversality condition is violated unless the value of debt is given by the present value relation

$$\frac{B_t}{P_t} = \int_{\tau=0}^{T} e^{-r\tau} s_{t+\tau} d\tau. \tag{5.47}$$

The transversality condition is a first-order condition for consumer optimization. We conclude that the price level adjusts so that the valuation equation holds.

Passive policy results if the stream of surpluses adjusts so that (5.47) holds for any price level P_t. Surplus policies that react to debt are one way to produce a passive policy. If the primary surplus responds to the value of debt,

$$\tilde{s}_t = s_{0,t} + \gamma \frac{B_t}{P_t}, \ \gamma > 0,$$

then we have

$$\frac{d}{dt}\left(\frac{B_t}{P_t}\right) = s_{0,t} + (r - \gamma)\frac{B_t}{P_t}.$$

Again integrating forward,

$$\frac{B_{t+T}}{P_{t+T}} = e^{(r-\gamma)T}\left[\frac{B_t}{P_t} - \int_{\tau=0}^{T} e^{-(r-\gamma)\tau} s_{0,t+\tau} d\tau\right].$$

If $\gamma > 0$ and $\{s_{0,t}\}$ is bounded, real debt grows more slowly than the real interest rate, and the transversality condition and valuation equation hold *for any* P_t. Again, the last integral has no particular interpretation and the valuation equation (5.47) discounts the entire surplus, including the $\gamma B_t/P_t$ term. If $\gamma > r$, then real debt is also bounded for any P_t.

This observation looks pretty damning for the fiscal theory, and several authors have interpreted it that way. Don't responsible governments raise surpluses to pay off debts, at least until they run into Laffer limits?

But active fiscal policy can respond to debt. It need only not respond to arbitrary variation in the price level. Define a price level target P_t^*. Let the government follow

$$\tilde{s}_t = s_{0,t} + \alpha V_t^* \tag{5.48}$$

$$\frac{dV_t^*}{dt} = rV_t^* - \tilde{s}_t \tag{5.49}$$

$$V_0^* = \frac{B_0}{P_0^*},$$

while the flow equation remains

$$\frac{d}{dt}\left(\frac{B_t}{P_t}\right) = r\left(\frac{B_t}{P_t}\right) - \tilde{s}_t. \tag{5.50}$$

If $\alpha > 0$ the latent variable V_t^* grows more slowly than the interest rate, and if $\alpha > r$, V_t^* is bounded. To see this, write

$$\frac{d}{dt}V_t^* = (r - \alpha) V_t^* - s_{0,t}$$

$$V_{t+T}^* = e^{(r-\alpha)T}\left[V_t^* - \int_{\tau=0}^{T} e^{-(r-\alpha)\tau} s_{0,t+\tau} d\tau\right].$$

Integrating (5.49) forward, then V_t^* is the present value of surpluses,

$$V_t^* = \int_0^\infty e^{-r\tau} s_{t+\tau} d\tau + \lim_{T \to \infty} e^{-rT} V_{t+T} = \int_0^\infty e^{-r\tau} s_{t+\tau} d\tau.$$

Differencing (5.49) and (5.50),

$$\frac{d}{dt}\left(\frac{B_t}{P_t} - V_t^*\right) = r\left(\frac{B_t}{P_t} - V_t^*\right)$$

then the real value of debt B_t/P_t grows at the interest rate, violating the consumer's transversality condition, unless

$$\frac{B_t}{P_t} = V_t^*.$$

Only one value of the price level, $P_t = P_t^*$, is consistent with the transversality condition. Fiscal policy is active, although the surplus responds to the value of debt as in (5.48). Again, we can also have an s-shaped surplus and an apparent response to debt via an s-shaped $\{s_{0,t}\}$.

5.4.3   Is It Reasonable?

Once one considers its possibility, specifying that fiscal policy responds to changes in the value of debt that result from accumulated deficits and (later) from changes in the real interest rate, but does not respond to revaluation of the debt stemming from arbitrary unexpected inflation or deflation, is not unreasonable or artificial.

Yes, governments often raise surpluses after a time of deficits, which builds up their debt. Doing so makes good on the explicit or implicit promise made when borrowing, and sustains the reputation needed for future borrowing. Governments often raise revenue from debt sales, and the value of debt increases after such sales, which essentially proves that investors believe surpluses will rise to pay off new debts. We see many institutions in place to try to precommit to repayment, rather than default or inflation. Those institutions help the government to borrow in the first place.

But the same governments may well and sensibly refuse to accommodate changes in the value of debt that come from arbitrary unexpected inflation and deflation, and people may well expect such behavior. Should, say, a 50% cumulative deflation break out, likely in a severe recession, does anyone expect the U.S. government to sharply raise taxes or to drastically cut spending, to pay an unexpected real windfall to nominal bondholders— Wall Street bankers, wealthy individuals, and foreigners, especially foreign central banks? Will not the government regard the deflation as a temporary aberration, prices "disconnected from fundamentals," like a stock market "bubble," that fiscal policy should ignore until it passes? Indeed, isn't the response to such an event more likely to be fiscal stimulus, unbacked fiscal expansion, and helicopter money, not heartless austerity?

Concretely, Cochrane (2017c) and Cochrane (2018) argue that this expectation is why standard new-Keynesian models' predictions of a large sharp deflation, and old-Keynesian predictions of a "deflation spiral," did not happen when the United States hit the zero bound on nominal interest rates in 2008–2009, and Japan two decades earlier. Such deflation requires a large "passive" fiscal tightening that would be anything but "passively" regarded in a stimulus-minded Congress and Administration.

Many economists call for governments to pursue helicopter-drop unbacked fiscal stimulus in response to below-target inflation. (Benhabib, Schmitt-Grohé, and Uribe (2002) is an influential example.) Such a policy likewise represents a refusal to adapt surpluses to deflation, but to repay debts incurred from deficits in normal circumstances. Conversely, is not fiscal "austerity" a common response to inflation or currency devaluation? Rather than enjoy the debt devaluation that inflation or devaluation offer, governments increase fiscal surpluses, often at great pain.

We can see institutions and reputations at work to communicate these intentions and turn them into commitments. A gold standard is a commitment to raise surpluses to buy gold or to borrow gold against credible future surpluses, rather than to enjoy the bounty of an inflation-induced debt reduction. A foreign currency peg or foreign currency borrowing commits the government to raise surpluses as needed to repay debt at the pegged exchange rate, no more and no less. Both commitments suffer because of variation in the relative price of goods and services to gold or foreign currency, which force a fiscal response to undesired inflation and deflation. The implied inflation target π_t^* is unnecessarily volatile. But both contain a devaluation escape clause, which is a deeper refusal to adapt fiscal policy to undesired deflation.

When governments in the 1930s abandoned the gold standard, they abandoned exactly a commitment to repay debt in higher real terms after undesired deflation. Jacobson, Leeper, and Preston (2019) argue persuasively that the Roosevelt administration, in its abandonment of the gold standard during the deflation of 1933, refused to raise surpluses after a deflation-induced increase in the real value of the debt. The rise in the real relative price of gold would otherwise have triggered an automatic fiscal response, paying greater than expected real returns to bondholders. Moreover, by separating the budget into an "emergency" and "regular" budget, the Roosevelt administration preserved its reputation for repaying debt once the price level returned to the administration's desired target, a reputation that allowed the U.S. government to borrow in real terms for WWII.

An inflation target agreement between government and central bank includes, explicitly or implicitly, the government's fiscal commitment to pay off nominal debt at the inflation target, neither more nor less, as much or more than it signals the government's desired value for coefficients in a central bank Taylor rule. Many economists have suggested an analogous fiscal rule that runs unbacked deficits in the event of deflation, commits to surpluses to fight inflation, but still repays debts incurred from past deficits should inflation come out on target. The latter provision allows the government to borrow, promising repayment, in normal times.

Committing to repay debts is wise, as it allows governments to borrow. Committing *not* to accommodate revaluation, due to any value of unexpected inflation and deflation that comes along, is also wise because it allows the government to produce a stable price level and also to avoid volatile taxes and spending.

Admittedly, appealing to episodes bends the rules about on and off equilibrium. It is useful though if both behaviors point in the same direction. Formally, one can identify off-equilibrium behavior if one can credibly say that the off-equilibrium behavior corresponds to some observable behavior. Governments that run stimulus when they see low inflation "in equilibrium" credibly would also do so if a "multiple equilibrium" inflation were to emerge.

There is also a long and useful tradition of breaking the equilibrium wall a bit, and treating observed behavior in rare events or moments in which policy rules are changing as indications of off-equilibrium behavior, either directly or how off-equilibrium behavior might look once a new regime is in place, though a strict reading of a rational expectations paradigm says we should never see off-equilibrium events.

We do not need to interpret the stochastic inflation target π_t^* as a value happily chosen, proudly announced, easily enforced, and exactly implemented. It may vary with external shocks. It may represent the value of inflation that the government acquiesces to, not the value it desires. Observed low inflation in the 2010s can represent a low π_t^*, though central banks' official inflation targets and government desires were higher, just as deficit projections are largely aspirational. Central banks and governments could have done a lot more to raise inflation, but saw those steps as too costly. The same is true of the spurt of inflation in 2021, which the Fed and Treasury did not intend but ignore as "transitory." The Fed and Treasury acquiesced to this inflation, as we see from the fact that they took no action in 2021 to do anything about it. Central banks routinely describe their official targets as aspirations, toward which they wish to nudge the economy. That's a different kind of target.

This parametric model and my interpretation that the variables v_t^* and $\Delta E_{t+1} \pi_{t+1}^*$ encode a set of institutions and policy reputations is attractive, I think, but it is not the only way to write active fiscal policy. It may prove more intuitive or consonant with institutions to write surplus rules that react directly to inflation or the price level; for example, mandating greater surplus if inflation breaks out. Latent variables that are not point-by-point equal to debt in equilibrium may eventually be more useful. Writing the inflation target as a long-run goal, similar to central banks' 2% inflation goals, is possible as well. I return to these ideas below.

5.4.4   Thinking about the Parameters

The parameter β_s in $\Delta E_{t+1} \pi_{t+1}^* = -\beta_s \varepsilon_{s,t+1}$ is convenient for the modeler, as it directly controls unexpected inflation and the cumulative surplus response $a(\rho)$. However, β_s is best regarded as a reduced-form parameter, a modeling convenience rather than an independent policy lever or a description of the mechanics of fiscal or monetary policy. The parameter β_s lets the modeler control $a(\rho)$. In reality the government does the hard work of raising surpluses, and $\beta_s = a(\rho)$ is the result.

By analogy, consider an AR(1) surplus $\tilde{s}_{t+1} = \eta_s \tilde{s}_t + \varepsilon_{s,t+1}$ in the flexible price model, producing $\Delta E_{t+1} \pi_{t+1} = -a(\rho)\varepsilon_{s,t+1} = -\varepsilon_{s,t+1}/(1 - \rho\eta_s)$. This algebraic specification invites an economically sensible modeling procedure: Specify the surplus process, and then find the unexpected inflation produced by the model. We could proceed backward: Specify unexpected inflation and then reverse engineer the surplus process parameter η_s

that produces it. But the algebra of the model does not suggest this unnatural procedure. A practical defect of my v_t^*, π_t^*, β_s model is that it is parameterized in a way that invites this sort of reverse logic. We want instead to specify sensible economic and policy primitives and then *derive* the model's prediction for unexpected inflation. To do that, we have to reverse engineer the $\Delta E_{t+1}\pi_{t+1}^*$ result that produces primitives of fiscal policy that we think are sensible.

Concretely, though one can estimate β_s in $\Delta E_{t+1}\pi_{t+1}^* = -\beta_s\varepsilon_{t+1}$, or one may specify it in a model, it typically does not make sense to hold β_s constant as one examines alternative values for other parts of the fiscal and monetary policy specification, as one might vary η_s or $\sigma(\varepsilon_{s,t})$ independently in an AR(1) surplus model. That is what I mean by calling β_s a "reduced form" parameter. Keeping β_s constant while moving other parameters of the policy process typically does not ask an interesting or sensible question. In practical terms, β_s directly controls unexpected inflation. If you hold β_s constant as you move other parameters of the policy process, those parameters cannot produce a different value of unexpected inflation.

In the simple v^*, π^* model (5.29)–(5.34), the persistence η_s of the surplus disturbance is the main other policy parameter. As persistence η_s rises, cumulative deficits rise, and one would naturally expect the government to inflate away more of this cumulatively larger fiscal shock. But if we keep the same value of β_s, we always find the same unexpected inflation by construction.

In keeping β_s constant as we raise η_s, we assume that the government inflates away the same fraction of the *initial* deficit shock. It is arguably more interesting to compare the inflationary effects of two values of η_s by specifying that the government inflates away the same fraction of the *overall* deficit shock. The overall deficit shock is $-a_u(\rho) = \sum_{j=1}^{\infty}\rho^{j-1}u_j = 1/(1-\rho\eta_s)$. Thus, it seems more interesting to specify a larger value $\beta_s = \beta_{s,0}/(1-\rho\eta_s)$; or equivalently that $a(\rho)$ is the same fraction of $a_u(\rho)$, not the same number, while varying η_s. We would then naturally conclude that if deficit shocks become more long-lasting, unexpected inflation is larger.

There is no right or wrong here, there are only interesting and uninteresting values of policy parameters to compare with each other. Interesting policy experiments invite us to change β_s along with other parameters.

5.5   Responses and Rules

I add monetary and fiscal policy rules to the model,

$$i_t = \theta_{i\pi}\pi_t + \theta_{ix}x_t + u_{i,t}$$

$$\tilde{s}_{t+1} = \theta_{s\pi}\pi_{t+1} + \theta_{sx}x_{t+1} + \alpha v_t^* + u_{s,t+1},$$

and put all the ingredients together. I calculate responses to fiscal and monetary policy shocks. I first calculate responses to shocks with no output and inflation reactions in the policy rules, $\theta = 0$. Then I calculate responses with those reactions in place. Policy rules buffer the effect of shocks by moving inflation forward. The responses to monetary policy shocks show a disinflation and recession, followed by Fisherian responses in the very long run.

Last, I add policy rules to the model and I put all of these ingredients together. Yes, we can ignore policy rules and study the response of inflation and output to specified paths or processes for interest rates and surpluses, which are after all what we observe. But it's often more interesting to model policy rules.

To ask what happens if the Fed raises interest rates, it is really not interesting to hold the path of surpluses constant. Surpluses naturally rise when output and inflation rise. We, or the Fed, would likely want to include such predictable reactions in an evaluation of the effects of monetary policy. Likewise, to ask for the consequences of a fiscal shock, it is really not interesting to imagine that the Fed keeps interest rates fixed. The Fed routinely raises interest rates in response to inflation and output. An interesting analysis of how the economy will evolve following a fiscal shock surely takes account of that fact. We may not always want to include policy reactions, but we sometimes do, so let's see how to do it and how they affect the results.

The model, from Cochrane (2021b), adds fiscal and monetary policy rules to the sticky price model with long-term debt and fiscal theory:

$$x_t = E_t x_{t+1} - \sigma (i_t - E_t \pi_{t+1}) \tag{5.51}$$

$$\pi_t = \beta E_t \pi_{t+1} + \kappa x_t \tag{5.52}$$

$$i_t = \theta_{i\pi} \pi_t + \theta_{ix} x_t + u_{i,t} \tag{5.53}$$

$$\tilde{s}_{t+1} = \theta_{s\pi} \pi_{t+1} + \theta_{sx} x_{t+1} + \alpha v_t^* + u_{s,t+1} \tag{5.54}$$

$$\rho v_{t+1}^* = v_t^* + r_{t+1}^n - \pi_{t+1}^* - \tilde{s}_{t+1} \tag{5.55}$$

$$\rho v_{t+1} = v_t + r_{t+1}^n - \pi_{t+1} - \tilde{s}_{t+1} \tag{5.56}$$

$$E_t \pi_{t+1}^* = E_t \pi_{t+1} \tag{5.57}$$

$$\Delta E_{t+1} \pi_{t+1}^* = -\beta_s \varepsilon_{s,t+1} - \beta_i \varepsilon_{i,t+1} \tag{5.58}$$

$$E_t r_{t+1}^n = i_t \tag{5.59}$$

$$r_{t+1}^n = \omega q_{t+1} - q_t \tag{5.60}$$

$$u_{i,t+1} = \eta_i u_{i,t} + \varepsilon_{i,t+1} \tag{5.61}$$

$$u_{s,t+1} = \eta_s u_{s,t} + \varepsilon_{s,t+1}. \tag{5.62}$$

The monetary policy rule (5.53) is conventional and straightforward. The Fed raises interest rates in reaction to inflation and to the output gap. The monetary policy disturbance $u_{i,t}$ is serially correlated, following an AR(1). When the Fed deviates from a rule, typically in reacting to some other variable like the exchange rate or a financial crisis, it does so for some time.

The fiscal policy rule starts analogously. Primary surpluses are likely to react to output and inflation for both mechanical and policy reasons. Tax receipts are naturally procyclical, as tax rate times income rises with income. Spending is naturally countercyclical, due to entitlements such as unemployment insurance and deliberate but predictable stimulus programs. Chapter 4 shows a strong correlation of surpluses with the unemployment rate and GDP gap. Imperfect indexation potentially makes primary surpluses rise with inflation. Beyond fitting current data and the current policy regime, we want to think about fiscal policy rules that can better stabilize inflation or avoid deflation, especially in a period of zero bounds or other constraints on monetary policy. Such rules may introduce a greater sensitivity of surpluses to inflation or react to the price level.

The latent variable v_t^* works much as in the simple model of the last few sections. Now the rate of return r_{t+1}^n appears in both v_{t+1} and v_{t+1}^* equations. A higher ex post return on government debt raises the value of debt. By including $r_{t+1}^n - \pi_{t+1}^*$ in the v_{t+1}^* equation, I specify that fiscal policy raises surpluses in reaction to such changes in the value of debt. One can make the opposite assumption, and such variations bear exploration. In (5.58), with β_s and β_i terms, the unexpected inflation target is correlated with the interest rate shock as well as the surplus shock.

Like the rest of the model, this surplus process can and should be generalized toward realism in many ways. News about future surpluses and historical episodes are likely not well modeled by AR(1) shocks. It is likely that the government's split between inflating away debt and borrowing against future surpluses to fund a deficit varies over time or state of the economy and nature of the fiscal shock.

Differencing (5.55) and (5.56), we obtain again

$$\rho \left(v_{t+1}^* - v_{t+1} \right) = \left(v_t^* - v_t \right) - \left(\pi_{t+1}^* - \pi_{t+1} \right). \tag{5.63}$$

The parameter $\rho \leq 1$, so this equation has a forward-looking or unit root. Therefore, the unique stationary equilibrium of the model includes $v_t = v_t^*$, $\pi_t = \pi_t^*$, and thus $\Delta E_{t+1} \pi_{t+1} = \Delta E_{t+1} \pi_{t+1}^*$.

The pair (5.51)–(5.52) has two expectational errors, one to output and one to inflation, but only one forward-looking root. The combination (5.55)–(5.56) then provides the extra forward-looking root, which is the fiscal theory's job. Equations (5.55)–(5.56) determine unexpected inflation, while (5.51)–(5.52) then determine unexpected output.

While we can feed the computer the entire system (5.51)–(5.62), and it will figure out $v_t = v_t^*$, $\pi_t = \pi_t^*$ along the way, we can also now just eliminate the $*$ variables, citing (5.63). Reordering them, the equilibrium conditions (5.51)–(5.62) reduce to

$$x_t = E_t x_{t+1} - \sigma (i_t - E_t \pi_{t+1}) \tag{5.64}$$

$$\pi_t = \beta E_t \pi_{t+1} + \kappa x_t \tag{5.65}$$

$$i_t = \theta_{i\pi} \pi_t + \theta_{ix} x_t + u_{i,t} \tag{5.66}$$

$$u_{i,t+1} = \eta_i u_{i,t} + \varepsilon_{i,t+1} \tag{5.67}$$

$$\Delta E_{t+1} \pi_{t+1} = -\beta_s \varepsilon_{s,t+1} - \beta_i \varepsilon_{i,t+1} \tag{5.68}$$

$$\tilde{s}_{t+1} = \theta_{s\pi} \pi_{t+1} + \theta_{sx} x_{t+1} + \alpha v_t + u_{s,t+1} \tag{5.69}$$

$$u_{s,t+1} = \eta_s u_{s,t} + \varepsilon_{s,t+1} \tag{5.70}$$

$$\rho v_{t+1} = v_t + r_{t+1}^n - \pi_{t+1} - \tilde{s}_{t+1} \tag{5.71}$$

$$E_t r_{t+1}^n = i_t \tag{5.72}$$

$$r_{t+1}^n = \omega q_{t+1} - q_t. \tag{5.73}$$

The group (5.64)–(5.68) can be solved for inflation, output and interest rates. Equations (5.69)–(5.73) then let us find surpluses, debt, and bond prices and returns. There is nothing deep or general about this separation between the first and second halves of the model. Many models include ingredients such as government spending or distorting taxes in consumer first-order conditions, by which fiscal events feed back to the output and inflation equilibrium. I have kept those out of the model so we see the minimum *necessary* feedback from fiscal to inflation and output affairs. This setup shows that we *can* extend a standard model to an explicit description of fiscal policy without changing the standard model at all, but we do not *have to* extend it in that way, and doing so rules out many interesting phenomena relevant to both facts and policy. This is the first, not the last step.

The whole v_t versus v_t^* business just justifies that (5.68) is the unique value of unexpected inflation, that the apparently passive fiscal policy of (5.69)–(5.71) is in fact active, because surpluses do not react to other values of unexpected inflation.

Again, we do not see $v_t \neq v_t^*$ or $\pi_t \neq \pi_t^*$ in equilibrium, so that part of this model is not testable by examining time series of these variables drawn from an equilibrium. Again, an "active money" specification can also deliver (5.68) with no other restrictions on the observable time series by specifying a different explosion for $\pi_t \neq \pi_t^*$. Observational equivalence is a feature not a bug: It means all of the armchair refutations of fiscal theory are false. The fiscal theory model is capable of producing any data that the active money specification of the same model can produce. Observational equivalence also makes it easy to translate any active money model to active fiscal policy and then change parameters if one wishes to improve its performance.

5.5.1 The Unexpected Inflation Parameters

As in the simple model, linking the unexpected inflation target directly to policy shocks in (5.57) is a convenient reduced-form simplification but the β_s, β_i parameters should not be seen as independent or economically interesting policy levers. We can estimate them in fitting data, but in doing policy experiments one should consider changing β_s and β_i as we change other parameters in order to make interesting comparisons of policy settings. We should think of the government choosing the underlying surplus process and β_i, β_s as its consequence.

In Section 5.4, we saw how we want to modify β_s as we make surplus shocks more persistent, raising η_s. Here, we also want similar modifications to the β parameters as we change policy rules θ. For example, we might want to specify the first part of the unexpected inflation target as

$$\Delta E_{t+1} \pi_{t+1}^* = -\hat{\beta}_s \Delta E_{t+1} \tilde{s}_{t+1} \tag{5.74}$$

in place of (5.58). Now $\hat{\beta}_s$ specifies how much of an unexpected deficit will be met by unexpected inflation, not how much of the *shock* to the surplus disturbance will be so met. Since there are other variables in the surplus rule that move contemporaneously, the two shocks are not the same. To see the effect of (5.74), use the surplus policy rule (5.54) and also simplify to $\theta_{sx} = 0$, yielding

$$\Delta E_{t+1} \tilde{s}_{t+1} = \theta_{s\pi} \Delta E_{t+1} \pi_{t+1} + \varepsilon_{s,t+1}.$$

Equation (5.74) then implies

$$\Delta E_{t+1} \pi_{t+1} = -\hat{\beta}_s \left(\theta_{s\pi} \Delta E_{t+1} \pi_{t+1} + \varepsilon_{s,t+1} \right)$$

and thus

$$\Delta E_{t+1} \pi_{t+1} = -\frac{\hat{\beta}_s}{1 + \hat{\beta}_s \theta_{s\pi}} \varepsilon_{s,t+1} = -\beta_s(\theta_{s\pi}) \varepsilon_{s,t+1}.$$

We're back to where we started, but the parameter β_s of the original specification depends on the $\theta_{s\pi}$ parameter.

So, if it is interesting to think of a government policy that splits a constant fraction of shocks to actual deficits between repayment and inflation, rather than so splitting shocks to the disturbance part of a policy rule, then we want to specify (5.74). Equivalently, we recognize that the parameter β_s is a reduced-form parameter, and we change β_s as we change $\theta_{s\pi}$ in thinking about the effects of alternative policies.

5.5.2   Deficit Shocks without Policy Rules

I plot responses to unexpected fiscal u_s and monetary u_i disturbances, in each case holding the other disturbance constant. I start with no policy reactions $\theta = 0$, which helps to see what responses are due to the economics of the model, rather than due to endogenous policy reactions. Then I add policy reactions $\theta \neq 0$, which lets us see how systematic policy rules modify the effects of fiscal and monetary policy shocks. I use an s-shaped surplus process induced by $\alpha \neq 0$ in both calculations. The comparison is only between policy rules that do and don't react to inflation and output.

Throughout I use $\rho = 0.99$, $\beta = 0.99$, $\sigma = 0.5$, $\kappa = 0.5$, $\alpha = 0.2$, $\omega = 0.9$, $\eta_i = 0.7$, $\eta_s = 0.5$. I pick the parameters to illustrate mechanisms, not to match data.

Figure 5.6 presents the responses of the variables in this model to a deficit shock $\varepsilon_{s,1} = -1$, with no policy reactions $\theta = 0$ and no monetary disturbance $u_{i,t} = 0$.

I choose the value of β_s, with the weighted inflation identity (3.20) in mind, so that the ω-weighted sum of current and expected future unexpected inflation relative to the overall size of the fiscal shock is 0.4,

$$\frac{\sum_{j=0}^{\infty} \omega^j \Delta E_1 \pi_{1+j}}{\sum_{j=0}^{\infty} \rho^j \Delta E_1 u_{s,1+j}} = 0.4. \tag{5.75}$$

I use the same ratio to infer β_s for the following calculation with $\theta \neq 0$ policy rule parameters. The numerator can be interpreted as the reduction in real face value of the bond portfolio, the total amount that time 0 bondholders will eventually lose due to inflation. The denominator is the amount of inflation that the surplus shock would produce on its own absent all policy rules including αv_t^*, and with constant discount rates. In that

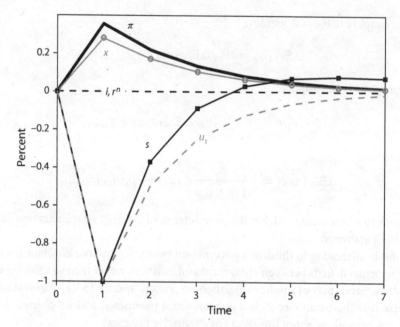

FIGURE 5.6. Responses of the Sticky Price Model to a Fiscal Shock with No Policy Rules

case, the surplus equals the disturbance $\tilde{s}_t = u_{s,t}$ and the discount rate terms in the inflation identities vanish. Fundamentally then, I choose β_s by specifying that the government meets the fiscal shock with a 40% state-contingent default via inflation. This value is likely a significant overstatement of U.S. data. I choose a larger value so inflation shows up on the graphs. The choice (5.75) produces $\beta_s = 0.36$ for the calculation with no rules $\theta = 0$ in Figure 5.6. Consequently, unexpected inflation at time 1 is 0.36%.

Inflation then decays with an AR(1) pattern. The deficit shock results in drawn-out inflation, not just a one-period price level jump. Output rises, following the forward-looking Phillips curve that output is high when inflation is high relative to future inflation. This deficit stimulates.

Drawn-out inflation is more realistic than a one-period price level jump. It is entirely the effect of sticky prices. Inflation is a two-sided moving average of the interest rate, with a geometrically decaying transient (see (5.5)). We're just seeing that transient, after an initial shock.

With neither monetary policy shock nor rule, the interest rate i_t and therefore long-term nominal bond return r_{t+1}^n do not move. Long-term debt therefore has no influence on these responses, which are the same for any bond maturity ω. The real rate falls exactly as inflation rises.

The surplus $\tilde{s}_t$ and the AR(1) surplus disturbance $u_{s,t}$ are not the same. The surplus initially declines, but resulting deficits raise the value of debt. Larger debt in turn raises subsequent surpluses. A long string of small positive surplus responses on the right side of the graph then partially repays the debt incurred from initial deficits. Lower real bond returns also bring down the value of debt. It would be easy to mistake this surplus process for an AR(1).

TABLE 5.1. Inflation and Bond Return Decompositions

Shock and model	$\sum_{j=0}^{\infty} \omega^j \pi_{1+j}$	=	$-\sum_{j=0}^{\infty} \rho^j \tilde{s}_{1+j}$	$+\sum_{j=1}^{\infty} (\rho^j - \omega^j) r_{1+j}$
Fiscal, no θ	(0.79)	=	$-(-0.90)$	$+(-0.11)$
Fiscal, yes θ	(0.79)	=	$-(-0.82)$	$+(-0.02)$
Monetary, no θ	(0.00)	=	$-(2.58)$	$+(2.58)$
Monetary, yes θ	(0.00)	=	$-(0.28)$	$+(0.28)$

Shock and model	π_1	$-r_1^n$	=	$-\sum_{j=0}^{\infty} \rho^j \tilde{s}_{1+j}$	$+\sum_{j=1}^{\infty} \rho^j r_{1+j}$
Fiscal, no θ	(0.36)	$-(0.00)$	=	$-(-0.90)$	$+(-0.55)$
Fiscal, yes θ	(0.14)	$-(-0.63)$	=	$-(-0.82)$	$+(-0.04)$
Monetary, no θ	(-0.65)	$-(-2.43)$	=	$-(2.58)$	$+(2.04)$
Monetary, yes θ	(-0.69)	$-(-1.75)$	=	$-(0.28)$	$+(1.34)$

Shock and model	r_1^n	=	$-\sum_{j=1}^{\infty} \omega^j r_{1+j}$	$-\sum_{j=1}^{\infty} \omega^j \pi_{1+j}$
Fiscal, no θ	(0)	=	$-(-0.44)$	$-(0.44)$
Fiscal, yes θ	(-0.63)	=	$-(-0.02)$	$-(0.66)$
Monetary, no θ	(-2.43)	=	$-(0.64)$	$-(0.64)$
Monetary, yes θ	(-1.75)	=	$-(1.06)$	$-(0.64)$

That inflation rises at all comes from the specification $\beta_s = 0.36$. With $\beta_s = 0$, the long-run surplus response would be higher, the discounted sum of all future surpluses would be exactly zero, and there would be no inflation. Conversely, the government may inflate away more debt in response to this deficit shock, which we would model with a higher value of β_s, capturing lower subsequent surpluses. Again, we should think of β_s as a consequence, not a cause, of this surplus behavior. At a minimum, if we regard unexpected inflation as a conscious movement of an unexpected inflation target, such surplus movements are necessary to implement that target.

The "Fiscal, no θ" rows of Table 5.1 present the terms of the unexpected inflation decompositions (3.20) and (3.22) and the bond return decomposition (3.21) for these responses.

The cumulative fiscal disturbance is $\Delta E_1 \sum_{j=0}^{\infty} \rho^j u_{s,1+j} = 1/(1 - \rho\eta_s) = -1.98\%$, which on its own would—with $\tilde{s}_t = u_{s,t}$ and no discount-rate change—lead to 1.98% inflation. Two mechanisms buffer this fiscal shock. First, the s-shaped endogenous response of surpluses to accumulated debt pays off about one percentage point of the accumulated deficits, leaving a $\Delta E_1 \sum_{j=0}^{\infty} \rho^j \tilde{s}_{1+j} = -0.90\%$ unbacked fiscal expansion. Second, higher inflation with no change in nominal rate means a lower real interest rate, which raises the value of debt, a deflationary force. This discount rate effect offsets another 0.11% of the fiscal inflation in the top row, leading to 0.79% ω-weighted inflation.

5.5.3   Deficit Shocks with Policy Rules

Next, add fiscal and monetary policy reaction functions. I use values

$$i_t = 0.8\,\pi_t + 0.5\,x_t + u_{i,t} \tag{5.76}$$

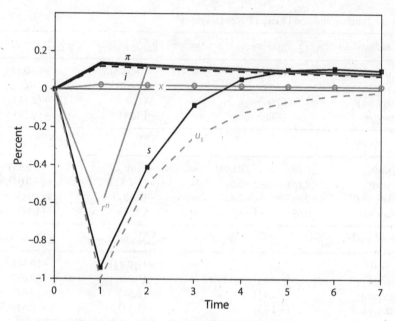

FIGURE 5.7. Responses of the Sticky Price Model to a Fiscal Shock, with Policy Rules

$$\tilde{s}_{t+1} = 0.25 \, \pi_{t+1} + 1.0 \, x_{t+1} + 0.2 \, v_t^* + u_{s,t+1} \tag{5.77}$$

$$u_{i,t+1} = 0.7 \, u_{i,t} + \varepsilon_{i,t+1} \tag{5.78}$$

$$u_{s,t+1} = 0.5 \, u_{s,t} + \varepsilon_{s,t+1} \tag{5.79}$$

$$\beta_s = 0.14. \tag{5.80}$$

Figure 5.7 plots responses that include these policy rules. This plot presents the responses to a deficit shock $\varepsilon_{s,1} = -1$, holding constant the monetary policy *distur-bance* $u_{i,t}$ but now allowing interest rates and surpluses themselves to change. Table 5.1 quantifies the corresponding decompositions, in the "Fiscal, yes θ"rows.

These parameters are also intended only as generally reasonable values that illus-trate mechanisms clearly in the plots. Estimating policy rules is tricky, as the right-hand variables are inherently correlated with errors.

I specify an interest rate reaction to inflation $\theta_{i\pi}$ less than 1, to easily generate a sta-tionary passive-money model. The monetary policy parameter $\theta_{i\pi}$ can in principle be measured in this fiscal theory, since it relates equilibrium quantities rather than describes off-equilibrium threats, so regression evidence is relevant. But the evidence for $\theta_{i\pi}$ sub-stantially greater than one in the 1980 to 2008 data, such as Clarida, Galí, and Gertler (2000), is sensitive to specification, instruments, and sample period. OLS regressions lead to a coefficient quite close to 1—the "Fisher effect" that interest rates rise with inflation dominates the data. Regressions of interest rates on inflation can have a coefficient greater than 1, even with $\theta_{i\pi} < 1$ (Cochrane (2011b)). But, as I do not try to match regressions and independent estimates of the other parameters of the model, I leave estimation of the policy response functions along with those other parameters for another day.

I use a surplus reaction to output $\theta_{sx} = 1.0$. The units of surplus are surplus/value of debt, or surplus/GDP divided by debt/GDP, so one expects a coefficient of about this magnitude. For example, real GDP fell 4 percentage points peak to trough in the 2008 recession, while the surplus/GDP ratio fell nearly 8 percentage points. Debt to GDP of 0.5 (then) leads to a coefficient 1.0. Surpluses should react somewhat to inflation, as the tax code is less well indexed than spending, but it's hard to see that pattern in the data. Surpluses were low coincident with inflation in the 1970s. An OLS regression that includes both inflation and output, though surely biased, gives a negative coefficient. (The Appendix to Cochrane (2021b) presents simple OLS regressions, which also suggest $\eta_s = 0.4$.) I use $\theta_{s\pi} = 0.25$ to explore what a small positive reaction to inflation can do.

I use $\beta_s = 0.14$ in this case, in order to produce the same 0.4 ratio of ω-weighted cumulative inflation to the fiscal shock, as in (5.75).

The fiscal shock now induces a monetary policy reaction. Higher inflation and output lead to a higher interest rate. (The nominal interest rate, labeled i, is just below the inflation π line.) This unexpected interest rate rise pushes inflation forward and thereby reduces current inflation. It produces a negative ex post bond return that soaks up inflation in the one-period accounting.

The inflation rate is now only slightly larger than the nominal interest rate, so real rates move much less. By making inflation persistent, nearly a random walk, and by reducing real rate variation, the endogenous monetary policy response almost entirely eliminates the output response to the fiscal shock. The policy rules produce even more drawn-out inflation in response to a fiscal shock.

Greater inflation and output also raise fiscal surpluses through the θ_{sx} and $\theta_{s\pi}$ parts of the fiscal policy rule. The surplus line is slightly higher in Figure 5.7 than in Figure 5.6. (Look hard. Small changes add up.) These higher subsequent surpluses also reduce the inflationary effects of the fiscal shock.

In the decompositions of Table 5.1, the shock to ω-weighted inflation with rules is the same as without rules, 0.79%, by construction. Instantaneous inflation of 0.14% is less than half its previous value of 0.36%, reflecting how inflation is now smoothed forward. The weighted sum of surpluses is slightly smaller in absolute value, a result of several offsetting forces. Since the interest rate moves with the inflation rate, there is much less real interest rate and discount rate variation, only 0.02% and 0.04%, not 0.11% and 0.55% deflationary pressure. The monetary policy reaction $\theta_{i\pi}$ nearly eliminates the real interest rate and consequent output response of the fiscal shock. In the second and third panels, a 0.63% negative bond return, reflecting future inflation, now soaks up the fiscal shock in the mark-to-market accounting. This is a measure of how much monetary policy smoothed the inflation shock by moving inflation forward.

The endogenous policy responses smooth forward and thereby reduce the inflation response, produce offsetting future surpluses, and nearly eliminate the output and real interest rate responses. Policy rule reactions to endogenous variables help to buffer shocks, reducing inflation and output volatility. This is an important and novel argument in favor of such policy rules, and we will see it in many different responses.

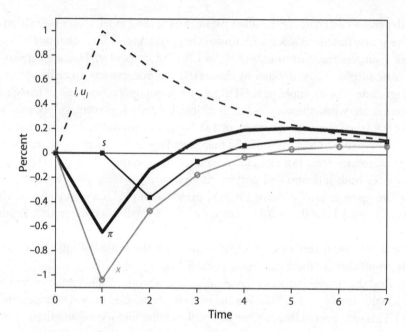

FIGURE 5.8. Responses to a Monetary Policy Shock with No Policy Rules

5.5.4   Monetary Policy Shocks without Policy Rules

Figure 5.8 presents responses to a monetary policy shock $\varepsilon_{i,1}$, with no policy rule reactions to endogenous variables $\theta = 0$.

Again, the tricky question in this response is what value of β_i to specify. What is the most interesting way to define a monetary policy shock that does not move fiscal policy? I already specify that the monetary policy shock comes with no direct fiscal shock, $u_{s,t} = 0$. But monetary policy may still have fiscal consequences: Following the systematic part of the fiscal policy rule, surpluses react to changes in output, inflation, and the value of debt that are induced by monetary policy changes. Even with no fiscal policy reactions, $\theta_{s\pi} = \theta_{sx} = 0$, when we choose a β_i, or equivalently first-period inflation, we choose the response of the value of debt, v_1, to the monetary policy shock. Larger debt sets off larger subsequent surpluses via $s_{t+1} = \ldots + \alpha v_t + \ldots$. Economically, of course, it is the larger surpluses that cause the lower unexpected inflation.

So, we want to pick β_i in a way that, beyond $u_{s,t} = 0$, expresses the idea that monetary policy does not move fiscal policy. Mirroring the treatment of the surplus shock (5.75) and with the weighted inflation decomposition (3.20) in mind, I choose β_i so that the weighted sum of inflation responses is zero,

$$\sum_{j=0}^{\infty} \omega^j \Delta E_1 \pi_{1+j} = 0. \tag{5.81}$$

Interpreting this quantity as the total reduction in the real value of debt, I thereby specify that the government reacts to a monetary policy shock with no state-contingent inflationary default at all. Any fiscal policy responses are backed. Any induced deficits are repaid by subsequent higher surpluses, not by inflating away initial debt. Obviously one may make lots of other choices. The point is that we have to make some choice and the answers depend on it, so we need to think about it.

With no policy rule reactions $\theta = 0$, the nominal interest rate i_t in Figure 5.8 just follows the AR(1) shock process $u_{i,t}$.

Inflation π declines initially, and then rises to meet the higher nominal interest rate. Output also declines, following the Phillips curve in which output is low when inflation is lower than future inflation.

The response of the expected nominal return r_{t+1}^n follows the interest rate i_t, as this model uses the expectations hypothesis. That rise in expected returns and bond yields sends bond prices down, resulting in the sharply negative instantaneous bond return r_1^n. Subtracting inflation from nominal bond returns, the expected real interest rate, expected real bond return, and discount rate rise persistently.

In sum, this model can produce a negative response of inflation to a monetary policy shock, and with it a contraction, negative ex post bond return, a lower market value of debt, and a rise in expected real bond returns. Long-term debt is the crucial ingredient in this model and parameterization for these results.

The left-hand side of the weighted inflation identity (3.20) is constant, by construction (5.81), and seen in the "Monetary, no θ" row of Table 5.1, top panel. With this parameter choice, monetary policy can rearrange inflation, lowering current inflation by raising future ω-weighted inflation but monetary policy cannot create less inflation overall without a fiscal response. The surplus and discount rate terms offset. The positive interest rate and negative inflation responses lead to higher real interest rates, giving a 2.58% inflationary discount rate effect. Though we see large initial deficits, those turn around to persistent surpluses past the right end of Figure 5.8, both to repay the initial deficits and in response to the increase in debt coming from high interest rates, generating an overall offsetting 2.58% surplus rise.

I have, perhaps unwisely, turned off two interesting pathways for fiscal–monetary interaction. The value of debt declines, which leads to lower surpluses, which might raise inflation. The higher expected real return, a higher discount rate, might lower inflation. But by choosing β_s so that there is no change in ω-weighted inflation, I specify that these responses to monetary policy all add up to naught: Every deficit-induced or return-induced change in value of debt is repaid in full by a subsequent change in surplus, and so cannot contribute to unexpected inflation. I rule out here all of the tantalizing deflationary effects of monetary–fiscal interactions that I argued for in Section 2.5.1. Specifying that some of the endogenous fiscal response is unbacked would change matters and potentially restore these channels.

I tried choosing β_s so that the market value of debt does not move, $\Delta E_1 v_1 = 0$. One can think of that specification as implementing the view that monetary policy does not change fiscal policy. Via $s_{t+1} = \ldots + \alpha v_t + \ldots$, no change in v_1 means no induced change in surpluses. However, interest rate hikes do seem to lower the market value of debt, and that assumption leads to a decline in ω-weighted inflation. I start instead with a calculation that shows some inflation decline with the most conservative assumption, but leave as a suggestion that a better definition of monetary–fiscal interactions could deepen the inflation decline.

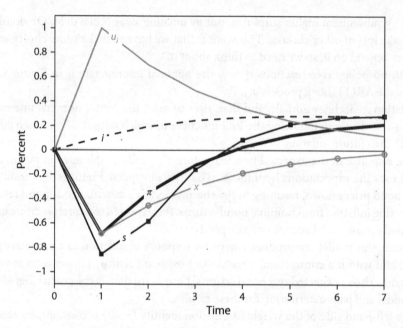

FIGURE 5.9. Responses to a Monetary Policy Shock with Policy Rules

Perhaps specifying that fiscal responses are partially unbacked, with the same (0.4 here) ratio of weighted inflation to surplus movement as one uses for fiscal policy is a more sensible approach. That approach would also allow the fiscal responses to affect inflation.

Rather than a definitive answer, we see once again just how important endogenous fiscal responses are to the effects of monetary policy. It matters not only how surpluses react to inflation and output, which we capture via θ_{is} and $\theta_{i\pi}$, but whether induced surpluses and deficits are backed by subsequent deficits and surpluses. In this parameterization, we capture these effects indirectly, and obscurely, via β_s.

5.5.5   Monetary Policy Shocks with Policy Rules

Figure 5.9 plots responses to the monetary policy shock, now adding fiscal and monetary policy rules θ that react to output and inflation.

The monetary policy reactions to inflation and growth push the interest rate i initially below its disturbance u_i. I held down the coefficient $\theta_{i\pi} = 0.8$, rather than a larger value, to keep the interest rate response from being negative, the opposite of the shock. Such responses are common, but confusing. (Cochrane (2018) p. 175 shows some examples.) The interest rate response is then quite flat. The policy rule times lower inflation and output offset the higher interest rate disturbance $u_{i,t}$. Long-term bonds again suffer a negative return on impact, due to the persistent rise in nominal interest rate. Expected bond returns then follow interest rates with a one-period lag, under the expectations hypothesis. The real rate, the difference between interest rate and inflation, again rises persistently.

Output and inflation responses have broadly similar patterns as without policy rules, but with more persistent dynamics. Since inflation is more persistent, the output response is smaller.

The surplus, reacting to low output and inflation, now declines sharply on impact and persists negatively for a few years before recovering. This persistent deficit could offset the monetary policy shock, had I not assumed otherwise by choice of β_i—that fiscal responses are financed by borrowing, fully repaid, and generate no shock to ω-weighted inflation or deflation. Likewise, the persistent rise in real interest rate would remain an inflationary force, had I not assumed otherwise. Other definitions of the monetary policy shock can again turn on these interesting mechanisms.

The "Monetary, yes θ" rows of Table 5.1 quantify these offsetting effects. The ω-weighted sum of inflation is again zero by assumption. Monetary policy only rearranges inflation. However, the offsetting surplus and discount rate effects are an order of magnitude smaller, 0.28 not 2.58, as we also see in the second and third panels.

As a second instance of a general pattern, policy rules smooth and therefore help to buffer the inflation and output responses to shocks. Taylor-type monetary policy rules and automatic stabilizers have a useful function here, having nothing to do with equilibrium selection and determinacy. Of course, if policy makers want their shocks to have big responses, the buffering properties of rules act against that desire.

5.5.6   Shock Definition

These calculations require us to think how we wish to define and orthogonalize monetary and fiscal policy disturbances. In the simplest model, I defined monetary policy as a movement in interest rates that does not change surpluses. In this more general model, that definition does not seem interesting. Here I define a monetary policy shock as a movement in the policy rule residual $u_{i,t}$ that does not affect the fiscal policy *disturbance* $u_{s,t}$. But monetary policy nonetheless has fiscal consequences: Surpluses respond to output, to inflation, to changes in the value of debt induced by varying real interest rates, unexpected inflation, and past surpluses.

Should an analysis of the effects of monetary policy include such systematic fiscal policy responses? In many cases, yes. If one is advising Federal Reserve officials on the effects of monetary policy, they likely want to know what happens if the Fed were to raise interest rates persistently $u_{i,t}$, but the Treasury takes no unusual action. But they would likely want us to include "usual" fiscal actions and responses, as we include the usual behavioral responses of all agents.

Perhaps not, however. Perhaps the Fed officials would like us to keep fiscal surpluses constant in such calculations, so as not to think of "monetary policy" as having effects merely by manipulating fiscal authorities into austerity or largesse. An academic description of the effects of monetary policy might likewise want to turn off predictable fiscal reactions, again to describe the monetary effects of monetary policy on the economy, not via manipulation of fiscal policy. In that case, even if one estimates $\theta_{s\pi}$ and θ_{sx} response parameters in the data, one should turn them off to answer the policy question.

There is no right and wrong in specifying policy questions, there is only interesting versus uninteresting, and transparent versus obscure. Calculations of the effects of monetary policy must and do, implicitly or explicitly, specify what parts of fiscal policy are held constant or allowed to move. This eternal (and often forgotten) lesson is especially important in this context.

Though orthogonal shocks are interesting for policy experiments, if we are describing history, estimating the model, or thinking about how external shocks affect the economy, we will surely confront monetary $u_{i,t}$ and fiscal $u_{s,t}$ disturbances that occur at the same time, and coincident with other shocks to the economy, as both authorities respond to similar events. For this reason, the responses I calculate holding one of the fiscal $u_{s,t}$ and monetary $u_{i,t}$ disturbances constant in turn are surely unlikely guidelines to interpreting historical episodes. Even the classic "monetary policy shock" of the early 1980s involved joint monetary, fiscal (deficits, two rounds of tax reform), and regulatory (supply or marginal cost shock) reforms. At a minimum, this fact means that estimating policy shocks with a fiscal sensibility needs one more difficult orthogonalization. The VAR literature has had a hard enough time finding movements in interest rates not taken in response to macroeconomic variables and forecasts. Now we need to find such movements that are also orthogonal to fiscal policy in some interesting sense. And perhaps the Fed officials, since they are seeing events that make them consider raising interest rates, *do* want you to put in whatever fiscal policy disturbance Treasury officials are likely to pursue in the same circumstance, in order to figure out what is likely to happen now.

These calculations are also important rhetorically and methodologically. Yes, one can include such endogenous reactions or policy rules. There is nothing in fiscal theory that requires "exogenous" surpluses.

5.6   Alternative Surplus Processes

The v^*, π^* surplus process, in which $v_t = v_t^*$ and $\pi_t = \pi_t^*$ in equilibrium, is particularly convenient for showing the potentially close relation between new-Keynesian and fiscal theory models, highlighting their essential differences, for importing new-Keynesian models to fiscal theory, for seeing how broadly fiscal theory can apply, for exploring observational equivalence, and for identifying assumptions that might surmount it. However, as my tussles with the β parameters indicate, it may not be the best structure to use for fiscal theory models going forward, once one has accepted all those previous points. Choosing β parameters, the nature of the stochastic inflation target π_t^*, specifying what parts of fiscal policy are backed and what parts are unbacked, and integrating sticky price models with more standard and microfounded models of public finance all may push us in the direction of alternative parameterizations of fiscal policy.

Identifying the inflation target with actual inflation point by point, and identifying the latent variable v_t^* with the value of debt point by point, are convenient for the former purposes, but not necessary. Abandoning those equalities may help to create more transparent models of fiscal policies, whose mathematical expression lies closer to the decisions of actual policy.

For a simple example, revert to one-period debt and flexible prices, and consider this modification of the simple model (5.29)–(5.34):

$$i_t = E_t \pi_{t+1}$$

$$\rho v_{t+1} = v_t - \Delta E_{t+1}\pi_{t+1} - \tilde{s}_{t+1}$$

$$\tilde{s}_t = s_t^* + \hat{s}_t \tag{5.82}$$

$$s_{t+1}^* = \alpha v_t^* + u_{s^*,t+1} \tag{5.83}$$

$$\rho v_{t+1}^* = v_t^* - s_{t+1}^* \tag{5.84}$$

$$\hat{s}_{t+1} = u_{\hat{s},t+1}$$

$$u_{s^*,t+1} = \eta_{s^*} u_{s^*,t} + \varepsilon_{s^*,t+1}$$

$$u_{\hat{s},t+1} = \eta_{\hat{s}} u_{\hat{s},t} + \varepsilon_{\hat{s},t+1}.$$

Starting in (5.82) I write a two-component model of the surplus. The surplus has a backed component s_t^*, and an unbacked component $\hat{s}_t$. The backed component has, by construction, $a(\rho) = 0$, and shocks $\varepsilon_{s^*,t+1}$ cause no unexpected inflation. The unbacked component has whatever $a(\rho)$ emerges from its process, $1/(1 - \rho\eta_{\hat{s}})$ here. Thus the inflationary effect of an overall $\tilde{s}_t$ surplus shock will depend on the extent to which it comes from each of the two surplus components.

The latent variable structure (5.83)–(5.84) offers a different intuition than before. Here, we can think of the government's "inflation target" as an unchanging value, 2%, say, and hence it disappears from (5.84). Actual inflation now differs from that target. We can think of the government committing to repay completely debts generated under the backed component of the budget, but not debts generated by the unbacked component of the budget. The Jacobson, Leeper, and Preston (2019) separation of a budget into "regular" and "emergency" components could be written this way. One could imagine (or hope!) that entitlement, military, and infrastructure spending go into the backed component, and stimulus spending, anti-inflation austerity, state-contingent default spending, or a $\theta_{s\pi}$ rule designed to stabilize inflation go into the unbacked component.

The moving average representation for this surplus process is, using (5.26)

$$\tilde{s}_{t+1} = \frac{(1 - \rho^{-1}L)}{[1 - (1 - \alpha)\rho^{-1}L]} \frac{1}{(1 - \eta_{s^*}L)} \varepsilon_{s^*,t+1} + \frac{1}{(1 - \eta_{\hat{s}}L)} \varepsilon_{\hat{s},t+1}.$$

You can verify that $a(\rho) = 0$ for the first term and $a(\rho) = 1/(1 - \rho\eta_{\hat{s}})$ for the second term. Thus,

$$\Delta E_{t+1}\pi_{t+1} = -\frac{1}{1 - \rho\eta_{\hat{s}}} \varepsilon_{\hat{s},t+1}.$$

The state variable v^* follows

$$v_{t+1}^* = -\frac{\rho^{-1}}{[1 - (1 - \alpha)\rho^{-1}L]} \frac{1}{(1 - \eta_{s^*}L)} \varepsilon_{s^*,t+1} = E_{t+1} \sum_{j=0}^{\infty} \rho^j s_{t+1+j}^*,$$

while the value of debt follows

$$v_{t+1} = \frac{\eta_{\hat{s}}}{(1 - \rho\eta_{\hat{s}})} \frac{1}{(1 - \eta_{\hat{s}}L)} \varepsilon_{\hat{s},t+1} - \frac{\rho^{-1}}{[1 - (1 - \alpha)\rho^{-1}L]} \frac{1}{(1 - \eta_{s^*}L)} \varepsilon_{s^*,t+1}$$

$$v_{t+1} = E_{t+1} \sum_{j=0}^{\infty} \rho^j \hat{s}_{t+1+j} + E_{t+1} \sum_{j=0}^{\infty} \rho^j s^*_{t+1+j}.$$

The state variable is not equal to the value of debt, and each value of debt cumulates its own surplus.

Online Appendix Section A2.4 outlines a surplus process with an s-shaped moving average representation composed of a transitory $AR(1)$ in one direction plus a persistent $AR(1)$ in the opposite direction, which may be useful for some purposes.

This is a barebones beginning. The point is that one can also construct models of this sort to represent s-shaped surplus processes, and for quantitative work within fiscal theory, models of this form may be more fruitful in the future.

Other aspects of the surplus process may be important for realism, and for today's policy issues. For example, it is attractive to specify that governments respond to *interest costs* on the debt rather than to the value of debt directly. One might write

$$\tilde{s}_{t+1} = \alpha \left[E_t \left(r^n_{t+1} - \pi_{t+1} \right) v^*_t \right] + \theta_{s\pi} \pi_{t+1} + \theta_{sx} x_{t+1} + \ldots + u_{s,t+1}.$$

This specification would account for the alacrity with which United States, European, and Japanese governments treat 100% debt-to-GDP ratios at very low real interest rates, compared to earlier eras. This change may produce interesting dynamics. In particular, a resurgence of real interest rates would provoke a sharp fiscal contraction, made worse by the debt accumulated in a previous period of low real interest rates.

Politicians seem to respond to nominal, not real, interest costs, which we could also model, eliminating the π_{t+1} in the above equation, and replacing the correct $E_t(r^n_{t+1})$ with the conventional accounting of interest costs. These considerations could add an important mechanism by which central banks affect fiscal policy via purely nominal or debt-structure changes.

I have specified that surpluses respond to the real *market* value of debt. Since U.S. debt accounting measures face value of principal, not market value, it may make more sense to model fiscal rules that respond to face values, not marked to market. For example, the regular debt ceiling fracas occurs when the face, not market, value of debt hits a limit.

5.7   Continuous Time

I introduce the simple sticky price model in continuous time.

$$dx_t = \sigma (i_t - \pi_t)dt + d\delta_{x,t}$$
$$d\pi_t = (\rho \pi_t - \kappa x_t)\, dt + d\delta_{\pi,t}$$
$$dv_t = (rv_t + i_t - \pi_t - \tilde{s}_t)dt.$$

It is useful to express the sticky price model in continuous time. Continuous time formulas are often simpler, as they avoid the timing conventions of discrete time, what variables are dated at t versus $t + 1$. Continuous time also forces us to think more carefully about which variables can and can't jump, or follow diffusions. The price level jumps of the frictionless model are unattractive. Do we need them? The answer turns out to be no, a major point of this section. Taking the flexible-price limit makes that point clear.

The models in this section and the following build on Cochrane (2017e) and Sims (2011). Cochrane (2015a) is a short introduction to continuous time stochastic models, dz versus dt, Ito's lemma, and so forth. Cochrane (2012) shows how to do linear operator mechanics in continuous time—how to write the equivalent of $a(L)x_t = \varepsilon_t$, how to invert $a(L)$ to a moving average representation, and so forth.

I start with a continuous time equivalent of the standard IS and Phillips curve model, with instantaneous debt:

$$dx_t = \sigma(i_t - \pi_t)dt + d\delta_{x,t} \tag{5.85}$$

$$d\pi_t = (\rho\pi_t - \kappa x_t)\,dt + d\delta_{\pi,t} \tag{5.86}$$

$$dp_t = \pi_t dt \tag{5.87}$$

$$dv_t = (rv_t + i_t - \pi_t - \tilde{s}_t)dt \tag{5.88}$$

$$di_t = d\varepsilon_{i,t} \tag{5.89}$$

$$d\tilde{s}_t = d\varepsilon_{s,t}. \tag{5.90}$$

These equations are linearized and all variables are deviations from steady-state. Here dx_t, roughly the limit of $dx_t = x_{t+\Delta} - x_t$, is the forward differential operator used in continuous time with either diffusion or jump shocks.

Equations (5.85) and (5.86) are the continuous time equivalents of the IS and Phillips curves (5.1) and (5.2). Equation (5.85) is the consumer's first-order condition, linearized, and using the absence of price level jumps or diffusion terms. It is usually written $E_t dx_t = \sigma(i_t - \pi_t)dt$. I add the expectational shock $d\delta_{x,t} = dx_t - E_t dx_t$ to write an equation with the outcome dx_t on the left-hand side. It is easiest to see this equation's analogy to its discrete time counterpart (5.1) by integrating forward to

$$x_t = -\sigma E_t \int_{\tau=0}^{\infty} (i_{t+\tau} - \pi_{t+\tau})d\tau.$$

This is the obvious analogue of the integrated version of the discrete time IS equation, (5.3). Consumption and therefore output are low if future real interest rates are high, driving the consumer to substitute intertemporally from present to future. Equation (5.86) is the continuous time version of the new-Keynesian Phillips curve. The analogy to the discrete time version is again easiest to see in integral form,

$$\pi_t = \kappa E_t \int_{\tau=0}^{\infty} e^{-\rho\tau} x_{t+\tau} d\tau,$$

which parallels the discrete time version (5.4). Inflation is high if current and future output gaps are high. As $\kappa \to \infty$, output variation becomes smaller for given inflation variation, so $\kappa \to \infty$ is the frictionless limit.

Equation (5.87) specifies that though inflation may move unexpectedly with a jump or diffusion component, the price level is continuous, differentiable, and hence completely predictable, $dp_t = E_t dp_t$. If a fraction λdt of producers changes price in each instant dt, the aggregate price level cannot jump or move unexpectedly. The previous discrete time one-period debt models include a price level jump that devalues short-term nominal debt. That mechanism is ruled out here, and our first task is to see what takes its place. While one can write models of price stickiness that allow for price level jumps and diffusions, and hence for inflation to devalue instantaneous debt, it is interesting to focus on the case in which this cannot happen. We see that the fiscal theory does not need such effects. The resulting model is elegant and intuitive.

Equation (5.88) is the linearized evolution of the real market value of government debt, from (3.42), with $i_t dt = dR_t^n$ since we have short-term debt and without rdt since variables are deviations from steady-state. Debt grows with the real interest rate, and declines with primary surpluses.

I use ρ to denote the discount rate in the Phillips curve (5.86), and r for the steady-state real interest rate in the debt accumulation equation (5.88), in place of $\beta = e^{-\rho}$ in the discrete time Phillips curve and a different $\rho = e^{-r}$ in discrete time debt accumulation equation and consequent forward-looking linearized identities. This is a standard notation in continuous time, so I use it despite recycling symbols.

The $d\varepsilon_t$ shocks are structural shocks, exogenous to this model. We can quickly generalize to serially correlated disturbances and policy rules that respond to endogenous variables. One should add structural shocks to the IS and Phillips curves as well, and study responses to such shocks. As in discrete time, solving the model involves solving the $d\delta_t$ expectational errors in terms of the $d\varepsilon_t$ shocks. Both $d\delta_t$ and $d\varepsilon_t$ may be diffusions or compensated jump processes. (A "compensated" jump process has mean-zero innovations.) Since the model is linearized, we can compute impulse-response functions as responses to "MIT shocks," one-time unexpected shocks $d\varepsilon_0$ at time 0, and perfect foresight thereafter.

5.7.1   An Analytic Solution

I solve the model analytically, giving inflation as a two-sided moving average of interest rates with a transient selected by the government debt valuation equation. I work out an example response to fiscal and monetary policy shocks. The government debt valuation equation selects equilibria. The valuation equation adjusts entirely via discount rate variation. Unexpected time 0 inflation does not instantly devalue outstanding debt. Instead, the path of inflation adjusts until the real interest rate brings the unchanged value of debt into line with the discounted value of surpluses. A period of low real returns devalues outstanding debt smoothly. The frictionless limit of discount rate variation to a price level jump is smooth.

In this section, I solve this simplest version of the model analytically. This analysis is the continuous time equivalent of Section 5.1.1. This analytical solution shows how the continuous time model works. In particular, we see how it can work with no price level jumps or diffusion terms, and how it smoothly approaches a frictionless solution that does have price level jumps or diffusions.

Before time 0, all variables are at the steady-state, so deviations from steady-state are zero. At time 0, people learn new paths for interest rates and surpluses, starting with $\tilde{s}_0$ and i_0. There is perfect foresight for $t > 0$ after one unexpected initial movement

$(d\delta_0, d\varepsilon_0)$ at time 0. In the perfect foresight region $t > 0$, we solve

$$\frac{dx_t}{dt} = \sigma(i_t - \pi_t) \qquad (5.91)$$

$$\frac{d\pi_t}{dt} = \rho\pi_t - \kappa x_t \qquad (5.92)$$

$$\frac{dv_t}{dt} = i_t - \pi_t + rv_t - \tilde{s}_t. \qquad (5.93)$$

The solutions to the pair (5.91)–(5.92) are

$$\pi_t = C_0 e^{-\lambda_2 t} + \left(\frac{1}{\lambda_2} + \frac{1}{\lambda_1}\right)^{-1} \left[\int_{\tau=0}^{t} e^{-\lambda_2 \tau} i_{t-\tau} d\tau + \int_{\tau=0}^{\infty} e^{-\lambda_1 \tau} i_{t+\tau} d\tau\right] \qquad (5.94)$$

where

$$\lambda_1 \equiv \frac{\rho + \sqrt{\rho^2 + 4\kappa\sigma}}{2}; \lambda_2 \equiv \frac{-\rho + \sqrt{\rho^2 + 4\kappa\sigma}}{2}$$

and C_0 is an arbitrary constant. (Algebra in Online Appendix Section A1.7.) As in discrete time, equilibrium inflation is a two-sided average of equilibrium interest rates, plus an exponentially decaying transient. There is a family of stable solutions, indexed by C_0, or equivalently by the initial value of inflation π_0.

The solution to the debt evolution equation (5.93) is

$$v_0 = \int_{\tau=0}^{\infty} e^{-r\tau} \left[\tilde{s}_\tau - (i_\tau - \pi_\tau)\right] d\tau. \qquad (5.95)$$

This is our usual linearized present value formula. The real value of debt is the present value of surpluses, discounted at the real interest rate. We substitute (5.94) into (5.95) to solve for the initial π_0 or C_0, thereby completing the solution.

In the flexible price case, (5.94) becomes $\pi_t = i_t$, (5.95) becomes

$$v_0 = \int_{\tau=0}^{\infty} e^{-r\tau} \tilde{s}_\tau d\tau,$$

so the price level must move unexpectedly, with a jump or diffusion component if the right-hand side does so. Since B_0 is predetermined, the denominator P_0 of $V_0 = B_0/P_0$ must jump.

In this model of price stickiness, we can no longer have price level jumps or diffusion terms. However, the model allows for an unexpected persistent rise in *inflation* starting at time $t = 0$. The *discount rate path* $(i_\tau - \pi_\tau)$ on the right-hand side of (5.95) adjusts until there is no need for the left-hand side to jump. Each of the possible inflation paths in (5.94) implies a different path of real rates in (5.95), corresponding to different values of the initial constant C_0 or initial inflation π_0.

For example, fixing the nominal rate path, a negative surplus shock leads to more inflation, which lowers the discount rate, restoring the time 0 real value of debt. After some time, higher inflation, generating a lower real rate of return, erodes the real value of debt.

With flexible prices and therefore constant real interest rates, expected inflation cannot devalue debt. The nominal interest rate rises one for one with inflation, protecting bondholders, so there must be a price level jump. But with sticky prices, a protracted inflation can lower real returns, so even holders of instantaneous debt lose the value of their investments.

- *With sticky prices and instantaneous debt, a fiscal shock leads to a protracted inflation, and a protracted period of low real interest rates. This discount rate change absorbs the entire fiscal shock in accounting for the present value of surpluses at time 0, with no change in the market value of debt. There is no price level jump devaluing outstanding debt. A period of low real returns and steady inflation takes its place.*

The story and economic mechanism are different than that of a price level jump. In turn, that fact tells us to interpret the price level jumps of the discrete time model as a view of this slow erosion over an interval of time, rather than a literal overnight or instantaneous price level jump. This is a fundamentally different and, I think, better parable to tell for the fiscal theory of the price level.

To work out a simple example, start at a steady-state with interest rate $i = r$, debt v_0, and surplus $\tilde{s} = r v_0$. Consider a permanent and unexpected monetary policy shock to i_0 at time 0, and a fiscal policy shock to $\tilde{s}_0$ at time 0. We can parameterize the family of solutions (5.94) by initial inflation π_0,

$$\pi_t = (\pi_0 - i_0) e^{-\lambda_2 t} + i_0.$$

The government debt valuation equation (5.95) then becomes

$$v_0 = \frac{\tilde{s}_0}{r} + \frac{\pi_0 - i_0}{r + \lambda_2}.$$

With no price level jumps, v_0 is predetermined, so we solve the second equation for π_0 and the first equation gives the path of inflation over time. Doing so, the unique path for inflation is

$$\pi_t = (r + \lambda_2)\left(v_0 - \frac{\tilde{s}_0}{r}\right) e^{-\lambda_2 t} + i_0. \tag{5.96}$$

A fiscal shock, a decrease in surplus with no interest rate change, moves the first term but not the second. It results in a transitory rise in inflation, melting away at $e^{-\lambda_2 t}$, but no price level jump. The value of debt evolves as

$$v_t - \frac{\tilde{s}_0}{r} = \frac{\pi_t - i_0}{r + \lambda_2} = \left(v_0 - \frac{\tilde{s}_0}{r}\right) e^{-\lambda_2 t}.$$

The value of debt is initially unchanged. It then erodes over time, until we reach the new steady-state $v_t = \tilde{s}_0/r$. The first interval of this erosion looks like a price level jump to discrete time analysis.

The responses are similar but prettier than those of the discrete time case, Figure 5.3. In that case we thought of an initial devaluation and then a discount rate effect. Here we see it's really all a discount rate effect.

Suppose there is no fiscal shock, $\tilde{s}_0 = \tilde{s}$, so the first term of (5.96) is zero, but the interest rate i_0 rises. The response is perfectly Fisherian: Inflation π_t rises immediately by exactly the interest rate rise i_0 and stays there.

This is qualitatively different behavior than the discrete time case of Figure 5.1. In that case, we saw inflation rise immediately when the interest rate rose, but it did not fully rise to match the interest rate unless prices were completely sticky. We see now that this behavior is an artifact of discrete time. In that case, an increase in time 1 inflation devalued outstanding one-period debt. Had inflation risen immediately to match the interest rate, one-period debt would have been devalued, but there would not have been any corresponding change in discount rate or surpluses. The halfway inflation response balanced a higher discount rate with debt devaluation. In continuous time, even an instantaneous rise in *inflation* has no effect on the *price level*, and thus does not devalue debt v_0. With no change in surplus, there now needs to be no change in discount rate either, so inflation jumps immediately and completely.

One should worry about a model that has no price level jump for nonzero price stickiness, but requires a price level jump at the frictionless limit point. In fact, the frictionless limit is well behaved. As $\kappa \to \infty$, $\lambda_2 \to \infty$. The path (5.96) has a larger and larger rise in inflation, but one that lasts a shorter and shorter time. The price level path smoothly approaches the jump of the truly frictionless model. Cumulative inflation is

$$\int_{t=0}^{\infty} \pi_t dt = (r + \lambda_2)\left(v_0 - \frac{\tilde{s}_0}{r}\right)\int_{t=0}^{\infty} e^{-\lambda_2 t} dt = \left(\frac{r}{\lambda_2} + 1\right)\left(v_0 - \frac{\tilde{s}_0}{r}\right),$$

so

$$\lim_{\kappa \to \infty} \int_{t=0}^{\infty} \pi_t dt = v_0 - \frac{\tilde{s}_0}{r},$$

exactly the size of the price level jump of the frictionless model. Figure 5.10 plots an example of this limit, described in the next section.

In reality one does not solve the model this way, solving forward one or groups of equations at a time. One uses matrix methods on the system (5.91)–(5.93), solving the unstable roots of the whole system forward and the stable roots backwards, as detailed in Online Appendix Section A1.7. One ends up at the same solution, but not an analytic expression.

5.7.2   S-Shaped Surpluses

I add the s-shaped surplus process in continuous time.

$$\tilde{s}_t = \alpha v_t^* + u_{s,t}$$
$$dv_t^* = \left(r v_t^* + \beta_s d\varepsilon_{s,t} - \tilde{s}_t\right) dt.$$

We can write the s-shaped surplus process in continuous time analogously to the discrete time version. Start with a simple example. Let the surplus have an AR(1) shock, but the surplus then responds to a state variable v_t^*,

$$\tilde{s}_t = \alpha v_t^* + u_{s,t} \tag{5.97}$$

$$dv_t^* = \left(r v_t^* + \beta_s d\varepsilon_{s,t} - \tilde{s}_t\right) dt \tag{5.98}$$

$$du_{s,t} = \eta u_{s,t} dt + d\varepsilon_{s,t}. \tag{5.99}$$

The state variable v_t^* is, in equilibrium, the value of debt in a flexible price version of the model, featuring a constant real rate r and allowing a price level diffusion or jump $dP/P = -\beta_s d\varepsilon_{s,t}$, which can devalue debt. We will adapt the surplus process in the next section to the sticky price model. The disturbance $u_{s,t}$ is a continuous time AR(1), with solution

$$u_{s,t} = \int_{\tau=0}^{\infty} e^{-\eta\tau} d\varepsilon_{s,t-\tau}.$$

Solving (below), the implied surplus process is the difference between two AR(1) processes. In operator notation with $D = d/dt$:

$$\tilde{s}_t = \left[\frac{\eta+r}{\eta+r-\alpha} \frac{1}{\eta+D} - \left(\frac{\alpha}{\eta+r-\alpha} - \alpha\beta_s\right) \frac{1}{(\alpha-r)+D} \right] D\varepsilon_{s,t}, \tag{5.100}$$

or explicitly,

$$\tilde{s}_t = \frac{\eta+r}{\eta+r-\alpha} \int_{\tau=0}^{\infty} e^{-\eta\tau} d\varepsilon_{s,t+\tau} - \left(\frac{\alpha}{\eta+r-\alpha} - \alpha\beta_s\right) \int_{\tau=0}^{\infty} e^{-(\alpha-r)\tau} d\varepsilon_{s,t+\tau}. \tag{5.101}$$

The first term is a multiple of the driving AR(1) in (5.97). The second term captures debt repayment, which goes in the opposite direction. Since we generally write $\eta \gg \alpha - r$, the first term is larger, but decays more quickly. The second, opposite term is smaller but longer lasting. Thus, we have a pretty s-shaped response formed by offsetting AR(1) processes. A negative shock $d\varepsilon_{s,t}$ sets off persistent deficits in the first term. Those deficits eventually turn to surpluses when the second term takes over. Eventually, the surpluses die off as well.

As in discrete time, we can regard the moving average representation (5.101) as primitive, or we can regard the government as "reacting to" the state variable v_t^*, which is the value of debt in equilibrium.

Hansen-Sargent prediction formulas capture present values in continuous time as well. If we write the surplus moving average such as (5.100) in operator form as

$$\tilde{s}_t = \mathcal{L}(D) D\varepsilon_{s,t},$$

then

$$E_t \int_{\tau=0}^{\infty} e^{-r\tau} \tilde{s}_{t+\tau} d\tau = \frac{\mathcal{L}(D) - \mathcal{L}(r)}{r - D} D\varepsilon_{s,t}.$$

The shock, loosely speaking $E_{t+\Delta} - E_t$ of the present value, is given by

$$\Delta_t \left(\int_{\tau=0}^{\infty} e^{-r\tau} \tilde{s}_{t+\tau} d\tau \right) = \mathcal{L}(r) D\varepsilon_{s,t}$$

which in this case is just $\mathcal{L}(r) = -\beta_s$. Here I use the notation $\Delta_t(x_t) = dx_t - E_t(dx_t)$ to denote an innovation in continuous time, equivalently the jump or diffusion component of a process. Thus, the price level diffusion/jump is given by

$$-\frac{\Delta_t(1/P_t)}{1/P_t} = -\left[\frac{d(1/P_t)}{1/P_t} - \frac{E_t d(1/P_t)}{1/P_t}\right] = -\mathcal{L}(r)d\varepsilon_{s,t} = \beta_s d\varepsilon_{s,t}.$$

$\mathcal{L}(r)$ is the continuous time equivalent of $a(\rho)$. With $\beta_s = 0$, deficits are fully repaid.

To derive (5.101), as in discrete time, first substitute (5.97) in (5.98) to find the v_t^* process, then substitute back in to (5.97) to find the $\tilde{s}_t$ process. The algebra is much easier with operator notation, which avoids messy double integrals. In operator notation, the model is

$$\tilde{s}_t = \alpha v_t^* + u_t \tag{5.102}$$

$$u_t = \frac{1}{\eta + D} D\varepsilon_{s,t} \tag{5.103}$$

$$Dv_t^* = rv_t^* + \beta_s D\varepsilon_{s,t} - \tilde{s}_t, \tag{5.104}$$

where, loosely, $Dx_t \equiv (1/dt)dx_t$, and dx_t is the forward differential operator.

First eliminate $\tilde{s}_t$ in (5.104),

$$Dv_t^* = -(\alpha - r)v_t^* + \beta_s D\varepsilon_{s,t} - u_t$$

$$v_t^* = -\frac{1}{D + (\alpha - r)}\left(-\beta_s D\varepsilon_{s,t} + u_t\right).$$

Then, substituting back in (5.102),

$$\tilde{s}_t = \left[1 - \frac{\alpha}{D + (\alpha - r)}\right]u_t + \frac{\alpha}{D + (\alpha - r)}\beta_s D\varepsilon_{s,t}$$

$$\tilde{s}_t = \frac{D - r}{D + (\alpha - r)}\frac{1}{D + \eta}D\varepsilon_{s,t} + \frac{\alpha\beta_s}{D + (\alpha - r)}D\varepsilon_{s,t}.$$

Decomposing the last expression by partial fractions,

$$\tilde{s}_t = \left[\frac{\eta + r}{\eta + r - \alpha}\frac{1}{\eta + D} - \frac{\alpha}{\eta + r - \alpha}\frac{1}{D + (\alpha - r)} + \frac{\alpha\beta_s}{D + (\alpha - r)}\right]D\varepsilon_{s,t},$$

and simplifying we obtain (5.100).

This section is an advertisement for operator methods in continuous time to manipulate linear models, analogously to discrete time. Cochrane (2012) is a reference.

5.7.3 Long-Term Debt and Policy Rules

I add long-term debt and monetary and fiscal policy rules to the model.

Next, I add long-term bonds and monetary and fiscal policy rules, mirroring the discrete time treatment. The model becomes

$$dx_t = \sigma (i_t - \pi_t) dt + d\delta_{x,t}$$

$$d\pi_t = (\rho \pi_t - \kappa x_t) dt + d\delta_{\pi,t}$$

$$dp_t = \pi_t dt$$

$$dq_t = [(r + \omega) q_t + i_t] dt + d\delta_{q,t} \tag{5.105}$$

$$dv_t = (rv_t + i_t - \pi_t - \tilde{s}_t) dt + d\delta_{q,t} \tag{5.106}$$

$$di_t = -\zeta_i [i_t - (\theta_{i\pi} \pi_t + \theta_{ix} x_t + u_{i,t})] dt + \theta_{i\varepsilon} d\varepsilon_{i,t} \tag{5.107}$$

$$\tilde{s}_t = \theta_{s\pi} \pi_t + \theta_{sx} x_t + \alpha v_t^* + u_{s,t} \tag{5.108}$$

$$dv_t^* = (rv_t^* + i_t - \pi_t^* - \tilde{s}_t) dt + (r + \omega) d\delta_{q,t} \tag{5.109}$$

$$E_t d\pi_t^* = E_t d\pi_t \tag{5.110}$$

$$d\pi_t^* - E_t d\pi_t^* = -\beta_s d\varepsilon_{s,t} - \beta_i d\varepsilon_{i,t} \tag{5.111}$$

$$du_{i,t} = -\eta_i u_{i,t} + d\varepsilon_{i,t} \tag{5.112}$$

$$du_{s,t} = -\eta_s u_{s,t} + d\varepsilon_{s,t}. \tag{5.113}$$

Again, the equations are linearized and all variables in the model are deviations from steady-state with $\pi = 0$, $i = r$, $\tilde{s} = rv$.

I use a geometric maturity structure as described in Section 3.6.3. A bond at time t pays coupon $e^{-\omega\tau} d\tau$ at time $t + \tau$. A nominal perpetuity that pays a constant \$1 coupon forever, with $\omega = 0$, is an important limit. The bond yield is y_t, and the bond price is $Q_t = 1/(y_t + \omega)$.

Equation (5.105) derives from the linearized bond pricing equation (3.48),

$$dq_t = (dR_t^n - rdt) + (\omega + r)(q_t - 1)dt.$$

I impose the expectations hypothesis so that $E_t (dR_t^n) = i_t$, and I denote the unexpected bond price

$$d\delta_{q,t} \equiv dR_t^n - i_t. \tag{5.114}$$

In steady-state, $dR_t^n = rdt$ and $q = 1$. The model describes deviations from steady-state while (3.48) describes the actual variables, so the rdt and $1dt$ terms drop.

Equation (5.106) derives from the linearized debt accumulation equation (3.42),

$$dv_t = rv_t dt + dR_t^n - (r + \pi_t) dt - \tilde{s}_t dt.$$

I make the same substitution (5.114). I drop rdt to take deviations from steady-state. Debt grows with the real interest rate, and declines with primary surpluses. A shock to bond prices $d\delta_{q,t}$ raises the real value of debt, so the same expectational error appears in both equations. The only difference between long-term and instantaneous debt is this term $d\delta_{q,t}$, just as $r^n_{t+1} \neq i_t$ distinguishes long-term debt in discrete time.

Equations (5.107) and (5.112) comprise a monetary policy rule. The parameter ζ_i describes a partial adjustment process, in which interest rates move slowly toward the policy rule. In discrete time, this rule is

$$i_t - i_{t-1} = -\zeta_i \left[i_t - \left(\theta_{i\pi} \pi_t + \theta_{ix} x_t + u_{i,t} \right) \right] + \theta_{i\varepsilon} \varepsilon_{i,t}$$
$$u_{i,t+1} - u_{i,t} = -\eta_i u_{i,t} + \varepsilon_{i,t}.$$

This is equivalent to a rule with a lagged interest rate and a serially correlated disturbance,

$$i_t = (1 - \zeta_i) i_{t-1} + \zeta_i \left(\theta_{i\pi} \pi_t + \theta_{ix} x_t \right) + \zeta_i u_{i,t} + \theta_{i\varepsilon} \varepsilon_{i,t} \qquad (5.115)$$
$$u_{i,t+1} = (1 - \eta_i) u_{i,t} + \varepsilon_{i,t}.$$

I add a direct impact of the shock $d\varepsilon_{i,t}$ in (5.107). Without it, the interest rate itself does not jump or have diffusions. The federal funds rate does jump when the Fed changes its target. This is a helpful first step, but to accurately model high-frequency federal funds rate behavior, one should follow the sort of time-series specification in Piazzesi (2005). I include $u_{i,t}$ at all in order to to investigate the difference between partial adjustment and serially correlated disturbances, and to produce a model that looks like the discrete time model above. One could also view partial adjustment as being enough, and write instead

$$di_t = -\zeta_i \left[i_t - \left(\theta_{i\pi} \pi_t + \theta_{ix} x_t \right) \right] dt + d\varepsilon_{i,t}.$$

A partial-adjustment dynamic formulation is important in continuous time. Recall the discrete-time flexible-price model with a monetary policy rule $i_t = \theta_\pi \pi_t$ and $i_t = E_t \pi_{t+1}$, so dynamics are $E_t \pi_{t+1} = \theta_\pi \pi_t$. In continuous time with differentiable prices, as here, $i_t = E_t \pi_{t+1}$ becomes just $i_t = \pi_t$. If we specify $i_t = \theta_\pi \pi_t$ without dynamics, we get $\pi_t = \theta_\pi \pi_t$, so $\pi_t = 0$ with instant dynamics. Instead, if we write

$$di_t = -\psi_i (i_t - \theta_\pi \pi_t) dt$$

together with $i_t = \pi_t$, we have

$$d\pi_t = -\psi_i (1 - \theta_\pi) \pi_t dt$$

and thus

$$\pi_t = \pi_0 e^{-\psi_i (1 - \theta_\pi) t},$$

a dynamic model that resembles the discrete time result.

This is a nice example of how continuous time helps to clarify ideas and distinguish economics from timing conventions. In discrete time we get into trouble if we specify a rule that responds (sensibly) to expected inflation, $i_t = \theta E_t \pi_{t+1}$. Then with $i_t = E_t \pi_{t+1}$ we obtain a silly equilibrium condition $E_t \pi_{t+1} = \theta E_t \pi_{t+1}$, so $E_t \pi_{t+1} = 0$. The discrete time model implicitly introduces dynamics via the policy rule in which interest rates i_t respond to *today's* inflation π_t, while the Fisher relation relates i_t to *tomorrow's* expected inflation $E_t \pi_{t+1}$. In continuous time, we build in the same lag consciously, which is good for clarity of what we are doing. (Cochrane (2011b) explores the effects of timing conventions on the Taylor rule in a discrete time, new-Keynesian model in some detail.)

Equations (5.108) and (5.113) specify a fiscal policy rule, in analogy to the similar rule in discrete time of Section 5.5. The surplus responds to inflation and output, via proportional taxes, an imperfectly indexed tax code, countercyclical spending, and so forth. The surplus disturbance $u_{s,t}$ is positively correlated, modeled as an AR(1). The surplus responds to the state variable v_t^* that evolves just as does the value of debt, except that it substitutes the stochastic inflation target π_t^* for inflation π_t.

Equation (5.110), specifying that the expected inflation target must equal expected inflation, captures a lot. The inflation target π_t^* is not arbitrary. The target π_t^* must be a candidate equilibrium of the model. Given the interest rate path, the only degree of freedom in the choice of π_t^* is its innovation. We could express this idea by writing out the whole model with π_t^* and then finding the needed i_t^*. Equation (5.110) has the same effect more simply.

Equation (5.111) expresses the relation between the inflation innovation and innovations in the structural shocks of the model. As in discrete time, this formulation invites abuse, and requires thought about what β values to specify as we change other parameter values. We should regard the time 0 inflation shock as a result of fiscal and monetary policy rather than as a policy lever.

As in discrete time, we can quickly difference (5.106) and (5.109) to obtain

$$d\left(v_t^* - v_t\right) = \left[-\left(\pi_t^* - \pi_t\right) + r\left(v_t^* - v_t\right)\right] dt.$$

The transversality condition ruling out debt explosions then implies $v_t = v_t^*$ and $\pi_t = \pi_t^*$. We can now simplify equations (5.108)–(5.111) to eliminate all the starred variables,

$$\tilde{s}_t = \theta_{s\pi}\pi_t + \theta_{sx}x_t + \alpha v_t + u_{s,t}$$
$$d\delta_{\pi,t} = -\beta_s d\varepsilon_{s,t} - \beta_i d\varepsilon_{i,t}.$$

5.7.4 Response Functions and Price Level Jumps

I plot responses to monetary and fiscal shocks in continuous time, with long-term debt. The basic patterns are the same as in discrete time but prettier.

The price level does not jump. Inflation, driving real discount rate changes, brings the present value relation in line. As pricing frictions are removed, the inflation or deflation becomes larger and shorter-lived, smoothly approaching a price level jump.

I compute responses using the full model (5.85)–(5.90), including long-term debt and policy reactions. Mirroring the discrete time treatment, I solve the model by writing it in standard form,

$$dz_t = Az_t dt + Bd\varepsilon_t + Cd\delta_t.$$

Solving the unstable eigenvalues forward we find expectational errors $d\delta_t$ in terms of structural shocks $d\varepsilon_t$. Then we have a standard autoregressive representation driven by the structural shocks $d\varepsilon_t$. Online Appendix Section A1.7 gives details.

I start without monetary or fiscal policy rules, turning off all the θ parameters. I also set $\alpha = 0$. The surplus does not respond at all to interest rate shocks, and follows an exogenous AR(1) with no debt repayment or s-shape. I use $\omega = 0$, a perpetuity. The top panel of Figure 5.10 shows the responses to an unexpected interest rate rise with no change in surpluses $d\varepsilon_{s,t} = 0$ for this case. The responses are essentially the same as the corresponding Figure 5.4 for discrete time, only smoother since we have a value at every point, and since shocks are instantaneous jumps. Long-term debt means that higher nominal interest rates can produce lower inflation. The response to an expected interest rate rise, not shown, is essentially the same as the discrete time case shown in Figure 5.2, as are responses to fiscal shocks and other exercises.

The bottom panel of Figure 5.10 plots the *price level* response to the unexpected interest rate increase for a variety of price stickiness parameters. The disinflation shown in the top panel of Figure 5.10 results in a protracted price level decline, which recovers when the disinflation turns to inflation. Sensibly, as prices become stickier, as κ declines, the period of disinflation lasts longer.

As prices become less sticky, as κ increases, the price level response approaches the downward jump followed by inflation shown in the frictionless model of Figure 5.4. *The fiscal theory of monetary policy has a smooth frictionless limit.* This point is important by contrast with some standard new-Keynesian models, which, as we will see, blow up as you remove price stickiness, though their frictionless limit point is well behaved.

The smooth frictionless limit means that the simple frictionless models provide a useful approximation. The frictionless model generates a downward price level jump, followed by inflation. The sticky price model generates a period of deflation followed by slowly emerging inflation. Price stickiness just drags out and makes more realistic the dynamics suggested by the stark frictionless model.

Higher interest rates lower inflation, but by a seemingly different mechanism than we are used to. With perfect foresight, the government debt valuation equation is

$$V_t = \frac{Q_t B_t}{P_t} = \int_{\tau=t}^{\infty} e^{-\int_{w=t}^{\tau}(i_w - \pi_w)dw} s_\tau \, d\tau. \qquad (5.116)$$

Higher interest rates give rise to a downward bond price Q_t jump. In a flexible price model, that jump is matched by a downward price level P_t jump. With sticky prices and varying real rates in discrete time, some of the lower bond price is absorbed by higher real interest rates and some is absorbed by a smaller downward price level jump. In continuous time with no price level jumps, the discount rate effect is the *entire* mechanism. In turn, we can think of the discrete-time price level jump as an artifact of looking coarsely at the time path of the economy.

The response to a fiscal policy shock with constant nominal rate is likewise nearly identical to the discrete time case, Figure 5.3, though again slightly prettier. Again, *inflation* jumps down but the *price level* does not jump at time 0, unlike discrete time which combines the two effects. If there is a decline in expected surpluses on the right-hand side

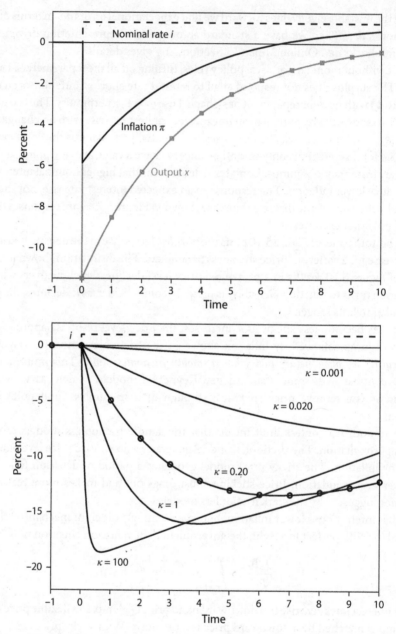

FIGURE 5.10. Responses to an Unexpected Permanent Interest Rate Shock. Model with long-term debt. Top: inflation and output response. Bottom: price level response with varying price stickiness parameters κ. Parameters $r = 0.05$, $\kappa = 0.2$, $\sigma = 0.5$, $\omega = 0$, $\alpha = 0$, $\theta = 0$.

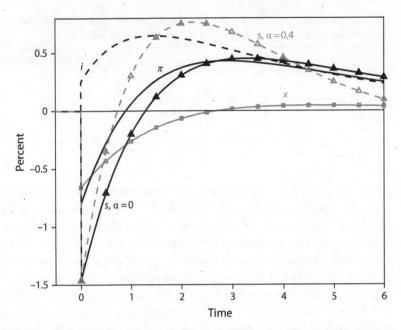

FIGURE 5.11. Responses to an Interest Rate Shock with a Surplus Rule. The surplus follows $\tilde{s}_t = 1.0x_t + 1.0\pi_t + \alpha v_t$. In the solid line, $\alpha = 0$. In the dashed line, $\alpha = 0.4$, $\beta_i = 0.8$. Short-term debt $\omega = \infty$. Other parameters are $\kappa = 2, r = 0.05, \rho = 0.05, \theta_{ix} = \theta_{i\pi} = 0, \theta_{i\epsilon} = 0.25, \zeta_i = 1, \eta_i = 0.3$.

of (5.116), we get a period of high inflation, lowering the discount rate of government debt so that the present value is unchanged despite the decline in surpluses. Equivalently, there is a period of low real returns that devalue debt. As we reduce price stickiness, the period of low inflation gets shorter and more dire, smoothly approaching the price level jump.

There is not much point in recreating the previous graphs with prettier continuous time versions, so instead I use the model to explore novel issues.

5.7.5   Monetary–Fiscal Coordination

With a fiscal policy rule that reacts to inflation and output, higher interest rates can produce lower inflation, even with short-term debt. Higher long-run inflation produces higher long-run surpluses, which push the economy to a path with lower short-run inflation. For this effect to work, however, the fiscal response must be "unbacked." It must produce a change in the weighted sum of surpluses. A rule that pays off deficits with higher later surpluses has no effect on inflation, even when those deficits react to inflation and output. In the parametric model of surpluses generated by α, θ, and β parameters, the weighted sum of surpluses is now controlled by a mixture of parameters, not just β.

Figure 5.11 shows how a surplus rule that reacts to inflation and output can induce a negative inflation response to higher interest rates, even with no long-term debt, and no direct response or correlation between monetary and fiscal policy shocks.

TABLE 5.2. Inflation Decompositions. Table entries give the terms of the weighted inflation identity (5.117) for the responses of Figures 5.11, 5.12, and 5.13.

Model	0	=	$-\int e^{-r\tau}\tilde{s}_\tau d\tau$	$+\int e^{-r\tau}(i_\tau - \pi_\tau)d\tau$
$\alpha = 0$	0	=	-1.28	$+1.28$
$\alpha = 0.4, \beta_i = 0.8$	0	=	-1.28	$+1.28$
$\alpha = 0.4, \beta_i = 0$	0	=	-0.50	$+0.50$
$\alpha = 0.4, \beta_i = -0.91$	0	=	0	$+0$

To produce the graph, I use a surplus rule that reacts strongly to output and to inflation, but does not respond to debt at all, $\tilde{s}_t = 1.0x_t + 1.0\pi_t + u_{s,t}$ with $\alpha = 0$. This is a larger value of $\theta_{s\pi}$ than I use elsewhere, in order to show the effect more clearly. With $\alpha = 0$, the whole starred set of equations drops from the model, so β_i in particular is now irrelevant and does not select unexpected inflation. I graph the response to a moderately persistent interest rate shock. I use $\eta_i = 0.3$, corresponding to an 0.7 disturbance ($u_{i,t}$) autocorrelation in annual data, and $\zeta_i = 1$, so the interest rate converges to the rule with a one-year half-life. I specify $\theta_{i\varepsilon} = 0.25$, so a 1% monetary policy shock $\varepsilon_{i,t}$ starts with an 0.25% shock to interest rates. In order to focus on the fiscal policy rule, monetary policy has no reaction to inflation and output, $\theta_{ix} = \theta_{i\pi} = 0$, so the interest rate just follows the graphed path exogenously. Other parameters are $r = 0.05$, $\rho = 0.05$, $\theta_{ix} = \theta_{i\pi} = 0$. In order to make a pretty graph, I use a large value of $\kappa = 2$.

Higher future nominal interest rates eventually produce higher inflation. The higher inflation produces larger surpluses, a fiscal tightening through $\theta_{s\pi}$. Though the short-term disinflation and recession—lower x—produce short-term deficits, these deficits are more than made up by the subsequent surpluses to create an overall fiscal tightening contemporaneous with the monetary policy shock. Inflation falls immediately with the higher interest rate, even though there is no long-term debt. This is the main point of the graph:

- *A fiscal rule in which surpluses respond to inflation can induce a negative response of inflation to higher interest rates.*

Despite low price stickiness, the real interest rate rises substantially for four years.

To better understand the mechanisms, Table 5.2 presents the terms of the linearized identity (3.51) for this and following impulse-response functions. Applied to a response function ($t = 0$, $x_\tau = \Delta_0 x_\tau$), and with short-term debt so $dR_\tau = (i_\tau - \pi_\tau)d\tau$, that identity is

$$\int_{\tau=0}^{\infty} e^{-(r+\omega)\tau}\pi_\tau d\tau = -\int_{\tau=0}^{\infty} e^{-r\tau}\tilde{s}_\tau d\tau + \int_{\tau=0}^{\infty} \left(e^{-r\tau} - e^{-(r+\omega)\tau}\right)(i_\tau - \pi_\tau)d\tau.$$

$$(5.117)$$

With short-term debt $\omega = \infty$, the left-hand side is zero. Future expected inflation cannot devalue long-term bonds, and the value of debt cannot change on impact. Thus, the weighted sum of future surpluses must equal the weighted sum of future real interest rates.

By raising the sum of surpluses, with a constant nominal interest rate, the economy must settle on an equilibrium path with lower inflation.

In the first row of Table 5.2, the weighted sum of surpluses rises by 1.28 percentage points, a deflationary shock. The weighted sum of discount rates must then rise by a matching 1.28 percentage points. Cumulative inflation must decline 1.28 percentage points, selecting an equilibrium path with low immediate inflation.

This example shows again that the fiscal regime is crucial to the effects of monetary policy. Fiscal authorities here do not react directly to the monetary policy change, nor do they react passively to a price level or unexpected inflation chosen by monetary authorities. The fiscal policy rule reflects how fiscal authorities habitually react to inflation and output, and it reflects the effect of endogenous inflation and output on tax receipts, benefits, and other payments. It represents people's expectations of such endogenous responses. Its presence causes inflation and output to decline in response to higher interest rates. Without the fiscal rule, inflation rises uniformly.

It is central to the result that this fiscal rule represents "unbacked" variation in surpluses and deficits. If surpluses respond to inflation and output, but all such induced higher surpluses correspond to subsequent lower surpluses, then the induced overall fiscal contraction vanishes.

I show two variations to explore this issue and to give some additional intuition for how the surplus process parameterized by v^* and π^* via α and β_i work. In this model with time-varying returns, backed versus unbacked fiscal policy is no longer as simple as $a(\rho) = 0$ or $\beta_i = 0$.

First, I use a value $\alpha = 0.4$, so the surplus rule is now $\tilde{s}_t = 1.0x_t + 1.0\pi_t + 0.4v_t$. This is an unrealistically high value for α, but it helps to keep the graphs clear. I use $\beta_i = 0.8$, in order to produce the same time 0 unexpected inflation as in the first case.

Since unexpected inflation at time 0 is unchanged, the whole path of inflation and output are unchanged, as shown in Figure 5.11. The interest rate path sets the family of solutions. Fiscal policy chooses only unexpected inflation at time zero. If that does not change, the inflation and output paths do not change. In more general models, different fiscal policy can change the equilibrium path, but not here where the model separates.

The change from $\alpha = 0$ to $\alpha = 0.4$, $\beta_i = 0.8$ produces a different surplus process, shown in the dashed line of Figure 5.11 marked "s, $\alpha = 0.4$." The initial deficits increase the value of debt (not shown), which in turn leads to lesser deficits in the medium run. As debt builds up, surpluses stay persistently larger to pay off the larger debt. As we see in the second row of Table 5.2, however, the weighted sum of surpluses does not change at all. The larger earlier surpluses are matched by lower long-term surpluses. Raising α and choosing $\beta_i = 0.8$ to leave unexpected inflation unchanged merely changes the *timing* of surpluses. This is an example of a "backed" change in surpluses that has no effect on inflation or output. Multiple fiscal policies can produce the same inflation and output paths. If the weighted sum of surpluses does not change, their effect on inflation and output does not change in this model.

Next, Figure 5.12 shows responses for $\beta_i = 0$, keeping $\alpha = 0.4$. The parameter β_i controls unexpected inflation at time 0 when $\alpha > 0$, so unsurprisingly unexpected inflation at time 0 is now 0, and inflation rises smoothly after that. We lose the negative inflation response of inflation to higher interest rates.

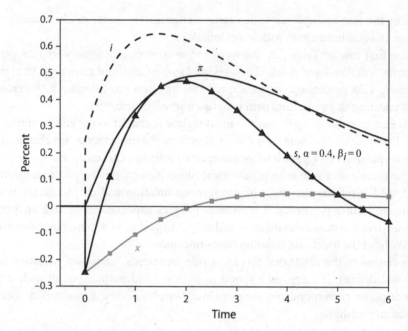

FIGURE 5.12. Responses to an Interest Rate Shock with a Surplus Rule. The surplus follows $\tilde{s}_t = 1.0x_t + 1.0\pi_t + 0.4v_t$, with $\beta_i = 0$. Short-term debt $\omega = \infty$. Other parameters are $\kappa = 2$, $r = 0.05$, $\rho = 0.05$, $\theta_{ix} = \theta_{i\pi} = 0$, $\phi_i = 0.3$, $\zeta_i = 1$, $\theta_{i,\varepsilon} = 0.25$.

Again, we should regard the surplus process as creating β_i and unexpected inflation, not the other way around, so the point of this graph is to look at the surplus process that produces no unexpected inflation. Aside from the initial period of deficits, the surplus is lower throughout than in Figure 5.11, and declines more swiftly. (Note the different vertical scales.) As measured in the third row of Table 5.2, the weighted sum of surpluses is 0.50, not 1.28. The left-hand side is still zero, so the smaller sum of surpluses is matched by smaller discount rates. Smaller discount rates mean that the selected inflation path rises, closer to the unchanged interest rate path, as we can see in the graph.

It is initially surprising that the weighted sum of surpluses is not zero in Table 5.2. In the original analysis of this surplus rule, in the context of the flexible price model of Section 5.7.2, setting $\beta_i = 0$ not only set unexpected inflation to zero, it also set to zero the weighted sum of surpluses $\mathcal{L}(D) = 0$. Here we see that while the former feature is general, the latter is not. With policy rules $\theta_{sx} \neq 0$ and $\theta_{s\pi} \neq 0$, the parameters that lead to a zero weighted sum of surpluses are not the same parameters that lead to zero unexpected inflation, and vice versa.

In this example, I do not change the inflation and output reaction parameters $\theta_{s\pi}$ and θ_{sx}. By changing α and β_i, I change how much of an induced surplus or deficit is backed or unbacked, how much it corresponds to subsequent deficits or surpluses. Both aspects of fiscal policy are important for driving an inflationary or disinflationary fiscal effect.

The monetary policy shock, parameters, and interest rate path are unchanged. The contrast between Figure 5.11 and 5.12 makes again the central point: The economy's

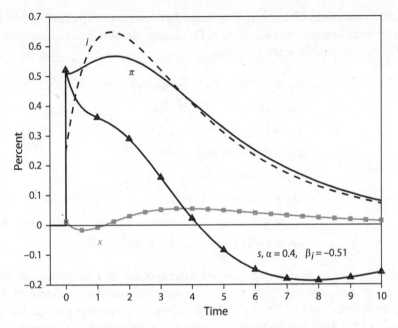

FIGURE 5.13. Responses to an Interest Rate Shock with a Surplus Rule. The surplus follows $\tilde{s}_t = 1.0x_t +$ $1.0\pi_t + 0.4v_t$, with $\beta_i = -0.5085$. Short-term debt $\omega = \infty$. Other parameters are $\kappa = 2, r = 0.05, \rho = 0.05$, $\theta_{ix} = \theta_{i\pi} = 0, \zeta_i = 1, \theta_{i\varepsilon} = 1, \eta_i = 0.3$.

response to monetary policy depends on the fiscal policy rule; in this case to what extent current fiscal reactions are backed or not by changes in later fiscal policy.

In Figure 5.13 and the last row of Table 5.2, I search for the value of β_i that along with $\alpha = 0.4$ produces a zero weighted sum of surpluses $\mathcal{L}(D) = 0$ and $\int_{\tau=0}^{\infty} e^{-r\tau}\tilde{s}_\tau d\tau = 0$. The consequent value of β_i is -0.51, generating a *positive* 0.51 percentage point unexpected inflation. By the identity, if it produces no weighted sum of surpluses, the model produces no weighted sum of discount rates. You can see dynamics in the difference between interest rate and inflation line, but they must stay relatively close together to produce no weighted sum of their difference. In the family of solutions to this model with a given interest rate path, there are no solutions with inflation strongly below interest rates early and strongly above interest rates later. The early surpluses, driven by the reaction of surplus to inflation and output, pay down debt. The α term then quickly allows the government to run deficits to offset the decline in debt, which balance out the early surpluses. The parameter configuration that produces both no weighted sum of surpluses and no discount rate effects is essentially Fisherian, with inflation quickly rising to match interest rates.

5.7.6 Sims's Model

I add habit persistence in consumption. The model produces more realistic hump-shaped impulse-response functions.

Sims (2011) is a model of this form that illustrates the sorts of steps one can take toward realism by including standard elements of DSGE models. Sims's linearized model is, in my notation, and with a few modifications,

$$di_t = -\zeta_i \left(i_t - \theta_{i\pi}\pi_t - \theta_{ix}x_t\right) dt + d\varepsilon_{i,t} \tag{5.118}$$

$$d\pi_t = \left(\rho\pi_t - \kappa x_t\right) dt + d\delta_{\pi,t} \tag{5.119}$$

$$dq_t = \left(rq_t + i_t\right) dt + d\delta_{q,t} \tag{5.120}$$

$$d\tilde{s}_t = \theta_{sx}\dot{x}_t dt + d\varepsilon_{s,t} \tag{5.121}$$

$$dv_t = \left(rv_t + i_t - \pi_t - \tilde{s}_t\right) dt + d\delta_{Q,t} \tag{5.122}$$

$$d\lambda_t = -\left(i_t - \pi_t\right) dt + d\delta_{\lambda,t} \tag{5.123}$$

$$dx_t = \dot{x}_t dt \tag{5.124}$$

$$d\dot{x}_t = \left(\psi\lambda_t + \sigma\psi x_t + r\dot{x}_t\right) dt + d\delta_{\dot{x},t}. \tag{5.125}$$

Equation (5.118) is a monetary policy rule. Sims specifies that the policy rule reacts to output gap growth, $di_t = \ldots \theta_{ix}\dot{x}_t \ldots$. I use a more conventional response to the output gap itself. Equation (5.119) is the Phillips curve. Sims specifies perpetuities, $\omega = 0$. Equation (5.120) describes the perpetuity price under the expectations hypothesis. Sims uses the bond yield $y_t = 1/Q_t$ rather than bond price q_t as the state variable, which is prettier but requires one to approximate away an Ito or jump nonlinearity term. Fiscal policy (5.121) responds to output growth, but does not contain a response to debt $\alpha \neq 0$. The model needs that extension. Equation (5.122) is the fiscal flow condition with long-term debt.

The last three equations are the novelty relative to the previous models in this book. Preferences include a cost of quickly adjusting consumption, a sort of habit. Equation (5.123) describes the evolution of the marginal utility of wealth. But now it is connected to output via (5.124) and (5.125). The appendix to Cochrane (2017e) contains a derivation. A term of this sort is a common ingredient to generate hump-shaped dynamics. I use ψ in place of Sims's $1/\psi$ to make the equation prettier.

Figure 5.14 and Figure 5.15 present responses to an unexpected monetary policy shock and to a fiscal shock, respectively, in this model. You can see similar qualitative lessons of previous graphs, but with prettier dynamics. The monetary policy shock leads to an extended disinflation and recession, with a nice hump-shaped output response. But inflation eventually rises. This model is Fisherian in the long run, which was Sims's point in writing this model. Sims's "stepping on a rake" is similar to the Sargent and Wallace (1981) "unpleasant monetarist arithmetic," in warning that monetary tightening without fiscal support can only help temporarily and will make matters worse in the long run. One might easily miss the inflation rise in VAR estimates. The model is important beyond this specific point, however.

The positive fiscal shock leads to a recession with disinflation. The Fed lowers interest rates endogenously to fight the recession, which as before raises short-run inflation over what it would otherwise be, reducing the output decline.

This sort of response function starts to look very much like what comes out of standard new-Keynesian model-building exercises, and standard views of the effect of monetary

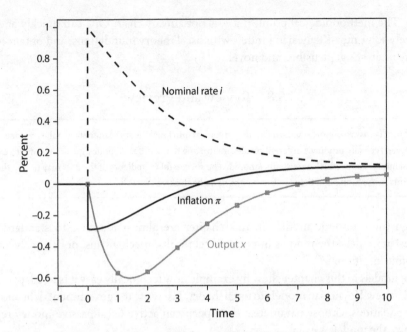

FIGURE 5.14. Response to an Unexpected Monetary Policy Shock in the Modified Sims Model

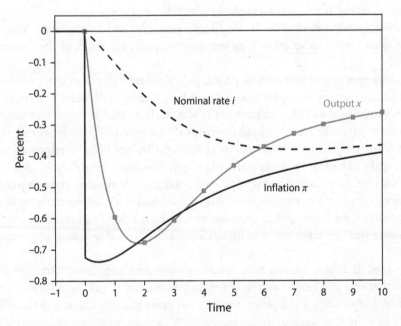

FIGURE 5.15. Response to a Fiscal Shock in the Modified Sims Model

policy. The methodological point, if it was not already clear: One can quickly and productively solve new-Keynesian models with fiscal theory foundations, and obtain results
that are interesting, plausible, and novel.

5.8   Review and Preview

It is technically easy to import standard DSGE ingredients into fiscal theory of monetary policy models. Doing
so, however, typically produces different results, invites one to ask different policy questions, and to examine
the fiscal implications, which are usually ignored. The successful ingredients of the past may not be the same
ingredients in the future and the results are unlikely to be the same as well.

Though the economic models in this chapter are almost identical to standard new-
Keynesian models, the models uncover novel results, mechanisms, policy analyses, and
economic intuition.

The models in this chapter show by example how technically easy it is to adapt current
DSGE or new-Keynesian models to fiscal theory. Just write the government debt and fiscal
policy equations, choose parameters that specify an active-fiscal passive-money regime,
and solve the model as usual.

Though the model is little changed, what one regards as a sensible policy question
may change. For example, it is natural here to think of a "monetary policy" shock as
somehow holding fiscal policy constant, where the passive-fiscal assumption in standard new-Keynesian models leads one to pair monetary and fiscal shocks. That difference in what counts as an interesting question accounts for much of the difference in
results.

Once we specify and take seriously fiscal policy, we are induced to write different and
more realistic fiscal policy specifications, as I have begun to do here, and to check fiscal predictions in data. That elaboration is also likely to lead to important differences
in specification, parameters, and policy analysis. At a minimum, the fiscal theory effort
should invite passive-fiscal modelers to check whether the fiscal implications of their
models make any sense. For example, when new-Keynesian models predict a disinflation, they implicitly predict a sharp "passive" increase in lump-sum taxes to pay off the
now more valuable government debt. We should look for that austerity in the data,
and question it for future policy interventions. Even if I do not persuade the reader to
write active fiscal policies, the tour invites a reevaluation and rewriting of passive-fiscal
models.

The models I have treated here remain simple and unrealistic. One hungers for
models that one can bring to data, estimate parameters, match impulse-responses to
well-identified structural and policy shocks, and make credible analysis of the effects of
policies or structural changes in the economy. We see an invitation to import many of
the ingredients of the vast new-Keynesian and DSGE effort. Since the results will almost
certainly change, this will not just be a relabeling or better-footnote exercise. Rather, we
have scattered around the floor well-understood ingredients that will likely produce new
and different results when imported to a fiscal theory framework. Which ingredients to
include, with which parameters, will certainly change.

More realistic IS and Phillips equations—the economic heart of the model—are an obvious need, and a long literature has investigated alternatives. The effect of shocks to those equations needs investigation.

One active branch of the new-Keynesian literature basically looks for foundations to make the IS and Phillips curves look more like traditional IS-LM equations. Rule-of-thumb or hand-to-mouth investors or sophisticatedly irrational expectations can make current income appear in the IS curve, and discount future inflation in the Phillips curve. (See Gabaix (2020), Cochrane (2016), García-Schmidt and Woodford (2019)). The standard version here, $x_t = E_t x_{t+1} - \sigma r_t$, captures only intertemporal reallocation of consumption around the steady-state, and thus has zero marginal propensity to consume and produces no traditional multiplier. Current heterogenous agent (HANK) models are particularly active here, including Kaplan, Moll, and Violante (2018), Auclert, Rognlie, and Straub (2020), and Alves et al. (2020).

It is likely that the form of these equations that best fits the facts will be different in a fiscal model than in a standard new-Keynesian model. New-Keynesian lessons about which ingredients produce a tastier soup are likely not to hold. For example, new-Keynesian models have a lot of trouble at the zero bound, detailed in Chapter 20. Complex alternatives to rational expectations emerged to repair these problems. The fiscal theory version of the simple models does not display zero-bound troubles. You are not likely to be led to drastic surgery of basic ingredients to fix nonexistent problems.

Asset-pricing research emphasizes that time-varying risk premiums rather than time-varying risk-free rates are the central feature of asset price variation over the business cycle, and that Q theory linking investment to stock market risk premiums rather than risk-free interest rates is central to understand cyclical variation in investment. (For an overview, see Cochrane (2017a).) Recessions *are*, at heart, times when people's and institutions' willingness and ability to bear risk and to make risky investments changes, not times when people desire consumption today less than consumption in the future. (Di Tella and Hall (2021) is a good example of the nascent risk premium based literature in macroeconomics.)

The Phillips curve has always stood on shaky theoretical ground. It makes intuitive sense that firms produce more when prices are higher, but that intuition links higher output to higher prices *relative* to wages, not to higher prices and wages together. Similarly, it makes intuitive sense that people work harder when wages are higher, but that intuition links more work to higher wages *relative* to prices, not higher prices and wages together. Lucas (1972) famously solved this conundrum with imperfect information: People misperceive unexpected inflation as higher relative prices and wages. But linking output only to unexpected inflation does not produce persistent output and unemployment variation. Microfoundations of new-Keynesian Phillips curves don't withstand a casual look out the window at the costs of changing prices or the slope of individual businesses' demand curves. They are a parable for something else. Maybe a good parable, but a parable nonetheless.

The Phillips curve stands on increasingly shaky empirical ground as well. The large rise in unemployment during the 2008 recession, with little price or wage deflation, and the long, slow recovery with high unemployment but steady inflation leads to the impression that the Phillips curve has become flat. Another interpretation is that the Phillips curve has become a meaningless cloud of points, not a flat but exploitable curve; that a tiny bit of inflation would not suddenly cure unemployment, or that inflation can move without immense employment or unemployment that a flat curve requires. (See Hall and Kudlyak (2021) for a search theory account of the 2008–2019 recovery, which basically says a standard Phillips curve is misspecified.) A huge microeconomic effort to understand and model product-level prices has not yet resulted in a better aggregate Phillips curve. The common habit of viewing the Phillips curve as a causal link, either that the Fed causes unemployment that causes inflation, or that the Fed causes inflation that causes unemployment, is also questionable.

Much of the history of macroeconomics comes down to shifting the time index in the reference point π_t^e of the Phillips curve $\pi_t = \pi_t^e + \kappa x_t$. The original Phillips curve sported a constant $\pi_t^e = \pi$. Adaptive expectations had a lag, $\pi_t^e = \pi_{t-1}$ or $\pi_t^e = a(L)\pi_{t-1}$. Rational expectations models move the index forward to $\pi_t^e = E_{t-1}\pi_t$ (Lucas (1972)). The new-Keynesian form uses expected future inflation, $\pi_t^e = E_t\pi_{t+1}$. While it makes great economic sense that expected future inflation should shift the Phillips curve, that specification means that output is high when inflation is declining, not when inflation is rising (Mankiw and Reis (2002)). The latter seems to fit the facts better, though as always that conclusion depends on the process driving inflation expectations (Cogley and Sbordone (2008)): If past inflation forecasts future inflation, then rational expectations look adaptive. And adaptive expectations start adapting much more quickly as inflation looms.

Much effort goes into justifying lagged inflation terms, again reviving IS-LM tradition and also fitting existing U.S. time series somewhat better, though in the same breath abandoning the triumph of Lucas's formulation that also fits times of high inflation (Lucas (1973)), ends of inflation, and currency reforms, when inflation has little output effect. The new-Keynesian theory also really wants marginal cost, not output or unemployment on the right-hand side. Marginal cost measures can show little correlation with output or employment, perhaps rescuing the curve but reducing its utility to understand recessions of output and employment. Empirically oriented new-Keynesian models emphasize wage stickiness, not price stickiness, thereby allowing profit to be procyclical.

In sum, the IS and especially Phillips curves of the models in this book surely need much improvement. However, standard more successful alternatives have not yet emerged, especially forms that are likely to be stable across policy rule and regime changes. And as always, what works in one model may not work in another model. We don't have solid evidence on individual equations separate from how they function in the context of a full model.

A long list of additional ingredients beckons, including habits or other dynamic preferences, human, physical, and intangible capital accumulation, investment with adjustment costs, individual and firm heterogeneity, varying risk aversion and risk premiums, labor market search, real business cycle production-side elaboration, financial frictions, lower bounds on interest rates, and so forth. Technically, one can simply import standard specifications of all of these generalizations from the existing new-Keynesian and real business cycle literature.

So, I do not stop here with models that ignore these features because I think these toy models are the end. They are the beginning.

Two key properties bear watching. First, in the simple models of this book, long-term debt or a fiscal policy rule are needed to produce an even temporary decline in inflation after an interest rate rise. But other ingredients including IS (preference) modifications, investment reactions, and financial frictions may contribute to such effects. Searching for more potential reasons behind this cherished belief is worthwhile.

Second, this book is really about the broad determinacy and stability properties of monetary models. In one sense, the conclusions of these simple models are likely to be robust because stability and determinacy depend on which eigenvalues are greater or less than 1. As long as a model modification does not move an eigenvalue across that boundary, the stability and determinacy conclusions are not changed. But once a modification moves an eigenvalue across that boundary, it can change a new-Keynesian model—stability, indeterminacy—to an old-Keynesian model—instability, determinacy—or have other large consequences.

The specification of monetary and fiscal policy in these simple models can and should be improved. My monetary policy rule is simplistic, needing at least lags and a lower bound, plus matching policy rule regressions, VARs, and full model estimates. The surplus process, which allows governments to borrow to finance deficits and to promise partial repayment in an active fiscal regime, is the most novel ingredient here. But it is only a first stab at the specification. News about future surpluses and historical episodes are likely not well modeled by AR(1) shocks to the surplus disturbance $u_{s,t}$. Specifying and estimating the fiscal policy rule responses to inflation, output, and other variables, is a challenge of similar order, not yet started. Parametric models other than my v versus v^*, π versus π^* may be empirically more productive and transparent, as I suggested above. The right specification of just how our institutions and leaders are likely to respond "off equilibrium" clearly needs more thought. The parameters of both fiscal and monetary policy rules are likely to change over time, and people expect such shifts when deciding what to do. In particular, the choice to finance deficits by inflating existing debt versus borrowing against future surpluses is likely to change over time and in response to state variables.

On the other hand, much of the fiscal policy rule might be estimated from knowledge of the tax code and the rules for automatic stabilizers, where the monetary policy rule consists only of modeling the human decisions of central bankers. Estimating the parameters $\theta_{s,}$. of fiscal policy may thus be easier than running regressions with dubious instruments that pervades monetary policy rule estimation.

More deeply, it is clearly better to specify fiscal policy via tax rates and spending decisions, both entitlement and discretionary, rather than to model primary surpluses. I have avoided all the economically important ways that fiscal policy feeds back into the economic portion of the economic model, in order to focus on the determinacy issues and the similarity with new-Keynesian models. But once we agree that the fiscal part of the model is important, it cries for integration with the standard public finance approach. All-in marginal tax rates are high, including the marginal tax rates associated with benefit phase-outs. They distort physical and human capital investment, labor supply, and more. The government buys goods and services that subtract from output and some purchases may enter utility functions in a way that affects other margins. Once fiscal policy enters macroeconomics, fiscal distortions should enter as well, not just via multipliers and government debt valuation considerations. Incentives matter, not just income and wealth.

It's possible that the distorting and wealth effects separate, so the two investigations can remain simple by remaining separate. But we won't know that until we look.

Linearization is an important weakness of these models and the surrounding literature. Now, one should be wary of this common complaint. Underlying economic models are nonlinear, but we don't necessarily know which nonlinearities are the right ones. Linearization can be more robust than a wrong nonlinear model. However, a few linearizations stand out as important. Linearization about a steady-state debt-to-GDP ratio raises the problem that the debt-to-GDP ratio has varied widely. This is a nonlinear effect: Terms such as $v_t r_t$ expand to $v(r_t - r) + r(v_t - v)$ but leave out $(v_t - v)(r_t - r)$, the fact that a response of a variable to r_t is different for low rather than high debt-to-GDP ratios. Monetary policy with a debt-to-GDP ratio of 25% in 1980 may be quite different from monetary policy with a debt-to-GDP ratio of 100% in 2021. The interest costs of a higher interest rate are four times larger.

But nonlinear models are hard to solve, and more importantly hard to understand once one has solved them. Black boxes are not yet useful in macroeconomics. The black-box approach, useful in meteorology or engineering, requires one to know the ingredients with great precision. We do not have that knowledge, so we must preserve an intuitive understanding of the whole model as a quantitative parable. A useful first step may be to linearize models around different points; for example, linearize around a lower debt-to-GDP ratio to analyze the 1970s, and a higher one today.

One may wish to pursue a medium-scale macro model, something like a Smets and Wouters (2007), or Christiano, Eichenbaum, and Evans (2005), adapted to fiscal theory as I have adapted the textbook new-Keynesian model here. Or one may wish to aim even larger. Adapting the large-scale models such as the Fed's FRBUS model to fiscal theory is not technically hard. Getting sensible answers out of such a project may be hard, however, but getting sensible answers out of the current model isn't easy either. The project of constructing large, general purpose macroeconomic models that can simultaneously fit data, explain history, forecast the future, and evaluate policies has been going on since the 1960s. It peaked in the 1970s, fell out of favor, and has never really recovered. Much policy evaluation remains tied to smaller purpose-built models and, in the end, back-of-the-envelope intuition. But this is a larger observation about model building, not specific to fiscal theory.

In sum, one *can* quite easily adapt current macroeconomic models to fiscal theory foundations. There are many ingredients to explore, and models that include them are likely to behave differently in a fiscal theory context than their original context. As a recipe for writing papers, this is great news. Of course, we do not build complexity for complexity's sake. We do not often write good economic research by randomly mixing ingredients. Computing models is easy. Finding the *right* model is hard, and understanding its central message is harder. That 30-year and ongoing specification search has not been so easy for standard new-Keynesian models either.

Not all of this speculation describes the future. More complex and therefore potentially more realistic models have been built in the fiscal theory tradition, combining fiscal price determination, detailed fiscal policy rules, interest rate targets, and many of the above ingredients. Chapter 23 includes a critical review, with speculation about where this important investigation may go in the future.

6

Fiscal Constraints

THIS CHAPTER takes a closer look at the present value relation and the nature of fiscal constraints. Inflation depends on the present value of surpluses, so I start with the present value Laffer curve. Tax rates may have no effect on labor supply, but by reducing economic growth can run into a long-run or present value Laffer curve. Other policies that influence growth are potentially even more important than tax rates for driving surpluses and hence inflation.

I analyze an instructive example in which the surplus is limited, say by a Laffer curve. Inflation is steady despite debt and deficits, and higher interest rates lower inflation. As debt and deficits build, however, a moment comes when the long-run Laffer limit is reached. Inflation suddenly breaks out, deficits cause more inflation, and monetary policy loses its power. Further interest rate hikes raise future inflation rather than lower current inflation.

I tackle the troublesome possibility that the rate of return on government debt may be less than the economy's growth rate, in which case fiscal theory seems to stop working, and government debt seems to become a free lunch. Much of the case stems from mixing up average returns in our stochastic economy with the constant risk-free rate of a perfect foresight economy.

Finally, I think about how productively to include promises such as Social Security and assets such as national parks and federal lands in the valuation equation.

6.1   The Present Value Laffer Curve

There is always a fiscal limit, at which governments can no longer raise tax revenue. The usual discussion of the Laffer curve is static, and centers on the tradeoff of work versus leisure. The fiscal theory responds to the *present value* of surpluses. Small effects of tax rates on growth have large effects on the present value of surpluses, even if tax rates have no immediate effect on labor supply, tax avoidance, or other reductions in the flow of tax revenue. Microeconomic and growth-oriented policies also affect long-term growth and thus can have profound effects on the present value of surpluses and the sustainability of debt.

As we think about surpluses and fiscal rules, it is natural to jump to tax rate and spending policy decisions. In fact, for the present value of surpluses that matters in the fiscal theory, economic growth is likely to be more important. Figure 4.1 reminds us that output is the primary determinant of the surplus-to-GDP ratio: Tax revenue grows in expansions and falls in contractions, spending does the opposite. And more GDP raises the surplus for any given surplus-to-GDP ratio.

Economic policies that change growth by a small amount can cumulate to large changes in tax revenue, even if they have little short-run impact. Poorly crafted "austerity" policies in particular run this danger: Raising marginal tax rates may bring a short-run revenue increase, but by decreasing growth such policies can lower long-run revenues and the present value of surpluses. The *present value* Laffer curve may bite at lower tax rates than the usual flow Laffer curve, and for different taxes.

Alesina et al. (2019) document that fiscal contractions focused on lower spending have better growth outcomes than those focused on higher marginal tax rates. The "Laffer curve" is popularly associated with its maximum, and the possibility that higher tax rates lower revenue. I use the word to refer to the whole curve.

The usual Laffer curve analysis focuses on static labor supply. Higher marginal tax rates are, effectively, lower wages. Wages have income and substitution effects: Lower income induces people to work harder, but a lower return to work encourages people to substitute from work to leisure, and to more pleasant or personally rewarding but less productive work. The latter effect is less commonly modeled in economics. The substitution and income effects are usually thought to roughly offset, hence the usual view that higher tax rates do not significantly dampen labor supply, output, and tax revenue. Our high taxes on labor are the result of this belief.

This simple parable is a poor approximation to the U.S. tax system. U.S. tax rates are highly progressive, not a flat tax on wages. Overall incentives include all taxes, including state and local taxes, payroll taxes, sales and property taxes, as well as federal income taxes. Overall incentives also include the income effect of benefits and the implied marginal tax rates from the fact that benefits phase out with income. Mankiw (2018) makes a simple calculation that based on tax and income data, "the effective marginal tax rate when a person moves from the bottom to the middle quintile is . . . 76 percent." Mulligan (2012) documents the details of many programs, especially health insurance, finding even larger marginal tax rates, and many cliffs of tax rates far above 100% when a benefit phases out suddenly. Transfers and benefits combined with high marginal tax rates unite the income and substitution effects against work. The opportunities to work are nonlinear, with minimum and maximum hours for most jobs, straight time versus overtime, one or both spouses working, and so forth.

The central question for us is, how will this situation *change* when the government wishes to raise more revenue or lower expenditure, by raising tax rates or increasing the means-testing of benefits?

The main worry for fiscal theory, and debt sustainability more generally, is that the long-run or present value Laffer curve may pose a harsher tradeoff than this static analysis suggests. This consideration is not commonly included in "dynamic scoring" analysis of tax and spending policy. The effect on overall surpluses of spending policy disincentives is usually left out as well.

The long run offers more room for tax-avoiding, GDP-lowering, and tax-revenue-lowering adjustment. In the short run, most people have settled into careers and jobs. Labor market regulation and custom make it hard for most people to raise or lower work hours. The "extensive margins" of joining or leaving the labor force or changing careers are small in the short run. But give it a decade or so. A higher marginal tax rate may not cause a doctor, lawyer, or entrepreneur to change hours of work that much, or to become an artist or activist. But high and progressive marginal tax rates influence people's career choices, willingness to take unpleasant and difficult college majors, invest in education, work up the job ladder, innovate new products, or invest time and effort in starting businesses; rather than to skip school, take fun majors, settle into easier or more enjoyable jobs. A convex tax code lowers the incentive for entrepreneurial risks whose upside is taxed away, toward safer human and physical investments. These margins can take a generation to take effect.

Disappointing revenue from tax rate increases also comes from tax avoidance. Tax avoidance takes time, as we can witness from the steady accretion of patches to our insanely complex tax code. Estate tax sheltering takes decades to have an effect.

Capital taxes are different from labor income taxes. The capital gains tax cuts of the late 1980s unequivocally raised revenue. Corporate taxes lead to different margins of avoidance, like moving to Ireland.

Raising capital taxes is a classic temptation and a classic example of the difference between current and long-run or present value revenue calculations. Unexpected capital taxes hit irreversible investments today, so generate revenue without distortion. But capital taxation removes the incentive to create tomorrow's capital, and thus can fail to raise the *present value* of tax revenue. High and progressive labor or total income taxation acts as a tax on human and intangible capital, with the same tradeoff. As the sorry history of rent controls illustrates, taxing capital can seem to work for a while, but in a few decades there is nothing left. The classic Judd (1999) and Chamley (1986) result states that the optimal capital tax rate is zero. Higher capital taxes just lead to lower capital until the after-tax marginal product of capital is unchanged. Like all classic results, it spawned a long debate; for example, Straub and Werning (2020). But it also captures a robust channel for revenue disappointment.

There is a worse possibility: What if high marginal tax rates lower the incentives to innovate, to create productivity-enhancing ideas and the firms that embody them, and thereby lower the economy's long-run growth rate? Jones (2020b) presents some sobering analysis in an endogenous growth model with distorting taxation, finding much lower Laffer limits than in standard analysis. Integrating fiscal theory or debt sustainability with endogenous growth theory is an obvious important step.

For a simple calculation, consider a flat income tax at rate τ. The conventional Laffer curve calculation asks for the effect on tax revenue of a change in the tax rate:

$$\frac{\partial \log(\tau y)}{\partial \log \tau} = 1 + \frac{\partial \log y}{\partial \log \tau}.$$

The second term is typically negative, as a higher tax rate lowers output and therefore lowers tax revenue from what it would otherwise be. But that elasticity is usually thought to be less than -1, so raising taxes raises some revenue, just less than static analysis predicts.

But write the present value of tax revenue

$$PV_t = \int_{u=0}^{\infty} e^{-ru} \tau y_{t+u} du = \tau y_t \int_{u=0}^{\infty} e^{-(r-g)u} du = \frac{\tau y_t}{r-g}.$$

Here g denotes the output growth rate. Now the elasticity of the *present value* of surpluses with respect to the tax rate τ is

$$\frac{\partial \log (PV_t)}{\partial \log \tau} = 1 + \frac{\partial \log y_t}{\partial \log \tau} + \frac{1}{r-g}\frac{\partial g}{\partial \log \tau}.$$

We have a second dynamic effect. Since $r - g$ is a small number, small growth effects can have a big impact on the fiscal limit. For example, if $r - g = 0.01$, 1%, then $dg/d\log \tau = -0.01$ puts us at the top of the present value Laffer curve, even with no static effect. Thus, if a tax rate τ rise from 50% to 60%, which is a 20% rise in tax rate, implies $0.01 \times 20 = 0.2$ percentage point reduction in long-term growth, then we are at the fiscal limit already. A value of r closer to g seems nice, as it produces a larger present value for a given stream of surpluses. But r closer to g also makes the present value more sensitive to variation in either r or g. Smaller growth effects then imply larger reductions in the present value of tax revenue.

The point here is not to argue quantitatively where the United States or other advanced economies are on the present value Laffer curve. The point is that there is a distinct present value Laffer curve that describes fiscal limits; and that present value Laffer curve may be more stringent than the static curve most commonly discussed. The danger of high tax rates is decades of sclerosis, not an immediate vacation.

Tax revenues are tax rate times income, τy, so the more general point is that GDP growth matters a lot to the present value of surpluses. Economic regulation is potentially a larger disincentive to growth than tax policy and social program disincentives. Keeping the taxi monopoly in and Uber out does not help government finances, but it lowers economic activity and thus the tax base. The vast array of protection and regulation of labor, health care, housing, education, banking, energy and more, largely focused on transferring resources from one group to another, retards economic activity without even a direct benefit to tax collection. Ease of doing business indices correlate well with enormous differences in GDP per capita, and thus tax revenue, across countries. The license Raj, not marginal tax rates, kept India poor for generations. Communism, not high marginal tax rates, kept China poor.

In thinking about the fiscal theory, then, we must broaden our vision from just tax and spending policies. Pro-growth *regulatory* economic and financial reforms are likely to raise the present value of surpluses and thereby help to lower inflation, potentially as or more effectively than pro-growth reduction in marginal taxation.

This beneficial effect of microeconomic reform, or "structural adjustment," is an important part of many successful disinflation plans. They are plausibly part of the story of the 1970s and 1980s in the United States and United Kingdom as well. The 1970s endured a productivity slowdown and growth malaise as inflation broke out. In the early 1980s, the United States and United Kingdom embarked on tax reform, sharply lowering marginal rates but broadening the base; and also regulatory reform, starting with trucks, airlines, and telephones. The later 1980s saw robust growth that eventually led to unprecedented surpluses.

6.2   Discount Rates

Lower growth may come with lower real interest rates, partially offsetting the present value Laffer curve effect, and vice versa. Higher real interest rates without higher growth—a sovereign credit spread—pose a larger danger of inflation. The debt crisis mechanism that causes default and currency crashes can also cause inflation.

The present value of surpluses also depends on the discount rate. And discount rates are related to growth. Higher growth g may bring higher real interest rates r, offsetting some of growth's beneficial properties for the present value of surpluses. Conversely, the ill effects of lower growth on government finances may be tempered by lower interest rates, secularly as they are in recessions. Discount rate variation unrelated to growth, or growth variation without a change in discount rates, has more potent effects than when growth and discount rates change together. Thus, the source of changes in growth and interest rates matters a lot.

A natural force connects real interest rates to growth. When real interest rates are higher, people consume less today and more tomorrow. Formally, the first-order condition for a representative dynastic (cares about children) consumer says that the real interest rate equals the subjective discount rate δ plus the inverse of the intertemporal substitution elasticity γ times the growth rate g,

$$r = \delta + \gamma g. \tag{6.1}$$

Higher growth usually comes with, or is caused by, a higher marginal product of capital, $r = f'(k)$, which also translates to higher real interest rates.

The simplest fiscal theory in steady-state with a constant surplus/GDP ratio says

$$\frac{B_t}{P_t y_t} = \int_{u=0}^{\infty} e^{-ru} \frac{s}{y} \frac{y_{t+u}}{y_t} du = \frac{s}{y} \int_{u=0}^{\infty} e^{-(r-g)u} du = \frac{s/y}{r-g}. \tag{6.2}$$

So, a real interest rate rise accompanying more growth tempers the long-run or present value effect of growth.

If $\gamma = 1$, then r and g rise and fall one for one, and higher or lower growth has no effect on the value of debt. We typically think $\gamma > 1$, in which case higher growth *lowers* the value of debt and vice versa. The discount rate effect is larger than the cash flow effect.

6.2.1   Sources of Low Interest Rates and Their Durability

As I write in 2021, real interest rates have been on a steady downward trend since 1980. Why did real interest rates decline? How long will low interest rates and consequent low interest costs last? The answer to the former is key to speculating on the latter.

Long-run growth also slowed down, tragically, with an especially clear decline since 2000. A benchmark that r fell because g fell, as described by (6.1) with $\gamma \approx 2$ makes sense to consider. The rise in the value of government debt, the steady decline in inflation, the decline in long-run growth and the somewhat larger decline in real interest rates, all fit together in this interpretation.

The reverse of this story suggests a paradoxical worry. Suppose growth were to return to its previous level, up from 2% to 4%. That happy event would, in this story, result in a greater rise in real interest rates. The present value of surpluses would then *fall*, requiring either inflation or a fiscal adjustment.

Should we fear a return to growth? I think not, because of the most important point left out so far: The surplus-to-GDP ratio is much improved by a higher level of GDP. If we write $s(y)/y$, not s/y, we may make the intuitive case that a return to strong growth would be a fiscal bonanza, despite the higher discount rates and interest costs that such an event would imply. Strongly growing countries seldom have fiscal troubles or inflation.

A lower marginal product of capital, $r = \theta f'(k)$ is the first place to look for a lower interest rate and lower growth rate. Ultimately, changes in technology θ are the central driving force of long-run economic growth. Why might the marginal product of capital be declining? Why is growth declining? There are lots of stories. Perhaps the shift of the economy to information and services means we need less capital than we needed in the era of steel mills and car factories. But the cries for languishing infrastructure, for massive green investments, as well as a quick look at any less developed country suggests plenty of need for capital. Moreover, a shift to less capital-intensive production should increase output, as products need fewer inputs. Less productivity growth θ is a more natural cause, but why? It could be the result of increasing regulation and barriers to entry and competition. Or, if the techno-pessimists are right (Bloom et al. (2020), Gordon (2016)), it could be that we are just running out of ideas, either temporarily or permanently. However, this is all shaky speculation for government debt, as capital is risky, and its expected return depends more on the risk premium than on the level of real interest rates.

The changing risk of nominal bonds is a second basic force for a low government debt discount rate. This and remaining forces are unrelated to growth, so lower rates are a directly deflationary force and vice versa. Since the sharp inflation decline in the 1980s, and especially since 2000, government debt has become a reliable negative-beta security. Recessions see deflation or disinflation and lower long-term nominal interest rates, and thus a positive ex post real return for government bonds when everything else is collapsing. Such a negative beta results in average returns *below* the real risk-free rate.

Much discussion of declining interest rates focuses on more novel ideas, such as a "savings glut," demographic changes, central bank interest rate and quantitative easing policy, special demands for U.S. government debt by foreign central banks, "exorbitant privilege" stemming from the fact that much trade is invoiced in dollars, a liquidity premium due to the usefulness of Treasury securities as collateral in financial transactions, or a more general "scarcity" of "safe assets" despite the rapidly rising supply of government debt. (Bansal and Coleman (1996); Krishnamurthy and Vissing-Jorgensen (2012) is a classic.)

All are contentious. The trend to lower interest rates has been steady since 1980, with no sign of the interventions of central banks, QE, or any other actions to artificially hold down rates. (Cochrane (2018) Figure 1 makes this clear.) And just how central banks could drive a 40-year trend in real interest rates, or decade-long risk premiums requires novel monetary and financial economics. The "safe asset" demand does not appear in portfolio theory, so it must be somewhat psychological. Assets can be risky yet instantly liquid; for example, stock index ETFs. Goods may be invoiced or paid for in dollars, but those dollars bought seconds before the transaction. U.S. Treasuries are useful collateral, but the spread between Treasury and corporate AAA or other illiquid debt securities is less than one percent, and Euro and Japanese debt has lower yields still than in the United States. Old people usually dissave. Still, each of these frictions offers the chance to add a few basis points, or interesting spreads, on top of the bigger picture, and in a manner unrelated to growth g.

Once we state economic forces that may lie behind the trend to lower interest rates, however, we see many forces that could rapidly reverse rather than an immutable law of nature.

The financial, friction-based, or policy-based stories can change especially quickly. Negative bond beta and flight to quality is not written in stone. In an economy subject to stagflation, such as the United States in the late 1970s, or in countries subject to frequent debt and currency crises and flights from, rather than to, local currency in bad times, we see higher inflation in bad times, not the current opposite correlation. In countries where bad times coincide with periodic government crises, interest rates may rise, not fall, in recessions. (Campbell, Pflueger, and Viceira (2020) document a shift in bond beta from positive to negative around 1980. However, they focus on high-frequency financial correlations. A business cycle frequency investigation of my consumption-beta speculation beckons.) If it's all central banks' doing, then it will reverse as soon as central banks change policy.

It is remarkable in the broad sweep of history that advanced country nominal bonds are considered default-free, markets seem to believe they will never be inflated away, and they consequently enjoy such low interest rates, compounded by liquidity premiums. This situation reverses centuries of experience with sovereign debt and the experience of most of the rest of the world. Doubts about the sanctity of sovereign debt in an economic, medical, or military crisis, with the background of so much debt and so many unfunded promises, could rapidly change the return investors require to roll over that debt.

6.3 Crashes and Breakouts

Inflation and currency crashes are asymmetric. I explore a little model of this asymmetry, which also shows how inflation and loss of monetary control can emerge suddenly. Governments promise to repay debt at a price level target, but face an upper limit on surpluses. In the unconstrained region, the price level is unaffected by surpluses and deficits, and higher interest rates lower inflation. In the constrained region, deficits cause immediate inflation, and higher interest rates only raise future inflation. The economy switches endogenously from the unconstrained to constrained region as debts or deficits build up, or when monetary policy tries a large interest rate increase.

Currency devaluations and sudden inflations are more common than upward jumps in currency values and sudden deflations. Miller (2021) presents a simple model that produces this behavior. The model also offers a useful warning for the current situation: how larger debts may sneak up and suddenly lead to inflation and powerless monetary policy.

Use the two-period model with a fiscal rule as in Section 2.5.1. The surplus s_1 pays off debt B_0 at a price level target P^*, but now there is a maximum surplus the government can or is willing to raise,

$$s_1 = \min\left(\frac{B_0}{P^*}, s_1^{\max}\right).$$

Equilibrium still consists of

$$\frac{B_0}{P_1} = s_1$$

$$\frac{B_{-1}}{P_0} = s_0 + \beta E_0 s_1.$$

The central bank sets an interest rate target i_0.

The two regimes of Section 2.5.1 now emerge endogenously. So long as $s_1 < s_1^{\max}$, we have $P_1 = P^*$, $P_0 = P^*/[\beta(1 + i_0)]$, unaffected by fiscal shocks. Additional deficits s_0 are financed by greater bond sales B_0 and repaid by greater surpluses s_1 with no effect on P_0, P_1. Monetary policy works in the standard way: If the central bank raises the interest rate target, it lowers P_0, leaving $P_1 = P^*$ alone.

Once over the limit, with $s_1 = s_1^{\max}$, we have

$$\frac{B_{-1}}{P_0} = s_0 + \beta s_1^{\max}$$

$$\frac{B_0}{P_1} = s_1^{\max}.$$

Any s_0 flows immediately into inflation P_0. Larger nominal rates i_0 have no effect on P_0 and just increase inflation P_1.

The condition $s_1 < s_1^{\max}$ occurs for

$$\beta(1 + i_0)\frac{B_{-1}}{P^*} - s_0 < \beta s_1^{\max}.$$

A lot of outstanding debt B_{-1}, big deficits s_0, or a large nominal interest rate forcing a low P_0 can push the economy over the limit.

So, slowly increase debt B_{-1} or deficits s_0. We have no inflation despite deficits. When the central bank wants to lower inflation, it raises the interest rate i_0, and inflation P_0 dutifully declines.

At some point, though, the wall is breached. Perhaps debt B_{-1} has grown too large. Perhaps the deficit s_0 is too large. Perhaps the Congress's willingness to fight future inflation with austerity $s_1^{\max}$ declines. Perhaps the central bank raises rates too much, asking for too much fiscal backing via a too-large rise in i_0. Now, all of a sudden, deficits s_0 cause inflation, and further central bank interest rate increases i_0 do nothing to stop it, and just fuel later inflation. The story is an obvious warning.

Miller adds a probability distribution over $s_1^{\max}$, and specifies that people can learn the value of $s_1^{\max}$ at a cost. As the probability of $s_1 > s_1^{\max}$ increases, people suddenly pay the cost to learn the true state. If it is the bad state, the price level jumps up discontinuously.

We have an apparent run or multiple equilibrium jump to inflation and currency crash, despite no current deficits or big news about the future.

6.4   What If $r < g$?

What if the rate of return on government debt is lower than the economy's growth rate, $r < g$? Is the present value infinite and fiscal theory either invalid, or predicts immense deflation? No, or at least not necessarily.

What if $r < g$? With a constant surplus-to-GDP ratio s/y, and an economy that grows at rate g, with perfect foresight and real interest rate r, the government debt valuation equation is

$$\frac{b_t}{y_t} = \frac{B_t}{P_t y_t} = \int_{\tau=0}^{\infty} e^{-(r-g)\tau} \frac{s}{y} d\tau = \frac{1}{r-g} \frac{s}{y}. \tag{6.3}$$

With $r < g$, the present value of surpluses is then apparently infinite. Is this a case in which the fiscal theory must give up? The rest of this section argues no.

The $r < g$ question is central in current debates over whether U.S. fiscal policy is sustainable. The question for us is whether $r < g$ is an empirically relevant trouble for fiscal theory. The questions are related, but not identical.

Generally, fiscal theory applies so long as government debt is not a free lunch, so long as greater debts today must be repaid by greater surpluses in the future, so long as the present value of surpluses is well defined. Whether that is true or not depends on the source of $r < g$. If we see $r < g$ because of liquidity or uncertainty, then present values can remain well defined and fiscal theory applies. In these cases, the average return on government bonds is misleading, as the properly discounted value of government surpluses converges and behaves well.

6.4.1   Sustainability and Fiscal Theory in Risk-Free Analysis

In a perfect foresight frictionless fiscal theory model, $r < g$ implies price-level indeterminacy, not infinity. However, $r < g$ must be truly permanent. A long period of $r < g$ makes debt easier to repay, but the present value still holds. With permanent $r < g$ and stochastic surpluses, an upper bound on debt-to-GDP ratio restores the present value and fiscal theory.

The debt-to-GDP ratio evolves as

$$\frac{d}{dt}\left(\frac{b_t}{y_t}\right) = (r_t - g_t)\frac{b_t}{y_t} - \frac{s_t}{y_t}. \tag{6.4}$$

$r < g$ seems to offer a delicious scenario: Run a sequence of large primary deficits $s_t < 0$, which increase the debt. Then, just keep rolling over the debt without raising surpluses. Debt grows at r, GDP grows at g, and the debt-to-GDP ratio slowly declines at rate $r - g$.

With $r < g$, the debt-to-GDP ratio converges on its own, with no additional surpluses. The fiscal expansion apparently has no cost.

Indeterminacy, not infinity, is the potential problem for fiscal theory when $r < g$. A deflation raises the initial value of nominal debt, $b_0 = B_0/P_0$. Again, the larger debt-to-GDP ratio melts away, for any price level P_0, with no change in primary surpluses. Technically, if $r < g$, we should solve the differential equation (6.4) backward,

$$\frac{b_t}{y_t} = \int_{\tau=0}^{t} e^{(r-g)\tau} \frac{s_{t-\tau}}{y_{t-\tau}} d\tau + e^{(r-g)t} \frac{b_0}{y_0}. \tag{6.5}$$

The integral tells us what the value of debt is for any *history* of surpluses and initial value of the debt.

For these arguments to work, the $r < g$ opportunity must truly be permanent. If the $r < g$ opportunity fades away, fiscal theory reemerges. In the same scenario, suppose that after 20 years of $r - g = -1\%$, the economy returns to $r - g = +1\%$. Then in order to avoid a debt-to-GDP explosion, we return to solving the differential equation forward,

$$\frac{b_t}{y_t} = \int_{\tau=0}^{20} e^{0.01\tau} \frac{s_{t+\tau}}{y_{t+\tau}} d\tau + e^{0.01 \times 20} \int_{\tau=20}^{\infty} e^{-0.01(\tau-20)} \frac{s_{t+\tau}}{y_{t+\tau}} d\tau.$$

The debt-to-GDP ratio converges for 20 years, but then values of debt different from this forward-looking integral lead to explosions.

Sustainability and determinacy differ in this case. In the same situation, one could well argue that while the fiscal expansion is not entirely cost free, it's a good deal. The debt-to-GDP ratio declines for 20 years, requiring only $e^{-0.2} = 80\%$ repayment. One might argue likewise that fiscal theory has less force if large changes in value of debt today respond to small declines in far-future surpluses. But the point here is just to understand the technical fact of determinacy. If we wish quantitative assessment, especially of the force of equilibrium conditions—tail versus dog arguments—we need a richer model.

Basic economics tells us there must be a limit to the opportunity offered by even permanent $r < g$. Can the government really borrow, send us money, and never raise taxes, simply rolling over the debt and watching GDP grow faster? If our government can borrow arbitrarily, and never repay debts, why should any of us repay debts? The government could borrow to pay our debts too. Why should we pay taxes? Why should we work or save? Let the government borrow, send us checks, and we can all just stay home and order from Amazon. Obviously not. But why not?

Well, obviously, because someone has to work at Amazon, and at the companies that make things that Amazon sells. The government can send us *cash*, but it does not send us real resources. We have to trade cash for real resources, to someone who wants that cash. If the government sends us real resources it too has to buy them. The real supply side of the economy limits the opportunity for a consumption bonanza. If nobody works, g declines. If nobody saves, or if government debt issues absorb all savings, the capital stock depreciates and the marginal product of capital and interest rate r rise, "crowding out." Marginal $r - g$ is not average $r - g$. As the government exploits it, the $r < g$ opportunity vanishes.

If r is low because of a liquidity premium, a money-like demand for government debt, "exorbitant privilege," that opportunity also swiftly declines as debt increases. Large debt-to-GDP ratios also leave the government more open to a doom loop, absent from this perfect certainty theorizing. If markets sniff a default or inflation in the future, they demand higher real interest rates. Higher rates raise interest costs, which means a faster rise in debt/GDP. Investors get more nervous still, and eventually the feared default or inflation happens.

Without writing down a full general equilibrium model, especially one with these sorts of frictions, we can think through some of these economic limitations by imposing an upper limit on the debt-to-GDP ratio. Then, even permanent $r < g$ does not imply an economic perpetual motion machine, or a globally indeterminate price level. In reality, there is no precise, hard and fast limit. High debt-to-GDP ratios can persist a long time, see Japan, while other countries have experienced debt crises with quite low debt-to-GDP ratios. Investors' willingness to roll over debt combines current debt and the likelihood of fiscal sobriety ahead, expectations of which can change quickly.

The delicious opportunity is first reduced to a local possibility: The U.S. government could borrow an additional finite amount, until r rises to meet g, or until we reach the debt-to-GDP limit. For fiscal theory, we might see a local indeterminacy as long as the value of debt is below that upper bound, and thus a limit on potential deflation.

But this view relies on permanent zero surpluses as well as a permanent $r < g$. Suppose we generate the surplus by an AR(1), $ds_t = -\eta(s_t - \bar{s}) + \sigma_s dz_s$. An AR(1) ranges over the entire real line, as does the integral of an AR(1) (6.5). So at some point the future debt-to-GDP ratio following (6.5) will eventually exceed any bound. That fact means that the initial value of debt b_0/y_0 in (6.5) is not sustainable. People will not lend to the government knowing that a default, inflation, or whatever happens at the upper bound is coming sooner or later. Even if we limit the support of the surplus distribution, but let it follow a stationary process, the integral of the surplus eventually exceeds any bound. You eventually flip 100 heads in a row.

The result now seems to be that *no* value of debt b_0/y_0 is sustainable. But the conclusion I take is that with an upper limit on debt-to-GDP ratio, we must already imagine a managed surplus process. As debt starts to grow, the government increases surpluses so as to avoid the boundary. A higher value of debt, induced by deflation, will push the government over the boundary absent a rise in future surpluses. A plan that exceeds the bound by a finite amount will lead to an initial price level rise, lowering the initial value of debt, until the government is again able to keep debt below the boundary. We are back to global determinacy of the price level and fiscal theory.

Limited debt and limited time act in much the same way. They restore the proposition that deficits must be repaid by future surpluses, lacking which the value of debt must fall to reestablish a sustainable path.

6.4.2 Flows and the $r = g$ Discontinuity

Present values seem discontinuous at $r = g$. The flow of surplus or deficit that $r - g$ requires or can fund is smooth across the $r = g$ boundary, so sensible economic interpretation of the formulas should also be smooth. Small $r < g$ is unlikely to undermine the need to repay debt, present values, and fiscal theory.

It seems that a theoretical cliff separates $r > g$ from $r < g$. If r is one basis point (0.01%) above g, we solve the differential equation forward to a present value, debts must be repaid, and fiscal theory applies. If r is one basis point below g, we solve the differential equation (6.4) backward, public debts never need to be repaid, and fiscal theory is empty. Obviously not. So why not?

Looking at flows makes sense of this apparent $r = g$ discontinuity. The steady-state of (6.4) features a surplus equal to $r - g$ times the value of debt. As we move from $r - g = 0.01\%$ to $r - g = -0.01\%$ at 100% debt-to-GDP ratio, we move from a steady 0.01% of GDP ($2 billion) surplus, to a steady 0.01% ($2 billion) of GDP deficit. That's not going to finance anyone's spending wish list! *This* transition is clearly continuous. Likewise, the opportunity to grow out of debt with $r - g = -0.01\%$, means 150% debt to GDP will, with zero primary surpluses, resolve back to 50% debt to GDP in $-\log(0.5/1.5)/0.0001 = 11,000$ years. On the other hand, $r - g = +0.01\%$ means an "explosive" debt-to-GDP ratio, starting at the same 150%, it only explodes to $150 \times e^{0.0001 \times 11,000} = 450\%$ after the same 11,000 years.

Thus, a sensible understanding of how equations map to the economy is continuous as r passes g. If there is a "wealth effect," a transversality condition violation in a debt-to-GDP ratio that rises by a factor of three from 150% to 450% in 11,000 years, then there is surely a "wealth effect" in a debt-to-GDP ratio that takes 11,000 years to decay by a factor of three from 150% to 50% in the same time period.

6.4.3   The Empirical Relevance of $r < g$

Credible values of $r < g$ cannot fund the U.S. structural primary deficits. $r < g$ offers the chance of a small persistent average primary deficit, but realistic variation in deficits still must be repaid, or cause inflation.

The $r < g$ debate is questionably relevant to current (2021) U.S. fiscal policy issues, and thus the related question whether fiscal theory applies to the U.S. economy. The U.S. government is running $1 trillion deficits in good times, 5% of GDP, and a cumulative $5 trillion, 25% of GDP, in each decade's crises. And then in about 10 years, unfunded Social Security, Medicare, and other entitlements really kick in. The debt-to-GDP ratio is growing exponentially, and forecast to continue to do so. (See, for example, the Congressional Budget Office (2020) long-term budget outlook.)

The $r < g$ scenario starts with zero surpluses and therefore slowly declining debt to GDP. It then allows for a "one-time" fiscal expansion, or a one-time deflation that increases the value of debt, followed by decades-long mean reversion of debt/GDP with zero primary surpluses. But zero primary surpluses—taxes equal spending for two generations, and gently declining debt-to-GDP ratios—are a debt hawk's dream come true. That's not our situation.

In flow terms, $r < g$ of 1% with 100% debt/GDP allows a 1% of GDP steady primary deficit, not 5% in good times, 25% in bad times, and then pay for Social Security and health care. If we had $r < g$ of 5% or more, if the debt-to-GDP ratio were already following a declining path that could be bumped to a higher level, we would tell a different story. But that's not the size of the problem or the nature of the opportunity.

The U.S. fiscal path of large permanent primary deficits is unsustainable, even if low interest rates last another 50 years, with $r < g$ of 1% or so. Our fiscal path must end in default, inflation, higher surpluses, or higher growth. Even default or inflation would not solve the fiscal problem, as the fiscal path of continued deficits would remain unsustainable. Sharply higher surpluses or higher growth would have to follow default or inflation.

So what does $r < g$, by something on the order of 1%, mean for the United States and similar western economies? $r < g$ may shift the *average* surplus to a slight 1% of GDP or so perpetual deficit, just as seigniorage allows a slight perpetual deficit. But any substantial *variation* in deficits about that average—large business cycles, crises, wars, the U.S. green new deal or the European green deal—must be met by a substantial period of above-average surpluses, to bring back debt to GDP in a reasonable time. The *variation about the average* remains well described by the standard forward-looking model.

The same insight applies to fiscal theory. With small $r < g$ that may not last forever, and with limits on the debt-to-GDP ratio, variation in the value of debt still has to be met by variation in subsequent surpluses. If surpluses are not sufficient, the initial debt will still devalue via inflation. The linearized identities can apply to deviations about a small negative average surplus.

6.4.4   Population, Demographics, and Dynamic Efficiency

Growth theory struggles to produce a permanent $r < g$. Population growth helps, but population growth must eventually end.

The basic representative agent, perfect foresight growth model does not easily deliver $r < g$. With utility function $\int e^{-\delta t} c_t^{1-\gamma}/(1-\gamma)dt$, the dynastic (cares about their children) representative agent's first-order conditions give

$$r = \delta + \gamma g. \tag{6.6}$$

We usually think that $\delta > 0$, people prefer the present to the future, and that $\gamma \geq 1$. Hence $r > g$.

One can deliver $r < g$ with small δ, $\gamma < 1$ and low g. However, in this case the transversality condition is more stringent than a nonexplosive debt-to-GDP ratio. Using even $\delta = 0$,

$$\lim_{T \to \infty} u'(c_T)b_T = c_T^{1-\gamma}\frac{b_T}{c_T}.$$

For $\gamma > 1$, steady b_T/c_T and growth in c_T implies the transversality condition. But for $\gamma < 1$, the right-hand side continues to grow as consumption grows. A steady debt/GDP ratio is not enough.

Population growth n allows $r < g$ more easily. If people do not care about their children or immigrants, the consumer's first-order conditions are

$$r = \delta + \gamma(g - n).$$

Government finances get the benefit of more people, and thus an income stream that grows faster than the individual income stream that is connected to the interest rate. Jones (2020a) links population growth to the long-term growth rate, multiplying its effect. Again, sustainability, fiscal theory, and endogenous growth need to be better integrated.

Still, the U.S. population growth rate was only 0.4% in 2020. Population growth has been trending downwards along with the real interest rate, so cannot account for the interest rate decline. And all estimates say population growth will slow further, raising r or lowering g. Barring interstellar colonization, with trade to send resources back to us, population growth must eventually end.

Demographics are sometimes said to drive the decline in real interest rate. The baby-boom generation entered their high saving years. If so, $r < g$ will soon pass, as the United States, Europe, Japan, and China age and people start to draw down savings.

Population growth can allow the government to take a little from each generation and give it to the previous one, which can be implemented by government debt. The government can run a slow Ponzi scheme, giving each generation a rate of return equal to the population growth rate. In such dynamically inefficient overlapping generations models, the present value condition fails. Government debt is not infinitely valuable however, and cannot overcome production limitations. Beware models that imply we can all stop working, and government debt is a free lunch. Even without a free lunch, population growth must go on literally forever for this Ponzi scheme to raise welfare. For this reason I don't pay much attention to dynamic inefficiency in fiscal theory. But I acknowledge the lacunae. Investigation of nominal debt in a dynamically inefficient environment seems still an interesting theoretical question.

These thoughts may all be reasons that the $r < g$ debate has focused on frictions rather than simple growth theory.

6.4.5   Liquidity

Measuring $r < g$ from our world and applying perfect foresight frictionless models is dangerous. Liquidity, a money-like aspect to government bonds, can lower their rate of return and produce $r < g$. This phenomenon can only be exploited in a limited amount. A government may enjoy seigniorage, but printing more money leads only to inflation. Marginal r is higher than average r, so substantial deficits still must be repaid. The present value relation and fiscal theory still hold, discounting by marginal utility. Attempting to discount using rates of return on government debt leads to misleading formulas that blow up.

Liquidity, a money-like aspect to government bonds, can produce $r < g$. But present values hold, and the fiscal theory continues to work. It is dangerous to discount at the government bond return rather than the stochastic discount factor.

A government that finances itself entirely by non-interest-bearing money is a clear and simple example. This government can run slight deficits forever, earning a steady seigniorage revenue proportional to GDP growth. But this opportunity does not scale. If the government tries a large fiscal expansion by printing money, it creates inflation, and real money demand falls. In the extreme, additional money printing raises inflation and lowers real money demand so much that it generates less revenue. For this economy, the rate of return on government debt is the negative of the inflation rate $r = -\pi$ so $r < g$. Yet the present value relation is well defined and determines the price level.

To see how these statements work, suppose the real risk-free rate r^f satisfies $r^f > g$. The government finances itself entirely from money, so the rate of return on government debt is $r = -\pi < g$. There is a demand for non-interest-bearing money

$$MV(i) = Py.$$

Differentiating, steady-state (constant i) money growth equals inflation plus economic growth,

$$\frac{1}{M}\frac{dM}{dt} = \pi + g.$$

Deficits financed by printing money are

$$\frac{dM_t}{dt} = -P_t s_t. \tag{6.7}$$

There is a steady-state with constant money-to-GDP ratio, $M/(Py)$, at which

$$(\pi + g)\frac{M}{Py} = -\frac{s}{y}. \tag{6.8}$$

The government can finance a steady deficit equal to inflation + growth times real money demand.

Now, how do we think of this money-financed government and its price level in terms of present values? Recall (3.54), the present value relation with money and debt. I specialize to certainty, a real interest rate r^f, no interest on money $i^m = 0$, and an endowment y_t growing at rate g. Expressing debt as a fraction of GDP we then have

$$\frac{M_t + B_t}{P_t y_t} = E_t \int_{\tau=t}^{\infty} e^{-(r^f - g)(\tau - t)}\left(\frac{s_\tau}{y_\tau} + i_\tau \frac{M_\tau}{P_\tau y_\tau}\right) d\tau. \tag{6.9}$$

The value of debt is the present value of surpluses, plus the interest savings due to the fact that money provides a stream of liquidity benefits.

In (6.9) we see also that in the steady-state with $i > 0$, the government can run a steady primary deficit, $s_\tau < 0$. You may have scratched your head about a positive present value with perpetually negative surpluses, but the combined middle term of (6.9) is positive. With surpluses given by (6.8) and $i = r^f + \pi$, that middle term is

$$\frac{s}{y} + i\frac{M}{Py} = (r^f - g)\frac{M}{Py}.$$

The seigniorage term is larger than the deficit term, and "pays back" the initial value of debt at the real rate of interest.

Yes, fiscal theory applies even with non-interest-bearing money that is never formally retired or repaid. The value of money is the present value of its benefits.

Equation (6.9) makes clear that if the government does not want inflation, any additional deficits must be paid for by issuing interest-bearing debt, which pays $r^f > g$, and repaid by subsequent larger surpluses discounted at r^f. We have an example in which the marginal $r = r^f > g$, though the average rate of return on government debt $r = -\pi < g$.

Now, what happens if we try to discount using the rate of return $r = -\pi < g$ on the government bond portfolio? The steady-state real money-to-GDP ratio follows[1]

$$\frac{d}{dt}\left(\frac{M_t}{P_t y_t}\right) + \frac{M_t}{P_t y_t}(\pi + g) = -\frac{s_t}{y_t} \tag{6.10}$$

or equivalently

$$\frac{d}{dt}\left(\frac{M_t}{P_t y_t}\right) + \frac{M_t}{P_t y_t}(i - r^f + g) = -\frac{s_t}{y_t}. \tag{6.11}$$

From (6.11), and with $r^f > g$ so integrating forward, we get (6.9), discounting using r^f and counting the interest rate term as seigniorage. But we can also integrate forward the equivalent (6.10), effectively using $r = -\pi$ as a discount rate, yielding

$$\frac{M_t}{P_t y_t} = \int_{\tau=t}^{T} e^{(\pi+g)(\tau-t)} \frac{s_\tau}{y_\tau} d\tau + e^{(\pi+g)(T-t)} \frac{M_T}{P_T y_T}. \tag{6.12}$$

Here, the terminal condition explodes for the steady-state. Since the left-hand side is finite, the present value integral also explodes negatively. The value of government debt is the same, but we express it with a present value and a terminal condition that each explode in opposite directions.

Now compare (6.12) with (6.9), including a terminal condition and without debt,

$$\frac{M_t}{P_t y_t} = \int_{\tau=t}^{T} e^{-(r^f-g)(\tau-t)} \left(\frac{s_\tau}{y_\tau} + i_\tau \frac{M_\tau}{P_\tau y_\tau}\right) d\tau + e^{-(r^f-g)(T-t)} \frac{M_T}{P_T y_T}. \tag{6.13}$$

Both the present value and the terminal condition converge.

Both (6.13) and (6.12) are correct. We just integrate forward differently. The question is, which expression is more useful or insightful? Is it more useful to think of the liquidity services of money as providing a convenience yield flow, seigniorage in the form of a lower interest cost of debt, which we discount at the real interest rate? Or is it more insightful to think of the liquidity services of money as lowering the discount rate, thereby thinking of a present value and terminal condition that explode in opposite directions?

---

1. To get to (6.10), differentiate

$$\frac{d}{dt}\left(\frac{M_t}{P_t y_t}\right) = \frac{M_t}{P_t y_t}\left(\frac{1}{M_t}\frac{dM_t}{dt} - \pi - g\right).$$

Then use (6.7) to get

$$\frac{d}{dt}\left(\frac{M_t}{P_t y_t}\right) = -\frac{M_t}{P_t y_t}\left(\frac{P_t}{M_t}s_t + \pi + g\right),$$

and rearrange.

I prefer the former. The latter can quickly lead to mistakes. You may take the terminal condition limit first, and conclude that the value of debt is infinite. You may think that the terminal condition is a "bubble" that is "mined" for surpluses. (The terminology is from Brunnermeier, Merkel, and Sannikov (2020), who explore a related model.) You may forget about the present value integral and conclude that the value of debt is infinite. You can miss the fact that additional surpluses still need to be repaid and conclude that money-financed expansion is painless.

The central difference between the two expressions is that in (6.9) and (6.13) we discount using the consumer's marginal rate of substitution,

$$e^{-\rho(\tau-t)}\frac{u'(c_\tau)}{u'(c_t)} = \frac{\Lambda_\tau}{\Lambda_t} = e^{-r^f(\tau-t)}.$$

The terminal condition in (6.9) converges because the transversality condition specifies discounting with the marginal rate of substitution,

$$\lim_{T\to\infty}\left[e^{-\rho(T-t)}\frac{u'(c_T)}{u'(c_t)}\frac{M_T}{P_T}\right] = \lim_{T\to\infty}\left[e^{-r^f(T-t)}\frac{M_T}{P_T}\right] = 0.$$

Even when the transversality condition holds, the terminal condition does not necessarily hold discounting with the ex post return, as it does not in this example.

If we ignore the terminal condition in (6.12), we see a clear mistake. Since the expression is a present value discounting at the government bond return, we can phrase the mistake as using a rate of return measured in a world with a liquidity premium, and applying a frictionless present value formula.

I reiterate the main point: By conventional sustainability accounting, this is an "$r < g$" example, since the rate of return on government debt is less than the growth rate. Yet the value of debt is finite, transversality conditions hold, government debt is not a free lunch, and the fiscal theory determines the price level. That fact is easiest to see if we discount surpluses and the convenience yield of government debt with the stochastic discount factor, and only use alternative discount factors when they happen to converge and therefore give the same result.

6.4.6   Discount Rates versus Rates of Return

One-period substitute discount factors, such as the inverse rate of return, may not work in an infinite period context. One can still use such formulas, including in our linearizations, if one checks that the terms converge.

This example illustrates a more general theoretical subtlety. One can always discount one-period payoffs with the ex post rate of return. It is trivially true that

$$1 = E_t\left(R_{t+1}^{-1}R_{t+1}\right).$$

It does not follow that one can always discount infinite streams of payoffs with the ex post return. It can happen that the present value of cash flows, discounted by the stochastic discount factor, is finite and well behaved, that both terms of

$$p_t = E_t \left(\sum_{j=1}^{T} \frac{\Lambda_{t+j}}{\Lambda_t} d_{t+j} \right) + E_t \left(\frac{\Lambda_{t+T}}{\Lambda_t} p_{t+T} \right)$$

converge, yet if we attempt to discount using returns $R_{t+1} = (p_{t+1} + d_{t+1})/p_t$,

$$p_t = E_t \left(\sum_{j=1}^{T} \prod_{k=1}^{j} \frac{1}{R_{t+k}} d_{t+j} \right) + E_t \left(\prod_{k=1}^{T} \frac{1}{R_{t+k}} p_{t+T} \right), \tag{6.14}$$

the present value term and the limiting term explode in opposite directions. Moreover, where my money example generated this behavior from a convenience yield, this explosion can happen in a frictionless market when all assets are priced by the stochastic discount factor. Two examples follow.

It is not *always* wrong to discount by the ex post return. The present value discounted at the ex post return is correct, if the sum and terminal value converge. When they do converge, discounting with returns is quite useful. For example, it underlies the linearizations. But that the sums converge is an extra assumption, not guaranteed by transversality conditions. And the condition that the second term in (6.14) converges is a stochastic version of $r > g$.

Thus, we have a warning that the *linearizations*, which use ex post returns to discount, may show a nonconverging present value term and a nonconverging terminal term. But we don't need general theorems. We can examine that convergence directly, and use the return-based linearizations when sums converge and not use them when they don't converge. Moreover, the linearizations apply to deviations from the mean. So when we subtract a mean surplus-to-GDP ratio, potentially negative, the linearizations may converge for deviations about that mean, and remain valid.

The issue is a bit open in asset pricing. For one-period returns, it is convenient to construct alternative discount factors, especially linear discount factors, in this one-asset case $\Lambda_{t+1}/\Lambda_t = R_{t+1}/E_t(R_{t+1}^2)$. Cochrane (2005a) is full of such tricks. But these alternative discount factors do not always deliver convergent terminal conditions in infinite-period settings. Extending the substitute discount factors to infinite sums is a potentially useful investigation in theoretical asset pricing, opening the door to a view focused on streams of payoffs rather than one-period returns.

6.4.7   Aggregate Uncertainty

Measuring $r < g$ from our world and applying perfect foresight models is dangerous. With aggregate uncertainty, precautionary saving can drive down the interest rate to $r < g$. Discounting using marginal utility, the present value formulas hold and fiscal theory works. Discounting using the average return on government debt leads to misleading formulas that blow up.

In perfect foresight models with no liquidity distortions, all discount factors are the same. Uncertainty opens wedges between the risk-free rate, the average return on government bonds, the physical rate of return from capital investment, and the consumer's marginal rate of substitution. With uncertainty, we again can have an average return on government bonds $E(r)$ that is less than the average rate of economic growth $E(g)$, yet the properly discounted present value of government debt is well defined, debts must be repaid by surpluses, and the fiscal theory applies. Here too it is a tempting mistake to take the average return and average growth rate, plug them into a perfect certainty model, and come falsely to the opposite conclusion.

We can see the issue in a simple model. Write the equation that debt equals the present value of surpluses as

$$\frac{b_t}{y_t} = E_t \left[\sum_{j=1}^{\infty} \beta^j \frac{u'(c_{t+j})}{u'(c_t)} \frac{y_{t+j}}{y_t} \frac{s_{t+j}}{y_{t+j}} \right]. \tag{6.15}$$

It is tempting but incorrect to move the expectation sign inside the sum, effectively using averages from an uncertain world as parameters in a perfect foresight formula. If we do that, we obtain

$$\sum_{j=1}^{\infty} E_t \left[\beta^j \frac{u'(c_{t+j})}{u'(c_t)} \right] E_t \left(\frac{y_{t+j}}{y_t} \right) E_t \left(\frac{s_{t+j}}{y_{t+j}} \right) = \sum_{j=1}^{\infty} \left(\frac{1+g}{1+r} \right)^j E_t \left(\frac{s_{t+j}}{y_{t+j}} \right), \tag{6.16}$$

where the right-hand equality specifies that consumption and GDP growth are independent over time.

But this is incorrect. It leaves out the covariance terms. The true present value can converge while this mistaken one explodes. For example, consider power utility and log-normal consumption, $c = y$ and a constant s/y. Now the terms of the correct formula (6.15) are

$$E_t \left[\frac{u'(c_{t+j})}{u'(c_t)} \frac{y_{t+j}}{y_t} \right] = E_t \left[\left(\frac{c_{t+j}}{c_t} \right)^{1-\gamma} \right] = e^{\left[(1-\gamma)g + (1-\gamma)^2 \sigma^2/2 \right] j},$$

while the terms of the incorrect $r - g$ version (6.16) are

$$E_t \left[\frac{u'(c_{t+j})}{u'(c_t)} \right] E_t \left(\frac{y_{t+j}}{y_t} \right) = E_t \left[\left(\frac{c_{t+j}}{c_t} \right)^{-\gamma} \right] E_t \left(\frac{c_{t+j}}{c_t} \right) = e^{\left[(1-\gamma)g + \gamma^2 \sigma^2/2 \right] j}.$$

With $\gamma > 1$ we have $(1 - \gamma)^2 < \gamma^2$. Thus, it is entirely possible that

$$e^{-\delta(1-\gamma)g + (1-\gamma)^2 \sigma^2/2} < 1 < e^{-\delta(1-\gamma)g + \gamma^2 \sigma^2/2},$$

where $\delta \equiv -\log(\beta)$. In this circumstance, using the risk-free rate r and average GDP growth g to discount indicates an explosive present value, where the correctly discounted present value is finite.

You may still be puzzled. After all, the rate of return on government debt is here the risk-free rate r. It is lower than the average growth rate of the economy g. If the government borrows and rolls over debt, the economy should outpace the growth of debt. And it will, *on average*. But the states of nature in which growth is bad, and debt outpaces growth, are states with high marginal utility, high contingent claims prices. These are exactly the states in which it is particularly painful to face fiscal austerity. Weighting states by marginal utility, we see a finite present value. The situation is similar to the classic finance trick of writing out-of-the money index put options and calling it arbitrage. It will work most of the time and on average. But when it fails, it fails at the most painful moment possible.

Bohn (1995) offers an example that connects well to the circumstance of government debt. (Cochrane (2021c) covers Bohn's example in more detail.) Consumption equals income. Growth is i.i.d., and a representative consumer has power utility. Growth is volatile enough to drive the risk-free rate below the growth rate. In the linearized formula,

$$r = \delta + \gamma g - \frac{1}{2}\gamma(\gamma - 1)\sigma^2 < g.$$

We had trouble above generating $r < g$ from a representative agent model. With uncertainty, precautionary saving can drive down interest rates. This effect is small for power utility, with γ not too large, and $\sigma \approx 0.01$. But it is a theoretical possibility for other parameters. Other utility functions such as habits, rare disasters, or alternative devices to match the equity premium, effectively large γ, also raise this precautionary saving effect. As with this example, they emphasize that risk premiums are first-order effects, and we need generally to discount in a way that recognizes risk premiums. If the real rate is 1% and the equity premium is 5%, discounting at the real rate is a major error.

Suppose the government keeps a constant debt/GDP ratio. At each date t the government borrows an amount equal to GDP, c_t, and then repays it the next period, paying $(1 + r)c_t$ at time $t + 1$. The primary surplus is then

$$s_t = (1 + r)c_{t-1} - c_t.$$

Now, the end-of-period value of government debt at time t, just after the government has borrowed c_t, is obviously, $b_t = c_t$. (It is more convenient for this example to look at end-of-period debt, which is the usual timing in asset pricing formulas.) Our job is to express that fact in terms of sensible present value relations.

If we construct a present value, discounting with marginal utility, we obtain

$$b_t = E_t\left[\sum_{j=1}^{T}\beta^j\left(\frac{c_{t+j}}{c_t}\right)^{-\gamma}s_{t+j}\right] + E_t\left[\beta^T\left(\frac{c_{t+T}}{c_t}\right)^{-\gamma}c_{t+T}\right]$$

$$= E_t\left\{\sum_{j=1}^{T}\beta^j\left(\frac{c_{t+j}}{c_t}\right)^{-\gamma}\left[(1 + r)c_{t+j-1} - c_{t+j}\right]\right\} + E_t\left[\beta^T\left(\frac{c_{t+T}}{c_t}\right)^{-\gamma}c_{t+T}\right].$$

The intermediate consumptions all cancel, leaving

$$b_t = \left\{ c_t - E_t \left[\beta^T \left(\frac{c_{t+T}}{c_t} \right)^{-\gamma} c_{t+T} \right] \right\} + E_t \left[\beta^T \left(\frac{c_{t+T}}{c_t} \right)^{-\gamma} b_{t+T} \right] = c_t. \quad (6.17)$$

The present value of borrowing c_{t+j} and repaying $(1+r)c_{t+j}$ the next period $t+j+1$ is zero, so only the first term, the time t value of $(1+r)c_t$ paid at time $t+1$ survives. The last term converges to zero, via the transversality condition.

Now try to discount at the risk-free rate, which is the government bond return.

$$b_t = \sum_{j=1}^{T} \left(\prod_{k=1}^{j} \frac{1}{R_{t+k}} \right) s_{t+j} + \left(\prod_{k=1}^{T} \frac{1}{R_{t+k}} \right) b_{t+T} =$$

$$= \sum_{j=1}^{T} \frac{(1+r)c_{t+j-1} - c_{t+j}}{(1+r)^j} + \frac{1}{(1+r)^T} c_{t+T}$$

$$b_t = \left(c_t - \frac{c_{t+T}}{(1+r)^T} \right) + \frac{c_{t+T}}{(1+r)^T}.$$

Taking expected value,

$$b_t = c_t \left[1 - \frac{(1+g)^T}{(1+r)^T} \right] + c_t \frac{(1+g)^T}{(1+r)^T}. \quad (6.18)$$

With $r < g$ the present value of cash flows term builds to negative infinity, and the terminal value builds to positive infinity.

Again, compare the present value discounted using marginal utility, (6.17), to the present value discounted using the ex post return (6.18). Both equations are correct. Which is more useful? At a minimum, the latter invites mistakes. The present value equation without the offsetting exploding terminal condition is wrong.

In sum, we have an example in which government debt pays the risk-free rate, the risk-free rate is below the economy's growth rate $r < g$, yet the value of debt equals the present value of future surpluses, additional deficits must be repaid by surpluses, and fiscal theory applies if one generalizes to nominal debt. Debt sustainability analysis and a present value that discount at the risk-free rate or government bond return give the wrong answer, as they ignore the high state prices of poor outcomes. Don't mix perfect certainty modeling with return measurements from an uncertain world. When in doubt, discount with marginal utility.

6.4.8 Summary

The key insight for fiscal theory: Do not give up just because the average ex post return on government debt is persistently a bit below the economy's growth rate!

Plausible values for $r < g$ are small, like plausible values of seigniorage, meaning that substantial deficits must still be repaid with subsequent surpluses. The present value of surpluses may be well defined, correctly discounting using the stochastic discount factor or consumer's marginal rate of substitution, where present value formulas that use the risk-free rate or the ex post rates of return on government debt explode. And, as Irving Fisher famously found out when in 1929 he declared stocks at a permanently higher plateau, beware trends. Interest rates could rise or growth could further slow.

The intersection of low interest rates, fiscal sustainability, and fiscal theory constitutes an active research area, and one's wish for a more definitive treatment should be a spur to more work on the question. Most prominently, perhaps, Blanchard (2019) investigates $r < g$ and the consequent possibility for a large fiscal expansion that has no fiscal cost. Given on the eve of an immense fiscal expansion, Blanchard's address is destined to be influential. Blanchard carefully outlines limitations of the "no fiscal cost" view, including crowding out and doom-loop scenarios. He considers the optimal size of debt and models with fiscal multipliers that add to the benefits of debt. As his sympathies side with expansion, his address is likely to be remembered either as opening our eyes to an unprecedented opportunity or as stoking the fires of disaster.

Bassetto and Cui (2018) is an excellent clear statement of many cases when low interest rates do and do not trouble fiscal theory, covering most of my points and more. They emphasize as I do that *why* interest rates are low is a key question. They give an example with large risk premiums, in which debt corresponds to a well-defined present value of surpluses, even though expected surpluses are always negative. Surpluses are low in high marginal utility states. They give a sophisticated model with debt in the utility function, generating analysis similar to the simple case with money that I present. Contrariwise, they exhibit an overlapping generations dynamically inefficient economy in which government debt is a free lunch, and present values do not converge.

Cochrane (2021c) emphasizes the quantitative failure of the argument for fiscal largesse: $r < g$ of 1% cannot finance 5% of GDP structural deficits and 30% of GDP crisis deficits.

Reis (2021) gives a new example in which the return on government debt is different from the marginal product of capital in a risky economy. Reis investigates an economy with uninsured individual risk, despite no aggregate risk, which also can drive r below g and separate the returns on government bonds from the marginal product of capital. In oversimplified terms, the volatility of consumption needed to drive down the interest rate via precautionary savings is too large, given modest risk aversion, to match aggregate consumption. But individuals may experience more volatile consumption. Mehrotra and Sergeyev (2021) construct a model with aggregate risk and rare disasters, in which again the present value of debt is well defined though $r < g$. See also Berentsen and Waller (2018), Brunnermeier, Merkel, and Sannikov (2020) with liquidity distortions in government bonds, and Williamson (2018).

6.5   Assets and Liabilities

What about other liabilities, like Social Security, pensions, health care and so on? What about the national parks or other assets? By and large, I suggest including them on the right-hand side as streams of state-contingent surpluses rather than include them as debt.

What about all the other assets and liabilities of the government? Social Security, pensions, Medicare, Medicaid, and social programs are all promises to pay people that act in some ways like government debt. Adding them up, depending on how one takes present values, one can compute a "fiscal gap," an effective debt, of $70 trillion to over $200 trillion (Kotlikoff and Michel (2015)), dwarfing the official $20 trillion (in 2020) federal debt.

The federal government also makes a lot of state-contingent promises, or has contingent liabilities. It offers deposit insurance. It is likely to bail out private and state and local pension funds, and student debt, and these bailouts are more likely in bad states of the world. It offers formal credit guarantees, including those on home mortgages that pass through Fannie Mae and Freddie Mac. Credit guarantees are a favorite method of offering subsidies to businesses. Unemployment insurance, food stamps and other social programs automatically create additional spending in recessions. The U.S. government is more and more likely to bail out banks, other financial institutions, and large corporations including auto makers and airlines.

The government has assets as well, including national parks and vast swaths of the Western states, spectrum and oil drilling rights, and toll roads.

Where do we put these assets and liabilities in the valuation equation? Marketable assets are easy to include on the right-hand side. Federal Reserve assets—loans to banks, private securities—belong there, though corresponding Federal Reserve (liabilities—reserves—also) belong on the left-hand side. The assets of countries with sovereign wealth funds belong on the right-hand side. But the chance that the Federal government would sell the national parks, and that it could raise resources in the trillions by doing so, seems remote.

I think such assets and liabilities are better treated by adding them to the uncertain, managed, and state-contingent flow of surpluses rather than try to compute present values, for the purpose of applying fiscal theory.

Social Security, health, and pensions are promises to pay, as coupon and principal are promises to pay. Social programs are formally "entitlements" to receive payment. However, the government can at any time reduce those promises without formal default. Many governments around the world have reformed pension and health payment systems in response to fiscal pressures. The United States will, eventually, do the same. There is a qualitative difference between interest and principal on 30-year U.S. Treasury debt and the promises to keep raising Social Security and health benefits for 30 years, that should make one hesitate to throw them into the same bucket.

More importantly, perhaps, these promises are not marketable debt, and they are long-term debt. There is no way to run on promised pension and health care payments. If you think the government will default, inflate, cut benefits, or if you just want the cash now, you cannot demand your share of Social Security or Medicare in a lump sum. You cannot sell your share to someone else. More than anything else, this feature drives me to think of them as state-contingent flows of surpluses on the right-hand side rather than as a present value on the left-hand side.

The government writes many implicit put options. But figuring out a market value of state-contingent, option-like liabilities and treating them like debt does not seem that productive. Perhaps I am too leery of complex option-pricing models, but it seems more productive to keep track of them as state-contingent payments, while also keeping track of the higher state prices when spending must be cut back.

Forecasts of future health and retirement payments, along with forecasts such as those of the Congressional Budget Office (CBO) of the overall budget, are clearly not forecasts, conditional expected values. They are "here is what will happen if you don't do something about this" warnings. What is unsustainable eventually does not happen, so the CBO calculations simply tell us that somewhere down the road the U.S. government must reform its spending promises, reform its tax system, trade more growth for reformed regulation, and likely all three, or face a monumental debt crisis. One should definitely not use such projections as conditional mean forecasts.

This is not a right or wrong question, it is a question of what kind of accounting seems more productive to understand inflation and fiscal dynamics. Sometimes a state-contingent flow accounting is more useful than a present value accounting. The discount factor adds to the trouble. With r close to g, small changes in discount rates make huge changes in present values. As I did digesting the discontinuity of present values at the $r < g$ boundary, sometimes issues are clearer on a flow rather than present value basis. But one should understand the state-contingent nature of flows, and the state-dependent costs of changing them as well. The fact that so many state-contingent government liabilities come in bad times suggests their true value is larger than even discounting at a low risk-free rate suggests. On the other hand, bad fiscal times can often be met by borrowing, spreading out the pain over subsequent decades.

How surpluses depend on the price level matters. If government worker salaries are not indexed for inflation, then inflation reduces real government liabilities. Most medical prices are administered by the government, and they respond slowly to inflation, reducing real government expenditure. Non-neutralities in the tax code, including progressive tax brackets that are not indexed, taxation of nominal capital gains, and the fact that depreciation schedules are not indexed, all mean that inflation helps government finance, at least once, until people demand better indexation. On the other hand, Social Security payments are aggressively indexed for inflation, so Social Security is at least a real debt, or even a debt whose value increases with inflation.

In sum, government assets and liabilities matter. These considerations are all important for figuring out how sensitive inflation is to fiscal and other shocks, and how tempting it will be for the government to inflate rather than reform or default when in trouble. However, it is not necessarily best to take entitlement promises in current law, and take separate present value, as if they were formal debt, to try to understand the current price level and inflation.

7

Long-Term Debt Dynamics

LONG-TERM DEBT adds many wrinkles to the fiscal theory. Long-term debt is important to understanding policy choices, episodes, and patterns in the data.

Here I explore long-term debt in greater detail. I start by analyzing forward guidance, promises of future interest rates. I then analyze how changes in the quantities of long-term debt affect the path of inflation, and what pattern of debt sales support interest rate or price level targets. The result is a unified view of interest rate targets, forward guidance, quantitative easing, and fiscal stimulus, which can produce standard beliefs about the signs of these policies' effects. The mechanism behind such effects is utterly different from standard models, however, as are some ancillary predictions.

I examine these mechanisms in the flexible price constant real interest rate model, now with long-term debt. I ask the simple questions from the first chapters: What happens if the government sells more debt B, holding surpluses constant? What happens if the government sets an interest rate or bond yield target and offers any quantity of debt B at that price, holding surpluses constant? What happens if there is a shock to surpluses s? With long-term debt, the answers are richer.

This analysis is just a starting point. Pricing frictions will give output effects and more realistic dynamics, and will introduce real interest rate and discount rate variation. Monetary frictions, financial frictions, or liquidity effects of government bonds should add to those interesting dynamics. As usual though, it is best first to understand the simple model and see how many effects don't require frictions.

The tools are simple. With long-term debt, flexible prices, and a constant real interest rate, the flow condition is (3.2),

$$B_{t-1}^{(t)} = P_t s_t + \sum_{j=1}^{\infty} Q_t^{(t+j)} \left(B_t^{(t+j)} - B_{t-1}^{(t+j)} \right),$$

and the present value relation becomes (3.3)

$$\frac{\sum_{j=0}^{\infty} Q_t^{(t+j)} B_{t-1}^{(t+j)}}{P_t} = E_t \sum_{j=0}^{\infty} \beta^j s_{t+j}.$$

We can also eliminate bond prices

$$Q_t^{(t+j)} = E_t \left(\beta^j \frac{P_t}{P_{t+j}} \right)$$

to express the flow and present value relations between debt and price levels directly,

$$\frac{B_{t-1}^{(t)}}{P_t} = s_t + \sum_{j=1}^{\infty} \beta^j \left(B_t^{(t+j)} - B_{t-1}^{(t+j)} \right) E_t \left(\frac{1}{P_{t+j}} \right), \tag{7.1}$$

$$\sum_{j=0}^{\infty} \beta^j B_{t-1}^{(t+j)} E_t \left(\frac{1}{P_{t+j}} \right) = E_t \sum_{j=0}^{\infty} \beta^j s_{t+j}. \tag{7.2}$$

This is a useful step to understanding the relationship between debt quantities and the price level.

7.1   Forward Guidance and Bond Price Targets

Announcements of future interest rate changes can change bond prices and thus change the price level today. In this sense the model captures forward guidance. However, an announcement whose horizon exceeds the maturity of all outstanding bonds has no effect on the price level today. In this sense, fully expected interest rate increases have no temporary disinflationary effect.

The central bank can peg all nominal bond yields. That policy obtains the desired inflation effect without doubtful promises of future interest rates.

We have seen how a rise in an interest rate target can create higher expected inflation. With long-term debt we have seen how an unexpected persistent interest-rate rise produces a temporary disinflation. Here, I investigate forward guidance: If the central bank can credibly commit to higher or lower *future* interest rates, that announcement alone changes long-term bond prices, and changes the price level immediately, with no change at all in current short-term interest rates.

Figure 7.1 picks up where Figure 3.1 left off. Figure 3.1 plotted the effects of an immediate sustained interest rate rise. Figure 7.1 plots a forward guidance policy. At time 0, the government announces that interest rates will rise starting at time 3, and stay higher. This anticipated rise in interest rates induces long-term bond yields at time 0 to rise as indicated by "yields at t=0." (Yields are plotted as a function of maturity, interest rates as a function of time. The algebra for Figure 7.1 is in Online Appendix Section A1.3.)

The price level jumps down at time 0. Much "forward guidance" has been an announcement that future interest rates will be lower than expected, in an attempt to stimulate time 0 inflation. Just flip the graph for that experiment.

However, the price level drop in Figure 7.1 is smaller than that in Figure 3.1. Fewer bonds change price, and those that do so change price by a smaller amount.

- *An interest rate shock in the form of forward guidance has less effect than the same shock made immediately. The maturity structure of outstanding debt controls how the effect of forward guidance falls with the announcement horizon.*

An announcement today of a future interest rate change only affects the value of debt whose maturity exceeds the time interval before rates change. This forward guidance

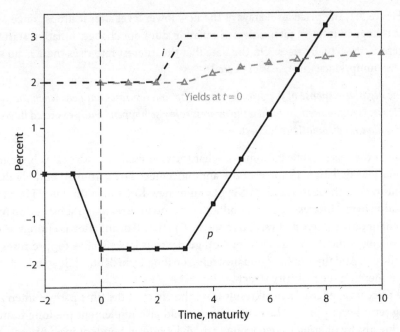

FIGURE 7.1. Price Level Response to a Forward Guidance Interest Rate Rise. At time 0, the government announces that interest rates will rise at time 3, and stay higher. Long-term debt with a geometric maturity structure $\omega = 0.8$ is outstanding.

mechanism eventually loses its power altogether once the guidance period exceeds the longest outstanding bond maturities.

To see these points, suppose that at time 0, the government announces unexpectedly that interest rates will rise starting at time T onward, and bonds of maturity up to $k > T$ are outstanding (30 years in the United States). Nominal bond prices fall, and the price level P_0 must fall since surpluses are not affected. Only bond prices of maturity $T + 1$ or greater are affected. In the present value relation

$$\frac{\sum_{j=0}^{T} Q_0^{(j)} B_{-1}^{(j)} + \sum_{j=T+1}^{k} Q_0^{(j)} B_{-1}^{(j)}}{P_0} = E_0 \sum_{j=0}^{\infty} \beta^j s_j, \qquad (7.3)$$

only the second term in the numerator on the left-hand side is affected by this forward guidance shock. Furthermore, for a given interest rate rise, bond price declines in that second term are smaller: For a permanent rise from r to i starting at time T, the prices of bonds that mature at $j \leq T$ are unaffected, and the prices of bonds that mature at $T + j$ are only affected by interest rates later in their lives. The bond price reaction is

$$Q_0^{(T+j)} = \frac{1}{(1+r)^T} \frac{1}{(1+i)^j} > \frac{1}{(1+i)^{T+j}}.$$

If $T > k$, and forward guidance exceeds the longest outstanding maturity, the price level P_0 does not decline at all, as was the case with one-period debt.

In Figure 7.1, the price level stays at the new lower level after it drops, since with no current change in interest rate, expected inflation does not change. Inflation starts when the interest rate actually rises. On the date that the interest rate rises there is no second price level jump, since this rise is expected.

- *The negative response of the price level to higher interest rates happens when the interest rate rise is announced, not when the interest rate rise happens. Fully expected interest rate rises have no disinflationary effect.*

Though the *answer* reflects some of what forward guidance advocates hope for, the inflationary or deflationary force of the announcement flows from an entirely different mechanism than those in standard Keynesian or new-Keynesian thinking. Here there is no variation in real interest rates, no Phillips curve, no intertemporal substitution reacting to current or future interest rates, and so forth. The time 0 disinflation is entirely a "wealth effect" of government bonds. This forward guidance is less effective for promises in the further future. And this forward guidance relies on long-term debt, while standard analysis does not mention the maturity structure.

The price level effects here all result from the effect of the time path of interest rates on long-term bond prices. The central bank could also implement the long-term bond prices directly, by offering to freely buy and sell long-term bonds at fixed prices, with no change in surpluses, in exactly the same way as we studied a short-term interest rate target achieved by offering to buy and sell short-term bonds at a fixed rate.

Thus we can read Figure 7.1 as the answer to a different question: Rather than promise and try to commit to the plotted path of future short-term rates, suppose the central bank at time 0 announces a full set of bond prices or the plotted yields as a function of maturity, and offers to buy and sell bonds of any maturity at those prices. By doing so, the central bank immediately creates the plotted yield curve and obtains the plotted disinflation. I verify below that such bond price targets work. Central banks shy away from direct yield control by announcing and trading at fixed prices but in this analysis there is no reason for them to do so.

7.2   Bond Quantities

What price level paths follow from given bond quantities? What bond quantities support a given price level path?

What are the effects of *long-term* bond sales on the sequence of prices, given surpluses? What is the effect of surplus shocks on the sequence of prices, with fixed long-term bond supplies? What happens if the government offers bonds for sale at fixed prices? How many bonds does it sell?

The answers to these questions turn out to be algebraically challenging in the presence of long-term debt. We want to solve the sequence (for each t) of flow conditions

$$\frac{B_{t-1}^{(t)}}{P_t} = s_t + \sum_{j=1}^{\infty} \beta^j \left(B_t^{(t+j)} - B_{t-1}^{(t+j)} \right) E_t \left(\frac{1}{P_{t+j}} \right) \tag{7.4}$$

or present value conditions

$$\sum_{j=0}^{\infty} \beta^j B_{t-1}^{(t+j)} E_t \left(\frac{1}{P_{t+j}} \right) = E_t \sum_{j=0}^{\infty} \beta^j s_{t+j} \tag{7.5}$$

for $\{P_t\}$, given $\{s_t\}$ and $\{B_t^{(t+j)}\}$. (The notation $\{x_t\}$ denotes the sequence x_0, x_1, $\ldots, x_t, \ldots$) Alternatively, given a path of $\{P_t\}$ and $\{s_t\}$ we search for corresponding debt policies $\{B_t^{(t+j)}\}$.

In the one-period bond case, the present value relation (7.5) by itself provides such a solution. There is only one price level, P_t, on the left-hand side, so we find that price level given debt and surplus policy settings. Now we have to solve the system of such equations simultaneously at each date to find the solution.

These operations are not mathematically hard. These are linear equations. But the general formulas don't lead to much intuition, so I start with a set of examples that isolate some important channels. I turn on three important pieces of long-term debt policy one by one. First, I consider a government that inherits a maturity structure $\{B_{-1}^{(j)}\}$ at time 0 and simply pays off this outstanding long-term debt as it matures. Next, I consider the effects of purchases or sales at time 0 across the maturity spectrum, $\{B_0^{(j)} - B_{-1}^{(j)}\}$, holding constant future purchases and sales as well as surpluses. I consider the effects of expected *future* purchases and sales, $\{B_t^{(t+j)} - B_{t-1}^{(t+j)}\}$. Finally, I present general-case formulas.

7.2.1 Maturing Debt and a Buffer

The government inherits a maturity structure $\{B_{-1}^{(j)}\}$ and pays off outstanding long-term debt as it matures. The price level each period is then determined by that period's surplus and maturing debt only. Bond prices in the present value of nominal debt, reflecting future price levels, adjust completely to news in the present value of future surpluses, and the current price level no longer adjusts. In this way, long-term debt buffers shocks to expected future surpluses.

I start with a simple case: Turn off sales or repurchases, the right-hand side of the flow condition (7.4). The government pays off outstanding long-term bonds by surpluses $\{s_t\}$ at each date as the bonds mature. Figure 7.2 illustrates the example.

Without subsequent sales or repurchases, the bond $B_{-1}^{(t)}$ outstanding at time 0 becomes the bond $B_{t-1}^{(t)}$ maturing at time t. The government prints up money, M in the picture, to redeem the bond, and then soaks up the money with a surplus s_t, neither selling nor redeeming additional debt. The price level at each date t is then set by debt coming due at that date, and that date's surplus,

$$\frac{B_{-1}^{(t)}}{P_t} = \frac{B_{t-1}^{(t)}}{P_t} = s_t. \tag{7.6}$$

Each date becomes a version of the one-period model.

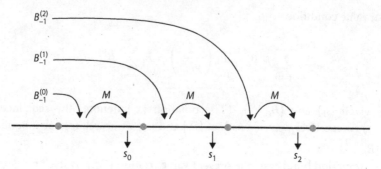

FIGURE 7.2. Example with Outstanding Debt, and No Subsequent Sales or Purchases

There is still a full spectrum of bonds outstanding, $\{B_{t-1}^{(t+j)}\}$ at each date. Their presence just doesn't affect the price level until they come due. There is a stream of subsequent surpluses and deficits $\{s_{t+j}\}$ at each date too, but they don't affect the price level at time t either.

The linkage between the price level and future surpluses seems to have disappeared in this example. What's happening? The present value condition is still valid,

$$\frac{\sum_{j=0}^{\infty} Q_t^{(t+j)} B_{t-1}^{(t+j)}}{P_t} = \sum_{j=0}^{\infty} \beta^j B_{t-1}^{(t+j)} E_t \left(\frac{1}{P_{t+j}} \right) = E_t \sum_{j=0}^{\infty} \beta^j s_{t+j}.$$

From (7.6), bad news about a future surplus s_{t+j} raises the *future* expected price level, lowering $E_t(1/P_{t+j})$ and hence lowering the bond price $Q_t^{(t+j)}$. So the real value of nominal debt at time t still equals the present value of future surpluses at time t. But the market value of debt in the numerator does all the adjusting to lower future surpluses, needing no help from the price level in the dominator. Taking innovations of both sides, *all* of the impact of a shock to future surpluses shows up in today's bond prices and *none* of it shows up in the price level. This is the exact opposite of the case with one-period debt that is constantly rolled over. A surprise fall in the present value of surpluses still results in an unexpected devaluation of bondholder value. But that devaluation shows up entirely in bond prices today and future inflation, rather than showing up entirely in today's inflation.

In this way, long-term debt can be a useful buffer against shocks to expectations of future surpluses, allowing their effects to be absorbed by bond prices today and expected future inflation rather than force an adjustment in the price level today.

(Cochrane (2001) finds long-term debt optimally smooths inflation. Lustig, Sleet, and Yeltekin (2008) give a sophisticated analysis of the term structure, in a model with nominal debt, distorting taxes, sticky prices, and financial frictions. They find that optimal policy "prescribes the almost exclusive use of long-term debt" because it allows "the government to allocate [fiscal shocks] efficiently across states and periods." Angeletos (2002) also argues for what I characterize as the smoothing and doom-loop prevention characteristics of long-term debt. He shows how buying and selling long-term debt can implement state-contingent payoffs.)

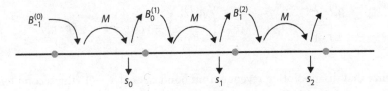

FIGURE 7.3. Short-Term Debt, Rolled Over

7.2.2 Intertemporal Linkages, Runs, and Defaults

With the long-term debt case in front of us, in which future surpluses have no effect on today's inflation, I return to the mechanics of inflation under one-period debt. Future surpluses affect today's inflation through a rollover process. People become concerned about repayment in year 30. They then fear bond sales in year 29 will not yield enough revenue, and thus inflation in year 29. This process works its way back so that people try to sell government debt today on fear the government will not be able to roll it over next year. People investing today fear that other investors will not be there to roll over their debt, rather than necessarily holding precise expectations about far-off events. The mechanism is similar to that of a financial crisis or run. It is inherently unpredictable, and its fiscal roots are hard to see.

It is initially puzzling that *short*-term debt leads to a present value formula, and *long*-term debt leads to a one-period formula. We are used to thinking of long-term assets leading to a long-term present value relation, and short-term assets valued by short-term present value relations.

Short-term assets lead to a long-term present value relationship because short-term bonds are rolled over. That rollover provides the intertemporal linkage. The present value relation describes the portfolio of government bonds, or a strategy that invests dynamically in that portfolio, not the value of an individual security. The individual short-term bond issued at time t is repaid at time $t + 1$, but the portfolio then buys additional bonds issued at time $t + 1$.

Figure 7.3 reminds us of the mechanics of short-term debt, in contrast to Figure 7.2. In this case, money printed to redeem bonds each day is soaked up by selling new bonds as well as by primary surpluses.

The present value relation comes from the flow relation

$$\frac{B_{t-1}^{(t)}}{P_t} = s_t + Q_t^{(t+1)}\frac{B_t^{(t+1)}}{P_t} = s_t + E_t\left(\beta\frac{B_t^{(t+1)}}{P_{t+1}}\right). \tag{7.7}$$

The second term on the right represents revenue from new debt sales.

Suppose people become worried that there will be inadequate surpluses s_T far in the future. They then worry that $B_{T-1}^{(T)}/P_T = s_T$ will result in a high price level P_T. Given that fear, they reason that investors won't want to pay a lot for debt at time $T - 1$, so revenue from bond sales at time $T - 1$ will be disappointing. With

$$\frac{B_{T-2}^{(T-1)}}{P_{T-1}} = s_{T-1} + E_{T-1}\left(\frac{B_{T-1}^{(T)}}{P_T}\right) = s_{T-1} + E_{T-1}\left(\beta s_T\right),$$

they realize that disappointing revenue from bond sales at $T-1$ (the second term) will lead to a greater price level at time $T-1$. Working backwards, investors are reluctant to hold government bonds at time 0 because they fear that the government will have trouble rolling them over at time 1. People at time 0 try to get rid of the bonds and drive up the time 0 price level.

Short-term financing is fragile. As in a bank run, people do not need direct and precise expectations of far-future surpluses. The fear that leads to inflation need not be about a specific time, just that eventually the government will run into an intractable fall in surpluses, or default explicitly.

The fear need not directly involve future surpluses. If people worry that other people won't be there to roll over debt tomorrow, for whatever reason, people don't buy debt today. The government then prints up money to pay off current bonds, but it is unable to raise enough revenue from bond sales to soak up that money, so inflation breaks out today. The soothing present value formula and law of iterated expectation hides a great fragility.

The mechanism is really a rollover crisis. As usual, it is easy in the event to miss its fiscal roots. Commenters, not seeing obvious fundamental news, will be tempted to attribute the inflation to sunspots, self-confirming expectations, multiple equilibria, contagion, irrational markets, bubbles, sudden stops, or other chimeras from the colorful menagerie of economic synonyms for "I don't understand it."

Stopping such events requires a display of fiscal force. The government must undertake a reform or other durable commitment that allows it to soak up money by selling debt.

This run-like nature of inflation is useful when thinking about events. Why does inflation seem to come so suddenly and unexpectedly? Well, for the same reason that financial crises come suddenly and unexpectedly. If people expect a run tomorrow, they run today. If people expect a fiscal inflation tomorrow, it happens today.

Why, conversely, can economies go on for years with economists scratching their heads over large debts and deficits, but no inflation? Well, like short-term debt backed by mortgage-backed securities in 2006, or Greek debt before 2009, it all looks fine until suddenly it doesn't. The United States, Europe, and Japan easily have the means to pay off their debts if they choose to do so. The question is whether our governments will choose to undertake the straightforward tax, pro-growth economic, and entitlement spending reforms that will let them pay down the debt, or whether the United States and other advanced economies will really careen to an unnecessary debt crisis sometime in the next few decades.

Government bonds are a bet against extreme events and political dysfunction. Do not look for a marker such as a precise value of debt-to-GDP ratio or sustained primary deficits that signals that event in the minds of bond investors. Do not look for warnings in long-term interest rates. Interest rates did not forecast the inflation of the 1970s, the disinflation of the 1980s, the debt crises of 2008, or the subsequent euro crisis.

Long-term debt offers a contrary buffer. In the simplest case of a government that just pays off long-term debt, bad news about future surpluses causes inflation on the future

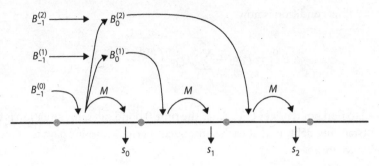

FIGURE 7.4. Long-Term Debt Example. The government may buy or sell debt at time 0, but not subsequently.

date only, and lowers the bond price today. Long-term debt defuses crises in government finance as it does in private finance.

7.3   Bond Sales and Bond Price Targets

We consider the effect of sales or repurchases of long-term debt at time 0, with no change in surpluses, and with no subsequent purchases or sales of debt.

If there is no long-term debt outstanding at time 0, then the real revenue raised by selling long-term debt is independent of the amount of debt sold. Additional debt sales lower bond prices and raise the future price level, but raise no additional revenue and have no effect on the current price level. They act just as in the two-period model.

In the presence of outstanding long-term debt, additional debt sales raise revenue, and therefore such sales can lower the price level. Debt sales dilute outstanding claims to future surpluses.

The government can target long-term bond prices by offering to freely buy or sell long-term debt at fixed prices. Monetary policy can target long-term rates. Bond purchases can lower long-term interest rates, and they can produce immediate inflation.

A state-contingent debt policy, unexpectedly buying or selling long-term debt, can offset surplus shocks and stabilize inflation – though at the cost of future expected inflation.

Expected future sales add to current sales of long-term debt to drive the final price level, and thus the bond price. With no long-term debt outstanding, a bond sale that is expected to be reversed has no effect.

With long-term debt outstanding, expected future bond sales have an interaction effect on the initial price level. An expected future bond sale changes the total amount of debt coming due at a future date, that a current debt sale may dilute.

We started fiscal theory in a two-date model, and considered the effects of selling more nominal debt B_0 at the end of the first day, with no change in surpluses. We return to that question with long-term debt, and find much more interesting answers.

Now, I modify the long-term debt setup of Section 7.2.1, by allowing the government to buy or sell some extra long-term debt $B_0^{(j)} - B_{-1}^{(j)}$ at time 0, potentially on top of outstanding debt $B_{-1}^{(j)}$. $B_0^{(j)}$ is the total amount of time j debt outstanding at the end of period 0, so $B_0^{(j)} - B_{-1}^{(j)}$ is the amount of time j debt sold at time 0. For now, I still suppose that the government never buys or sells debt at subsequent dates. Figure 7.4 illustrates the example.

The $t = 0$ flow condition is now

$$B_{-1}^{(0)} = P_0 s_0 + \sum_{j=1}^{\infty} Q_0^{(j)} \left(B_0^{(j)} - B_{-1}^{(j)} \right). \tag{7.8}$$

We need to find bond prices $Q_0^{(j)}$. After the time 0 bond sales, the situation is the same as with outstanding debt, in that each subsequent period's surplus pays for that period's bonds. We have for $j > 0$

$$\frac{B_0^{(j)}}{P_j} = s_j \tag{7.9}$$

and hence bond prices and the revenue from bond sales are

$$Q_0^{(j)} = \beta^j E_0 \left(\frac{P_0}{P_j} \right) \tag{7.10}$$

$$\frac{Q_0^{(j)} B_0^{(j)}}{P_0} = \beta^j E_0(s_j). \tag{7.11}$$

Equation (7.11) tells us that if surpluses are fixed, the *total* end-of-period real value of date j debt is independent of the total amount.

Substituting bond prices from (7.10) and (7.9) into (7.8),

$$\frac{B_{-1}^{(0)}}{P_0} = s_0 + \sum_{j=1}^{\infty} \beta^j \frac{\left(B_0^{(j)} - B_{-1}^{(j)} \right)}{B_0^{(j)}} E_0(s_j). \tag{7.12}$$

The right-hand term in (7.12) is the real revenue raised at time 0 by selling *additional* date j debt. We want to find the price level effects of these additional bond sales $B_0^{(j)} - B_{-1}^{(j)}$. You can already see that additional sales matter as a proportion of the total amount of debt $B_0^{(j)}$ that is a claim to the surplus s_j.

(Leeper and Leith (2016) interpret the debt terms in (7.12) as a discount factor. However, in this economy with constant real rates, I think a better interpretation is that they represent dilution, the fraction of the future surpluses that are devoted to repaying debts to new versus initial bondholders.)

7.3.1   No Outstanding Debt

Start with the case that no long-term debt is outstanding, so $B_{-1}^{(j)} = 0$ for $j > 0$. Equation (7.12) reduces to

$$\frac{B_{-1}^{(0)}}{P_0} = s_0 + \sum_{j=1}^{\infty} \beta^j E_0(s_j). \tag{7.13}$$

(I assume the government sells some debt $B_0^{(j)} > 0$ for all $j > 0$.) With no long-term debt outstanding, P_0 is still determined by fiscal shocks alone, independently of any sales $B_0^{(j)}$. We then have a natural generalization of the two-period results:

- *If there is no long-term debt outstanding, $B_{-1}^{(j)} = 0$ for $j > 0$, then the real revenue raised by selling long-term debt $B_0^{(j)}$ with no change in surplus s_j is independent of the amount of debt sold. Additional sales lower bond prices $Q_0^{(j)}$, raise the yield of long-term bonds, and cause future inflation $E_t(1/P_j)$, but they have no effect on the current price level P_0.*

We also have in (7.13) again the familiar present value statement of the fiscal theory with one-period debt, even though the government now rolls the one-period debt over to long-maturity debt which it then leaves outstanding.

Long-term debt sales begin to resemble quantitative easing. The nominal debt market appears "segmented" across maturity. Each bond maturity is a claim to a specific surplus, and no other. The government can change, say, the 10-year bond price, with no effect on the 9-year price or the 11-year price. These results depend on the assumption that the government does not change surpluses s_j along with a debt sale, and does not use future debt sales to spread inflation across dates. The usual theory of bond markets makes the opposite assumption, that expected surpluses move one for one with debt sales, which is why it usually sees flat demand curves. The usual theory also concerns real, not purely nominal, interest rate variation.

Sales of maturity j debt reduce maturity j bond prices $Q_0^{(j)}$. Conversely, then, the government can fix long-term bond prices by offering to sell any amount of debt at fixed prices, and the resulting demands will be finite:

- *The government can target long-term bond prices $Q_0^{(j)}$, by offering to freely buy or sell long-term debt at fixed prices. Equation (7.11) then says how much debt the government will sell.*

In quantitative easing, central banks changed bond supplies $B_0^{(j)}$ with the hope of changing long-term interest rates. It is a bit puzzling that they did not just announce the interest rate they wanted, and offer to freely buy and sell long-term bonds at that rate, rather than leave us with endless debate whether they moved bond prices at all. They may have worried that huge demands would ensue, or that they secretly had no power to change rates and would have been revealed as wizards of Oz. This observation extends to long-term debt the reassurance that fixed nominal bond prices can result in finite and limited bond sales. A one percentage point bond price change implies a one percentage point change in the nominal bond supply, so the quantities are small and the (unit) elasticity large.

However, for this proposition to hold, people must again expect that surpluses do not change with bond sales. Communicating unchanged surpluses when people are used to sober debt management may be just as hard as communicating that debts will be repaid after multiple inflations and defaults. Putting the bond sales in the central bank's hands helps, but inventing new institutions is not instantaneous. Also, this proposition holds in this flexible price world, but sticky prices may modify it.

The Bank of Japan has recently experimented with a long-term bond price target, offering to freely buy and sell, and the U.S. Federal Reserve targeted bond prices in the years after WWII, so there is also some historical precedent for the viability of long-term bond price targets by the central bank.

7.3.2   Outstanding Debt

Now suppose there is some long-term debt outstanding at time 0 as well, $B_{-1}^{(j)} > 0$. The government may sell additional long-term debt at time 0, $B_0^{(j)} - B_{-1}^{(j)}$, but still refrains from subsequent sales. We have an additional effect: Long-term bond sales, with no change in surpluses, *can* raise revenue, and can affect the price level P_0. Equation (7.12) offers this novel result:

- *In the presence of outstanding long-term debt, $B_{-1}^{(j)} > 0$, additional debt sales $B_0^{(j)} - B_{-1}^{(j)}$ with no change in surplus raise revenue, and therefore such sales lower the price level P_0 immediately, as well as raise future price levels.*

New long-term debt sales dilute existing long-term debt as a claim to future surpluses. Selling such debt transfers value from existing bondholders to the new bondholders. Consequently, the government raises revenue by selling additional debt, and with no change in surplus that revenue can lower the time 0 price level.

This debt operation adds a second important element of quantitative easing or tightening. Now a long-term debt purchase at time 0 stimulates inflation at time 0 as well as lowers long-term interest rates. Such bond purchases or sales can, for example, implement the price level paths of Figure 3.1 or Figure 7.1.

In the presence of outstanding long-term debt, the revenue resulting from additional debt sales can also help to fund a deficit at time 0 and thereby avoid immediate inflation. The innovation version of (7.12) is

$$\frac{B_{-1}^{(0)}}{P_{-1}} \Delta E_0 \left(\frac{P_{-1}}{P_0} \right) = \Delta E_0 s_0 + \sum_{j=1}^{\infty} \beta^j \Delta E_0 \left[\frac{\left(B_0^{(j)} - B_{-1}^{(j)} \right)}{B_0^{(j)}} s_j \right].$$

A shock $\Delta E_0 s_0$ could be balanced by a shock to bond sales without current inflation. Of course, such sales raise future inflation. These operations shift inflation around and potentially smooth it, offering a longer period of smaller inflation, but they do not eliminate inflation. They let the government choose which bonds will be inflated away and when.

- *A state-contingent debt policy, unexpectedly buying or selling long-term debt $B_0^{(j)} - B_{-1}^{(j)}$, can offset surplus shocks and reduce current inflation, at the cost of higher future expected inflation.*

7.3.3   Future Bond Sales

Expected future bond sales, still with no change in surpluses, can affect the current price level and interest rates. The algebra is not enlightening, so I relegate it to Online Appendix Section A1.8. There I pursue a three-period example, in which period 0, 1, 2, debt is outstanding at period 0, the government may sell additional period 1, 2 debt at period

0, and the government may also sell additional period 2 debt at period 1—the expected future sale—all with no change in surplus.

With no long-term debt outstanding at time 0, expected future bond sales do not affect the price level P_0. There must be debt outstanding for any dilution effects to operate. Expected future sales add to current sales of long-term debt to drive the final price level, and thus the bond price. Thus, with no long-term debt outstanding, a QE sale that is expected to be reversed has no stimulative effect.

With long-term debt outstanding, expected future bond sales can affect the initial price level P_0 as well. They operate only through an interaction term. An expected future bond sale changes the total amount of debt coming due at a future date, that a current debt sale may dilute.

7.4   A General Formula

I display a general formula for finding the price level P_t given paths of debt $\{B_t^{(t+j)}\}$ and surpluses $\{s_t\}$.

Again, our task is to solve the sequence of flow relations

$$\frac{B_{t-1}^{(t)}}{P_t} = s_t + \sum_{j=1}^{\infty} \beta^j E_t \left(\frac{1}{P_{t+j}} \right) \left(B_t^{(t+j)} - B_{t-1}^{(t+j)} \right) \tag{7.14}$$

or present value relations

$$\sum_{j=0}^{\infty} \beta^j E_t \left(\frac{1}{P_{t+j}} \right) B_{t-1}^{(t+j)} = E_t \sum_{j=0}^{\infty} \beta^j s_{t+j} \tag{7.15}$$

for $\{P_t\}$ on one side and all the $\{B\}$ and $\{s\}$ on the other side.

The problem is not mathematically difficult. These are linear equations. Suppressing expectations E_t to simplify notation, we can write (7.15) as

$$
\begin{bmatrix}
B_{-1}^{(0)} & \beta B_{-1}^{(1)} & \beta^2 B_{-1}^{(2)} & \beta^3 B_{-1}^{(3)} & \cdots \\
 & B_0^{(1)} & \beta B_0^{(2)} & \beta^2 B_0^{(3)} & \cdots \\
 & & B_1^{(2)} & \beta B_1^{(3)} & \cdots \\
 & & & B_2^{(3)} & \cdots \\
 & & & & \ddots
\end{bmatrix}
\begin{bmatrix}
1/P_0 \\
1/P_1 \\
1/P_2 \\
1/P_3 \\
1/P_4 \\
\vdots
\end{bmatrix}
=
\begin{bmatrix}
1 & \beta & \beta^2 & \beta^3 & \cdots \\
 & 1 & \beta & \beta^2 & \cdots \\
 & & 1 & \beta & \cdots \\
 & & & 1 & \cdots \\
 & & & & \ddots
\end{bmatrix}
\begin{bmatrix}
s_0 \\
s_1 \\
s_2 \\
s_3 \\
s_4
\end{bmatrix}.
$$

We could write this equation as

$$Bp = Rs \tag{7.16}$$

and hence write its solution as

$$p = B^{-1} Rs.$$

The problem is just that the inverse B matrix doesn't yield very pretty answers.

My best attempt at a pretty formula, from Cochrane (2001), has again the form of a weighted present value:

$$\frac{B_{t-1}^{(t)}}{P_t} = E_t \sum_{j=0}^{\infty} \beta^j W_t^{(j)} s_{t+j}. \tag{7.17}$$

The weights are defined recursively. Start by defining the fraction of time $t+j$ debt sold at time t,

$$A_t^{(t+j)} = \frac{B_t^{(t+j)} - B_{t-1}^{(t+j)}}{B_{t+j-1}^{(t+j)}}.$$

Then, the weights are

$$W_t^{(0)} = 1$$
$$W_t^{(1)} = A_t^{(t+1)}$$
$$W_t^{(2)} = A_{t+1}^{(t+2)} W_t^{(1)} + A_t^{(t+2)}$$
$$W_t^{(3)} = A_{t+2}^{(t+3)} W_t^{(2)} + A_{t+1}^{(t+3)} W_t^{(1)} + A_t^{(t+3)}$$
$$W_t^{(j)} = \sum_{k=0}^{j-1} A_{t+k}^{(t+j)} W_t^{(k)}.$$

These formulas likely hide additional interesting insights and special cases.

One can see just from the fact that B is a matrix and p is a vector that

• *There are many debt policies that correspond to any given price level path.*

We have already seen how either expected sales of one-period debt or initial sales of long-term debt can determine any sequence of expected price levels. Many paths involving dynamic buying and selling of debt can support the same sequence of price levels. This insight leads me to focus on interest rate targets once we have reassurance that there is at least one debt policy that supports the target, and to spend less attention on the effects of given debt operations with constant surpluses. Also, in practice, debt and surpluses generally move together. The exercises of moving B fixing s and moving s fixing B are useful conceptual exercises, but likely poor guides to history, events, or policy.

7.5   Constraints on Policy

The present value condition at time 0

$$\sum_{j=0}^{\infty} \beta^j B_{-1}^{(j)} E_0 \left(\frac{1}{P_j}\right) = E_0 \sum_{j=0}^{\infty} \beta^j s_j$$

acts as a "budget constraint" on the price level sequences that surplus-neutral debt policy—changes in $\{B_t^{(t+j)}\}$—or interest rate policy—changes in $\{Q_t^{(t+j)}\}$—can accomplish. There is a debt policy and interest rate policy that achieves any price level path consistent with this formula, and debt policy cannot achieve price level paths inconsistent with this formula. Debt policy can raise or lower P_0 in particular, by accepting contrary movements in future price levels.

Fixing surpluses, the end-of-period real value of the debt

$$\frac{\sum_{j=1}^{\infty} B_0^{(j)} Q_0^{(j)}}{P_0} = \sum_{j=1}^{\infty} \beta^j B_0^{(j)} E_0\left(\frac{1}{P_j}\right) = E_0 \sum_{j=1}^{\infty} \beta^j s_j$$

is independent of the quantity of debt $B_0^{(j)}$.

What price level paths can debt policy—changes in debt without changes in surpluses—accomplish? The present value condition provides this general result directly:

$$\frac{\sum_{j=0}^{\infty} Q_0^{(j)} B_{-1}^{(j)}}{P_0} = \sum_{j=0}^{\infty} \beta^j B_{-1}^{(j)} E_0\left(\frac{1}{P_j}\right) = E_0 \sum_{j=0}^{\infty} \beta^j s_j. \tag{7.18}$$

- *There is a debt policy—a set of debt sales or purchases with no change in surpluses—that achieves any path of price levels consistent with (7.18). There is no debt policy that can achieve a price level path inconsistent with (7.18).*

The maturity structure of outstanding debt $\{B_{-1}^{(j)}\}$ acts as a "budget constraint" for the sequence of expected future price levels achievable by debt policy or interest rate policy. This is the *only* constraint on debt policy.

The attractive part of this statement is what's missing. It is an existence proposition. It tells you there *is* a debt policy that achieves a given set of expected price levels, but it does not tell you *which* debt policy generates the sequence of price levels. In general, there are many: One can achieve a price level sequence consistent with (7.18) by time 0 sales of long-term debt, by expected future sales of long and short-term debt, or by combinations of those policies. Similarly, it tells you that there is an interest rate policy that achieves the given set of price levels—there is a set of interest rate or bond price targets $Q_t^{(t+j)} = \beta^j E_t(P_t/P_{t+j})$, enforced by passive bond sales at those targets—without specifying just which bonds the government must offer to sell.

To prove existence of a debt policy that achieves a price level path, we can just give an example. To show there are multiple debt policies that support a price level path, we can show two examples.

We already have two examples of a debt policy that generates *any* sequence of price levels for times greater than zero, $\{E_0(1/P_j); j > 0\}$. First, the government can sell long-run debt at the end of period 0 in the quantity $B_0^{(j)}$ given by

$$B_0^{(j)} E_0\left(\frac{1}{P_j}\right) = E_0(s_j); \quad j > 0 \tag{7.19}$$

and then not buy or sell any more. Second, the government can buy back all the outstanding long-term debt $B_{-1}^{(j)}$ at time 0, and then issue and roll over short-term debt in the right quantity to set P_1, P_2, etc. as desired via

$$\frac{B_{j-1}^{(j)}}{P_j} = E_j \sum_{k=0}^{\infty} \beta^k s_{j+k}. \tag{7.20}$$

More realistic alternatives exist between these two extremes. But to prove that multiple debt policies *exist* to support the price level path, two unrealistic examples are enough.

Given this sequence of price levels P_1, P_2, etc., the present value relation (7.18) tells us what the price level P_0 must be. Any debt policy that generates a given $\{E_0(1/P_j); j > 0\}$ must generate this P_0. By construction, the example policies satisfy the period j flow and present value constraints for every j, so there are no other constraints.

This statement and equation (7.18) have a number of useful implications.

If only one-period debt is outstanding at time 0, then $B_{-1}^{(0)}/P_0$ is the only term on the left-hand side. The government can achieve any sequence of price levels $E_0(1/P_j)$ it wants in the future. But changes in future price levels have no effect on the time 0 price level P_0. Only surplus shocks can change the price level P_0.

If long-term debt $\{B_{-1}^{(j)}\}$ is outstanding, then (7.18) describes a binding trade-off between future and current price levels. I typically use it to find the implied jump in P_0 that results from the government's choices of $\{E_0(1/P_j)\}$, since the latter are unconstrained.

The interest rate policy and forward guidance examples of Figures 3.1 and 7.1 involve raising $\{P_j\}$ and thereby lowering P_0, and vice versa. We see in (7.18) attractive generalizations of those results. For example, if you want to create a quantitative easing policy that raises the price level for some interval of time between 0 and T, (7.18) shows what the options are for lower price levels at other dates.

A QE policy that raises near-term price levels with no decline in future price levels is not possible. Equation (7.18) generalizes Sims's (2011) "stepping on a rake" or Sargent and Wallace's (1981) "unpleasant arithmetic"—a lower price level today must result in higher future price levels—to say that lower price levels at some dates must be accompanied by higher price levels at some other dates, all weighted by the maturity structure of outstanding debt. Debt policy or interest rate policy can only shift the price level around.

Debt policy can offset fiscal shocks as well. In response to a negative fiscal shock, debt policy can eliminate current inflation $\Delta E_0(1/P_0) = 0$, at the cost of accepting larger future inflation. It can allow a short, swift inflation or a long, slow inflation. Debt policy can affect the *timing* of fiscal inflation, but cannot eliminate inflation entirely.

Section 7.2.1 showed how long-term debt can be a passive buffer, absorbing surplus shocks into the price of bonds rather than the price level, and thereby postponing the inflationary effect of surplus shocks. Here we see a complementary "active buffer" mechanism as well. By selling long-term debt in response to shocks, the government can additionally smooth inflation forward.

The end-of-period valuation formula

$$\frac{\sum_{j=1}^{\infty} B_0^{(j)} Q_0^{(j)}}{P_0} = \sum_{j=1}^{\infty} \beta^j B_0^{(j)} E_0\left(\frac{1}{P_j}\right) = E_0 \sum_{j=1}^{\infty} \beta^j s_j \tag{7.21}$$

offers additional insights. The real end-of-period value of debt is the same, no matter how much is outstanding at the end of time 0, $\{B_0^{(j)}\}$. Here we see a simple generalization of the unit elasticity of the one-period debt model in which the value of end-of-period debt is set by the present value of subsequent surpluses, independent of how much debt is outstanding.

In the model with short-term debt, it was convenient to view fiscal policy as setting unexpected inflation, and monetary policy as setting expected future inflation. I warned that generalizations would appear, and here we see one. More deeply here, fiscal policy sets the overall amount of inflation and monetary policy sets the timing of inflation.

7.6   Quantitative Easing and Friends

I construct a more realistic quantitative easing example. Long-term debt is outstanding with a geometric maturity structure. The central bank modifies this maturity structure with short-term or overnight debt sales and purchases, and quantitative-easing long-term bond sales and purchases. The resulting intervention, combining long-term bond purchases, short-term issues, promises not to quickly repurchase the long-term debt, and promises about the path of interest rates, looks more like quantitative easing.

In quantitative easing policies, central banks buy long-term debt, issuing short-term debt (interest-paying reserves) in return. They hope to lower long-term interest rates, and to stimulate current aggregate demand and inflation by so doing. Central banks offer stories for this policy firmly rooted in frictions—segmented bond markets, preferred habitats, and IS-LM-style Keynesianism, augmented a bit with expectations "anchored" by sufficiently stirring central-banker speeches. Still, let us ask to what extent and under what conditions the simple frictionless model here can offer something like the hoped-for or believed *effects* of a quantitative easing policy, or to what extent we obtain neutrality results that negate QE and therefore guide us to models with such frictions if we think QE indeed has an effect.

Suppose the central bank wishes to follow the policies graphed in Figure 3.1 or Figure 7.1: a period of lower price level followed by steady inflation, or a period of higher price level followed by a steady lower inflation. We know the bank can do it, and that there is a debt policy to achieve this price level path. But is there a debt policy that supports these price level paths, that features an immediate (time 0) lengthening or shortening of the maturity structure, an exchange of short-term debt for long-term debt, as in a QE or open market operation? I work out a few examples in which there is such a policy.

In this analysis, I make a crucial assumption, that Treasury and central bank debt issues carry the same expectation of repayment. Quantitative easing is no more than a rearrangement of the maturity structure, with no change in surpluses. From the beginning, however, we have thought about a different specification, that Treasury debt is expected to be repaid, but central bank debt sales carry no expectations of higher surpluses. If by buying Treasury debt and issuing central bank debt the central bank changed the expectation that the debt will be repaid, then QE would have a powerful inflationary effect. That is a mechanism by which the central bank operation does change surpluses. It does not, however, seem a reasonable assumption of the 2010–2020 QE operations. Most of all, central banks announced that those operations would be temporary, the balance sheet eventually "normalized," and the asset purchases reversed. The debt would go back to being debt and repaid. Again, but by a different mechanism, whether a QE operation is expected to be reversed matters.

This form of fiscal–monetary operation might make sense of traditional central banks that issue only cash and non-interest-bearing reserves. Then, we might think that an open market operation changes debt that will be repaid (Treasury debt) to debt that will not be repaid (money). The *fiscal* loosening of such an open-market operation gives it an inflationary force. In Chapter 21, I speculate that such an interpretation might make sense of the huge increase in reserves during 2020–2021, which did create inflation.

7.6.1   QE with a Separate Treasury and Central Bank

Suppose the Treasury keeps a geometric maturity structure $B_{t-1}^{(t+j)} = \omega^j B_{t-1}$. Suppose the central bank adjusts this structure by selling or buying long-term debt $\tilde{B}_t^{(t+j)}$, and by issuing or borrowing reserves $M_t^{(t+1)}$. Reserves here are just additional one-period debt, with face value $M_t^{(t+1)}$ payable at time $t+1$. I use the notation $\tilde{B}_t$ and M_t to distinguish the central bank's modifications of the debt from the Treasury's original issues. Long-term debt in private hands is $B_t^{(t+j)} + \tilde{B}_t^{(t+j)}$ and short-term debt in private hands is $B_t^{(t+1)} + \tilde{B}_t^{(t+1)} + M_t^{(t+1)}$.

Start at a steady-state with $\tilde{B}_t = 0$ and $M_t = 0$ and a constant surplus s. From the present value equation (7.18), the steady-state obeys

$$\sum_{j=0}^{\infty} \beta^j \frac{\omega^j B}{P} = \frac{B}{P} \frac{1}{1 - \beta\omega} = \frac{1}{1-\beta}s. \qquad (7.22)$$

Suppose that the Treasury keeps this nominal debt quantity unchanged so $B_t = B_{-1} = B$, and all adjustments come from the central bank's M_t and $\tilde{B}_t$ modifications. Let the central bank engage in long-term bond sales or purchases once at time 0, and then let those bonds roll off,

$$\tilde{B}_t^{(j)} = \tilde{B}_{t-1}^{(j)} = \tilde{B}_0^{(j)}, j = 1, 2, 3 \dots$$

This is the central bank's quantitative-easing intervention. In addition, the central bank maintains a one-period interest rate target by reserve supply $\{M_t\}$.

At each date $t > 0$ the present value relation reads

$$\frac{M_{t-1}^{(t)}}{P_t} + \sum_{j=t}^{\infty} \beta^{j-t} \frac{\omega^{j-t}B + \tilde{B}_0^{(j)}}{P_j} = \frac{1}{1-\beta}s.$$

Using (7.22), we can write this present value relation as

$$\frac{M_{t-1}^{(t)}}{B} \frac{P}{P_t} + \sum_{j=t}^{\infty} \beta^{j-t} \left(\omega^{j-t} + \frac{\tilde{B}_0^{(j)}}{B} \right) \frac{P}{P_j} = \frac{1}{1 - \beta\omega}. \qquad (7.23)$$

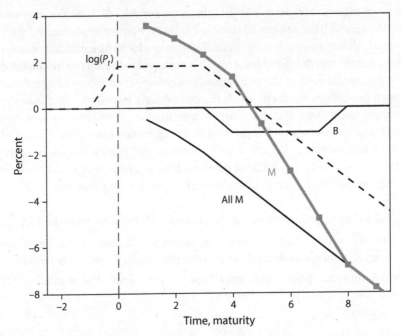

FIGURE 7.5. Debt Policies to Support a Stimulus with Geometric Long-Term Debt. "All M" gives the path of $M_{t-1}^{(t)}$ with no debt sales $\tilde{B}_0^{(j)}$. The "B" line plots debt sales—long-term debt sold at time 0, $\tilde{B}_0^{(j)}$, as a function of maturity j. The negative value means a debt purchase. "M" gives the path of $M_{t-1}^{(t)}$ with debt sales as given by "B." The "All M" is an alternative to the combination of "M" and "B" policies that produce the same price level path "$\log(P_t)$." M and B are expressed as percentages of the steady-state nominal market value of debt, $B \sum_{j=0}^{\infty} \beta^j \omega^j = B/(1 - \beta\omega)$.

I drop E_0 in front of $1/P_j$ as we are looking at a perfect foresight path after a one-time shock. Now, for a desired price level path and a choice of one of monetary $M_{t-1}^{(t)}$ or QE purchases $\tilde{B}_0^{(j)}$, (7.23) gives us the other one. We have reverse engineered monetary or QE policies that deliver the desired price level path.

Figure 7.5 plots two debt policies corresponding to a quantitative easing, monetary policy, or forward guidance stimulus. The "$\log(P_t)$" line plots the price level path. The objective is to stimulate, to raise inflation in the near term. We know we can't have a permanently higher price level with no change in surpluses, so the near-term price level rise must be matched by longer-horizon price level fall.

The "M" and "B" lines together offer a quantitative easing-like debt policy to produce the price level path. Here, the central bank at time 0 buys zero-coupon bonds that mature at times 4, 5, 6, and 7, and lets the bonds mature. The "B" line graphs the face value of these bonds as a function of their maturity at time 0, $B_0^{(j)}$ as a function of j. The B line is negative, since the policy is a bond purchase. The "M" line displays the monetary policy $M_{t-1}^{(t)}$ at each date t required along with these debt purchases to produce the given price level path, by (7.23).

The central bank purchases long-term debt $\{\tilde{B}_0^{(j)}\}$ and it issues one-period debt $\{M_{t-1}^{(t)}\}$, as in a quantitative easing operation. The result is a stimulus, a period of higher price level despite no change in short-term interest rates from period 1 to 3. As the long-term debt rolls off, the central bank returns to standard monetary policy implemented with short-term debt M_t alone to target interest rates. This looks a lot like quantitative easing.

In these definitions, the rise in reserves M_t is not equal to the change in value of debt $\tilde{B}_t$, and debt B_t remains held by the public. You might hope for a model of quantitative easing or open market operations in which the central bank buys bonds and issues reserves of exactly the same value. But the point of open market operations or quantitative easing is to change prices. So a successful model of open market operations and quantitative easing must involve some element of price pressure, not just exchanges at given prices. Any difference between a central bank debt purchase and its overnight debt issue is made up by cash. People don't want to hold that cash overnight, and the price level adjusts, as usual.

The "All M" line produces the same price level path by short-term debt $M^{(t)}_{t-1}$ alone; (7.23) with $\tilde{B}^{(j)}_0 = 0$. The central bank can announce an interest rate target and offer interest-bearing reserves as desired, or by reserves supply target. It is initially surprising that the monetary policy does not follow the price level. But remember $M^{(t+1)}_t$ is short-term debt sold *on top of* the Treasury's debt.

We can write (7.23)

$$\frac{M^{(t)}_{t-1} + \sum_{j=t}^{\infty} \left(B\omega^{j-t} + \tilde{B}^{(j)}_0 \right) Q^{(j)}_t}{P_t} = \frac{1}{1 - \beta\omega} \frac{B}{P} \qquad (7.24)$$

and $\tilde{B}^{(j)}_0 = 0$ in this case. Since the value of surpluses is constant in this exercise, changes in the total market value of debt (numerator on left-hand side) at each date must match changes in the desired price level at that date (denominator of the left-hand side). Given the price level path as plotted, and its implication for bond prices, we can choose any combination of M and $\tilde{B}$ in the numerator of (7.24) to produce that price level path.

That observation also explains the patterns of debt that we see in Figure 7.5. When bond prices rise at time 0, the Treasury's long-term debt jumps up in value. The rise is large enough that the central bank must reduce the value of nominal debt with a negative M. As the day of disinflation and lower short-term rates gets closer, the value of the Treasury's debt grows larger, requiring more negative M to control the overall value of the numerator. This trend accounts for the decreasing M in periods 1–3. Once the period of lower interest rates and deflation starts, the Treasury's debt has a constant value, so now the central bank alone changes the value of debt, which must decline to match the declining price level.

7.6.2   *Quantitative Easing and Maturity Structure*

I present an argument for the irrelevance of maturity structure, and its limits. The QE approach may offer some precommitment. Long-term debt matters as a buffer to future shocks. Actual QE may have had smaller effects than we see here.

In these examples, there are lots of ways to produce a given price level path. The present value relation states

$$\frac{\sum_{j=0}^{\infty} B_{t-1}^{(t+j)} Q_t^{(t+j)}}{P_t} = E_t \sum_{j=0}^{\infty} \beta^j s_{t+j}.$$

Fixing surpluses, the *only* restriction on debt to produce a price level path $\{P_t\}$ is that the total nominal market value of debt at each date moves proportionally to the desired price level at that date. The maturity structure at each date is irrelevant. The last section provides an example: We achieve the same price level path with a policy that modifies only short-term debt, and a different QE-like policy involving long-term debt. The maturity structure $B_{-1}^{(j)}$ outstanding at time 0 matters, but only to determine the price level jump P_0.

Maturity structure can still matter for other reasons. A maturity structure rearrangement alters the timing of debt policy actions. It therefore may help the government to offer some signaling or precommitment, features outside this model. Contrast the first example, in which the government sells long-term bonds at time 0, with the short-term debt example, in which the government adjusts the price level at each time t with debt at $t - 1$. Both examples produce the same price level path. But the short-term debt policy requires expectations of future actions. The long-term debt policy offers a fire-and-forget policy, taken at time 0 and then left alone.

Lack of commitment is a central problem with monetary policy, since so much of the effects of monetary policy depends on expectations of future actions. The central bank may say in the depths of a recession that it will keep interest rates low after the recession is over, lower than it will prefer to do ex post once the recession is over. But will it carry out the promise ex post? And will people believe such promises?

It's not quite so easy, of course. These QE policies require that the government not undo the policy later, either by selling off the long-term debt or by later short-term debt policies. But it is plausibly easier to commit not to *undo* an action taken today, than it is to commit to *take* an action tomorrow that may seem ex post undesirable. Inaction bias is a form of precommitment.

In these examples, QE operations still require forward guidance of the interest rate target, and for the central bank to state that it will let QE bonds mature, or reinvest them rather than resell them if the central bank changes its mind. Both promises were prominent features of QE operations, which the model makes sense of.

Also, we are only considering the impulse-response function question, how expectations of the future adapt to a single shock. A longer maturity structure changes the response of the price level to *future* shocks. Resilience to future shocks is a key question for maturity structure.

With this theory in mind, we might wonder why actual quantitative easing in the United States, Europe, and Japan seemed so *ineffective*. It is hard to see any lasting effect of QE on either bond prices or inflation. (See Cochrane (2018) and Greenlaw et al. (2018).) Central banks argue, naturally, that without their courageous action things would have been worse, but that is as always a weak argument.

We started with a strong QE: $B_0^{(j)} = P_j s_j$ means that a 1% decrease in bond supply gives a 1% decrease in future price level and a one percentage point increase in bond price. But subsequent analysis gives plenty of reasons for a weaker QE. Though the Federal Reserve in its quantitative easing operations announced its plan to let long-term debt roll off the balance sheet naturally, and that it would keep interest rates low for a long time, people may have believed that QE would be reversed, that the Treasury would take a contrary action, or that central banks would raise interest rates at the customary rate ex post. Surely if conditions improve, the hawks at the Fed will press for selling off the bond portfolio before it matures and raising rates. They did so argue, in fact, and it's hard to tell whether all the forward guidance promises in the early 2010s delayed the 2016–2019 interest rate liftoff at all.

Most of all, "debt policy" as analyzed in this chapter requires people to expect that changes in debt quantities do not correspond to *any* changes in surpluses. As I have emphasized, while changing debt with fixed surpluses and vice versa are useful conceptual exercises for understanding fiscal theory mechanics, it is dangerous to apply these partial derivatives to events. Perhaps people thought QE-induced variation in debt would, like Treasury-induced variation in debt, correspond to changes in surpluses. Greenwood et al. (2015) show that Fed purchases have a larger effect on bond prices than the same bonds issued by the Treasury, suggesting that Fed operations do lead to somewhat different expectations of future surpluses, but not necessarily zero. In addition, with sticky prices, changes in nominal interest rates move real interest rates, so even if surplus expectations were unaffected by QE, the present values of those surpluses are affected. The whole *point* of QE, for the Fed, was to move real interest rates. A serious fiscal theory analysis of QE needs to integrate both features. Finally, the Treasury was selling even more long-term debt than the Fed was buying. At a minimum, its contemporary reactions to events need to be included to evaluate history.

7.6.3 *Summary*

In sum, fiscal theory offers a framework that can begin to describe quantitative easing and open market operations, in the same breath as it can describe interest rate targets and forward guidance about those targets, even in this completely frictionless environment, without price stickiness, monetary frictions, liquidity premiums for special assets, segmented bond markets, or other financial frictions. It offers insights: Promises not to quickly resell debt are important, combining quantitative easing with forward guidance is important, long-term nominal bond price targets can work, and, as always, it is vital to clarify the fiscal foundations of central bank actions, how surpluses react directly or endogenously to monetary policy.

The mechanism for quantitative easing here has nothing to do with the usual analysis. The usual motivation is that via segmented markets for real debt, central bank bond-buying lowers long-term interest rates even though future surpluses rise one for one with debt sales. Markets are just unsegmented enough, however, that those lower long-term Treasury rates leak to corporate and household borrowing rates and stimulate investment, and thereby output. The mechanism here is entirely a wealth effect of government debt. And the different mechanism makes important predictions. Here, a stimulative QE requires outstanding long-term debt, for example. Last, of course, without some real/nominal interaction there is no reason to want inflation in the first place.

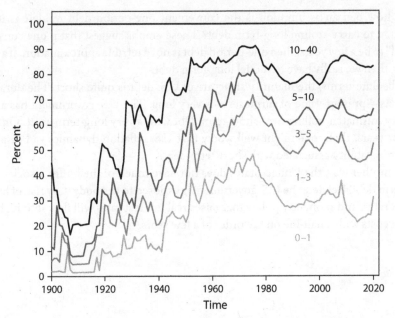

FIGURE 7.6. Face Value of U.S. Treasury Debt by Maturity. Zero coupon basis, $B_t^{(t+j)}$. Data courtesy of George Hall.

7.7 A Look at the Maturity Structure

The U.S. maturity structure is quite short, with half of all debt rolled over in three years or less. The maturity structure has changed a good deal over time. WWII debt was considerably longer.

Figure 7.6 presents the maturity structure of U.S. Treasury debt on a zero-coupon basis. (Data from Hall, Payne, and Sargent (2018).) The U.S. Treasury sells long-term bonds, which combine a large principal and many coupons. I break these up here into their individual components. This is the quantity $B_t^{(t+j)}$ of the theory, expressed as a fraction of the total, $B_t^{(t+j)} / \sum_{j=1}^{\infty} B_t^{(t+j)}$. These are face values, not market values.

The maturity structure is relatively short, with about a third of the debt due in a year or less, and half the debt due and largely rolled over every three years. Reality is even shorter, as this data includes debt held by the Federal Reserve, but does not count the Fed's liabilities, cash, and reserves. Ideally, one should consolidate the Fed and Treasury balance sheets, subtracting Fed holdings and adding cash and reserves as debt held by the public. The graph suggests that a geometric maturity structure $B_t^{(t+j)} = \omega^j B_t$ is not a terrible first approximation or point of linearization.

The maturity structure has changed over time. Keep in mind though that so has the amount of debt. The pre-WWI debt looks very long, but there is very little of it. Some of the gradual shortening of the maturity structure between WWII and 1980 comes simply from paying off long-term debt used to finance that war.

Just how bad an assumption is the convenient one-period debt model? Is it really important to carry around long-term debt? These graphs suggest that if one considers a "period" to be a few years, then one-period debt is not a terrible approximation. If a period is a day, then we really have to model long-term debt.

In absolute terms, the maturity structure of U.S. debt is quite short. The duration of the assets—present value of surpluses—is very long. The U.S. government has a classic maturity mismatch, rolling over short-term debt with a very long-term asset. On a scale of a few years, then, one might well worry that U.S. inflation dynamics can display the run-like instability associated with short-term debt.

Put another way, the United States does not have much of the buffer associated with long-term debt. Related, the U.S. government is exposed to the budgetary risk of high real interest rates, and monetary policy that raises real interest rates will flow into higher real interest costs with a half-life on the order of a few years.

PART II

Assets, Rules, and Institutions

8

Assets and Choices

SOCIETIES CAN CHOOSE a wide range of assets and institutions with which to run their fiscal and monetary affairs. In this chapter, I examine some possibilities, how the fiscal theory generalizes to include these possibilities, and some thoughts on which choices might be better than others in different circumstances.

Fiscal and monetary policy face many trade-offs. A government facing a fiscal shock may choose inflation, explicit partial default, partial defaults on different classes of debt held by different investors, distorting taxes, capital levies, spending cuts, or other measures. Each of these options has welfare and political costs. Each decision is also dynamic, as actions taken this time influence expectations of what will happen next time, and constraints on later actions. Expectations of rarely observed, or "off-equilibrium" behavior matter. Precommitment, time-consistency, reputation, moral hazard, and asymmetric information are central considerations in a monetary and fiscal regime. For this reason, fiscal and monetary policy is deeply mediated by laws, constraints, rules, norms, customs, and institutions.

A theme recurs throughout this part: How can the government commit to surpluses that underlie a stable price level, and communicate that commitment? The expectation on the right-hand side of the valuation equation is otherwise nebulous and potentially volatile. Most governments would like to precommit and communicate that they will manage surpluses to defend a stable price level or inflation rate—no more, and no less. That inflation is much less volatile than stock prices suggests that our governments have been able to make such commitments, at least partially and implicitly. Examining and improving the institutions that allow such commitment is an important task.

The government might like a more sophisticated commitment: that it will manage surpluses to defend stable inflation, but with escape clauses in war, deep recession, and so forth when it might like to implement a state-contingent default, or redistribution from savers to borrowers, via inflation. In the 2010s, our governments struggled to deliberately create modest inflation. Institutions designed to contain inflation struggled to make the necessary commitment to a limited reduction in backing.

These chapters pull together ideas from monetary theory, corporate finance, dynamic public finance, and sovereign debt and default, in a fiscal theory context.

8.1   Indexed Debt, Foreign Debt

I extend fiscal theory to include real debt—indexed debt, or debt issued in foreign currency. Such debt acts as *debt*, where nominal debt acts as *equity*. If the government is to avoid explicit default, it must raise surpluses sufficient to pay off real debt. With only real debt outstanding and surpluses independent of the price level, the price level is not determined by the valuation equation.

Governments often issue indexed debt—debt issued in another country's currency or, historically, debt redeemable in gold. Such debt acts like corporate or individual debt. It must be repaid or default. Government-issued nominal debt functions like corporate equity. Its price—the price level—can adjust in response to lower surpluses, just as corporate equity prices can adjust in response to lower dividends. As a corporation does not have to adjust its dividends upward to match an increase in its stock price, neither does a government that has issued nominal debt have to adjust surpluses to follow changes in the price level.

Indexed debt pays $\$P_t$ rather than $\$1$ when it comes due at time t. If the price level rises from 100 to 110, an indexed bond pays \$110. Denote the quantity of one-period indexed debt issued at time $t - 1$ and coming due at time t by b_{t-1}. Suppose the government finances itself entirely with indexed debt. The government must then pay $b_{t-1}P_t$ dollars at time t. It collects $P_t s_t$ dollars from surpluses. Likewise, each bond sold at the end of t promises P_{t+1} dollars at time $t + 1$. With a constant real rate, risk-neutral pricing, and discount factor β, the flow condition becomes

$$b_{t-1}P_t = P_t s_t + E_t \left[\beta \frac{P_t}{P_{t+1}} \times P_{t+1} \right] b_t$$

$$b_{t-1} = s_t + \beta b_t.$$

The term in square brackets in the first equation is the nominal price of indexed bonds. Iterating forward, we obtain

$$b_{t-1} = \sum_{j=0}^{\infty} \beta^j s_{t+j}. \tag{8.1}$$

If real surpluses s_t are independent of the price level, the price level disappears from the valuation equation. The fiscal theory is not an always and everywhere theory. For the fiscal theory to determine a price level, we need an equation with something nominal and something real in it. However, surpluses that respond to the price level $s(P)$ can lead to a determinate price level even with real debt.

(The timing of this equation is a bit unusual, to preserve the analogy with the B_{t-1} notation for nominal debt. The quantity b_{t-1} is the real value of debt at the beginning of time t. It is known at time $t - 1$, and hence the subscript is not inaccurate. Its real value at time $t - 1$ is βb_{t-1}.)

If the government is to avoid default, equation (8.1) now describes a restriction on surpluses, essentially that surpluses must rise to fully pay off past deficits with interest;

$a(\rho) = 0$ in our earlier moving average notation or $a_s(\rho) - a_r(\rho) = 0$ with varying real interest rates. Though equation (8.1) is often called "the government's intertemporal budget constraint," it is in reality a no-default condition, at least in models as well as reality in which default can happen.

Cash still exists in this indexed debt story, and indexed debt is settled with cash. Write the nominal equilibrium flow condition

$$P_t b_{t-1} = P_t s_t + P_t \beta b_t.$$

The government prints up cash to pay $\$P_t$ to each maturing indexed bond. It soaks up those dollars with primary surpluses, and by selling indexed debt. If surpluses obey (8.1), then this flow condition holds for any price level. If not, then we see instant hyperinflation or hyperdeflation.

Which kind of debt *comes due* is the key question. The amount raised by the debt sale equals the present value of subsequent surpluses, whether the government sells real or nominal bonds. Thus, if real debt is outstanding, but the government issues nominal debt, the price level is still undetermined. If nominal debt is outstanding and the government issues real debt,

$$\frac{B_{t-1}}{P_t} = s_t + \beta b_t = s_t + \beta \sum_{j=0}^{\infty} \beta^j s_{t+1+j}$$

then the price level is determined, at least for this one time period.

Foreign currency debt works in a similar way. Suppose the government dollarizes, or proclaims a permanent foreign exchange peg. This case can be handled with the usual valuation equation, denominating everything in foreign currency:

$$\frac{B_{t-1}}{P_t^*} = E_t \sum_{j=0}^{\infty} \beta^j s_{t+j}. \tag{8.2}$$

Now, P_t^* represents the price of goods in terms of the foreign currency, and s_t is the surplus measured in the same units. Equation (8.2) is again a constraint on surpluses that the government must run in order to avoid default.

The same logic applies to a country in an idealized currency union. Greece uses euros, and agrees to pay its debts in euros. Therefore, (8.2) requires that Greece either run surpluses to pay its debts, or default. The European price level need not adjust in response to Greece's debts.

The situation is the same as the debt of a company, household, or state and local government denominated in dollars. These borrowers must repay or default. If the dollar price level falls, they must raise additional real resources to avoid default.

Many real-world arrangements occupy a muddy middle. Bailouts to people, banks, companies, EU member states, and U.S. state and local governments link public and private debts. For now the point is just to accommodate idealized indexed and foreign debt into fiscal theory.

8.2   Currency Pegs and Gold Standard

Exchange rate pegs and the gold standard are really fiscal commitments. Foreign currency or gold reserves don't matter to first order, as governments do not have enough reserves to back all of their nominal debt. If people demand foreign currency or gold, the government must eventually raise taxes, cut spending, or promise future taxes to obtain or borrow reserves. The peg says "We promise to manage surpluses to pay off the debt at this price level, no more and also no less." The peg makes nominal debt (equity) act like real debt (debt). Unlike full dollarization, a peg gives the country the right to devalue without the costs of explicit default. But the country pays the price for that lesser precommitment. Likewise, a gold standard offers the option of temporary suspension of convertibility and permanent devaluation or revaluation. Both gold and foreign exchange rate pegs suffer that the relative price of goods and gold, or foreign currency, may vary.

In an exchange rate peg or under the gold standard, the country issues its own currency, and borrows in its own currency. But the government promises to freely exchange its currency for foreign currency or for gold, at a set value.

These arrangements suggest that money gains its value from the conversion promise. But exchange rate pegs and the gold standard are in fact *fiscal* commitments. The value of the currency comes ultimately from that fiscal commitment. They are instances of, not alternatives to, fiscal theory. To peg to gold, the government must have or be able to get the gold. To peg to foreign currency, the government must have or be able to get the foreign currency.

Analysis of the gold standard and exchange rate pegs often focuses on whether the government has enough reserves to stand behind its conversion promise. Enough has not always been enough, though, and gold promises and foreign exchange rate pegs have seen "speculative attacks" and devaluations. (Switzerland in 2015 experienced the rare opposite possibility, a speculative attack leading to an undesired *rise* in currency value, and challenging the country's ability to run fiscal *deficits*.) A currency board takes the reserves logic to its limit: It insists that all domestic currency must be backed 100% by foreign currency assets. One hundred percent gold reserves against currency issue are a similar and common idea.

But reserves are, to first order, irrelevant. It is the ability to *get* reserves when needed that counts. Countries, even those on currency boards, do not back all of their *debts* with foreign assets or gold. If a country could do so, it wouldn't have needed to borrow in the first place. When those debts come due, if the government cannot raise surpluses to pay them off or roll them over, the government must print unbacked money or default. When the government runs into fiscal trouble, abandoning the gold standard or currency board and seizing its reserves will always be tempting. Argentina's currency board fell apart this way in a time of fiscal stress. (Edwards (2002) includes a good history.) Moreover, if people see that grab coming, they run immediately, leading to inflation and devaluation.

Conversely, if the government has ample ability to tax or borrow reserves as needed, credibly promising future taxes or spending cuts, then it can maintain convertibility with few reserves. Sims (1999) cites a nice example:

From 1890 to 1894 in the U.S., gold reserves shrank rapidly. U.S. paper currency supposedly backed by gold was being presented at the Treasury and gold was being requested in return. Grover Cleveland, then the president, repeatedly issued bonds for the purpose of buying gold to replenish reserves. This strategy eventually succeeded.

Cleveland persuaded bond buyers that the United States would run larger future fiscal surpluses. The United States' final abandonment of gold promises in 1971 followed a similar outflow of gold to foreign central banks, presenting dollars for gold. The Nixon administration was unable or unwilling to take the fiscal steps necessary to buy or borrow gold.

Reserves may matter to second order, if financial frictions or other constraints make it difficult for the government to tax or borrow needed gold or foreign exchange quickly. But they only matter for that short window. Likewise, solvent banks do not need lots of reserves because they can always borrow reserves or issue equity if needed. Insolvent banks quickly run out of even ample reserves.

With reserves, we can write the government debt valuation equation as

$$\frac{B_{t-1}}{P_t} = G_t + E_t \sum_{j=0}^{\infty} \beta^j s_{t+j}.$$

Here, P_t is the price of goods in terms of gold or foreign currency, and G_t is the quantity of gold or foreign currency reserves. Reserves per se are irrelevant. They are one fiscal resource to back the issue of currency and nominal debt, but they enter in parallel with the usually larger present value of surpluses.

Foreign exchange pegs or the gold standard, when successful, are thus primarily *fiscal commitments* and *communication devices*. If P_t is going to be constant, then the government must adjust surpluses s_t on the right-hand side as needed, not too little (inflation) but not too much (deflation) either. The peg says, "We will manage our taxes and spending so that we can always pay back our debts in foreign currency or gold at this fixed exchange rate, no more and no less." When that promise is credible, it removes the uncertainty of a present value of surpluses and stabilizes the price level. In the language of Section 4.2, they are a precommitment to an active surplus process with $a(\rho) = 0$. In the language of Section 5.4 they are a v versus v^* fiscal policy that precommits to repay debts but not to respond to unanticipated inflation or deflation of the currency relative to gold. Free conversion helps to enforce and make visible this commitment.

This sort of fiscal commitment and communication is valuable. If the government left the price level to the vagaries of investor's expectations about long-run surpluses, inflation could be as volatile as stock prices. But if governments offer and communicate a commitment that surpluses will be adjusted to defend a given price level, and debt will be paid off at that price level, no more as well as no less, the price level is stabilized. A successful currency peg or gold standard produces what looks like a passive fiscal policy, but is in fact an active fiscal policy arranged to determine a steady price level.

Conversely, abandoning the gold standard or revaluing an exchange rate peg can create a defined amount of inflation or deflation by defining the change in surpluses. If the government says, rather than $20 per ounce, the dollar will now be pegged at $32 per ounce, that means that the government will only run enough surpluses to pay off existing debt at $32 per ounce, not $20. But people may lend new money to the government with confidence that the dollar will not quickly fall to $50 an ounce. A devaluation is a way of announcing a partial default via inflation, and its exact amount. Like all capital levies, of course, the trick is to convince people that sinning once does not portend a dissolute life; that this is a once-and-never-again devaluation or at best a rare state-contingent default, not the beginning of a bad habit.

The gold standard or exchange rate peg thus offer a fiscal commitment with an escape clause. The government can enjoy in normal times the advantages of a fiscal precommitment, giving a steady price level and anchored long-term expectations, while leaving open the option of state contingent default achieved through devaluation in emergencies. The government also pays the price of an interest rate premium when people think it likely to use the escape clause too lightly.

A large disadvantage of the gold standard and exchange rate peg is that the relative price of goods and gold varies, and the relative price of domestic and foreign goods, the real exchange rate, varies. Pegging the currency in terms of gold, there was still unpleasant inflation and deflation in the price of goods and services. Exchange rate pegs turn real exchange rate variation into inflation or deflation.

This variation has fiscal consequences. Define the price level in terms of a price index for all goods and services, as we normally do. Specifically, define the price level in the formulas as the relative price of currency versus goods and services, not the relative price of currency versus gold. That's the price level we care about. If the price of gold and currency together relative to goods and services rises, if there is a deflation under the gold standard, the government must raise the present value of surpluses in terms of goods and services to accommodate that deflation. If the relative price of domestic to foreign goods declines—if demand for a country's commodity exports declines, for example—a government on an exchange rate peg must pay off debt with surpluses that are more valuable in terms of domestic goods and services.

A gold standard is an *active* fiscal policy with respect to deviations of the value of currency from gold, but a *passive* fiscal policy with respect to deviations of the price level from the joint value of currency and gold. A foreign-currency peg is active with respect to deviation of the value of domestic from foreign currency, but passive with respect to deviations of the price level from that joint value.

That is pretty much what happened to the gold standard in the 1930s. The price level fell, the value of gold rose, and the value of the currency relative to goods and services rose with it. If the government was going to maintain the gold standard, it would have to cut spending or raise taxes to pay a real windfall to bondholders.

Countries either devalued or abandoned the gold standard. The result, and to us the key mechanism, is that they thereby abandoned a fiscal commitment to repay nominal debt at the now more valuable gold price. This step occasioned lawsuits in the United States, which went to the Supreme Court. The court said, in essence: Yes, the United States is defaulting on gold clauses; yes, this means the government does not have to raise taxes to pay bondholders in gold; and yes, the U.S. government has the constitutional right to default (Kroszner (2003), Edwards (2018)). The government also abrogated gold clauses in private contracts, to avoid a transfer from borrowers to lenders, which the court also affirmed as constitutional. Jacobson, Leeper, and Preston (2019) describe the 1933 revaluation in this way, as a device to allow a defined fiscal devaluation when the gold standard demanded fiscal austerity.

The gold standard is well designed to prevent long-term fiscal inflation. It is much less well designed to prevent deflation.

This episode is also important for forming the expectations underlying today's formally unbacked regime. If a 1933 deflation were to have broken out in 2008, standard passive-fiscal analysis, explicit in new-Keynesian models and IS-LM stories, states the government would dutifully raise taxes and cut spending to pay an unexpected real windfall to bondholders, just as it would have had to do under the gold standard. Obviously, expectations were strong that the government would respond instead exactly as it did: Ignore the "temporary" price level drop, and run a large fiscal expansion under the guise of stimulus until the emergency ended. The memory of 1933 certainly did not hurt in forming that expectation. Consequently, the deflation of 1933 did not repeat.

The shackles of the gold standard can be useful when loosened. When a country devalues, it makes clear the *fiscal* loosening will happen, and its amount. Attempts at unbacked fiscal expansion during the recent zero bound era were not able to communicate that debts would not be repaid. Tying yourself to a mast has the advantage that it is clear when you tie yourself to a shorter mast, and just how much shorter the mast is.

This analysis is simplistic, emphasizing the fiscal points. Thorough analysis of the gold standard takes into account its many frictions: the costs of gold shipment, the way coins often traded above their metallic content (Sargent and Velde (2003)), limits on convertibility, trade frictions, financial frictions, multiple goods, price stickiness, the fee to turn gold into coins, and so forth. Gold standard governments also ran interest rate policies, and raised interest rates to attract gold flows. That combination is initially puzzling. Doesn't the promise to convert gold to money describe monetary policy completely? It merits analysis in the same way we added interest rate targets to the fiscal theory.

A foreign exchange peg begs the question, what determines the value of the foreign currency? Not everyone can peg. The obvious answer is, fiscal theory in the primary country, and we have to investigate fiscal commitments in the primary country or the institutions of the currency union.

The parallel question arises regarding gold: What determines the value of gold in the first place? We often tell a story that the value of gold is determined by industrial uses or jewelry independent of monetary policy. But this story is clearly false. Almost all gold was used for money and is now stored underground, in vaults rather than mines. Based only on industrial use, its value would be much lower.

The gold standard was built on economies that used gold coins. Gold coins are best analyzed, in my view, as a case of $MV = Py$, rather than a case in which money has value because it carries its own backing as an independently valuable commodity. Gold is in sharply limited supply, with few substitutes, especially for large denomination coins. A transactions and precautionary demand for gold, in a world in which gold coins were widely traded, gave gold its value. A gold standard piggybacks on *that* value to generate a value of currency. Think of gold-standard currency then as inside money.

The gold standard has many faults. I do not advocate its return, despite its enduring popularity as a way to run a transparent rules-oriented monetary policy that forswears fiscal inflation, at least inflation of the currency relative to gold.

Most of all, a gold or commodity standard requires an economic force that brings the price level we *do* want to control into line with the commodity that can be pegged. In the gold standard era, gold and gold coins continued to circulate. If the price of gold and currency relative to other goods rose—if there was deflation—then people had more money than they needed. In their effort to spend it on a wide variety of assets, goods, and services, the price level would return. The $MV = Py$ of gold coins made gold a complement to all goods and services. But if the price of gold relative to other goods rises now, this mechanism to bring the relative price of gold to goods back in line is absent. Gold is just one tiny commodity. Tying down its nominal price will stabilize the overall price level about as well as if the New York Fed operated an ice-cream store on Maiden Lane and decreed that a scoop of chocolate fudge ice cream shall always cost a dollar. Well, yes, a network of general equilibrium relationships ties that price to the CPI. But not very tightly. One may predict that ice cream on Maiden Lane will be $1 but the overall CPI will wander around largely unaffected by the peg.

Conventional analysis predicts that if we moved back to a gold standard, the CPI would inherit the current volatility of gold prices. But if the Treasury returned to pegging the price of gold, it is instead possible that it, well, pegs the price of gold, but the CPI wanders around unaffected. The relative price of gold to CPI would lose its current high frequency volatility, but the CPI would wander off.

Foreign exchange rate pegs suffer some of the same disadvantage. The economic force that pulls real exchange rates back, purchasing power parity, is weak. At a minimum, that's why countries peg to their trading partners, and pegs are more attractive for small open economies.

There is evidence that as I hypothesized for gold, the real relative price of foreign and domestic goods depends on the regime. Mussa (1986) pointed out a fact that's pretty clear just looking out the window: Real exchange rates are much more stable at high frequency under a nominal exchange rate peg than under floating rates. The real relative price of a loaf of bread in Windsor, Ontario versus Detroit is more volatile when the U.S. and Canadian dollars float than when they are pegged. This stabilization of real exchange rates is an important argument in favor of exchange rate pegs and common currencies. But it undermines the argument for an exchange rate peg for an individual country's price level control when countries are not well integrated. Countries face a tradeoff between inflation volatility and real exchange rate volatility.

8.3   The Corporate Finance of Government Debt

I import concepts from corporate finance of equity versus debt to think about when governments should issue real (indexed or foreign currency) debt, when they should have their own currencies and nominal debt, and when they might choose structures in between, like an exchange-rate peg or gold standard that can be revalued without formal default.

Governments issue more real debt when they cannot precommit by other means not to inflate or devalue, and when their institutions and government finances are more opaque. To issue nominal debt, governments must offer something like control rights of equity. In modern economies, many voters are mad about inflation, which helps to explain that stable democracies have the most successful currencies.

Should a government choose indexed or nominal debt? Or should it construct contracts and institutions that are somewhat in between, such as the gold standard, foreign exchange peg, or price level target, which are like debt with a less costly default option? Corporations also fund themselves with a combination of debt, equity, and intermediate securities, so we can import much of that analysis.

The government faces shocks to its finances and trade-offs between (at least) three ways of addressing those shocks: formal default (b, B), default via inflation (B/P), and raising taxes or cutting spending (s). Formal default is costly. Unexpected inflation and deflation is also destructive with sticky prices, nominal rigidities, or unpleasant effects of surprise redistributions between lenders to borrowers. Distorting taxes are costly, and governments regard "austerity" spending cuts as costly too. Each option has dynamic and moral-hazard implications. Lucas and Stokey (1983) argue for state contingent partial defaults to minimize tax distortions. Schmitt-Grohé and Uribe (2007) add price stickiness and argue for more tax variation and less inflation variation. But clearly the optimum is an interior combination depending on the costs.

Governments may issue a combination of real and nominal debt. With such a combination, the valuation equation becomes

$$b_{t-1} + \frac{B_{t-1}}{P_t} = E_t \sum_{j=0}^{\infty} \beta^j s_{t+j}. \tag{8.3}$$

The price level is determined by the ability to devalue the nominal debt only.

A corporation that finances itself by more debt and less equity increases the volatility of its stock returns, and is at greater risk of default. Likewise, a government that issues more real debt and less nominal debt, other things constant (they never are), increases the volatility of inflation and raises the chance of explicit default.

That consideration suggests that governments issue more nominal debt and less real debt. Even a country such as Norway that has a substantial sovereign wealth fund may wish to continue to issue extra nominal debt and buy additional real assets, as it has done.

On this basis, Sims (2001) argues against Mexico adopting the dollar or issuing dollar-denominated debt. Dollarization means that fiscal problems must be met with distorting taxes, spending cuts, or costly explicit default. A floating peso and peso-denominated debt allows for subtle devaluation via inflation. More peso debt allows Mexico to adapt to adverse fiscal shocks with less inflation, and lower-still costs of explicit default or devaluation, just like a corporation that finances itself with equity rather than debt.

The same argument lies behind a fiscal theoretic interpretation of the widespread view that countries like Greece should not be on the euro. Currency devaluation and inflation implements state contingent default, perhaps less painfully than explicit default or "austerity" policies to raise surpluses.

On the other hand, corporate finance also teaches us that debt helps to solve moral hazard, asymmetric information, and time consistency or precommitment problems. An entrepreneur may not put in the required effort, may be tempted to divert some of the cash flow due to equity investors, or may not be able to credibly report what the cash flow is. Debt leaves the risk and incentive in the entrepreneur's hands, helping to resolve the agency problems. So, despite the risk-sharing and default-cost reductions of equity financing, the theory of corporate finance predicts and recommends widespread use of debt. Equity only works when the issuers can certify performance, through accounting and other monitoring, and by offering shareholders control rights.

Real government debt is a precommitment device. The legal structure of real debt, and the actual and reputational cost of default, help the government to produce surpluses that repay debt, even if doing so involves unpleasant taxation or spending cuts.

Default also has costs. If it did not, real debt would not offer any precommitment. Those costs are regretted ex post. Greece is a good example: By joining the euro, so its bonds were supposed to default if Greece could not repay them, Greece precommitted against default. That precommitment allowed Greece to borrow a lot of euros at low interest rates, and to avoid the regular bouts of inflation and devaluation that it had suffered previously. Alas, when Greece finally did run into a rollover crisis, it discovered just how large those costs might be.

Sims's (2001) argument, like that for the drachma, does not consider the possibility of mismanagement, the difficulty of fiscal probity, and the need for fiscal precommitments, evident in decades of deficits, crises, devaluations, wasted spending, and inflation around the world. It neglects that surpluses are a choice, not an exogenous shock. The properties of the surplus process $\{s_t\}$ are not independent of real versus nominal financing. Evaluating Sims's advice for Mexico, one might consider the comparative fiscal and monetary history of Ecuador and Panama, fully dollarized; Argentina, with bouts of dollar pegs; and Venezuela, with its own currency (Buera and Nicolini (2021), Restuccia (2021)). I'm cherry-picking of course, and repeated crises of exchange rate pegs and formal defaults on dollar debt are also painful. But a precommitment value of dollarization exists. A weaker but substantial precommitment value of a peg exists as well. Issuing and borrowing in a national currency and then quickly inflating to solve every fiscal shock is not always optimal.

Nominal government debt, like corporate equity, works better when government accounts are more trustworthy and transparent. Nominal debt works better when the country has other means to commit to an s-shaped surplus process.

Corporate equity requires some mechanism to guarantee dividend payments in place of the explicit promises offered by debt, backed by law, collateral, or other penalties and punishments. For corporate equity, control rights are that mechanism. If the managers don't pay dividends or seem to be running the company badly, the shareholders can vote them out and get new management. What are the equivalent of control rights for nominal debt, which behaves like government equity? Most naturally in the modern world, *voters*. If nominal government debt gets inflated away, a whole class of voters is really mad. Inflation is even more powerful than explicit default in this way. If the government defaults, only bondholders lose, and a democracy with a universal franchise may not care. Or the bondholders may be foreigners. If the government *inflates*, every private contract is affected. The government's debt devaluation triggers a widespread private devaluation, and everyone on the losing end of that devaluation suffers. The chaos of inflation hurts everyone. Alexander Hamilton is justly famous for the insight that a democracy needs widespread ownership of government debt, by people with the political power to force repayment. Widespread pain of inflation is even more powerful. Why do we use government debt as our numeraire, thus exposing private contracts to the risks of government finances? Well, the fact that we do, and we vote, means that there is a large group of voters who don't like inflation.

The standard ideas of corporate finance thus suggest that countries with precommitment problems, poor fiscal institutions, and untrustworthy government accounts, who tend to issue and then default or inflate, should or have to issue real or foreign currency debt. To borrow at all they may even have to offer collateral or other terms that make explicit default additionally painful. Countries that have alternative precommitment mechanisms, strong institutions, and stable democracies with a widespread class of people who prefer less inflation, are able to issue government equity. Such countries have their own currencies and borrow in those currencies.

Confirming this view, dollarization, currency pegs, and indexed and foreign debt are common in the developing and undemocratic world. Nominal debt and local currencies here often come with stringent capital controls, financial repression, wage and price controls, and frequent inflation. Successful non-inflating currencies and large domestic currency debts seem to be the province of stable democracies.

Though we appear to determine the price level via (8.3) with an arbitrarily small amount of nominal debt, we should as always be cautious about such limits. Consider smaller and smaller amounts of nominal debt in (8.3), with more and more real debt, and coupled with a surplus process that steadily pays back more debt, approaching $a(\rho) = 0$, so that inflation remains the same as we make this change in debt. The price level is determinate all the way along at the limit, but not the limit point. This is a fiscal theory version of the cashless limit puzzle. Yes, when debt is down to the $10 in pennies in your sock drawer plus $20 trillion of indexed debt, and the expected surpluses decline by $1, there should be a 10% inflation. But the economic force for that inflation is clearly weak. You might just leave the pennies in your sock drawer. The wealth effect of nominal government bonds is weaker as the size of nominal debt declines. If we wish to think about a backing theory of money for small amounts of nominal debt, backing that debt with a visible set of real assets and an explicit redemption promise offers a greater force to value adjustment. That may be a reason for gold standards in the previous era of small government debt. I take up below how one might construct such an institution today.

The sovereign debt literature studies the extent to which reputation and other punishments can induce repayment, since governments are difficult to sue and sovereign debt typically does not offer collateral. This theory is useful for us to import, thinking about inflation in place of default.

In the history of government finance, it took centuries for governments to somewhat credibly promise repayment, and thereby to borrow in large quantities at low rates. The parallel development of paper currencies that did not quickly inflate took hundreds of years as well. Government debt is full of institutions that help to precommit to repayment and limit ex post inflation and default. The Bank of England and parliamentary approval for borrowing, taxation, and expenditures were seventeenth-century institutions that limited the sovereign's authority to default. That limit allowed the U.K. government to borrow more ex ante. The French absolute monarch, being more powerful, could not precommit to repay, so he could not borrow as much. This deficiency has long been regarded an important factor in France losing the wars of the eighteenth century and eventually the French revolution itself (Sargent and Velde (1995)). Imperial Britain used force to get other sovereigns to repay. Today, sovereign debt includes many institutions beyond reputation to try to force repayment, including third-country adjudication, the right of creditors to seize international assets, and threats by international institutions to cut defaulters off. All have partial success, but also partial failures given the repeated foreign debt crises of the last several decades.

8.4   Maturity, Pegs, Promises, and Runs

Long-term debt can offer a buffer against surplus shocks and real interest rate shocks. Long-term debt opens the door to policies that resemble quantitative easing. Long-term debt insulates the government, and inflation, from the run-like dynamics of short-term debt. However, all insurance invites moral hazard. Short-term debt and pegs may impose a commitment to fiscal discipline.

Should governments choose long-term or short-term financing? This choice has varied a great deal over time. The Victorian United Kingdom was largely financed by perpetuities, preceded by centuries in which perpetual debt was a common instrument. The current U.S. government has, as above, a quite short maturity structure, rolling over about half the debt every two to three years. Governments in fiscal trouble find themselves pushed to shorter and shorter maturities by higher and higher interest rates for longer-term debt. Markets think default or inflation more likely than the government wishes, and attempts to buy lots of insurance in the form of long-term debt just raise suspicions further.

Why governments chose long-term debt and why they have moved to short-term debt is an interesting open question. In part, the less developed financial and communication technology of the time may have played a part. Rolling over a large principal payment might have been difficult. In part, long-term price stability under the gold standard made long-term financing relatively cheaper. In part, we may simply have lost some of our ancestors' wisdom.

Sections 3.5.2, 7.2.1, and 7.6 showed ways in which long-term debt can offer a buffer against fiscal shocks. The linearization (3.22) shows some mechanisms compactly,

$$\sum_{j=0}^{\infty} \omega^j \Delta E_{t+1} \pi_{t+1+j} = - \sum_{j=0}^{\infty} \rho^j \Delta E_{t+1} \tilde{s}_{t+1+j} + \sum_{j=1}^{\infty} (\rho^j - \omega^j) \Delta E_{t+1} r_{t+j}. \quad (8.4)$$

If $\omega = 0$, short-term debt, then the entire revision in the present value of surpluses must be met by immediate inflation $\Delta E_{t+1} \pi_{t+1}$. The longer the maturity of debt ω, the more the revision in present value of surpluses can be spread to future inflation, though at the cost of more total inflation. In many views of price stickiness, a protracted small inflation is better than a short large inflation. Long-term debt empowers monetary policy to reduce current inflation when it spreads inflation forward.

On a flow basis, long-term debt leaves the budget and hence the price level less exposed to real interest rate variability. If the government borrows short term, then a rise in the interest rate raises real interest costs in the budget and necessitates tax increases or spending decreases, or results in inflation. If the government borrows long term, then the increase in interest cost only affects the government slowly. The tradeoff is familiar to any homeowner choosing between a fixed and floating rate mortgage. If interest rates rise, the floating rate borrower has to pay more immediately. The fixed rate borrower pays the same amount no matter what happens to interest rates.

We can see this effect in identity (8.4) as well. An increase in real interest rate is an increase in the expected real bond return on the right-hand side. The larger ω, the smaller the weights $\rho^j - \omega^j$. In the limit $\omega = \rho$, a real-rate increase has no inflationary effect. The rate rise still makes unexpected future deficits more costly to finance, but it means the government can pay off current debt with the currently planned surpluses, ignoring interest costs.

In this case, the linearization is a bit misleading. It values discount rate effects at the average surplus, and surplus effects at the average discount rate. The obvious proposition, that the government is insulated from real rate shocks when the maturity of debt matches the maturity of surpluses, requires the interaction term. We can see the effect more clearly with the continuous time present value relation

$$\frac{\int_{\tau=0}^{\infty} Q_t^{(t+\tau)} B_t^{(t+\tau)} d\tau}{P_t} = E_t \int_{\tau=0}^{\infty} e^{-\int_{j=0}^{\tau} r_{t+j} dj} s_{t+\tau} d\tau.$$

Using the expectations hypothesis for bond prices,

$$Q_t^{(t+\tau)} = E_t \left(e^{-\int_{j=0}^{\tau} r_{t+j} dj} \frac{P_t}{P_{t+\tau}} \right),$$

we have

$$\int_{\tau=0}^{\infty} E_t e^{-\int_{j=0}^{\tau} r_{t+j} dj} \frac{B_t^{(t+\tau)}}{P_{t+\tau}} d\tau = E_t \int_{\tau=0}^{\infty} e^{-\int_{j=0}^{\tau} r_{t+j} dj} s_{t+\tau} d\tau.$$

Now, if today's debt maturity $B_t^{(t+\tau)} E_t (1/P_{t+\tau})$ matches the path of expected real surpluses $s_{t+\tau}$ as a function of τ, then real interest rate changes r_{t+j} cancel from both sides. The stream of assets matches the stream of liabilities. Otherwise, the mismatch between the maturity of debt and the usually much longer maturity of the surplus determines how the price level reacts to real interest rates.

Section 7.2.2 emphasized how the intertemporal linkages of the present value relation come from rolling over short-term debt. Short-term investors hold government debt because they believe other short-term investors will buy their debt. A rollover crisis or run on nominal debt causes a sudden inflation or devaluation. Long-term debt cuts off this crisis or run-like mechanism entirely. Sovereign debt crises too are (almost) always and everywhere crises of short-term debt.

All of these considerations point to long-term debt for its buffering properties. But again they take the surplus process as given. Corporate finance also points us to *incentive* properties of short-term debt. Making things worse ex post gives an incentive for, and precommitment to, more careful behavior ex ante. Governments that issue short-term debt will, the theory goes, be more attentive to fiscal policies, to maintaining their ability to borrow, and will be forced to take painful fiscal adjustments sooner. In return, markets will offer better rates to governments who bind themselves via short-term debt in this way, unless the governments have other commitment devices. Diamond and Rajan (2012) argue that run-prone short-term debt disciplines bankers. Run-prone short-term debt might discipline governments as well.

Long-term debt offers insurance. All insurance risks moral hazard. The more long-term debt, the easier it is for the government to put off a fiscal reckoning, letting it fall on long-term bond prices rather than current budgets, refinancing, or interest costs. In turn, that expectation leads to higher interest rates for long-term debt, so that a sober government feels it pays too much. Greenwood et al. (2015), for example, advocate that the U.S. Treasury borrow short to save interest costs. Like not buying insurance, if the event does not happen the premium is a waste. If markets look at who is buying insurance and charge higher rates still, insurance is doubly expensive. And if the absence of insurance prods one to more careful behavior, insurance can be additionally expensive.

The conversion promise of a gold standard and foreign exchange peg, rather than the more elastic guidepost of a gold price or foreign exchange target, which can be missed temporarily, adds an additional invitation to run, and thereby another precommitment to sober fiscal policy. Offering that anyone can bring in a dollar and receive gold, or everyone can bring in a peso and get a dollar, immediately, invites an instantaneous run when, as always, governments do not back currency 100% with reserves, or when they have additional debt or a temptation to grab the reserves. In turn, a government that offers such a right ties itself even more strongly to the mast to always maintain plenty of fiscal space.

I offer benefits and costs on both sides, to frame the long versus short discussion, not to answer it. As I judge the maturity issue, a U.S. or global advanced-country sovereign-debt rollover crisis, though unlikely, would be an immense economic and financial catastrophe. The U.S. Congress, though not unable to reform, needs time to do it and not to bungle the process. A small insurance premium seems worth it. Long-term nominal interest rates of 1.5%, slightly negative in real terms as I write in late 2021, seem a low premium for the insurance they provide. True, if 0% short rates continue for 30 years, the interest costs of short-term debt will turn out to have been even lower. Also true, I offered the same advice 10 years ago, and short rates have been lower that whole time. I have also, by this ex post logic, wasted 35 years of fire insurance premiums on my house. It's a judgment, and the probability of the event and risk aversion must matter. I note however, that terrorist attacks, housing price collapses, and a global pandemic were all thought to have lower probability ex ante than they do now.

Whether markets would still offer 1.5% long rates should the U.S. federal government wish to buy a lot more of that insurance is also an interesting question. It would be enlightening to find out, as it would measure just how insatiable demand for U.S. debt is, and how ironclad markets' faith in U.S. finances really is.

Whether the additional precommitment of run-inviting short-term debt or pegs is useful is also debatable. I judge not, but that too is a judgment, awaiting more careful research. Just how strong is the fiscal precommitment value of government debt structure that is prone to inflation runs or rollover runs? Are there not other precommitment devices that are not so dangerous when they fail? Peltzman (1975) famously argues for spikes on the dashboard to encourage safer driving. But we chose seatbelts and other incentives instead.

In this context, the Diamond and Rajan (2012) analysis of bank capital structure, advocating run-prone debt for its incentive properties, is controversial. In fact, equity holders can and do monitor and punish bank managers as they do for all other corporations. In fact, most holders of short-term debt do no fundamental analysis of borrowers' cash flows. Short-term debt is an "information insensitive" security designed so that its holders *do not* do any monitoring, in the contrary Gorton and Metrick (2012) view of banking, until all of a sudden they wake up and run. To be fair, Diamond and Rajan emphasize short-term financing offered by big investment banks and broker-dealers, rather than bank deposits or the commercial paper market. Monitoring is more plausible in that case. But that story then applies even less to government debt. Short-term government debt is the paradigmatic "risk-free" security, held as cash, by investors doing no "fundamental" analysis of long-run government fiscal affairs. Until they wake up and run.

As equity-financed banking has a good point (Cochrane (2014c)), despite the need for equity rather than short-term debt holders to monitor management, so government finance based on long-term nominal debt and targets rather than pegs, monitored by grumpy voters, may have a point as well.

Greece not only signed up for euro-denominated debt, it rolled over short-term debt. It failed in a rollover crisis. Apparently, the discipline of run-prone debt was not large enough for Greece to mend its fiscal affairs.

The history of the gold standard and foreign exchange pegs is replete with crisis after crisis, as the history of banking funded by immediate service, run-prone deposits is one of crisis after crisis, in which the disciplinary forces failed.

The end of the Bretton Woods era in 1971 offers an example of a peg gone awry.[1] In the Bretton Woods era, foreign central banks could demand gold for dollars, though people and financial institutions could not do so. Exchange rates were fixed, and capital markets were not open as they are today. A persistent trade deficit could not easily result in devaluation, or be financed by a capital account surplus, or foreigners using dollars to buy U.S. stocks, bonds, or even government debt. Trade deficits had to be financed by paper dollars, and gold if foreign central banks did not want those dollars. Bretton Woods was simply not designed for a world with large persistent trade deficits and surpluses and capital flows. Instead, the persistent trade deficit, fueled by persistent fiscal deficits, resulted in foreign central banks accumulating dollars. The banks grew wary of dollars and started demanding gold. The resulting run on the dollar precipitated the U.S. abandoning Bretton Woods and the gold standard entirely, allowing the dollar to devalue, and inaugurating the inflation of the 1970s. It was a classic sovereign debt crisis. With the remaining tie of dollars

---

1. Shlaes (2019) tells the history well, as do Bordo (2018) and Bordo and Levy (2020) with more economic analysis. Rueff (1972), writing at the time, emphasizes the link between the trade deficit and inflation in the Bretton Woods system:

> The trouble that I denounced in 1961 has brought about all the consequences I had foreseen: a perennial deficit in America's balance of payments, inflation in creditor countries, and in the end, disruption of the monetary system by requests for reimbursement of the dollar balances so imprudently accumulated. (p. 179.)

The dollar nonetheless remained the reserve currency despite the end of Bretton Woods.

to gold at a fixed price, Bretton Woods was fundamentally incompatible with steady, even small, inflation.

The fiscal deficits of the Vietnam War and Great Society and the era's trade deficits were large by the standards of the time. Both are smaller than we have grown accustomed to today. Why did those deficits cause a great crisis and inflation, while post-2000 immense trade and fiscal deficits resulted in nothing, at least until 2021? Well, the institutional framework matters. The combination of a gold promise to foreign central banks, fixed exchange rates, and largely closed capital markets shut off today's adjustment mechanisms.

In one sense our mechanisms are much better. Our government can now borrow immense amounts of money, and our economy can run immense trade deficits, financed in capital markets, not by gold flows. In another sense, our mechanisms expose us to a much bigger and more violent reckoning if and when the reckoning comes.

Just why did the Johnson and Nixon administrations not borrow, and buy gold, as Grover Cleveland did, to stem the gold flows? Sure, they were already borrowing a lot, but it's hard to argue that the United States was unable to borrow more, and pledge higher future surpluses in so doing. Or were the restrictions in international capital markets tight enough to turn off this saving mechanism?

The gold standard retains an allure. The government freely exchanges money for gold, thereby transparently and mechanically determining the value of money, without the need for central banker clairvoyance. As we have seen, it is at heart a fiscal commitment, which is both good and bad. It rules out the option to devalue via inflation, which helps the government to borrow ex ante and resist inflationary temptation ex post. But at times inflation is a better option than sharp tax increases, or spending cuts. It also signals that surpluses will *only* be large enough to pay off debt at the promised gold peg, thus precommitting against deflation of currency relative to gold.

But in its failures, more frequent than usually remembered, the gold standard leads to explicit default, chaotic devaluation, speculative attack when devaluation looms, or a suspension of convertibility with uncertain outcomes. A gold standard, as opposed to a gold price target, introduces run-like commitments. These further bind the government to fiscal probity to avoid runs, but make crises worse when runs do break out. The gold standard was not as mechanical as advocates remember, including in the United Kingdom with an active central bank also setting interest rates. And, most of all, the gold standard allows inflation and deflation when the price of gold and currency rise or fall together relative to goods and services. The gold standard imposes a passive fiscal commitment to tighten fiscal policy in the event of such deflation, or to loosen fiscal policy to validate such inflation. Such volatility is more likely now that gold is disconnected from the financial system and hence other prices.

8.5 Default

Fiscal theory can incorporate default. An unexpected partial default substitutes for inflation in adapting to a fiscal shock. A preannounced partial default creates a defined fiscal inflation. It is analogous to a gold parity devaluation, or devaluing a currency peg.

Fiscal theory can easily incorporate default. We do not need to assume that governments always print money to devalue debt via inflation rather than default.

Suppose that the government at date t writes down its debt: It says, for each dollar of promised debt, we pay only $D_t < 1$ dollars. Now, we have

$$\frac{B_{t-1} D_t}{P_t} = E_t \sum_{j=0}^{\infty} \beta^j s_{t+j}. \tag{8.5}$$

The price level is still determined. An unexpected partial default allows the government to adapt to a negative surplus shock with less or no inflation. Fiscal theory does *not* require that governments always inflate rather than default.

With short-term debt and no change in surpluses, a pure *expected* partial default has no effect on the current price level, but it can influence future inflation. It works analogously to bond issues. With the possibility of future partial default, and simplifying with no current default $D_t = 0$, the flow condition remains

$$\frac{B_{t-1}}{P_t} = s_t + \frac{Q_t B_t}{P_t} = s_t + E_t \sum_{j=1}^{\infty} \beta^j s_{t+j}. \tag{8.6}$$

The bond price becomes

$$Q_t = \frac{1}{1 + i_t} = E_t \left(\beta \frac{P_t}{P_{t+1}} D_{t+1} \right). \tag{8.7}$$

If at time t people expect a partial default $D_{t+1} < 1$, with no change in surpluses, this change has no effect on the current price level P_t, by (8.6). An expected partial default just lowers bond prices, and thus lowers the revenue the government raises from a given amount of nominal bonds. With the same surpluses, the government must sell more nominal bonds to generate the same real revenue.

The effect of an expected partial default on the future price level P_{t+1} and expected inflation $E_t(P_t/P_{t+1})$ depends on monetary policy—how much nominal debt B_t the government sells, or how it sets the interest rate target i_t. If the government allows the interest rate to rise, fully reflecting the higher default-risk probability, then neither P_t nor P_{t+1} is affected by the announced partial default. The government just sells more nominal debt B_t. Selling two bonds when people expect a 50% haircut is exactly the same as selling one bond when people expect no haircut, except nominal bond prices fall by half. It generates the same revenue, and results in the same future issue of \$1 to pay off the debt. However, if the government sticks to the nominal interest rate target, requiring that i_t and Q_t are unchanged, then the expected future price level P_{t+1} declines. It's equivalent to selling less nominal debt or lowering the interest rate target.

But an announced partial default with no surplus news is a strange and unrealistic intervention. When we think of a default, we think that the government is *not* going to raise surpluses to repay some debt. Thus, a more realistic story pairs an expected future default with bad news about future surpluses.

So, suppose at time t, the government announces a 10% haircut for $t + 1$, $D_{t+1} = 0.90$. People infer that surpluses from $t + 1$ onwards $E_t \sum_{j=1}^{\infty} \beta^j s_{t+j}$ will be 10% lower; not, as in our last example, that surpluses are unchanged. This expected future default then raises the price level today by 10%.

• *Expected future default can trigger current inflation in the fiscal theory.*

Monetary policy still determines the expected future price level. If the government allows the interest rate to rise, to follow the increased default premium, then by (8.7), the expected price level at $t + 1$ is also 10% higher.

Really the *point* of this announced default is a commitment and communication device that the government really will lower future surpluses, and will not, as customary, repay debts without causing inflation. A preannounced partial default, along with monetary policy that allows nominal interest rates to rise, is analogous to a 10% devaluation under a gold standard or foreign exchange peg. Those are likewise good devices to communicate a fiscal commitment and produce 10% cumulative inflation, and only 10% cumulative inflation.

Many governments at the zero bound and with inflation stubbornly below their central banks' 2% inflation targets have *wanted* to inflate, but to inflate only a little and in a controlled fashion. They turned to fiscal stimulus with little effect. Evidently, bond markets did not lightly abandon government's hard-won reputations for repaying debt. "Unbacked fiscal expansion" is easy to say, but hard to do, and hard to do in a limited way. A preannounced partial default could raise inflation by reducing fiscal backing, and by a clear and calibrated amount. Like all devaluations, just how to communicate that this is a one-time policy and not the beginning of a regular pattern is the hard part.

8.6   Central Bank Independence

An independent central bank is a fiscal commitment. Independent central banks make it difficult to finance deficits with non-interest-bearing money, thereby forcing the fiscal authorities to raise current or future surpluses, or to default.

So far, I have integrated central bank and treasury. In the end, central bank and treasury are part of the same government. Their finances are united, as are the finances of members of a family. If the treasury issues debt and the central bank buys that debt and issues reserves or cash, it is the same as the treasury issuing reserves or cash directly. In this section, I consider some ways in which the separation between central bank and treasury matters.

Central bank independence is usually thought of in terms of monetary control, with the price level set by $MV = Py$ or by interest rate policy. Giving an independent central bank control of M or interest rates helps the government to precommit against goosing the economy or lowering interest rates for short-term political reasons; for example, ahead of elections.

An independent central bank can act as an important *fiscal* commitment, in a fiscal theory of the price level. It is part of a larger institutional structure that tries to precommit the government against inflationary finance, and more generally commit to debt repayment and s-shaped surpluses so the government can borrow in the first place.

Most of all, since the central bank alone controls the issuance of currency and reserves, the treasury may not print currency or issue reserves to repay debt or to finance deficits. To do that, the treasury must issue debt, and the central bank must buy that debt. When a debt-limit default loomed in 2009, it surprised many commentators that the U.S. Fed cannot monetize deficits to continue spending, even to avoid default, as much as the mantra is repeated that a country that defines its own currency need never default.

The Federal Reserve may not buy Treasury securities directly from the Treasury. Treasury securities promise reserves, not more Treasury securities. The Treasury may not legally grab assets from the Fed's balance sheet. Additionally, central bankers have a certain amount of political independence, both in law and custom.

We should not assume that central bankers always dislike inflation. Many, viewing themselves as macroeconomic planners, would choose more inflation in order to achieve other goals. Many would like to use the central bank's great financial and regulatory power to pursue policy objectives unrelated to inflation. Removing the inflation punch bowl just as the party gets going, as William McChesney Martin put it, doesn't get anyone cheers at Davos or more glamorous political positions. Part of the institutional structure therefore also precludes the *central bank* from fiscal policy and fiscal inflation: Central bank helicopter drops are illegal; central banks must always lend or buy assets. Central banks cannot give out money, and they are often limited in the range of assets they can buy; including, traditionally, not providing subsidized credit to favored businesses and industries. Central banks are given limited mandates. Mandates are as important for what they omit and forbid as for what they include and command. Mandate limitations and political autonomy give central bankers the authority to resist political pressure for inflation or to finance deficits. They also limit central bankers who might prefer inflation, or to use the central bank's tools for their own political and policy priorities, and might misuse independence to do so.

Independence and mandates are limited in their anti-inflationary effect. The Federal Reserve's official mandate also includes "maximum employment," and some sort of "financial stability" mandate is widely agreed on. No agency can or should be totally independent in a democracy. Federal Reserve officials are appointed by the President and confirmed by Congress. Central bankers who wish to be reappointed tend to bend to the desires of the administration and Senate. Mandate limitations only matter if Congress and the administration object when the Federal Reserve goes boldly where it has not gone before.

The point, for us: An independent central bank, with monopoly on the issuance of reserves and currency, that cares about inflation either from its own preferences or by paying attention to a mandate, that can refuse to purchase more than a certain amount of government debt, can force a recalcitrant treasury and government to pay back its debt with surpluses, to credibly promise future surpluses to roll over the debt, or to default, rather than inflate. Even in my simple frictionless models, inflation in the end comes from too much cash. The "government" prints money to redeem debt and soaks money up with surpluses and more debt. If the central bank controls the printing press, the government can be precluded from the first step, and thereby from fiscal inflation.

Independent central banks and rules against deficit finance have been important parts of inflation control, and more generally for ensuring that governments repay debt, for centuries. The Bank of England was founded in 1694, as a private company with a monopoly on the issuance of bank notes, precisely to buy government debt and ensure its repayment. Restoring central bank independence has been an important element of fiscal–monetary stabilizations from the Fed–Treasury accord of 1951, to inflation-targeting episodes, to the end of inflations and hyperinflations (Section 14.2), and to stabilizations under inflation-targeting regimes (Section 9.1).

Central bank independence is important for many additional reasons unrelated to the price level and fiscal issues of this book. Central banks have enormous regulatory power to tell banks who to lend to and who not to lend to, how banks operate, and how much to pay depositors. Central banks can directly lend or buy assets at inflated prices. Precommiting not to use central banks' tools for such inherently political acts, and keeping independent central bankers from following their own policy preferences with such acts, have historically been important for sound economic performance where successful, and damaging outcomes when unsuccessful.

I do not emphasize a separate balance sheet, independence, and other aspects of central bank versus treasury tensions in this book. There is a huge literature on the subject. Most of the analysis applies quickly to fiscal theory, and I don't have much novel to say about it. Once central bank and treasury play whatever the game between them is, we can draw again a circle around the government, and model the government's decisions and its unified balance sheet. It's really a part of the larger political economy question *how* the government makes decisions about surpluses and debt or interest rates, and thus a theory of what sorts of decisions it is likely to make. Like other theories of preference formation, we don't *have* to look under the hood in order to analyze how the effects of government policy—treasury and central bank together—affect the economy.

9

Better Rules

LEAVING SURPLUSES to expectations or implicit commitments is clearly not the best institutional structure for setting a monetary standard. If only the government could commit
and communicate that the present value of surpluses shall be this much, neither more nor
less, then it could produce a more stable price level. It could also quickly produce inflation or deflation when it wishes to do so. Historically, committing and communicating
against inflationary finance was the main problem. In the Great Depression and the 2010s,
committing and communicating that surpluses will not rise, to combat deflation, became
important as well.

The gold standard offers this kind of commitment: The present value of future surpluses shall be just enough to pay back the current debt at the gold peg, neither more
nor less. Alas, the gold standard suffers the above list of problems that make it unsuit-
able for the modern world. I examine here alternative institutions that may analogously
communicate and commit the government to a present value of surpluses.

The fiscal theory of monetary policy combines fiscal policy that determines surpluses
and monetary policy that implicitly sets the path of nominal debt. We have grown accustomed to monetary policy that consists of nominal interest rate targets, set by hopefully
wise central bankers. I investigate alternative monetary rules, including a target for the
spread between nominal and indexed debt.

9.1   Inflation Targets

Inflation targets have been remarkably successful. I interpret the inflation target as a fiscal commitment. The
target commits the *legislature and treasury* to pay off debt at the targeted inflation rate, and to adjust fiscal
policy as needed, as much as it commits and empowers the central bank. This interpretation explains why the
adoption of inflation targets led to nearly instant disinflation, and that central banks have not been tested to
exercise the toughness that conventional analysis of inflation targets says they must occasionally display.

Inflation targets have been remarkably successful. Figures 9.1 and 9.2 show inflation
around the introduction of inflation targets in New Zealand and Canada. On the
announcement of the targets, inflation fell to the targets quickly, and stayed there, with
no large recession, and no period of high interest rates or other monetary stringency, such
as occurred during the painful U.S. and U.K. stabilizations of the early 1980s. Sweden had
a similar experience. Just how were these miracles achieved?

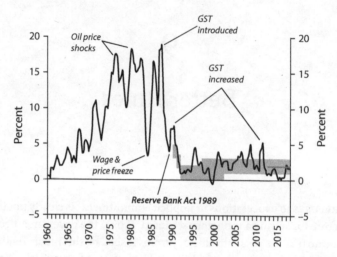

FIGURE 9.1. Inflation Surrounding the Introduction of a Target in New Zealand. Shading indicates the inflation target range. Source: McDermott and Williams (2018). Figure courtesy of Rebecca Williams.

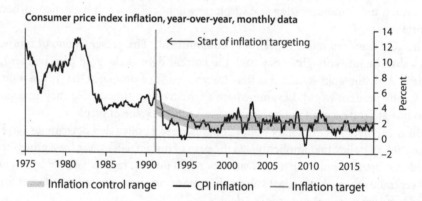

FIGURE 9.2. Inflation Surrounding Canada's Introduction of an Inflation Target. Source: Murray (2018).

Inflation targets consist of more than just promises by central banks. Central banks make announcements and promises all the time, and people regard such statements with skepticism well-seasoned by experience.

Inflation targets are an agreement between central bank, treasury, and government. The conventional story of their effect revolves around central banks: The inflation target agreement requires and empowers the central bank to focus only on inflation. The agreement gives the bank greater independence. It typically does not spell out a rule, rather giving the bank relatively free rein in how it is to achieve the inflation target. Central bankers are evaluated by their performance in achieving the inflation target, which is a commitment by the government *not* to complain about other objectives.

These stories are wanting. Did previous central banks just lack the guts to do what's right, in the face of political pressure to inflate? Did they wander away from their clear institutional missions and need reining in? Moreover, just what does the central bank *do* to produce low inflation after the inflation target is announced? One would have thought, and most people did think, that the point of an inflation-targeting agreement is to insulate the bank from political pressure during a long period of monetary stringency. To fight inflation, the central bank would have to produce high real interest rates and a severe recession such as accompanied the U.S. disinflation during the early 1980s. And the central bank would have to repeat such unwelcome medicine regularly. For example, that is the diagnosis repeated by McDermott and Williams (2018) of the 1970s and 1980s.

Nothing of the sort occurred. Inflation simply fell like a stone on the announcement of the target, and the central banks were never tested in their resolve to raise interest rates, cause recessions, or otherwise squeeze out inflation. Well, "expectations shifted" when the target was announced, and became "anchored" by the target, people say, but why? The long history of inflation certainly did not lack for speeches from politicians and central bankers promising future toughness on inflation. Why were *these* speeches so effective? Why did they produce anchors and not sails?

Figure 9.1 provides a hint, with the annotation "GST [goods and services tax] introduced" and "GST increased." Each of these inflation targets emerged as a part of a package of reforms including fiscal reforms, spending reforms, financial market liberalizations, and pro-growth regulatory reforms. McDermott and Williams (2018), though focusing on central bank actions, write "A key driver of high inflation in New Zealand over this period [before the introduction of the inflation target] was government spending, accommodated by generally loose monetary policy." It follows that a key driver of non-inflation afterwards was a reversal of these policies, not just a tough central bank.

I therefore read the inflation target as a bilateral commitment. It includes a commitment by the *legislature and treasury* to 2% (or whatever the target is) inflation. They commit to run *fiscal* and economic affairs to pay off debt at 2% inflation, no more, and no less. People expect the legislature and treasury to back debt at the price level *target*, but not to respond to changes in the real value of debt due to changes in the price level away from the target. Above-target inflation will lead to fiscal stringency. Below-target inflation will lead to inaction or stimulus. The inflation target captures the π^* and v^* of my simple fiscal models.

The inflation target functions as a gold price or exchange rate target, which commit the legislature and treasury to pay off debt at a gold or foreign currency value, no more and no less. But the inflation target aims at the CPI directly, not the price of gold or exchange rate, eliminating that source of relative price variation. And the inflation target avoids the run-inducing promise to freely trade cash for gold or foreign currency.

One can read the success of inflation targets as an instance of the Sargent (1982b) analysis of the ends of inflations, which I review in Section 14.3. When the long-run *fiscal* problem is credibly solved, inflation drops on its own, almost immediately. There is no period of monetary stringency, no high real interest rates moderating aggregate demand, no recession. Interest rates fall, money supply may rise, and deficits may rise temporarily as well, with the government newly able to pledge surpluses. As such, inflation targeting episodes are as revealing about lack of mechanical stickiness in expectations, specifically in the Phillips curve, as they are about the fiscal foundations of those inflation expectations.

Berg and Jonung (1999) discuss another example, from an earlier period in history, Sweden's price-level target of the 1930s. It called for systematic interest-rate increases if the price level increased and vice versa, answering the question of what action the central bank was expected to take. Like the modern experience, the central bank never had to do it, and actually pegged the exchange rate against the pound during the period.

An inflation target failed instructively in Argentina 2015-2019. In the analysis of Cachanosky and Mazza (2021) and Sturzenegger (2019), the basic problem was that the necessary fiscal commitment was absent. The latter also points out interesting fiscal dynamics:

> After an initial success, each program was discontinued because of a distinct form of fiscal dominance: as pensions are indexed with a lag and represent a large portion of spending, quick disinflations jeopardize fiscal consolidation.

Argentina's failure reinforces my point that a successful inflation target is as much a commitment by treasury as a commitment by and commandment to the central bank.

This sort of fiscal commitment is not written in official inflation targeting agreements, nor is it (yet) much discussed in the surrounding literature. But it surely seems like a reasonable expectation of what the commitments to fiscal reform in inflation-targeting legislation mean. And writing a model of an inflation target that ignores the fiscal reforms, and the financial and regulatory reforms that grow the tax base, putting in a footnote about passive fiscal policy and lump sum taxes, seems to miss a central part of the historical lesson.

Still, that commitment is implicit. If my reading of the inflation target is right, a more formal fiscal rule, announcing how fiscal policy will and won't react to inflation, would make sense.

9.2   A Simple Model of an Inflation Target

I construct a model of an inflation target. The surplus responds to pay off higher debts at the price level target, $s_t = s_{0,t} + \alpha V_t^*$, where V_t^* accumulates deficits at the price level target P_t^*. Together with an interest rate target $Q_t = \beta E_t(P_t^*/P_{t+1}^*)$, the price level is determined and equal to $P_t = P_t^*$. The government commits to pay back any debt incurred by deficits $s_{0,t}$, at the price level target. But the government commits not to respond to off-target inflation or deflation.

To construct a simple dynamic model of the inflation target, I use the same π^*, v^* idea as in Section 5.4 and Section 5.5, which generalize the $s_1 = B_0/P_1^*$ idea from the two-period model in Section 1.6.

Define a state variable V_t^* by

$$V_1^* = \frac{B_0}{P_1^*}, \tag{9.1}$$

$$V_{t+1}^* = \frac{1}{Q_t} \frac{P_t^*}{P_{t+1}^*} \left(V_t^* - s_t \right). \tag{9.2}$$

One-period debt follows the flow condition

$$\frac{B_{t-1}}{P_t} = s_t + Q_t \frac{P_{t+1}}{P_t} \frac{B_t}{P_{t+1}}$$

and hence

$$\frac{B_t}{P_{t+1}} = \frac{1}{Q_t} \frac{P_t}{P_{t+1}} \left(\frac{B_{t-1}}{P_t} - s_t \right). \tag{9.3}$$

Comparing (9.2) and (9.3), the state variable V_t^* represents what the real value of debt would be if the price level were always equal to the target. It accumulates past deficits, but does not respond to arbitrary unexpected inflation and deflation.

Fiscal policy follows a rule that responds to the state variable V_t^*, thereby ignoring changes in the value of the debt that come from off-target inflation,

$$s_t = s_{0,t} + \alpha V_t^*. \tag{9.4}$$

In this example, consider an exogenous process for $\{s_{0,t}\}$.

Monetary policy sets an interest rate consistent with the price level target,

$$Q_t = \frac{1}{1+i_t} = \beta E_t \left(\frac{P_t^*}{P_{t+1}^*} \right). \tag{9.5}$$

With a time-varying real rate, the central bank has a nontrivial job to do. It must try to figure out the correct real rate, and adjust the nominal rate to mirror that real rate plus the inflation target. As above, the interest rate must obey the equilibrium conditions of the model given the price-level target, a nontrivial job. Errors result in monetary policy shocks.

In this setup $P_t = P_t^*$ is the unique equilibrium price level. To show that, I first establish that V_t^* is the present value of surpluses. Substituting (9.5) in (9.2) and taking expectations,

$$\beta E_t \left(V_{t+1}^* \right) = V_t^* - s_t. \tag{9.6}$$

Using (9.4),

$$\beta E_t \left(V_{t+1}^* \right) = (1-\alpha)V_t^* - s_{0,t}.$$

For bounded $\{s_{0,t}\}$, the V_t^* variable converges,

$$\lim_{T \to \infty} \beta^T E_t \left(V_{t+T}^* \right) = 0.$$

Thus, we can iterate (9.6) forward, and the limiting term drops out, leaving us

$$V_t^* = E_t \sum_{j=0}^{\infty} \beta^j s_{t+j}.$$

Since the real value of nominal debt is also the present value of surpluses, we have $B_{t-1}/P_t = V_t^*$ at all dates. From (9.1) we have $P_0 = P_0^*$. With (9.2) and (9.3), $P_t = P_t^*$ then implies $P_{t+1} = P_{t+1}^*$ so we have $P_t = P_t^*$ at all dates.

This result requires both the surplus rule (9.4) and the interest rate target (9.5), which is the main point of this section. *An inflation target consists of a monetary policy rule and a fiscal commitment.* The interest rate target alone is insufficient. The surplus rule alone is also insufficient. Even with the rule (9.4), a decision to double nominal debt without changing surpluses will have the usual effect of doubling the future price level. So the surplus rule needs to be paired with some rule for setting the quantity of nominal debt, which sets expected inflation. Here I write the more conventional interest rate target. Other monetary policy rules could also work.

9.3   Fiscal Rules

The government could systematically raise and lower surpluses in response to inflation and deflation, in a sort of fiscal Taylor rule, $s_t = s_t(P_t)$. Such fiscal rules can determine the price level with purely indexed debt. They can also be a helpful part of a monetary–fiscal regime with nominal debt.

9.3.1   Indexed Debt in a One-Period Model

In a one-period model, $b_{T-1} = s(P_T)$ can determine the price level P_T. Better, $s_T(P_T) = b_{T-1} + \theta_{sp}(P_T - P_T^*)$ determines $P_T = P_T^*$. Fiscal theory does not require nominal debt.

A fiscal rule can determine the price level even with fully indexed debt.

In a one-period model, suppose indexed debt b_{T-1} is outstanding at time T, but the government follows a rule or systematic policy in which the surplus rises with the price level, $s_t(P_t)$ with $s_t'(P_t) > 0$. Then, the equilibrium condition at time T is

$$b_{T-1} = s_T(P_T).$$

This condition can determine the price level P_T, although the debt is fully indexed. Better, suppose the government commits to repay real debts, but also reacts to the price level,

$$s_T(P_T) = b_{T-1} + \theta_{sp}(P_T - P_T^*). \tag{9.7}$$

Then the equilibrium price level is $P_T = P_T^*$.

Continuing the usual story, in the morning of time T, the government prints up $P_T b_{T-1}$ dollars to pay off the outstanding indexed debt. The government then commits to raising sufficient taxes to soak up the money, thereby paying off the debt, and additionally that any spending at time T is also financed by taxes at time T, so there is no additional primary surplus or deficit. But if the price level is below P_T^*, the government commits to money-financed expenditures or tax cuts, an unbacked fiscal expansion, while if the price level is too high the government commits to a fiscal austerity, raising taxes and cutting spending to soak up money.

The fiscal theory only needs something real and something nominal in the same equation. The fiscal rule can be the something nominal. *Fiscal theory does not require nominal debt*, as this example shows.

I started this book with a simple example of a constant tax rate and no spending, $P_t s_t = \tau P_t y_t$, to establish that the real surplus does not naturally *have* to depend on the price level. But surpluses can and do depend on the price level. Tax brackets, capital gains, and depreciation allowances are not indexed. Government salaries, defined-benefit pensions, and medical payments are at least somewhat nominally sticky. All of these forces should result in somewhat higher surpluses with inflation $s'_t(P_t) > 0$. So this mechanism should already be part of an empirical investigation of price level determination.

More importantly, the government can *intentionally* vary surpluses with inflation or the price level to improve price level control, as central banks following a Taylor rule or inflation target intentionally vary the interest rate with inflation or the price level to improve their control. And governments do routinely tighten fiscal policy as part of inflation-fighting efforts, and loosen fiscal policy when fighting deflation.

In a dynamic model, the main issue is to convince people that the latter fiscal changes are really unbacked, that today's inflation-fighting surpluses or deflation-fighting deficits will not be repaid.

9.3.2 A Dynamic Fiscal Rule with Indexed Debt

In a dynamic model with surplus rule $s_t = s_{0,t} + \theta_{sp}(P_t - P_t^*)$, the valuation equation is

$$b_{t-1} = \sum_{j=0}^{\infty} \beta^j s_{0,t+j} + \theta_{sp} \sum_{j=0}^{\infty} \beta^j (P_{t+j} - P_{t+j}^*).$$

With $s_{0,t} = a(L)\varepsilon_{s,t}$ and $a(\beta) = 0$, this rule determines the weighted sum $\sum_{j=0}^{\infty} \beta^j P_{t+j}$. A debt policy $\beta b_t = b_{t-1} - s_{0,t}$ or an interest rate target $1/(1 + i_t) = \beta E_t(P_t^*/P_{t+1}^*)$ can complete the regime and determine $P_t = P_t^*$.

Next, think about this fiscal rule in a dynamic context. As usual, since the quantity of debt must come from somewhere, we need both fiscal and monetary policy.

Continuing our flexible price, constant real rate model, the flow equilibrium condition with indexed debt states that old debt is paid off by surpluses or new debt,

$$b_{t-1} = s_t(P_t) + \beta b_t. \tag{9.8}$$

Iterating forward and imposing the transversality condition,

$$b_{t-1} = \sum_{j=0}^{\infty} \beta^j s_{t+j}(P_{t+j}).$$

This expression holds ex post. Real debt must be repaid or default. Any shocks to surpluses must be met by subsequent movement in the opposite direction. Now the price level can vary to cause that surplus movement, and in so doing we help to determine the price level.

Now consider the surplus rule

$$s_t = s_{0,t} + \theta_{sp}(P_t - P_t^*)$$

in this dynamic context. The valuation equation is

$$b_{t-1} = \sum_{j=0}^{\infty} \beta^j s_{0,t+j} + \theta_{sp} \sum_{j=0}^{\infty} \beta^j (P_{t+j} - P_{t+j}^*).$$

(9.9)

The valuation equation and the surplus rule determine the value of the sum $\sum_{j=0}^{\infty} \beta^j P_{t+j}$ but not the shape of that path and hence the price level at each date.

To keep the example simple, assume that $\{s_{0,t+j}\}$ follows a process with moving average representation $s_{0,t} = a(L)\varepsilon_{s,t}$ and $a(\beta) = 0$. Debt incurred to finance this component of primary deficit is paid off by following surpluses. The next section writes a more realistic model with this feature. With real debt and no defaults, the overall surplus $\{s_t\}$ must follow the analogous restriction. Now we *can* have $P_t = P_t^*$ at every date. As there are no innovations to the first term on the right-hand side of (9.9), there are no innovations to the second term as well. But that term is the weighted sum of deviations from target. Individual price levels may deviate from their targets.

Write the flow budget constraint

$$b_{t-1} = s_{0,t} + \theta_{sp}(P_t - P_t^*) + \beta b_t + \frac{M_t}{P_t}.$$

(9.10)

In equilibrium, $M_t = 0$. Now if the price level P_t is below the target P_t^*, the government sells additional debt b_t. The following path of prices has $P_{t+j} > P_{t+j}^*$, to generate surpluses that pay off this additional debt.

We can determine the price level at each date by enlarging the regime to cut off the latter possibility. If the government holds real debt sales fixed at the value needed to roll over real debt and to finance the underlying real deficit,

$$\beta b_t = b_{t-1} - s_{0,t},$$

(9.11)

then from the flow equilibrium condition (9.8), we must have $P_t = P_t^*$. In the flow budget constraint (9.10), $P_t < P_t^*$ must now result in $M_t > 0$, the familiar mechanism that produces fiscal inflation. In words, *the government commits that in the event of a too-low price level it will embark on printed-money fiscal expansion. It will not soak up extra money with sales of (indexed) debt,* and vice versa. The "fiscal rule" for debt sales b_t can be the residual of a money-printing rule.

It should not be surprising that in order to fully determine the price level, we need a surplus policy and a debt sale policy. The lesson applies to real as it does to nominal debt.

As before, we do not have to interpret this model as precise adherence to an inflexible target, exactly 2% per year inflation for example. We can interpret the stochastic P_t^* target to allow inflation to rise and fall, and as what the government is willing to put up with rather than what it aspires to. We can interpret the stated 2% per year target as a long-run value of P^*, not its precise value on each date.

I have pushed the example hard, to show that a fully fiscal model of price level determination is possible with indexed debt. Rather than select the price level path with the fiscal rule (9.11), however, or its equivalent money printing rule, we can rely as usual on an interest rate target to set the price level path. An interest rate target i_t requires

$$\frac{1}{1+i_t} = \beta E_t \left(\frac{P_t}{P_{t+1}} \right). \tag{9.12}$$

Thus, if the interest rate target is set by

$$\frac{1}{1+i_t} = \beta E_t \left(\frac{P_t^*}{P_{t+1}^*} \right),$$

then only the sequence $P_t = P_t^*$ satisfies both (9.9) and (9.12).

9.3.3   A Better Fiscal Rule

I write the fiscal rule as a combination of a regular, backed budget, and an emergency or price level stabilization, unbacked budget. The two budgets follow $s_{r,t} = s_{0,t} + \alpha_r b_{r,t}$ and $s_{p,t} = \theta_{sp}(P_t - P_t^*)$, respectively. This separation allows the government to communicate how much debt is backed and unbacked, and to deliberately inflate while also retaining its commitment to repay regular debts and thereby borrow when needed. The α_r term generates repayment of the $s_{r,t}$ component without requiring an exogenous s-shaped moving average.

The model in the last section is a little strained. I specify an exogenous surplus process $\{s_{0,t}\}$ with $a(\beta) = 0$. It is prettier, more intuitive, more practical, and more realistic to produce this feature with a fiscal rule rather than a direct s-shaped moving average. This section presents such a rule.

I phrase this model in the language of Jacobson, Leeper, and Preston (2019), who describe the Roosevelt administration's separation of finances into a "regular" budget whose debts are repaid and an "emergency" budget that is unbacked. The Roosevelt administration was battling deflation. They first devalued the dollar relative to gold. This step already changes the backing of nominal debt, which should create inflation—it changes expected surpluses. But they wanted to do more: They wanted to undertake an unbacked fiscal expansion to create additional inflation. They wanted to increase nominal debt without promise of additional surpluses. At the same time, they did not want to turn the United States into a hyperinflationary basket case. They wanted to maintain the U.S. government's reputation so that if it wished to borrow in the future, when the Depression was over, it could pledge surpluses to that future borrowing. That reputation would soon be needed, in large measure. How do you run a little bit of state contingent default and unbacked fiscal expansion, yet retain a reputation for backing your future fiscal expansions after the threat of deflation has ended?

To accomplish this feat of expectations management, the Roosevelt administration separated the budget into a "regular" budget whose debts are repaid and an "emergency" budget that is unbacked. The administration proposed to fund the emergency budget entirely by borrowing until the Depression ended, but then to end the practice. Separating the items on the regular versus emergency budget, and tying the emergency budget to visible economic conditions neatly unties the Gordian knot.

This brilliant idea (or, more accurately, this brilliant reinterpretation of the Roosevelt administration's actions) forms the basis not just of a deflation-fighting scheme, but of a broader fiscal rule that works under indexed debt or gold standard debt. Let the "regular" budget surplus be

$$s_{r,t} = s_{0,t} + \alpha_r b_{r,t},$$

and the corresponding portion of the debt $b_{r,t}$. Let the price stabilization surplus be

$$s_{p,t} = \theta_{sp}(P_t - P_t^*), \tag{9.13}$$

with corresponding portion of the debt $b_{p,t}$. The total surplus and debt are

$$s_t = s_{r,t} + s_{p,t}$$
$$b_t = b_{r,t} + b_{p,t}.$$

Each debt accumulates separately,

$$b_{r,t} = R\left(b_{r,t-1} - s_{r,t}\right)$$
$$b_{p,t} = R\left(b_{p,t-1} - s_{p,t}\right).$$

One might implement this idea with distinct debt issues, as public debt is distinct from debt sold to the Social Security trust fund.

With $\alpha_r > 0$, the regular surplus repays its debts automatically, without an extra $a(\beta) = 0$ assumption,

$$b_{r,t-1} = \sum_{j=0}^{\infty} \beta^j s_{r,t+j},$$

and ignoring the price level completely. The regular part of the deficit and its repayment drop completely out of price level determination.

The price level stabilization budget separately obeys

$$b_{p,t-1} = \sum_{j=0}^{\infty} \beta^j s_{p,t+j} = \theta_{sp} \sum_{j=0}^{\infty} \beta^j (P_{t+j} - P_{t+j}^*). \tag{9.14}$$

The price level control part of the surplus does not feature automatic repayment. There is no α_p term in (9.13). The whole point of this budget is to threaten unbacked fiscal expansion or contraction, or money left outstanding, and to force the price level sequence to adjust.

As before, the price level budget (9.14) only sets this weighted sum of the price level path, but not each element. To continue in a realistic way, as above, we can pair this fiscal policy with a debt target, here $b_{p,t} = 0$, an equivalent money printing policy or, better, with a monetary policy that controls the nominal interest rate and therefore the price level path.

These examples need elaboration. We need to include nominal as well as indexed debt, sticky prices or other important frictions, and a realistic distinction between aspirations— a steady 2% inflation, or steady price level—and the equilibrium inflation that the rule is willing to tolerate in the presence of shocks.

9.3.4 A Fiscal Rule with Inflation and Interest Rates

I introduce a model with an interest rate rule $i_t = \theta_{i\pi} \pi_t + u_t$ and a surplus that reacts to inflation, $s_t = s_{0,t} + \theta_{s\pi} \pi_t$. We have

$$b_{t-1} = \frac{\theta_{s\pi}}{1 - \beta\theta_{i\pi}} \pi_t + \frac{\beta\theta_{s\pi}}{(1 - \beta\theta_{i\pi})(1 - \beta\eta)} u_t + E_t \sum_{j=0}^{\infty} \beta^j s_{0,t+j},$$

so inflation is determined.

I pursue a little model that merges fiscal and monetary policy to determine inflation, rather than the price level, with indexed debt. Monetary policy picks the inflation path, while the fiscal policy rule sets the level of inflation. The model is expressed in a form that more easily invites adaptation to linearized sticky price models.

Monetary policy follows an interest rate target,

$$i_t = \theta_{i\pi} \pi_t + u_t$$

$$u_t = \eta u_{t-1} + \varepsilon_t$$

with $\theta_{i\pi} < 1$. The economy has flexible prices and a constant real rate so

$$i_t = E_t \pi_{t+1}.$$

Inflation therefore follows

$$E_t \pi_{t+1} = \theta_{i\pi} \pi_t + u_t. \tag{9.15}$$

Fiscal policy follows a rule that responds to inflation,

$$s_t = s_{0,t} + \theta_{s\pi} \pi_t.$$

Only indexed debt is outstanding. The government debt valuation equation reads

$$b_{t-1} = E_t \sum_{j=0}^{\infty} \beta^j \left(s_{0,t+j} + \theta_{s\pi} \pi_{t+j} \right).$$

Using (9.15) to eliminate expected future inflation, we have

$$b_{t-1} = \frac{\theta_{s\pi}}{1 - \beta\theta_{i\pi}} \pi_t + \frac{\beta\theta_{s\pi}}{(1 - \beta\theta_{i\pi})(1 - \beta\eta)} u_t + E_t \sum_{j=0}^{\infty} \beta^j s_{0,t+j}. \tag{9.16}$$

This equation now determines inflation at each date π_t, despite completely indexed debt.

The surplus response to inflation $\theta_{s\pi}$ is key to the result. Without this response, π_t drops from the equation. The monetary response to inflation $\theta_{i\pi}$ is not essential. With

$\theta_{i\pi} = 0$ we have $i_t = u_t$ and

$$b_t = \theta_{s\pi}\pi_t + \frac{\beta\theta_{s\pi}}{1-\beta\eta}i_t + E_t\sum_{j=0}^{\infty}\beta^j s_{0,t+j}.$$

An interest rate target is essential. Without it, the expected future inflation that drives expected future surpluses is not pinned down. (This example modifies Sims (2013). Section 16.10.8 summarizes Sims's point, which is different.)

9.3.5   Fiscal Rules with Nominal Debt

Surplus rules that respond to the price level can be useful parts of a fiscal regime that also includes nominal debt. They add to the force of price level determination, valuable if nominal (own-country) debt is small. They offer fiscal austerity/stimulus in place of the outstanding debt devaluation as a fundamental mechanism.

Now, consider mixed real and nominal debt with a fiscal rule. As usual, the basic ideas are easiest to see in the simple one-period model. With mixed real and nominal debt, we have

$$b_{T-1} + \frac{B_{T-1}}{P_T} = s(P_T).$$

Ruling out the passive possibility, which requires $s'(P) < 0$, the price level is determined.

With any nominal debt, a surplus rule is not strictly needed for determinacy. But $s'(P) > 0$ helps. The stronger the divergence in price level dependence between the left- and right-hand sides of the valuation equation, the better price level determination must be.

In Section 8.3, we worried about the cashless limit problem, in which a small amount of nominal debt tries to determine the price level. A surplus rule addresses that problem. If nominal debt is only 10% of all debt, then a 10% change in the price level only affects the value of government bonds by 1%. A larger change in $s(P)$ on the right-hand side can make up for that weakness.

The fiscal rule also changes the nature of price determination. The stronger $s'(P)$, the more that inflationary fiscal shocks are met by an induced fiscal tightening, and the less they are met by inflating away outstanding nominal government debt.

A little bit of nominal debt, or money, also is useful to allow monetary policy to set the nominal interest rate, an issue I glossed over above.

9.4   Targeting the Spread

Rather than target the nominal interest rate, the central bank can target the *spread* between indexed and non-indexed debt. This policy determines expected inflation, while letting the level of interest rates rise and fall according to market forces. The policy can be implemented by allowing people to trade indexed for nominal debt, or by offering inflation swaps, at fixed rates. A spread target, like a nominal interest rate target, only nails down expected inflation. Actual inflation also depends on fiscal policy.

Rather than target the level of the nominal interest rate, suppose the central bank targets the *spread* between indexed and nonindexed debt. The nominal rate equals the indexed (real) rate plus expected inflation, $i_t = r_t + E_t \pi_{t+1}$. So, by targeting $i_t - r_t$, the central bank can target expected inflation directly.

This target can also be implemented as a peg, like an exchange rate peg or gold standard, by offering to freely trade indexed for nonindexed debt. Bring in a one-year, zero-coupon indexed bond, which promises to pay $\$1 \times \Pi_{t+1}$ at maturity, where Π_{t+1} is the gross inflation rate. You get in return Π^* zero-coupon nominal bonds, each of which pays $\$1$ at maturity, where Π^* is the inflation target. If inflation comes out to $\Pi_{t+1} = \Pi^*$, the two bonds pay the same amount. This policy will drive the spread between real and nominal debt to Π^*, so inflation expectations settle down to Π^*. We have to check the latter statement—that the economy is stable and determinate under a spread target. That analysis follows.

The central bank could also target rather than peg the real–nominal spread by conventional instruments of monetary policy. It could adjust the level of nominal interest rates in order to achieve its desired value for the real–nominal spread, as some central banks adjust nominal interest rates to target the exchange rate without actually pegging or buying and selling foreign currency, or as historically monetary policy chased a gold price target without offering to buy and sell gold.

Why target the spread? I have simplified the discussion by leaving out real interest rate variation, and treating the real interest rate as known. To target expected inflation by targeting nominal interest rates, the central bank just adds the real rate r_t to its inflation target $E_t(\pi^*_{t+1})$, and sets the nominal interest rate at that value $i_t = r_t + E_t(\pi^*_{t+1})$. But in reality, the real rate varies over time. The real rate is naturally lower in recessions: People want to save more but invest less; consumption growth is low; the marginal product of capital is low. The real rate is naturally higher in expansions, for all the opposite reasons. But there is no straightforward way to measure the natural, neutral, correct, or proper real rate. With sticky prices, the real rate varies as the central bank varies the nominal rate, so the bank partially controls the thing it wants to measure. There is currently a big discussion over lower frequency variation in the natural real rate, whether "r^*" is lower. Even with complex models, the Fed struggles to measure r^* (see Holston, Laubach, and Williams (2017)), as the Fed struggles to define and measure the "natural" rate of unemployment. Measuring business cycle or higher frequency in the "natural" rate is an order of magnitude harder. Yet that is, essentially, what central banks try to do in order to figure out what nominal interest rate to set.

Economic planners have had a tough time setting prices. Economic philosophers have had a tough time proclaiming the just price for centuries. Real interest rates are no exception. If the underlying or natural interest rate is like all other prices, especially asset prices and exchange rates, it moves a lot in response to myriad information that planners do not see, befuddling even ex post rationalization.

In this context, then, if the central bank targets the *spread* between indexed and nonindexed debt, and thereby targets expected inflation directly, it can leave the *level* of real and nominal interest rates entirely to market forces. This policy leaves the central bank in charge of the nominal price level only, and can get it out of the business of trying to set the most important real price in the economy.

The spread target can also vary over time or in response to the state of the economy, if one wishes to accommodate, rather than eschew, central banks' macroeconomic planning tendencies. Rather than view its "stimulus" or cooling efforts through desired nominal or real interest rates, a central bank could stimulate by raising expected inflation directly, and vice versa. Such efforts might also be more effective at raising or lowering expected inflation than moving nominal rates, or making forward guidance promises about such movements.

The idea can extend throughout the yield curve. The central bank can target expected inflation at any horizon, and it can implement that target by offering to trade indexed for nonindexed debt at any maturity. Thus, the spread target also offers a way to directly "anchor" long-run inflation expectations. The central bank could operate a short-run interest rate target, QE, and other interventions, while also targeting the spread between indexed and nonindexed long-term debt to better anchor long-run expectations. Since prices are sticky and short-run inflation is hard to control, such a separation between conventional short-run policy and long-term expectations management may prove useful.

The practical effect on monetary policy of this change may not be great, in equilibrium, and in response to the usual shocks. If the central bank follows a Taylor rule, $i_t = (r + \pi^*) + \theta_\pi \pi_t + \theta_x x_t$, and if the real interest rate tracks inflation and output, $r_t = r + \theta_\pi \pi_t + \theta_x x_t$, then the spread target produces the same result as the Taylor rule. But targeting the spread is clearer, and helps better to set inflation expectations. A spread target may perform better when the economy is hit by a different set of shocks, so the historical correlation of the real rate with the Taylor rule changes. Rules developed from history and experience have a certain wisdom but that wisdom often reflects correlations that change over time.

In my storytelling, I offer a year or more horizon. Why not a day, you might ask, and let the central bank target daily expected inflation? Well, prices are sticky, so one should not expect that the central bank can control daily expected inflation. A year seems to me about the shortest horizon at which one might expect inflation to be able to move in response to the spread rather than vice versa. But this intuition needs to be spelled out.

A spread peg can be implemented via CPI futures or swaps rather than, or in addition to, trading underlying bonds. In an inflation swap, parties agree to pay or receive the difference between realized inflation and a reference rate set at the beginning of the contract period. They pay or receive $P_{t+1}/P_t - \Pi_t^*$. No money changes hands today. The reference rate Π_t^* adjusts to clear the market, and is equal to the risk-neutral expected inflation rate. If the central bank targets or pegs the inflation swap rate Π_t^*, expected inflation adjusts. Entering an inflation swap is the same thing as buying one indexed bond that pays P_{t+1}/P_t in one period, and selling nominal bonds that pay Π_t^*. (Dowd (1994) describes a peg to a contract similar to CPI futures.)

Indexed debt (TIPS) in the United States is currently rather illiquid, and it suffers a complex tax treatment. Simplifying the security would make it far more liquid, transparent, and reflective of inflation expectations. Cochrane (2015b) contains a detailed proposal for simplified and more liquid federal debt, consisting of tax-free indexed and nonindexed perpetuities and swaps between these simple securities. Fleckenstein, Longstaff, and Lustig (2014) document arbitrage between TIPS and CPI swaps, a sure sign of an ill-functioning market. Central banks should work with treasuries more broadly to modernize and simplify the latter's offerings, and of indexed debt in particular. The absence of significant inflation up to 2021 may have removed the incentive for institutional change, but that incentive may reappear.

Central banks can also create and offer more extensive real and nominal term liabilities, which is a good idea for many reasons. Banks offer certificates of deposit, why not the central bank? Central bank liabilities are really liquid. And, at least initially, CPI swaps or futures may end up being the most liquid and forceful implementation of these ideas.

Obviously, central banks would inch their way to such a proposal. Start by paying a lot more attention to the spread. Work to get the markets more liquid and implement better securities. Start gently pushing the spread to where the central bank wants the spread to go with QE-like purchases in fixed amounts. Get to a flat supply curve at the spread target slowly. And allow time and experience so people understand the regime.

Targeting the spread is really only a small step from the analysis so far. If the government can target the nominal interest rate i_t, and then expected inflation will adjust in equilibrium to $E_t\pi_{t+1} = i_t - r_t$ with r_t the real interest rate determined eventually elsewhere, then the economics of a spread target are really not fundamentally different from those of an interest rate target. This statement needs to be verified, and the next two sections do so.

9.4.1   Fiscal Theory with a Spread Target

I write the spread target in the sticky price fiscal theory of monetary policy model to verify that it works, and how it works. A spread target determines expected inflation, while the government debt valuation equation determines unexpected inflation. The spread target works just as the interest rate target works in the sticky price model. The spread target leads to i.i.d. inflation around the target, and leads to endogenous real interest rate variation that offsets IS shocks. We can also support a spread target with active monetary policy—the idea is not intrinsically tied to fiscal theory.

Writing $i_t - r_t = E_t\pi_{t+1}$, and concluding that if the central bank pegs the left side, the right side will adjust, may seem straightforward. The condition $i_t - r_t = E_t\pi_{t+1}$ is a steady-state of practically every model. But one may worry that this steady-state may be unstable, that pegging the spread between real and nominal bonds may lead to spiraling inflation or deflation rather than inflation or deflation that converges to the spread. *Can the government even force the spread to be 2% without trading infinite quantities?* The spread between indexed and nominal bonds *measures* inflation expectations, but silencing the canary does not make the mine safe. Which way is it? That's what we need models for.

With flexible prices, the real interest rate is independent of inflation, so the spread target is stable and determinate when an interest rate target is stable and determinate, and vice versa. In old-Keynesian adaptive expectations models, an interest rate peg leads to unstable inflation, and a spread target has the same outcome. In new-Keynesian models, an interest rate peg leads to indeterminate inflation, and one can anticipate the same result of a spread target. But in fiscal theory of monetary policy, an interest rate peg can be stable and determinate. If that is true, a spread peg is also stable and determinate.

Let us put a spread target in the standard sticky price fiscal theory of monetary policy model, in place of a nominal interest rate target. I start with an even simpler version of the model,

$$x_t = -\sigma(i_t - E_t\pi_{t+1}) \tag{9.17}$$

$$\pi_t = E_t\pi_{t+1} + \kappa x_t. \tag{9.18}$$

Here I delete the $E_t x_{t+1}$ term in the first equation, so it becomes a static IS curve, in which output is lower for a higher real interest rate. This simplification turns out not to matter for the main point, which I verify by going through the same exercise with the full model. But it shows the logic with much less algebra. Section 17.1 uses this simplified model extensively to cleanly exposit new-Keynesian and old-Keynesian versus fiscal theory of monetary policy approaches.

Denote the real interest rate

$$r_t = i_t - E_t\pi_{t+1}. \tag{9.19}$$

We can view the spread target as a nominal interest rate rule that reacts to the real interest rate,

$$i_t = \theta r_t + \pi^{e*}, \tag{9.20}$$

rather than react to inflation. (I add e for expected and $*$ for target to π.) The spread target happens at $\theta = 1$, but the logic will be clearer and the connection of an interest rate peg and interest spread peg clearer if we allow $\theta \in [0, 1]$ to connect the possibilities and track the limit as $\theta \to 1$.

Eliminating all variables but inflation from (9.17)–(9.20), we obtain

$$E_t\left(\pi_{t+1} - \pi^{e*}\right) = \frac{1-\theta}{1-\theta+\sigma\kappa}\left(\pi_t - \pi^{e*}\right). \tag{9.21}$$

When the coefficient on the right-hand side is less than 1, inflation is stable but indeterminate, as $\Delta E_{t+1}\pi_{t+1}$ can be anything. We complete the model with the government debt valuation equation, in linearized form

$$\Delta E_{t+1}\pi_{t+1} = -\Delta E_{t+1}\sum_{j=0}^{\infty}\rho^j\tilde{s}_{t+1+j} + \Delta E_{t+1}\sum_{j=1}^{\infty}\rho^j(i_{t+j} - \pi_{t+1+j}), \tag{9.22}$$

which determines unexpected inflation.

We can substitute (9.19) and (9.20) into (9.21), iterate forward, and solve (9.22) to find unexpected inflation,[1]

$$\Delta E_{t+1}\pi_{t+1} = -\frac{(1-\rho)(1-\theta)+\sigma\kappa}{(1-\rho)(1-\theta)+\sigma\kappa+\rho}\varepsilon_{\Sigma s,t+1}. \tag{9.23}$$

---

1. Algebra: Uniting (9.19) and (9.20),

$$r_t = \frac{1}{1-\theta}\left(\pi^{e*} - E_t\pi_{t+1}\right).$$

Equations (9.21) and (9.23) now completely describe the solution—expected and unexpected inflation.

Starting at the familiar $\theta = 0$, an interest rate peg, we have

$$E_t \left(\pi_{t+1} - \pi^{e*} \right) = \frac{1}{1 + \sigma \kappa} \left(\pi_t - \pi^{e*} \right)$$

$$\Delta E_{t+1} \pi_{t+1} = -\frac{1 - \rho + \sigma \kappa}{1 + \sigma \kappa} \varepsilon_{\Sigma s, t+1}.$$

There are only fiscal shocks, which cause unexpected inflation. That inflation settles down to the inflation target with an AR(1) response driven by price stickiness.

As we raise the real interest rate response $0 < \theta < 1$, the solution (9.21) and (9.23) remains qualitatively the same. As θ rises, the dynamics of (9.21) happen faster, and expected inflation converges more quickly to the target.

At $\theta = 1$, the spread target $i_t - r_t = \pi^{e*}$ nails down expected inflation. Equivalently, expected inflation settles down to the target infinitely fast. Equation (9.21) becomes

$$E_t \pi_{t+1} = \pi^{e*}.$$

Equation (9.23) becomes

$$\Delta E_{t+1} \pi_{t+1} = -\frac{\sigma \kappa}{\sigma \kappa + \rho} \varepsilon_{\Sigma s, t+1}.$$

In sum, the model obeys

$$\pi_{t+1} = \pi^{e*} - \frac{\sigma \kappa}{\sigma \kappa + \rho} \varepsilon_{\Sigma s, t+1}.$$

Inflation is not equal to the target period by period. But inflation is uncorrelated over time, which is as close as we can get with an expected inflation target. Output and real

---

From (9.21)

$$\Delta E_{t+1} \pi_{t+1+j} = \left(\frac{1 - \theta}{1 - \theta + \sigma \kappa} \right)^j \Delta E_{t+1} \pi_{t+1}.$$

We can then write (9.22)

$$\Delta E_{t+1} \pi_{t+1} = -\varepsilon_{\Sigma s, t+1} + \sum_{j=1}^{\infty} \rho^j \Delta E_{t+1} \left[\frac{1}{1 - \theta} \left(\pi^{e*} - \pi_{t+j+1} \right) \right]$$

$$\Delta E_{t+1} \pi_{t+1} = -\varepsilon_{\Sigma s, t+1} - \frac{1}{1 - \theta} \sum_{j=1}^{\infty} \rho^j \left(\frac{1 - \theta}{1 - \theta + \sigma \kappa} \right)^j \Delta E_{t+1} \pi_{t+1}$$

and solving, we get (9.23).

and nominal rates then follow

$$x_t = \frac{1}{\kappa} \left(\pi_t - \pi^{e*} \right)$$

$$r_t = -\frac{1}{\sigma \kappa} \left(\pi_t - \pi^{e*} \right)$$

$$i_t = \pi^{e*} - \frac{1}{\sigma \kappa} \left(\pi_t - \pi^{e*} \right).$$

A fiscal shock leads to a one-period inflation, and thus a one-period output increase. Higher output means a lower interest rate in the IS curve, and thus a lower nominal interest rate. Real and nominal interest rates vary due to market forces, while the central bank does nothing more than target the spread.

We may wish for more variable expected inflation, and central banks may wish for something to do. Many models find that it is desirable to let a long smooth inflation accommodate a shock. Both desires can be accommodated by varying the expected inflation target. The central bank could follow $\pi_t^{e*} = E_t \pi_{t+1} = \theta_\pi \pi_t$ to produce persistent inflation. Or, the central bank could follow $\pi_t^{e*} = p^* - p_t$ to implement an expected price level target p^* with one-period reversion to that target. Or the bank could follow $\pi_t^{e*} = \theta_\pi \pi_t + \theta_x x_t + u_{\pi t}$ in Taylor rule tradition, including discretionary responses to other events in the $u_{\pi t}$ term. The point is not tied to a desire for a constant expected inflation peg, nor to require central bank inaction. The point is only that a spread target is possible and will not explode.

One may be a bit surprised that expected inflation is exactly equal to the spread target, even though prices are sticky. But the definition $r_t = i_t - E_t \pi_{t+1}$ guarantees that unless the model blows up, expected inflation must instantly equal the spread target. When prices cannot move, the real interest rate moves. The danger is that the real interest rate might explode in the attempt. It does not do so.

The same behavior occurs in the full new-Keynesian model. I simultaneously allow shocks to the equations and a time-varying spread target. The model is

$$x_t = E_t x_{t+1} - \sigma \left(i_t - E_t \pi_{t+1} \right) + u_{x,t} \tag{9.24}$$

$$\pi_t = \beta E_t \pi_{t+1} + \kappa x_t + u_{\pi,t}. \tag{9.25}$$

Write the spread target as $i_t - r_t = \pi_t^{e*}$. With the definition $r_t = i_t - E_t \pi_{t+1}$, we simply have $E_t \pi_{t+1} = \pi_t^{e*}$. As in the simple model, the spread target directly controls equilibrium expected inflation. Unexpected inflation is set by the same government debt valuation equation (9.22), now with discount rate terms. I won't write out the solution for unexpected inflation, as it is algebraically large and unenlightening.

Given inflation, output and the real rate follow from (9.25) and (9.24),

$$x_t = \frac{1}{\kappa} \left(\pi_t - \beta \pi^{e*} - u_{\pi,t} \right) = \frac{1}{\kappa} \left[(1-\beta)\pi^{e*} + \Delta E_t \pi_t - u_{\pi,t} \right]$$

$$r_t = \frac{1}{\sigma \kappa} \left(\Delta E_t \pi_t + \kappa u_{x,t} + u_{\pi,t} - E_t u_{\pi,t+1} \right). \tag{9.26}$$

These are the case of a constant target, $\pi_t^{e*} = \pi^{e*}$. Changes in that target add additional dynamics, and are now the response to monetary policy, so worth pursuing. In this simple case, output again follows inflation with serially uncorrelated movements, plus Phillips curve disturbances. The real rate and nominal interest rate also follow inflation with a serially uncorrelated movement, plus both IS and Phillips curve shocks. The IS shock does not appear in equilibrium output. Endogenous real rate variation $\sigma r_t = u_{x,t}$ offsets the IS shock's effect on output in the IS equation $x_t = E_t x_{t+1} - \sigma r_t + u_{x,t}$. This is an instance of desirable real-rate variation that the spread target accomplishes automatically.

This discussion is obviously only the beginning. We need to see the spread target at work in more realistic models. The sense in which it is desirable, adapting automatically to shocks that the central bank cannot directly observe, needs to be expressed formally. Optimal monetary policy sets the interest rate, in a conventional policy, and the spread target, in this policy, as a function of the underlying shocks. But the central bank cannot see those shocks. How does the spread target compare to other rules in approximating the ideal response to shocks that the central bank cannot see? Clearly something about the Phillips curve makes this a sensible idea for targeting long-run inflation expectations, but not at a monthly or daily horizon. What is that something?

I phrase the spread target in the context of the fiscal theory of the price level, choosing unexpected inflation from the government debt valuation equation (9.22), because that is the point of this book. However, targeting the spread rather than the level of interest rates does not hinge on active fiscal versus active monetary policy. In place of (9.22), one could determine unexpected inflation by adding a monetary equilibrium-selection policy instead. The central bank can threaten to let the spread diverge explosively for all but one value of unexpected inflation, in classic new-Keynesian style. In place of $i_t = i_t^* + \phi(\pi_t - \pi_t^*)$, write $\pi_t^{e*} = i_t - r_t = \pi_t^* + \phi(\pi_t - \pi_t^*)$, where π_t^* is the full inflation target, obeying $\pi_t^{e*} = E_t \pi_{t+1}^*$.

Hetzel (1991) is the earliest suggestion of a spread target I am aware of. Milton Friedman (1992, p. 229) mentions a spread target approvingly, as a way to accommodate the hands-off philosophy of money growth rules in an interest rate targeting environment. Holden (2020) presents the spread target idea, in the latter new-Keynesian context, showing that the rule $i_t = r_t + \phi\pi_t$ with $\phi > 1$ achieves a determinate price level.

9.4.2   Debt Sales with a Spread Target

Would the offer to trade real for nominal debt at fixed prices lead to explosive demands? The mechanics are a straightforward generalization of the effect that selling additional nominal debt raises the future price level. If the government offers more nominal bonds per real bond than the market offers, people will take the government's offer, thereby creating the change in debt that raises the expected price level. The offer to exchange indexed for nominal debt at a fixed rate is stable, with finite demands, and drives expected inflation to the target.

A second worry one might have about a spread peg, which implements a spread target by offering to sell real for nominal bonds at a fixed rate, is that the bond demands might explode. We need to verify that this is not the case; that the bond demands which support a spread target are well defined.

The argument is analogous to the case of an interest rate peg. We saw that by selling nominal bonds without changing the surplus, the government raises the expected future price level. We then saw that by offering bonds at a fixed nominal rate, again holding surpluses constant, people would buy just enough bonds so that the expected future price level is consistent with that nominal rate. Bond demand is well defined with a flat nominal supply curve. The mechanics of targeting expected inflation via a real for nominal debt swap is a simple extension of the same idea. In both cases, the caveat "holding surpluses constant" is key, and the hard work of institutional implementation. If people read changes in future surpluses into today's nominal bond sales, when offered in exchange for real bonds, reactions are different and an offered arbitrage opportunity could indeed explode. As in the case of nominal debt and an interest rate target, this observation offers a reason for the central bank, rather than treasury, to operate the spread target.

Start with the government debt valuation relation with both indexed and nominal debt,

$$b_{t-1} + \frac{B_{t-1}}{P_t} = E_t \sum_{j=0}^{\infty} \beta^j s_{t+j}.$$

An indexed bond pays $\$P_{t+1}$ at time $t + 1$ and is worth βP_t dollars at time t. The real interest rate is constant, which hides the usefulness of the idea, but clarifies the mechanics. Express the valuation equation in terms of end of period values, after bonds are sold,

$$\beta b_t + \beta B_t E_t \left(\frac{1}{P_{t+1}} \right) = \beta b_t + Q_t \frac{B_t}{P_t} = E_t \sum_{j=1}^{\infty} \beta^j s_{t+j}. \qquad (9.27)$$

If the government offers to exchange each real bond for $E_t(1/P_{t+1})$ nominal bonds, or if it exchanges real for nominal bonds at market prices, the left-hand side does not change, so the real versus nominal structure of the debt is irrelevant to the expected price level. People are indifferent at market prices.

Now let us see that selling more real and fewer nominal bonds with a trade-off different from market prices affects the future price level. Suppose the government sells $b_{0,t}$ and $B_{0,t}$ real and nominal debt, and then modifies its plan, selling P^* additional nominal bonds in return for each real bond,

$$- (B_t - B_{0,t}) = (b_t - b_{0,t}) P^*.$$

Plug into (9.27),

$$\beta \left(b_{0,t} - \frac{B_t - B_{0,t}}{P^*} \right) + \beta \left[B_{0,t} + (B_t - B_{0,t}) \right] E_t \left(\frac{1}{P_{t+1}} \right) = E_t \sum_{j=1}^{\infty} \beta^j s_{t+j}$$

$$\beta b_{0,t} + \beta B_{0,t} E_t \left(\frac{1}{P_{t+1}} \right) + \beta (B_t - B_{0,t}) \left[E_t \left(\frac{1}{P_{t+1}} \right) - \frac{1}{P^*} \right] = E_t \sum_{j=1}^{\infty} \beta^j s_{t+j}.$$

It's easiest to see the effect of exchanging real for nominal debt by taking derivatives,

$$dB_t \left[E_t \left(\frac{1}{P_{t+1}} \right) - \frac{1}{P^*} \right] + B_t d \left[E_t \left(\frac{1}{P_{t+1}} \right) \right] = 0$$

$$d \left[E_t \left(\frac{1}{P_{t+1}} \right) \right] = - \left[E_t \left(\frac{1}{P_{t+1}} \right) - \frac{1}{P^*} \right] \frac{dB_t}{B_t}.$$

If $1/P^* = E_t(1/P_{t+1})$, then the expected price level is independent of the real/nominal split. If $1/P^* < E_t(1/P_{t+1})$—if the government offers more nominal bonds per real bond than the market offers—then as nominal debt B_t rises, $E_t(1/P_{t+1})$ falls, and, roughly, the expected future price level rises. The previous description of monetary policy was in effect $P^* = \infty$; the government simply increased nominal debt with no decline in real debt, and that change resulted in next-period inflation. This case is a generalization. The government sells more nominal debt but undoes some of the dilution by taking back real debt. But if it takes back less real debt than the current market price trade-off, then increasing B_t nominal debt still lowers $E_t(1/P_{t+1})$; that is, raises the future price level.

Now, what happens if the government offers people the option to trade real for nominal bonds at a fixed relative price? If $1/P^* < E_t(1/P_{t+1})$, if the government gives more nominal bonds per real bond than offered by the market, it's worth exchanging a real bond for a nominal bond. But as people exchange real bonds for nominal bonds, they drive down $E_t(1/P_{t+1})$ until $1/P^* = E_t(1/P_{t+1})$ and the opportunity disappears. Likewise, if $1/P^* > E_t(1/P_{t+1})$, then people will exchange nominal bonds for real bonds, driving up $E_t(1/P_{t+1})$ until $1/P^* = E_t(1/P_{t+1})$ again.

In sum,

- *Offering to freely exchange real debt for nominal debt at the rate P^*, while not changing surpluses, drives the expected price level to $E_t(1/P_{t+1}) = 1/P^*$.*

This operation simply generalizes offering nominal debt at a fixed nominal interest rate, without any real debt in return.

The real versus nominal debt split, even at market prices, still matters for how future unexpected inflation reacts to future shocks. The government can retain control of the real versus nominal split of its debt in equilibrium. Trades of real for nominal debt *at the* market price have no effect on the price level. In our equations, the value of $B_{0,t}$ versus $b_{0,t}$ has no effect on the price level. That the treasury sells debt via auctions, but the central bank offers fixed interest rates, makes additional sense.

9.5 A Price Level Target via Indexed Debt

If the government targets the nominal price of indexed debt, then the price level is fully determined. This target can be accomplished by a peg: Offer to freely buy and sell indexed debt at a fixed nominal price. Its operation is analogous to a gold standard, commodity standard, or foreign exchange rate peg. It offers free conversion of dollars into a valuable commodity, next period's consumption. This peg determines the price level, but real interest rate variation induces price level volatility.

Suppose the government targets the nominal price of indexed debt. Indeed, suppose the government pegs that price, committing to trade any quantity of cash or reserves for indexed debt at a fixed price. This policy can nail down the price level. It combines fiscal and monetary policy into one rule. In essence, the government runs a commodity standard, with next-period consumption being the commodity.

Here, the government pegs the *level* of the indexed bond nominal price, rather than the *spread* between indexed and nonindexed debt. The advantage is that this peg determines the price level rather than the expected future price level, and includes the fiscal commitment that fully determines that level. The disadvantage is that real interest rate variation now adds to price level volatility, unless the central bank artfully adjusts the peg; whereas the spread target nails down expected inflation, allowing the real rate to vary according to market forces.

To be concrete, a one-period indexed bond pays $\$P_{t+1}$ at time $t+1$. Maintaining the constant real rate and flexible prices, indexed bonds have real time t value β and nominal time t value βP_t. Suppose the government pegs the nominal value of such bonds at βP_t^*; that is, it says you can buy or sell indexed bonds for βP_t^* dollars at time t. Then we must have an equilibrium price level $P_t = P_t^*$. We fully determine the time t price level, not just expected inflation.

As one way to see the mechanism, note that with the peg in place buying bonds gives a real return $1/(1 + r_t) = \beta P_t^*/P_t$. If $P_t < P_t^*$, then the real interest rate is too low and the bond price is too high. At a too-low interest rate, people want to substitute from future to present consumption. More demand for consumption today is more aggregate demand, which pushes the price level up.

Specifically, suppose that the government only issues real debt. The government sells bonds b_t at nominal price βP_t^*, real bond price $q_t = \beta P_t^*/P_t$, and soaking up $\beta P_t^* b_t$ dollars. The real flow condition is

$$b_{t-1} = s_t + q_t b_t = s_t + \beta \cdot \frac{P_t^*}{P_t} b_t. \tag{9.28}$$

In our frictionless model with a constant endowment, with the opportunity to buy and sell indexed debt at the fixed nominal price, people's demands for consumption and government debt follow the first-order condition and budget constraint (with $M_t = 0$),

$$\frac{\beta P^*}{P_t} u'(c_t) = \beta E_t u'(c_{t+1}) \tag{9.29}$$

$$y + b_{t-1} = c_t + s_t + \beta \frac{P_t^*}{P_t} b_t.$$

Consider a one-period deviation from the equilibrium price level path, with $P_t \neq P_t^*$ but $P_{t+j} = P_{t+j}^*$ for all $j > 0$. Then the first-order condition (9.29) for all future time periods gives $c_{t+j} = c_{t+j+1}$, so any extra or lesser wealth is spread evenly across all future consumption. As the price level P_t falls, consumption demand c_t rises, and demand to invest in bonds $\beta(P_t^*/P_t)b_t$ and therefore bonds themselves b_t and future consumption smoothly decrease. With demand c_t greater than supply y_t, the price level must rise. Price level determination comes by equilibrium—aggregate demand equals aggregate supply—not by arbitrage. With concave utility, consumption and bond demands do not explode at off-equilibrium prices.

Thus the nominal peg of a real bond is like a gold or commodity standard, or foreign exchange peg. It pegs the dollar in terms of an imperfect substitute for the general consumption basket: gold, foreign goods, or in this case, next-period consumption. A marginal real bond gives the consumer a marginal unit of next period consumption. By selling a real bond at nominal price βP_t^*, the government allows the consumer to trade one unit of future consumption for $\beta = 1/R$ units of consumption today, at the equilibrium price $P_t = P_t^*$. If the actual price level is lower, consumption today is more attractive. In a commodity standard, the government allows the consumer to trade one unit of the commodities for P_t^* dollars and hence P_t^*/P_t units of consumption immediately. If the actual price level is lower, total consumption is more attractive, and the consumer substitutes away from the commodities in the standard to the other goods in the total basket. Doing so drives down the commodity price and up the price level until equilibrium is reestablished. Only if the commodity standard includes all consumption goods, or perfect substitutes, is it an arbitrage.

This is still fiscal theory. When the government issues additional real debt, it must promise additional surpluses to repay that debt. Money today, used to pay off today's maturing indexed debt, and soaked up by today's indexed debt issues, is automatically backed by the present value of surpluses.

The indexed debt peg continues to determine the price level in the presence of nominal debt. However, nominal debt functions differently in this regime than before. Since $P_{t+1} = P_{t+1}^*$ is set, selling more nominal debt B_t cannot raise P_{t+1}. And selling more nominal debt cannot change the current price level P_t. Thus, as the government sells more nominal debt B_t, it simply ends up selling less real debt b_t. The split between real and nominal debt remains in the government's control.

Nominal debt still functions as a buffer, and can play an important part in price level determination. Suppose the government unexpectedly devalues at time t, raising the price level target P_t^* and therefore raising the price level P_t. This action devalues outstanding nominal debt B_{t-1}, and the present value of surpluses still declines by the amount of that devaluation. In the absence of nominal debt, the higher price level has no fiscal consequences. In return, without nominal debt outstanding, the government cannot react to an adverse fiscal shock by raising the price level target, and thereby inflating away some outstanding debt. Thus, though the decision to sell more nominal rather than real debt does not affect the current or expected future price levels, that decision sets up a state variable that affects the response of inflation to future shocks.

The central bank need not vanish. The government may wish to devolve debt management to the central bank. The central bank can manage the indexed debt peg, exchanging reserves for indexed debt according to the peg, as a corridor central bank pegs a nominal interest rate or as a gold standard bank exchanges cash for gold. The bank could buy and sell nominal treasury debt B_t to accommodate maturity and liquidity demands for nominal debt versus reserves. The central bank could be in charge of setting a time-varying bond price target. And when we introduce frictions to the model, the central bank may set interest rates or quantities of various kinds of debt, as central banks also set interest rates in the gold standard era. Whether all this activity is desirable is another issue, but it is certainly possible.

As we add realism to the model, this policy will not in practice completely fix the price level, for several reasons. First, the real interest rate varies over time, in ways the government is not likely to understand. (In this frictionless model, imagine variation in the endowment $\{y_t\}$.) This variation motivated the spread target above. With a fixed nominal bond price target Q^* we have

$$Q^* = \frac{1}{1+r_t}P_t^*,$$

so real interest rate variation will result in price level variation, unless the government or central bank knows the correct real interest rate and artfully changes its bond price target. Another reason for a central bank appears, the same one that holds with a nominal interest rate target. Likewise, a gold standard, commodity standard, or foreign exchange rate peg induces price level variation, unless the government artfully changes the conversion price to match the market-clearing relative price. No government tried to do so on a regular basis, leaving devaluation and revaluation for rare extreme circumstances, a fact that may reflect precommitment problems and the value of a stated peg as a commitment device. Tomorrow's consumption is likely more closely linked to today's consumption basket than are gold, foreign goods, or the sorts of baskets of commodities of such proposals, so this proposal improves on those standards. But it remains imperfect as a means for exactly targeting the price level.

Second, prices are sticky. One might think of stabilizing the actual price level by using this proposal at the highest possible frequency. Real interest rate variation from today to tomorrow is next to nothing. But obviously targeting the overnight indexed debt rate will not cause the price level today to change, because prices are sticky for a day. Intuitively, this proposal must act on a time scale in which prices are free to move. Like the spread target, that horizon is at least a year and potentially more. Thus, this proposal may end up being a long-term fiscal rule and commitment coexisting with shorter-term interest rate, spread, or other targets. But this conclusion is speculative, and needs analysis within explicit models with sticky prices. One may expect that just how prices are sticky will matter.

Third, the fiscal underpinnings are vital as always. To see this and the last point, imagine we speed up the process to a five-minute horizon. Suppose the CPI is 250, but the government wishes to hit a price level target of 200. So, for $200 you can buy a contract that pays $250 in five minutes. Buy! Now, to buy bonds you have to reduce consumption. But a five-minute reduction in consumption demand is, in our world, not likely to reduce the price level from 250 to 200 in five minutes. So, the government maintains the offer. You can use the $250 to buy more bonds that pay $312.50 in five more minutes, and so on. Something seems to be going wrong. The indexed debt peg was supposed to be soaking up money, causing disinflation, but instead money is exploding.

What's wrong? Well, in the first five minutes, the policy does soak up money in exchange for indexed debt, and that may even give some downward price level pressure in the first five minutes. Cancel dinner reservations, we're buying bonds. Each five minutes that one keeps holding and rolling over the indexed debt, one consumes less and drives down the price level. This process does in the end soak up money and keep it soaked up into indexed debt.

When the government issues more indexed debt, it also promises larger subsequent surpluses to pay off that debt. Each step in this story raises expected surpluses by just as much as the additional issuance of long-term debt. Eventually, when the price level reaches 200, the merry-go-round stops, and government gets to work steadily paying off the astronomical accumulated debt with astronomical surpluses. People have a lot of government debt, but also a lot of taxes to pay, so the day does not end with a bonanza in which people spend the money on nonexistent goods and services. But like any promise to deliver something real in exchange for money, like any rule promising future surpluses to retire debt, the scheme works only so long as that fiscal promise remains credible. The five-minute promise would break down long before the price level declines, as the debt issue and promised surpluses would be immense.

Thus, this story at a longer horizon may describe how an indexed debt target would work with sticky prices. The price level could be persistently above target; during that period people persistently accumulate indexed debt, forcing a fiscal contraction, and slowly drive the price level back to target.

The example also suggests why one might wish to target longer-term debt in the presence of sticky prices. At a one-year horizon, the offer to buy indexed debt at $200 when the price level is 250 is a $100 \times (250/200 - 1) = 25\%$ real interest rate. That's a good incentive to consume less and drive down aggregate demand. At a one-day horizon, the offer is a 25% overnight return; that is, a $100 \times [(250/200)^{365} - 1] = 2.3 \times 10^{37}\%$ annualized interest rate. That offer, especially if persistent, sends consumption demand essentially to zero. Well, all the better for getting the price level down to 200 in the next five minutes. But when prices cannot move in the next five minutes, there is no point to doing so, or to force a $2.3 \times 10^{37}\%$ rise in indexed debt via intermediate payments on indexed debt.

The last few paragraphs are clearly speculative. One should develop this idea in the context of explicit price stickiness, as well as in the context of an inflation target rather than a price level target.

9.6 A CPI Standard?

A CPI standard that mimics the gold standard, by offering instant exchange of cash for some financial contract linked to the CPI, is an intriguing idea. The spread target and indexed debt target take us halfway there.

A gold standard remains attractive in many respects: It represents a mechanical rule, embodying both fiscal and monetary commitments, that determines the price level without requiring prescient central bankers. Nostalgia for the gold standard, and even advocacy for its return, remains active in many quarters. Yet, as we have seen, the actual gold standard will not work well for a modern economy. The relative price of gold and everything else varies over time, so the gold standard leaves substantial inflation volatility. More importantly, in my view, the price of gold is poorly connected to the price of goods and services. The relative price of gold will change once it is pegged, so a new gold standard may settle down the price of gold but leave the price of goods and services unmoored. A gold price peg leads to runs and crashes.

Is there a way to have the advantages of a gold standard or currency peg, without unwanted inflation or deflation when the relative price of gold or foreign currency moves, and in a way that actually will control the price level, not just the price of the commodity? How can a government peg the consumer price index?

Most of the components of the CPI are not tradable, so the government cannot just open a huge Walmart and trade the components of the CPI for money, though it is fun to think of such a scheme. We must design a commitment that trades a dollar for some cash-settled financial contract. I use the term "CPI standard" to refer to such a scheme.

Many authors have suggested commodity standards: In return for one dollar you get a basket of short-dated, cash-settled commodity futures—wheat, pork bellies, oil, metals, and so on, or commodities that are physically traded. But the value of any commodity basket is also volatile relative to other goods and services, and they are only a bit more connected to the general price level than is the value of gold. Crude oil futures and health insurance premiums may diverge for quite a while. Given that loose connection, like gold and foreign exchange pegs, targeting commodity values might stabilize the prices of those commodities, but not have much effect on the overall price level.

One might consider an adaptation of the Modern Monetary Theory proposal for a federal jobs guarantee: Peg the price of unskilled labor at $15 per hour, by offering a job to anyone who wants it at $15 an hour and, on the margin, printing money to do so. But unskilled labor is also a small part of the economy, not well linked to the general level of prices and wages. And such a program presents obvious practical difficulties. From an inflation control point of view, the government must leave the wage at $15 an hour in the event of stagflation, having low-skilled labor lead other prices and wages down, where the government will naturally wish to raise the wage to help struggling people on the bottom end of the labor market. Gold mining provided a similar channel: When the price level declined, the value of time spent mining gold rose, encouraging people to trade time for creating money. But that too is an imperfect and slow mechanism, and all that work is a social waste.

One might peg the dollar to a basket of real assets including stocks, corporate bonds, and real estate, as well as commodities. But then variation in the relative price of real assets to consumption, so-called "asset price inflation," would show up in the price level. When the real interest rate declines, long-term real asset prices rise relative to the consumption basket, much more so than the price of a one-year indexed bond.

The spread peg and indexed debt peg can be thought of as improvements in this scheme. The spread peg ties down the expected future price level, the expected future rate of exchange between dollars and the entire basket of goods. The indexed debt peg ties down today's price of next year's basket of goods. The value of next year's CPI basket is more tightly tied to the value of today's CPI basket than gold, commodities, foreign goods, and so forth.

The question remains, is there a way to peg the dollar to *today's* basket of goods via a cash-settled financial contract? I don't have the answer, but as I ponder the question I believe it has to be answered in the context of somewhat sticky prices. The CPI standard must allow actual prices to deviate from the target and move slowly toward it, without offering arbitrage opportunities that imply infinite fiscal commitments. If the government offers to trade $250 for a CPI-linked bet that pays off today, and the CPI is 260, people will trade infinite amounts; buying at $250, getting $260, reinvesting, and so forth; my example of the last section speeded up to infinity.

The basic structure of the fiscal theory, and its interpretation of our current institutions, already addresses much of the commodity standard desideratum. Taxes are based on the entire bundle of goods and services, not one or a few specific goods. Thus the essential promise of the fiscal theory—bring us a dollar and we relieve you of a dollar's worth of tax liability—functions as a commodity standard weighted by the whole bundle of goods, not one particular good such as gold, and without requiring delivery of that bundle of goods.

Still, a CPI standard would be an important addition to our understanding of theoretical possibilities. Perhaps there is a better structure than the indexed debt peg or spread target.

10

Balance Sheets and Pots of Assets

THE FISCAL THEORY is at heart a backing theory. Money is valued as a claim to something real. In this chapter, I think about monetary systems in which money is a claim to a pot of assets, isolated from general government finances.

Central banks appear to be set up this way. They have assets matching their liabilities— reserves and currency.

The Federal Reserve can be seen as a huge money market fund. Its shares are pegged at a dollar each, and pay interest. The shares are backed by a portfolio composed mostly of government and agency securities. It also has an implicit equity tranche and credit back-stop, via its tradition of remitting profits to the Treasury and the possibility of Treasury recapitalization. Unlike money market funds, the Fed's liabilities are dollars, which it can create, rather than promises to pay dollars, making the Fed immune to runs.

For example, total Federal Reserve assets on November 3, 2021, were $8.5 trillion (Statistical Release H.4.1). Of this, $5.5 trillion were Treasury securities, and $2.5 trillion were mortgage-backed securities. Liabilities included $4.1 trillion in bank reserves, $1.6 trillion in reverse repurchase agreements, which are essentially a device to let money market funds hold reserves, and $2.2 trillion of currency. The Fed's balance sheet does not include an explicit shareholder equity line, and does not report market values of either assets or liabilities.

The Fed's assets seem to back its liabilities. We have, so far, ignored that fact, noting the many ways in which central bank assets and liabilities are really not distinct from those of the general government. Here, we start to bring the balance sheet back into the analysis.

By imagining a central bank isolated from government finances, we can think about how an independent central bank with a separate balance sheet helps to resist inflation or commit to inflation. We can think about an ideal European Central Bank (ECB); a supranational central bank divorced from government debts, which other countries or groups of countries might want to set up, and we can think about the actual ECB. We can think about how a greater separation of treasury and central bank might work. We can think about private currencies, defined by shares of funds, or backed cryptocurrencies.

10.1   Three Pots of Assets

We think about money, a central bank liability, valued by backing, as a claim to central bank assets. To determine the price level, the assets must be real.

We want to describe a central bank, which could also be a private institution, fund, or cryptocurrency. I write "central bank" to avoid endlessly repeating the latter possibilities. The central bank is the only issuer of numeraire assets, currency and reserves. The central bank is set up to give value to those liabilities by backing them with a pot of assets.

It is straightforward to describe money backed by assets when the numeraire is defined elsewhere. Banks issue notes or checking accounts, money market funds issue shares, a backed cryptocurrency issues tokens, each backed by portfolios of assets. Each of these moneys has value determined by its backing. But the money so created and the assets that back it are claims to a numeraire defined elsewhere—government currency or, historically, coins. This is a story of liquidity transformation, not a story of numeraire definition and price level determination.

It is also straightforward to describe a standalone central bank if the price level is determined by $MV = Py$ for central bank liabilities. The central bank's job is then to expand or contract its balance sheet just enough to produce the correct quantity of money M. Assets on the balance sheet help to ensure that the central bank can always and quickly soak up excess money by selling assets. But money gains value from its special demand and scarcity, not from its backing. Central banks with assets worth less than liabilities, or less than 100% reserves, would still work.

Here, I pursue a different question: How can we set up money backed by assets, to determine the price level, and to define the numeraire itself? We abstract from the liquidity transformation business of central and private banks.

In reality, the two goals are mixed. A shortage of inside money can push down the price level. Central banks are set up to liquefy government debt. The real world has frictions, and realistic extensions of the theory should include them. But they are separate issues. I focus here on the price level and numeraire definition questions, clarifying that issue by starting without frictions.

The two functions of backing differ immediately on the nature of central bank assets. If central bank assets are entirely nominal debt, then a higher price level lowers the value of assets and liabilities equally. When the numeraire and price level are set elsewhere, such as by $MV = Py$, a currency peg, or a gold standard, the price level is still determined. But nominal assets and nominal liabilities cannot define a numeraire or determine the price level without frictions. Numeraire and price level determination by backing requires real assets.

Additionally, as in the discussion of a CPI standard, it is not practical for the assets to be actual real commodities. The assets have to be cash-settled and tradable financial contracts, that themselves only promise more central bank liabilities. We have to show that such a system can bootstrap itself to define a price level.

I describe here three general financial structures by which a pot of financial assets can form the backing for money as numeraire, and determine the price level. These examples reinforce a general point: *The real backing stream that appears in the fiscal theory does not have to be government surpluses.* Of course, then we should probably find a better name than "fiscal" theory.

10.1.1   Nominal Debt and Real Assets

The central bank issues nominal liabilities B_t, and holds real assets with value b_t. The price level is determined by $B_{t-1}/P_t = b_t$. Only central bank liabilities are numeraire. Governments or private asset issuers must repay their debts by delivering central bank reserves.

Suppose the central bank issues nominal debt B_t, and holds assets whose real value at the beginning of period t is b_t. The price level is determined, by

$$\frac{B_{t-1}}{P_t} = b_t.$$

We can write this relation as the usual present value formula, replacing b_t by the discounted present value of its real dividend or coupon stream $\{s_t\}$.

To determine the price level, the assets on the right-hand side need not be entirely real. We can have $b_t(P_t)$. It is enough that their value does not decline one for one with the price level, mirroring the left-hand side. As usual, though, the greater the difference between left- and right-hand sides as a function of the price level, the stronger the force for price level determination. We also wish for a stable value, so short-term indexed debt is a natural candidate.

The central bank can set expected inflation as before, by varying nominal debt B_t without changing the amount of real securities—effectively by share splits—or equivalently via a nominal interest rate target that offers nominal liabilities at fixed price without changing real assets. Central banks already pay interest on reserves by creating new reserves from thin air, thereby raising the value of nominal debt with no change in backing. Given the incoming B_{t-1}, shocks to the value of real assets b_t drive unexpected inflation, as fiscal shocks did previously. Now the bank alone determines both expected and unexpected inflation.

The B_{t-1} on the left-hand side includes only the central bank's nominal debt issue. The numeraire in this economy is maturing central bank nominal debt only; that is, central bank reserves and cash. Governments may issue nominal debt, but their debt is a promise to deliver central bank reserves, just as corporate nominal debt promises to deliver central bank reserves. This is our current institutional structure: Treasuries have renounced the right to print money (other than coins in the United States). Private issuers such as banks and money market funds may issue money-like securities, fixed value liquid deposits, or even notes. But those are also promises to pay central bank money, if requested. So reality departs from this ideal primarily on the asset side of the central bank balance sheet.

The key point: This setup creates a numeraire and determines its value. It determines the price level even though b_t consists of securities that pay cash, and do not deliver actual commodities. To see this fact, write the nominal value of dividends or indexed debt coupons paid to the central bank's real assets as $P_t s_t$ each period. Then we recover our old friend

$$B_{t-1} = P_t s_t + Q_t B_t = P_t s_t + \beta E_t \left(\frac{P_t}{P_{t+1}} \right) B_t.$$

It has a new interpretation: Each period, the central bank prints up money or creates reserves to redeem its debt B_{t-1}. The nominal debt B_{t-1} can be interest-paying reserves. Such nominal debt automatically becomes money, intraday reserves, without a separate morning redemption step. We can also imagine longer-term nominal liabilities that are converted to reserves in the morning. (The ECB already has term financing, and the Fed ought to implement it, among other reasons to lengthen the maturity structure of its liabilities.) Since central banks allow free conversion of cash to reserves, I write "cash" meaning the sum of the two. Next, in $P_t s_t$, the issuers of the real assets must come up with enough cash to pay the central bank. They get cash either by selling goods or by taxation, if the asset is indexed government debt. Overall, nominal debtholders get cash from the central bank. They pay taxes or pay firms for goods and services with that cash. The government or security issuers pay coupons or dividends to the central bank with cash. These payments soak up money. The bank also then sells new debt B_t, either fixing a quantity or via a nominal interest rate target. As with reserves, this need not be an extra step: Intraday money can simply turn into overnight reserves.

The quantity of real assets need not be constant. The central bank may buy and sell real assets, expanding and contracting its balance sheet, without affecting price level determination. By doing so, it provides more or less nominal debt, which is useful to make sure the economy is satiated in any liquidity demands. To verify, let $\hat{s}_t$ denote the dividends per share of the central bank's asset holdings. Let

$$\hat{q}_t = E_t \sum_{j=1}^{\infty} \beta^j \hat{s}_{t+j} \tag{10.1}$$

denote the real price per share and let $\hat{b}_{t-1}$ denote the number of shares that the central bank holds at the end of period $t-1$ and thus beginning of period t. The value of the bank's asset portfolio is now $\hat{b}_{t-1}(\hat{q}_t + \hat{s}_t)$, rather than b_t, at the beginning of period t. The flow equilibrium condition is

$$\frac{B_{t-1}}{P_t} = \hat{b}_{t-1}\hat{s}_t + \beta E_t \left(\frac{B_t}{P_{t+1}} \right) - \hat{q}_t \left(\hat{b}_t - \hat{b}_{t-1} \right). \tag{10.2}$$

Money printed up to pay nominal debt is soaked up by the dividend the central bank receives, by sales of new nominal debt, and now by sales of real assets. (The sign is negative on the last term, since $\hat{b}_t$ represents central bank assets, while B_t denotes liabilities.)

In equilibrium, the value of nominal debt is still equal to the present value of payments to the original portfolio.

$$\frac{B_{t-1}}{P_t} = \hat{b}_{t-1} E_t \sum_{j=0}^{\infty} \beta^j \hat{s}_{t+j} = \hat{b}_{t-1} \left(\hat{s}_t + \hat{q}_t \right). \tag{10.3}$$

Any increase in real assets, the last term of (10.2) is matched exactly by an increase in the value of nominal liabilities, the middle term of that equation.

One might think that asset purchases $\hat{b}_t - \hat{b}_{t-1} > 0$ would introduce extra money into the economy at time t, thereby raising the price level, and (10.2) suggests that outcome if you move the right-hand term and leave the second to last term alone. But a larger $\hat{b}_t$ implies more assets backing nominal debt B_t, which thus raise the amount of money soaked up by nominal debt sales.

To get to (10.3), substitute (10.1) in (10.2) and rearrange,

$$\frac{B_{t-1}}{P_t} - \hat{b}_{t-1} E_t \sum_{j=0}^{\infty} \beta^j \hat{s}_{t+j} = \beta E_t \left(\frac{B_t}{P_{t+1}} - \hat{b}_t E_{t+1} \sum_{j=0}^{\infty} \beta^j \hat{s}_{t+1+j} \right). \tag{10.4}$$

To avoid an explosion, a transversality condition violation, both sides must be zero.

Since it does not matter for price level determination, the bank could offer people the right to exchange money for the real asset, and vice versa, a sort of real bills doctrine. In that way, the bank would passively accommodate liquidity demands for nominal debt. Control of the size of the balance sheet is not necessary or desirable for price level determination.

10.1.2   A Right to Trade Real Assets

The value of central bank assets might become disconnected from the value of its liabilities, like closed-end fund shares. Allowing free conversion of each dollar to a proportionate share of bank assets, as mutual funds and exchange-traded funds do, can bring the value of assets and liabilities more closely in line.

Since central banks hold portfolios of long-term debt and mortgage-backed securities, the value of central bank assets changes a good deal on a mark-to-market basis. These changes have no discernible effect on inflation or anything else. Central banks do not even typically bother to report mark-to-market values.

This fact might just reflect the underlying unity of central bank and treasury balance sheets. Any gains eventually go to the treasury, and sufficient losses lead to treasury recapitalizations. Reported balance sheets exclude these implicit transfers, which we can consider an implicit equity tranche or credit backstop. The value of private banks' debt liabilities similarly does not vary with the mark-to-market value of their assets, because equity soaks up the difference. With largely nominal assets, the price level adjustment mechanism is currently weak.

One can think of reasons that the price level might not be tightly controlled, even in this theory, with flexible prices, real assets, and a rigorously separate central-bank balance sheet. The central bank can behave like closed-end funds whose value of liabilities can drift away from the value of assets (Zweig (1973)). Long-term arbitrage of the closed-end fund discount or premium is costly. All you can do about it is to buy the cheaper of fund or synthetic shares, long only, and enjoy the dividends at a lower initial price. This is a weak mechanism for bringing prices into line.

The pot of assets central bank faces an additional impediment: In order to change the value of the central bank's liabilities, reserves and short-term debt, the price level of *all other* goods and services must move. The price of the closed-end fund shares can move relative to the numeraire, but the bank's liabilities are the numeraire.

One can and perhaps should think of this issue by studying the model's equilibrium after adding sticky prices and financial frictions. Here I think about it in terms of the forces that drive us to equilibrium in the simple model, as before.

The pot of assets central bank suffers relative to our previous models that unite central bank and treasury balance sheets, because its assets and liabilities are smaller than overall government debt and the present value of surpluses. That fact means that two of the three mechanisms for moving to equilibrium are weaker.

A wealth effect is one of our forces: If the price level is too low, central bank liabilities are over-valued, and they feel like extra wealth. People spend more, driving up the price of goods and services. But if central bank liabilities are 1/10 the size of government debt, then a given change in the price level has only 1/10 of the effect on consumer's perceived wealth, and this mechanism is proportionally weaker. Likewise, if extra money is piling up, only 1/10 as much is piling up.

It is therefore desirable for the central bank to have a large balance sheet. We seem to be moving to that world. The Fed's $8 trillion 2021 balance sheet is more than a quarter of all public debt ($22 trillion). On December 27, 2007, just before the 2008 financial crisis, the balance sheet was only $880 billion. Liabilities were almost all currency, $830 billion, and reserves were a paltry $5 billion.

A large balance sheet has desirable features, in its other role of supplying liquidity. Our world still features a demand for fixed-value liquid assets. If those assets are provided directly, rather than by large inside-money creation leveraging a small quantity of reserves, we can eliminate private sector financial crises. Cochrane (2014c) expands on this view.

By contrast, the force of intertemporal substitution is unchanged and independent of the size of the assets and liabilities concerned. If the price level is 10% too low this year, but that deviation lasts one year only, the resulting 10% negative expected real return offers the same incentive to substitute consumption from future to present, no matter the size of the balance sheet.

The scenario of concern, then, is a persistent deviation of the price level from its equilibrium value, that does not greatly alter the real rate of return on the bank's liabilities. One step to address that concern is to more tightly tie the value of assets to liabilities, and therefore to determine the price level more tightly. Mutual funds sell securities to meet redemptions at net asset value. Exchange-traded funds allow investors to deliver securities in exchange for shares and vice versa. They deliberately make arbitrage between fund shares and fund assets easy. Consequently, the value of shares tracks the value of assets closely.

So, let us allow people to exchange central bank debt or reserves for central bank assets. At any moment, in return for one dollar of central bank liabilities (currency or reserves), the central bank will give you a fraction of its asset portfolio proportional to the number of dollars outstanding at that moment. The central bank portfolio could be formally organized as a fund with traded shares, to facilitate such conversion.

How would this provision work to stabilize the price level? There is one equilibrium, and a thousand ways to be out of equilibrium. I'll describe one. Markets clear, and consumption equals endowment each period. Period by period supply equals demand is a strong force. A violation of the flow budget constraint is impossible, and a violation of intertemporal substitution is not the core problem. So, imagine a violation of the transversality condition. Write the equilibrium condition (10.4) as

$$\frac{B_{t-1}}{P_t} - \hat{b}_{t-1}E_t \sum_{j=0}^{\infty} \beta^j \hat{s}_{t+j} = \beta E_t \left[\frac{B_t}{P_{t+1}} - \hat{b}_t \sum_{j=0}^{\infty} \beta^j \hat{s}_{t+1+j} \right] \quad (10.5)$$

$$\frac{B_{t-1}}{P_t} - \hat{b}_{t-1}(\hat{s}_t + \hat{q}_t) = \beta E_t \left[\frac{B_t}{P_{t+1}} - \hat{b}_t(\hat{s}_{t+1} + \hat{q}_{t+1}) \right]. \quad (10.6)$$

If P_t is too low and B_{t-1}/P_t is too high, then the sequence P_{t+j} must also also decline relative to equilibrium value, so the net value grows at the real interest rate.

The central bank assets $\hat{b}_{t-1}(\hat{s}_t + \hat{q}_t)$ are private sector liabilities. They are either assets—stocks and indexed bonds—sold by the private sector to the central bank, or tax payments that flow through government to the central bank. Thus, the quantity on the left-hand side of (10.6) is apparent excess private sector wealth.

If the price level is too low, people should consume more. They can raise consumption at time t by the quantity on the left-hand side of (10.6). Or they can raise consumption at all time periods so that the present value of such additional consumption equals the left-hand side of (10.6). An attempt to do so violates supply equals demand, and pushes the price level to equilibrium.

The worry, though, is that consumers might not act quickly on this opportunity, especially when both terms on the left-hand side of (10.6) are small. Suppose, for instance, that the central bank loses mark-to-market value of its portfolio $\hat{q}_t$, but the price level does not change. It might take a long time for a consumer to figure out that the present value of his or her liability stream is reduced. If, say, the central bank holds stock, and expected dividends and stock prices decline, the consumer has to feel *wealthier* than he or she would otherwise feel because he or she indirectly owes less to the central bank.

Add the right to trade. For example, in the "morning," just before or after nominal debt B_{t-1} is redeemed, B_{t-1} liabilities are outstanding. Let people trade each dollar or maturing bond for $\hat{b}_{t-1}/B_{t-1}$ shares of the asset portfolio, or vice versa. We now have a peg, not just backing, like a gold standard or foreign exchange rate peg. And it is 100% backed—the central bank can exchange all debt this way, or arbitrarily expand the balance sheet.

Suppose again that the price level is too low, so the value of central bank liabilities B_{t-1}/P_t is larger than the value of its assets $\hat{b}_t(\hat{q}_t + \hat{s}_t)$. Each share sold to the central bank gives more dollars than one can obtain in private markets. People would rush to sell shares to the central bank, increasing its holdings beyond $\hat{b}_{t-1}$ and increasing dollars outstanding beyond B_{t-1}. People who do so are individually, immediately, wealthier. They spend this wealth, driving up the price level.

In this way, the offer to trade assets for dollars makes immediate the difference between private sector asset B_{t-1}/P_t and liability $\hat{b}_{t-1}(\hat{s}_t + \hat{q}_t)$ values. We worried that an individual consumer might not see the private sector's collective liability to the central bank. By allowing a trade, the difference between collective assets and liabilities is immediate and potentially in each consumer's hands.

The central bank here offers an arbitrage opportunity. Until the price level rises, people would keep selling unlimited assets to the bank. What happens when prices are sticky? The discount rate and hence asset price $\hat{q}_t$ might temporarily rise as well. As pegging gold might peg the gold price more effectively than it pegs the price level, pegging the asset price might peg that price more effectively than the price level. We also don't desire asset price fluctuations to translate immediately to the price level. So a more limited version of this right might be desirable, slowly pulling the price level back but not demanding immediate equality.

In this example, the bank's liabilities are worth more than its assets. It is technically insolvent. Yet I write that people bring assets to the bank and demand more of its liabilities. Don't people run from, not to, insolvent banks? Not in this case. The run-prone bank offers a dollar for each deposit, so if the bank is insolvent and everyone accepts the offer, it runs out of dollars. This central bank offers one share of the assets for each dollar. Every dollar can be redeemed, and any amount can be printed. Giving assets to this bank in return for its liabilities is a good deal.

Didn't we just show in the last section that central bank asset purchases and sales have no effect on the price level? Those purchases are made at market prices, in equilibrium. These are made away from market prices, out of equilibrium.

The opposite case, that the price level is too high, works differently. People should feel poorer, and correspondingly lower consumption, sending the price level down. Offered the chance to trade dollars for assets, they would, however, buy assets from the central bank, making them individually richer, and everyone else poorer still.

However, the scenario is no longer realistic, because the transversality condition is asymmetric. Positive net wealth builds up at the interest rate. Ignoring it, and failing to raise consumption, is possible but suboptimal. Negative net wealth also builds at the interest rate, but is eventually ruled out by a budget constraint. So, while there are feasible price level sequences for which consumers intertemporally optimize and obey budget constraints, consumption equals endowment, and the value of private wealth grows, there are no feasible price level sequences in which the value of private wealth starts negative and grows ever more negative. An interesting negative example must violate intertemporal substitution, not the transversality condition.

So, we must imagine a scenario in which the price level is temporarily too high and the value of central bank debt temporarily too low, and consequently the expected return on central bank liabilities is greater than market expected returns. Consumers should try to consume less, and save more, lowering the price level.

10.1.3   Shares as Money

We could use central bank shares, giving the right to $1/N$ of the central bank portfolio, or shares of a large index fund, as money. I check that this idea works: that if companies sell products in return for shares and pay dividends in shares, the price level is determined.

We can eliminate nominal debt entirely. Suppose the bank simply sells shares in its portfolio, and we use those shares as money. Money is *defined* as $1/N$ of the central bank's asset portfolio. We could also use shares of a large index fund.

Such shares clearly have a value, except for the numeraire and cash-settlement problem. If a company pays dividends that are just more shares of the same company, can those shares have value? The answer is yes.

To keep it simple, build our monetary system on a potato farm. The farm has N shares outstanding. The farm sells s_t potatoes each day, in return for its own shares. Let P_t denote the number of shares per potato in the potato (goods) market. Each day, consumers use $P_t s_t$ shares to buy and eat the day's potatoes, leaving $N - P_t s_t$ shares outstanding. The farm then gives the $P_t s_t$ shares to its investors as dividends. The same number N of shares are outstanding at the end of the day.

The real value of a share, in terms of potatoes, at the beginning of period t (including s_t) is

$$E_t \sum_{j=0}^{\infty} \beta^j \left(\frac{P_{t+j} s_{t+j}}{N} \right) \frac{1}{P_{t+j}} = \frac{1}{N} E_t \sum_{j=0}^{\infty} \beta^j s_{t+j}.$$

Though shares only give the right to receive more shares, one can use shares to buy potatoes. Therefore, the value of shares is the same as if dividends delivered potatoes.

The real value of a share in the goods market must be the same as the real value of a share in the asset market. Thus, the price of potatoes in terms of shares is determined by

$$\frac{N}{P_t} = E_t \sum_{j=0}^{\infty} \beta^j s_{t+j}.$$

In sum, yes, the price level is determined if we simply use shares of a real asset, and those shares only promise more shares.

The potato farm shares might be volatile, as the potato crop waxes and wanes, inducing price level volatility. We can split the potato farm into an indexed debt tranche and an equity tranche, and define the numeraire by the indexed debt tranche.

Start with indexed perpetuities. An indexed perpetuity that pays a real $1 forever is worth $\sum_{j=0}^{\infty} \beta^j = (1+r)/r$, a large number. Perpetuities, like all bonds, are usually therefore quoted in terms of yield rather than price. So, let the numeraire be $y/(1+y)$ perpetuities where y is a small number, and call these "dollars." Obviously the special case $y = r$ will be convenient, but I don't want to assume that the risk-free rate is constant over time, so I let the story build toward that case. Potatoes cost P_t dollars, $P_t y/(1+y)$ perpetuities, by definition of P_t.

Period t dawns with M indexed perpetuities outstanding. Consumers pay the potato farm $P_t s_t$ dollars in return for its crop. The farm pays P_t dollars to the holder of each perpetuity, MP_t dollars in total. It pays the remainder to its stockholders, each of which receives $1/N(P_t s_t - MP_t)$ dollars. The real value of each perpetuity, at the beginning of period t, is thus the right-hand side of

$$\frac{1+y}{y} \frac{1}{P_t} = E_t \sum_{j=0}^{\infty} \beta^j \frac{P_{t+j}}{P_{t+j}} = \frac{1}{1-\beta} = \frac{1+r}{r}. \tag{10.7}$$

The nominal value of a perpetuity is $(1 + y)/y$, as the dollar is defined as the inverse of that many perpetuities. The real value of a perpetuity is thus the left-hand side of (10.7), and the price level is determined by this equation. All in all,

$$P_t = \frac{(1+r)y}{(1+y)r}.$$

Obviously, it is convenient to define $y = r$ so $P_t = 1$, or close to it.

The potatoes seem to have vanished, but they have not. Even if we allow occasional negative dividends, the value of equity must be positive, so the value of the perpetuity is limited by the present value of potato sales.

If we had defined the dollar as a potato or a claim that delivers one potato, we would have gotten to a unit price level more quickly. If we had defined the perpetuity as the right to receive one potato per year and the dollar equal to $r/(1+r)$ perpetuities, we would again have gotten to a unit price level more quickly. The point is that the same result holds with a purely financial contract.

When interest rates vary, perpetuity prices vary, so this structure may still lead to a variable price level. We can alternatively construct a system that defines a one-period indexed bond as numeraire, producing less price level variation.

At time $t + 1$, the farm will sell s_{t+1} potatoes for price $P_{t+1}s_{t+1}$. A quantity M_t of indexed bonds is outstanding. The farm will give $M_t P_{t+1}$ of the time-$t + 1$ numeraire to the bondholders, and $P_{t+1}s_{t+1} - M_t P_{t+1}$ to the stockholders. The real time t value of the indexed bonds is thus $M_t \beta E_t(P_{t+1}/P_{t+1}) = \beta M_t$.

If people use these indexed bonds as numeraire at time t, the price level is $P_t = \beta$. Backing still matters. Most simply, we can require that payments to stockholders are non-negative, so the farm defaults if $s_{t+1} < M_t$. Then, we either value the bonds including the probability of default, or we add $M_t < \min(s_{t+1})$.

Now, let M_{t-1} one-period indexed bonds be outstanding at the beginning of period t. Each bond is redeemed for $P_t = \beta$ new indexed bonds, enough to buy one potato. The farm prints up and issues those bonds, instantly rolling over the debt. The farm sells potatoes for $P_t s_t$ bonds, again sending any extra bonds so earned to the stockholders, who get $P_t s_t - M_{t-1}$ bonds. Since each bond delivers enough numeraire to buy a potato, the time-t indexed bonds are worth β at time $t - 1$, and around we go. Additional bond issues come by reducing the amount of stock.

Again it would be prettier, if less clear, to define the numeraire as $1 + y$ indexed bonds with $y \approx r$ a small number, so the price level is closer to one.

In the end, the economy works as in the indexed debt target of Section 9.5, but now privately run.

One can also specify that the potato farm sells unlevered equity, and a downstream fund buys that equity, issuing the indexed debt and levered equity tranches. It is not necessary to have a monopoly of numeraire issuers either. If we standardize the portfolio of assets, multiple issuers can hold shares of the asset portfolio and issue liabilities, competing on transactions costs and other conveniences.

All of these ideas need elaboration with sticky prices. Since central bank liabilities are typically overnight debt, we really are talking about a day. Price level jumps are unrealistic, so it is likely to be more fruitful to pursue these ideas with the continuous time framework, in which a period of inflation leads to a period of low real returns that devalue even overnight debt without price level jumps. Discount rate variation and variation in the asset price on the right-hand side will then appear. I also left out the distinction between zero-rate currency and interest-paying reserves, and zero bound or negative interest rate issues.

10.2   A Managed Central Bank Portfolio

Pots of assets ideas are useful to understand central bank balance sheets when banks hold treasury securities and are part of the government. Central bank assets provide a clearer and potentially more stable backing, while overall government debt, surpluses, and deficits vary.

Now return to thinking about the institutional separation between treasury and central bank, with the central bank part of the government and holding government debt. Why bother with a balance sheet?

We can think of a central bank that is the only issuer of cash and reserves, backed by an asset portfolio of government debt, as a fiscal rule, a way of managing and guaranteeing the stream of surpluses that determines the price level, while remaining surpluses vary more, and other debts may even default.

The art of inflation control, by *controlling* the stream of surpluses that back nominal debt, has been with us for several chapters. We started by thinking about how the government can commit to repay all its debts, or not—how to commit to $a(\beta) = 0$, or how to commit to $a(\beta) \neq 0$ by a specified amount; how to commit to a steady $E_t \sum_{j=0}^{\infty} \beta^j s_{t+j}$ or a defined rise or fall in that quantity.

With a separate central bank that holds a balance sheet of assets, the government instead carves out a stream of surpluses, apart from general surpluses and debt, dedicated to price level control. The government need only control and communicate a steady value of *central bank* assets in order to produce a quiet price level, while the rest of the governments' surpluses, deficits, and debts may vary widely. Moreover, we can *observe* the value of a central bank asset portfolio. We don't have to guess about future surpluses.

In our picture of the government debt valuation equation,

$$\frac{B_{t-1}}{P_t} = E_t \sum_{j=0}^{\infty} \beta^j s_{t+j},$$

a typical government goes through waves of larger and smaller debt, occasioned by periods of deficits followed by periods of surpluses. Debt B_{t-1} on the left-hand side and the present value of surpluses on the right-hand side each vary through time, with most of their variation offsetting. We have to cut through this large joint variation to see the small changes in debt that are not backed by surpluses, or the small unbacked deficits that result in inflation. And so do people in the economy.

With a central bank that has its own balance sheet, however, the government can back reserves and cash by a stable and visible quantity of assets. Keeping a steady $20 in your right pocket and letting debts and repayments accumulate in your left pocket can assure the recipient of a $20 IOU that it will be repaid.

Separation of central bank and general government finances remains key to this system. The central bank must not print up money to redeem general government debt, and the government must refrain from grabbing central bank assets. On the other hand, topping up central bank assets would be a way to slow inflation, and confiscating those assets would be a way to create inflation. Like capital levies or subsidies, though, these would have to be done unexpectedly, which is always a tricky matter.

It would be useful in this vision to have an institutional structure in which the central bank's holdings of government debt are special. The bank could hold distinct debt issues. The government could then discriminate between the government debt held by the central bank and other government debt, or it could more easily make contingent payments to and from the central bank differentially from other bond holders. Discrimination between categories of debtholders is commonplace in defaults. Hall and Sargent (2014) give a lovely account of defaults and inflation that discriminated between categories of debt in U.S. history.

That arrangement could allow the government to partially default on non-central bank debt without causing inflation. If we *want* inflation, we might want the opposite, for general government debt to be fully repaid, preserving the reputation needed for borrowing, while inflating the central bank's liabilities.

The separation of central bank debt from general treasury debt mirrors the previous idea of a "regular" and "emergency" or "price level control" budget, each with separate classes of debt and distinct traditions of repayment.

10.3   Balance Sheets, Contingent Transfers, and the ECB

Why are central bank and treasury balance sheets integrated in the first place? Contingent transfers—profit rebates and recapitalization—central bank purchases of government debt, and debt monetization unite the balance sheets. Separate balance sheets are part of an institutional structure that tries to resist inflation. We live in an uncomfortable middle ground. However, it is always true that the price level adjusts to set the real value of all government debt to the value of surpluses. With a completely walled-off central bank, that view only adds debt and the surpluses that repay it to left- and right-hand sides.

Since central banks have separate balance sheets, one may wonder why we haven't been analyzing inflation this way all along. Just why does the previous analysis unite money and government debt as claims to general government surpluses? The answer is, because appearances deceive, and several forces unite the balance sheets.

Central banks usually profit from the interest spread between assets and liabilities. Central banks rebate this profit to the treasury, or spend it directly by employing economists and other staff. Increasingly, they use it to make subsidized loans. If interest income increases, central banks rebate more to the treasury or spend more directly. If interest income declines, they rebate less to the treasury or spend less. If they lose a lot, central banks are recapitalized by treasuries.

For example, the ECB website[1] explains that profits are used first of all to fund its operations. Assets are then held as a provision against future losses.

But after that, any remaining ECB profits go to the national central banks of the euro area countries, as the shareholders of the ECB. . . . profits usually go to the country's government, thus contributing to its budget. . .

The U.S. Federal Reserve also funds its operations from the interest spread between assets and liabilities, and rebates the rest to the Treasury. (What will happen if interest rates on the ECB's assets continue to be negative, with a lot of cash outstanding, if economies go cashless so zero interest liabilities disappear, or if the yield curve reverts to a downward slope as in the nineteenth century, are interesting questions.)

In the other direction, the ECB has the right to demand recapitalization from EU governments. This provision, and the parallel possibility of recapitalization of the Federal Reserve from the U.S. Treasury, also addresses substantial defaults that would imperil the value of central bank assets. This event is less and less impossible as the ECB adds sovereign, corporate, and deliberately overvalued (i.e., regarded by the ECB as "underpriced") green bonds to its portfolio. Those debts are either in the end backed by general EU taxes, or will be inflated away. (Bassetto and Caracciolo (2021) have an excellent exposition of the obscure fiscal connections between ECB, country central banks, and their treasuries.) Unlike the ECB, the Federal Reserve typically buys risky securities in partnership with the U.S. Treasury, in which the Treasury takes the first tranche of losses. But larger losses are always possible.

These contingent assets and liabilities, not reported on a balance sheet, make up the difference between mark-to-market asset and liability values. Their presence is a good thing too, as it provides a stabilization of the asset values. They act as a loss-absorbing equity tranche that insulates private banks' deposit and short-term debt liabilities from changes in the value of their assets, or the credit backstop used by money market funds and special purpose vehicles.

Most of all, a unified treasury and central bank balance sheet represents a view that when the chips are down, the central bank will print money or create reserves to allow the treasury to repay its debts and to finance deficits, rather than force a default or rollover crisis. We have seen inflation, but default on domestic currency debt is rare. Relatively small turmoil in the U.S. Treasury market in March 2020 led the Federal Reserve to finance broker-dealer purchases and start buying the majority of new Treasury issues. Other governments have forced central banks to buy debt directly at inflated prices, or grabbed central bank assets to stave off default.

The ECB was supposed to be a central bank divorced from government budgets. Initially it created money, lent it to banks, and counted the loans as the corresponding assets. It now has a large securities portfolio. The ECB was explicitly not supposed to monetize sovereign debts. In a currency union without fiscal union, insolvent countries are supposed to default, just as insolvent corporations default, or obtain direct fiscal support from generous neighbors, or from the IMF. This provision was always a bit in doubt.

---

1. https://www.ecb.europa.eu/explainers/tell-me-more/html/ecb_profits.en.html

Companies are not required to have debt and deficit limits to operate in the dollar zone, because they default if in trouble. (Well, ideally. Corporate bailouts are becoming more common too.) That the Eurozone put debt and deficit limits in place was already a sign that a hard-nosed attitude toward sovereign default might not prevail, and that the ECB would rather not face the temptation. The Greek affair, "whatever it takes" support for Italian and Spanish sovereign debt, and subsequent sovereign and corporate bond purchases show that the rule against monetizing debts, or bringing them on to a general EU balance sheet, is more elastic. The ECB is becoming a more classic fiscal theory of the price level operation, money backed by collective general government surpluses, not a separate institution with a segregated asset base. The collective nature of the surpluses backing the euro still invites countries to race to the bottom of deficits. Those of us in the United States should not sneer, as bailouts of student debts, pensions, housing, state and local governments, banks, insurance companies, financial institutions, and corporate debts loom similarly.

But central banks and central bank balance sheets exist. Somewhat independent central banks that don't like inflation and resist monetizing debts are an important part of inflation control, devices to force the government to repayment rather than inflation, and to help the government to precommit to that outcome in order to borrow in the first place. A separate balance sheet is part of that architecture.

How do we model the situation? In one sense it doesn't matter. In any case, the price level still adjusts so that the value of overall government liabilities is equal to the present value of overall surpluses. That relation is not wrong, it is just harder to measure since we needlessly add a component of debt and an offsetting component of surpluses. But we can get a better measurement by recognizing the presence of the central bank balance sheet. It is useful to study tensions between central banks and governments and the somewhat effective commitments that independence, mandates, and balance sheets provide. Likewise, it is useful to study household conflicts that produce household-level preferences, or the internal conflicts that lead to corporate decisions. We lie in a middle space: The Fed's and the ECB's liabilities and potential asset losses are partially backed by general government transfers. Much general government and pan-European debt will, in the end, be monetized by the Fed and ECB if the debt threatens default. But central bank resistance will be an important force to a fiscal adjustment rather than quick resort to inflation.

Del Negro and Sims (2015) study this situation, showing that even apparently independent central banks, with access to seigniorage and term premium profits and ostensibly separate balance sheets, must have access to fiscal support. Bassetto and Messer (2013) model explicitly the situation of a central bank that issues interest-bearing reserves as well as non-interest-bearing currency, noting in extremis "the CB faces two options: either it is recapitalised by Treasury or it increases its monopoly profits by raising the inflation tax." Bassetto and Sargent (2020) have an excellent discussion, "two government budget constraints" of a central bank with a balance sheet that is at least in theory separate from the treasury. In their analysis, summarizing also Sims (2004), Sims (2005), a central bank that holds nominal government debt cannot determine the price level. "Only the Treasury can provide a fiscal backstop." A central bank that holds real assets, gold reserves in their case, can determine the price level.

As I write in late 2021, inflation is rising in Europe, and the ECB is facing a classic fiscal theory challenge. Italy's debt is 160% of GDP, so raising interest rates will raise Italy's debt service costs. Where will the fiscal resources come from?

10.4   Assets

For a pot-of-assets central bank to determine the price level, the assets should have stable value and be real. Short-term indexed debt is ideal. Foreign debt, currency swaps, diversified debts, and contingent transfers do not move one for one with the price level, however, and contribute to price level determination. Central banks do not currently hold much indexed debt, most likely because they are set up to provide liquidity, not to determine the price level.

We want the assets on the right-hand side of $B_{t-1}/P_t = b_t$ to be real, or at least to have a nominal value that does not rise one for one with the price level. It is also desirable for the assets on the right-hand side to have a stable value, so as not to induce inflation volatility. To tie the value of assets to the value of liabilities, assets whose value is clear, transparent, and reported are advantageous, rather than, say, shares of privately held businesses or real estate. If we allow conversion, assets should be liquid and tradable as well. Short-term, default-free indexed debt seems ideal. The preference for central banks holding debt rather than equity, and short-term debt at that, makes a lot of sense.

Assets can include private securities, stocks, bonds, or indexed debt, as well as government securities. The U.S. Fed was originally set up to buy "real bills," short-term commercial paper, not U.S. Treasury securities. There are many political problems with central banks buying private assets, and obvious need for restrictions on the practice; for example, rules about buying index funds rather than individual securities. The issue here is only price level determination, abstracting from those valid political economy concerns. This "central bank" can also be entirely separate from government, a fund or cryptocurrency.

Foreign currency debt, private debt, and debt from several governments in a currency union can provide diversification. Diversification solidifies backing of nominal debt even if the general government runs into trouble. This thought also suggests that central banks should diversify their assets more when their general governments have greater fiscal problems, as they seem to do.

Though central banks do not hold much indexed debt, the value of their assets also does not rise mechanically one for one with the price level. Foreign currency debt and currency swaps are essentially real, at least to the individual country. Central banks typically hold longer term assets than their liabilities, whose response to inflation is complex depending on the stochastic process of inflation and its joint movement with bond risk premiums.

Given the paucity of indexed debt, it is not currently feasible for central banks to buy a lot of it. CPI swaps could offer a cheap way to turn nominal assets into real assets. And it would be a good idea for treasuries to offer better indexed debt products, including CPI-linked perpetuities. A bigger central bank demand, as well as indexed reserves, could thicken the market.

The government could manage the value of the portfolio of assets, by topping up or reducing the quantity of nominal assets, rather than count on their nominal price rising and falling, to create backing that is stable in real terms. Of course, benign topping up and eliminating central bank assets in an effort at inflation control looks a lot like merging balance sheets and grabbing assets for fiscal purposes, so such a structure is delicate. Varying the interest payments rebated by central banks to the treasury, varying the recapitalization flows from treasury to central banks, or varying central bank expenditures systematically with the price level also create effectively real assets.

Why do central banks not hold more real assets? The answer seems clear: Central banks are not currently set up with this form of price level determinacy in mind. Their balance sheets are designed to provide liquidity, with $MV = Py$, interest rate control, gold standard, or other theories of numeraire definition and price level determination in mind. The last item includes classic fiscal theory in which the balance sheet is irrelevant, though today's central banks are surely not constructed with fiscal theory in mind. With this intellectual framework, central banks don't need to hold real assets, and the nominal bond market is much larger.

But institutions evolve. A bout of fiscal inflation, that conventional tools seem powerless to stem, may interest people again in setting up a more independent central bank. If deflation is again a problem, finding ways to communicate that assets are *not* there to back liabilities may return to the agenda. And once those in charge shed the intellectual force of $MV = Py$ or interest rate control, and come to view price level determination rather than liquidity provision as a key objective of central bank balance sheets, it will quickly be obvious that real assets are a good idea.

10.5   Backing

Many different kinds of backing have been tried. Government debt has advantages in principle over mortgages and other private loans: It is now larger, the stream of surpluses has longer duration, and a fiscally solvent government can adapt the stream of surpluses. Backing that defines the numeraire can avoid explicit default.

Many different kinds of backing have been tried, to give value to paper money or to define a numeraire. Some of the earliest money consisted of clay tokens, representing commodities stored in granaries or at ports. Naturally, we start the analysis of the value of such tokens by the real value of the commodities that back them. However, cowrie shells, wampum, and other objects that are arguably intrinsically worthless but in limited supply have also circulated for millennia.

Gold coins are, in a sense, money that carries with it its own backing. Coins are often traded at a premium to their metallic value. Backing theories allow for a medium-of-exchange premium on top of backing. Fiscal theory allows for money to pay no interest if money provides liquidity services.

In 1716, John Law directed one of the most notorious first efforts to use paper money. It was backed by government debt and then by shares in the Mississippi company, which was to make huge profits in Louisiana. The system failed when that backing proved illusory, and too many notes were printed.

Sargent and Velde (1995) describe a number of monetary innovations in the French Revolution, including assignats: The revolutionary government had seized church property. The government needed revenue, but it would take time to sell off the church property. It issued assignats, backed by the proceeds of eventual church asset sales. Assignats circulated as money. They maintained their value for several years until they too eventually hyperinflated from printing too many of them.

Rabushka (2008) tells the history of the first paper money issued in the Americas by the Massachusetts Bay Colony starting in 1690 (p. 357 ff.). The money was issued as circulating government debt ("bills") to finance military expenditures. It quickly traded at a "discount of 30–40 percent." On February 3, 1691, the legislature "decreed that bills would be accepted by the government for tax payments," as in my first fiscal theory story. Indeed, the government offered "a 5 percent advance or premium." The result, "as the deadline for tax payments approached, bills became 5 percent more valuable than . . . other forms of money." That provision also means that bills paid 5 percent interest, so the legislature in one fell swoop invented paper money, backed by taxes, and money that pays interest. However, bills were denominated in sterling. This is backed paper money, not a new numeraire.

Initially, "with each issue of bills, the legislature authorized specific taxes equal to the size of the note issue." Then, "to retire this debt, the law of May 21 required that bills remitted in taxes to the Treasury were to be destroyed each year," an interesting fiscal commitment.

The money grew popular, and many holders quickly rolled over the notes rather than used them to pay taxes. In 1692, the legislature decreed the bills legal tender for public and private debts, despite "England's prohibition against the printing of paper money in the colonies."

However, the colony soon issued too much money, largely to finance military expenditures.

> The fears of the English government and creditors materialized. As the supply of bills increased, the value of Massachusetts money depreciated. . . The legislature quickly discovered that postponing the redemption of bills enabled it to spend money it did not have, while deferring the collection of taxes to a later date, a practice that was popular with voters.

While backing with a long-deferred stream of surpluses can work, apparently faith that long-deferred taxes would materialize was not strong. Since bills did not pay interest, they could not become long-term government debt held in a quantity larger than money demand would accommodate.

The Bank of England, on its founding in 1694, bought government securities and issued notes. It had a monopoly on both. Under the gold standard, the point was to make government debt more liquid, as well as to organize a force for its repayment. Both features helped the government to borrow. The bank's monopoly on note issue helped to prevent the swift fiscal inflation of other paper monies.

Banks, expanding in the nineteenth century, backed notes and deposits by loans and mortgages. Such backing is a reasonably good arrangement. There are a lot of loans and mortgages, real estate is a large element of the capital stock, so a large quantity of money and liquid deposits can be issued backed by real estate. Furthermore, two layers of equity stabilize the value of resources that back money: Bank assets are loans, collateralized by real estate, and the bank has an equity claim to absorb losses. Loans and real estate are long-lived assets.

Under the gold standard, these arrangements were primarily aimed only at the first goal of backing, to provide a means of issuing liquid notes while maintaining the value of notes relative to gold.

The present value of future fiscal surpluses has advantages over backing by real-estate loans. First, it is even longer lived.

Second, mortgages are illiquid. If the time comes that people test the backing, banks have to sell mortgages or foreclosed property. Solvent banks can borrow against their assets, but it's hard to tell illiquid from insolvent. In any case, this expedient does not increase the overall stock of money in a systemic run. This asset illiquidity is a central ingredient in all our financial crises.

The government, by contrast, has a unique ability to adjust the revenue stream that backs its money, so long as there is some fiscal space to the top of the present value Laffer curve or some political and economic space to cut expenditures. That attribute allows the government to promise a steadier path of surpluses than backing by private assets can do. The events in which real estate loans default, and bank equity is wiped out, are potentially more common than the events in which the government cannot raise surpluses and its money must inflate. Or so it has been in most of the postwar history of advanced countries.

Third, government debt is only a promise to pay more government debt. It can be uniquely free of explicit default. Bank deposits and notes promise payment in some other currency. They don't try to define a numeraire.

Fourth, government debt is now in abundant supply. One might have worried in the past that there simply was not enough government debt to back liquidity needs, that banks were necessary on top of a government currency to "transform" illiquid real estate assets into a pool of liquid liabilities. No longer.

All of these are good reasons that we have evolved from money defined by gold and backed by loans, to short-term government debt as numeraire, backed by fiscal surpluses.

But primary surpluses are not a perfect backing either. Governments occasionally default or inflate. Our governments may be headed in that direction. Historically, over the last 1000 years, government debt has been quite risky. The placid monetary experience since 1980, and even that restricted mostly to the United States, Europe, and Japan, may not last forever.

The general principle of the fiscal theory remains—a numeraire can be valued by its backing—but perhaps we can find sources of backing are better than the arrangement we seem to have evolved toward, that short-term nominal government debt is numeraire, and money is backed by a stream of fiscal surpluses via an effectively integrated central bank and government balance sheet. The euro is already an innovation relative to national currencies, and at least in its original design provided a second buffer between the assets pledged to back money and general government surpluses. Other possibilities beckon.

10.6   After Government Money

We have converged on a monetary system in which short-term nominal government debt is the numeraire, unit of account, and by and large medium of exchange. Most transactions that are not simply netted between banks involve the transfer of interest-paying reserves. Government debt is the "safe asset" and best collateral in financial transactions. I have structured most of the fiscal theory discussion around this institutional reality.

It was not always so, and it may not always remain so. I doubt that our economy will transition to another system before a crisis, as it is human nature not to embark on grand adventures when the current system is working reasonably well. But in the event that happens, or in the rare event that innovation precedes a crisis, it's worth thinking about alternative arrangements. Competition from crypto or other private payments providers may spur changes, especially if they try to define a numeraire as Bitcoin does.

10.6.1　Government Debt Is Not Perfect

Backing by government debt is not perfect either. Such systems have crashed before, and our fiscal situation may lead to a debt crisis. That would be a financial catastrophe. It would motivate a search for better alternatives.

A failure of our fiscal–monetary arrangements is not unimaginable. The United States has had inflation. Other countries have had more severe inflations. Many countries, even advanced Western countries, have had debt crises and exchange rate crises. The United Kingdom had repeated crises in the 1950s through 1970s. The United States had a debt and currency crisis in the early 1970s when it abandoned gold, floated the dollar, and exited the Bretton Woods agreement. Many advanced countries have 100% or larger debt to GDP ratios, persistent deficits, health care and pension promises that they cannot keep, and sclerotic growth. Debt service is not a problem with r as low or lower than the discouraging g, but a rise in r or further fall in g would force a reckoning.

In the aftermath of the 2008 crisis and 2020 pandemic, it now seems that any crisis will be met by immense bailout and stimulus spending, based on newly borrowed debt or newly created reserves. Imagine that a new global recession, pandemic, or war breaks out. The U.S. federal government will try to borrow additional trillions or tens of trillions of dollars to bail out banks, businesses, households, state and local governments, pension funds, retirement funds, and student debts; plus stimulus spending, pay for the war or other direct crisis expenses; plus, as usual, roll over something like half the stock of debt each year. All of this in a steep recession, while other countries are facing their own sudden fiscal problems. China's debt might blow up, Italy default, and they and other countries might sell rather than buy U.S. Treasurys. But this time, it all starts from a more than 100% debt to GDP ratio, with large structural deficits, unreformed entitlements, even more polarized politics and even less idea how any of it will be paid back. At some point, bond and currency markets say no, even to the United States.

The best situation is that nobody counts on a bailout and it comes. The worst situation is that everyone expects a bailout and it does not come. If the Treasury cannot borrow, and banks don't want trillions more reserves, the town is on fire and the firehouse has burned down.

An actual default, haircut, or restructuring of U.S. debt is not inconceivable. In the midst of a crisis, will our Congress really prioritize interest and principal payments to what it will surely regard as Wall Street fat cats, wealthy individuals, foreign financial institutions and central banks, over sending checks to needy Americans? As an indication, in the debate over the debt ceiling increase of summer 2021, all commentators, and the Treasury Secretary in particular, stated as if fact that hitting the debt ceiling must imply a default on Treasury principal and interest obligations. Nobody stated the simple accounting fact that the United States could avoid such default by spending less. Nobody whispered that repayment of U.S. debt should be sacrosanct, coming before the first dollar of spending. Yes, the spending cuts would have been severe, and one may defend that choice. The point is that default is a choice. If the U.S. government is likely to make that choice facing the mild constraint of a debt limit snafu with a rapidly growing economy, think what it would do in a real rollover crisis accompanied by an economic crisis.

But an actual default, even a small haircut, on U.S. Treasury debt would cause chaos in a financial system that treats such debt as safe collateral. It would likely cause a profound restructuring of monetary and financial arrangements. If the result were only inflation, we would be lucky.

If the government fails to bail out banks and financial institutions as expected, the credit card and ATM machines could go dark. A hint of such default in the future would cause inflation, devaluation, and chaos right away. The possibility that the United States might not be *able* to bail out all and sundry would likewise cause an intense panic. Such an event would indeed provoke radical change.

Moreover, even substantial inflation or default will not cure U.S. fiscal problems. The central U.S. fiscal problem is not outstanding debt. The central fiscal problem is large and growing structural deficits, fueled by entitlement promises substantially larger than the revenues that support them. If the tax and entitlement reform does not come before and in time to stem the debt crisis, it will come chaotically and painfully afterwards.

The event is unlikely and unnecessary. A little more growth-oriented policy, simple reforms to tax and entitlement systems, and dedication to end the bailout and stimulus response to every crisis would solve the looming problem. But it could happen. It is also not obvious that we will turn to private money rather than a reformed government money in its wake. But that could happen as well.

Our monetary system has evolved from its predecessors, but evolution is not perfection. Many past monetary systems seemed to work well for a while, and ended with rather spectacular failures, starting with John Law's. They left substantially different monetary arrangements in their wake.

Less darkly, perhaps a spirit of free-market reform will emerge. Perhaps competition in financial arrangements will lead to the emergence of an alternative standard, emerging from payments system, fintech, or cryptocurrency innovations. Many less developed countries seem to lurch from crisis to inflation to crisis. They seem unwilling to dollarize or euroize. They might lead on monetary innovation. El Salvador's adoption of Bitcoin is an innovation, though one I suspect will not end well.

Or perhaps perpetual deflation and "secular stagnation" will become the problem. Our institutions evolved to control inflation, not deflation.

So, what are the alternatives to a monetary system based on short-term nominal government debt as numeraire, backed by general government surpluses, managed by a central bank following an interest rate target?

The most obvious alternatives further separate monetary backing from general government finance. In this vision, we continue to have a government-provided numeraire, currency or reserves. The official meter sits in Paris, defining the unit of length. The official euro sits in Frankfurt, defining the unit of value, well backed, and this time insulated from government finances. Sovereigns default if they get in trouble, or offer more equity-like securities such as GDP-linked bonds that fluctuate in relative value without the legal distress of actual default.

This vision eschews the advantage of soft default via inflation over explicit default, and the corporate finance advantage of an equity-like nominal debt. It eschews the conventional arguments for local monetary policy to offset local shocks by inflation and devaluation, and it certainly does not appeal to the grand aspirations of central bankers to direct the economy and financial system. The U.S. Fed is in no hurry to adopt a digital dollar, and is actively blocking narrow banks, institutions that take deposits, service payments cheaply, and invest the proceeds entirely in reserves. *Après le déluge*, perhaps devaluation and stimulus will not seem such useful tools, and price stability may reappear as a primary and difficult goal of monetary institutions. If sticky prices and wages are the core social problem preventing swift macroeconomic adjustment to shocks, perhaps governments will be encouraged to remove the legal and regulatory restrictions that make prices and wages more sticky, rather than to encourage central banks to manipulate stickiness to our supposed benefit. Or, countries can establish pegs to the standard of value and devalue when they think appropriate.

10.6.2   Private Currency and Cryptocurrency

How could a private currency work? Cryptocurrencies are rediscovering old monetary ideas, implemented with new technology. Bitcoin is fiat money with a strong supply rule, emulating gold. But it does not limit substitutes or inside moneys. Backed cryptocurrencies can replicate bank deposits or money market funds. As such they can provide liquidity and payments services, but they do not define a numeraire. Pots of assets structures can implement a private numeraire.

What other alternatives can we think of? Can a private standard of value function? This question may be, at the moment, a bit of libertarian fantasizing. But it is a line of thought brought to the fore by the cryptocurrency movement. And to round out our understanding of monetary theory, we should at least ponder if a completely private standard of value *can* work in a modern economy, or whether it is an essentially government function.

The basic lesson, I think, of the fiscal theory and the last several hundred years' experience is that *only a backed money can have a long-term stable value*, and especially so in our era of rampant financial innovation. Cryptocurrencies feature great technical innovation, but as far as I can see no monetary or financial innovation.

Bitcoin is fiat money, with no backing or intrinsic value. There is a demand, despite a low long-run expected return, similar to the transactions demand for money, though in this case fueled by the relative anonymity of Bitcoin transactions more than by their convenience. If supply asymptotes to a constant, then from $MV = Py$, Bitcoin's return could be positive, equal to GDP growth. The return can also be temporarily positive if demand increases and V declines. "Speculative" demand anticipates that event. Crucially, Bitcoin supply is limited. Provision against oversupply is its major monetary feature. Sadly, like gold, the supply is limited by wasted resources to create it. Its value is determined by $MV = Py$. It's fascinating technology, but a classic *monetary* vision. We can also consider Bitcoin equivalent to gold coins, in my view that the value of gold coins really comes from $MV = Py$, not an independent value of gold.

Bitcoin already visibly suffers the first defect of gold: that its value relative to goods and services fluctuates widely. This volatility might be reduced if sticky prices were quoted in Bitcoin but not eliminated, as the volatile inflation of the gold standard era teaches us.

More deeply, though the supply of Bitcoin is limited, there is no limit to the supply of substitutes or of derivative claims and inside moneys. You cannot freely create more Bitcoins, but you can create Ethereum, Ripple, Bitcoin cash, EOS, Stellar, Litecoin, Basecoin and so forth. You can fork Bitcoin and start over. And you can create Bitcoin derivatives, promises to pay Bitcoin. Bitcoin "checking accounts," electronic Bitcoin IOUs, themselves cryptocurrencies, or Bitcoin futures (which exist already) can satisfy Bitcoin money demands. Indeed, they can be more liquid and faster-transacting than Bitcoin itself. With a flat supply curve of substitutes at zero marginal cost, the long history of unbacked money suggests the long-term value of any unbacked cryptocurrency must be zero. $(M^b + M^i + M^f)V = Py$, with M^b = base, M^i = inside, and M^f = foreign or substitute moneys, no control over the latter two, is also a classic monetary story. To Silicon Valley purists who respond "first mover advantage," I answer: Netscape, Yahoo, AOL.

Cryptocurrency innovators are beginning to understand this reality, and to offer cryptocurrencies that are backed or partially backed. In the first instance, they are reinventing the nineteenth-century bank, which issued fixed value notes backed by loans and other investments, with an equity cushion to stabilize the value of resources backing the notes. Many of these cryptocurrencies are only partially backed. Others, like Tether and the initial description of Libra, offer backing but no conversion promise to that backing, like a closed-end fund. If I print up a bunch of money and swear I have a pot of gold in my basement, but money holders have no individual right to the pot of gold, that value can fluctuate too.

While prices remain quoted in dollars, the safest and most stable backing today is short-term government bonds, with 100% reserves. Reinventing the bank, or the federal money market or exchange-traded fund (funds that hold only Treasury securities and offer free conversion) remains an interesting innovation, if the cryptocurrency can offer better transactions facilitation than current funds can do. Cryptocurrency startups by and large resisted that hard realization, as the profits from printing unbacked or partially backed money are so much larger than the profits from offering 1% deposits backed by 1.01% Treasurys or reserves, or the small fees that transactions facilitators might earn.

Such cryptocurrencies compete with improvements in digital payments systems; faster and cheaper movements of an account on a central ledger. Such accounts also can be 100% backed, in narrow banks or money market funds. Most payment innovations are of this form, since central ledgers are computationally more efficient.

But a stable-value cryptocurrency, promising dollars, and backed by Treasurys or reserves, cannot replace U.S. dollars as numeraire.

Likewise, central bank digital currencies, implemented via cryptocurrency or trans-ferrable accounts at the central bank, can offer speedier and lower-cost transactions. But these are just reserves with better technology. They do not change the basic fiscal theory picture of price level determination. ·

Central bank digital currency faces the difficult trade-off of privacy versus anonymity. We don't want the government surveilling every transaction we make, but low-cost anony-mous transactions facilitate tax evasion and illegal activity. In my view, this conundrum is best handled by private narrow banks. These offer payment services 100% backed by reserves or short-term Treasurys, and the government must subpoena their data. Whether these banks offer central ledgers, accounts, or cryptocurrency tokens is a purely techno-logical question, not a financial one. Private banks are also much more likely to generate a low-cost and pleasant consumer experience. The Federal Reserve is poorly situated to run a consumer-facing website, let alone to try to implement its own regulations. But this question is outside the price level determination agenda of this book.

Do not take this as a negative commentary. The U.S. digital payments system is ineffi-cient, expensive, and antiquated. Two to four percent credit card and debit card fees, and typing in your numbers on websites, need to go the way of the dinosaurs. Private, 100% backed, competitive payments operators would not only be a boon, they could undermine the case for the sea of inside short-term debt that periodically suffers a run and crisis. But again, that change has little effect on the fiscal theory of the price level.

How could we set up a private standard of value that includes a numeraire? The most obvious solution is to implement one of the pot of assets ideas from Section 10.2, in particular the last in which indexed bonds backed by ownership shares are numeraire. Again, whether the shares are traded as a cryptocurrency or as accounts on a centralized computer makes little financial or monetary difference.

10.7   How Much Money Do We Need, Really?

Does the numeraire need to be provided in large quantity? In principle, a small amount of numeraire can sup-port a large amount of inside money. But such inside moneys have been prone to runs and crises. If a large stock is required, government debts equal to 100% of GDP could back a huge stock of fixed value, interest-paying money without inflation, and drive out run-prone inside moneys. Modern financial, computational, and com-munication technology severs the link between *liquidity* and *fixed value*. We could accomplish transactions with tiny amounts of numeraire. That evolution could underpin alternative moneys.

It is tempting to add size to the list of requirements: A numeraire provider must be able to provide a large amount of liquid assets with fixed nominal value. But it's not obvious that requirement remains true, given the large advances in financial, computational, and information technology.

Our financial system currently includes vast quantities of liquid short-term debt, with liquidity demands bleeding into longer-term Treasurys. Many economists feel that any numeraire must be provided in large quantity to satisfy this demand.

As a matter of economics, the numeraire itself need not be in huge supply. People can create inside moneys. Notes promised gold coins. Bank deposits and repurchase agreements promise dollars. Modern financial technology could support a much larger expansion. A relatively small private or semiprivate institution, as above, could define the numeraire. A small government—Switzerland, say—could offer a stable money, backed by a managed pot of assets or an ironclad fiscal commitment. We do not need each to *hold* a large quantity of Swiss francs, we can hold accounts denominated in Swiss francs. As we only need one official meter or kilogram housed in Paris, the rest of an electronic economy could manage well with a relatively small standard of value. People often repeat that no currency can replace the dollar because there is not enough of any other currency to go around. But we do not need to hold a lot of Swiss francs, individually or collectively, for them to serve as numeraire.

This is not an ideal answer, however. In repeated crises, there isn't enough to go around when everyone wants to run from those derivative claims to the real thing.

Size then argues for government debt. U.S. government debt is passing $25 trillion, 100% of GDP as I write in 2021. A $25 trillion stock of nominally risk-free liquid assets could be 100% backed claims to government debt. The Fed still has lots of room to expand its balance sheet. Better, the Treasury could directly issue fixed value, floating rate overnight debt directly, using swap contracts to manage maturity risks to the budget. The more we eliminate run-prone inside money, the less the chance of a private sector financial crisis, though the more we become dependent on the absence of a government financial crisis. Fiscal theory assures us that even 100% of GDP in completely liquid fixed value, floating rate money need not cause inflation.

But why do people hold so much low-yielding fixed value debt in the first place? Given current financial, computational, and information technology, there is no longer any fundamental economic reason why our payments and financial system requires such a large stock of nominally risk-free assets. And any remaining reason is quickly evaporating.

You could pay for a coffee by tapping a cellphone, which sells an S&P500 index fund, and transfers the proceeds to the seller's mortgage-backed security fund, all in milliseconds. Even the last milliseconds of holding the numeraire are really not necessary, as financial institutions can net most transactions without transferring anything. The S&P index fund and mortgage-backed security fund have floating values. They do not promise a fixed value, payment in numeraire, and first come first serve, so they are immune to runs. Yet today they can be instantly liquid. In this world, you do not need a checking account, or any stock at all of fixed value low-return money. Your retirement savings can be completely liquid.

In the classic Baumol-Tobin or cash in advance stories, you need to settle transactions with cash, and it's expensive and time-consuming to get cash. But today you don't need to settle transactions with cash, and you can get cash quickly and cheaply. Tomorrow, the Baumol-Tobin trip to the bank will take 20 milliseconds and cost a tiny fraction of a basis point. And money demand is then effectively zero.

We needed to hold a stock of fixed value claims to provide liquidity in the 1930s, when our banking system was fundamentally conceived, and in the 1960s when $MV = Py$ was developed. If you offered shares of stock to pay for coffee, the coffee shop owner would not know what they're worth, might suspect asymmetric information, and it would take days to transfer ownership. Only a fixed value claim could be liquid. Communications, computational, and financial technology—the exchange-traded index fund—open up this possibility. Crypto technology may open up the possibility even further. *Liquidity* no longer requires a fixed value claim. You could make all the purchases you want by transferring shares of your retirement portfolio.

If we move further to such a financial or transactions system, then we could get by with a small amount of numeraire, and no run-prone inside moneys. A necessarily smaller private money could then emerge.

Obstacles remain. Regulation and accounting demand fixed value assets, which drives continued demand and paradoxically fills the financial system with run-prone liabilities. The government tends to bail out holders of fixed value run-prone assets, precisely to stop runs, but thereby subsidizing those assets. Securities markets still take a day or more to settle, not the milliseconds that are technically possible. But on a technical and economic basis, the economy could easily leverage a very small provision of actual numeraire assets *without* vastly increasing run-prone inside debt claims. Those numeraire assets could more easily be privately provided, or provided by an entity completely walled off from government finances.

PART III

Monetary Doctrines, Institutions, and Some Histories

MONETARY THEORY is often characterized by doctrines, statements about the effects of policy interventions or the operation of monetary and fiscal arrangements and institutions. Examples include "Interest rate pegs are unstable," "The central bank must control the money supply to control inflation." These propositions are not tied to particular models, though many models embody standard doctrines. The doctrines pass on in a largely verbal tradition, much like military or foreign policy "doctrines," more durably than the models that embody them.

Reconsidering classic doctrines helps us to understand how fiscal theory works and matters, how fiscal theory is different from other theories, and which might be the right theory. By observational equivalence, fiscal and conventional theories can each give an account of events. But fiscal theory suggests different results of policy interventions, different sets of preconditions for different outcomes, different results of changed institutional arrangements, different views of fiscal–monetary institutions, different "doctrines." As we see the results of different policy institutions, as we organize experience on the doctrines, we can also learn which theory is right. (Ljungqvist and Sargent (2018), Section 27.3, also list 10 related monetary "doctrines.")

Experience is ripping out the underpinnings of classic doctrines, and thereby putting them to the test. The distinction between "money" and "bonds" is vanishing, undermined by rampant financial innovation. Money pays interest. Central banks target interest rates, not monetary aggregates. Interest rates were stuck near zero for most of a decade in the United States, more than a decade in the European Union, and nearly a quarter century in Japan, yet inflation remained quiet. Under quantitative easing, central banks undertook open market operations thousands of times larger than ever contemplated before, with no effect on inflation. The clash of doctrines in such events can provide nearly experimental, or cross-regime, evidence on fiscal versus classic theories of inflation.

This part contrasts core doctrines under the fiscal theory with their nature under classic monetary theory, in which the price level is determined by money demand $MV = Py$ and control of the money supply, and under interest rate targeting theory, in which the price level is determined by an active interest rate policy. I develop those alternative theories in detail in later chapters. However, since the point now is to understand what the fiscal theory says rather than to understand those alternative theories in detail, and since these doctrines are likely familiar to most readers and stand apart from specific models, we can proceed now to discuss classic doctrines and later fill in details of models that capture alternative theories.

11

Monetary Policies

I START with doctrines surrounding monetary policies, in the traditional sense of the word: operations that affect the supply of money.

11.1   The Composition versus the Level of Government Debt

Monetarism states that $MV = Py$ and control of money M sets the price level. Surpluses must then adjust to satisfy the government debt valuation equation. The split of government liabilities between debt B and money M determines the price level, and must be controlled.

Fiscal theory states that the overall quantity of government liabilities relative to surpluses sets the price level, and the split between M and B is irrelevant to a first approximation. The split must passively accommodate money demand. Fiscal theory rehabilitates a wide swath of passive money policies and institutions, which we observe along with quiet inflation.

An important exception to the rule: If, as hypothesized, the central bank is set up to issue debt that will not be repaid, and the treasury debt is repaid, then the split between central bank and treasury issuance is central to the price level. However, this split has nothing to do with the monetary nature of central bank liabilities.

The monetarist tradition states that $MV = Py$ sets the price level P. The *split* of government liabilities M versus B determines the price level, because only the M part causes inflation. This theory requires a money demand—an inventory demand for special liquid assets, a reason M is different from B—and also a restricted supply of money. Monetarist tradition emphasizes that this split must not be passive, responding to the price level, or the price level becomes unmoored.

In this view, fiscal policy must be passive, adjusting surpluses to pay off unexpected inflation- or deflation-induced changes in the value of government debt. "Passive" fiscal policy is not always easy. Many inflations occur when governments cannot raise surpluses and instead print money to repay debts or to finance deficits. Monetarist thought recognizes that monetary–fiscal coordination is important, and that monetary authorities must have the fiscal space to abstain from repaying debts or financing deficits by printing money. The "passive" word comes from the fiscal theory tradition; monetarists use words like monetary–fiscal coordination, or fiscal support for monetary policy.

In the fiscal theory, the total quantity of government liabilities $M + B$ matters for the price level. The split of government liabilities between M and B, to first order, is irrelevant. If people have a demand for money as distinct from bonds due to liquidity, transactions, or other reasons, supply of that money must be passive. Fiscal policy must be active, refusing to adjust surpluses to changes in the value of government debt that flow from any arbitrary change in the price level.

So, fiscal theory rehabilitates passive money policies. Passive money comes in many guises. The following sections illustrate a variety of passive money policies and institutions that have been followed in the past, or are followed or considered now, and that are critiqued as undermining price level stability. The fact that inflation has often been quiet under passive monetary policies and institutions is a point in favor of fiscal theory.

A few equations help to make this and the following discussion concrete. The simple fiscal theory with one period debt, interest-paying money and a constant discount rate from Section 3.4 states

$$\frac{B_{t-1}+M_{t-1}}{P_t} = E_t \sum_{j=0}^{\infty} \beta^j \left[s_{t+j} + \frac{i_{t+j}-i_{t+j}^m}{\left(1+i_{t+j}\right)\left(1+i_{t+j}^m\right)} \frac{M_{t+j}}{P_{t+j}} \right]. \tag{11.1}$$

Add a money demand function,

$$M_t V(i_t - i_t^m, \cdot) = P_t y_t. \tag{11.2}$$

To first order, ignore seigniorage, with $i - i^m$ small, or imagine a fiscal policy that changes surpluses to account for seigniorage. In monetarist thought, control of M and $MV = Py$ determines P in (11.2), and then surpluses s must adjust to validate any changes in the price level in (11.1). In fiscal theory, the government debt valuation equation (11.1) sets the price level, and then monetary policy must "passively" accommodate the money demand requirement in (11.2).

11.2   Open Market Operations

Classic doctrine: Open market purchases lower interest rates and then raise inflation. The composition, not quantity, of government debt matters for inflation.

Fiscal theory: Open market operations have no first-order effect on the price level or interest rates. The composition of government debt (B versus M) is irrelevant to first order. Differences in liquidity lead to interest rate spreads between various kinds of debt.

Seigniorage and liquidity demands, and the effects of changing the maturity structure of debt, add second-order effects to fiscal theory. An open market operation with no other change in policy is not a well-posed question. Observational equivalence reminds us that empirical evaluation of open market operations will not settle the issue.

The open market operation is the textbook instrument of classical monetary policy. The central bank buys government bonds, issuing new money in return, or vice versa. It is a change in the *composition* of government debt, which does not change the overall quantity of government debt. By increasing the supply of money M, an open market operation is inflationary in standard monetarist thought.

Since $M + B$ appears on the left-hand side of the government debt valuation equation, to first order, an open market operation swapping M for B has no effect in fiscal theory. Think of money as green m&ms, and debt as red m&ms. If the Fed takes some red m&ms and gives you green m&ms in return, this has no effect on your diet. To monetarists, only the green m&ms have calories.

Now, there is potentially an important exception to this rule. Early on, I hypothesized that central banks are set up distinctly from treasuries, to signal "share split" debt issuance, without change in surpluses versus "equity issue" debt issuance that comes with the expectation and reputation of future surpluses, if not an explicit promise. Below, I speculate that the 2021 fiscal expansion was inflationary in part because so much of it came from newly created reserves.

If this is the case, a change in the composition of government debt from treasury debt to central bank reserves is inflationary. However, that effect comes entirely from different *fiscal* foundations and commitments of central bank reserves versus treasury debt, not from their liquidity, money-like nature, status in the banking system, convertibility to cash, and so forth. Central bank versus treasury debt becomes regular versus emergency budget debt, unbacked versus backed debt. In this analysis, an open market operation, buying treasury debt and issuing reserves, converts some debt from backed to unbacked. However, as in our analysis of QE, the inflationary effect of such reserves depends on whether people expect the central bank to undo reserve issuance, by selling treasurys in its portfolio and converting reserves back to backed debt. Pointing to 2021 is too easy, as we need a story why 2021 was inflationary and QE was not.

In the monetarist view, any effect of monetary policy comes entirely from the quantity of money. The fact that the bond supply B decreases in an open market operation is irrelevant. In particular, if an open market sale (less M, more B) raises interest rates, that rise comes from an interest-elastic money demand $MV(i) = Py$, not from greater bond supply. A helicopter drop of more M with no decline in B has the same effect as an open market operation in which B declines.

Bond supply ideas are often used to analyze quantitative easing. That view is centered on frictions such as segmented bond markets, which are not part of the traditional monetarist view. The bond supply channel turns monetarism on its head, viewing the increase in interest-paying reserves as irrelevant. The central bank is thought to lower long-term interest rates by "removing duration" from the bond market. This bond supply view also requires purchases that are a nonnegligible fraction of the bond supply. Open market operations were traditionally tiny. Before 2008, total reserves were on the order of $10 billion dollars, open market purchases an order of magnitude smaller, and all of this a drop in the ocean of bond supply. Quantitative easing operations are thousands of times larger.

The simple fiscal theory of monetary policy has a bond supply channel, but it is entirely a *nominal* bond supply channel. The central bank and treasury together sell bonds with no change in surpluses, to raise expected inflation. This is a frictionless model with no segmentation, only changing real rates if there is some stickiness to prices.

I hedge these statements with "first order" to acknowledge several second-order possibilities and other caveats.

These statements are clearest when money pays full interest $i_t = i_t^m$, or interest rates are zero. When there is an interest spread, an open market operation creates seigniorage on the right-hand side of the valuation equation (11.1), which can affect the price level. I argued that seigniorage is tiny for advanced economies in normal times. Fiscal policy may also adapt, offsetting the $i - i^m$ term in (11.1), without becoming passive. But seigniorage is not small when governments are financing large deficits by printing non-interest-bearing money, and we should include this channel when thinking about large fiscal inflations.

Seigniorage effects can go either way. If the interest elasticity of money demand is low, as in the monetarist tradition, raising future M adds future seigniorage revenue, which *lowers* the initial price level. It trades future inflation for current deflation. But once past the hyperinflationary point on the inflation-tax Laffer curve, raising M lowers seigniorage revenue and creates both current and future inflation.

An open market operation also changes the maturity structure of government debt. The analysis of maturity structure rearrangements from Chapter 7 applies. This consideration was minor with the small open market operations of the small reserves regime, but the trillions of dollars of quantitative easing asset purchases substantially shorten the maturity structure of government debt. The Treasury could offset these changes by issuing longer debt, or engaging in swap contracts. The Treasury and Federal Reserve need to come to a new accord about who is in charge of the maturity structure and hence interest rate risk exposure of the debt. It seems a bit dysfunctional that the Treasury issues long-term debt to lengthen the maturity structure, and the Fed quickly snaps that debt up and turns it into overnight debt.

Today, almost all money other than cash pays interest. With $MV(i - i^m) = Py$, an exchange of B for M can result in a change in the interest rate paid to money i^m, with little effect on anything else. Then velocity takes up the slack of an open market operation. In the old days with $i^m = 0$, the interest rate on everything else had to change in order to satisfy money demand.

With $MV(i - i^m) = Py$ describing money demand, we can satisfy the money demand curve by letting the interest rate spread $i - i^m$ vary; we do not need "passive" supply of money itself. This statement includes a substantial generalization of what "passive" monetary policy means for fiscal theory. The price of money can be passive rather than the quantity of money.

More generally, variation in the composition of government debt of varying liquidity, including reserves, on the run versus off the run, treasury versus agency, high or low coupon issues, and so forth, can just result in a change in interest rate spreads between the various flavors of government debt, with no effect on the underlying interest rate i that governs intertemporal substitution and is connected to inflation. The central bank can control the relative quantities of money, liquid and illiquid bonds, if it wishes to do so, even in fiscal theory.

Short-run endogenous velocity and a fuzziness to the money demand function is a more general possibility. Even a die-hard monetarist would not predict from $M_t V = P_t y_t$ that if the money supply increases at noon on Monday, nominal GDP must rise proportionally Monday afternoon. There are "long and variable lags." Velocity is only "stable" in a "long run." Short-run elasticities are different than long-run elasticities. It takes a while for people to adjust their cash management habits in response to changes in the interest costs of holding money. If the Fed buys bonds, even in a fiscal theory world, it's sensible that people just hold the extra money for a while, and velocity (a residual) moves. The pressures from money supply greater than money demand can take months or even years to appear. This endogenous velocity result is even more likely when the interest cost of holding money is small, and when money and bonds become nearly perfect substitutes. The requirement to satisfy money demand under fiscal theory can be elastic. (These thoughts are formalized in Akerlof and Milbourne (1980) and Cochrane (1989).)

We cannot easily settle which theory holds by estimating the effect of open market operations, however. Observational equivalence tells us that must be the case. Specifically, if a rigid money demand relation $M_t V = P_t y_t$ applies, an open market exchange of M_t for B_t that changes nothing else—neither surpluses nor overall quantity of debt—is not a well-posed policy. In the monetarist view, pay attention to the footnote about passive fiscal policy or fiscal coordination. An open market operation that reduces inflation must come with a fiscal contraction to pay off the larger value of debt. If that monetary fiscal coordination does not happen, we have uncoordinated or overdetermined policy, equations that contradict each other. In a fiscal theory view, the government must adopt a passive monetary policy to ensure $MV = Py$ is satisfied, so changing M versus B without changing anything else likewise makes no sense. To accomplish the open market operation, the government must tighten fiscal policy. Then the "passive" monetary policy exchanges some M for B. Both theories describe an identical fall in money M, rise in debt B, and a rise in surpluses s. Time series tests will not tell them apart.

11.3   An Elastic Currency

Classic doctrine: Elastic money supply leaves an indeterminate price level, so it leads to unstable inflation or deflation.

Fiscal theory doctrine: Elastic money supply is consistent with and indeed necessary for a determinate price level.

Suppose monetary policy offers the split between bonds and money passively: The central bank assesses Py, and issues the appropriate M in response. It responds to perceived "tightness" in money and credit markets, or to its perception of how much money people and businesses demand. It provides an "elastic currency" to "meet the needs of trade."

From a monetarist perspective, you can see the flaw. If the price level starts to rise, the central bank issues more money, the price level keeps rising, and so forth. Any P is consistent with this policy. The central bank must control the quantity of monetary aggregates.

Yet even the title of the 1913 Federal Reserve Act states that the Fed's first purpose is to "furnish an elastic currency." Congress mandated passive money supply. The price level was considered to be determined at least in the long run by the gold standard, not by the Fed. The Act does not task the Fed with controlling inflation or the price level at all. It was viewed that banks, private debt markets, and the Treasury's currency issues did not sufficiently adjust money supply to match demand. There were strong seasonal fluctuations in interest rates (Mankiw and Miron (1991)) as around harvest time, and a perceived periodic and regional scarcity of money. Financial crises smelled of a lack of money then as now. The Fed was founded largely in response to the 1907 financial crisis. So, the Fed's main directive was to supply money as needed.

Monetarists acknowledge that money supply should accommodate supply-based changes in real income y, so that higher output need not cause deflation. Money supply should also accommodate shifts in money demand—shifts in velocity V—rather than force those to cause inflation, deflation or output fluctuation. The central bank should and does accommodate seasonal variation in money demand around Christmas and April 15. The trouble is as always to distinguish just where a rise in money demand comes from; for the Fed to react to the "right" shifts deriving from real income, seasonals, and panics, but not to the "wrong" shifts in money demand that result from higher inflation or expected inflation or, in the conventional view, "excess" aggregate demand, "inflationary pressures," and so forth. Milton Friedman argued for a 4% money growth rule not because it is full-information optimal, but because he thought the Fed could not distinguish shocks in this way, or implement an activist strategy in real time.

Fiscal theory frees us from this conundrum. The price level is fixed by fiscal surpluses and the overall supply of government debt, the latter either directly or via an interest rate target. A passive policy regarding the split of the *composition* of government debt between reserves and treasury securities does not lead to inflation.

11.4   Balance Sheet Control

Should central banks control the size of their balance sheets? Or should they allow banks and other financial institutions to trade securities versus reserves at will?

Conventional doctrine: The central bank must control the size of its balance sheet, or it will lose control of the price level.

Fiscal theory doctrine: The central bank may offer a flat supply of reserves, and any size balance sheet, with no danger of inflation. Such a policy can be desirable, as it implements passive money without conscious intervention.

Contemporary central bank doctrine: Central banks think that balance sheet size matters, though not through traditional monetary channels. The Fed controls that size, and nature of assets, as well as target interest rates by the rate it pays on excess reserves.

The Federal Reserve balance sheet contains Treasury and other securities (mostly mortgage-backed securities) as assets, and the monetary base equal to reserves plus cash, as liabilities. Open market and quantitative easing operations increase the size of the balance sheet. The "size of the balance sheet" is often used as a synonym for the stimulative stance of monetary policy. The word choice is interesting for focusing attention on how many and which assets the central bank holds, rather than just the liability side, the monetary base, or the broader money supply.

Should central banks control the size of their balance sheets, offering a vertical supply of reserves, holding a fixed quantity of assets for long periods of time, and using the size of the balance sheet as a policy instrument, distinct from the level of the nominal rate?

Or should central banks offer a horizontal supply of reserves, letting people freely trade Treasury or other qualifying debt for reserves, borrow reserves against specified collateral, or lend to the central banks, holding reserves, each at fixed rates?

The conventional monetarist answer is that the central bank must control the size of its balance sheet, or risk inflation. If anyone can bring a Treasury security in and get money, then the money supply—the split between M and B—is not controlled.

In fiscal theory, the central bank can open its balance sheet completely. The split of government liabilities between reserves and treasurys in private hands has no effect on the price level. A flat reserve supply easily achieves the passive money that a fiscal regime requires.

A flat reserve supply and a passive balance sheet solve the primary practical problem with my description of elastic currency: How does the central bank know it should supply more or less money? By allowing people (financial institutions) to get money any time they need it, in exchange for Treasury debt, the central bank accomplishes mechanically the passive money that must accompany the fiscal theory: It "provides an elastic currency," to "meet the needs of trade," without itself having to measure the sources of velocity, the split of nominal income between real and inflation, or to decide on open market operations.

Balance sheet control has been a central part of Federal Reserve policy for a long time. Before the 2008 move to interest on reserves, the New York Fed's trading desk tried to forecast each morning how many reserves were needed to hit the interest rate target for that day, supplied those via open market operations, and then closed up shop for the day. There were often interest rate spikes later in the day if banks turned out to need more reserves than had been supplied (Hamilton (1996)). During the day, at least, the supply curve was vertical. Over horizons longer than a day, however, hitting an interest rate target required adjusting the size of the balance sheet, effectively providing a flat supply curve. Just why the Fed thought this necessary, and why many economists yearn for a return to these operating procedures, is unclear to me. There is something faintly monetarist about it; controlling the money supply, if only for a day.

Other central banks have followed a corridor system since the 1990s, lending and borrowing throughout the day at fixed rates and thus leaving the size of the balance sheet open. I see no evidence that the corridor system led to less control over interest rates or the economy.

In 2008 the Fed started paying interest on reserves, and using interest on reserves as its main tool for setting interest rates. The Fed soon exploded reserves from $10 billion to trillions of dollars in quantitative easing operations. Yet, though the size of the balance sheet no longer has anything to do with controlling interest rates, the Fed has also maintained strict control over the total size of the balance sheet, with assets that do not change at all for long periods of time, and grow or decline linearly when they do change. The Fed raises and lowers the balance sheet by trillions of dollars in the belief, echoed widely on Wall Street, that such changes stimulate or cool the economy. Some of the feeling is related to the idea that the Fed thereby affects financial market risk premiums.

Fixing both a price (interest rate) and a quantity is tricky. Unlike most price pegs, it's possible. See Section 2.9 and Cochrane (2014b). Why try? As with the earlier operating procedures, some Cheshire-cat residual monetarism remains, I think, in central bankers' doctrines: a view that a large balance sheet is permanently stimulative by itself, for the same level of interest rates, even if reserves are held in superabundance compared to reserve requirements and other regulations, and even if reserves pay *more* interest than short-term Treasurys, as they frequently did. The Fed's view of "stimulus" seems to combine the interest on reserves and federal funds, a direct effect of the quantity and the nature (maturity, Treasury versus mortgage versus commercial paper etc.) of balance-sheet assets, and "forward guidance" speeches about future intentions with regard to all of the above. From 2018 to 2020, the Fed deliberately reduced the size of the balance sheet and reserves, eventually provoking a resurgence of spikes in overnight rates, a characteristic of the earlier daily fixed supply regime (Hamilton (1996)), as new liquidity regulations started to bite (Copeland, Duffie, and Yang (2021), Gagnon and Sack (2019)). Opening up the discount window, or a standing repo facility that would allow banks to immediately get reserves, would quiet those spikes. Fiscal theory says this sort of policy poses no danger for price level control.

11.5   Real Bills

The real bills doctrine states that central banks should lend freely against high-quality private credit.

    Classic doctrine: A real bills policy leads to an uncontrolled price level.

    Fiscal theory doctrine: A real bills policy is consistent with a determinate price level.

The real bills doctrine states that central banks should lend money freely against high-quality private credit. Bring in a "real bill," private short-term debt, either as collateral or to sell to the central bank, and the central bank will give you a new dollar in return, expanding the money supply. The Federal Reserve Act's second clause says "to afford means of rediscounting commercial paper," essentially commanding a real bills policy, though the Fed does not now follow such a policy. The classic doctrine specified private rather than government debt. Thus, it combines two separate ideas: backing by real assets, and a flat supply curve or open balance sheet. The classic doctrine also distinguished between bills that finance "real" production versus bills that finance "speculation."

A real bills doctrine endogenizes the money supply as well, so in classic monetarist thought it therefore destabilizes the price level. As P rises, people need more M. They bring in more real bills to get it, and M chases Py.

Under the fiscal theory, the price level is determined with a real bills doctrine. If the central bank accepts private "real bills" in return for new M, that action expands total government liabilities on the left side of the valuation equation, but it equally expands assets on the right-hand side of the valuation equation, either directly or in the stream of dividends such assets provide.

Real bills' force for price stability is strong, because real bills are salable assets. If people don't want the money any more, they can have the real bills back. The government need not tax or borrow against future surpluses to soak up extra money. "Real" bills are not typically indexed, so this is not a "pot of assets" regime in which assets = liabilities determines the price level. But real bills insulate the backing of money for liquidity provision from government finances. The real bills mechanism is usually thought of as a way to trade something less liquid, the real bill, for something more liquid, government money. But it is also a way to replace a government liability, backed by the government's willingness and ability to tax or abstain from spending, for a private liability, backed by real assets, a stream of private cashflows, and legal contract enforcement.

In the fiscal theory, a real bills doctrine can be a desirable policy, as it is one way to automatically provide the passive money that fiscal price determination requires. It is especially useful in a situation in which there is little treasury debt outstanding, so that providing needed monetary base is difficult by a similar promise to exchange treasury debt for money. That is not our current situation, but government debt was not so large in the early 1900s and not so liquid. Perhaps someday we will return to a small amount of government debt, as appeared briefly possible in the late 1990s. Real bills may also be useful to isolate money from government finance if government debt threatens default.

The real bills doctrine raises many issues beyond inflation control. Private debt has credit risk, which raises financial stability, political, and economic questions. Whether the central bank or treasury takes the credit risk is unimportant for the rest of the economy but important for the political independence of the central bank. Today, the Fed typically buys or lends against private securities in a special purpose vehicle in which the Treasury takes the first losses.

Much motivation for real bills purchases or direct central bank lending to private institutions and people concerns the supply of credit and avoiding financial panics, flights from risky securities to government debt. Since 2008, the Federal Reserve and other central banks have expanded their assets beyond Treasurys to include agency securities, mortgage-backed securities, state and local government debt in the United States, member state debt in Europe, commercial paper, corporate bonds, stocks, "toxic assets," and "green" bonds. The Fed typically offers to buy or to lend against collateral a limited though large amount. Up to that amount, it looks a lot like a real-bills policy.

Central bank purchases are aimed to prop up the prices of those assets, and to encourage borrowers to issue such assets so those borrowers can make real investments, not to increase the supply of reserves, which today could easily be accomplished by buying or lending against some of the immense supply of Treasurys. Such central bank purchases of private and nonfederal government securities can also easily cross the line to bailouts, price guarantees, and subsidized central bank financing of low-value and politically favored investments. This only risks *inflation* if the central bank overpays, but the practice has obvious risks and benefits from other points of view. A central bank may well wish to insulate itself against moral hazard and malfeasance by announcing a fixed quantity of such operations rather than an unlimited flat supply curve.

12

Interest Rate Targets

CENTRAL BANKS TODAY do not stimulate or cool the economy by increasing or decreasing the monetary base or monetary aggregates. Most central banks follow interest rate targets. Interest rate pegs or targets that vary less than one for one with inflation are criticized by traditional doctrine, as letting inflation get out of control. The fiscal theory allows pegs or sluggish targets. That fact opens the door to analyzing many periods in which we observe poorly reactive interest rate targets, including zero bound periods.

12.1 Interest Rate Pegs

Classical doctrine: An interest rate peg is either *unstable*, leading to spiraling inflation or deflation, or *indeterminate*, leading to multiple equilibria and excessively volatile inflation.

Fiscal theory: An interest rate peg can be stable, determinate, and quiet (the opposite of volatile).

An interest rate peg is another form of passive money supply that standard monetary theory has long held leads to a loss of price level control.

First, as crystallized by Friedman (1968), an interest rate peg is thought to lead to *unstable* inflation. In "What Monetary Policy Cannot Do," the first item on Friedman's list is "It cannot peg interest rates for more than very limited periods." (By "peg" in this context, Friedman means a target that is constant over time, not necessarily an offer to buy and sell bonds at a fixed price, or to borrow and lend at a fixed rate.)

Friedman starts from the Fisher relationship $i_t = r_t + \pi_t^e$, where π_t^e represents expected inflation. One of the two great neutrality propositions of his paper is that the real interest rate is independent of inflation in the long run. (The other proposition is that the unemployment rate is also independent of inflation in the long run.) Thus, higher nominal interest rates must eventually correspond to higher inflation.

But to Friedman, this Fisher equation describes an unstable steady-state. The central bank cannot fix the nominal interest rate i_t and expect inflation to follow. Instead, if, say, the interest rate peg i_t is a bit too low, the central bank will need to expand the money supply to keep the interest rate low. More money will lead to more inflation, and more expected inflation. Now the peg will demand an even lower real interest rate. The central bank will need to print even more money to keep down the nominal rate. In Friedman's description, this chain does not spiral out of control only because the central bank is not that pig-headed. Eventually, the central bank abandons the low interest rate peg, bringing back the Fisher equation at a higher level of interest rate and inflation. Yes, inflation and interest rates move together in the long run, but like balancing a broom upside down, the central bank cannot just move interest rates and count on inflation to follow.

Friedman's prediction comes clearly from adaptive expectations:

> Let the higher rate of monetary growth produce rising prices, and let the public come to expect that prices will continue to rise. Borrowers will then be willing to pay and lenders will then demand higher interest rates—as Irving Fisher pointed out decades ago. This price expectation effect is slow to develop and also slow to disappear. (Friedman 1968, p. 5–6.)

Standard IS-LM thinking with adaptive expectations gives the same result, though through a different mechanism that de-emphasizes the money supply. In that view, the real interest rate directly affects aggregate demand. So a too-low nominal rate implies a too-low real rate. This low rate spurs aggregate demand, which produces more inflation. When expectations catch up, the real rate is lower still, and off we go. Section 17.3.2 models these views with simple equations and a graph.

These views predict an uncontrollable deflation spiral when interest rates are effectively pegged by the zero bound. Such a spiral was widely predicted and widely feared in 2008 and following years, correctly following the logic of these views. The spiral did not happen.

When rational expectations came along, a different problem with interest rate pegs emerged, as crystallized by Sargent and Wallace (1975). An interest rate peg leads to *indeterminate* inflation. Under rational expectations, expected inflation is $\pi_t^e = E_t \pi_{t+1}$. The Fisher equation $i_t = E_t \pi_{t+1}$ is stable: If the central bank pegs the interest rate i, then $E_t \pi_{t+1}$ settles down to $i - r$ all on its own. With sticky prices the real interest rate r may move for a while, but the real interest rate eventually reverts, and inflation follows the nominal interest rate. However, unexpected inflation $\Delta E_{t+1} \pi_{t+1}$ can be anything; it is indeterminate.

Though indeterminacy means that the model has nothing to say about unexpected inflation, most authors writing about such policies such as Clarida, Galí, and Gertler (2000) and Benhabib, Schmitt-Grohé, and Uribe (2002) equate indeterminacy with excess inflation *volatility*, as unexpected inflation jumps around following sunspots or some other economically irrelevant coordination mechanism. The difference between stability, volatility, and determinacy is subtle, and not all authors use the words as I do here.

Indeterminacy counts as a "doctrine" as it is a robust characterization of many models. But most central bankers and commenters continue to think in old-Keynesian or monetarist adaptive-expectations terms, and don't worry about multiple equilibria and sunspots. So indeterminacy can only be said to be a doctrine among modelers who really understand rational expectations.

The fiscal theory of monetary policy contradicts these doctrines. An interest rate peg can leave the price level and inflation stable, determinate, and quiet (the opposite of volatile). Even a peg at zero interest rate can work. If the economy demands a positive real rate of interest, a slight deflation would emerge to produce it.

The classic doctrines are not logically wrong, they just make an opposite assumption. They explicitly or implicitly assume passive fiscal policy—that the government will adapt surpluses to unexpected revaluations of nominal debt due to inflation or deflation. Active fiscal policy cuts off this possibility.

Stability and determinacy at an interest rate peg is clearest when we marry fiscal theory with a rational expectations model of the economy, as I mostly do in this book. The rational expectations part gives stability, and fiscal theory adds determinacy. Yet stability at an interest rate peg is a troublesome doctrine, contradicting much intuition. It leads to the Fisherian proposition that raising nominal interest rates must eventually raise inflation. All that comes from the rational expectations part of the model, not from fiscal theory per se.

One can also marry fiscal theory with adaptive expectations models. Fiscal theory can help to cut off inflation and deflation spirals in those models. A deflation spiral requires fiscal austerity to pay a real windfall to bondholders in those models as well. No austerity, no spiral. I don't pursue fiscal theory with adaptive expectations in this book. I stop here to emphasize the "can" in my restatement of the doctrine. It is clearest with rational expectations, and worked out here. It is suggestive with adaptive expectations, but needs working out.

That inflation has been quiet despite long periods of constant near-zero interest rates in the United States, Europe, and Japan is a feather in the fiscal cap, and the sort of observation that helps us to surmount observational equivalence questions.

I emphasize "can" here, because a stable, determinate, and quiet peg requires fiscal policy as well as the interest rate peg. Countries with unsustainable deficits cannot just lower interest rates and expect inflation to follow! Countries with volatile fiscal policies, or who suffer volatile discount rates, will see volatile unexpected inflation under a peg.

Though a peg is *possible*, a peg is not necessarily *optimal*. Under a peg, variation in the real rate of interest r_t, due to variation in the marginal product of capital, for example, must express itself in varying expected inflation. When prices are sticky, such variation in expected and therefore actual inflation will produce unnecessary output and employment volatility. A central bank that could assess variation in the natural rate r_t and raise and lower the nominal interest rate in response to such real interest rate variation, could produce quieter inflation and by consequence quieter output. We have also seen that varying the nominal interest rate in response to output and inflation can help to smooth fiscal and other shocks. Of course, a central bank that is not very good at measuring variation in the natural rate may induce extra volatility by mistimed stabilization efforts. So the case for a peg is something like Milton Friedman's case for a 4% money growth rule—not full information optimal, but a robust strategy for a controller with limited information or decision-making ability. My previous suggestion to peg the spread rather than the level of nominal rates addresses some of these concerns.

12.2   Taylor Rules

The Taylor principle states that interest rates should vary more than one for one with inflation.

Conventional doctrine: Interest rates must follow the Taylor principle, or inflation will become unstable or indeterminate, and therefore volatile.

Fiscal theory: Inflation can be stable and determinate when interest rates violate the Taylor principle, as they are under a peg.

A strong reaction of interest rates to inflation may nonetheless remain wise policy, exploiting a negative short-run inflationary effect.

Beginning in the 1980s, academics started to take seriously the fact that central banks control interest rates, not money supplies, and theories about desirable interest rate targets emerged. The Taylor principle is the most central doctrine to emerge from the experience of the early 1980s and this investigation: Interest rates should vary more than one for one with inflation. An interest rate rule that follows the Taylor principle cures instability in adaptive expectation, IS-LM, old-Keynesian models and it is thought to cure indeterminacy in rational expectation new-Keynesian models. (I write "thought to" because I take issue with that claim below.)

So, standard doctrine now states that interest rate targets should vary more than one for one with inflation. If it does not do so, instability (adaptive expectations) or indeterminacy (rational expectations) will result, and inflation will be volatile.

Fiscal theory contradicts this doctrine. Insufficiently reactive interest rates, like a peg, can leave stable and determinate, hence quiet, inflation.

The fiscal theory doctrine is helpful for us to address the many times in which interest rate targets evidently did not move more than one for one with inflation, including the recent zero bound period, the 1970s, the postwar interest rate pegs, and interest rate pegs or passive policy under the gold standard.

Still, an interest rate target that follows something like a Taylor rule, raising interest rates when inflation or output rise, can be a good policy even in an active fiscal, passive money regime. A Taylor-type rule can implement the idea that the central bank should raise the nominal rate when the "natural rate" is higher. As the natural interest rate, output, and inflation all move together, we are likely to see nominal interest rates that rise with output and inflation. Taylor-like responses to output and inflation smooth shocks, leading to smaller output and inflation variance than we would otherwise see.

In the simple models we have examined, under fiscal theory the response of interest rate to inflation should be less than one for one, "passive." That seems to contradict the view that sometimes, as in the early 1980s, interest rates rise more than one for one with inflation. In the simple fiscal theory model, with $i_t = \phi \pi_t$ and $i_t = E_t \pi_{t+1}$, equilibrium is $E_t \pi_{t+1} = \phi \pi_t$. If $\phi > 1$, inflation is determinate but unstable.

First, regression evidence is actually not that clear. Second, the greater than one-for-one response of the Taylor principle is not visible in equilibrium of new-Keynesian models, as it represents an off-equilibrium threat. Regression estimates, which relate observed equilibrium quantities, should show a coefficient less than one. (Equations are in Section 16.5.) Third, interest rates may rise more than one for one with inflation, even in a well-run, active fiscal, passive money regime. The key property is the number of system eigenvalues greater or less than one. What matters, here, is the ϕ in $E_t \pi_{t+1} = \phi \pi_t$, not the ϕ in $i_t = \phi \pi_t$. The response of interest rates to inflation does not generically control that eigenvalue. It does so in the simple model of the last paragraph. The simple sticky price model we have studied is also Fisherian. But in more complex models, the eigenvalue can be stable while the coefficient of interest rate on inflation is greater than one. What matters in the new-Keynesian view is that the central bank commits to explode *inflation* for all but one initial value of inflation. The Taylor principle is a means to that end in some models, but not always.

One of Taylor's central and robust points is the advantage of rules—any rules—over the shoot-from-the-hip discretion that characterizes much monetary policy. Rules help to stabilize expectations, reducing economic volatility.

13

Monetary Institutions

IF THE PRICE LEVEL is determined ultimately by the intersection of money supply and demand, the government must engage in a certain amount of financial repression. It must ensure a substantial demand for money, and it must limit supply. It must control the creation of inside money, it must regulate the use of substitutes including foreign currency or cryptocurrency, it must restrict financial innovation that would otherwise reduce or destabilize the demand for money, it must maintain an artificial illiquidity of bonds and other financial assets lest they become money, it must forbid the payment of interest on money, and it must stay away from zero interest rates. None of these restrictions are necessary with fiscal price determination.

13.1 Inside Money

Classic doctrine: The government must control the quantity of inside money or the price level becomes indeterminate.

Fiscal theory doctrine: The price level can remain determinate with arbitrary creation of inside moneys. Reserve requirements and limitations on the creation of liquid inside assets are not needed.

Reserve requirements and restrictions on the private issuance of liquid short-term debt remain useful for the separate question of financial stability, preventing runs.

Currency and reserves are not the only assets that people can use for transactions and other money-related activities. Checking accounts are the easiest example of inside money. When a bank makes a loan, it flips a switch and creates money in a checking account.

More generally, short-term debt can circulate as money. If I write an IOU, say "I'll pay you back $5 next Friday," you might be able to trade that IOU to a friend for a beer this afternoon, and your friend collects from me. Nineteenth-century banks issued notes. Commercial paper and other short-term debts have long been used in this way, essentially writing a tradable IOU. Money market funds offer money-like assets, backed by portfolios of securities. Inside money can help to satisfy the transactions, precautionary, liquidity, etc. demands that make "money" a special asset.

Recognizing this fact, we should write money demand as

$$(Mb + Mi) \, V = Py,$$

distinguishing between the monetary base Mb and inside money Mi. More sophisticated treatments recognize that liquid assets are imperfect substitutes for money rather than simply add them together.

Again, the monetarist view determines the price level from the intersection of such a money demand with a limited supply. To that end, it is not enough to limit the supply of the monetary base Mb. The government must also limit the supply of inside money Mi. Reserve requirements are a classic supply-limiting device. To create a dollar in a checking account, the bank must have a certain amount of base money. If the reserve requirement is 10%, then checking account supply is limited to 10 times the amount of reserves. Other kinds of inside money are regulated to limit their liquidity or quantity, or illegal. Bank notes are now illegal.

In sum,

- Classic doctrine: The government must control the quantity of inside money.

In the fiscal theory, the price level is fundamentally determined by the value of government liabilities. Hence there is no need, on price level determinacy grounds, to limit inside money at all.

- Fiscal theory doctrine: The price level can remain determinate with arbitrary creation of inside moneys. Reserve requirements and limitations on the creation of liquid inside assets are not needed for price level determination.

This doctrine is fortunate. Inside moneys have exploded. In January 2020, reserves were $1,645,384 million, though required reserves were only $158,765 million. (Federal Reserve H.3.) The reserve requirement, which is the classic constraint on the supply of demand deposit money, was slack by one and a half trillion dollars. In March 2020, the Fed eliminated reserve requirements altogether. Commercial paper, repurchase agreements, money market funds, and other highly liquid financial instruments, whose supply is not controlled at all, dominate the "cash" holdings of financial institutions along with Treasury securities.

My point here is narrow, about price level determination. There are excellent financial-stability reasons to limit inside moneys. A financial institution that issues short-run liquid debt against illiquid assets is prone to a run. In the financial stability context, I argue for much stronger regulation against inside money than we have now (Cochrane (2014c)). I argue that the government should indeed take over entirely the business of providing fixed value, run-prone electronic money. The government analogously took over the business of note issuance in the nineteenth century, thereby ending runs on privately issued bank notes. Interest-paying central bank digital currency, or its equivalent provided by the Treasury, are under discussion as modern equivalents. In my view, it would be better for the government to allow 100% backed narrow banks, as private institutions are likely to operate customer-facing payments software more efficiently. Traditional banks should finance risky investments with equity and long-term debt. Such a system would eliminate private financial crises forever, leaving us only with sovereign debt to worry about.

Reserve requirements were instituted to forestall runs, and may retain that role in fiscal theory. They were only repurposed to have a money supply and inflation control function much later.

The inside money question illuminates a key distinction between fiscal theory and a fiat money theory based on transactions demand. One might look at $MV = Py$ and $B = P \times EPV(s)$, where $PV(s)$ means present value of s, and conclude they are basically the same. In place of money we have all government debt, and in place of a transactions demand related to the level of output, we have the present value of surpluses. But here we see a big difference: Only direct government liabilities appear on the left-hand side of the fiscal theory, while private liabilities also appear in M.

By analogy, consider the question whether short sales, futures, and options affect the value of a stock. By uniting a put and call option, you can buy or sell a synthetic share of the stock. These are "inside shares" in that they net to zero. For every synthetic purchaser there is a synthetic issuer. They impose no liability on the corporation. Do these "inside stock shares" compete with "real stock shares" to drive down the value of stocks? Well, in the baseline frictionless theory of finance, no. The company splits its earnings among its real owners only, and doesn't owe anything to the owners of inside shares. Therefore, we begin the theory of valuation with price times company-issued shares = present value of company-paid dividends, ignoring inside shares.

Likewise, primary surpluses repay only holders of actual government debt, not those who have bought private assets that promise to pay government debt, such as checking accounts. So, to first order, the value of government debt is not affected by inside claims. For every private buyer of inside money, there is a private issuer, so the number of such claims, or their valuation, has no aggregate wealth effect.

There can be secondary effects. In finance, scarcity of share supply can affect asset prices, and supply of inside shares due to short-selling, futures, or options can satisfy a demand for shares (Lamont and Thaler (2003), Cochrane (2003)). In monetary affairs, liquidity demands can potentially affect the price level. Gold and silver coins often circulated at values above their metallic content (Sargent and Velde (2003)). So too can government debt, or equivalently the discount rate in the valuation formula can be low. In such a situation, the provision of inside money substitutes can reduce that valuation difference, and affect the price level. My statement that only government liabilities appear on the left-hand side also is not so crisp in a world of deposit insurance, bailouts, and implicit and explicit credit guarantees. Private debt does compete a bit for government surpluses.

Money substitutes, though not promises to deliver dollars, function in much the same way. Money substitutes, including foreign currency, help to facilitate transactions and compete with government money. Financial repression is often used to reduce that competing demand. In times of monetary shortages, stamps, bus tokens, cigarettes, and other commodities have circulated as money. That even persistent monetary shortages have usually not led to deflation, which would restore the real value of money and end its shortage, is a fact suggestive of a fiscal or backing value of money.

13.2   Financial Innovation

Classic doctrine: Regulation must limit financial innovation and transactions technologies to maintain control of the price level.

Fiscal theory doctrine: The price level is determined with arbitrary financial innovation, and even if no transactions are accomplished using the exchange of government liabilities.

For monetary price level determination to work, it must remain costly to hold money. Money must pay less interest than other assets. But the cost of holding money gives people an incentive to economize on money holding by financial innovation, which increases and destabilizes velocity. Even when money needs to be used for transactions, the key to money demand and $MV = Py$ is that one must hold that money for a discrete amount of time before making transactions. If one could obtain money a few milliseconds before buying, and the seller could redeposit that money in a few additional milliseconds, money demand would vanish; velocity would explode.

Thus monetary price level determination needs constraints on financial innovation. Yet our economy is evolving with rampant financial innovation, which reduces the need to hold money. Better electronic payment systems are obvious cases. Interest-bearing inside money and repo can be seen as such a money-saving, transactions-facilitating innovation rather than a competing form of private money. If we write $Mb \times V = Py$, checking accounts raise the velocity of base money.

We already live in a surprisingly money-free system. If I write you a $100 check, and we use the same bank, the bank just raises your account by $100 and lowers mine by the same. No actual money ever changes hands. If we have different banks, our banks are most likely to also net our $100 payment against someone else's $100 payment going the other way. The banks transfer the remainder by asking the Fed to increase one bank's reserve account by $100 and decrease the other's. That operation still requires banks to hold some reserves. But by 2008, banks were able to accomplish the transactions in the (then) $10 trillion economy, including the massive volume of financial transactions, with only $10 billion or so of non-interest-paying reserves, an impressive velocity indeed.

Credit cards, debit cards, and electronic funds transfers allow us to accomplish the same transactions, as well as to enjoy the other features of "money," without holding government money, and without suffering the lost interest that an inventory of money represents. Electronic payments systems in many countries are ahead of those in the United States, and avoid the holding and exchange of government money. Cryptocurrency enthusiasts think they will provide payments systems that leave the government out altogether.

As a first abstraction, our economy looks a lot more like an electronic accounting system, an electronic barter economy, than it looks like an economy with transactions media consisting of cash and checking accounts, which suffer an important interest cost, are provided in limited supply, and are rigidly distinguished from illiquid savings assets such as bonds and savings accounts.

But it is a logical consequence of monetarism that all this must be stopped. If V goes through the roof, then $MV = Py$ can no longer determine P. If V becomes unstable, so does Py. Chicago monetarists were pretty free market, and in favor of an efficient and innovative financial system as in other parts of the economy. This circumstance posed a conundrum. The fiscal theory liberates us to consider financial innovation on its merits, without worrying about price level control.

Sure, one might think that as V increases, M can decrease, from $10 billion to $1 billion, and finally to an economy of quickly circulating electronic claims to the last $1 bill—the puzzle that started me on this whole quest. But as velocity explodes, the power of money to control the price level must surely also disappear. If you hold still the last hair on the end of the dog's tail, it is unlikely that the dog will wag. When suboptimal behavior has trivial costs, don't expect quick adjustments. Surely, velocity becomes endogenous instead. When the whole economy is operating at the 1 cent interest cost of holding one dollar bill, it will happily just pay 2 cents if the Fed wishes the economy to hold two dollars, at least for quite some time.

Such endogenous velocity likely holds on the way to this limit. At a velocity of 10, typical of the pre-zero-bound era, and at a 2% nominal interest rate, the cost of holding money is 0.2% of income. If money increases 10%, which ought to lead to a substantial 10% inflation, the interest cost of not maximizing is 0.02% of income. And since money has benefits too, the overall cost of not maximizing is an order of magnitude lower.

A theory that works at the limit *point*, zero money demand, not just in the limit with one last dollar of money demanded and supplied, is better adapted to an economy that is moving toward that limit.

The money demand story and Baumol-Tobin model are still repeated to undergraduates. You go to the bank once a week to get cash, and then use cash for all transactions. That model may reasonably describe the 1960s. But it must sound like ancient history to those undergraduates. If the people have no cash, let them use a credit card or Apple Pay, the undergraduate might say. If you ask an economist from Mars to choose a simple model to describe today's financial system, and the choice is Baumol-Tobin versus Apple Pay, linked to a cashless electronic netting system based on short-term government debt, I bet on Apple Pay.

The money supply and demand story falls apart if people can use assets they hold entirely for savings or portfolio reasons, without suffering any loss of rate of return, to accomplish transactions, precautionary, and other motivations for money demand. If you could costlessly wire around claims to the stocks in your retirement portfolio, or if you could sell stocks and refill your checking account one second before using it to wire out a transaction, you wouldn't need to hold money at all. Monetary price level determination falls apart. We are rapidly approaching that world too.

I argued against inside money on financial stability grounds, though inside money does not undermine the price level. The instant exchange of *floating* value securities can give us the best of both worlds—immense liquidity, and no more private sector financial crises.

Yes, a great deal of cash remains. But more than 70% of U.S. cash is in the form of $100 bills, and most is held abroad. Cash supports the illegal economy, tax evasion, undocumented workers, illegal drugs, sanctions evasion, and U.S. financing of various groups abroad. Cash, and U.S. cash especially, is a store of value around the world where governments tax rapaciously and limit capital movement. Cryptocurrency may undermine some of these demands. One could, I suppose, found a theory of the price level on the illegal demand for non-interest-bearing cash, but I doubt this approach would go far. Federal Reserve writings and testimony arguing for continued illegal activity to bolster money demand and allow inflation control are a humorous idea to contemplate. Perhaps most importantly, monetary price level control requires limited supply. But the U.S. Fed and other central banks freely exchange cash for reserves. So if we base a theory of the price level on illegal cash demand, we instantly face a flat supply curve.

In sum,

- Classic doctrine: For the price level to be determined, regulation must stop the introduction of new transactions technologies, which threaten to explode V.
- Fiscal theory doctrine: The price level is determined with arbitrary transactions technologies, and even if no transactions are accomplished using the exchange of government liabilities.

13.3   Interest-Paying Money and the Friedman Rule

Classic doctrine: Money must not pay interest, or at least it must pay substantially less interest than risk-free short-term bonds. If the interest rate is zero, or if money pays the same interest as bonds, the price level becomes undetermined. We cannot have the Friedman optimal quantity of money. Money and competing liquid assets must be artificially scarce to control the price level.

Fiscal theory doctrine: The price level is determined even if money pays exactly the same interest as bonds, either directly or if the interest rate is zero. We can have the Friedman optimal quantity of money; we can be satiated in liquidity, using assets held and valued only for savings purposes to make transactions and fulfill other liquidity demands.

The possibility of zero interest rates, or that money pays the same interest as bonds, undermines $MV = Py$ price level determination. When there is no interest cost to holding money, money and bonds become perfect substitutes. Now V is Py divided by whatever M happens to be. A switch of M for B has no effect at all. When money pays the same interest as other assets, money demand ceases to be a function, but is instead a correspondence, with any amount of money consistent with a zero interest cost. With no interest costs, money becomes an asset held as part of an investment portfolio. One gets the liquidity services of an asset held for other reasons, for free. Monetary price determination fails.

The fiscal theory offers the opposite conclusion. If money M_t pays the same interest as B_t, if M_t and B_t are perfect substitutes, we're simply back to $(B_t + M_t)/P_t = E_t \sum_{j=0}^{\infty} \beta^j s_{t+j}$ with no money, no seigniorage, and no other change. The price level is easily determined.

The famous Friedman (1969) optimal quantity of money states that zero nominal interest rates, so non-interest-bearing money and bonds have the same rate of return, is optimal. Slight deflation gives a positive real rate of interest. Since printing more money costs society nothing, we should have as much of it as we want. At a minimum, we save on needless trips to the cash machine. Zero also means no hurry to collect on bills or other contracts that do not include interest clauses, and no need to write interest clauses into such contracts. Cash management to hold less money, and thereby save on interest costs, is a social waste. Money is like oil in the car. We don't slow down a car by deliberately starving it of oil, especially if we can print oil for free.

As money becomes interest-bearing checking accounts, money market funds, or similar securities, and as transactions become electronic using such funds, we can generalize the Friedman optimum to say that the supply of money-like liquid, transactions-facilitating assets should be so large that they pay the same return as illiquid assets. They should also be allowed to pay such rates contra decades of regulation forbidding interest payments on checking accounts. In particular, reserves should be abundant and pay the same interest as short-term Treasurys.

But Friedman did not argue for an interest rate peg at zero or for interest-paying money. He never took the optimal quantity of money seriously as a policy proposal. He argued for 4% money growth. Why not? I speculate because, if the price level comes from money supply and money demand, it becomes unmoored by interest-paying money or a peg at zero. Society must endure the costs of an artificial scarcity of liquid assets, in order to keep inflation under control. If the gas pedal is stuck to the floor, and the brakes don't work, you have to slow the car by draining oil.

The fiscal theory denies this doctrine. Summing up,

- Classic doctrine: Money must not pay interest, or at least it must pay substantially less interest than risk-free short-term bonds. We must stay away from the zero interest liquidity trap. We cannot have the Friedman optimal quantity of money.
- Fiscal theory doctrine: The price level is determined even if money pays exactly the same interest as bonds. That interest rate can be zero, or money may pay the same interest as bonds. We can have the Friedman optimal quantity of money, we can be satiated in liquidity, using assets held and valued only for savings purposes to make transactions and fulfill other liquidity demands.

Again, this is a fortunate prediction because our world looks less and less like one that meets the classical requirements. Reserves pay interest, at times larger than short-term Treasurys, and are thousands of times larger than required. Checking accounts can pay interest. Money market funds, repos, and other interest-paying money abounds. Treasurys themselves are liquid and a money-like store of value for financial institutions. To the extent that these instruments do not pay interest, it is because the United States, Europe, and Japan were stuck at the zero bound for so long, equally troubling to classic doctrine.

The monetarist position is more nuanced. Zero nominal rates, as observed in the Great Depression, sparked a central and classic controversy. Keynesians view the situation as a "liquidity trap" in which monetary policy loses its power. Money and bonds are perfect substitutes, so trading M for B does nothing, and interest rates cannot be lowered below zero.

Monetarists often counter with a view that more money M can still stimulate nominal income Py at the zero bound. The issue comes down to the behavior of velocity V. If money and bonds are truly perfect substitutes, then V is meaningless. It adapts to whatever split of M versus B that the government chooses, with no effect on Py. But monetarists argue that velocity V is not so infinitely adaptable, even at the zero bound. Velocity is "stable" or stable in some "long run," so more money and less bonds will still encourage more spending.

This view that more M for less B does any good at the zero bound requires some *upper* limit on money demand, not a lower limit or some residual transactions value. It requires some reason people would want to get rid of "too much money" in favor of bonds that pay exactly the same amount. It neglects that zero interest rates are a *consequence* of liquidity satiation: If, unlike car oil, arbitrarily large money holdings still provide marginal liquidity services, then it would have taken an infinite amount of money to drive the interest rate on money and bonds to the same value. That we observe equal rates between money and bonds, or even lower rates on bonds (Treasurys have paid less than reserves in the United States, bonds paid negative rates in Europe for long periods) means directly that, like a car with oil, the economy can be satiated with liquidity.

The intuition remains strong that "helicopter drops" of money can stimulate inflation at the zero bound. Fiscal theory agrees: More M with no change in B and no change in future s creates inflation. But that fact and intuition does not tell us that open market operations, more M and less B, do any good.

The last section concluded with a vision of a nearly cashless economy, in which we handle all transactions by wiring around claims to a stock portfolio. This section concludes with a vision of an abundant cash economy, in which interest-bearing money is the same as short-term bonds, held also for investment purposes, and we handle transactions by wiring around claims to that portfolio. Either one works under fiscal theory. Ether one undermines the price level for a monetary theory.

13.4   Separating Debt from Money

Classic doctrine: Bonds must be kept deliberately illiquid, or the price level will not be determined. Bonds may not be issued in small denomination, discount, bearer, fixed value, or cheaply transferable form.

Fiscal theory doctrine: An artificial separation between "bonds" and "money" is not necessary for price level determination. The Treasury can issue fixed value, floating rate, electronically transferable debt. Savings vehicles may be allowed to be as liquid as technology can make them.

In $MV = Py$, we need to have a definite separation between "liquid," or transactions-facilitating assets M and "illiquid" savings vehicles B. Control of M and the split between M and B gives control over the price level. This is the reason for banning interest-paying money, so that money does not become a savings vehicle like bonds. Here, I discuss the complementary doctrine: Bonds should not become a transactions vehicle like money. It is important to deliberately limit the liquidity of public and private debt issues.

Bank notes are illegal, though they are just zero maturity, zero interest, small denomination bearer bonds issued by banks. They are illegal for good financial stability reasons, but the doctrine states that they must remain illegal, or supply limited, for price control reasons. Corporations and state and local governments must not issue small denomination or bearer bonds that might circulate. (Bearer bond principal and coupons are paid to whoever shows up with them, and are not registered. They gradually fell out of favor and are now illegal for a host of reasons.) Even the U.S. Treasury must deliberately hobble the liquidity of its securities, the doctrine says, despite the lower interest rates that doing so could produce. It must sell illiquid securities and let the Fed buy them to issue a limited quantity of liquid debt—cash and reserves—in its place.

Indeed, the U.S. Treasury does not issue bonds in denomination less than $1,000— only recently reduced from $10,000—and not in anonymous (bearer) form. The shortest Treasury maturity is a month, and the Treasury does not issue fixed value, floating rate debt. The Treasury sells securities via its website treasurydirect.gov but does not buy them or allow transfers from one account to another as banks can do with reserves at the Fed. Treasury sells hundreds of distinct securities rather than bundle its debt into two or three issues that would be vastly more liquid.

This deliberate illiquidity, keeping "bonds" separate from "money," is crucial in the $MV = Py$ world:

- Classic doctrine: Bonds must be deliberately illiquid, and separate from money, or the price level will not be determined. Bonds may not be issued in small denomination, discount, bearer, fixed value, or cheaply transferable form that might be used for transactions demand.

The fiscal theory denies this proposition. The maturity, denomination, transaction cost, bearer form, or other liquidity characteristics of private or government debt make no difference to price level determination. To the extent that such features lower Treasury interest costs overall, so much the better for government finances and liquidity provision to the economy.

- Fiscal theory doctrine: An artificial separation between "bonds" and "money" is not necessary for price level determination.

In a more detailed proposal (Cochrane (2015b)), I argue that the Treasury should offer to all of us fixed value, floating rate, electronically transferable debt, in arbitrary denominations. This is the same security that the Fed offers to banks as reserves. Treasury electronic money might be a good name for it. I also argue that the Treasury should supply as much of this security as people demand. Roughly the same structure is advocated as central bank digital currency, opening up reserves to all; see, for example, Duffie and Economy (2022). But central banks are set up to serve banks, and already reluctant to allow nonbank institutions to hold reserves, as well as resistant to financial innovation that would undermine bank profits. The Treasury already sells debt to the public. The Treasury can manage its duration and interest rate risk exposure with longer maturities or swaps. I also argue that the Treasury and Fed should allow narrow banks and private nonbank payment processing companies to operate, using this security as 100% reserves, since private institutions are likely better at operating low-cost transactions and intermediation services, interacting with retail customers. Finally, the Treasury should offer nominal and indexed perpetuities, and thereby dramatically reduce the number of its distinct long-term debt issues. This move would increase the liquidity of long-term debt.

The Federal money market fund—a private mutual fund that offers fixed value, floating rate, electronically transferable investments, backed by a portfolio of short-term Treasurys—should be a threat to price level control. After all, the Federal Reserve itself is such a fund. Such funds are already widespread. They don't yet have immediate electronic transfers, ATM machines, and link to a debit card, in part to avoid being regulated as "banks," and that regulation serves to reduce competition for bank deposits. But that is a legal limitation, not a technological limitation. Add that feature and we have already completely circumvented the Federal Reserve's intermediation of Treasury debt to electronic money. If control of the size of the Fed's balance sheet matters, money market funds undermine that control.

Such a proposal is anathema in a monetarist view, as the price level would be unmoored. The relative quantity of B and M would become endogenous, and the character of B and M (reserves) would become identical.

13.5   A Frictionless Benchmark

Classic doctrine: We must have monetary frictions to determine the price level.

Fiscal theory doctrine: The price level is well defined in an economy devoid of monetary or pricing frictions, and in which no dollars exist. The dollar can be a unit of account even if it is not the medium of exchange or store of value. The right to be relieved of a dollar's taxes is valuable even if there are no dollars.

The frictionless model is a benchmark on which we build models with frictions as necessary. But unlike standard monetary economics, frictions are not *necessary* to describe an economy with a determinate price level. And the simple frictionless model can provide a first approximation to reality.

In classical monetary theory, some monetary friction is necessary to determine the price level. In a completely frictionless economy, with no money demand, money can have no value.

As we have seen, fiscal theory can determine the price level even in a completely frictionless economy. We do not need liquidity demands, transactions demands, speculative demands, precautionary demands, incomplete markets, dynamic inefficiency (OLG models), price stickiness, wage stickiness, irrational expectations, and so forth. Such ingredients make macroeconomics fun, and realistic. We can and do add them to better match dynamics, as I added price stickiness in previous chapters. But the fiscal theory does not *need* these ingredients to determine the price level.

We can even get rid of the "money" in my stories. People can make transactions with maturing government bonds, in Bitcoin, with foreign currency, by transferring shares of stock, or by an accounting and netting system. The "dollar" can be a pure unit of account. Government debt can promise to pay a "dollar," even if nobody ever holds any dollars at all. The right to be relieved of one dollar's worth of tax liability establishes its value as numeraire and unit of account.

This frictionless view describes the frictionless *limit point*, not just a frictionless limit. A theory that holds at the limit point is more reliable to describe economies that are near the limit, avoiding the tail wags the dog problem.

Frictionless valuation is a property of a backing theory of money. If dollars promised to pay gold coins, then we could establish the value of a dollar equal to one gold coin, also if nobody used dollars in transactions. Money may gain an *additional* value if it is specially liquid and limited in supply, or it may pay a lower rate of return. But in a backing theory, a fundamental value remains when the liquidity value or supply limits disappear. Entirely fiat money loses all value in that circumstance.

To summarize, continuing my list of doctrines,

- Classic (fiat-money) doctrine: We must have some monetary frictions to determine the price level.
- Fiscal theory doctrine: We can have a well-defined price level in an economy devoid of monetary or pricing frictions, and in which no dollars exist. The dollar can be a

unit of account even if it is not medium of exchange or store of value. The right to be relieved of a dollar's taxes is valuable even if there are no dollars.

This observation really sums up previous ones – interest-paying money, abundant inside money not constrained by reserve requirements, debt that can function as money, and financial innovations that allow us to make transactions and satisfy other demands for money without holding money are all different aspects of the march to a frictionless financial system, which we now need not fear.

14

Stories and Histories

A FEW SIMPLE stories, histories, and conceptual experiments quickly come up when we think of any monetary theory. It's important to see how fiscal theory is consistent with and interprets these monetary stories.

14.1 Helicopters

Dropping money from helicopters surely raises inflation. Does this story establish that money causes inflation? No. Fiscal theory also predicts that prices rise under a helicopter drop. The drop is an expansion of nominal debt with no change in surpluses. It does not follow that more M with less B creates inflation. A helicopter drop is a brilliant device for communicating a fiscal commitment, that surpluses will not be raised to pay off the new debt.

Milton Friedman famously proposed that if the government wishes inflation, it should drop money from helicopters. People will run out and spend the money, driving prices up. Doesn't this, one of the most famous gedanken experiments in economics, prove that in the end money causes inflation?

No. The government debt valuation equation has money and bonds $M + B$ on the left-hand side. Dropping money M from helicopters with no change in surpluses s and no change in debt B raises the price level P in the fiscal theory too. The sign of the response to this conceptual experiment does nothing to distinguish monetary from fiscal theories of inflation.

The helicopter drop remains a key conceptual experiment. But first of all, recognize this is not what central banks do. Central banks do not print money (create reserves) and hand it out. They always *exchange* money for something else. A helicopter drop is fiscal policy, or at least a joint fiscal–monetary policy operation. To accomplish a helicopter drop in our economy, the Treasury must borrow money, hand it out, record it as a transfer payment, and the central bank must buy the Treasury debt. Even when the Fed simply prints money and hands it out, it must make a loan not a gift, and book a promise to repay. Central banks do not print M and hand it out, they exchange M for B.

Yes, the central bank, charged with controlling inflation, is forbidden this one most obvious tool for creating inflation. It is even more forbidden the single most obvious tool for stopping inflation: helicopter vacuums, confiscating money. There are excellent reasons for this institutional limitation. An independent agency in a democracy should not print money and give it to voters, or to chosen businesses and asset holders. It certainly should not confiscate or tax wealth. Those are the jobs of the politically accountable Treasury, administration, and Congress. Even in the extreme measures of the financial crisis and COVID-19 recession, the U.S. Fed carefully structured its massive interventions as plausibly risk-free lending, with the Treasury taking credit risk.

Suppose that while the Fed helicopter-drops $1,000 of cash in your backyard, the Fed burglars come and take $1,000 of Treasury bills from your safe. How much would that combined operation make you spend? The answer is not so obvious, and "nothing" is reasonable. You, and the economy as a whole, have more transactions balances than you need. But you're also no better off. You have correspondingly less savings than you had before, so you feel no wealthier, no drive to spend to increase consumption.

The helicopter drop story artfully leads you to jump from intuition about a wealth effect, increasing the overall amount of government liabilities with no promise of future surpluses, to a composition effect, more money relative to bonds. This conflation is not dishonest. In monetarist thinking, only $MV = Py$ matters to the price level. Whether the money supply increases because the Fed buys bonds, buys stocks, lends it to banks, or simply drops it from helicopters makes no difference at all to inflation. The wealth effect is tiny or irrelevant in monetarist thinking. But your intuition may be guided by the wealth effect, not by an excess of transactions balances. If so, you're thinking in fiscal theory terms. Likewise, many monetary models specify money "injections" or "transfers" in which the central bank just hands out or confiscates money, and then draw implications for open market operations.

Imagine that the government drops cash from the sky, with a note that says, "Good news: We have dropped $1 trillion from the sky. Bad news: Next week taxes go up $1 trillion. See you in a week!" Now how much will people spend? In the fiscal theory, this is a parallel rise in M_t and s_{t+1}, which has no effect on the price level.

Dropping cash from helicopters is a brilliant way to communicate a *fiscal* expectation: We're dropping this cash on you, and we will *not* raise taxes to soak it up. Go spend it.

Imagine that the government drops newly printed one-month Treasury bills from the sky. Would that have a much different effect than dropping the corresponding cash? The monetarist interpretation says that this operation would have no effect on inflation. The frictionless fiscal theory would say that the Treasury bill drop could well have the same effect as the money drop, if people think the debt, like the money, will not be repaid. (In both cases, the people initially receiving the bounty may spend it. The question is whether the private sector as a whole does so; what do the ultimate bond buyers or money holders believe? The representative agent sums over a lot of heterogeneity.)

The latter is the key question. Is dropping securities, whether cash or bonds, from helicopters, the key innovation that changes people's expectations? Or is it the nature of the dropped security, and it doesn't matter how people get it? Tobin (1980) (p. 53) considers this "bond rain." In his view, the monetarist says it has no effect, because the monetarist is Ricardian: People expect that bonds are repaid by subsequent surpluses, and money is not. The nature of the security, not the mechanism of its dropping, is what matters. But perhaps your intuition says yes: Bonds dropped from helicopters would be interpreted just like money dropped from helicopters, as unbacked. Perhaps the same rhetorical reason that Friedman chose to say helicopters, not stimulus checks, applies to bonds.

We commonly think that bonds, sold to investors, even if used to finance cash transfers to consumers, are less likely to be inflationary, because the institutional structure of bond sales is set up to communicate the expectation of surpluses. Both the security (bonds) and the method (sales, transfers via legislated social programs, not helicopters) engenders that expectation. That view helps to explain why supposed "helicopter drops" of the zero bound, fiscal stimulus, QE era did not do much to inflate. The main difference above between Treasury issues, like stock issues, and central bank actions, like share splits, is that institutional setting.

Tobin wrote that the bond rain would be stimulative, and eventually inflationary, because people ignore Ricardian equivalence. Fiscal theory, with nominal rather than real debt, allows such a "non-Ricardian" bond sale without change in future surpluses, without needing to invoke short-sighted investors. Or the opposite. Expectations of future surpluses are not always the same for issues of the same security. Tobin went on to write that the open market operation would have little effect because money and bonds have roughly the same fiscal backing; but Friedman would have said he ignored how money is special.

In sum, a good reason for the power of Friedman's parable is that helicopters signal fiscal expectations differently. We have struggled with institutions to communicate fiscal expectations and our governments struggled during the 2010s to create inflation. Alas, literal helicopters (or, today, drones) are not a practical idea. However, in 2020 the Federal Reserve and Treasury got together, created about $2.5 trillion of new reserves, and sent people checks. This move arguably set off the 2021 inflation, surveyed below. So perhaps we have, unintentionally, found our helicopter.

Magnitudes may distinguish the monetarist and fiscal theory answers to the helicopter drop experiment. Suppose each family has $100,000 savings in Treasury bonds, and earns $100,000 a year. They hold an additional $1,000 in cash to make transactions. The government drops $1,000 per household in cash. How much does the price level rise? A fiscal theory answer is, 1%. Overall Treasury debt just got diluted 1%. The monetarist answer is 100%. The money supply doubles, so the price level must double. You may spend your extra $1,000, but then someone else has $2,000. People only want 1% of their income in cash. People collectively keep trying to spend their extra cash until they have doubled the price level, doubled nominal income, and the $2,000 in cash per person is 1% of the now $200,000 per household nominal GDP. The fact that this doubling of the price level wipes out half of the real value of $100,000 of Treasury savings has no effect on the price level. Passive fiscal policy means that the present value of taxes has declined $50,000.

14.2 Hyperinflations and Currency Crashes

Governments print a lot of money in hyperinflations, but this fact does not prove that money causes inflation. Hyperinflations involve intractable fiscal problems. A central bank that refuses to print money would not likely stop a fiscal hyperinflation.

Governments print huge amounts of money in hyperinflations. Doesn't that fact prove that money causes inflation?

No. Every hyperinflation has indeed occurred when governments print money. But the governments printed money to finance intractable deficits, expanding the amount of total government debt, with no surpluses in sight. No hyperinflation has occurred from central bank policy errors in a government with healthy finances.

Imagine that a central bank of a hyperinflation-ridden country refuses to print more money, and the government funds its deficits by issuing one-month bonds instead, paying suppliers with such bonds, and rolling over old bonds with new bonds directly. Would that stop the inflation? Likely not. People would still try to unload government debt by buying real assets, foreign assets, and goods and services.

If the central bank creates a means of payment shortage in this situation, people will use foreign currency, barter, credit, government bonds, put in more effort to hold money for the least possible time, and so forth. At best, the central bank can try to force a fiscal reform by its refusal to print more money. This refusal can put pressure on fiscal authorities. A commitment not to monetize debt can help a new regime to get going. But if the fiscal problem is not cured, the bank can at best force a default. Thus, stronger central bank commitments seem to be most useful with explicit fiscal reform, and seldom successful on their own. Without fiscal reform, changing the composition of government debt has little effect.

A similar situation occurs when the currencies of countries having fiscal and balance of payments crises start to collapse. The central bank may try to fight the crisis by soaking up domestic currency in return for nominal bonds. But nobody wants the nominal bonds either, and high interest costs worsen the deficit. Governments in both cases try financial repression and capital controls to force people to hold their debt. That too eventually fails.

Monetarist analyses have long recognized fiscal limits, and that successful control of the money supply requires a solvent fiscal policy, monetary–fiscal coordination. But the fact that hyperinflating countries do typically print up a lot of money does not tell us that money printing alone causes inflation, that inflation could be stopped by more spine at central banks, or that an *exchange* of money for bonds has the same effect as printing money to finance deficits.

14.3   Ends of Inflations

Inflations have been ended by solving the underlying long-run fiscal problem, and by changing the fiscal and monetary *regime*. Ends of inflations have included printing *more* money, *lower* interest rates, continued deficits and little or no output loss. I review Tom Sargent's classic studies and their place in history. Many inflations have not ended in response to monetary tightening alone or temporary fiscal measures.

Hyperinflations end when the underlying fiscal problem is solved. Monetary reforms are often involved, so we should call them joint fiscal–monetary reforms.

The ends of large inflations typically involve printing *more* money. Real money demand expands when the interest costs of holding money decline. People start holding money for weeks, not hours, so the economy needs more of it. The nominal interest rate *declines*

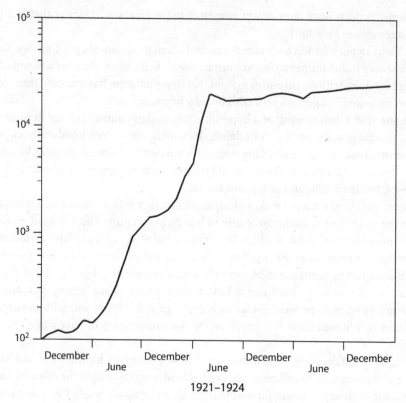

FIGURE 14.1. Wholesale Prices in Austria, 1921–1924. Source: Sargent (1982b)

when the fiscal problem is solved. There is no period of monetary stringency. Near-term fiscal deficits may stay the same or increase. Fixing the long-run problems allows the government to borrow more. Inflations have ended with no rise in unemployment or decline in output, and quickly improving economies. Inflation, attendant demonetization, financial repression and the difficulty of finance during inflation, and fiscal chaos all drag down the economy, and are quickly improved when the stabilization package arrives.

Sargent (1982b) "The ends of four big inflations" is the pathbreaking study of the ends of hyperinflations and their fiscal roots. It set the sails of fiscal theory. It also shows by example how historical analysis of regime changes lets us surmount observational equivalence and Lucas critique concerns. It insists that good economics should describe the big events first and foundationally, not as outliers to be treated with different economics from more sedate times.

Sargent studied the immense hyperinflations of Austria, Germany, Poland, and Hungary in the early 1920s, and their abrupt ends, along with the placebo test of Czechoslovakia, which avoided inflation despite being surrounded by inflation.

Start with Austria, displayed in Figure 14.1. The inflation is dramatic and its end instantaneous. What happened? I quote from Sargent, in part to document the role of this foundational work in developing fiscal theory:

The hyperinflations were each ended by restoring or virtually restoring convertibility to the dollar or equivalently to gold.

This sounds like a monetary policy change, but it is not. Sargent states as I have that the gold standard is primarily a fiscal commitment:

> since usually a government did not hold 100% reserves of gold, a government's notes and debts were backed by the commitment of the government to levy taxes in sufficient amounts, given its expenditures, to make good on its debt. [Note debt, not just money.] In effect, the notes were backed by the government's pursuit of an appropriate budget policy. . . . What mattered was not the current government deficit but the present value of current and prospective future government deficits. The government was like a firm whose prospective receipts were its future tax collections. The value of the government's debt was, to a first approximation, equal to the present value of current and future government surpluses. . . . In order to assign a value to the government's debt, it was necessary to have a view about the fiscal policy regime in effect, that is, the rule determining the government deficit as a function of the state of the economy now and in the future. The public's perception of the fiscal regime influenced the value of government debt through private agents' expectations about the present value of the revenue streams backing that debt.

Sargent emphasizes the importance of a change in *regime*. To believe that the present value of surpluses has changed, people need to see that fiscal and monetary affairs have changed in a durable way. Announcements, decisions, and reversible policies by today's politicians don't often budge long-term expectations. I have used the word "institutions" that guide expectations in much the same spirit.

The new fiscal regime *allowed* the countries to restore convertibility:

> The depreciation of the Austrian crown was suddenly stopped by the intervention of the Council of the League of Nations and the resulting binding commitment of the government of Austria to reorder Austrian fiscal and monetary strategies dramatically.

This event included internal fiscal reform:

> Expenditures were reduced by discharging thousands of government employees. . . . Deficits in government enterprises were reduced by raising prices of government-sold goods and services. New taxes and more efficient means of collecting tax and custom revenues were instituted. . . . Within two years the government was able to balance the budget.

But a larger issue hung over Austria: whether it would continue as a nation, and repay its debts, and how much reparations the Allies would demand.

> The first protocol was a declaration signed by Great Britain, France, Italy, Czechoslovakia, and Austria that reaffirmed the political independence and sovereignty of Austria.
>
> At the same time, it was understood that the Reparation Commission would give up or modify its claim on the resources of the government of Austria.

This did the trick, and instantly stopped the inflation. Indeed,

> even before the precise details of the protocols were publicly announced, the fact of the serious deliberations of the Council brought relief to the situation.

Monetary policy alone did little. Yes,

> The Austrian government promised to establish a new independent central bank, to cease running large deficits, and to bind itself not to finance deficits with advances of notes from the central bank.

But such promises have been made hundreds of times in failed stabilizations. Unless you solve the structural problem, change the regime, swearing not to finance deficits is a pie-crust promise (easily made, easily broken). On the other hand, central bank reforms are a useful part of a joint monetary–fiscal stabilization; they help to prevent future inflationary finance, and they help the fiscal reform to stick.

Money supply expanded, and money-financed deficits continued. Neither monetary stringency nor an immediate end to deficit spending mattered. Curing the expectation of future deficits mattered.

> The Austrian crown abruptly stabilized in August 1922, . . . prices abruptly stabilized a month later. This occurred despite the fact that the central bank's note circulation continued to increase rapidly . . . from August 1922, when the exchange rate suddenly stabilized, to December 1924, the circulating notes of the Austrian central bank increased by a factor of over 6.

The key difference:

> Before the protocols, the liabilities of the central bank were backed mainly by government treasury bills; that is, they were not backed at all, since treasury bills signified no commitment to raise revenues through future tax collections. After the execution of the protocols, the liabilities of the central bank became backed by gold, foreign assets, and commercial paper, and ultimately by the power of the government to collect taxes. . . . The value of the crown was backed by the commitment of the government to run a fiscal policy compatible with maintaining the convertibility of its liabilities into dollars. Given such a fiscal regime, to a first approximation, the intermediating activities of the central bank did not affect the value of the crown . . .

It is striking that "backing" by treasury bills was regarded as no backing at all, relative to our current economies and financial systems that seem to regard backing by treasury bills as the safest kind of backing. That is not written in stone for us either. The calming effect of a real "pot of assets" in the central bank is also interesting.

Germany presents an even starker case. Figure 14.2 presents the German price level during its post-WWI hyperinflation. Notice the exponents on the vertical axis.

> After World War I, Germany owed staggering reparations to the Allied countries. This fact dominated Germany's public finance from 1919 until 1923 and was a most important force for hyperinflation . . . except for 1923, the budget would not have been badly out of balance except for the massive reparations payments made.

FIGURE 14.2. Wholesale Prices in Germany, 1919–1924. Source: Sargent (1982b)

For one thing, considerably larger sums were initially expected of Germany than it ever was eventually able to pay. For another thing, the extent of Germany's total obligation and the required schedule of payments was for a long time uncertain and under negotiation. From the viewpoint that the value of a state's currency and other debt depends intimately on the fiscal policy it intends to run, the uncertainty about the reparations owed by the German government necessarily cast a long shadow over its prospects for a stable currency.

Germany's hyperinflation stopped just as suddenly as Austria's, when the long-term fiscal problem was solved.

Simultaneously and abruptly, three things happened: additional government borrowing from the central bank stopped, the government budget swung into balance, and inflation stopped.

The fiscal trouble was not all reparations:

The government moved to balance the budget by taking a series of deliberate, permanent actions to raise taxes and eliminate expenditure . . . the number of government employees was cut by 25 percent; all temporary employees were to be discharged; all above the age of 65 years were to be retired. . . . The railways, overstaffed as a result of post-war demobilization, discharged 120,000 men during 1923 and 60,000 more during 1924. The postal administration reduced its staff by 65,000 men; the Reichsbank itself which had increased the number of its employees from 13,316 at the close of 1922 to 22,909 at the close of 1923, began the discharge of its superfluous force in December . . .

But reparations were a central component:

Substantially aiding the fiscal situation, Germany also obtained relief from her reparation obligations. Reparations payments were temporarily suspended, and the Dawes plan assigned Germany a much more manageable schedule of payments.

Again, the stabilization did not involve monetary stringency. The opposite occurred. While the inflation was going on, the usual substitution away from real money holdings took hold:

In response to the inflationary public finance and despite the efforts of the government to impose exchange controls, there occurred a "flight from the German mark" in which the real value of Reichsmark notes decreased dramatically. The fact that prices increased proportionately many times more than did the Reichsbank note circulation is symptomatic of the efforts of Germans to economize on their holdings of rapidly depreciating German marks. Toward the end of the hyperinflation, Germans made every effort to avoid holding marks and held large quantities of foreign exchange for purposes of conducting transactions.

When the inflation stopped, Germany printed *more* money:

a pattern that we have seen in the three other hyperinflations: the substantial growth of central bank note and demand deposit liabilities in the months after the currency was stabilized.

There was also no Phillips curve:

By all available measures, the stabilization of the German mark was accompanied by increases in output and employment and decreases in unemployment.

"Stopping Moderate Inflations: The Methods of Poincaré and Thatcher," Chapter 4 in Sargent (2013), covers the end of the much smaller French inflation of the 1920s. The same principles apply, which is important: Fiscal theory and fiscal–monetary interactions are often grudgingly acknowledged for hyperinflations and crashes, but said to be unimportant in less extreme events.

France had borrowed a large amount to fight WWI, and was hoping to repay that debt from German reparations. When it became clear that Germany would not pay, in 1924, the Franc started depreciating quickly. The period was volatile. Sargent's data includes years of surprising deflation as well. The period was

characterized by a massive flight of French capital abroad, partly an anxiety reaction to some of the tax proposals under discussion, such as a capital levy.

The *dénoument:*

> Poincaré was a fiscal conservative, . . . As soon as he assumed control of the govern-
> ment . . . the Franc recovered and inflation stopped.

Sargent details the subsequent tax changes (both increases and decreases), a return to
the gold standard at a low and thus more easily sustainable value, implying an 80% devaluation of wartime nominal debt, and limits on central bank finance. Sargent emphasizes
again the gold standard as a fiscal commitment. But the gold standard must be backed
up by fiscal possibility or it is an empty promise, not a commitment. Most importantly,
people believed that the change was permanent:

> there had been broad consensus both about the principal economic factors that had
> caused the depreciation of the Franc—persistent government deficits and the con-
> sequent pressure to monetize government debt—and the general features required
> to stabilize the Franc—increased taxes and reduced government expenditures suffi-
> cient to balance the budget, together with firm limits on the amount of government
> debt monetized by the Bank of France . . . a political struggled had been waged over
> *whose* taxes would be raised.

But now,

> all political parties except the socialists and communists gathered behind Poincaré.
> Five former premiers joined his government.

Sargent's point in this work was only half about the fiscal foundations of inflation. Much
of his point is about the Phillips curve. Sargent wrote in the early 1980s, in the context of
the U.S. and U.K. inflation stabilization, which at the time had only begun. At the time,
the conventional Keynesian consensus held that expectations are mechanically and slowly
adaptive, prices and wages are mechanically sticky, so it would take a prolonged and costly
depression to get rid of inflation. Sargent cites contemporary estimates that a 1 percentage
point reduction in inflation would cost 8% of GNP. And U.S. inflation peaked above 14%.
Conventional wisdom argued it was better to live with inflation, or pursue (again) wage
and price controls and jawboning, pressuring companies and unions not to raise prices
and wages, rather than to suffer such a fate.

In this context, Sargent argued for the possibility that if people see a new fiscal and
monetary regime in place, expectations of inflation and hence actual inflation can decline
quickly, with little output loss or even a gain. In the context of the Phillips curve we
have written down, $\pi_t = E_t \pi_{t+1} + \kappa x_t$, getting $E_t \pi_{t+1}$ to fall is the key to a recession-free
inflation reduction.

Most of Sargent's point is about how *hard* this outcome is to achieve and how per-
ilous the U.S. and U.K. stabilizations actually were. Today, economists tend to breezily
assert that central banks just need to give speeches to "manage" inflation expectations:
Announce a different inflation target, talk about "anchoring," give "forward guidance."
Driving down (or up) expected inflation is not nearly so easy, especially with three failed
attempts in the rearview mirror as was the case in 1980.

Sargent's point is that a swift and relatively painless end of inflation, a credible stick-to-it
reform, a change in Phillips curve expectations, can happen, but it will only happen with a

credible change of *regime*. The central lesson of intertemporal economics is that we cannot think about policy actions in isolation, as standard Keynesian economics does. Instead, we must think of regimes, policy rules and traditions, institutions and commitments, and through these expectations of future policy. Speeches, promises, and one-time policies do not reliably change expectations. In turn such a change in regime often needs a political realignment, a change in institutions and commitments they embody, or change of external circumstance. Per Sargent, "The change in the rule . . . [must be] widely understood, uncontroversial and unlikely to be reversed."

Sargent took a skeptical view of the U.S. and U.K. stabilization attempts, as of the time he wrote. Both the United States and United Kingdom had large deficits. The early part of the U.S. monetary tightening did not come with an immediate change in fiscal policy. Though we now see debts and primary deficits that are neither large by later standards, nor unusual given the size of the recession, the "Reagan deficits" were big and contentious in economic discussion at the time.

The central point of Sargent and Wallace's (1981) "Unpleasant Monetarist Arithmetic" (covered in detail in Section 19.6), as well as these historical writings, was to point out the fiscal underpinnings of inflation, and to argue that the United States and United Kingdom needed quickly to undertake fiscal reforms, or the stabilizations would fail. Being expected to fail, or at least with great uncertainty about whether the governments would or could stick with it, expectations in the Phillips curve would not shift, and the attempt would be unnecessarily costly in terms of output and employment.

Sargent's "Methods of Poincaré and Thatcher" was even harsher on likely success in the U.K. He wrote

> Mrs. Thatcher comes to power against the background of over twenty years of "stop-go" or reversible government policy actions. Her economic policy actions are vigorously opposed both by members of the Labour party and by a strong new party, the Social Democrats. . . . Mrs. Thatcher's party now runs third in the political opinion polls . . . speculation has waxed and waned about whether Mrs. Thatcher herself would be driven to implement a "U-turn". . . there is widespread dissent from Thatcher's actions among British macroeconomic scholars [an understatement, and equally true of President Reagan among U.S. scholars.] . . . for all these reasons it is difficult to interpret Thatcher's policy actions in terms of the kind of once-and-for-all, widely believed, uncontroversial and irreversible regime change that rational expectations equilibrium theories assert can cure inflation at little or no cost in terms of real output . . . and employment.

Sargent writes at greater depth about the "gradualism" of U.K. policy. Gradualism is always an invitation to renegotiation.

The U.S. and U.K. stabilizations did not fail. The Reagan administration did not choose short-term fiscal austerity, raising taxes and cutting spending in the middle of the 1982 recession. But in 1982 and especially 1986, the United States passed a profound fiscal reform, lowering marginal rates and broadening the tax base. The United States and United Kingdom left behind the malaise of the 1970s, at least in part due to less distorting taxes and microeconomic deregulation, and embarked on two decades of strong growth. By the late 1990s, the United States was running large primary surpluses, and economists were debating what to do when the federal government had paid down all the debt. Surpluses did rise, and their present value bore out the disinflation. Surpluses repaid the Reagan deficits, the larger real value of 1980 nominal debt, and the high real interest costs of the 1980s. Surpluses rose with greater delay and a different mechanism—more growth and wider base, not higher tax rates or programmatic spending cuts. Sargent did not clairvoyantly foresee just what an Iron Lady Mrs. Thatcher turned out to be, persisting through the disinflation despite political and economic storms, or that Reagan and Volcker would similarly persist. Indeed, one might view the election of Reagan, or his acceptance of the remarkable Schultz et al. (1980) stick-to-it memorandum, as an event like the election of Poincaré. It made the outcome clear, if not the path by which the country would get there.

Sargent was right that the 1980s disinflations were not painless, however. The recessions of 1980 and 1982 were severe. The United States and United Kingdom experienced high ex post real interest rates for a further decade, arguably in part reflecting continued doubt that the countries would once again give up and return to inflation. But Sargent was also right that the disinflations were nothing like the dire predictions offered by contemporary Keynesians. From 14.4% in May 1980, inflation fell to 2.35% in July 1983. Inflation and its expectation did drop, in the end quite suddenly, without decades of pain. Unemployment was severe, but recovered with remarkable speed, especially relative to the subsequent "jobless recoveries." The disinflations could well have been swifter still, less costly, had they come with a clear, contemporaneous and permanent change in fiscal, monetary, and (importantly) microeconomic and regulatory regime. However, profound reforms like that of 1986 do not happen overnight, as evidenced by the United States' inability to do anything like it in the following 35 years. Later inflation stabilizations involving inflation targets and explicit coordination between fiscal monetary and microeconomic reforms, covered in Section 9.1, did achieve nearly painless disinflation.

This discussion is also tainted by selection bias. We study stabilizations that worked. A study of *failed* stabilizations might be more informative. And there are plenty of them. Latin American history is sadly full of such attempts (Kehoe and Nicolini (2021)). Typically, there is a monetary tightening or reform, together with promises of fiscal and microeconomic reforms. Inflation quiets down for a year or two. The fiscal and microeconomic reforms evaporate, and inflation takes off again. Viewed through this prism, the 1986 tax reform and the regulatory reforms of the Reagan era, continuing through Bush and Clinton, play a larger role. Had they not occurred, a purely monetary tightening might have failed in North America as well.

The lesson that only policy *regimes* durably change expectations remains foreign to most central bankers and many economists. The inconvenient lesson that only by constraining one's freedom to act ex post can one offer reliable promises ex ante is just as frequently ignored. Central bankers seem to think expectations are "anchored" by their speeches, not by repeated, credible actions and precommitments. "Forward guidance," in which the central bank promises today to take actions it will not want to follow next year—for example, keeping interest rates low despite a resurgence of inflation and strong output—is now considered by the Federal Reserve to be one of its most important "tools." Many economists advocate that central bankers announce new policies such as a higher inflation target, and expect people to immediately believe such promises. Indeed, the whole notion of rules as precommitments or regimes, not as descriptions of discretion, is foreign to the operation of most central banks, who simply wake up each day and make decisions. (Readers at the Fed may bristle at this characterization. Read the Federal Open Market Committee (2020) "strategy," however. Is there any decision the Fed could make that it could not justify as following this elastic description of its strategy?) We who must form expectations somehow are left with guessing the reputations and habits of central bankers.

As I write in Winter 2021, inflation is surging. It may pass, a one-time price level rise occasioned by stimulus payments and a negative, pandemic-induced, transitory, aggregate supply or Phillips curve shock. Or those payments, evidently unbacked fiscal expansion, may lead to continued inflation, if people see our continued structural deficits as more unbacked expansion. If the United States has to contain inflation once again, Sargent's message will resonate, especially with the larger debts and clearer fiscal roots of this inflation. Containing inflation will require a joint fiscal, monetary, and microeconomic reform, putting in place new commitments and institutions of sound fiscal policy, debt repayment, and higher economic growth that last a generation. Whether the U.S. political system is capable of such a reform will be a crucial test.

14.4   Episodes of War and Parity

Countries at war under the gold standard typically suspended convertibility and borrowed and printed money to finance the war. They promised to restore convertibility after the war, though whether they would do so remained uncertain and dependent on the outcome of the war. Fiscal backing is the obvious way to think about inflation and deflation in these episodes.

Countries under the gold standard financed war by suspending convertibility, issuing currency and nominal debt. There was an implicit promise that sometime after the war was over, the country would restore convertibility at the prewar level. Doing so is a promise to pay back rather than inflate away the debt. Whether that would happen, or what conversion rate would hold, was uncertain, and naturally depended on the outcome of the war, so there was often inflation and a fall in bond prices during the war, requiring deflation if parity were to be restored afterwards. But the reputation for returning to parity, for repaying currency as well as debt, allows the government to borrow and issue currency next time. The United Kingdom through the wars with France ending with victory over Napoleon is perhaps the paradigmatic example. Bordo and Levy (2020) give a good capsule account of inflation and war finance, including the Swedish Seven Years' War, the American Revolution, the Civil War, and World Wars I and II.

Rather obviously, inflation in such episodes reflects expected fiscal backing of nominal government debt, not supply versus demand of the medium of exchange or central bank management of currency versus debt.

The United States, though it famously followed Alexander Hamilton's advice to repay interest-bearing debt from the Revolutionary War, left the paper continental dollars inflated and ultimately redeemed them at one cent on the dollar. Hall and Sargent (2014) analyze this episode as a clever combination of a one-time capital levy on money and a successful reputation-buying investment by repaying debt. It offers a similar lesson to the

Jacobson, Leeper, and Preston (2019) story of the Roosevelt administration, which also inflated while preserving a reputation for future borrowing.

In the Civil War, the United States issued paper greenbacks, which inflated and lost value relative to gold coin dollars, perhaps in part from the example of continental dollars. But the United States after the Civil War eventually returned to par, repaying both greenback dollars and Civil War debt in full, though after a long debate only settled by President Grant. The "one-time" capital levy always beckons, especially ex post. The debate whether to return to parity or devalue after wartime inflation reignited in the United Kingdom and France after WWI. Understanding the inflation and deflation of greenbacks clearly starts with money and bond holders' evaluation of the U.S. fiscal commitment to repay Civil War debts.

Fiscal backing is even clearer in the correlation of currency value with battlefield outcomes. In their figure 11, Hall and Sargent (2014) plot the discount of greenbacks versus gold in the Civil War. They write "after a string of Union defeats in the Spring of 1863, 60 gold dollars bought $100 in greenbacks. The price rebounded to 80 after victories at Gettysburg and Vicksburg but fell again reaching its nadir in June 1864 at a price below 40 gold dollars." McCandless (1996) provides background and detail. McCandless quotes Mitchell (1903),

> While the war continued there could be no thought of redeeming the government's notes. Hence every victory that made the end of the hostilities seem nearer raised the value of the currency, and every defeat depressed it. The failures and successes of the Union armies were recorded by the indicator in the gold room more rapidly than by the daily press. . .

A nice comment on efficient markets. Mitchell continues, perfectly stating my main point:

> fluctuations in the premium on gold were so much more rapid and violent than the changes in the volume of the circulating medium that not even academic economists could regard the quantity theory as an adequate explanation of all the phenomena. (p. 188.)

He opined that these fluctuations

> followed the varying estimates which the community was all the time making of the government's present and prospective ability to meet its obligations. (p. 199.)

Mitchell describes the fiscal theory in a nutshell. Its essence has indeed been with us a long time.

McCandless investigates the value of Confederate currency. Confederate dollars also rose and fell with battlefield success and loss. The chance of Confederate currency being repaid if the South lost the Civil War was pretty clearly zero. But money supply versus transactions demand does not change the day after a lost battle.

Like all interesting episodes, Civil War inflation remains open to inquiry. Lerner (1956) and Friedman and Friedman and Schwartz (1963) provide classic accounts, emphasizing the immense printing of paper money. But money creation was also deficit finance, so they don't really address our crucial question, how much money demand was limited by quantity theory versus fiscal backing.

Burdekin and Weidenmier (2001) examine the consequences of the 1864 Confederate currency reform, in which the quantity of money differed dramatically between the eastern and western Confederacy. The price level differed, indicating an important liquidity value on top of a presumably uniform set of expectations about eventual redemption. Weidenmier (2002) is a nice review of the literature. Hall and Sargent (2014) artfully place Civil War inflation in the context of the modern theory of public finance.

The post-WWI history is more famous. The conventional view credits France, which went back on gold at 20% of the prewar parity, with wisdom for avoiding the deflation and recession suffered by the United Kingdom, which went back fully to the prewar parity. Fiscal affairs are complicated by the status of large international loans, especially from the United States, by prospective reparations from Germany, and by the British gold exchange system. Still, to our point, we would not begin to understand the price level in this era based on transactions demand and money supplies, or interest rate manipulations and a Phillips curve; rather than think about the gold standard, its fiscal backing, a nation's ability and will to establish one or another parity to gold, and the tradeoff between fiscal austerity and deflation against the reputation that repaying debt brings the next time a government wishes to borrow.

In which circumstances deflation or disinflation matters to output is another interesting question of these and other episodes. The post–Civil War United States had a steady deflation, especially of greenback values, with no obvious aggregate consequences. (Bryan's "cross of gold" consequences were distributional, borrowers versus lenders, not a Phillips curve of low aggregate output.) Hall and Sargent (2019) contrast the price level and output history of post–Civil War and post–WWI episodes. We add to our list of times when the Phillips curve seems to operate, and times including currency reforms, the ends of hyperinflations, and the introduction of inflation targets with fiscal reforms, when it seems completely absent.

Perhaps the fact that gold currency circulated in the United States during the Civil War and its aftermath helped people to adjust to the much larger greenback deflation. The numeraire matters. In the other direction, Velde (2009) gives a fascinating account of seventeenth-century France. There were two currencies, a numeraire and unit of account (livres) in which prices were quoted, and a distinct medium of exchange (ecus) held and used for all transactions. A revaluation of the unseen unit of account, needing a decline in quoted prices, led to a severe recession. Velde's article is also a testament that unit of account and medium of exchange may be completely separate, as in my stories of economies in which a "dollar" is valued, though people never hold any dollars.

Was the United Kingdom really unwise to restore gold parity, as Keynes so famously argued? Was there a way to do so and avoid a recession, as so many other stabilizations have done? Why was the post–WWI Phillips curve so severe in the United Kingdom? By restoring parity, the United Kingdom purchased a lot of debt repayment reputation. That hard-won reputation might have been valuable to finance World War II with more money or debt and lower taxes, had the United Kingdom not abandoned the gold standard in the 1930s. France might have needed such a reputation had it not lost the second war so quickly. Keynes might have been wrong. Perhaps "don't buy a reputation you won't keep," is the lesson, and "don't waffle about whether you are going to buy that reputation."

15

Esthetics and Philosophy

Keynesianism, new-Keynesianism, and monetarism were each useful theories, to then-current political debates or to the concerns of central bankers. Fiscal theory is currently less useful to those concerns but that may change. The fiscal theory, by allowing free financial innovation, may replace some of the usefulness of monetarism. It may rescue many useful properties of new-Keynesianism, by fixing the latter's foundations. Fiscal theory is simple and elegant. Simpler and more elegant theories are often correct.

THE OPPORTUNITY to base a theory of the price level on a perfectly frictionless supply and demand model, on which we build frictions as necessary, is also esthetically pleasing. Everywhere else in economics, we start with simple supply and demand, and then add frictions as needed. Monetary economics has not been able to do so. Now it can.

In this way, the fiscal theory fills a philosophical hole. It is initially puzzling that Chicago championed both monetarism and free markets. The traditional Chicago philosophy generally pushes toward a simple supply and demand explanation of economic phenomena, and generally tries where possible to arrive at solutions to social problems based on private exchange and property rights. Yet Chicago started its macroeconomics with one big inescapable friction separating money from bonds. Though Friedman advocated floating exchange rates and other financial innovations, monetarism cannot withstand financial innovation that makes bonds fully liquid, or money that pays full interest. This financial innovation only started in earnest in the 1980s.

That philosophy makes sense in historical context. The Chicago view was a lot less interventionist than the Keynesian view of the time. And at the time, there was no alternative for macroeconomic affairs. Fiscal theory as presented here did not exist. Fiscal theory needs intertemporal tools that had not been developed. The quantity theory tradition from Irving Fisher was well developed and ready to be put to use.

But now there is an alternative. The fiscal theory can offer a monetary theory that is more Chicago than Chicago. A monetary theory that allows a free market financial system, and allows us interest-paying money, liquidity satiation, and the Friedman-optimal quantity of money, might have been attractive to the Chicago monetarists.

Theories prosper when they are logically coherent and describe data. But empirically, theories also prosper when they are useful to understand important events, or a larger debate or political cause. Keynesianism in the 1930s has been praised for saving capitalism. Against the common view at that time that only Soviet central planning, fascist great-leader direction, or Rooseveltian NRA micromanagement could save the economy,

351

Keynesians said no: If we just fix a single fault, "aggregate demand," with a single elixir, fiscal stimulus, the economy will recover, without requiring a government takeover of microeconomics, or abolition of private property and markets. Even if one regards that Keynesian economics as a fairy tale, embodying in one place dozens of classic economic fallacies, it may have been a *useful* fairy tale as it emboldened resistance to total nationalization in the 1930s.

The tables turned in the postwar era. Now Keynesianism continued to be useful to the left of the U.S. political spectrum. Communist central planning was no longer on the table. But Keynesianism remained potent in U.S. economic debates, part of a softer paternalistic dirigisme. The Keynesians' vision of continual aggregate-demand management fit well with their advocacy of banking, financial and exchange controls, industrial policies, and wage and price controls, as well as extensive microeconomic government management in the postwar era.

In this context, monetarism was likewise *useful* to the free market resurgence in the 1960s. In the face of the then-dominant static Keynesian paradigm, Friedman and the Chicago school could not hope to prevail by asserting that recessions are the normal work of a frictionless market. The *possibility* of this view embodied in Kydland and Prescott (1982) was a long way away. Nobody had the technical skills to build that model, and the verbal general equilibrium assertions of the 1920s were generally dismissed with derision. Something obviously went very wrong in the Great Depression. Views of the 1930s driven by financial frictions following bank runs (see the influential literature starting with Bernanke (1983)) and views emphasizing the microeconomic distortions of misbegotten policies (see, for example, Cole and Ohanian (2004)) were simply not yet available by theory, historical analysis, or empirical work. The intellectual and political climate demanded that the government do *something* about recessions, that government should have done something about the Great Depression, and demanded a simple, understandable, unicausal theory without the subtleties of modern intertemporal economics. Intertemporal general equilibrium thinking is hard, harder still with frictions, and has little impact on policy to this day, which remains guided by the embers of hydraulic Keynesianism. When in trouble, reach for stimulus. The argument could be phrased as monetary versus fiscal stimulus, which at least removed the question of just what the government would spend money on from the imprimatur of macroeconomics. Monetarism was perfect to the purpose.

But as the set of facts we must confront has changed since the 1960s, the policy and intellectual environment has changed too. We don't *need* monetarism any more. Fiscal theory fits today's facts, it is adapted to our much-changed institutional and financial structure, and it's ready for today's evident challenge: price level control in the shadow of debt and deficits. And the fiscal theory fits much of Friedman's philosophical and intellectual purposes in today's environment, even if it turns many monetarist propositions on their heads. So, I hope that even Friedman might change his mind if he were around today.

I'm beating a dead horse. Monetarism is not a current force, though money supply equals demand shows a surprising resilience in economic theory articles that need to determine the price level somehow, and in commentary. Adaptive expectations IS-LM thinking dominates policy, untied from the quantitative models that gave it some rigor in the 1970s. New-Keynesian models featuring dynamic general equilibrium, explicit frictions, and explicit if not rational expectations, dominate in academia, combined with a Taylor-rule description of interest rate setting. These theories too grew out of empirical and practical necessity. Inflation surged under interest rate targets in the 1970s and declined under the same targets in the 1980s. Monetary aggregate-based policy fell apart in the early 1980s. We have to talk about interest rate targets. These are *useful* theories.

Moreover, they connect with the concerns of central bankers. If a central banker asks, "Should we raise or lower the interest rate?," and you answer, "You should control the money supply," you won't be invited back. If you answer, "Recessions are dominated by supply, credit, and other shocks with interesting dynamics, and monetary policy doesn't have that much to do with them," you won't be invited back. If you answer, "The price level is dominated by fiscal policy," you won't be invited back. If you answer, "Let's talk about the interest rate rule and regime," you might be invited back to a technical conference, but the banker will surely press, "Yes, yes, but what should we do *now*?" Central banks follow interest rate targets, and central banks are the central consumers of macroeconomic advice. A useful theory of monetary policy, that any central banker will pay any attention to, must model interest rate targets—even if, as here, it ends up suggesting there are better ways to run monetary policy.

The economic conceptual framework used by people in policy positions is often fundamentally wrong, of course. And one should say that. But if we want to understand why theories around us prosper, usefulness as well as pure scientific merit has strong explanatory power. And where possible without sacrificing scientific merit, trying to find common ground or speak to issues of the day is not a totally undesirable characteristic of an economic theory. Moreover, listening isn't a bad habit either. Sometimes the practical knowledge of people in the thick of things reveals facts and economic logic we have not considered.

This book takes its long tour of interest rate targets and central bank actions to offer supply to that demand as well. I have worked to show how fiscal theory can fill the gaping holes of new-Keynesian models, allowing at least continuity of methodology if not necessarily of results, and thereby making fiscal theory *useful* to researchers who want to improve new-Keynesian style models of monetary policy and to central bankers and treasury officials who wish to guide inflation. There are many other ways fiscal theory suggests that we might set up a monetary system in the future. But these considerations are not terribly useful right now, so I have spent less time on them in this book.

New-Keynesian economists are explicit in an intellectual goal, equally esthetic, philosophical, and useful to the larger debate: to revive the general flavor of IS-LM in a framework that survives the devastating Lucas (1976) critique of IS-LM theory, Sims's (1980) "Macroeconomics and Reality" critique of its empirical practice, and the evident grand failure of IS-LM in the inflationary 1970s and disinflationary 1980s. It is designed to be a theory of monetary policy, based on interest rate targets, more than it is designed to be a theory of recessions, which come from the same ephemeral "shocks" as in other theories. It gives the Fed something to do and a framework to think about the effects of its decisions, which the real business cycle theory of recessions does not offer. New-Keynesian economics is designed to be a theory that is both beautiful and useful. Fiscal theory of monetary policy is not likely to offer justification for

IS-LM thinking, but it turns out the actual equations of new-Keynesian models don't do so either.

Fiscal theory is not immediately useful to one side or another of today's economic, methodological, ideological, or political debates. Indeed, I have intentionally broadened its appeal to indicate how a wide variety of modeling philosophies can incorporate fiscal theory.

In my framing, fiscal theory takes on some of the mantle of monetarism. Fiscal theory offers a theory of inflation based on simple explainable supply and demand foundations. It stresses the underlying importance of stable monetary and fiscal institutions. Nothing is more forward-looking than a present value formula. I spend time using the fiscal theory to think about proposals and possibilities for a pure inflation target, a gold-standard-like, interest spread operating rule, and the possibility of private institutions taking over. I use it to embrace the possibilities that current communication, computation, and financial technology offer us today. But this pursuit reflects my economic philosophy. One could use fiscal theory in much different ways. One can use fiscal theory to patch up new-Keynesian theoretical holes, and proceed in a much more interventionist direction. One can more swiftly add layers of frictions for policy to exploit.

Esthetic and philosophical considerations don't make a theory right. Usually we pretend such concerns don't exist, so we do not write about them. But they shouldn't be ignored. Though economics is often criticized for playing with pretty theories rather than the "real world," the most successful theories of the past have been simple and elegant in economics as in the rest of science. Epicycles seldom survive, even if, as in Copernicus's case, they temporarily fit the data better than the simpler and eventually victorious theory (Kuhn (1962)). Supply and demand, comparative advantage, the burden of taxation, the great neutrality results—all have a decisive simplicity.

At least in the eyes of this beholder, the fiscal theory is truly beautiful. I hope by now to have infected you with that view as well. Fiscal theory can be expressed in a simple model, with a simple story. Nothing like the simplicity and clarity of the first chapter of this book underlies new or IS-LM Keynesian models, or even monetarism.

These are secondary concerns. The primary case for fiscal theory is that it holds together logically, it is consistent with the facts of our monetary and financial institutions, and it describes events such as the zero bound period in a way that monetarism or new and old Keynesianism do not do. If a surge of clearly fiscal inflation breaks out after this book is published, and if its insights help to address that surge, its need will be even clearer. These are the true tests of a useful theory.

PART IV

Money, Interest Rates, and Regimes

HAVING DESCRIBED the fiscal theory of the price level, I turn to the alternatives. As always, the case for a new theory is bolstered by flaws in old theories, in their internal logic as well as their ability to describe events.

The two most important alternative theories of inflation are fiat money with a controlled supply, and interest rate targets that move more than one for one with inflation. Each of these theories specifies an "active" monetary policy together with a "passive" fiscal policy, while the fiscal theory specifies some important "passivity" of these monetary arrangements, with its "active" fiscal regime. We have met both theories already, as well as the "regime" question. I return to these issues in a more comprehensive way.

I address three questions. First, *can* these alternative theories determine the price level or at least the inflation rate in an economy like ours? I conclude that they can't. The fiscal theory is the only viable theory we have that is broadly consistent with present institutions.

Since these theories wipe out one equilibrium condition, the valuation equation for government debt, they leave one object undetermined—the price level or the inflation rate—and thus they leave multiple equilibria. Therefore, they must add some new assumption to make up for the missing equilibrium condition. Broadly speaking, these assumptions amount to equilibrium selection threats by the government. The government threatens actions it would take in multiple equilibria, to rule out all but one. These actions include hyperinflating the economy, simultaneously following an inconsistent money supply and interest rate target, introducing an arbitrage opportunity, or some other device so that equilibrium cannot form—essentially, blowing up the economy. I review and argue that these threats are not even vaguely plausible, especially as descriptions of how people today expect government to behave. Nobody expects the government to react to off-target inflation by blowing up the economy. Central banks also do not restrict the quantity of money as specified by $MV = Py$. Our financial arrangements have thoroughly blurred the distinction between money and debt.

Second, can we tell theories apart? The two broadly related questions are *observational equivalence* and *identification*. One cannot measure behavior off equilibrium, or in other realizations of multiple equilibria, from data in one equilibrium. The crucial parameters, which specify reactions away from the observable equilibrium, are not identified. Thus, there is no time series test we can use to distinguish one from the other class of theory based on time series drawn from an economic equilibrium. At this level of generality, the new-Keynesian, monetarist and fiscal theory approaches are observationally equivalent.

Economics is full of nonidentification and observational equivalence theorems. They just mean we have to think about what we're doing, judge the plausibility of alternative stories, make identification assumptions and judge their plausibility. We have to examine monetary institutions, precommitments, and authorities' statements about how they would behave in different circumstances. Nonidentification and observational equivalence theorems are simply an important guide to our logic, as elsewhere in economics.

Third, how do the alternative theories account for events? Here I focus on the lessons of the zero bound decade and quarter century in Japan. Extant monetary and interest rate theories made definite and radical predictions for this episode—inflation or deflation spirals, indeterminacy and volatility. They required elaborate ex post epicycles to patch them up to be consistent with the quiet inflation of this period. They make dramatic policy prescriptions, such as arbitrarily large multipliers, or effects of forward guidance that are larger as the promise is made for dates further in the future, which are either appetizing or nonsense, depending on your view. Fiscal theory offers a clean, simple account of the episode, and normal analysis of policy options. These observations don't contravene observational equivalence, as each theory can be stretched to fit the facts. But the plausibility of such stretching is hard to digest for monetary and interest rate theories.

I conclude that the currently available alternatives don't work. The fiscal theory is all we have, at least for now. There are indeed many challenges in applying fiscal theory to the world, but until another theory comes along, the task at hand is to figure out how the fiscal theory works, not to test it against a viable alternative.

As usual, I survey the issues quickly in some stripped-down models, and then circle back for a fuller treatment.

16

The New-Keynesian Model

IN THE NEXT few chapters I examine the currently most popular approach to monetary policy, based on interest rate targets alone. The new-Keynesian dynamic stochastic general equilibrium (DSGE) approach summarized by Woodford (2003) describes the current academic theory. We'll also look at old-Keynesian IS-LM models, which pervade policy analysis though they have been absent from academic work for a generation. They turn out to be quite different from new-Keynesian models. Indeed, the label "new-Keynesian" is in many ways a misnomer. Woodford places his analysis in the tradition of Wicksell (1965) and Wicksell (1898), who pioneered the idea that the central bank could stabilize the price level by raising or lowering an interest rate target. New-Keynesian models emphasize the power of monetary policy, while traditional Keynesians argue for fiscal policy instead. "New-Keynesian" models are really a marriage of Wicksellian, monetarist, and rational expectations thought. But I won't try to change the label now.

I start with the simplest case of the new-Keynesian model, featuring constant real interest rates and flexible prices. It turns out that one can see all the important issues in this case, as we found with the fiscal theory. I then add price stickiness, which generates varying real interest rates and output, is more realistic, and is the form studied by most of the literature. Its study verifies that indeed the simple model does capture the important ideas.

We have used the model extensively in previous chapters. What's different here is not the model—the IS and Phillips curves, and an interest rate target—but a different approach to equilibrium selection.

My main point, of course, is to contrast the new-Keynesian model with the fiscal theory of monetary policy. The investigation leads to a different understanding of new-Keynesian models than is commonly presented, which is useful on its own.

16.1   The Simplest Model

I present the simplest new-Keynesian model,

$$i_t = E_t \pi_{t+1}$$

$$i_t = \phi \pi_t + u_t.$$

The model specifies $\phi > 1$, adds a rule against nominal explosions, and so determines inflation by

$$\pi_t = -\sum_{j=0}^{\infty} \frac{1}{\phi^{j+1}} E_t \left(u_{t+j}\right).$$

With an AR(1) process for the disturbance $u_t = \eta u_{t-1} + \varepsilon_t$, the model produces inflation and interest rates that follow an AR(1),

$$\pi_t = -\frac{1}{\phi - \eta} u_t; \; i_t = -\frac{\eta}{\phi - \eta} u_t.$$

Figure 16.1 plots these responses.

The simplest form of the standard new-Keynesian model, as set forth for example in Woodford (2003), consists of the same set of equations as the simplest fiscal theory of monetary policy model from Sections 2.5 and 2.6; equations (2.16), (2.17), and (2.22):

$$i_t = E_t \pi_{t+1} \tag{16.1}$$

$$i_t = \phi \pi_t + u_t \tag{16.2}$$

$$\Delta E_{t+1} \pi_{t+1} = -\varepsilon_{\Sigma s, t+1}. \tag{16.3}$$

I use notation ϕ rather than θ as it plays a different role in this model.

New-Keynesian modelers solve these same equations differently than we have. New-Keynesian modelers specify a passive fiscal policy, that (16.3) determines surpluses $\varepsilon_{\Sigma s, t+1}$ for any unexpected inflation. As (16.3) then does not influence the rest of the model, they often relegate it to footnotes, or drop it entirely. It is also typically absent from empirical evaluation of the models.

We then eliminate i_t from (16.1)–(16.2). Having wiped out (16.3), we have a single equilibrium condition

$$E_t \pi_{t+1} = \phi \pi_t + u_t. \tag{16.4}$$

We can then write the equilibria of this model as

$$\pi_{t+1} = \phi \pi_t + u_t + \delta_{t+1}; \; E_t \left(\delta_{t+1}\right) = 0, \tag{16.5}$$

where δ_{t+1} is any conditionally mean zero random variable. Multiple equilibria are indexed by arbitrary initial inflation π_0, and by the arbitrary random variables or "sunspots" δ_{t+1}.

If $\|\phi\| < 1$, this economy is *stable*. Expected inflation $E_t \pi_{t+j}$ converges going forward for any initial value. But it remains *indeterminate*. "Sunspot" shocks δ_{t+1} can erupt at any time, and fade away.

If $\|\phi\| > 1$, all of these equilibria except one are expected eventually to explode, as $\|E_t \left(\pi_{t+j}\right)\|$ grows without bound. New-Keynesians add a rule against such explosive solutions. Then, we find the "unique locally bounded equilibrium" by solving the difference equation (16.4) forward, to obtain

$$\pi_t = -\sum_{j=0}^{\infty} \frac{1}{\phi^{j+1}} E_t \left(u_{t+j}\right). \tag{16.6}$$

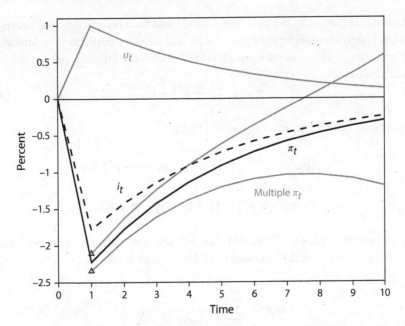

FIGURE 16.1. Response of the New-Keynesian Model to a Monetary Policy Shock $\varepsilon_{i,t}$. Gray lines give inflation in alternative equilibria. $\phi = 1.25$; $\eta = 0.8$.

With an AR(1) disturbance

$$u_t = \eta u_{t-1} + \varepsilon_{i,t},$$

(16.6) gives

$$\pi_t = -\frac{u_t}{\phi - \eta}. \tag{16.7}$$

Equivalently, by this criterion we select the variables π_0, $\{\delta_{t+1}\}$ that index multiple equilibria, as

$$\pi_0 = -\frac{u_0}{\phi - \eta}; \quad \delta_{t+1} = -\frac{\varepsilon_{i,t+1}}{\phi - \eta}. \tag{16.8}$$

Equilibrium inflation follows the same AR(1) process as the shock u_t,

$$\pi_{t+1} = \eta \pi_t - \frac{1}{\phi - \eta} \varepsilon_{i,t+1}. \tag{16.9}$$

The interest rate follows

$$i_t = -\frac{\eta}{\phi - \eta} u_t. \tag{16.10}$$

Figure 16.1 graphs the response of inflation and interest rates to a monetary policy shock, with parameters $\phi = 1.25$; $\eta = 0.8$. In response to a positive shock to the disturbance u_t, inflation π_t declines immediately, and then reverts slowly. That response looks surprisingly reasonable, for a model with no monetary or pricing frictions at all.

If one wishes to determine the price level rather than the inflation rate, let the interest rate policy rule be

$$i_t = \phi_p \left(p_t - p^* \right) + u_t. \tag{16.11}$$

Now, substituting into the Fisher equation (16.1),

$$E_t \left(p_{t+1} - p^* \right) - \left(p_t - p^* \right) = \phi_p \left(p_t - p^* \right) + u_t$$

$$E_t \left(p_{t+1} - p^* \right) = \left(1 + \phi_p \right) \left(p_t - p^* \right) + u_t.$$

Again, we have multiple equilibria. But if $\phi_p > 0$ and if we rule out explosive equilibria, then we have a unique locally bounded equilibrium price level,

$$p_t = p^* - \sum_{j=0}^{\infty} \frac{1}{(1 + \phi)^{j+1}} E_t \left(u_{t+j} \right).$$

Woodford calls this a "Wicksellian" regime, in honor of Wicksell (1898).

Thus we have it: If the central bank's interest rate target reacts sufficiently and if we rule out explosive equilibria, then it seems that a pure interest rate target *can* completely determine the inflation rate or price level, with no money demand, no money supply control, no gold, commodity, or other backing, and no redemption promise. Before criticizing, let us admire the edifice. This appears to be a truly novel theory of the price level. The list is short.

16.2   Inflation Targets and Equilibrium Selection

Writing the policy rule $i_t = i_t^* + \phi(\pi_t - \pi_t^*)$ with $i_t^* = E_t \pi_{t+1}^*$ clarifies how the model works. The central bank can achieve any path for inflation. Monetary policy has two distinct parts: interest rate policy i_t^*, which determines expected inflation; and equilibrium selection policy $\phi(\pi_t - \pi_t^*)$, which selects unexpected inflation.

The operation of the model is clearer if we write the policy rule in an equivalent form introduced by King (2000),

$$i_t = i_t^* + \phi(\pi_t - \pi_t^*). \tag{16.12}$$

Here, the interest rate target $\{i_t^*\}$ and the inflation target $\{\pi_t^*\}$ are the equilibrium interest rate and inflation rate the central bank wishes to produce. The targets must respect private sector equilibrium conditions, $i_t^* = E_t \pi_{t+1}^*$ in this simple model.

This form of the policy rule is equivalent to (16.2), $i_t = \phi \pi_t + u_t$. One can translate between the two representations by

$$u_t = i_t^* - \phi \pi_t^* = E_t \pi_{t+1}^* - \phi \pi_t^* \tag{16.13}$$

and, going in the other direction,

$$\pi_t^* = -\sum_{j=0}^{\infty} \frac{1}{\phi^{j+1}} E_t u_{t+j}; \; i_t^* = E_t \pi_{t+1}^*.$$

The i_t^*, π_t^* notation is just a different way of writing the disturbance term u_t.

Again eliminate i_t from the rule (16.12) and (16.1), $i_t = E_t \pi_{t+1}$. The equilibrium condition becomes

$$E_t \left(\pi_{t+1} - \pi_{t+1}^* \right) = \phi (\pi_t - \pi_t^*). \tag{16.14}$$

If the central bank follows $\phi > 1$, the only nonexplosive equilibrium is $\pi_t = \pi_t^*$. We reach this conclusion quickly, for any process of the monetary policy disturbance, not just an AR(1).

With the parameterization (16.12), we see quickly that the central bank can achieve any value of inflation it wishes in this model. The central bank announces its inflation target $\{\pi_t^*\}$, and announces a threat to hyperinflate or deflate for any other value of inflation $\phi(\pi_t - \pi_t^*)$. The bank sets the interest rate to $i_t^* = E_t \pi_{t+1}^*$, and the private sector jumps to the equilibrium π_t^* represented by the central bank's inflation target. That conclusion is also true of the conventional parameterization, but reverse engineering a $\{u_t\}$ to produce a given inflation path is more cumbersome.

The parameterization (16.12) separates monetary policy into *interest rate policy* i_t^*, and a distinct *equilibrium selection policy* $\phi(\pi_t - \pi_t^*)$. It thereby lets us see clearly which aspect of policy drives which result. Interest rate policy sets the path of interest rates that we observe in equilibrium $i_t = i_t^*$, and sets expected inflation via $i_t = E_t \pi_{t+1}$. Equilibrium selection policy $\phi(\pi_t - \pi_t^*)$ describes how the central bank would react to the emergence of a different equilibrium, and sets unexpected inflation in this model. These two aspects of the interest rate rule are tied together in the parameterization $i_t = \phi \pi_t + u_t$, and hard to distinguish. Indeed, it's not immediately clear from that representation that there is such a counterintuitive thing as "equilibrium selection policy," unknown in IS-LM thinking, underlying the model.

Finally, we see quickly how the new-Keynesian and fiscal theory of monetary policy are related in this simple model. The central bank determines the observed interest rate $i_t = i_t^*$ in both cases, and via $i_t = E_t \pi_{t+1}$ determines expected inflation. In fiscal theory, shocks to the present value of surpluses determine unexpected inflation. In new-Keynesian theory, the central bank's equilibrium selection policy determines unexpected inflation.

Interest rate policy i_t^* need not be a time-varying peg. Interest rate policy can include rules, such as $i_t^* = \theta \pi_t^* + u_t$. Then the full monetary policy rule is

$$i_t = \theta \pi_t^* + u_t + \phi (\pi_t - \pi_t^*).$$

Again, we are just pulling more out of the disturbance term, or putting correlations with other variables in that term.

The two notations are equivalent. In my view, this * notation makes the model's operation much clearer. However, I make the points of subsequent sections in both notations so you can be assured that the points really do hold even in the standard expression of the model.

With two simple expressions of the model before us, I turn to some of its major issues and problems. The model adds a rule against hyperinflations, but what's wrong with hyperinflations? The model specifies that the central bank selects equilibria by threatening hyperinflation in response to inflation. This threat is contrary to everything central banks say and any credible set of beliefs about central bank behavior. The parameter ϕ and the monetary policy disturbance are not identified. We cannot learn them, and agents in the model cannot learn them. The new-Keynesian and fiscal theory models are observationally equivalent using time series data from an equilibrium. The response to a monetary policy shock is the same as the fiscal theory of monetary policy response to a fiscal shock. Finally, the new-Keynesian model produces its response by equilibrium selection. The Fed does not raise and lower aggregate demand; it induces the private sector to jump from one to another of multiple equilibria.

16.3   What's Wrong with Hyperinflations?

Economics does not rule out nominal explosions. Ruling out such paths is an addition to the usual definition of equilibria. Many countries have seen hyperinflations. Fiscal theory rules out real explosions, by the transversality condition.

The model produces a unique equilibrium by ruling out hyperinflationary paths, or more generally by ruling out equilibria that are not "locally bounded." But what's wrong with inflationary, or non-locally-bounded paths? Transversality conditions can rule out real explosions, but not nominal explosions. There is no violation of the consumer's transversality condition in a path $\pi_t = \phi^t \pi_0$. Hyperinflations are historic realities. Recall post-WWI Germany in Section 14.3, or Venezuela or Zimbabwe.

The restriction to nonexplosive or locally bounded equilibria does not come from standard economics. It's a new and additional restriction. Without it, this model does not eliminate multiple equilibria and hence does not determine inflation or the price level. I conclude that the new-Keynesian model simply does not solve the multiple equilibrium problem. That we do not observe frequent hyperinflations simply means that the world, and especially the central bank, does not behave this way; the model is wrong.

One might object that I am taking the linearized model too seriously. Central banks don't push inflation to infinity, they just push it up to an uncomfortable level. The language "nonlocal" equilibria rather than "explosive" equilibria refers to that possibility. But now the logic of a rule against such solutions is even more tenuous. Why rule out solutions in which inflation runs up to 20% and stays there?

One might object that the fiscal theory approach to this model also describes an equilibrium in which a variable, the price level, is determined by a forward-looking expectation, and jumps to avoid an explosive root. But there is a fundamental difference: The transversality condition rules out *real* explosions, explosions of B_{t-1}/P_t. There is no corresponding economic condition forcing anyone to avoid nominal explosions, of P_t itself.

An economic mechanism drives unexpected inflation in fiscal theory: If the price level is too low, nominal government bonds appear as net wealth to consumers. They try to increase consumption. Aggregate demand pushes prices back up. In the new-Keynesian reading of these equations, there is no corresponding economic mechanism to push inflation to its target, (16.6). We are choosing *among* equilibria; we are finding the unique *locally bounded* equilibrium, not the unique equilibrium.

16.4   Central Bank Destabilization?

No central bank says that it deliberately destabilizes the economy, or selects from multiple equilibria. The $\phi > 1$ threat is disastrous ex post for the central bank, so people are not likely to believe the bank will do it. Since the response ϕ is not identified, there is no way for people to learn it.

Grant for the moment a rule against nominally explosive equilibria. The central bank *causes* these explosions. Real central banks don't do that.

In the central equilibrium condition $E_t\pi_{t+1} = \phi\pi_t + u_t$, with $\phi < 1$, this economy is stable. The central bank deliberately makes the economy unstable by following $\phi > 1$. When inflation breaks out, the bank raises interest rates more than one for one via $i_t = \phi\pi_t$. Via $i_t = E_t\pi_{t+1}$, the bank's rate rise *raises* subsequent inflation. In * notation, the central bank deliberately makes inflation diverge *away* from its target, $E_t(\pi_{t+1} - \pi_{t+1}^*) = \phi(\pi_t - \pi_t^*)$. Together with the rule against nominal explosions, the intentional destabilization captured by ϕ is the central bank's equilibrium selection policy.

Increasing inflation in response to current inflation is the key point, as that is what leads to equilibrium selection. The reaction of interest rates to inflation is only a means to that end. If by raising interest rates the bank lowered expected inflation, then the path would not be ruled out as an equilibrium. In more general models, the greater than one-for-one reaction of interest rates to inflation is neither necessary nor sufficient to the essential condition, which is one additional explosive eigenvalue in system dynamics.

No central bank on the planet describes its inflation control efforts this way: "We will respond to undesired inflation by forcing inflation to rise further without limit. We intentionally destabilize the economy to fight the scourge of multiple equilibria." Central banks uniformly explain the opposite: In response to inflation they will raise interest rates, yes, but by raising interest rates they *reduce* subsequent inflation, and vice versa. And if interest rates fail, they will do whatever it takes—asset purchases, credit controls, forward guidance, and so forth—to reduce inflation, or to raise inflation if it comes out below their target. Yes, it's all about inflation dynamics, not centrally about the interest rate response, but they do everything in their power to produce stable inflation dynamics, not the opposite. In this way, central bank descriptions of their policy lie firmly in the adaptive expectations IS-LM tradition. We don't necessarily have the wrong policy rule to describe their thinking and their clear explanation of their role; we have the wrong model. If you describe "equilibrium selection policy" as the essential task of a central bank, you will be met with blank stares.

Of course, people discount all sorts of central bank pronouncements. What matters in the model is what people believe about central banks. But that the central bank will react to inflation by pushing the economy to more inflation, or that it will react to deflation by pushing the economy to more deflation, is an even more outlandish specification of people's *beliefs*, today and in any sample period we might study, than it is about central bank behavior. Financial press commentary and policy discussion accords entirely with the central bank's contrary description of their behavior and function.

Large inflation or deflation are disastrous for the central bank's objectives. Even if central banks said they would do it, would they ex post really deliberately create their anathema just to punish people for the wrong equilibrium? Imagine a Fed chair reporting to an angry Congress that the Fed is deliberately inducing a large inflation or deflation, because it committed to do so in order to try to tame multiple equilibria a few years ago, and back then inflation came out one percent above its target. That time-inconsistency is ever more reason for people not to believe that central banks would do it, even if the bank were to announce such a threat.

In this model $\phi < -1$ is as good as $\phi > 1$ to produce local determinacy. Well, if the economy abhors growing inflation, oscillating inflation and deflation are even ghastlier. (King (2000), p. 78.) This example should drive home that the central bank is not stabilizing inflation, raising interest rates to tamp down future inflation, but destabilizing inflation in order to make all but one equilibrium unpleasant.

16.5   Identification

The parameter ϕ is not identified from observed equilibrium time series $\{i_t, \pi_t, s_t\}$. A regression $i_t = \phi \pi_t + u_t$ fails because the right-hand variable and disturbance are perfectly correlated. In equilibrium, $i_t = \eta \pi_t$, so the regression measures η not ϕ. In $i_t = i_t^* + \phi(\pi_t - \pi_t^*)$, there is no variation in the right-hand variable needed to measure ϕ. The parameter ϕ does not enter equilibrium dynamics. We cannot measure off-equilibrium threats from equilibrium time series.

You may object that we can just measure ϕ rather than argue about murky central bank statements and silly commentary in the financial press. This approach does not work because the parameter ϕ is not identified in the new-Keynesian model.

What about running a regression $i_t = \phi \pi_t + u_t$? That regression does not measure the parameter ϕ of the model, because the model predicts that u_t and π_t are correlated— perfectly negatively correlated in this case. Using (16.6) and either (16.1) or (16.2), the equilibrium relation between interest rates and inflation is

$$i_t = \eta \pi_t \qquad (16.15)$$

with no error. A regression of i_t on π_t in data from this model produces η not ϕ.

From (16.9), all we *observe* of the model is

$$\pi_{t+1} = \eta\pi_t + \varepsilon_{\pi,t+1} \tag{16.16}$$

$$i_t = \eta\pi_t \tag{16.17}$$

$$\varepsilon_{\pi,t+1} = -\varepsilon_{\Sigma s,t+1} \tag{16.18}$$

where I write $\varepsilon_{\pi,t+1} = \Delta E_{t+1}\pi_{t+1}$. The observable $\{i_t, \pi_t, s_t\}$ dynamics are the same for any value of ϕ. No instrument can help. The likelihood function does not involve ϕ. There is simply no way to measure ϕ from time series data on the observables $\{i_t, \pi_t, s_t\}$.

The monetary policy disturbances u_t are also not identified. We infer monetary policy disturbances from a regression residual. If you could observe the parameter ϕ, you could calculate $u_t = i_t - \phi\pi_t$. If you could observe monetary policy disturbances u_t directly, you could infer ϕ from $i_t = \phi\pi_t + u_t$ despite the correlation of u_t and π_t. Formulas such as (16.9) include parameters ϕ and shocks $\varepsilon_{i,t}$, so it seems that those parameters affect dynamics. But these parameters and variables always appear together, so there are different combinations of ϕ, u_t, $\varepsilon_{i,t}$ which give the same time series of interest rates and inflation.

Plots of the inflation, output, and interest rate responses to monetary policy disturbances u_t, such as Figure 16.1, are plots of responses to an unmeasurable quantity. This is one reason that I emphasize plotting and thinking about responses to *interest rates*, rather than responses to monetary policy *disturbances*.

The AR(1) is not central to nonidentification and observational equivalence. Choose any process $\{\pi_t\}$. An equilibrium must have $i_t = E_t\pi_{t+1}$. Choose any ϕ. Construct $u_t = i_t - \phi\pi_t$. These reverse-engineered assumptions about ϕ and u_t produce the chosen $\{\pi_t\}$ and its resultant $\{i_t\}$ as an equilibrium. Thus, observation of π_t and i_t cannot tell us ϕ and u_t, no matter what is the time series process of inflation.

The * notation (16.12),

$$i_t = i_t^* + \phi(\pi_t - \pi_t^*) \tag{16.19}$$

shows nonidentification of ϕ directly. The parameter ϕ only multiplies *deviations* from equilibrium $\pi_t - \pi_t^*$. In equilibrium, $\pi_t = \pi_t^*$, so there is no variation on the right-hand side with which to measure ϕ.

More deeply, there is no way to measure how the central bank would respond to an unobserved off-equilibrium inflation, using data drawn from an equilibrium. If a threat to inflate drives the economy to π_t^*, because we rule out explosive paths, just how fast the explosion comes – larger versus smaller ϕ – is irrelevant. If, to get the kids to eat spinach, you threaten no ice cream, and if the threat is effective, the data (spinach, ice cream; spinach, ice cream) do not reveal the threat. You cannot tell whether the threat was no ice cream for a day, a week, or a month (different values of ϕ).

In the last section, I opined that people are unlikely to believe $\phi > 1$. We economists also generally discount statements by central bankers, and instead think that people learn the structural parameters of rational expectations models from experience. But the fact that ϕ is not identified, that behavior away from equilibrium cannot be learned from time series drawn from equilibrium, means that agents in the model have no way of learning ϕ from experience any more than we econometricians looking at data can do.

16.6   Observational Equivalence

The new-Keynesian inflation response to a monetary policy shock is the same as the fiscal theory inflation response to a fiscal shock. Writing the policy rules $i_t = i_t^* + \phi(\pi_t - \pi_t^*)$ and $\tilde{s}_{t+1} = \alpha v_t^* + \gamma(v_t - v_t^*) + u_{s,t+1}$, we see a parallel logic and observational equivalence. The regimes are characterized by behavior away from equilibrium not visible in equilibrium. Neither γ nor ϕ is identified.

Observational equivalence clarifies implicit identifying assumptions of attempts to measure and test regimes. It opens the door to interpreting the entire sample with fiscal theory. It leads us to consider information other than equilibrium time series, such as statements, rules, institutions, laws, and other commitments.

The new-Keynesian inflation response to a monetary policy shock of Figure 16.1 is exactly the same as the fiscal theory inflation response to a fiscal shock $\varepsilon_{\Sigma s,t+1}$, graphed in Figure 2.2. Specifically, the fiscal theory equilibrium from Section 2.6 is (2.25),

$$\pi_{t+1} = \theta \pi_t + u_t - \varepsilon_{\Sigma s,t+1},$$

where the new-Keynesian model (16.9) gives

$$\pi_{t+1} = \eta \pi_t - \frac{1}{\phi - \eta} \varepsilon_{i,t+1}.$$

If we use an interest rate rule parameter θ equal to the disturbance correlation parameter η from the new-Keynesian model, and if we specify a fiscal shock $\varepsilon_{\Sigma s,t+1}$ equal to $\varepsilon_{i,t+1}/(\phi - \eta)$ from the new-Keynesian model, the fiscal theory model produces exactly the same time series as the new-Keynesian model.

This equivalence is economic, and not just formal. The fiscal equation (16.3) is still part of the new-Keynesian model. After the central bank engineers a monetary contraction, fiscal policy "passively" raises surpluses by $\varepsilon_{\Sigma s,t+1} = -\Delta E_{t+1} \pi_{t+1} = \varepsilon_{i,t+1}/(\phi - \eta)$. This value is exactly the same as the fiscal theory model's "active" fiscal shock. The new-Keynesian says the monetary equilibrium selection threat caused inflation to jump and fiscal policy followed. The fiscal theorist looks at the same data and says no, this fiscal shock caused the disinflation jump, and the observed interest rate followed inflation via a different policy rule. The observables are the same in each interpretation.

You may object that we can tell the models apart because they rely on different parameters ϕ and η. Just measure ϕ. But ϕ is not identified in the new-Keynesian model.

In both new-Keynesian and fiscal theory of monetary policy versions of this simple model, interest rate policy, setting i_t^*, controls expected inflation. In new-Keynesian models, an equilibrium selection policy $\phi(\pi_t - \pi_t^*)$ and a rule against nominal explosions determines unexpected inflation. In fiscal theory, fiscal policy chooses unexpected inflation with $\Delta E_{t+1} \pi_{t+1} = -\varepsilon_{\Sigma s,t+1}$.

A particular form of fiscal policy makes the parallel even clearer. In Sections 5.4 and 5.5 we wrote fiscal policy in a * notation parallel to (16.19). Adding that to the model, we can unite the two possibilities in a general specification,

$$i_t = E_t \pi_{t+1} \tag{16.20}$$

$$i_t = i_t^* + \phi(\pi_t - \pi_t^*)$$

$$\tilde{s}_{t+1} = \alpha v_t^* + \gamma(v_t - v_t^*) + u_{s,t+1}$$

$$\rho v_{t+1}^* = v_t^* - \Delta E_{t+1}\pi_{t+1}^* - \tilde{s}_{t+1} \tag{16.21}$$

$$\rho v_{t+1} = v_t - \Delta E_{t+1}\pi_{t+1} - \tilde{s}_{t+1}. \tag{16.22}$$

(Complete this model with a specification of its disturbances, i_t^*, π_t^*, $u_{s,t}$.) These parametric forms are not the *only* ways either active fiscal or active monetary policy can select equilibria. We have seen a variety of each and we will see more. But these are common parameterizations that fit nicely in the VAR(1) structure of standard models.

We specify an active-fiscal passive-monetary policy regime with $\phi < 1$, most simply $\phi = 0$ and $\gamma = 0$. We specify active-monetary passive-fiscal policy with $\phi > 1$ and $\gamma > 0$, most simply $\gamma = \alpha > 0$.

If we write the models without the * notation, we are tempted to try to estimate and test these "regimes." But the * notation makes clear that the regimes are observationally equivalent. We see $i_t = i_t^*$ and $\pi_t = \pi_t^*$. We see

$$i_t = E_t \pi_{t+1} \tag{16.23}$$

$$\tilde{s}_{t+1} = \alpha v_t + u_{s,t+1}$$

$$\rho v_{t+1} = v_t - \Delta E_{t+1}\pi_{t+1} - \tilde{s}_{t+1}. \tag{16.24}$$

The fiscal parameter γ is just as unidentified as the monetary parameter ϕ by time series drawn from equilibrium. The equilibrium conditions of the model are the same in active fiscal or active money regimes. All either "active" specification does is to give a reason why $\Delta E_{t+1}\pi_{t+1}$ in (16.24) is unique.

Observational equivalence is a very useful theorem. If one wants to estimate and test regimes, observational equivalence and this formalism are a useful starting point from which to state and understand identification restrictions, which are often implicit. Observational equivalence goes both ways. Any new-Keynesian model can be written as a fiscal theory model. Thus, observational equivalence opens the door to using fiscal theory always. You can always fit the data at least as well with a fiscal theory model as you can with an active money model. Writing the model in a form that expresses observational equivalence provides a recipe for that translation. Observational equivalence prods us to choose a regime based on evidence other than equilibrium time series. That evidence includes rules, statements, institutions, traditions, commitments, and responses to crisis events by which governments commit to and communicate fiscal support for the price level.

16.7 Responses

The inflation response of Figure 16.1 reflects equilibrium selection policy, not the conventional view that higher interest rates push down inflation. Interest rates and inflation move in the same direction throughout. The model can produce a super-Fisherian response and an open mouth operation, in which inflation moves with no movement in interest rates at all.

In the standard new-Keynesian story, unexpected inflation is just one of many equilibria, and the Fed coordinates expectations. The required "passive" fiscal adjustment provides an aggregate demand story. In this sense there is only fiscal theory, and the new-Keynesian story is just a way to produce the fiscal policy that actually lowers inflation.

Superficially, the Figure 16.1 inflation response looks promising relative to prior beliefs that tighter monetary policy should lower inflation. But on second glance, the responses do not embody common intuition.

Just why did inflation drop in response to the monetary policy tightening of Figure 16.1, and immediately, at the same time as the monetary policy shock? From (16.13), the $u_1 = 1$ shock is the same thing as a $\pi_1^* = -1/\phi$ shock. Inflation jumped down because the inflation target jumped down, the equilibrium-selection point jumped down, the central bank threatened hyperinflation or hyperdeflation for any other value, and we ruled out such equilibria. The inflation decline is entirely a result of equilibrium selection policy, not interest rate policy.

To visualize this point, the thin gray lines labeled "multiple π_t" in Figure 16.1 graph what would happen if inflation π_1 jumped to slightly higher or lower values. Any of these jumps are consistent with private sector behavior, which only ties down expected inflation $E_0\pi_1 = i_0 = 0$. But following dynamics $E_1\pi_{t+1} = \phi E_1\pi_t + E_1 u_t$ induced by the central bank's policy rule ϕ, these alternative equilibria spiral away. We rule out such spirals, to declare the solid line the unique equilibrium. Mechanically, the responses in this case are alternative solutions of $E_1\pi_{t+1} = \phi E_1\pi_t + E_1 u_t$, or

$$E_1\pi_{t+1} = -\frac{1}{\phi - \eta}u_{t+1} + \phi^{t+1}\left(\pi_1 + \frac{1}{\phi - \eta}u_1\right)$$

for different values of π_1. Inflation explodes for any value of π_1 but one.

The actual, observable interest rate *declines* throughout the episode. This model does not produce lower inflation in response to higher *interest rates*. The model is Fisherian $i_t = E_t\pi_{t+1}$ throughout. You can draw a horizontal line from each interest rate to the subsequent expected inflation, except for the unexpected shock at time 1. Interest rates fall on impact i_1 along with unexpected inflation π_1. Mechanically, though the disturbance u_t is positive, inflation π_t declines and the endogenous part of the policy rule $i_t = \phi\pi_t$ with $\phi > 1$ overwhelms the positive disturbance u_t to produce lower interest rates. Don't confuse a negative response to a monetary policy *disturbance* with a negative response to *interest rates* themselves. Someone observing data from this economy would see interest rates and inflation always moving in the same direction.

This is a strange monetary policy "tightening." If observed interest rates decline, suddenly and unexpectedly, on the date that the Fed takes action, I doubt the financial press would call it a tightening! To say monetary policy has tightened, you have to say that interest rates are not as low as they should be given low inflation and the Fed's policy to move interest rates more than one for one with inflation. But you have to know the policy and its parameter ϕ to say that.

In retrospect, of course the model is Fisherian. The model has a constant real rate and no monetary or pricing frictions. It *should* be neutral. It would be a miracle if it were not neutral. You may object that price stickiness will fix all this. It does not do so. Perhaps that is the real surprise, which comes later.

All of the inflation decline comes from the instant unexpected downward jump $\Delta E_1 \pi_1$ that happens *at the same time* as the policy shock $\varepsilon_{i,1}$ and interest rate decline i_1. This model does not embody the idea that tighter monetary policy slowly squeezes out inflation. That fact reinforces the view that equilibrium selection rather than monetary stringency is the central intuition of the response.

The inflation response can be super-Fisherian. To generate a super-Fisherian response, we want $\pi_1 = \pi_2 = \ldots = 1$. So set interest rate policy $i_1^* = i_2^* = \ldots = 1$, which sets $\pi_2 = \pi_3 = \ldots = 1$; and set equilibrium selection policy $\pi_1^* = 1$, so that $\pi_1 = 1$ immediately. Interest rates and inflation rise together, immediately and permanently, in lockstep.

We can describe this super-Fisherian response with a conventional rule, $i_t = \phi \pi_t + u_t$. Pick any ϕ. From (16.13) it follows that $u_t = i_t^* - \phi \pi_t^* = 1 - \phi$ to produce this result. Thus, we specify persistence $\eta = 1$, and a shock $\varepsilon_1 = u_1 = 1 - \phi$, and the response formulas (16.9) and (16.10) generate the super-Fisherian response.

The inflation response can be an open mouth operation. Inflation moves on the announcement of policy, with no change in interest rates at all. The price level takes a permanent jump. We wish $\pi_1 = 1$, $\pi_2 = \pi_2 = \cdots = 0$. So set $\pi_1^* = 1$, and $i_t^* = 0$ for all time. The central bank just announces a one-period change in its inflation target, without ever touching interest rates, and lo and behold, inflation moves.

We can describe an open-mouth operation with a conventional policy rule $i_t = \phi \pi_t + u_t$ as well. Pick any ϕ. Generate the disturbance following (16.13) by

$$u_1 = -\phi \pi_1^* = -\phi_1; \ u_2 = u_3 = \ldots = 0.$$

In time series language, we specify $\eta = 0$ and $\varepsilon_1 = -\phi$.

The open mouth operation is particularly beautiful as an example of pure equilibrium selection policy. The central bank has an awesome power to command prices to rise and fall at will, without taking any action. That same awesome power is why inflation declines in the more conventional response of Figure 16.1.

(New Zealand Reserve Bank Governor Donald Brash coined the term "open mouth operation" in Brash (2002), referring to his apparent ability to move interest rates by making announcements, but without open market operations or any other concrete action.)

As the $\eta = 0$ or open mouth case dramatizes, the pretty dynamics shown in Figure 16.1 come from the exogenous dynamics of the forcing process u_t, not from a delayed response of the economy to the monetary policy shock. In this model, anticipated interest rate changes move expected inflation with a one-period lag; $E_t \pi_{t+1} = i_t$ so $E_t \pi_{t+j+1} = E_t i_{t+j}$. That's it for the *economic* dynamics of the model. The long inflation response is entirely a one-period response to a long-lasting interest rate impulse, not a delayed response to the period 1 shock.

Old-Keynesian IS-LM intuition says that by raising nominal rates, the central bank raises real rates, which lowers aggregate demand and subsequent inflation. That's *not* this model. A neutral model, with flexible prices and constant real interest rates, cannot possibly embody IS-LM intuition. The monetary policy rule in this model does *not* say to raise real interest rates when inflation rises. The real rate is $i_t - E_t \pi_{t+1}$ not $i_t - \pi_t$. Such a rule, $i_t = \phi E_t \pi_{t+1}$ with $\phi > 1$, would lead to an equilibrium condition $\phi E_t \pi_{t+1} = E_t \pi_{t+1}$, which has no solution. Pasting IS-LM intuition on the response function of this model is a classic misreading of what its equations actually do.

New-Keynesian intuition views the unexpected inflation entirely as an equilibrium selection story. We could all drive on the right side of the street or the left side of the street. The Fed just says "everyone go to the right side" and it happens. The Fed is no longer in charge of "aggregate demand" and "stimulus" but it is merely our multiple equilibrium traffic cop.

One might leave that interpretation as it stands, and add it to the charges of unrealism at the feet of the new-Keynesian model, or at least dramatic change from old-Keynesian intuition that it was designed to formalize. But there is a more charitable and useful way to regard the new-Keynesian model, which brings aggregate demand back to the underlying story for inflation, and offers a unifying view. The pure multiple equilibrium view follows by erasing the government debt valuation equation from the analysis. But the government debt valuation equation is still there. The equilibrium selection policy disturbance—a decline in the inflation target π_t^*—must occasion a fiscal contraction, $\varepsilon_{\Sigma s, t+1} = -\Delta E_{t+1} \pi_{t+1}$, which leads to a decrease in aggregate demand. Contrariwise, if this "passive" fiscal contraction does not or cannot happen, the unexpected inflation cannot happen. Really, answering the question of this section, the monetary policy shock lowers inflation *because* it induces a fiscal contraction, and only because it induces a fiscal contraction.

Thus, one can interpret the new-Keynesian model response more simply: The central bank lowers its inflation target π_t^*. The fiscal authorities "passively" raise taxes to validate the lower inflation target, to pay off nominal bonds at the lower inflation. The lower aggregate demand resulting from the fiscal contraction pushes prices down. Monetary policy is a carrot in front of the fiscal horse, and the fiscal horse pulls the inflation cart.

This story gives, I think, a much more coherent description of the new-Keynesian model mechanism. Inflation *is* too much money chasing too many goods, aggregate demand caused by a flight from government debt. It is not just a jump between equally plausible equilibria, followed by a fiscal mopping-up operation.

In this view, however, there really is nothing *but* fiscal theory. Central bank equilibrium-selection policy works, if and only if it can force the treasury to the needed fiscal expansion or contraction. But the hyperinflation threat $\phi(\pi_t - \pi_t^*)$ seems even more unbelievable as a mechanism for the central bank to play a game of chicken to force the treasury to take fiscal action.

16.8   A Full Model and the Lower Bound

I present a full nonlinear model. Figure 16.2 plots the set of equilibria. The previous linearized analysis bears out near the active equilibrium Π^*. The zero bound forces us to consider another equilibrium Π_L. This equilibrium must violate the Taylor principle, with multiple locally bounded equilibria. In turn, the multiple equilibria to the left of Π^*, though not locally bounded, do not explode, reducing further any reason to rule them out. Consideration of the full nonlinear model only makes multiplicity worse.

One may worry that my simple example (16.1)–(16.3) is linearized and not fully spelled out. Let's write down a full model, and make sure there is not some left-out ingredient. (Here I simplify standard sources, in part to emphasize agreement on these points: Benhabib, Schmitt-Grohé, and Uribe (2001b), Benhabib, Schmitt-Grohé, and Uribe (2002), and Woodford (2003) Chapter 2.4 starting p. 123, and Chapter 4.4, starting on p. 311. This discussion is based on Cochrane (2011a).)

The setup is the same as the complete frictionless model of Section 2. The interest rate and inflation conform to the nonlinear Fisher relation,

$$\frac{1}{1+i_t} = \beta E_t\left(\frac{P_t}{P_{t+1}}\right) = \frac{1}{1+r}E_t\left(\frac{1}{\Pi_{t+1}}\right). \tag{16.25}$$

Equilibrium also requires our friend,

$$\frac{B_{t-1}}{P_t} = \sum_{j=0}^{\infty} \beta^j E_t\left(s_{t+j}\right). \tag{16.26}$$

The Fisher equation (16.25) and the government debt valuation equation (16.26) are the only two conditions that need to be satisfied for the price sequence $\{P_t\}$ to represent an equilibrium. The equilibrium is not yet *unique*, in that many different price or inflation paths will work. We need some specification of monetary and fiscal policy to determine the price level.

New-Keynesian analysis specifies a passive fiscal regime. Government surpluses s_{t+j} adjust so that the government debt valuation equation (16.26) holds given any price level. (See Woodford (2003), p. 124.) Yes, solutions of the simple model consisting of a Fisher equation and a Taylor rule (16.1)–(16.2), as I studied above, do in fact represent the full set of linearized equilibrium conditions of this explicit model. My linearized model didn't leave anything out.

To keep the equations as simple as possible, simplify further to perfect foresight equilibria, so that initial inflation Π_0 is the only indeterminacy. Write the interest rate policy rule

$$1 + i_t = (1+r)\Phi(\Pi_t); \quad \Pi_t \equiv P_t/P_{t-1}. \tag{16.27}$$

$\Phi(\cdot)$ is a function allowing nonlinear policy rules. With perfect foresight, the consumer's first-order condition (16.25) reduces to

$$\Pi_{t+1} = \beta(1 + i_t). \tag{16.28}$$

We are looking for solutions to the pair (16.27) and (16.28). As before, we substitute out the interest rate and study inflation dynamics,

$$\Pi_{t+1} = \Phi(\Pi_t). \tag{16.29}$$

This is the nonlinear, global (i.e., not local), perfect foresight version of the $E_t\pi_{t+1} = \phi\pi_t$ equilibrium condition of the last section. Figure 16.2 plots dynamics (16.29).

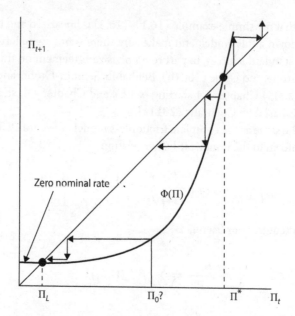

FIGURE 16.2. Dynamics in a Perfect Foresight new-Keynesian Model

The steady-state Π^* has $\Phi'(\Pi^*) > 1$. This is a region of local instability. The equilibrium Π^* is a unique "locally bounded" equilibrium because any Π_t that is ε above or below Π^* leads away from Π^*.

Nonlinearity and global solutions make one big difference: We must respect the zero bound on nominal interest rates. Consumers can hold money, and negative nominal interest rates offer arbitrage between bonds and cash. From (16.28), the bound $i \geq 0$ means we cannot have $\Pi_{t+1} \leq \beta$. Thus, the function $\Phi(\Pi)$ must also have another stationary point, labeled Π_L. This stationary point must be stable, with $\Phi'(\Pi_L) < 1$. Many paths lead to Π_L and there are "multiple local equilibria" near this point.

Yes, the unstable Π^* is the "good" equilibrium and the stable Π_L is the "bad" equilibrium, which authors try to remove. "Stability" near Π_L, which you might think a good thing, comes with "indeterminacy," multiple equilibria.

All of the paths graphed in Figure 16.2 are perfect foresight equilibria. Since these paths satisfy the policy rule and the consumer's first-order conditions by construction, all that remains is to check that they satisfy the government debt valuation formula (16.26). We check that there is a set of ex post lump-sum taxes with which that formula holds, and hence that consumer's transversality condition is satisfied. There are lots of ways the government can implement such a policy. We only need to exhibit one: If the government simply sets net taxes in response to the price level as

$$s_t = \frac{r}{1+r} \frac{B_{t-1}}{P_t}, \qquad (16.30)$$

then the real value of government debt is constant, and the valuation formula holds. (This is a particular case of the specification $s_t = \gamma (B_{t-1}/P_t)$ that produces passive fiscal policy.)

To see why this is true, start with the flow condition that proceeds of new debt sales plus taxes equals old debt redemption,

$$\frac{B_t}{1 + i_t} + P_t s_t = B_{t-1}.$$

With $1 + i_t = (1 + r)P_{t+1}/P_t$, this expression can be rearranged to track the real value of the debt,

$$\frac{B_t}{P_{t+1}} = (1 + r)\left(\frac{B_{t-1}}{P_t} - s_t\right).$$

Substituting the rule (16.30) we obtain

$$\frac{B_t}{P_{t+1}} = \frac{B_{t-1}}{P_t}.$$

We're done. With constant real debt, the transversality condition holds, and the flow condition implies the present value (16.26).

Overall, you can see that this explicit, complete, and exact model verifies the conclusions we drew from the simple linearized version in the vicinity of Π^*.

The nonlinear model and a global view make the equilibrium selection problems *worse*, however, because now we have the second, stable, steady-state Π_L. Deflationary equilibria that start anywhere below Π^* and approach Π_L are also valid equilibria, as is Π_L itself. Equilibria that start below Π^* do not lead to explosive deflation, but instead trundle down gently to the zero bound.

If $\Pi^* = 2\%$, for example, and the real interest rate is $r = 1\%$, then we have to rule out paths that start at $\Pi_t = 1.99\%$ and drift down to $\Pi_t = -1\%$, $i_t = 0\%$, and stay there. Well, these equilibria are "nonlocal" to $\Pi^* = 2\%$, since -1% is outside an ε interval of $\Pi = 2\%$. But that seems like a poor reason to rule them out, especially given the experience during the 2010s, a long period of near-zero interest rates with low inflation. And if negative real interest rates endure, Π_L may occur at, say, 1% inflation, only one percentage point below the 2% target, corresponding to a -1% real rate.

These equilibria are "globally bounded," though not "locally bounded around Π^*." We have to modify the equilibrium selection rule to rule out "non-locally bounded" equilibria around Π^*, and somehow to rule out also the multiple locally bounded equilibria around Π_L.

The criticism that no central bank follows a rule such as $\Phi(\Pi)$ remains. In the downward direction, it is no longer an explosive threat, but a commitment to drive inflation down to the zero bound, from Π^* to Π_L, as an equilibrium selection threat to enforce $\Pi = \Pi^*$. Central banks seemed rather desperate to *increase* inflation in the 2010s, with inflation running below target, rather than to deliberately drive inflation down. One might say we observed such a drift, but that would undermine the argument that such equilibria are so unpleasant that the economy would avoid them in the first place.

But even if central banks were to threaten such paths, and people were to believe them, the argument that something is wrong with the path and needs to be ruled out as an equilibrium is much weaker than the argument that something is wrong with an explosively deflationary equilibrium.

In recent years, many economists have advocated eliminating cash, so that central banks can impose arbitrarily negative overnight interest rates. (For example, Kimball (2020), Rogoff (2017).) This move might allow a rule with global instability $\Phi'(\Pi)$. However, none of those advocating negative rates have made this argument. The negative 50%, negative 100% and more interest rates that a globally unstable rule would require are beyond anything advocated by authors who argue for negative interest rates. Their argument is entirely for the stimulative possibilities of an interest rate policy with small observed equilibrium negative interest rates, not for an unobserved threat of immensely negative interest rates as an equilibrium selection policy.

16.9   Identification Patches

I survey attempts to overcome the nonidentification of the equilibrium selection rule. Each must tie equilibrium selection threats to some observable behavior. On examination, the assumptions don't make sense.

Observational equivalence and nonidentification mean that attempts to test one category of theory versus another must include identifying assumptions, and we should look carefully to understand and evaluate those identifying assumptions.

Nonidentification of the Taylor principle parameter ϕ in new-Keynesian models has important empirical consequences. For example, Clarida, Galí, and Gertler (2000) is one of the most important pieces of evidence for the new-Keynesian model. They estimate policy rules by regression. They find that the cumulative inflation response ϕ was below 1 in the 1970s, and rose to greater than 1 in the 1980s. They interpret this finding via a new-Keynesian model. They conclude that the economy shifted from indeterminate to determinate; that the volatile inflation of the 1970s came from multiple equilibrium $\phi < 1$ volatility, and this volatility was eliminated in the 1980s by shifting to active $\phi > 1$ policy. But since they measure a regression between observable equilibrium quantities i^* and π^*, their regression does not measure the central stability parameter ϕ of their model. The model parameter ϕ is not identified. The parameter ϕ represents an off-equilibrium threat not seen in equilibrium. This most classic estimate, though it establishes an interesting correlation in the data, does not, in fact, measure the structural parameter ϕ and thereby provide evidence in favor of the new-Keynesian model.

Now, identification is a property of a model, not of data. Clarida, Galí, and Gertler's regressions measure something. The question is, what parameter of which model do they measure? In my simple example, a regression of interest rate on inflation measures η, the persistence parameter of the monetary policy shock. Such a regression can identify the parameter ϕ in old-Keynesian models, where $\phi > 1$ brings stability. One may interpret the Clarida, Galí, and Gertler (2000) estimate in the light of the old-Keynesian model, to say that the Fed brought inflation stability from instability. One may interpret their estimate in light of the fiscal theory of monetary policy model, in which it can estimate the reaction of interest rates to inflation, subject only to the usual worries about error correlations. Add a different introduction and model, and all is well. But the regressions do not identify the ϕ of the new-Keynesian model, and we cannot take them as evidence for a new-Keynesian parameter $\phi > 1$ in the later period, or a victory of determinacy over indeterminacy, which was their objective.

This lack of identification pervades new-Keynesian empirical work. For example, the influential Smets and Wouters (2007) new-Keynesian model restricts the estimate of ϕ a priori to be greater than 1. The prior and posterior for the inflation response of monetary policy ϕ are nearly identical (Figure 1C p. 1147). The estimate is $\phi = 1.68$ relative to a prior mean of $\phi = 1.70$, suggesting that the policy rule parameters are at best weakly identified, even in a local sense (restricting $\phi > 1$).

One can of course identify anything by sufficient assumptions. For example, Giannoni and Woodford (2005) identify the policy rule parameters including ϕ by assuming that 1) the monetary policy disturbance $\varepsilon_{i,t}$ is i.i.d. and not predictable by any variables at time $t-1$, nor correlated with other shocks to the model; 2) the Fed does not react to expected future output, or wage or price inflation, or other state variables; 3) wages, prices, and output are fixed a period in advance. These are all unrealistic assumptions. Disturbances are persistent. Central banks deviate from rules for years at a time. The Fed reacts to expectations about the future, and wages and prices move within a quarter.

The logic of the new-Keynesian model is that some state variable must jump coincidentally with any shock, jumping the economy to the unique equilibrium that now (after the shock) does not explode, just as π_t jumps coincident with u_t in the simple model. If inflation π_t cannot jump, say if it is fixed one quarter in advance, then some other state variable must jump. Giannoni and Woodford (2005) assume that the central bank does not respond to that state variable.

One must achieve identification by tying the unmeasurable, unobserved behavior $i_t - i_t^* = \phi(\pi_t - \pi_t^*)$ to something observable. We could assume that if our parent has a glass of wine with dinner, then no spinach will be followed by no dessert. We measure a glass of wine, kids eating spinach, and conclude that the no-dessert threat did the trick. But there is no way to verify the assumption, especially with no confirming narrative evidence: The parent never audibly threatens no dessert, nor ties it to wine. We can, however, ask if the restriction is reasonable, if it is consistent with policy statements, rules, traditional norms, and the other range of evidence we have about central bank behavior.

If we write the policy rule

$$i_t = \theta \pi_t^* + \phi(\pi_t - \pi_t^*) + u_t,$$

we see that the identifying assumptions that let us measure ϕ start with $\theta = \phi$. The central bank reacts to inflation *in equilibrium* θ the same way that it reacts to *deviations from* equilibrium, or jumps to other equilibria, ϕ. That's an assumption, and it helps to identify ϕ, but is it a reasonable assumption? The parameter θ describes interest rate policy. It governs the correlation between interest rate and inflation in equilibrium. Its purpose is to minimize inflation and output variation in that equilibrium. The parameter ϕ describes equilibrium selection policy. Its purpose is to induce explosive dynamics and thereby scare the economy away from multiple equilibria. With such utterly different purposes and mechanism it is hard to think of a reason to tie the two parameters together.

We also need assumptions on the properties of u_t, since everything else can be swept in or out of that disturbance. The parameter ϕ is also identified if there is no disturbance in the policy rule $i_t = \phi \pi_t$ and there are shocks to other equations leading to some volatility in the right-hand variable π_t. This assumption also ties unobservable behavior to observable behavior, by assuming that the off-equilibrium reaction $(i_t - i_t^*) = \phi(\pi_t - \pi_t^*)$ is the same as the on-equilibrium relation $i_t^* = \theta \pi_t^*$, as well as by assuming no shock. But there really is no reason to make either assumption. There are always disturbances—no policy rule fits with 100% R^2.

We might try to assume that monetary policy disturbances u_t are orthogonal to disturbances to the other equations of the model, and those disturbances move inflation. Giannoni and Woodford (2005) is a case of this general idea. In $i_t = \phi \pi_t + u_t$, that assumption could give us an instrument, a movement in π_t orthogonal to the shock u_t. But why should the central bank not respond by deviating from the rule in response to other shocks, or to inflation resulting from such shocks? Optimal monetary policy (minimizing output and inflation variance) directs the central bank to respond to all shocks, to set u_t in response to other shocks in the economy. Written in the equivalent form $i_t = i_t^* + \phi(\pi_t - \pi_t^*)$, the "stochastic intercept" of the policy rule should respond to other shocks. Real central banks clearly describe *all* of their actions, especially deviations from policy rules, as responses to other shocks. Moreover, extending the $\theta = \phi$ argument, why should the central bank's rule respond to inflation that results from other shocks in the same way that it responds to inflation that results from multiple equilibria?

One may respond that "well, all identification involves assumptions," which is true. But most of the time in economics we are trying to identify things that are in principle measurable. Identifying a supply curve, and how firms would behave away from equilibrium prices, is hard because the data are driven by both supply and demand shocks. If the supply shocks would be quiet for a minute, or if we could isolate demand shocks that do not move the supply curve, we could measure the supply curve. And it is sensible to assume that suppliers respond in the same way to "off-equilibrium" prices provoked by price controls as they do to "equilibrium" prices provoked by a shift in the demand curve. But we are trying to measure something that is inherently unmeasurable, as in equilibrium there are no movements away from equilibrium. Here, there is less reason to tie in-equilibrium to off-equilibrium responses. And most of the time, identification assumptions and the behavior they isolate are somewhat plausible, which they are not here. The first lesson of a good econometrics class is that you may not simply write down "We assume that ε is orthogonal to x," you must state what are the economic forces that drive variation in x and ε and why it is sensible to believe them orthogonal.

Identification can use information other than parameter and statistical assumptions. We have a lot of information beyond the time series behavior of equilibrium quantities, including narrative, historical, legal, and institutional information. That information can tell us a lot about believable off-equilibrium behavior, as captured by parameters ϕ and γ.

16.10   Equilibrium Selection Patches

That the new-Keynesian model suffers multiple equilibria, that $\phi > 1$ with a rule against nonlocal equilibria is not a completely satisfactory answer, is now a well-known problem.

It has attracted an enormous number of attempts to fix it, while retaining the passive fiscal policy assumption that wipes out the government debt valuation equation.

Broadly, authors add restrictions to the definition of equilibrium or they add to the policy specification. It turns out to be harder to rule out equilibria than it appears. The government must basically threaten to blow up the economy in alternative equilibria. But the government does not threaten to blow up the economy, people do not expect the government to do so, the government will not choose to do so ex post, there are no institutions committing the government to do so, and in the conventional writing of policy the government *cannot* exercise these threats. (This section draws on the broader discussion in Cochrane (2011a).)

16.10.1   *Reasonable Expectations and Minimum State Variables*

Woodford argues that it is unreasonable for people to expect hyperinflation or deflation, so multiple equilibria should not break out. But what is unreasonable in our world is not so unreasonable in the model. McCallum argues for a "minimum state variable" criterion, which rules out multiple equilibria generically.

Why should we rule out inflationary or deflationary equilibria? Woodford (2003) (p. 128) argues that expectations should "coordinate" on the locally unique equilibrium, Π^* in Figure 16.2:

> The equilibrium $[\Pi^*]$ ... is nonetheless *locally* unique, which may be enough to allow expectations to coordinate upon that equilibrium rather than on one of the others.

Moreover,

> The equilibria that involve initial inflation rates near (but not equal to) Π^* can only occur as a result of expectations of *future* inflation rates (at least in some states) that are even *further* from the target inflation rate. Thus the economy can only move to one of these alternative paths if expectations about the future change significantly, something that one may suppose would not easily occur.

Similarly, King (2000) (p. 58–59) writes:

> By specifying $[\phi > 1]$ then, the monetary authority would be saying, 'if inflation deviates from the neutral level, then the nominal interest rate will be increased relative to the level which it would be at under a neutral monetary policy.' If this statement is believed, then it may be enough to convince the private sector that the inflation and output will actually take on its neutral level.

These paragraphs echo the fundamental role of equilibrium selection policy in the new-Keynesian model. The threat to raise inflation in response to current inflation is a coordinating device among multiple equilibria, not the conventional story by which higher interest rates lower aggregate demand.

But this logic seems a rather weak foundation for the basic economic question, what determines the price level? Is economics on its own really incapable of answering that question? Is there *no* simple supply and demand underlying the price level on which models can build?

Woodford has a point. We should read people's actions from expectation of the future to action today, not the other way around. It does seem unlikely that people wake up one morning and believe, with no other news, that a hyperinflation is coming in 10 years, so they should raise prices just a little today. It's a good deal more plausible that they wake up and decide that another slide to the zero bound is coming so they should lower prices just a little today, but even that case requires a bigger shift in expectations about the future than today's change.

But if we are to appeal to common intuition about reasonable beliefs, we have to separate reasonable beliefs of people who live in this model from reasonable beliefs of people who live in our world, from which intuition springs. In this model, the central bank is committed to react to inflation by driving the economy to hyperinflation, introducing instability. In this model, expected increases in interest rates raise expected inflation. If people lived in the world of this model, a belief that hyperinflation could suddenly arise seems pretty reasonable.

Our world and our central banks are populated by people who think that the central bank will respond to unexpectedly higher inflation by lowering subsequent inflation, through largely old-Keynesian logic. If that is our world, people are indeed unlikely to wake up and think hyperinflation is coming. If fiscal theory underlies price level determination, then people are also unlikely to wake up believing there will be a hyperinflation or deflation with no fiscal or discount rate news. But these are not the worlds of this model, so one cannot appeal to intuition formed in these worlds to say that such a belief is unreasonable in the world of the new-Keynesian model.

In a series of papers, summarized in McCallum (2003), McCallum argues for a related minimum state variable (MSV) criterion to pick from multiple equilibria. Endogenous variables in an economic model should only depend on the fundamental state variables of that model.

This criterion is a good technique for finding solutions to complex models, especially when state variables are Markovian; that is, state variables today capture all one needs to know about their expected future values. Look for $x_t = f(z_t)$ where z_t is a list of the state variables. This "method of undetermined coefficients" is often much easier than the matrix solution method, as I exposit in Online Appendix Section A1.5.

The minimum state variable criterion rules out the explosive and sunspot solutions of this model. In the simple linearized model of Section 16.1, the only exogenous variable is the monetary policy disturbance u_t, and it contains all information about future exogenous states of the economy. Hence, the minimum state variable criterion says to pick $\pi_t = f(u_t)$. The only such solution is the "locally bounded" choice (16.6) $\pi_t = -u_t/(\phi - \eta)$.

The minimum state variable and coordinated expectations ideas are related. The minimum state variable criterion argues that reasonable expectations of future inflation should be functions of underlying state variables, thus ruling out sunspot equilibria. However, McCallum (2003) (p. 1154) states that his proposal does not apply to selecting among nominal indeterminacies, and only applies to models with multiple real paths. Therefore, it appears that it does not apply to the frictionless models, but only to later models with nominal–real interactions.

Both of these approaches add something else to *economics*, to the definition of equilibrium, as the rule against nonlocal equilibria adds something to the economic definition of equilibria. If accepted, those principles should logically be applied to all models, not just as a patch for these models' pathologies. Such a program has far-reaching implications, as multiple equilibria and sunspots are often revealing and useful economic models. Multiple equilibrium models of bank runs such as Diamond and Dybvig (1983) and of doom-loop sovereign debt crises would have to go. One should be wary of far-reaching fixes for narrow problems. Do we really have to modify economics so fundamentally in order to determine the price level? If we are not willing to apply fundamental changes broadly, do we really take the model seriously? Most of all, again, is there really no simple, supply and demand, Walrasian equilibrium model of the price level?

To be clear, my point is not to defend as reasonable the multiple explosive equilibria generated by the simple model with $\phi > 1$. My point is that *if* the simple model were true, and if central banks acted this way, then we should take seriously these multiple explosive equilibria. Since we agree that the multiple explosive equilibria don't make a lot of sense, I conclude that the simple new-Keynesian model with $\phi > 1$ is wrong.

16.10.2   Stabilizations and Threats

I survey attempts to cut off multiple equilibria by adapting proposals to stop hyperinflations or deflations, by switching to a money growth target, commodity standards, or similar means. If an inflation breaks out, and the government stops it, that path remains an equilibrium. In fact, it is now more plausible.

These proposals in fact stop equilibria by specifying a period of inconsistent policy, in which equilibrium can't form. They are "blow up the world" threats. But it is not plausible that governments would do such a thing, or even that they can do such a thing.

Why not just blow up the world directly, rather than as part of an otherwise sensible stabilization? That these proposals modify sensible proposals to stop or stabilize inflations reveals a source of confusion about new-Keynesian models.

The next set of suggestions add something else beyond $i = \phi (\pi - \pi^*)$ to the policy regime in order to try to prune multiple equilibria, while maintaining passive fiscal policy and the conventional set of equilibrium selection rules.

These approaches adapt common ideas for stopping hyperinflations, deflations, or liquidity traps. If an inflation or disinflation breaks out, governments switch to another policy regime, including a money growth target, a commodity standard or foreign exchange peg, or an active fiscal regime, in order to stop the inflation or deflation. Examples include Woodford (2003) Section 4.3, Atkeson, Chari, and Kehoe (2010), Minford and Srinivasan (2011), and Christiano and Takahashi (2018).

It's a natural idea: Speculative inflations and deflations are the problem. If we add off-the-shelf policy prescriptions to stop inflations and deflations, we should solve the problem, no?

No. If a multiple-equilibrium inflation or deflation breaks out, and if the government successfully stops the inflation or deflation by these means, and is expected to do so, then the inflation or deflation and its end remain an equilibrium path. If anything, such proposals make multiple-equilibrium matters worse. To the extent that the prospect of never-ending hyperinflation or a perpetual liquidity trap made expectations of such events "unreasonable," or "coordinated" expectations against them, expectations that the government would likely stop the inflation or deflation make the paths more reasonable for people to expect in the first place.

To stop a multiple-equilibrium inflation or disinflation from breaking out in the first place, one must change the policy configuration so that the equilibrium cannot form. Policy must be such that private sector first-order conditions, budget constraints, or market clearing conditions are violated along the equilibrium path that we wish to rule out.

That is exactly what these proposals do, if you read very carefully and with this logic in mind. There is at least one period T of overlap between inflation and its stabilization, in which the central bank commits *both* to an interest rate rule $i_T = \phi \pi_T$ with still high π_T, requiring a high nominal interest rate, *and* to a low money growth target, a commodity standard, or active fiscal policy, to lower π_{T+1}, which requires a low nominal interest rate i_T or low money growth. Since the interest rate and money growth cannot be simultaneously high and low, since an interest rate target and an inconsistent money growth target or commodity standard cannot coexist, "equilibrium cannot form" in such periods. In a rational expectations dynamic economy, the equilibrium path leading to this event cannot then form either.

It is these periods of inconsistent policy that rule out the equilibrium, not the underlying idea of stopping an inflation or deflation on which the proposals build. Stopping inflation does not need inconsistent policy. If the government separates by one period the inflation and its stabilization, then the inflation is stopped, and equilibrium can form each period on the way. That's how inflations *are* stopped, with no period in which equilibrium "doesn't form" along the way. Conversely, to rule out an equilibrium, there is no need to appeal to the memory of policies that stop and stabilize inflations and deflations. Just set an inconsistent policy somewhere along the undesired equilibrium path.

Atkeson, Chari, and Kehoe (2010) recognize this fact, and offer a range of "sophisticated" policies to trim multiple equilibria without the smokescreen of induced inflations and inflation stabilization policy changes. The swifter and more severe the threat, the more likely it is to succeed. Rather than respond to an undesired equilibrium by gently leading the economy by $\phi > 1$ to an inflationary region, promise a cure by a money growth rule or other reform, but then blow up the economy at a roadside stop along the way; the government can simply threaten the economy with an immediate explosion should the wrong equilibrium appear.

The objections to these proposals are natural. What does it mean for a government to set policy so that "equilibrium cannot form?" Presumably it means that all economic activity stops? Even reversion to barter is an equilibrium of sorts. This sort of policy is a threat to blow up the world, or crash the economy, à la Dr. Strangelove. (In the movie, the Soviets devise a bomb that will destroy the world, including themselves, in the event of attack.)

But what government on earth would ex post embark on a policy so draconian that "no equilibrium can form," whatever that means? Carrying out such a threat is disastrous for the government's objectives. Therefore, ex ante, there is little reason for people to believe such threats. And our central banks and governments emphatically do not make such threats. They promise to stop and stabilize inflations, always to rescue the economy, not to set policy so "no equilibrium can form."

Is it even *possible* for the central bank or government to follow a policy that forces people to violate first-order conditions, markets not to clear, for equilibrium not to form? What would actually happen if the central bank were to announce simultaneously an interest rate target requiring high money growth and a money growth target demanding low money growth, or an interest rate target together with an inconsistent commodity standard requiring free exchange of money for the commodity? One instrument cannot achieve two targets, especially when the targets are far apart.

We usually think of governments acting in markets, just like everyone else. Governments may have monopoly powers, but even monopolies must respect demand curves and budget constraints. In the Ramsey tradition, most public finance studies government policy settings, taking private first-order conditions and market clearing as *constraints* on the government's policies. If the central bank wants to raise interest rates, it must respect the money demand curve—set an interest rate and provide money as demanded, or set money supply and accept the market interest rate. It is simply impossible for the central bank to simultaneously target interest rates and money supply in a way that violates the money demand curve. It is simply impossible for a Ramsey government to set policy so "equilibrium cannot form," just as it is impossible for you, me, or even a great monopoly to act in such a way. If it's *impossible* for the central bank to set policy so no equilibrium can form, as well as disastrous for its objectives, it seems even more dubious that people would expect such a thing, and hence rule the inflationary path out of their expectations.

Moreover, these are at best proposals for how some future central bank might act, not proposals for how we model our central banks, our governments, expectations people have now, or any sample period we may study. So proposals involving setting policy so "equilibrium cannot form" are not useful for studying history, data, or current policy choices.

In this whole literature, I am puzzled why there is so much attention to and controversy over equilibrium selection policies that our governments clearly do not follow. "Indeterminacy could be fixed if central banks changed policy to x" does not solve the problem of a model's indeterminacy in describing our current world and data.

In retrospect, the approach is puzzling. If the government, to rule out equilibria, makes some threat to blow up the world, why do authors write models in which such threats are buried in the timing of perfectly sensible policies to stop hyperinflations while keeping the world going, or even while minimizing output losses of the stabilization? Why talk about stopping hyperinflations at all? Well, the objective was not so clear when the papers were written. The difference between curing a hyperinflation and ruling out a hyperinflationary equilibrium is subtle. Again, understanding what the equations say is hard. But with the clear understanding of hindsight, we can say the effort fails.

Here are some specific examples. Woodford (2003) Section 4.3, p. 138, studies proposals to cut off inflationary equilibria to the right of Π^* in Figure 16.2:

> self-fulfilling inflations may be excluded through the addition of policy provisions that apply only in the case of hyperinflation. For example, Obstfeld and Rogoff (1986) propose that the central bank commit itself to peg the value of the monetary unit in terms of some real commodity by standing ready to exchange the commodity for money in the event that the real value of the total money supply ever shrinks to a certain very low level. If it is assumed that this level of real balances is one that would never be reached except in the case of a self-fulfilling inflation, the commitment has no effect except to exclude such paths as possible equilibria. . . . [This proposal could] well be added as a hyperinflation provision in a regime that otherwise follows a Taylor rule.

Obstfeld and Rogoff study models with a money growth target, not an interest rate target, so I defer a detailed description of their proposal. Here, let's think about whether reversion to commodity standard can trim equilibria under interest rate rules.

A backup commodity standard could certainly *stop* an inflation. But stopping the inflation does not rule out the inflationary equilibrium path and its end. Inflation rises, the government switches to gold, inflation stops. That commitment alone would not "exclude such paths as possible equilibria." The key in Woodford's quote must therefore be "otherwise follows a Taylor rule." If a government continues to follow the Taylor rule (Taylor principle, really) requiring high nominal interest rates, even after it has switched to a commodity standard that requires low nominal interest rates, then yes, no equilibrium can form. But how *could* a government both "stand ready to exchange the commodity for money," at a fixed rate, while also following an interest rate target by providing whatever money people want at the target interest rate? Even if it did work as a matter of theory, our central banks do not make such a commitment. Reversion to a gold standard in the event of inflation, with 100% reserves capable of soaking up the entire money stock, is not on the agenda, and is not expected. So it too is at best a proposal for future central banks, not a proposal one can appeal to in the analysis of current data or policies.

Atkeson, Chari, and Kehoe (2010), Minford and Srinivasan (2011), and Christiano and Takahashi (2018) give more explicit examples. In these papers, the central bank follows an active interest rate target, $i_t = \phi \pi_t$, $\phi > 1$, until inflation exceeds bounds $[\pi_L, \pi_U]$. When inflation exceeds those bounds, the government reverts to a money growth rule. They model an economy with constant velocity and hence money demand $M_t V = P_t y$. The central bank operates by setting the money supply in both interest rate target and money growth regimes.

Now, how does that policy configuration *rule out* multiple equilibria, rather than just stop, and thus solve, their inflations? Let period T be the first period in which inflation exceeds the upper bound π_U. During this period, the central bank follows an active interest rate target $i_T = \phi \pi_T$, $\phi > 1$, which requires a high nominal interest rate, *at the same time* as it implements the money growth rule $M_{T+1}/M_T = \mu = \Pi_{T+1}$, which lowers inflation Π_{T+1} and thus implies a low nominal interest rate i_T.

Well, that is indeed a policy configuration for which no equilibrium can form. One may say "agents cannot satisfy their intertemporal optimization condition," since a very high interest rate $i_T = \phi \pi_T$ is inconsistent with a low inflation $\mu = \pi_{T+1}$ and the condition $i_T = r + \pi_{T+1}$. One might equally say that agents satisfy intertemporal optimization, but agents cannot satisfy their money demand equation, or one might say that the economy cannot satisfy market clearing conditions. In any case, an equilibrium cannot form at period T, and therefore the inflationary path leading to T is not an equilibrium.

But just how could the central bank do it? How could a central bank, with one instrument, the money supply $\{M_T, M_{T+1}\}$, simultaneously set i_T to a large level and π_{T+1} to a low level? Perhaps the right view is that this path is impossible, not because the private sector is off a market clearing condition, but because it is impossible for the government to execute the specified policy path. That view does not make it a particularly effective threat!

In addition to the usual complaints, our central banks do not follow money growth rules, arguably cannot do so in the face of rampant financial innovation and abundant liquid assets, and velocity is interest elastic. With interest elastic money demand, a constant money growth rule leaves just as many indeterminacies as the interest rate rule, covered in Section 19.2 and following. So the solution of switching to money growth rules doubly does not and cannot apply to the actual economies we study. It doesn't even stop inflation, let alone rule out the equilibrium path.

16.10.3   Fiscal Equilibrium Trimming

A second group of proposals tries to trim equilibria by fiscal means: helicopter drops of money, deliberately unbacked fiscal expansions, or a contingent switch to fiscal theory. Again, if an inflation or deflation breaks out, and is stopped by fiscal means, then the inflation and its aftermath remain valid equilibrium paths. Again, the equilibria are ruled out by a period of inconsistent policy that blows up the economy.

Benhabib, Schmitt-Grohé, and Uribe (2002), mirrored in Woodford (2003) Section 4.2, try to trim equilibria by adding fiscal commitments to the Taylor rule. Their ideas are aimed at trimming deflationary liquidity trap equilibria that converge to Π_L in Figure 16.2, but the same ideas could apply to inflations as well, since hyperinflations are also stopped by fiscal reforms.

These proposals are inspired by many policy proposals to exit liquidity traps: helicopter drops of money and unbacked fiscal expansions. But here too, proposals that *fix* a liquidity trap do not *rule out* the trap or the equilibria leading to and out of the trap. If the government successfully exits a liquidity trap, that trap, and the inflation path leading to it, remains a valid equilibrium. The fix makes matters worse, because now there is less reason to disregard equilibria that lead to the trap. To *rule out* the trap and equilibria leading to it, one must specify an *inconsistent* policy; a policy regime so that no equilibrium can form somewhere along the path. It is the inconsistent policy, not the trap exit policy, that does the work.

Benhabib, Schmitt-Grohé, and Uribe (2002) specify that in low inflation states, near Π_L of Figure 16.2, the government switches to active fiscal policy. The government lowers taxes, real debt grows explosively, the consumer's transversality condition is violated, and the government debt valuation equation no longer holds at the original low price level.

Specifically, (their equations (18)–(20)) in a neighborhood of Π_L, the government commits to surpluses $s_t = \theta(\Pi_t)\,(B_{t-1}/P_t)$ with $\theta(\Pi_L) < 0$ in place of a passive rule such as $s_t = \gamma B_{t-1}/P_t$. They also suggest a target for the growth rate of nominal liabilities, a "4% rule" for nominal debt. If deflation breaks out with such a commitment, real debt explodes, violating the consumer's transversality condition. Woodford suggests this implementation as well (p. 132): "Let total nominal government liabilities D_t be specified to grow at a constant rate $\bar{\mu} > 1$ while monetary policy is described by the Taylor rule . . ." Since the resulting model does not work, he concludes, "Thus, in the case of an appropriate fiscal policy rule, a deflationary trap is not a possible rational expectations equilibrium."

These proposals are inspired by sensible and time-honored prescriptions to inflate the economy out of a liquidity trap. Benhabib, Schmitt-Grohé, and Uribe (2002) describe them this way (p. 548):

this type of policy prescription is what the U.S. Treasury and a large number of academic and professional economists are advocating as a way for Japan to lift itself out of its current deflationary trap. . . A decline in taxes increases the household's after-tax wealth, which induces an aggregate excess demand for goods. With aggregate supply fixed, the price level must increase in order to reestablish equilibrium in the goods market.

Zero interest rates and $1.5 trillion deficits soon followed in the 2008 recession, and larger and apparently more unbacked deficits in 2020–2021. This quote is, indeed, how a coordinated active fiscal regime works; it is good intuition for operation of the fiscal theory of the price level, and it is a good reading of what real-world proponents of these policies have in mind.

But that's *not* their, or Woodford's, equilibrium selection proposal. The point of their proposal is *not* to "lift the economy out of a deflationary trap" back to Π^*. The point of their proposal is for the economy to sit Π_L with an uncoordinated policy and to let government debt explode, violating a consumer optimization condition, so the economy cannot drift down to the liquidity trap Π_L in the first place. If their proposal *did* successfully steer the economy back to Π^*, then the whole path to Π_L and back would be an equilibrium. How do they rule out the equilibrium? In fact, Benhabib, Schmitt-Grohé and Uribe change tax policy *while also maintaining the Taylor rule* $\Phi(\Pi)$ and the dynamics of Figure 16.2. The government switches to an active fiscal regime, which demands higher inflation, while simultaneously keeping the interest rate rule in place, which demands continued low inflation. This impossible, inconsistent policy is what rules out the equilibrium.

16.10.4   Threaten Negative Nominal Rates

Why not just threaten substantially negative nominal rates—remove the lower equilibrium Π_L, and keep the active Taylor principle going throughout the negative interest rate range? No equilibrium can form with an arbitrage opportunity. In its cleanliness, this is a logically revealing proposal. Why insist that the government respect the arbitrage condition of money versus bonds, but then add specifications that violate first-order conditions in other dimensions? But it is no more possible or credible.

Once we see that central point, that the government or central bank eliminates multiple equilibria by threatening policies for which "no equilibrium can form," we can think of many monetary–fiscal policies that preclude multiple equilibria equivalently and more transparently. If inflation gets to an undesired level, tax everything. Burn the money stock. Introduce an arbitrage opportunity.

Cleanest of them all, specify a $\Phi(\Pi)$ function that includes negative nominal interest rates, while still allowing cash. Just eliminate the Π_L equilibrium in the first place by straightening out the policy rule in Figure 16.2. Bassetto (2004) suggests this insightful option. Since negative nominal rates introduce an arbitrage opportunity between debt and money, such a $\Phi(\Pi)$ function cleanly rules out deflationary equilibria. The minute we pass the zero bound, no equilibrium can form, and thus paths leading to that point are not equilibria.

In retrospect, why demand a Ramsey approach in setting up the problem—the policy rule must not prescribe negative nominal rates, because that would violate consumer optimality conditions—and then patch it up with policy prescriptions that deliberately *do* violate optimality conditions, budget constraints, or market clearing? Why not just commit to negative nominal rates that violate first-order conditions in the first place?

That would be too clear. We can see that the central bank cannot threaten large negative nominal rates, because the central bank must take private sector optimization as a constraint. But it is no harder to implement steeply negative nominal interest rates than it is to implement the other policies that prevent equilibrium formation. Negative nominal rates are just too obvious about it, rather than sneaking in on the coattails of a sensible stabilization policy. And again, our central banks clearly do not follow this policy, so it does not help us to analyze our economies.

16.10.5   Weird Taylor Rules

The Fed could threaten to blow up the economy by setting inflation to infinity above some value.

Woodford (2003) suggests (p. 136) a policy rule with a stronger threat. He suggests that the graph in Figure 16.2 becomes vertical at some finite inflation Π_U above Π^*, that the central bank will set an infinite interest rate target, promising infinite inflation, in response to a finite inflation, and therefore in finite time. Similarly, Alstadheim and Henderson (2006) remove the Π_L equilibrium by introducing discontinuous policy rules that jump from below to above the 45° line, or V-shaped rules that only touch the 45° line at the Π^* point. The above suggestion from Bassetto (2004) that the policy rule ignore the $i \geq 0$ bound and promise unboundedly negative nominal rates in a deflation also fits in this category.

These proposals blow up the economy directly, and in finite time. If $\phi > 1$ and a steady march to hyperinflation isn't quite enough to eliminate equilibria, then turn up the volume. Hyperinflating away the entire monetary system ($\Phi(\Pi)$ becoming vertical), introducing an arbitrage opportunity (allowing $i < 0$ in the policy rule), and so forth might remove equilibria more effectively.

But all the problems remain. Just how can a central bank set policy so equilibrium cannot form? Would it do so ex post? Does anyone believe our central banks currently do anything like this, so these proposals can rescue use of the models on current data?

16.10.6   Residual Money Demand

In monetary economies, the central bank could threaten infinite inflation indirectly, with finite interest rate targets.

Schmitt-Grohé and Uribe (2000) and Benhabib, Schmitt-Grohé, and Uribe (2001a) add money in such a way that the economy explodes to infinite inflation, despite finite interest rates. Thus, we do not have to appeal to a central bank setting infinite interest rates to generate an economic explosion. This idea is also reviewed by Woodford (2003) (p. 137), and has roots in the literature on hyperinflations with fixed money supply and interest elastic demand.

The idea is easiest to express with money in the utility function, so $u(c_t)$ becomes $u(c_t, M_t/P_t)$. In equilibrium with a constant endowment $c_t = y$, the intertemporal first-order condition becomes

$$1 + i_t = \Pi_{t+1} \frac{u_c(y, M_t/P_t)}{\beta u_c(y, M_{t+1}/P_{t+1})} = \Pi_{t+1}(1 + r_t), \tag{16.31}$$

where r_t denotes the real interest rate. This is a perfect foresight model, so the expectation is missing. Suppose the policy rule is

$$1 + i_t = \frac{1}{\beta}\Phi(\Pi_t).$$

Substituting i_t from this policy rule into (16.31), and expressing the money u_m versus consumption u_c first-order condition as $M_t/P_t = L(y, i_t)$, inflation dynamics follow

$$\Pi_{t+1} = \Phi(\Pi_t)\frac{u_c\left[y, L(y, \Phi(\Pi_{t+1}))\right]}{u_c\left[y, L(y, \Phi(\Pi_t))\right]} \tag{16.32}$$

instead of (16.29), $\Pi_{t+1} = \Phi(\Pi_t)$.

The difference equation (16.32) may rise to require $\Pi_{t+1} = \infty$ above some bound Π_U, even if the policy rule for nominal interest rates $1 + i_t = \Phi(\Pi_t)/\beta$ remains bounded for all Π_t. Woodford (2003) and Schmitt-Grohé and Uribe (2000) give examples of specifications of $u(c, M/P)$ for which this situation can happen.

Is this the answer? First, if we do not regard it reasonable that the central bank will directly hyperinflate the economy (i_t rises to ∞), it is just as unreasonable that the central bank will take the economy to a state in which the economy blows up all on its own—or, most importantly, that people believe such a thing could happen. Infinite inflation and finite nominal interest rates mean infinitely negative real rates; a huge monetary distortion.

Surely people believe the central bank would notice that real interest rates are approaching negative infinity and change its policy rule! This proposal is no different than a rule in which $\Pi_{t+1} = \Phi(\Pi_t)$ blows up the economy in finite time, as the central bank understands the money demand function. Indeed, if we change the definition of Φ to represent the mapping from inflation to future inflation rather than from inflation to interest rates, it is exactly the same. The central bank does whatever it takes to raise future inflation given current inflation.

Second, the proposal is delicate. This approach relies on particular behavior of the utility function or the cash-credit goods specification at very low real money balances. Are monetary frictions really important enough to rule out inflation above a certain limit, sending real rates to negative infinity, or to rule out deflation below another limit? We have seen some astounding hyperinflations such as post-WWI Germany or more recently in Zimbabwe. Real rates did not move with anything like the ten to the big power movements of inflation. At higher and higher inflations, the economy starts to look more and more neutral.

Sims (1994) pursues a similar idea. Perhaps there is a lower limit on *nominal* money demand. Everyone keeps one last penny in the sock drawer, no matter how low the price level and hence how valuable that penny. Then real money holdings explode in a deflation, violating the transversality condition and ruling out a perpetual deflation as an equilibrium.

But perhaps not. Perhaps the government can print any number it wants on bills, or the government runs periodic currency reforms, adding or subtracting zeros, and no longer honoring old currency. Perhaps real money demand is finite for any price level. Perhaps once a penny becomes worth a billion of today's dollars, people will look through their sock drawers and under their couch cushions, and try to spend that one last penny.

Overall, these proposals require two things: First, they require expectations that the government will follow a rule to explosive hyperinflations and deflations. Second, they require belief in a deep-seated monetary nonneutrality sufficient to send real rates to negative infinity or real money demand to infinity, though such events have never been observed, and that the central bank deliberately calibrates its interest rate rule to let this happen, as an equilibrium selection policy.

16.10.7   *Learning and Other Selection Devices*

I briefly discuss "learnability" and other equilibrium selection principles. Since we do not see $\pi \neq \pi^*$ and ϕ is not identified, I argue that the new-Keynesian equilibrium selection rule is not learnable.

Adding some concept of "learnability" on top of the standard Walrasian rules has been advocated to prune multiple equilibria. This idea reflects a long tradition in rational expectations theory, that studies whether people can learn what they need to know in order to sustain, or converge to, rational expectations.

McCallum (2009a) and McCallum (2009b), McCallum and Nelson (2005), and Christiano (2018) claim that applying the e-stability concept in Evans and Honkapohja

(2001) to our situation, the active, Π^* equilibrium of Figure 16.2 is learnable, while the passive Π_L equilibrium and the multiple equilibria leading to it are not learnable.

In Cochrane (2009), I argue that learnability leads to the opposite conclusion. As we have seen, the parameter ϕ and monetary policy disturbance u_t are not identified from time series data in the active monetary policy $\phi > 1$ equilibrium. The policy rule represents an off-equilibrium threat not measurable from data in an equilibrium. People in the economy cannot learn it any more than econometricians can learn it.

On-equilibrium parts of the interest rate rule are potentially identified and learnable. In the passive-money active-fiscal equilibrium, $\theta < 1$ of $i_t = \theta \pi_t + u_t$ is identified, and hence measurable by econometricians and learnable to agents. Cochrane (2011b) p. 2–6, and Cochrane (2018) p. 199–201, have an extended discussion of additional learnability concepts and their ability or not to prune equilibria.

The argument admittedly cuts both ways. Fiscal as well as monetary off-equilibrium behavior is not observable to agents in the economy as it is not observable to econometricians, if each views only time series from an equilibrium. But I don't advocate learnability as an equilibrium selection criterion, and I have emphasized other ways of forming expectations of fiscal policy.

There are dozens of other principles one can add to models to select among multiple rational expectations equilibria. There are also many different definitions of learnability. Different definitions can lead to different results. One would hope that equilibrium selection will be robust to which principle one uses. Here, my debate with McCallum is instructive. When researchers with different priors approach this question, they come to diametrically opposed conclusions about what is "learnable."

Most of all, I repeat the call: Is there not a simple supply and demand Walrasian equilibrium underlying price level determination? Is it *necessary* to add to the definition of equilibrium—"reasonable" expectations, no nonlocal equilibria, minimum state variables, learnability, and so forth—in order to determine the price level in *any* model of the economy, no matter how simplified?

16.10.8   A Tiny Bit of Fiscal Theory

Sims (2013) suggests a way to rule out multiple explosive equilibria in a new-Keynesian model, by putting a slight fiscal response to high inflation or deflation. The model becomes fiscal theory of monetary policy, with very small fiscal roots in normal times. However, the proposal still depends on the central bank to follow a deliberately explosive monetary policy.

Sims (2013) suggests a way to solve the multiplicity of equilibria with a light touch of an inflation-dependent surplus rule, of the sort analyzed in Section 9.3, also summarized in Cochrane (2015c). In essence, an inflation-dependent surplus rule turns active monetary policy into active fiscal policy, thus giving firm economic foundations to active monetary policy.

Sims writes in continuous time. I present the argument in discrete time as in the rest of this section. Use the simple environment

$$i_t = E_t \pi_{t+1}$$
$$i_t = \phi \pi_t.$$

Let there be real or indexed debt b_t. Let surpluses respond to inflation and debt,

$$s_t = \gamma b_t + \theta \pi_t. \tag{16.33}$$

Debt accumulates by

$$b_{t+1} = R b_t - s_t = (R - \gamma) b_t - \theta \pi_t = (R - \gamma) b_t - \theta \phi^t \pi_0. \tag{16.34}$$

(I leave out a constant or time-varying surplus, $s_{0,t}$ in $s_t = s_{0,t} + \gamma b_t + \theta \pi_t$, for simplicity as it does not affect the point here.) For simplicity, specialize to $\gamma > R - 1$ so debt is stationary rather than just growing more slowly than the interest rate, and specialize to $\phi > 1$, which is the point here. Look at perfect foresight solutions, so the problem is the initial inflation π_0. The solution to (16.34) is

$$b_t = (R - \gamma)^t b_0 - \theta \frac{1 - (R - \gamma)^t \phi^{-t}}{1 - (R - \gamma) \phi^{-1}} \phi^{t-1} \pi_0.$$

For any $\pi_0 \neq 0$, debt explodes, violating the transversality condition. Fiscal policy is active. The result that $\gamma > R - 1$ leads to passive policy needs a bounded external component of the surplus. The geometrically growing inflation term in (16.33) violates that restriction, so fiscal policy is active despite $\gamma > R - 1$.

We now have a real reason to rule out the nominally explosive equilibria, and an aggregate demand mechanism for establishing initial inflation.

This result holds for any arbitrarily small $\theta > 0$. Sims argues that such small reactions of the surplus to inflation might not be detectable in normal data. And we can imagine a model in which the inflation reaction only shows up nonlinearly, an austerity response to serious inflation or a fiscal expansion to serious deflation, but is exactly zero in normal times. Such a response—fiscal theory to the rescue in disasters but absent in normal times—is a common view of the whole enterprise. As Sims writes, "its $[\theta]$ presence would have no effect on the first two equations of the system or on the equilibrium time path of prices and interest rates, except for its elimination of the unstable solutions as equilibria of the economy."

Is this the answer? Back to new-Keynesian models with a little bit of fiscal theory so that the hyperinflationary threat really does rule out multiple equilibria? I think not. Most of all, this approach still requires us to believe that central banks deliberately destabilize the economy, that they respond to undesired inflation with increasing inflation, and to deflation with increasing deflation, that they turn stable eigenvalues into unstable eigenvalues, until fiscal policy comes to the rescue. It requires us to believe that 1982 was about forcing a jump to a different equilibrium by threatening to start a large inflation for a now lower inflation target. Central banks just don't take actions that *raise* expected inflation in response to current inflation. They do not deliberately destabilize the economy. They are not worried about determinacy.

This example does not revive the proposition that an active Taylor principle alone can determine the price level—it cleverly ties an active Taylor principle to active fiscal policy to determine equilibria, so this is a full-on case of fiscal theory of monetary policy. However, this example revives the spirit of new-Keynesian models, in which one does not need any serious analysis of fiscal policy to understand monetary affairs, except as a footnote about unverifiable ("hard to detect") assumptions that a theorist can add to trim multiple equilibria.

It seems a curious example, in the context of Sims's American Economic Association Presidential Address, which otherwise is all about how serious analysis of monetary policy must understand, measure, consider, and design appropriate fiscal backing. It seems that the fiscal–monetary coordination of this example is exactly the sort that Sims must argue is implausible, if the rest of his address and the research program that it advocates matters at all. Why give an AEA presidential speech about how new-Keynesians might adopt a better footnote about unobservable fiscal backing to justify locally unique equilibria as globally unique?

17

Keynesian Models with Sticky Prices

STICKY PRICES make the analysis more interesting, and more realistic. It may seem hard to believe that the previous discussion does justice to new-Keynesian models, whose whole point was to introduce nonneutralities via price stickiness. In the end, sticky prices just smooth out dynamics, and the fundamental ideas are represented by the frictionless equilibrium selection story I told above. We refine how the models work and we understand the points more clearly in the sticky price context. We also see how much confusion comes from mixing new-Keynesian models with old-Keynesian intuition.

17.1   New versus Old Keynesian Models

I analyze a simple model that includes sticky prices along with adaptive or rational expectations.

$$x_t = -\sigma (i_t - \pi_t^e)$$
$$\pi_t = \pi_t^e + \kappa x_t.$$

The model's equilibrium condition is

$$\pi_t = -\sigma \kappa i_t + (1 + \sigma \kappa) \pi_t^e.$$

With adaptive expectations $\pi_t^e = \pi_{t-1}$, the equilibrium condition is

$$\pi_t = (1 + \sigma \kappa) \pi_{t-1} - \sigma \kappa i_t.$$

An interest rate peg produces *unstable, determinate* inflation. With rational expectations $\pi_t^e = E_t \pi_{t+1}$, the equilibrium condition is

$$E_t \pi_{t+1} = \frac{1}{1 + \sigma \kappa} \pi_t + \frac{\sigma \kappa}{1 + \sigma \kappa} i_t.$$

Now, an interest rate peg produces *stable, indeterminate* inflation. The models have diametrically opposite dynamics. Much confusion results from mixing them up, and mixing up stability versus determinacy.

Write the standard new-Keynesian economic model from Section 5.1 as

$$x_t = E_t x_{t+1} - \sigma (i_t - \pi_t^e) \tag{17.1}$$
$$\pi_t = \pi_t^e + \kappa x_t. \tag{17.2}$$

The symbol π^e stands for expected inflation. Letting $\pi_t^e = E_t\pi_{t+1}$, we have a new-Keynesian rational expectations model. Letting $\pi_t^e = \pi_{t-1}$, we have an old-Keynesian adaptive expectations model. We can quickly contrast the two approaches.

To keep the algebra simple, I delete the $E_t x_{t+1}$ term in (17.1), so our model becomes

$$x_t = -\sigma(i_t - \pi_t^e) \tag{17.3}$$

$$\pi_t = \pi_t^e + \kappa x_t. \tag{17.4}$$

Equation (17.3) is now a static Keynesian IS curve, in which output is lower when the real interest rate is higher. This simplification allows us to see the important points without the considerable algebra that clouds the full model, presented later.

We can eliminate x_t from (17.3)-(17.4) to describe equilibria by a single equation,

$$\pi_t = -\sigma\kappa i_t + (1 + \sigma\kappa)\pi_t^e. \tag{17.5}$$

As before, start by characterizing the path of inflation and output for a given path of interest rates. This calculation gives us intuition about how the economic part of the model behaves, before we add policy rules.

The adaptive expectations model gives

$$\pi_t = (1 + \sigma\kappa)\pi_{t-1} - \sigma\kappa i_t. \tag{17.6}$$

Inflation is *unstable* but *determinate* under an interest rate peg. The coefficient $(1 + \sigma\kappa) > 1$. There is only one equilibrium. Higher real interest rates bring down subsequent inflation,

$$\pi_t - \pi_{t-1} = -\sigma\kappa(i_t - \pi_{t-1}),$$

which is the standard intuition.

The rational expectations model gives

$$E_t\pi_{t+1} = \frac{1}{1+\sigma\kappa}\pi_t + \frac{\sigma\kappa}{1+\sigma\kappa}i_t. \tag{17.7}$$

Inflation is *stable* but *indeterminate*. The coefficient $1/(1+\sigma\kappa) < 1$, but any value of unexpected inflation $\Delta E_{t+1}\pi_{t+1}$ is possible. Higher real interest rates *raise* subsequent expected inflation,

$$E_t\pi_{t+1} - \pi_t = \sigma\kappa(i_t - E_t\pi_{t+1}).$$

An interest rate equal to inflation $i = \pi$ remains a steady-state in both cases. But the dynamics around this steady-state are exactly opposite.

17.2   Responses to Interest Rate Changes

In response to a permanent interest rate change, inflation in the adaptive expectations model spirals away. The rational expectations model is Fisherian; inflation is slowly drawn to the new interest rate. However, any value of unexpected inflation can accompany the rise in expected inflation.

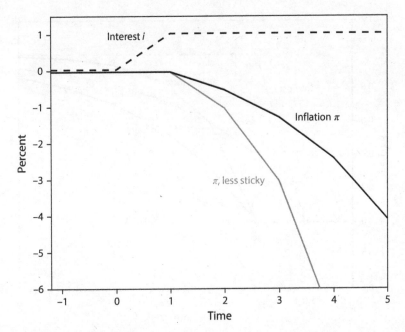

FIGURE 17.1. Inflation Response to a Permanent Interest Rate Rise. Simple old-Keynesian or adaptive expectations sticky price model. $\sigma = 1, \kappa = 0.5$, and 1.

Figure 17.1 presents the response to a permanent interest rate rise in the adaptive expectations model, using (17.6). Though the dynamics are unstable, we do not solve this model forward, since there is no expectational error and no variable that can jump to offset explosions.

The model captures traditional old-Keynesian and policy-world beliefs about monetary policy. Higher interest rates lower inflation. They do not do so immediately. They push inflation down over time. An interest rate peg invites an inflation or deflation spiral. There are no multiple equilibria. Of course, those beliefs are as much or more formed by decades of playing with this model as they are from experience, so conformity with traditional beliefs is not much independent confirmation.

The model captures a traditional mechanism. With adaptive expectations, a higher nominal interest rate means a higher real rate, $i_t - \pi_t^e = i_t - \pi_{t-1}$. The higher real rate means lower output via the IS curve, $x_t = -\sigma(i_t - \pi_t^e)$. Lower output x_t means declining inflation via the Phillips curve $\pi_t = \pi_{t-1} + \kappa x_t$. Persistently low nominal interest rates drive accelerating inflation, and persistently high interest rates drive inflation down, generating conventional stories about the 1970s and 1980s.

Turning to rational expectations, $\pi_t^e = E_t \pi_{t+1}$, the bounded solutions (17.7) express inflation as a backwards-looking moving average of the interest rate and inflation shocks $\delta_{t+1} = \Delta E_{t+1} \pi_{t+1}$,

$$\pi_{t+1} = \frac{\sigma \kappa}{1 + \sigma \kappa} \sum_{j=0}^{\infty} \left(\frac{1}{1 + \sigma \kappa} \right)^j i_{t-j} + \sum_{j=0}^{\infty} \left(\frac{1}{1 + \sigma \kappa} \right)^j \delta_{t+1-j}. \qquad (17.8)$$

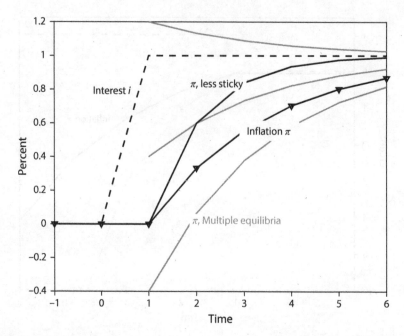

FIGURE 17.2. Inflation Response to a Permanent Unanticipated Interest Rate Rise. Simple rational-expectations new-Keynesian sticky-price model. Solid lines are $\delta_1 = 0$, gray lines give other equilibria. Parameters $\sigma = 1$ and $\kappa = 0.5$; the "less sticky" line uses $\kappa = 1.5$.

This expression simplifies the solution of the full model, equation (5.5) of Section 5.1.1, which has a two-sided moving average. It is a smoothed version of the frictionless solution $\pi_{t+1} = i_t + \delta_{t+1}$.

Figure 17.2 presents the inflation responses of this rational-expectations sticky-price model (17.7) to an unexpected permanent interest rate shock. Start with the solid lines, which give the $\delta_1 = 0$ case. The dynamics are *stable*—the interest rate rise eventually brings inflation up to meet it. The model remains Fisherian even with sticky prices, smoothing out the response we saw in the frictionless model $i_t = E_t \pi_{t+1}$. As we turn down price stickiness, raising the parameter κ, the dynamics happen faster, as graphed by the "less sticky" line. The model smoothly approaches the frictionless result, in which $\pi_1 = 1$ and stays there forever.

The equilibrium dynamics so far don't pin down unexpected inflation $\pi_1 = \delta_1$. The gray lines of Figure 17.2 present several possibilities for unexpected inflation. As before, we can select equilibria by either active monetary or active fiscal policy to choose one of these paths. If we rule out nominal explosions and add a policy rule of the form

$$i_t = i_t^* + \phi(\pi_t - \pi_t^*),$$

with $\phi > 1$, and if fiscal policy passively adapts to inflation $\Delta E_{t+1}\pi_{t+1} = -\varepsilon_{\Sigma s, t+1}$, the central bank can achieve any value of unexpected inflation, and any one of these paths can be equilibrium inflation $\{\pi_t^*\}$. Active fiscal policy likewise selects one equilibrium by specifying a fiscal shock (or the absence of one) that accompanies the interest rate rise.

The response to an *expected* interest rate rise at time 1 is the same, only that there can be no jump at time 1, as represented by the solid lines. Any unexpected movements must come on the day of the announcement. As in the frictionless case, expected monetary policy matters, and now for output as well.

17.3   Rational Expectations Responses with Policy Rules

With a policy rule,

$$i_t = \phi \pi_t + u_{i,t},$$

the model's equilibrium condition is

$$\pi_t = \frac{1 + \sigma\kappa}{1 + \sigma\kappa\phi}\pi_t^e - \frac{\sigma\kappa}{1 + \sigma\kappa\phi}u_{i,t}.$$

With adaptive expectations,

$$\pi_t = \frac{1 + \sigma\kappa}{1 + \sigma\kappa\phi}\pi_{t-1} - \frac{\sigma\kappa}{1 + \sigma\kappa\phi}u_{i,t}.$$

Passive policy $\phi < 1$ produces *unstable, determinate* inflation. A central bank following the Taylor rule $\phi > 1$ *stabilizes* an otherwise unstable economy. With rational expectations,

$$E_t\pi_{t+1} = \frac{1 + \sigma\kappa\phi}{1 + \sigma\kappa}\pi_t + \frac{\sigma\kappa}{1 + \sigma\kappa}u_{i,t}.$$

Passive policy $\phi < 1$ produces *stable, indeterminate* inflation. A central bank following the Taylor principle $\phi > 1$ *destabilizes* the economy, to render it determinate.

Now, add an interest rate policy rule

$$i_t = \phi \pi_t + u_{i,t}$$

to the model (17.1)–(17.2). Eliminating i_t, the equilibrium condition becomes

$$\pi_t = \frac{1 + \sigma\kappa}{1 + \sigma\kappa\phi}\pi_t^e - \frac{\sigma\kappa}{1 + \sigma\kappa\phi}u_{i,t}. \qquad (17.9)$$

With adaptive expectations $\pi_t^e = \pi_{t-1}$, this equilibrium condition becomes

$$\pi_t = \frac{1 + \sigma\kappa}{1 + \sigma\kappa\phi}\pi_{t-1} - \frac{\sigma\kappa}{1 + \sigma\kappa\phi}u_{i,t}. \qquad (17.10)$$

Any "passive" monetary policy $|\phi| < 1$ produces *unstable, determinate* inflation. The coefficient on lagged inflation is above 1. Inflation or deflation generically spiral away. But there is only one equilibrium.

The Taylor rule $|\phi| > 1$ *stabilizes* an otherwise unstable but determinate economy. Raising ϕ to a value greater than 1, the coefficient on lagged inflation in (17.10) becomes less than 1. Any shocks, such as induced by $u_{i,t}$, eventually die out. Spirals such as Figure 17.1 don't happen, because the central bank moves the interest rate down more than one for one, to push inflation back up.

This model captures in its simplest form the way Taylor introduced the Taylor rule, and how Taylor rules are thought to operate in central banks and policy circles. If inflation gets too big, then the central bank raises the nominal interest rate more than one for one with inflation. Via (17.3), that action lowers aggregate demand and output x_t, which via the Phillips curve (17.4) lowers inflation. Indeterminacy just isn't an issue.

Under rational expectations $\pi_t^e = E_t\pi_{t+1}$, the equilibrium condition (17.9) becomes

$$E_t\pi_{t+1} = \frac{1+\sigma\kappa\phi}{1+\sigma\kappa}\pi_t + \frac{\sigma\kappa}{1+\sigma\kappa}u_{i,t}. \qquad (17.11)$$

The frictionless case (16.4), $E_t\pi_{t+1} = \phi\pi_t + u_{i,t}$, is the $\kappa \to \infty$ limit. Now, passive policy $\phi < 1$, like a time-varying peg $\phi = 0$ produces *stable, indeterminate* inflation. The coefficient on lagged inflation in (17.11) is below 1. Any inflation or deflation is expected to melt away on its own. But the model is indeterminate, as we saw in the frictionless model. Unexpected inflation $\delta_{t+1} = \Delta E_{t+1}\pi_{t+1}$ can be anything.

In this case, a central bank following the Taylor principle $\phi > 1$ takes an economy that is already stable, and deliberately makes it unstable, in order to try to make it determinate. For all but one value of $\delta_{t+1} = \Delta E_{t+1}\pi_{t+1}$, the central bank deliberately leads the economy to hyperinflation. If we add a rule against hyperinflations as equilibria, then there is only one equilibrium.

The words sound repetitious. That's the point. The frictionless model did in fact capture the issues in this sticky price model. Sticky prices add realistic dynamics, but can hide the central issues.

Rational expectations are associated with stability, and adaptive expectations with instability. If you drive a car looking in the rearview mirror—adaptive road expectations— you will veer off course. If you drive looking through the front windshield—forward-looking, rational expectations—your car will be stable.

The nature and dynamic properties of the adaptive, old-Keynesian and rational expectations new-Keynesian models are exactly opposite. The equations look tantalizingly similar, but moving a subscript from π_{t-1} to $E_t\pi_{t+1}$ changes the sign of stability and determinacy properties.

Much of the confusion surrounding new-Keynesian models comes, I think, from trying to shoehorn new-Keynesian equations into old-Keynesian intuition. Though rescuing IS-LM provided much motivation for developing new-Keynesian models, the equations give utterly different models.

I generally avoid calling $\phi > 1$ the "Taylor rule" in a rational expectations context. I try to call it a "policy rule" following the "Taylor principle" instead. The Fed in Taylor's writings, Taylor (1999) for example, *stabilizes* inflation by raising interest rates more than one for one, in an adaptive expectations context. It does not deliberately introduce instability to ward off indeterminacy.

I use the word "spiral" to refer to instability as in Figure 17.1. The word is also used sometimes to talk about models with multiple equilibrium volatility, which may reflect confusion about the difference between instability and indeterminacy. The words "stability" and "instability" are used in many different ways. My use is neither universal nor perfect, though I hope it is consistent. One could say that the observed equilibrium of the new-Keynesian model is "stable" in that inflation does not veer away from the shocks. The full model also includes one "stable" and one "unstable" root. There is no standard terminology, so when in doubt refer to the equations.

17.3.1   Responses with Policy Rules

I calculate responses to an AR(1) monetary policy shock. A permanent shock $\eta = 1$ gives rise to a super-neutral response, even with sticky prices. The open mouth operation occurs for an intermediate value of persistence η. Now a sufficiently small η delivers a negative response of inflation to interest rates. However, once we generalize past the AR(1), there is no connection between the persistence of shocks and the sign of the inflation response. The long-run response is always positive. This model cannot generate the standard story for 1970s inflation resulting from persistently low interest rates or 1980s disinflation delivered by persistently high interest rates.

To calculate the new-Keynesian, rational expectations response to monetary policy shocks, we can solve the equilibrium condition (17.11) forward just as in the frictionless case. Applying the rule against nominal explosions,

$$\pi_t = -\frac{\sigma\kappa}{1+\sigma\kappa\phi} \sum_{j=0}^{\infty} \left(\frac{1+\sigma\kappa}{1+\sigma\kappa\phi}\right)^j E_t u_{i,t+j}.$$

In the AR(1) case, inflation then follows

$$\pi_t = -\frac{\sigma\kappa}{(1+\sigma\kappa\phi)}\frac{1}{\left(1-\eta\frac{1+\sigma\kappa}{1+\sigma\kappa\phi}\right)}u_{i,t} = -\frac{1}{\phi-\eta+\frac{1-\eta}{\sigma\kappa}}u_{i,t}. \tag{17.12}$$

The interest rate follows

$$i_t = \left(1-\frac{\phi}{\phi-\eta+\frac{1-\eta}{\sigma\kappa}}\right)u_{i,t} = -\left(\frac{\eta-\frac{1-\eta}{\sigma\kappa}}{\phi-\eta+\frac{1-\eta}{\sigma\kappa}}\right)u_{i,t}. \tag{17.13}$$

The frictionless limit $\kappa \to \infty$ reduces to the frictionless AR(1) responses, (16.6) and (16.10). Inflation and the interest rate are still proportional to the disturbance, but with different coefficients. The basic picture of the simple frictionless model continues to apply with price stickiness.

As in the frictionless case, a persistent shock $\eta = 1$ produces a super-Fisherian result.

$$\pi_t = -\frac{1}{\phi-1}u_{i,t}$$

$$i_t = -\frac{1}{\phi-1}u_{i,t}$$

or,

$$\pi_t = i_t.$$

Inflation rises *immediately*, the moment interest rates rise, even with sticky prices.

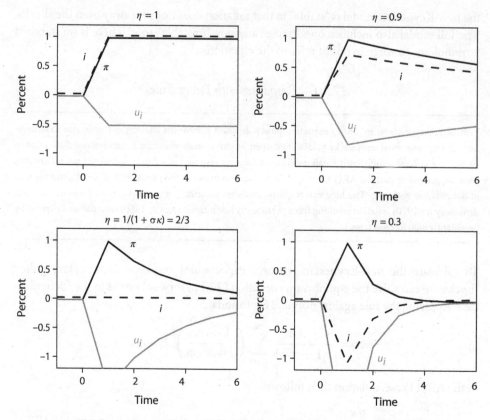

FIGURE 17.3. Response to a Monetary Policy Shock. Simple sticky price new-Keynesian model.

The top-left panel of Figure 17.3 presents this case, labeled $\eta = 1$. Inflation π_t and interest rates i_t move exactly one for one, in the opposite direction as the disturbance $u_{i,t}$. The top-right panel reduces persistence η somewhat. You can see that this model still produces the Fisherian result.

The bottom-left panel produces an open mouth policy. For

$$\eta = \frac{1}{1 + \sigma\kappa},$$

equations (17.12) and (17.13) produce

$$\pi_t = -\frac{1}{\phi}u_{i,t}; \ i_t = 0.$$

Inflation moves on the announcement of the shock, and interest rates never move. We saw that behavior in the frictionless model for $\eta = 0$. Here it appears for positive η. Open mouth policy is not a particularity of the frictionless model, though the parameter values at which it occurs change.

In the bottom-right panel of Figure 17.3, we see the standard result at $\eta = 0.3$. Finally, the actual interest rate goes in the direction of the disturbance, and inflation goes in the opposite direction. This result captures the usual wisdom: The standard new-Keynesian sticky price model can produce a negative response of inflation to interest rate shocks, but it only does so for sufficiently transitory shocks.

Even this result is not correct as stated, however, as it is tied to the AR(1) process for the shock. The possibility of a negative response has nothing fundamentally to do with the persistence of shocks. This fact is easiest to see by writing the policy rule in the form

$$i_t = i_t^* + \phi(\pi_t - \pi_t^*).$$

The central bank can, by its equilibrium selection policy, produce positive or negative responses π_t^* to an announcement at time 1, for any persistence of the interest rate policy i_t^*. Figure 17.2 offers one example: A permanent i_t^* shock can come with a negative π_t^* response, shown in the lowest gray line. Contrary examples, with transitory interest rates i_t^* or disturbances $u_{i,t}$ and positive inflation responses are just as easy to construct. They are not AR(1)s.

The inflation target π_t^* and the interest rate target i_t^* are again constrained by the equilibrium conditions of the model. In the frictionless case, we had $i_t^* = E_t\pi_{t+1}^*$. Here we have from (17.7) a natural generalization,

$$i_t^* = \left(1 + \frac{1}{\sigma\kappa}\right) E_t\pi_{t+1}^* - \frac{1}{\sigma\kappa}\pi_t^* \tag{17.14}$$

or

$$E_t\pi_{t+1}^* = \frac{\sigma\kappa}{1+\sigma\kappa} \sum_{j=0}^{\infty} \frac{1}{(1+\sigma\kappa)^j} i_{t-j}^*.$$

But even within this constraint, as with $i_t^* = E_t\pi_{t+1}^*$, the persistence of movements in i_t^* does not constrain the sign of $\Delta E_1\pi_1^*$ on the date 1 of a shock. Any value of *unexpected* inflation is consistent with any persistence of the interest rate target.

The long-run response of inflation to interest rates in this model is always positive. This model does *not* produce the old-Keynesian (or monetarist) story for the conquest of inflation in the 1980s—that persistently high interest rates, or persistently tight money growth, slowly drove inflation down. A persistently high interest rate still drives inflation *up* eventually in all equilibria of this model, as Figure 17.2 emphasizes. Only an unexpected shock, and the fiscal shock it "passively" engenders, can reduce inflation. To fit the 1980s, one has to imagine a sequence of unexpected shocks, all with the same sign.

17.3.2   Adaptive Expectations Responses with Policy Rules

In response to a positive Taylor rule disturbance $u_{i,t}$, interest rates rise and inflation declines. But interest rates then decline to catch and stabilize inflation, as graphed in Figure 17.4. This graph captures the standard view of monetary policy. If interest rates hit the zero bound or cannot move, the model predicts a deflation spiral.

To see conventional Taylor rule behavior, let us put an explicit Taylor rule $i_t = \phi\pi_t + u_{i,t}$, with an AR(1) monetary policy shock, in the adaptive expectations model. From (17.10), inflation follows an AR(2),

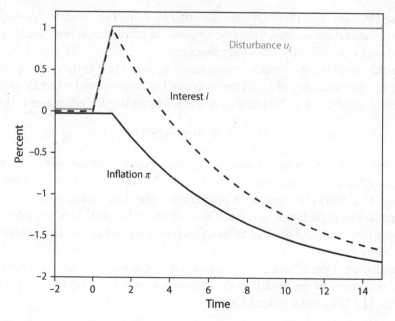

FIGURE 17.4. Response to a Monetary Policy Shock. Old-Keynesian model with a stabilizing $\phi > 1$ Taylor rule. $\sigma = 1, \phi = 1.5, \kappa = 0.5$.

$$\left(1 - \frac{1+\sigma\kappa}{1+\phi\sigma\kappa}L\right)\pi_t = -\frac{\sigma\kappa}{1+\phi\sigma\kappa}u_{i,t}$$

or

$$\left(1 - \frac{1+\sigma\kappa}{1+\phi\sigma\kappa}L\right)(1-\eta L)\pi_t = -\frac{\sigma\kappa}{1+\phi\sigma\kappa}\varepsilon_{i,t}.$$

Figure 17.4 plots the response to a permanent monetary policy shock, the case $\eta = 1$. Again, the interest rate rise sets off a disinflation. But now the endogenous response $\phi\pi_t$ means that the actual interest rate quickly reverses course and keeps the disinflation from spiraling away.

The economy is unstable, like a seal balancing a ball on its nose. The secret to stabilizing the economy is for the seal (the central bank) to move its nose more than one for one with movements of the ball.

This graph captures Milton Friedman's (1968) description of an attempt to peg interest rates, without Friedman's monetary mechanism. Friedman described the opposite sign, a too-low peg. Inflation begins to spiral upward. But then ever-increasing inflation forces the central bank to give up the peg and increase interest rates quickly, so that the attempt to lower interest rates in the end results in higher rates and more inflation.

Friedman's prediction is pretty much the conventional story of the emergence of U.S. inflation in the 1970s and the disinflation of the early 1980s. In the 1970s, the Fed kept interest rates too low, or followed $\phi < 1$, so an inflation spiral began. By a switch to $\phi > 1$ and a long-lasting monetary policy tightening, the Fed sharply raised nominal and real rates. As inflation declined, the Fed was able to lower nominal rates, though keeping real rates persistently high, and slowly squeezed inflation out of the economy.

17.4   Full Model Responses

The models of the last few sections are deliberately oversimplified. Here we look at new-Keynesian solutions to the full prototype new-Keynesian model. We verify that its qualitative behavior is described by the toy models of the last few sections, but we also learn some subtleties of its behavior. Slightly repetitive prose can help us to overcome more forbidding equations and see that their basic message is the same as with the much simpler models.

The economic model, which we first met in Section 5.1, is

$$x_t = E_t x_{t+1} - \sigma r_t + u_{x,t} \tag{17.15}$$

$$i_t = r_t + E_t \pi_{t+1} \tag{17.16}$$

$$\pi_t = \beta E_t \pi_{t+1} + \kappa x_t + u_{\pi,t}. \tag{17.17}$$

We can write $u_{x,t} = -\sigma u_{r,t}$ to interpret the IS disturbance in units of an interest rate distortion or discount-rate disturbance.

17.4.1   Interest Rates and Inflation

Inflation is a two-sided moving average of interest rates. Figure 17.5 plots the response of inflation to a permanent interest rate rise. Now inflation moves ahead of the interest rate rise as well as following it. There can also be an inflation jump on announcement, selected by the central bank's equilibrium selection policy. Each equilibrium has a fiscal counterpart. I calculate the fiscal policy change needed for several equilibria. Since real interest rates vary, there is now a discount rate or interest cost effect.

As with previous models, start by characterizing the relationship between equilibrium inflation and equilibrium interest rates. Eliminating x_t from (17.15)–(17.17), we can write

$$i_t = \frac{1}{\sigma \kappa} \left[-\beta E_t \pi_{t+2} + (1 + \beta + \sigma \kappa) E_t \pi_{t+1} - \pi_t \right]. \tag{17.18}$$

Here we see that sticky prices add dynamics to the Fisher equation $i_t = E_t \pi_{t+1}$ of the frictionless model. Inverting the lag polynomial, equation (5.5) of Section 5.1.1 expresses inflation as a two-sided moving average of interest rates, plus a moving average of past multiple equilibrium shocks δ_t, generalizing the frictionless model's $\pi_{t+1} = i_t + \delta_{t+1}$ and the one-sided moving average in (17.8).

Figure 17.5 presents the inflation response to a permanent interest rate increase, as given by the two-sided moving average (5.5). I plot the case with no additional unexpected shocks $\delta_t = 0$.

The solid inflation line gives the response to a fully expected interest rate rise. Since the solution is a two-sided moving average, inflation now rises before the interest rates rise. Expected future interest rate rises increase inflation today. This is a lovely forward guidance result, revealing of how the model works.

A preannounced interest rate rise increases inflation. Inflation rises ahead of the interest-rate rise. That prediction is either an exciting piece of novel economics, advice

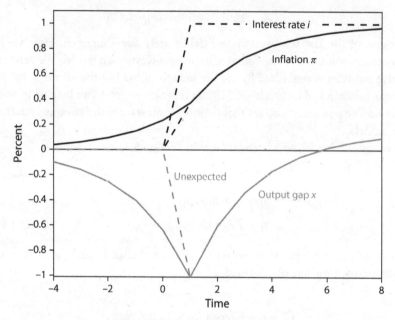

FIGURE 17.5. Response of the New-Keynesian Economic Model to a Permanent Interest Rate Rise. Solid: expected. Dashed: unexpected.

how central banks can lift themselves out of the zero bound "trap," or it is a disturbing characterization of the model, depending on your view. In either case, it is novel. Thirty years of playing with this model has not loudly announced this Fisherian property, because everyone is in the habit of only plotting responses to unexpected shocks.

The dashed line that joins the solid inflation curve from 0 to 1 gives the inflation response to an unexpected interest rate rise. The forward-looking terms are all zero until the day of the announcement. Then inflation joins the path given for the expected interest rate rise.

Inflation is thoroughly Fisherian so far—higher interest rates raise, not lower, inflation. As before, to get a negative response out of this model, we have to engineer a jump to a different equilibrium on the announcement date.

Output declines. In this model, output is low if inflation is low relative to expected future inflation; if inflation is increasing. Fully expected interest rate rises do lower output, contrary to the classic information-based models such as Lucas (1972). The conventional intuition that interest rate rises lower output and that there is little difference between announced and surprise interest rate rises is correct in this model.

What about multiple equilibria δ? Figure 17.6 graphs the response of inflation to the unexpected permanent interest rate rise, this time adding several possibilities for δ_1, which indexes multiple equilibria. If the rise were announced in advance, these jumps would take place on the announcement date, not the date of the interest rate rise.

The original $\delta_1 = 0$ equilibrium already had a little jump in inflation, resulting from the rise in future interest rates in the two-sided moving average representation of inflation given interest rates.

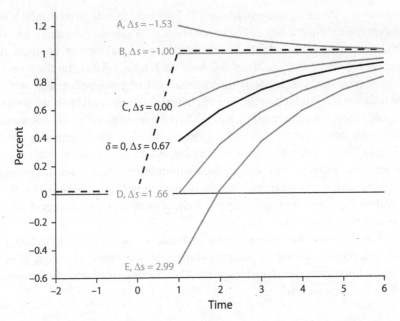

FIGURE 17.6. Response of the New-Keynesian Economic Model to a Permanent Unexpected Interest Rate Rise, with Multiple Equilibria. A, B, etc. identify equilibria in the text. Δs gives the percent change in fiscal surpluses in each equilibrium.

Equilibrium A has a positive additional inflation shock, $\delta_1 = 1\%$. Equilibrium B chooses δ_1 to produce 1% inflation at time 0, $\pi_1 = 1\%$. It shows that a super-neutral response is possible, in this full sticky price model. Equilibrium D chooses δ_1 to produce no time 1 unexpected inflation, $\pi_1 = 0$, to show that is possible.

Equilibrium E chooses $\delta_1 = -1\%$. By mixing a negative multiple equilibrium shock with the interest rate rise, we obtain a negative response of inflation to the permanent interest rate shock. As in the simplified model of the last section, there is no connection between the persistence of the interest rate shock and the sign of the inflation movement, once we generalize past AR(1) disturbances.

Next, we add active policy to select one of these equilibria. If we write an active money policy rule in the form

$$i_t = i_t^* + \phi(\pi_t - \pi_t^*),$$

then by choosing π_t^* as one of the plotted paths, and choosing i_t^* by (17.18), the central bank can, following new-Keynesian rules, choose any of these equilibria. Still, each equilibrium choice requires a fiscal policy reaction. We should check what the assumed "passive" fiscal policy is, and verify that it is reasonable. Alternatively, we can use the fiscal theory to select from these equilibria directly, specifying the fiscal policy shock that accompanies the monetary policy shock.

The Δs numbers in Figure 17.6 tell us by what percentage steady-state surpluses must change to produce each equilibrium, whether actively or passively accomplished. The $\Delta s = 0$ equilibrium is not the equilibrium with $\delta_1 = 0$ or with $\Delta E_1 \pi_1 = 0$. In making the surplus calculation, I recognize the discount rate in the government debt valuation equation to vary. In the $\pi_1 = 0$ equilibrium D, for example, real interest rates rise. That force lowers the right-hand side of the government debt valuation formula, which on its own produces inflation. In order to keep inflation from breaking out, the fiscal authorities must raise $\Delta s = 1.66\%$. Equilibrium C with $\Delta s = 0$ has inflation for the same reason: Real interest rates rise, which lowers the present value of government debt, so there is a surprise inflation. To produce equilibrium E, in which inflation declines, the government must supply a large fiscal contraction, enough to pay a windfall to bondholders and more, to pay larger real interest costs of the debt. (The Δs calculation is described in more detail in Cochrane (2017b).) Any of these jumps, and especially a negative effect of interest rates on inflation, must happen on the date of the announcement, not the day that interest rates rise. At a minimum, a new-Keynesian analysis should show these substantial fiscal requirements underlying monetary policy. Alternatively, of course, one could regard active fiscal policy as selecting the equilibrium.

Overall, sticky prices just smear out the frictionless model's description that inflation responds to interest rates with a one-period delay plus unexpected jumps, $\pi_{t+1} = i_t + \delta_{t+1}$, and the full sticky price model smears further the one-sided smooth response of the simplified sticky price model.

17.4.2   The Fiscal Underpinnings of New-Keynesian Models

New-Keynesian models have fiscal implications. For higher interest rates to lower inflation, there must be a fiscal contraction. Writing the policy rule in standard form $i_t = \phi\pi_t + u_t$, multiple disturbance paths u_t produce the same interest rate path, but they produce different inflation paths and require different fiscal support. In a new-Keynesian way of thinking about things, lacking fiscal support, the central bank is forced to choose a disturbance u_t path underlying its interest rate path that produces less or no disinflation. Even in the completely stock new-Keynesian model, considered and solved by new-Keynesian methods, fiscal constraints may make it impossible for the central bank to lower inflation by raising interest rates.

The standard new-Keynesian model does have a government debt valuation equation. The "passive" fiscal policy must happen. If higher interest rates are to provoke a disinflation, they must be accompanied with a fiscal contraction. If the fiscal contraction does not happen, the lower inflation will not follow.

This is a particularly important policy issue as I write in late 2021. If inflation persists and our central banks wish to contain inflation by raising interest rates, in this model, that monetary policy must induce a fiscal contraction. Absent the fiscal contraction, higher interest rates will not lower inflation. This proposition is just as true in new-Keynesian as in fiscal theory ways of solving the model.

Simplifying to one-period debt, write the unexpected inflation identity

$$\Delta E_{t+1}\pi_{t+1} = -\Delta E_{t+1}\sum_{j=0}^{\infty}\rho^j\tilde{s}_{t+1+j} + \Delta E_{t+1}\sum_{j=1}^{\infty}\rho^j r_{t+1+j}. \tag{17.19}$$

In this new-Keynesian model, this equation gives us the rise in surpluses, the fiscal tightening, that must happen if an unexpected inflation decline is to occur.

Equation (17.19) describes two mechanisms. First, an unexpected disinflation requires a surplus-financed windfall to nominal bondholders. Second, with sticky prices, higher nominal interest rates result in a period of higher real interest rates. We can say that higher real interest rates lower the present value of surpluses, requiring even more surpluses to lower inflation. Or, we can say that higher real interest rates raise interest costs on the debt. The government must pay those interest costs from current or future surpluses. It cannot just roll them over forever by issuing ever more debt. If the government does not back up the disinflation by repaying debt with more valuable dollars and repaying higher real interest costs of the debt, the disinflation must fail.

At 100% and rising debt-to-GDP ratio, with persistent primary deficits, these effects are not small, the type that one might relegate to footnotes in normal times. Since $\tilde{s}$ is surplus divided by the value of debt, a 100% debt-to-GDP ratio requires surpluses to rise one percentage point of GDP for every percentage point of unexpected inflation decline—$200 billion in 2021—before we add real interest rate effects. In 1980, the last great interest rate rise, debt was only 25% of GDP. Evidence from that era may not apply.

Imagine, if it has not happened by the time you read this, that the Federal Reserve wishes to raise interest rates 5 percentage points in order to fight inflation. The federal funds rate rose 15 percentage points from 1977 to 1981, so this is not an extreme example. Will our Congress and administration really "passively" go along with a $1 trillion, 5% of GDP fiscal austerity to pay larger interest costs on the debt, and follow it with similar or larger austerity to pay a windfall to bondholders? If "passive" fiscal policy runs into a brick wall, the Fed's attempt to lower inflation by raising interest rates must fail.

The following example makes the point concrete. I cast the example entirely in new-Keynesian language, for rhetorical reasons. Even if you are a die-hard new-Keynesian (and somehow you made it this far in this book), monetary policy needs fiscal backing. The "passive" fiscal backing may not materialize, and if so a monetary tightening will fail to lower inflation.

A die-hard new-Keynesian should at least take from this book an invitation to look at the "passive" fiscal policies of their models, and recognize that those fiscal requirements pose important constraints on monetary policy, constraints which may be more important now than in the past given large debts and no surpluses in sight. This section offers an example of how one might take that perspective.

The model is the standard new-Keynesian model

$$x_t = E_t x_{t+1} - \sigma (i_t - E_t \pi_{t+1})$$
$$\pi_t = \beta E_t \pi_{t+1} + \kappa x_t$$
$$i_t = \phi \pi_t + u_t$$

and the unexpected inflation identity (17.19), which we solve for the needed passive fiscal policy of surpluses, and using $r_{t+1} = i_t - \pi_{t+1}$.

Now, suppose the Fed raises interest rates by a positive and serially correlated disturbance u_t. Figure 17.7 presents the result.

The figure presents a surprise AR(1) rise in the interest rate, with serial correlation $\eta = 0.6$, a standard transitory monetary policy experiment. However, in this new-Keynesian

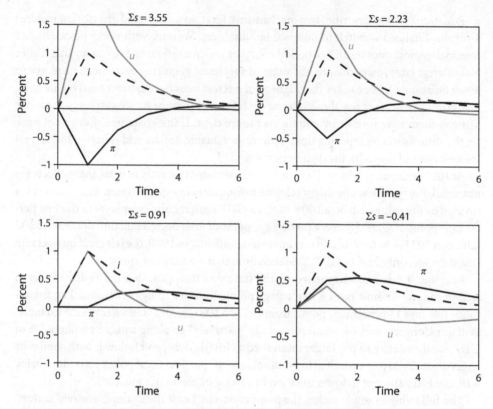

FIGURE 17.7. Inflation Response to an AR(1) Interest Rate Rise. New-Keynesian sticky price model. Each panel presents a different choice of the disturbance u_t which produces the same interest rate path. The title $\Sigma s = \ldots$ gives the percent change in the sum of surpluses required by passive fiscal policy for each case. Parameters are $\eta = 0.6$, $\sigma = 1$, $\kappa = 0.25$, $\beta = 0.95$, $\phi = 1.2$.

model, there are multiple disturbance paths $\{u_t\}$ that produce the same interest rate path but different inflation paths. In each case, I reverse engineer a $\{u_t\}$ disturbance to produce the same AR(1) interest rate path, and a chosen value of initial inflation π_1.

Start in the top-left panel. I choose the disturbance $\{u_t\}$ to produce the AR(1) interest rate and a -1% initial inflation. This panel gives the standard new-Keynesian result: A higher interest rate lowers inflation, here by exactly 1%. The disturbance u_t follows an AR(1)-like process. It moves more than the interest rate, since $\phi\pi$ and negative inflation drag the actual interest rate down below the disturbance u_t.

Fiscal policy is passive, but the fiscal response has to happen. Let's rescue it from footnotes and take a look at it. In this case, as reported in the figure title, cumulative surpluses have to rise 3.55 percentage points of GDP. (I use $\rho = 1$ and 100% debt-to-GDP ratio.) Surpluses have to rise one percentage point of GDP to pay the 1% deflationary windfall to bondholders. They have to rise an additional 2.55 percentage points of GDP because of the long period of high real interest rates, which you can see from a higher i_t line than π_t line, which represent a higher discount rate or higher real interest costs of the debt.

Multiplying by 5, a 5-percentage-point interest rate rise and 5-percentage-point disinflation require an 18% of GDP austerity program, $4 trillion. Will the administration and Congress passively accede to this request? If they do not, the attempt must fail; the path is not an equilibrium.

(This example is not the sort of permanent stabilization that the Fed will actually wish to do. The rhetorical experiment here asks only what are the fiscal foundations of the most textbook new-Keynesian result. The fiscal and monetary policy required for a permanent stabilization, as occurred in 1980, is a different and important question.)

What can the Fed do differently? It can follow a different disturbance $\{u_t\}$ that produces the same interest rate path, but requires less fiscal support. In the top-right panel, I reverse engineer a disturbance u_t that produces the same interest rate path, but only -0.5% disinflation. The disturbance is smaller and has different dynamics. Since this disturbance produces less disinflation, it also requires less fiscal austerity, 2.23 percentage points of GDP rather than 3.55 percentage points. But for a 5% interest rate rise, this path still requires Congress and the administration to cut back by $5 \times 2.23 = 11.5$ percent of GDP, or $2.2 trillion.

In the lower left-hand panel, I reverse engineer a disturbance u_t that produces the same interest rate path, but produces no disinflation at all. Though interest rates follow the same AR(1), inflation starts at zero and then slightly *rises*. But this path still requires passive fiscal policy to turn to austerity, by 0.91 percentage points of GDP. Higher real interest rates still provoke a discount rate effect, or higher real interest costs, which surpluses must overcome.

In the bottom-right panel, I reverse engineer a disturbance process u_t that produces +0.5% inflation, along with the same interest rate path. This time passive fiscal policy includes a slight fiscal loosening. Congress and administration cheer, but we clearly have done nothing to fight inflation.

The lesson of this example is that in the stock new-Keynesian model, thought of and solved in completely new-Keynesian fashion, the same interest rate path can occur with multiple disturbance paths. By changing the dynamic path of the disturbance, the central bank can fully choose the amount of unexpected inflation that accompanies an interest rate rise, from positive to negative. But each choice of disturbance serial correlation and inflation path has fiscal consequences. For a higher interest rate to disinflate, it must be accompanied by fiscal austerity. If that austerity does not or cannot happen, the Fed cannot lower inflation by raising interest rates. It must choose a different disturbance path u_t. This is not active fiscal policy. It is passive fiscal policy, up to a fiscal constraint. But the available passive fiscal response limits what the Fed can do.

My calculation is only slightly unusual in that I specify the path of interest rates and keep it the same across experiments rather than specify directly the path of disturbances u_t. It is not a widely appreciated fact that different u_t processes can generate the same path of interest rates. But interest rates are what we observe, and we want to know what are the effects of an observed *interest rate* tightening. The reverse engineered u_t processes are not AR(1), but AR(1) disturbances are not written in stone.

In order to reverse engineer a u_t disturbance process that gives a given interest rate path but different choice of initial inflation, I start by choosing i_t^* and π_t^* in the representation $i_t = i_t^* + \phi(\pi_t - \pi_t^*) = \phi\pi_t + u_t$. I pick i_t^* to follow the assumed AR(1). The inflation path π_t^* is then determined by the solution (5.5) up to an initial value. When I pick π_1^*, then, I pick a full path for inflation. Now, I pick an arbitrary $\phi = 1.2$, and I simply reverse engineer at each date $u_t = i_t^* - \phi\pi_t^*$. I used $\phi = 1.2$ rather than the traditional $\phi = 1.5$ to keep the disturbance u_t somewhat on the vertical scale of the graphs. If fed these $\{u_t\}$ paths, the model produces the given interest rate and inflation paths. Presenting it this way makes clear that this really is the standard new-Keynesian model and I'm not hiding something with the i_t^* and π_t^* business. You can reverse engineer by search and not breathe a word about stars.

Monetary and fiscal coordination do not go away in new-Keynesian models. They are brushed under the rug to footnotes, but they reappear if called on by theorist or hard reality. A 100% debt-to-GDP ratio, and a fiscal policy deep in perpetual primary deficits makes that event more likely. One usually thinks of fiscal consequences of monetary policy as being second order, so brushing them to footnotes does no harm. That is likely true of seigniorage, but the fiscal consequences of debt revaluation and of interest costs on the debt are large today. Whether the central bank *can* lower inflation by interest rate hikes, even if it could do so in fiscally happier times, is an important issue.

17.4.3 Responses to AR(1) Monetary Policy Disturbances

Figure 17.8 presents responses, including the open mouth case, and shows that the qualitative features of the simple sticky price model continue to hold.

I present calculations of the inflation and output responses of the standard new-Keynesian model (17.15)–(17.17), using the standard new-Keynesian expression of the policy rule and AR(1) disturbances,

$$i_t = \phi\pi_t + u_{i,t}, \tag{17.20}$$

$$u_{i,t} = \eta u_{i,t-1} + \varepsilon_{i,t}. \tag{17.21}$$

This traditional approach ties monetary policy to equilibrium selection policy and imposes AR(1) disturbances, which as we have seen can hide important lessons. Even here, however, how the results vary with shock persistence reveals the same unsettling behavior that we saw in simple models. Online Appendix Section A1.6 explains the solution methodology in more detail.

Figure 17.8 presents responses to monetary policy shocks in this model, for a variety of persistence parameters η. Contrast to Figure 17.2 of the simplified new-Keynesian model, or Figure 16.1 of the frictionless model, and you can see the behavior is qualitatively the same.

In the top-left panel, the persistent disturbance $\eta = 1$ again gives a super-Fisherian response, even though we use the full sticky price model:

$$\pi_t = -\frac{1}{\phi - 1}u_{i,t}$$

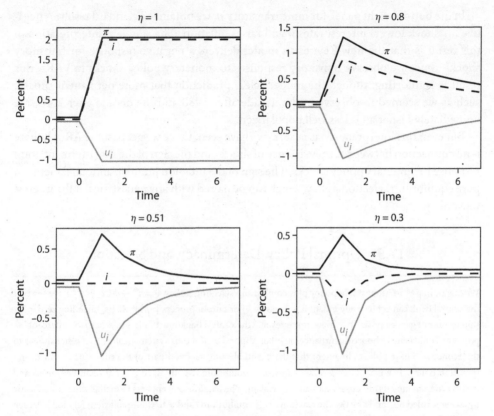

FIGURE 17.8. Response of the New-Keynesian Model to Monetary Policy Disturbances of Varying Persistence. $\beta = 0.95, \kappa = 1/2, \sigma = 1, \phi = 1.5$.

$$x_t = -\frac{1-\beta}{\kappa}\frac{1}{\phi-1}u_{i,t}$$

$$i_t = -\frac{1}{\phi-1}u_{i,t}.$$

The inflation rate moves immediately and matches the interest rate one for one. Output, not shown in the graph, rises by a small $(1-\beta$ is small) amount and stays there. A negative disturbance gives rise to positive interest rates, because the $\phi\pi_t$ term in $i_t = \phi\pi_t + u_{i,t}$ wins.

The bottom-left panel shows an "open mouth" value of the persistence parameter η. Output and inflation move with no actual movement of interest rates, where $\phi\pi_t$ and $u_{i,t}$ exactly balance. This situation occurs for η that solves

$$\eta - \frac{(1-\beta\eta)(1-\eta)}{\sigma\kappa} = 0.$$

(See Online Appendix equation (A1.87).)

In the bottom-right panel, for more transitory η, we obtain the standard result: A negative $u_{i,t}$ shock lowers interest rates i_t and raises inflation. The standard interpretation of this result is that the new-Keynesian model delivers a negative response for transitory shocks. Since we observe transitory responses to monetary policy shocks in VARs, this result is comforting, though the model's clear prediction that more permanent shocks, such as we seemed to observe in the decade after 1980 and the decade after 2008, are immediately Fisherian is less well popularized.

But even this interpretation is false, as we have seen. Once we get past the AR(1), there is no connection between the persistence of shocks and the sign of the short-term inflation response to monetary policy shocks. The sign of the inflation jump on announcement is a pure equilibrium selection policy, which can be paired with any persistence of the interest rate policy.

17.5 Optimal Policy, Determinacy, and Selection

Writing policy as an interest rate policy plus equilibrium selection policy, $i_t = i_t^* + \phi(\pi_t - \pi_t^*)$, we see that the central bank can achieve any inflation process $\{\pi_t^*\}$ or output process $\{x_t^*\}$ it wants, including zero inflation or output gap, ex post. To achieve these results, the central bank must follow a "stochastic intercept" i_t^* policy or equivalently choose disturbances $u_{i,t}$ that respond to and thus systematically offset other shocks to the economy. These policies highlight that the ϕ equilibrium selection part of the rule is irrelevant to stabilization policy. The parameter ϕ disappears from equilibrium dynamics, so it is not identified; fiscal and new-Keynesian models are observationally equivalent. The parameter ϕ appears to matter when a stochastic intercept is ruled out, and one ties the reaction of off-equilibrium i and π to the equilibrium relation between i^* and π^*.

As before, we gain a lot of intuition by expressing the policy rule as King (2000) suggests,

$$i_t = i_t^* + \phi(\pi_t - \pi_t^*). \tag{17.22}$$

We only observe $i_t = i_t^*$ and $\pi_t = \pi_t^*$ so ϕ disappears from equilibrium dynamics.

17.5.1 Optimal Policy

The central bank can achieve any $\{\pi_t^*\}$ or $\{x_t^*\}$ it wishes in this full model as well. It is easiest to calculate the required policy via i_t^* in (17.22). We can then re-express the answer as $i_t = \phi\pi_t + u_{i,t}$.

Two examples are interesting and instructive. Write (17.15)–(17.17) as

$$x_t^* = E_t x_{t+1}^* - \sigma(i_t^* - E_t \pi_{t+1}^*) + u_{x,t} \tag{17.23}$$

$$\pi_t^* = \beta E_t \pi_{t+1}^* + \kappa x_t^* + u_{\pi,t}. \tag{17.24}$$

Now, to achieve no inflation, to set $\pi_t^* = 0$, we need

$$x_t^* = -\frac{1}{\kappa} u_{\pi,t}$$

and hence

$$i_t^* = \frac{1}{\sigma\kappa}\left(-E_t u_{\pi,t+1} + u_{\pi,t}\right) + \frac{1}{\sigma}u_{x,t}. \tag{17.25}$$

To achieve no output gap, to set $x_t^* = 0$, we need

$$\pi_t^* = E_t \sum_{j=0}^{\infty} \beta^j u_{\pi,t+j}$$

and hence

$$i_t^* = E_t \sum_{j=0}^{\infty} \beta^j u_{\pi,t+1+j} + \frac{1}{\sigma}u_{x,t}. \tag{17.26}$$

In simpler models, we found that the central bank could hit whatever inflation it wished. Despite more equations and more shocks, monetary policy in this model can still attain either any given inflation path or any given output path exactly. In particular, it can make inflation or output constant.

One often asks optimal policy questions of new-Keynesian models (Woodford (2003), Chapter 6, for example). In Woodford's setup, maximizing welfare is equivalent to minimizing a weighted sum of output and inflation variation

$$\min \lambda\mathrm{var}(x_t^*) + (1 - \lambda)\,\mathrm{var}(\pi_t^*).$$

The choices $x_t^* = 0$ and $\pi_t^* = 0$ are simple examples of such policies.

We can compute the interest rate policy i_t^* that generates any desired inflation path $\{\pi_t^*\}$, not just zero. From (17.23)–(17.24),

$$i_t^* = \frac{1}{\sigma\kappa}\left[-\beta E_t\pi_{t+2}^* + (1+\beta+\sigma\kappa)E_t\pi_{t+1}^* - \pi_t^*\right] + \frac{1}{\sigma\kappa}\left[-E_t u_{\pi,t+1} + u_{\pi,t}\right] + \frac{1}{\sigma}u_{x,t}. \tag{17.27}$$

You can see here the generalization of $i_t^* = E_t\pi_{t+1}^*$, smeared out by dynamics and with the addition of shocks. To achieve a given inflation path, including zero, the interest rate target i_t^* generically reacts to shocks.

We can write the policy rules following from equations (17.25), (17.26), and (17.27) in more familiar forms as

$$i_t = i_t^* + \phi(\pi_t - \pi_t^*) = \left(i_t^* - \phi\pi_t^*\right) + \phi\pi_t = \phi\pi_t + \left(i_t^* - \phi\pi_t^*\right) = \phi\pi_t + u_{i,t}.$$

The first form reminds you of the i^*, π^* setup. The central bank sets interest rates to i_t^* and threatens explosions to enforce π_t^*. The second form thinks about $i_t^* - \phi\pi_t^*$ as a *stochastic intercept* to the rule. The third and fourth forms think about $i_t^* - \phi\pi_t^*$ as a *monetary policy disturbance* that reacts to other shocks.

Now we can state the general optimal policy point:

The stochastic intercept, monetary policy disturbance, or interest rate target and inflation target should react to, and offset, the other shocks in the economy.

In the $\pi_t^* = 0$ case (17.25) gives the disturbance/intercept $\left(i_t^* - \phi \pi_t^*\right)$ directly. In the $x_t^* = 0$ case,

$$i_t^* - \phi \pi_t^* = (1 - \phi) E_t \sum_{j=0}^{\infty} \beta^j u_{\pi,t+1+j} + \frac{1}{\sigma} u_{x,t}.$$

This result makes sense of the presence of monetary policy disturbances at all, and central bank's statements that they deviate from rules in order to address various shocks. If that is why we have monetary policy disturbances, however, the resulting disturbances are ipso facto correlated with other shocks of the model, so there is no instrument or independent monetary policy shock for VAR modelers and policy rule estimators to measure.

Offsetting shocks isn't as easy as it sounds. The u_π and u_x shocks are not directly measurable, by us or by central banks. The right-hand variables of those equations are correlated with their shocks too. The art of central banking consists of distinguishing "supply" from "demand" and other shocks (financial, international) and reacting accordingly, stimulating in response to deficient demand, abstaining from stimulus when it's deficient supply. Or at least that's how it should be. Most central banks seem only to recognize a demand side of the economy, or treat supply constraints superficially.

The ensuing debate whether central banks should fine tune has gone on, rightly, for decades if not centuries. Milton Friedman argued for a fixed money growth rule, not because he denied that optimal control of a perfectly understood model results in a time-varying and shock-dependent rule, but because his study of history persuaded him that central bankers, in real time, are not capable of measuring shocks and reacting appropriately and they are therefore more likely to do harm than good. Reacting to shocks that require central bank divination looks a lot like discretion, and raises the time consistency and rules versus discretion debate. I read in John Taylor's advocacy of an interest rate rule today much the same mistrust, along with a desire to stabilize expectations. Markets can't tell easily deviations that are responses to hard-to-measure shocks from deviations that are discretionary and unpredictable.

Current discussions of central bank policy might be phrased in terms of a rule

$$i_t = r_t^* + \pi^* + \theta_\pi \pi_t + \theta_x x_t + \phi_\pi \left(\pi_t - \pi^*\right) + u_{i,t}. \tag{17.28}$$

π^* is the central bank's long-run inflation target, 2%. r_t^* is a very long-run slow movement in the "natural rate," reflecting "global imbalances," demographics, trend growth, and so on. Central banks believe that this "supply" effect is slow moving, contra the real business cycle tradition. The debate over the path of "normalization" in the late 2010s concerned whether r_t^* declined from about 2% to 1% or less, and consequently whether nominal interest rates should asymptote to something like 4% or something like 2% or 3%. Systematic responses to endogenous variables $\theta_\pi \pi_t + \theta_x x_t$ in this framework generate useful responses to typical shocks. The disturbance $u_{i,t}$ then consists of short-run responses to other shocks, beyond what happens naturally via the rules $\theta_\pi \pi_t + \theta_x x_t$. Those shocks could include financial events such as 2008, 1987, international events, or supply shocks such as COVID-19. This discussion breaks the debate into three components $(r_t^*, \theta_\pi \pi_t + \theta_x x_t, u_{i,t})$ based on frequency and economic mechanism. All of this is a debate about how the observed equilibrium interest rate i_t^* should react to events.

This analysis is the same if fiscal theory selects equilibria rather than the final $\phi(\pi_t - \pi_t^*)$, $\phi > 1$ threat.

This optimal-policy digression has a larger point for us. In the context of the new-Keynesian model, we learn that the $\phi(\pi_t - \pi_t^*)$ *reaction part of the rule is completely irrelevant to stabilization policy*. The parameter ϕ does not enter equilibrium dynamics, so it cannot have anything to do with optimal policy.

So why is there so much study of optimal ϕ? For example, Woodford (2003) in Chapter 6 studies optimal ϕ extensively. The answer is that such optimal ϕ calculations rule out the stochastic intercept, and thereby tie equilibrium dynamics to the off-equilibrium threats. But if the central bank contemplates deviations from a rule, reactions to temporary disturbances, variation in the natural rate, or time-varying targets i_t^* and π_t^*, then these alone are powerful enough to accomplish everything the central bank can do in equilibrium. On the other hand, different values of ϕ without a time-varying intercept cannot fully stabilize inflation or output. There is no reason that a central bank would want to foreswear time-varying targets, or tie ϕ to θ irrevocably.

17.5.2   Determinacy

Determinacy depends on the eigenvalues of the full-model transition matrix. When it works, $\phi > 1$ exploits the Fisherian property of the model: Higher interest rates in response to inflation raise future inflation.

To study determinacy and stability in the full model, define *deviations* from a given equilibrium, following King (2000). Use tildes to denote deviations of an alternative equilibrium x_t from the $*$ equilibrium, $\tilde{x}_t \equiv x_t - x_t^*$. Subtracting, deviations must follow the same model as (17.15)–(17.17) and (17.22), but without constants or disturbances.

$$\tilde{\imath}_t = \tilde{r}_t + E_t\tilde{\pi}_{t+1} \tag{17.29}$$

$$\tilde{x}_t = E_t\tilde{x}_{t+1} - \sigma\tilde{r}_t \tag{17.30}$$

$$\tilde{\pi}_t = \beta E_t\tilde{\pi}_{t+1} + \kappa\tilde{x}_t. \tag{17.31}$$

$$\tilde{\imath}_t = \phi\tilde{\pi}_t. \tag{17.32}$$

In matrix notation,

$$\begin{bmatrix} E_t\tilde{x}_{t+1} \\ E_t\tilde{\pi}_{t+1} \end{bmatrix} = \frac{1}{\beta} \begin{bmatrix} \beta + \sigma\kappa & -\sigma(1-\beta\phi) \\ -\kappa & 1 \end{bmatrix} \begin{bmatrix} \tilde{x}_t \\ \tilde{\pi}_t \end{bmatrix}. \tag{17.33}$$

The eigenvalues are given in Online Appendix equation (A1.82). $\phi > 1$ generates two explosive ($\lambda > 1$) eigenvalues and $\|\phi\| < 1$ leaves one stable ($\lambda < 1$) eigenvalue.

Thus, if the policy rule is sufficiently active, any equilibrium other than $\tilde{\imath}_t = \tilde{y}_t = \tilde{\pi}_t = 0$ is explosive. Ruling out such explosions, we now have $\tilde{\imath}_t = \tilde{y}_t = \tilde{\pi}_t = 0$ as the unique locally bounded equilibrium. This is the matrix version of $E_t\pi_{t+1} - \pi_{t+1}^* = \phi(\pi_t - \pi_t^*)$. "Active" policy is the requirement to have two explosive eigenvalues, matching the two expectational errors. Active policy is now a property of the whole system, controlled by its eigenvalues, not just the parameter ϕ. In general, $\phi > 1$ is neither necessary nor sufficient for explosive eigenvalues. Adding $\phi_x x_t$ responses widens the range of parameters for which this is the case (Cochrane (2011b)).

As before, this expression makes it immediately clear that ϕ does not enter the equilibrium dynamics of the observed equilibrium variables i_t^*, π_t^*, x_t^*. The parameter ϕ lives only in (17.32), which reads $0 = 0$ in equilibrium. That equation and ϕ are entirely a threat used to select equilibria. *Interest rate policy* $\{i_t^*\}$, which may react and correlate with inflation and output π_t^* and x_t^* or structural disturbances u_t in all sorts of interesting ways, including observed Taylor rule regressions, is distinct from *equilibrium selection policy*, the reaction $\phi(\pi_t - \pi_t^*)$ never seen in equilibrium, by which the central bank makes threats to force a single equilibrium to emerge. As in the simple model, the point of equilibrium selection policy is to induce *explosive* dynamics, eigenvalues greater than one, not to "stabilize" so that the economy always reverts after shocks.

The Fisherian response to permanent and to expected interest rate rises of this three-equation model is a crucial part of this interpretation. If inflation rises, the central bank raises interest rates. But even in this full sticky price model, higher interest rates lead to *higher* long-run inflation. By this means the Taylor principle is destabilizing, not stabilizing as it is in IS-LM models.

With price stickiness, nominal explosions can also be real explosions, and they can induce real explosions faster than the interest rate so $E_t \beta^j x_{t+j}$ does not converge to zero. One might rule out such solutions by appeal to the real transversality condition. However, the model of price stickiness that turns a nominal explosion to a real explosion, and especially its linearization, is not designed to describe extreme inflation and deflation. In actual hyperinflations and deflations, output does not go to infinity or negative infinity. Barter or use of foreign currencies takes over. The Calvo fairy comes more frequently in Argentina. So, I have not seen appeal to this mechanism to resolve why the explosive inflation paths are not equilibria.

The analysis so far has mirrored my analysis of the simple model of Section 17.1. So in fact, that model does capture the determinacy issues, despite its absence of any frictions. Conversely, determinacy in the new-Keynesian model does not fundamentally rely on frictions, the Fed's ability to control real rates, or a Phillips curve.

18

History and Implications

18.1 New and Old Keynesian Confusion

Why have these issues been so confusing for so long? These points were not obvious at the time. The distinction between stability and determinacy is subtle. That central banks do not stabilize inflation, but instead destabilize it to fight multiple equilibria, is so unlike intuition and central bank statements that it was hard to recognize in the equations. The new-Keynesian model was developed, in part, to deliver IS-LM intuition. Recognizing that the resulting equations operate in a completely different way from IS-LM is therefore even harder. Active policy takes a stabilizing policy in old-Keynesian model and turns it into a destabilizing equilibrium selection threat. That it has this new and different role was not clear. But now that the distinction is clear, we should recognize just how the equations of the new-Keynesian model behave.

NEW-KEYNESIAN and old-Keynesian models are dramatically different. In old-Keynesian and monetarist thinking, the Taylor principle stabilizes an otherwise unstable, determinate economy. Higher interest rates lower inflation by reducing aggregate demand. In new-Keynesian models, the Taylor principle destabilizes an otherwise stable but multiple-equilibrium economy, to solve multiple equilibria. Higher interest rates lower inflation by forcing jumps between equilibria, a quite different mechanism. The new-Keynesian model includes a "passively" achieved fiscal contraction. In my interpretation, the latter—a wealth effect of government bonds—is the main source of aggregate demand that lowers the price level. It is clearly the only source of aggregate demand in the flexible price new-Keynesian model. With price stickiness, intertemporal substitution also occurs in the IS equation, but the similarity of results suggests that the fiscal contraction is still doing most of the work. But this interpretation is also not old Keynesian: Aggregate demand comes from a wealth effect, not from higher real interest rates that depress investment demand.

Perhaps most starkly, the new-Keynesian model does not produce the standard old Keynesian (and monetarist) narrative of the rise of inflation in the 1970s and its end in the 1980s. In the standard narrative, too-low interest rates, stemming from a policy rule that did not react enough to inflation, pushed inflation up in the 1970s. Then, years of high nominal and real interest rates, stemming from a more reactive policy rule, gradually pushed inflation and inflation expectations back down again. The new-Keynesian model, by contrast, can only say of the 1970s that inflation was indeterminate, subject to sunspot volatility. The new-Keynesian model can only say of the 1980s that inflation was determinate. But the model, at least in the simple forms studied here, is deeply Fisherian, and only produces a negative sign of inflation to interest rates for specific transitory interest rate movements. The Fisherian property should, if anything, mean that too low interest rates of the 1970s lead to low inflation. And one must account for the 1980s as a sequence of transitory interest rate shocks, not a persistent, dogged policy of high interest rates. They are profoundly different models.

As a reader with an ex post view of these issues, you may wonder why this difference took so long to figure out. Why does there remain so much confusion between new-Keynesian models and old Keynesian intuition? Why are we still writing down models that specify explosion-inducing central bank behavior? You may also be suspicious. In my reading, the new-Keynesian approach is fundamentally wrong, in a fairly elementary way. Could so many great economists really be so wrong for so long? By seeing the development of the ideas in historical context, you can see how it was perfectly sensible not to notice these problems. In turn, that observation should help to convince you that it really is wrong, and it's time to move on.

All ideas start complicated and confused and slowly become simple and clear over time. It takes a lot of reflection, digestion, and debate to understand what equations really say, and to figure out what is central, what is part of the parable, and what is technical detail or harmless simplifying assumption.

Friedman (1968) articulates most influentially the classic doctrine that inflation is *unstable* under an interest rate peg, spiraling away to hyperinflation or deflation. Already, Friedman's view was revolutionary as it brought money and economics back to thinking about inflation, which at the time was mostly relegated to "wage–price spirals," union negotiations, and a static Phillips curve with no economic underpinnings. Friedman's view that a nominal interest rate peg would not work, that the central bank could not forever move real interest rates or unemployment, that money is neutral in the long run, were dramatic news, for which Friedman's speech is justly famous. But his expectations were explicitly adaptive. He saw spirals, not sunspots.

The Taylor principle emerged in the 1980s, and solved Friedman's conundrum. If the central bank *moves* the interest rate in response to inflation, following a rule such as $i_t = \phi \pi_t$ with $\phi > 1$, then the instability of adaptive expectations (old-Keynesian and monetarist) models is cured. This was a central result because central banks do follow interest rate targets. Reiterating that they should adopt money growth rules does not let us confront data or policy. McCallum (1981) is the first paper I know in the modern literature with the result that raising interest rates more than one for one with inflation either stabilizes inflation or renders it determinate. Carlozzi and Taylor (1985) is the first paper by John Taylor with the result (I asked Taylor). This paper has the "Wicksellian" form that the interest rate should increase with the price level to stabilize the price level. Taylor (1993) and Taylor (1999) are more famous for really bringing the importance of the Taylor rule to life.

In conversation, Taylor reports that the general idea was in the air previously. Many people realized that a money growth target would result in higher interest rates when inflation is higher, though not necessarily more than one for one. Many economists felt that interest rates should have been raised more aggressively in the 1970s to fight inflation. The concept that the Fed should raise the nominal interest rate enough to raise the real interest rate in response to inflation—a nominal rate that rises more than one for one—seems simple within standard IS-LM thinking, yet an expression of the idea with that clarity emerged slowly. The deeper view that such active interest rate policy might itself determine inflation, not just by indirectly controlling the money growth rate, took even longer. Hall (1984) comes close, writing "In the long run, control over the Treasury Bill rate gives the Fed control over the price level. Whenever the price level is a little to high, the Fed should raise interest rates, and whenever it is too low, it should lower them . . ."

Wicksell (1898), republished as Wicksell (1965), first wrote that raising or lowering the interest rate target alone could stabilize the price level. The United States-based academic literature largely forgot about him until Woodford (2003) credited him with the idea. However, that idea is a long way from its modern model-based expression, as the fiscal theory is a long way from the Adam Smith quote that begins this book. In particular, Wicksell (of course) did not use rational expectations, microfoundations, market clearing, or express the model in quantitative terms.

Sargent and Wallace (1975) show that with rational expectations, the problem is indeterminacy, not instability. As we have seen, from the rational expectations Fisher equation, $i_t = r + E_t\pi_{t+1}$, pegging the interest rate i_t can determine expected inflation $E_t\pi_{t+1}$, but unexpected inflation $\delta_{t+1} = \pi_{t+1} - E_t\pi_{t+1}$ can be any unpredictable random variable, with $E_t\delta_{t+1} = 0$.

That summary, however, is an ex post interpretation benefiting from much hindsight. Sargent and Wallace's paper uses overlapping generations, so one might have thought it really about money or dynamic inefficiency. And the crucial difference between indeterminacy and instability was not really clear in most people's minds for decades afterwards. One might have thought that Sargent and Wallace just formalized Friedman's view. I did, for decades.

New-Keynesian models were developed starting in the late 1980s. Michael Woodford summarizes his own and many others' contributions in the seminal Woodford (2003). (Galí (2015) is an excellent and updated treatment.) As we now know, the Taylor principle in new-Keynesian models serves to rule out Sargent-Wallace indeterminacy, not Friedman instability, by having the central bank induce instability and a rule against explosive solutions.

The new-Keynesian literature had an explicit goal: to rescue IS-LM intuition and monetary policy recommendations from the empirical failures of IS-LM models, the theoretical destruction brought by the rational-expectations general-equilibrium revolution and the rise of real business cycles.

IS-LM models failed to capture the rise of inflation in the 1970s or the swift decline of inflation in the 1980s. One might avoid that failure with patches and epicycles, and go along another 40 years leaving theorists to fruitlessly search for "microfoundations" of Keynesian economics (a large, long-running, and now mostly forgotten enterprise). But the rational expectations revolution destroyed IS-LM as a coherent theoretical enterprise. Most effectively, perhaps, in his famous "critique," Lucas (1976) pointed out that the models could not be used for analyzing policy, as coefficients such as the marginal propensity to consume change when policy changes.[1] By modeling "consumption," "investment," and

---

1. For example, in the rational expectations permanent income model, consumption follows $c_t = rk_t + r\beta \sum_{j=0}^{\infty} \beta^j y_{t+j}$. If income follows an AR(1), $y_t = \eta y_{t-1} + \varepsilon_t$, then

so forth, the models left out people, who simultaneously decide how much to consume and invest, face budget constraints, and look to the future while deciding what to do today. Modern macroeconomics is inherently intertemporal, linking decisions about the present to decisions about the future, and produces cross-equation restrictions as emphasized by the devastating critiques in Sims (1980) and Lucas and Sargent (1981).

Meanwhile, Kydland and Prescott (1982), King, Plosser, and Rebelo (1988), and Long and Plosser (1983) started the real business cycle revolution, which showed how the cross-sectional and time series correlations of recessions—many industries rise and fall together, investment, employment, and output move together and more than consumption—could result from supply-side disruptions, leaving aggregate demand and monetary and fiscal policy out altogether as a first approximation.

As unfashionable as RBC models are these days, VAR estimates still do not assign much inflation, output, or employment volatility to monetary policy shocks. Most inflation comes from inflation shocks; equivalently, shocks to the Phillips curve. Friedman's view that most fluctuations come from monetary policy mistakes is not reflected in contemporary VAR or model-based shock accounting. Though the underlying shocks of twentieth-century recessions remain a bit of a mystery, the 2008 and 2020 recessions have clear underlying shocks—a mortgage meltdown and a pandemic—having nothing to do with surprise increases in the federal funds rate.

At best, monetary policy helps to smooth shocks that come from somewhere else, or fails to do so, and its rule or deviations from the rule that respond to other shocks is now the focus of attention. A detailed production side, elaborate preferences, tax, financial and other "wedges," and important non-policy shocks have snuck back into the new-Keynesian DSGE exercise without the real business cycle name.

New-Keynesian models were built on optimal price-setting with frictions, intertemporal optimization with budget constraints, rational expectations, and market clearing. Market clearing with sticky price setting was a key innovation relative to the previous best attempt to forge a rigorous general equilibrium understanding of Keynesian economics, epitomized by the Barro and Grossman (1971) general disequilibrium view, in which rationing in one market spills over to supply and demand in other markets.

But, again, their explicit goal was to rationalize IS-LM-style monetary policy analysis in a Lucas critique-proof model. Many authors illustrate new-Keynesian models with IS-LM-like graphs. Introductions and conclusions try to interpret new-Keynesian results with old-Keynesian intuition. In one sense, they are "new monetarist" not "new Keynesian," since at least until the zero bound era they focused on monetary policy rather than fiscal stimulus. They can be seen as an effort to add monetary frictions and some real effect of interest rate policy to a fundamentally real business cycle model of the economy.

Why did it take so long to figure out that the equations of new-Keynesian models are diametrically opposed to IS-LM intuition? Why has the difference between stability and

---

$$c_t = rk_t + \frac{r\beta}{1 - \beta\eta} y_t = rk_t + \frac{r}{1 + r - \eta} y_t.$$

We see a Keynesian consumption function. But if policy changes the persistence of income, say by smoothing recessions, then the marginal propensity to consume changes. The marginal propensity to consume is a "mongrel," reflecting shock persistence, not a structural parameter.

determinacy, between aggregate demand and equilibrium selection been so confusing? Why is it still so confusing? I devote many pages of this book to the mechanics of what are now 25-year-old models because in my view just how these simple equations work is still not clear to many active researchers, let alone struggling graduate students. Why?

Well, first, since the explicit motivating goal of the new-Keynesian enterprise was to produce IS-LM intuition with proper microfoundations, one tends to find what one is looking for. Columbus went to his grave thinking he had found Japan.

Second, a rigorous set of equations that embody IS-LM intuition would be enormously *useful*, and it's hard to discard something so useful. The policy world employs back-of-the-envelope static or hydraulic Keynesianism, filling "gaps" with monetary and fiscal "stimulus," 40 years after its demise in publishable academia. Look at all the discussion of the 2008 and 2020 fiscal stimulus bills: The "gap" is x percent of GDP; the "multiplier" is m. The deficit should be x/m. The basic insights that decisions are made across time and markets, that expectations are not a third force but rather depend on policy, so we can only think of policy as a rule or regime, has made essentially no impact at the top levels of economic policy making. Modern macroeconomics still has a difficult marketing job to do.

Moreover, central banks need advice and something to do. They want to know, "What happens if we raise interest rates?" Telling them to control money supplies, or writing models in which they have no effect on anything, is not useful to their concerns.

So if you're a young central bank researcher and you describe your model in terms of equilibrium selection and determinacy, your superiors are not likely to pay much attention. If you write old-Keynesian equations, you'll never get the paper published. So, you walk the line: new-Keynesian equations, old-Keynesian introduction, intuition, and policy implications.

Third, the new-Keynesian equations look a lot like IS-LM equations. Subtle timing differences, π_{t+1} in place of π_{t-1}, make a huge difference to stability and determinacy properties, but it's easy to miss that fact.

Fourth, new-Keynesians started with complex models that include price stickiness, changing real interest rates, something like interest-rate induced aggregate demand, spelled-out microfoundations, and so forth. Nobody would have been silly enough to investigate a model with flexible prices. You "know" from your IS-LM training that such an approach won't go anywhere. The instability, equilibrium selection, and identification issues that are so obvious in the stark frictionless model I start with here are much harder to see in more complex models. Even the linearized three-equation model I ended up with is greatly simplified relative to the models new-Keynesians were working with. Only after the fact and much digestion did the simple model emerge as a paradigm for the behavior of the more complex model. Woodford (2003) did the world a great favor by developing the flexible price new-Keynesian model and advancing it as a simple environment to understand the model with price stickiness. I would never have understood these issues even in the three-equation model, and if I had advanced the frictionless model in a critique I would have been laughed at. In my own thinking, the frictionless model in Benhabib, Schmitt-Grohé, and Uribe (2002) was the lightbulb that allowed me to understand instability versus indeterminacy. If I had presented these chapters backwards, as theory developed historically, and started with long discussion of the eigenvalues of the three-equation model, or the stability and determinacy properties of more complex nonlinear models, it would have been terribly confusing.

Rightly, most papers in the new-Keynesian enterprise focused on microfoundations of each equation, which is an immense effort that I have glossed over by just presenting simple linearized equations, on the project of fitting the model to data, on enlarging the model so it can fit the data, and on deriving advice for politicians and central bankers. Stability, determinacy, and equilibrium selection seem like boring technical issues compared to this much more exciting and productive effort. Of course you rule out weird solutions that blow up. Let's get to work with the one sensible solution, and not get bogged down. I long regarded transversality conditions and rules to rule out hyperinflationary equilibria as pointless technicalities and didn't pay too much attention as well. I was wrong. I still likely don't pay enough attention to foundations of equilibria beyond the Walrasian–Ramsey tradition, as in Bassetto (2002).

Fifth, the distinction between instability and indeterminacy is a difficult concept and was confused for a long time. Instability—eigenvalues greater than one—is not the same thing as indeterminacy—multiple equilibria. Both can give rise to volatility, but they are different forces. It took a long time to understand the difference. Like everything else, it's only obvious in retrospect.

We can see the slow process of discovery, of confronting what the equations are saying with what researchers want them to say, in policy prescriptions to trim multiple equilibria. I surveyed these prescriptions in detail above in part to make this point. If the point is equilibrium selection, making a blow up the world, equilibrium can't form threat to rule out multiple equilibria, why build that threat in a subtle transition period in an otherwise sensible existing policy idea, advocated to cure inflation or deflation? Well, clearly, the distinction between "stabilize inflation," or "stop a hyperinflation or deflation," and "rule out an inflationary equilibrium in the first place" was not clear.

Active policy itself was part of this discovery process. The original Taylor rule described how the Fed behaves empirically, and as such includes output responses,

$$i_t = \phi_\pi \pi_t + \phi_x x_t + u_{i,t}. \tag{18.1}$$

Empirical rules, designed to be even more realistic, include inertia and responses to expected values, say

$$i_t = \phi_i i_{t-1} + \phi_\pi \pi_t + \phi_x x_t + \phi_{\pi,1} E_t \pi_{t+1} + \phi_{x,1} E_t x_{t+1} + u_{i,t}. \tag{18.2}$$

Around 1980 the U.S. Fed seemed empirically to raise its inflation coefficient, and inflation dropped like a stone in 1982. These Taylor rules naturally morphed into a recommendation how the central bank *should* behave. These sorts of rules make lots of sense in old-Keynesian, stabilizing models.

So imagine that you're constructing an early new-Keynesian model. What will you use for monetary policy? Well, the Taylor rule (18.1) with $\phi_\pi > 1$ seems to fit and work pretty well, and both Taylor's work and the IS-LM intuition we want the model to capture say it works well. So of course you put it in the model. You discover playing with hard equations that $\phi_\pi > 1$ gives the eigenvalue you need for a unique linearized solution. Presto! On we go to calculating impulse-response functions. Since $\phi > 1$ rules out volatility induced by multiple equilibria, it is natural to write an introduction that says $\phi > 1$ expresses "stabilization" in the new model. The policy rule is the same in new and old Keynesian models. The change in the rest of the model alters the policy rule's role from stabilizing and inflation control to destabilizing and equilibrium selection. It's natural not to notice that one is assuming radically different central bank behavior, by using the same equation in a different model.

As these issues are much clearer in the frictionless model, otherwise hiding in the eigenvalues of big matrices, they are equally much clearer when we write the policy rule in the equivalent King (2000) formulation,

$$i_t = i_t^* + \phi(\pi_t - \pi_t^*). \tag{18.3}$$

But until King, nobody wrote the policy rule this way. And why would you? If you plug (18.1) into the model, which usually requires numerical solution, and you rule out explosions, you get a unique solution and pleasant-looking response functions. Why look harder? Taylor didn't write it this way. Unless you're really thinking hard about multiple equilibria, you wouldn't think to write it this way. Indeed, King's expression of the rule seems to bring up multiple equilibrium and identification questions that are absent in the hidden identification assumptions of the conventional writing. Write it King's way, and the likelihood function will be flat and the computer program won't estimate ϕ. Why ask for trouble? While you're constructing models to make policy predictions and fit data, multiple equilibria are just one of hundreds of annoying technical details.

Clarida, Galí, and Gertler (2000) is a good example halfway through the discovery process. They estimate policy rules, and find $\phi_\pi < 1$ before 1980, and $\phi_\pi > 1$ afterwards. They interpret this finding in terms of the new-Keynesian model, so that $\phi_\pi < 1$ means multiple-equilibrium volatility, and $\phi_\pi > 1$ means determinacy, which should reduce the volatility of inflation. Read carefully: This is not the conventional wisdom that $\phi_\pi < 1$ means IS-LM instability and $\phi_\pi > 1$ restores stability. That's the old-Keynesian interpretation of the coefficient. Indeed, they write (p. 150)

> the pre-Volcker rule leaves open the possibility of bursts of inflation and output that result from self-fulfilling changes in expectations . . . On the other hand, self-fulfilling fluctuations cannot occur under the estimated rule for the Volcker-Greenspan era since, within this regime, the Federal Reserve adjusts interest rates sufficiently to stabilize any changes in expected inflation.

The last sentence is revealing. In their model, the Federal Reserve adjusts interest rates to *destabilize* expected inflation. But "stable" can also mean "less volatile." Then it also harks back to old-Keynesian intuition, which does not describe the model. This is all only clear in retrospect.

Is the Taylor rule valuable because it delivers stability or because it delivers determinacy? Well, both, if you ask Taylor. The fact that it delivers good, if not exactly optimal, results across a wide range of models including such drastically different models as new-versus old-Keynesian is a point in its favor. For an articulation of this view, see most recently, Cochrane, Taylor, and Wieland (2020). We have seen that fiscal theory of monetary policy models add to that list, though with coefficients just below one rather than just above one in these simple models. Interest rate responses to inflation and output smooth the economy's response to shocks, and reduce inflation and output volatility. But to say that policy rules give a pretty good answer no matter the question does not help us much, because we are interested in just which is the right question.

So do not read old papers harshly, or my conclusion that they are fundamentally wrong as criticism of the authors. It has taken me two decades to figure out what I now think the much simpler equations in this book are telling us, and you will see many confusions in my early papers too.

But, now we do understand what the equations mean. And I can only conclude that all of these efforts to trim multiple equilibria of the new-Keynesian model without active fiscal policy have failed. The natural economic model gives us an equation that determines the price level and unexpected inflation, namely the government debt valuation equation. If we throw out that equation by assuming globally passive policy, that equation can't be replaced, and we lose the ability to determine one endogenous variable: the price level and consequently unexpected inflation. So put the equation back in.

As a critique, realize too that most of the new-Keynesian DSGE effort survives unscathed. The issue is equilibrium selection, and taking seriously the fiscal equations that are already present in the same models, if only in footnotes. Observational equivalence is an open door and an invitation. Compared to, say, Keynesians versus monetarists, the technical differences are small.

The new-Keynesian model set out to provide microfoundations to IS-LM intuition about monetary policy. Once we really listen to the equations, we see it ended up creating something entirely different. That's fine. New models should embody new mechanisms and make new predictions! That's far more interesting than finally, half a century later, justifying IS-LM. But that creation has a fundamental flaw: It does not surmount the equilibrium selection problem. This flaw is easy to fix: Add back active fiscal policy. The result, however, is even less likely to confirm IS-LM intuition. Well, so much for IS-LM intuition. It is for many macroeconomists a treasured memory of their first undergraduate class, but comfortable nostalgia is not a reason to keep hanging on.

18.2   Adaptive Expectations?

Why not just retreat to adaptive expectations? First, that model fails empirically. Second, it means there really is no economic, Lucas-critique proof model of the price level. Adaptive expectations produce a negative response of inflation to interest rates by changing the stability and determinacy properties of the model, thereby walling themselves off from the flexible price limit. Enhancing short-run frictions—financial frictions, lending channel, irrational expectations—while maintaining the basic stability and determinacy properties seems more fruitful. Such a model can capture the hoped-for negative sign, while accounting for the zero bound. One can, however, merge fiscal theory with adaptive or irrational expectations models. The core fiscal interactions remain.

Why not just return to adaptive expectations, one might reasonably ask? It produces a set of equations that embody central bankers' belief that higher interest rates lower inflation, and it gives us a model with determinate inflation, if not quite a price level, and no multiple equilibrium problems.

The first reason not to follow this path is empirical. This traditional view predicts that if the interest rate does not or cannot move more than one for one with inflation, inflation or deflation should be unstable. Yet in 8 years of interest rates stuck at the zero bound in the United States, 13 years so far in Europe, and a quarter century in Japan, inflation stayed remarkably quiet, and no spiral emerged. (Chapter 20 treats this episode in detail.) Adaptive expectations fell apart when those models failed to predict the rise of inflation in the 1970s, a second time in the relatively quick end of inflation in the 1980s, again in the rapid stabilizations under inflation targets, again confronting the history of hyperinflations, and once more at the zero bound. At best it is a contingent, occasionally and in a few places theory, not an always and everywhere theory.

A second reason is more esthetic or philosophical, but esthetics are important. Somewhat irrational expectations and mechanically sticky prices may be useful ingredients as icing on a cake, as epicycles to understand dynamics of episodes, or to understand never before seen policies and events. But if we follow the old-Keynesian path, we put irrational expectations and mechanically sticky prices squarely in the foundations of monetary economics. We then *cannot* understand the basics of price level determination or the basic sign and stability properties of monetary policy, *without* irrational expectations or mechanically sticky prices. We say there is no truly economic theory by which the price level is determined. Monetary policy is all a conjuring trick, by which clever bureaucrats exploit our foibles to fool a naive populace. And if people ever wake up and figure out what's going on, if more volatile inflation attracts more attention, the whole edifice falls apart and we have no theory of the price level at all.

IS-LM, with all forward-looking behavior turned off, isn't really an economic model at all. It is at best a set of equations that captures historical correlations. It is not "policy invariant." It does not survive the Lucas (1976) critique. Its parameters will not stay still if they are regularly and systematically exploited for policy. People may not be "rational," but they are not permanently, systematically, and exploitably "irrational" either. Such a model does not allow us to ask structural questions such as, what if the Fed stops paying interest on reserves? What if people start using a lot of Bitcoin? What if the internet makes prices less sticky, or people more attentive? What happens at negative interest rates? It needs perpetual patching up with each failure. We want a theory that works beyond the relatively quiet (so far) postwar U.S. time series. A theory of the price level should extend to currency crashes, hyperinflations, currency reforms, and so on, and not treat those as somehow fundamentally different.

Creating an economic, microfounded, Lucas-critique-proof theory was the whole point of the new-Keynesian agenda. It was constructed to satisfy this esthetic principle, not directly to solve empirical problems with IS-LM models. I choose so far to cheer and fix the effort, not to abandon it.

If the choice were only between new- and old-Keynesian models, one might choose the adaptive expectations model at least for a restricted range of observations like postwar U.S. business cycles. But the new-Keynesian model, with fiscal theory in place of central bank equilibrium-selection threats, provides an economic model that is simple, complete, Lucas-proof, and so far consistent with evidence. That surely is worth exploration before giving up on the "economics" part of "monetary economics," before giving up hope that one can *start* to analyze the price level with a coherent supply and demand model.

The recent new-Keynesian literature, recognizing difficulties at the zero bound episode and some of these theoretical issues, has moved toward adaptive expectations, while steadfastly avoiding active fiscal policy or even looking at fiscal implications. Two excellent examples are García-Schmidt and Woodford (2019), and Gabaix (2020). Both are instructively difficult and complex. What is the minimum we need to understand the price level? Apparently, hundreds of pages and dozens of difficult equations. Changing the treatment of the government debt valuation equation, already part of the model, seems a lot easier.

The adaptive expectations model is not a perfect fit to central banker intuition either. It says higher interest rates lower inflation, but it also uncomfortably requires central bankers to raise interest rates promptly and more than one for one with inflation, a position central bankers resist. And adaptive expectations are immune to central banker speeches, forward guidance, and so forth.

The models before us offer an uncomfortable choice. The rational expectations model is deeply Fisherian, and struggles to produce a negative inflation response to interest rates, especially in the long run. The new-Keynesian model produces that negative reaction with a contemporaneous fiscal contraction. I add long-term debt. Both are unsatisfactory mechanisms. The adaptive-expectations model produces the desired sign by changing the entire stability and determinacy properties of the model, changing eigenvalues greater than one to eigenvalues less than one. It thereby erects a wall between sticky and unsticky prices. In addition to empirical troubles, that is also unsatisfying.

The ingredient—rational, adaptive, or complex expectations—is not really important. The basic stability and determinacy properties of the model are more important. Fundamentally, I think it will be more productive, if we wish to produce a model in which higher interest rates have a larger negative effect on inflation, to add ingredients such as financial frictions or a small amount of irrational expectations, that retain the basic stability and determinacy properties of the flexible-price rational-expectations model. That approach would allow us the negative sign, while also not necessarily requiring the central bank to move interest rates more than one for one to keep inflation from exploding. Fisherian long-run results would remain, but central banks might well want to move inflation around more quickly by exploiting the negative opposite relation.

Fiscal theory does not have to be paired with rational expectations, or even models with the stability and determinacy properties of this rational expectations model. Merging adaptive or irrational expectations models, or determinate/unstable models with fiscal theory is an interesting research question. Long-neglected fiscal constraints abound for any economic model. If the Fed wishes to raise interest rates, and for those to lower inflation, Congress will have to finance higher interest costs on the debt, a windfall to bondholders, and lost seigniorage, at a minimum. The vision that stabilization of an indebted, stagnating, and inflating economy needs joint monetary, fiscal, and microeconomic reform holds as well.

Mixing less than rational expectations with modern general equilibrium models, including an asset pricing equation such as the government debt valuation equation, is hard. Does one get rid of rational expectations in intertemporal substitution and price setting, but not in the asset pricing formula that values government debt? That seems silly. But how is government debt valued with irrational expectations? But answering such questions is possible, especially with an explicit theory of expectation formation more founded than just plonking last year's inflation in the place of π_t^e. Adding fiscal theory to the Garcia-Schmidt and Woodford or Gabaix frameworks is a straightforward research investigation. Sims (2016) adds fiscal theory to an entirely backward-looking model, with a wealth effect in the consumption function. With fiscal theory, inflation is stable at an interest rate peg.

In sum, in this book so far, there are really two core assumptions: Fiscal theory, and a forward-looking economic model, especially its Phillips curve, that maintains the determinacy and stability of a frictionless benchmark. One can use either ingredient without the other. You can easily take the message of this book to join fiscal theory, or at least a close look at fiscal requirements of monetary theory, with a different kind of economic model.

18.3 Interest Rate Targets: A Summary

I conclude that active interest rate targets, with a globally passive fiscal policy, are not, in fact, a coherent complete alternative theory of inflation or the price level. Replacing $\phi\,(\pi_t - \pi_t^*)$ or related equilibrium selection threats with the government debt valuation equation can maintain all the great accomplishments of the new-Keynesian DSGE structure, selecting equilibria in a different way.

We need a theory of inflation under interest rate targets. Central banks follow interest rate targets, not money supply rules.

It seemed that active $\phi_\pi > 1$ interest rate targets, with globally passive fiscal policy, could completely determine the price level or inflation rate, overcoming the indeterminacy or instability of interest rate targets from classical theory. I conclude after this tour, however, that active interest rate targets with passive fiscal policy are not successful in that endeavor. Central banks don't threaten to blow up the economy, and if they did the economy might well blow up. New-Keynesian models do not successfully surmount indeterminacy. And old Keynesian models aren't economic models.

The old and new-Keynesian models are also not quite complete theories of the price level. First, since central banks are not specified to follow Wicksellian policies in which interest rates react to the price level—sensibly, as central banks do not follow such policies—these models give a theory of inflation, but the price level is cumulated inflation plus whatever it was in the Garden of Eden. Second, they do not yet include an independent theory (other than $MV = Py$ at microscopic scale) of how central banks determine interest rates, analogous to the sales of nominal debt with fixed surplus and the flat supply curve of Section 2.9.

The fix is easy. Adding fiscal theory to new-Keynesian models, or really restoring the fiscal theory that was there all along, easily handles determinacy issues and produces the kind of theory we need. The observational equivalence and nonidentification theorems make that fix even easier than it may have seemed before, at least technically.

Even if all this is not convincing, I hope at least a die-hard new-Keynesian will be inspired to look at the "passive" fiscal underpinnings of those models. The required fiscal adjustments are large. One may rightly have felt that seigniorage is small, so one can ignore monetary–fiscal interactions. But revaluation of nominal debt and interest costs are large. Fiscal–monetary interactions are important to the results. They do not occur by lump-sum taxes one finds in theoretical footnotes. By observational equivalence, just how one writes equilibrium selection parts of the model is not in the end terribly important. But, for example, the observation that a purely new-Keynesian analysis of whether higher interest rates can lower inflation falls apart without a large and unlikely fiscal austerity, is genuine news that one can analyze with a fully active-money passive-fiscal outlook.

19

Monetarism

THE MOST DURABLE current theory of inflation is based on money supply and demand. In this theory, money is intrinsically worthless. People need money to buy things, so they are willing to hold some of it despite a rate of return less than that of bonds. The central bank controls and limits the supply of money. Money demand $MV = Py$ intersected with a limited supply $M = M^s$ leads to a determinate P. I'll lump these ideas together under a common term, "monetarism," despite important differences between early quantity theorists such as Irving Fisher; Milton Friedman and his followers, whose views today define classic "monetarism;" and cash in advance, money in utility, overlapping generations, search theoretic, and related formal theories of money.

I have deferred a detailed discussion because monetarism manifestly does not apply to current institutions. The distinction between money and bonds is evaporating, and whatever money is, our central banks do not control its supply. However, monetarism is a vital piece of history, history of thought, and economics that a student of inflation should understand. Its insights matter to many historical episodes. And to understand fiscal theory we need to understand how it is different from monetarism.

In this chapter I look more deeply at monetary price level determination. The main technical point is that monetarism suffers from multiple equilibrium problems analogous to those of the new-Keynesian model. $MV(i) = Py$, a fixed money supply, and globally passive fiscal policy does not determine P, except in one special and unrealistic case, that money demand does not depend on interest rates. Fiscal theory cures that indeterminacy. This point buttresses my claim that the fiscal theory is really the only theory we have. However, for practical application, the fact that the separation between money and bonds is evaporating and central banks don't limit money supply is more important. Even if you adhere to one or another alternative method for pruning monetary equilibria, our economy does not have the preconditions for monetarism to work.

I develop two standard models of money: money in utility and cash in advance. I show how cash in advance turns into our basic fiscal theory model, when asset markets reopen in the afternoon and with active fiscal policy. We see how fiscal theory handles cash in advance but zero interest rates or money that pays the same interest rate as bonds. I include a comparison of fiscal theory with the Sargent and Wallace (1981) "unpleasant monetarist arithmetic" model. It is a central precursor, but fiscal theory is more general.

Some Cheshire-cat intellectual remnants of monetarism remain in thinking about current policy. We still call it "monetary policy," not "interest rate policy" or "government debt management." In the end, once an interest rate target discussion gets too confusing, many economists retreat to $MV = Py$ as a foundation for price level determination, regarding the interest rate target as an indirect way of setting the money supply M. An active discussion surrounds central bank operating procedures. Should the Fed return to a small amount of reserves that pay no interest, and implement interest rate targets by controlling the daily quantity of reserves, as it did before 2008? Why does the Fed target the level of reserves at all, controlling the size of the balance sheet, rather than run a pure corridor or peg, in which people can borrow or lend to the bank freely at the targeted rate? Some feeling remains that QE "works" by increasing reserve supply, not by reducing bond supply and that this source of "support," "easing," "accommodation," or "stimulus" is important, if not by increasing transactions balances then by "injecting liquidity" into financial markets. Should central banks reestablish control of monetary aggregates, say by tightening reserve requirements or by limiting financial and payments system innovations? Do open market operations stimulate at the zero bound by raising M even though the overnight interest rate does not change? Some economists still argue that central banks *should* target monetary aggregates. Others analyze events and the impact of interest rate targets by measuring monetary aggregates. A good deal of commentary periodically looks at M2 and warns of inflation to come. Viewing the world through fiscal theory lenses, I view all of these arguments as historical remnants or second-order effects, but the discussion is still alive, and second-order effects are important.

19.1 Equilibria and Regimes

Money demand equals money supply and the government debt valuation equation are both equilibrium conditions. Monetary analysis says that the money supply, and in particular the split of liabilities between money and bonds, determines the price level. Surpluses adjust passively so that the valuation equation holds. Fiscal theory says that the government debt valuation determines the price level, so money supply must be passive. The two views are observationally equivalent. Monetary analysis often considers needed fiscal backing.

A reminder: In Section 3.4, we added money demand,

$$M_t V_t = P_t y_t, \tag{19.1}$$

to the fiscal theory. With money that does not pay interest, and ignoring inside money, we saw that the government debt valuation equation becomes

$$\frac{B_{t-1}}{P_t} = E_t \sum_{j=0}^{\infty} \frac{\Lambda_{t+j}}{\Lambda_t} \left(\frac{M_{t+j} - M_{t+j-1}}{P_{t+j}} + s_{t+j} \right) \tag{19.2}$$

or

$$\frac{B_{t-1} + M_{t-1}}{P_t} = E_t \sum_{j=0}^{\infty} \frac{\Lambda_{t+j}}{\Lambda_t} \left(\frac{i_{t+j}}{1 + i_{t+j}} \frac{M_{t+j}}{P_{t+j}} + s_{t+j} \right). \tag{19.3}$$

We considered an active-money passive-fiscal regime, in which a fixed money supply $M_t = M_t^s$ and money demand (19.1) determine the price level. In that case, the government must adjust surpluses ex post so that the government debt valuation equation holds—it must follow a passive fiscal policy.

Fiscal theory looks at the same equilibrium conditions. Surpluses $\{s_t\}$ and the overall quantity of debt $M_{t-1} + B_{t-1}$ in the government debt valuation equation set the price level P_t. Then monetary policy must be passive, providing the money that people demand. Seigniorage muddies the picture, but the logic remains intact, as we have seen.

Monetarist analysis focuses on management of the money supply M by an *exchange* of money for government bonds, more M and less B, a change in the composition of government debt, rather than focus on the overall supply of government debt, $M + B$. Monetarist analysis also focuses on restrictions on the creation of inside money.

If monetary and fiscal policy are both passive, then the price level is undetermined. For this reason, monetarists have long bemoaned the fact that central banks so often follow apparently passive policies. Inflation is always *something*, so it's hard to know what "undetermined" means as an empirical prediction. In the event, inflation has often been remarkably quiet under passive monetary policies. If a monetarist observes passive monetary policy and quiet inflation, perhaps this is an invitation to strengthen the fiscal part of the theory rather than argue that the world is wrong.

The fiscal and monetary regimes are observationally equivalent. All we see in equilibrium are the two equilibrium conditions, (19.1) and (19.2) or (19.3). As always, this observation invites us not to take pure active versus passive, or games of chicken descriptions too seriously, but instead understand coordinated policies.

Monetary–fiscal coordination has always been part of fully described monetarist ideas. In any well-written article, you will find, perhaps in a footnote, an assumption that the government raises or lowers surpluses as necessary so that the present value condition holds. Monetary analysis of events and institutions takes fiscal coordination seriously. Looking at the required fiscal policy to see if it is there is more common in monetary analysis than it is to date in new-Keynesian analysis. In part, monetary analysis has been around longer and covered a wider range of times, places, and episodes. Monetary analysis of disinflations usually includes the requirement for long-term fiscal reform to replace seigniorage revenue. Monetary analysis of large inflations notices that money is often printed to pay intractable government deficits, not because central bankers were too stupid to see the error of their ways, nor just to satisfy political demands for stimulus despite healthy government finances. Contrariwise monetarists recognize that in order to contain inflation, the government must run sufficient surpluses to allow monetary restraint. One may think of the thousand-year history of paper money as, basically, a long voyage of discovery of institutional and legal constraints that keep fiat money from being quickly inflated away by fiscally pressed governments.

But as long as the government has adequate fiscal space, and seigniorage is a small part of the budget, the fiscal part lies in the background of monetarist analysis of advanced economies.

19.2 Interest Elastic Money Demand and Multiple Equilibria

With interest elastic money demand, money supply control is not enough to determine the price level. Multiple inflationary or deflationary equilibria can emerge. Adding fiscal theory solves the multiple equilibrium problem.

Money demand $M_t V = P_t y_t$ and money supply control seem to determine the price level. However, money demand is interest elastic. V is not a number, but a rising function of the nominal interest rate. We really should write

$$M_t V(i_t) = P_t y_t$$

with $V'(i) > 0$. When nominal interest rates are higher, the opportunity cost of holding money is larger. People go to the ATM machines more often and hold less real money on average. Financial institutions put more effort into cash management. Interest elastic money demand means that even a fixed money supply is not sufficient to determine the price level with passive fiscal policy. Monetarism suffers the same indeterminacy problems as we saw for interest rate targets.

To exhibit the problem, consider first a simple example. Let output be constant, and let money demand be a declining function of interest rates,

$$M_t = P_t Y V^{-\alpha i_t}, \tag{19.4}$$

or in logs

$$m_t - p_t - y = -\alpha i_t v.$$

(Here, V and v are parameters; numbers, not functions of other variables. I temporarily use Y for the level and y for the log of real output.) Introduce the Fisher equation

$$i_t = r + E_t \pi_{t+1} = r + E_t p_{t+1} - p_t.$$

The price level paths $\{p_t\}$ are then given by

$$m_t - p_t - y = -\alpha v \left(r + E_t p_{t+1} - p_t \right). \tag{19.5}$$

$$E_t p_{t+1} = \frac{1 + \alpha v}{\alpha v} p_t - \frac{1}{\alpha v} (m_t - y) - r.$$

$MV(i) = Py$ is now a difference equation for the sequence of prices, not a single equation for the price level at one date.

Suppose that money is constant $m_t = m$. There is a steady-state price level

$$p = m - y + \alpha v r. \tag{19.6}$$

The steady-state price level is higher as the real interest rate is higher, because then the nominal rate is higher and money demand is lower.

There are other equilibria. From (19.5), the full set of equilibrium price levels is any sequence with

$$E_t p_{t+1} - p = \theta \left(p_t - p \right), \tag{19.7}$$

where

$$\theta \equiv \frac{1 + \alpha v}{\alpha v} > 1.$$

There is a family of solutions. Writing (19.7) as

$$\left(p_{t+1} - p \right) = \theta \left(p_t - p \right) + \delta_{t+1},$$

the model restricts $E_t \delta_{t+1} = 0$, but the expectational error δ_{t+1} can take any value ex post. The full set of solutions is

$$p_t - p = \theta^t \left(p_0 - p\right) + \sum_{j=1}^{t} \theta^{t-j} \delta_j.$$

The alternative solutions are explosive. At any date for $p_t \neq p$, people expect explosive hyperinflation or hyperdeflation. But nothing in the specification of the model so far rules out these alternative solutions, just as we could not rule out nominal explosions $E_t \pi_{t+1} = \phi \pi_t, \phi > 1$ in the simple new-Keynesian model.

These multiple paths are often called "speculative hyperinflations." If one reads causality from future to present, changing expectations of future price levels causes the price level today to jump. A hyperinflation breaks out on its own with no external shock.

For a general money supply process $\{m_t\}$, we can solve (19.5) forward, to

$$E_t p_{t+1} = \theta p_t - (\theta - 1) \left(m_t - y + \alpha vr\right)$$

$$p_t = \left(1 - \frac{1}{\theta}\right) \left(m_t - y + \alpha vr\right) + \frac{1}{\theta} E_t p_{t+1}$$

$$p_t = \left(1 - \frac{1}{\theta}\right) E_t \sum_{j=0}^{\infty} \frac{1}{\theta^j} \left(m_{t+j} - y + \alpha vr\right) + \lim_{T \to \infty} \frac{1}{\theta^T} E_t \left(p_{t+T}\right). \tag{19.8}$$

It is tempting to set the last term on the right-hand side to zero and to declare a unique forward-looking equilibrium. The price level then depends beautifully on a forward-looking moving average of money rather than today's money alone, just as in the simple new-Keynesian model, we found inflation depends on a forward-looking moving average of monetary policy disturbances. But there is again no reason to set to zero the last term of (19.8).

As with interest rate targets, most papers simply pick the bounded solution without further ado. But this is an extra criterion, not (yet) part of the economic model.

The fiscal theory solves this multiple equilibrium problem. Reverse the passive fiscal assumption. With perfect foresight, (19.2) reduces to

$$\frac{B_{-1}}{P_0} = \sum_{j=0}^{\infty} \beta^j s_j.$$

This condition picks the one missing element, P_0, and we now fully determine the price level.

In the stochastic case, similarly,

$$\frac{B_t}{P_t} \Delta E_{t+1} \left(\frac{P_t}{P_{t+1}}\right) = \Delta E_{t+1} \sum_{j=0}^{\infty} \beta^j s_{t+1+j}$$

picks unexpected inflation at each date, and

$$\frac{B_t}{P_t} E_t \left(\frac{P_t}{P_{t+1}} \right) = E_t \sum_{j=0}^{\infty} \beta^j s_{t+1+j},$$

with expected inflation picked by (19.7), determines nominal bond sales B_t. (As usual, either add a seignorage term or assume that surpluses offset seignorage. I keep the equation simple to focus on the point.) Bond sales B_t are no longer an independent policy lever. Fiscal theory of monetary policy contains a monetary policy to set expected inflation, but only one monetary policy—either control of the interest rate, of nominal debt, or, in this model, money supply.

The solution picked in this way will generically be one of the explosive solutions, not the steady-state or bounded solution. One might object that we don't routinely see explosive inflation. But governments are not so pig-headed as to set constant money forever in the face of exploding inflation. They are not so pig-headed as to set m, B_0 and the path of surpluses randomly, and independently of the price level they wish to produce. They are not so pig-headed as to follow fiscal policies that validate any inflation or deflation that comes along. They meet inflation with austerity and deflation with stimulus.

In sum, with interest-elastic money demand, money supply control is not enough to determine the price level. If we add fiscal theory, we can solve this indeterminacy problem, and produce a sensible monetary–fiscal regime, as fiscal theory plus interest rate targets does. A coordinated policy sets surpluses, money, and the nominal quantity of debt to avoid explosive solutions. I don't pursue this example further because no government these days controls monetary aggregates, nor plans to do so.

This section stems from the famous Cagan (1956) analysis of hyperinflations. Cagan uses adaptive expectations. Sargent and Wallace (1973) and Christiano (1987) use rational expectations, which leads to these forward-looking solutions and determinacy issues.

Monetarists talk about how velocity is "stable" at least in a "long run." One point of that talk is to brush under the table this multiple equilibrium problem stemming from interest elastic money demand. (The other purpose is to assert that $MV = Py$ still allows M to raise Py when interest rates are zero, to deny a "liquidity trap.")

19.3   Money in Utility

We examine the classic money in the utility function model. This section introduces the utility function and budget constraints, and defines equilibrium.

I review two standard explicit models for producing a money demand and monetary price level determination: the money in the utility function model here and the cash in advance model in Section 19.5.

The models serve an immediate purpose, to examine more carefully the analysis of the last section. $MV = Py$ and passive fiscal policy really do not determine the price level, if we spell out a model completely. Indeed, the full nonlinear model adds a second stable steady-state, as we found for the nonlinear interest rate rule model. Adding fiscal theory, however, the models are useful workhorses for studying monetary–fiscal policies when there are special liquid assets.

The representative household maximizes

$$\max E \sum_{t=0}^{\infty} \beta^t u\left(c_t, \frac{M_t}{P_t}\right). \tag{19.9}$$

Money in the utility function stands in for the fact that holding money makes it easier to purchase goods and services. Models that detail the search, information, transactions or shopping frictions that really motivate holding liquid assets usually end up with something like this indirect utility function.

The day follows our usual timing. The household holds nominal one-period government bonds B_{t-1} and government money M_{t-1} overnight. I keep the model simple with no inside money. Then the household receives an endowment y_t, consumes c_t, pays net real taxes s_t, and buys new bonds B_t at price Q_t. The household's period budget constraint is

$$B_{t-1} + M_{t-1} + P_t(y_t - c_t) = Q_t B_t + M_t + P_t s_t. \tag{19.10}$$

The household operates in complete contingent claim markets with state price Λ_t.

Money and debt holdings must also satisfy a lower bound, $M_{t-1} + B_{t-1} > -B$, and their optimal choices include transversality conditions. Thereby the household must satisfy the present value budget constraints, either

$$\frac{B_{t-1}}{P_t} = E_t \sum_{j=0}^{\infty} \frac{\Lambda_{t+j}}{\Lambda_t}\left(\frac{M_{t+j} - M_{t+j-1}}{P_{t+j}} + s_{t+j} + c_{t+j} - y_{t+j}\right) \tag{19.11}$$

or

$$\frac{B_{t-1} + M_{t-1}}{P_t} = E_t \sum_{j=0}^{\infty} \frac{\Lambda_{t+j}}{\Lambda_t}\left(\frac{i_{t+j}}{1 + i_{t+j}}\frac{M_{t+j}}{P_{t+j}} + s_{t+j} + c_{t+j} - y_{t+j}\right). \tag{19.12}$$

The government sets a sequence $\{M_t^s, B_t^s, s_t\}$. The government obeys a flow constraint, that money not soaked up is left over:

$$B_{t-1}^s + M_{t-1}^s = P_t s_t + Q_t B_t^s + M_t^s.$$

The government does not need to obey a transversality condition or present value budget constraint. If people wish to paper their caskets with money, and absorb an ever increasing amount of it, no budget constraint stops the government from satisfying this need.

An equilibrium is a set of $\{M_t, B_t, s_t, c_t, y_t, \Lambda_t\}$ that satisfy consumer optimality, the government flow constraint, and equilibrium $c_t = y_t$, $M_t^s = M_t$, $B_t^s = B_t$. The eventual government debt valuation equation results from the consumer's budget constraint, and equilibrium $c_t = y_t$.

19.3.1   First-Order Conditions and Money Demand

The first-order conditions in equilibrium $c_t = y_t$ give a money demand function,

$$\frac{u_m(y_t, M_t/P_t)}{u_c(y_t, M_t/P_t)} = \frac{i_t}{1 + i_t}$$

or

$$M_t = P_t L(y_t, i_t).$$

The first-order conditions for maximizing (19.9) subject to (19.12) are[1]

$$\beta^t u_c\left(y_t, \frac{M_t}{P_t}\right) = \Lambda_t \tag{19.13}$$

$$\beta^t u_m\left(y_t, \frac{M_t}{P_t}\right) = \Lambda_t \frac{i_t}{1 + i_t}. \tag{19.14}$$

Here, I save a later step, substituting $y_t = c_t$ to characterize the equilibrium.

We can rewrite these equations in several useful and intuitive ways. From the consumption condition we have the standard asset pricing formula,

$$\frac{\Lambda_{t+1}}{\Lambda_t} = \frac{\beta u_c(t+1)}{u_c(t)}$$

where I use the notation $(t) \equiv \left(y_t, \frac{M_t}{P_t}\right)$. Bond prices follow the standard formula

$$Q_t = \frac{1}{1 + i_t} = E_t\left(\beta \frac{u_c(t+1)}{u_c(t)} \frac{P_t}{P_{t+1}}\right). \tag{19.15}$$

---

1. To derive these first-order conditions easily, consider each item as a function of state x^t in the time zero problem. Think of c_t as $c_t(x^t)$ and so forth in

$$\max \sum_{t=0}^{\infty} \sum_{x^t} \beta^t pr(x^t) u\left(c_t, M_t/P_t\right)$$

s.t.

$$\frac{B_{-1} + M_{-1}}{P_0} = \sum_{t=0}^{\infty} \sum_{x^t} pr(x^t) \frac{\Lambda_t}{\Lambda_0}\left[\frac{i_t}{1+i_t} \frac{M_t}{P_t} + s_t + c_t - Y_t\right].$$

I use x for state and pr for probability as conventional symbols s and π are already in use. Now introduce a Lagrange multiplier λ on the constraint and take the derivative with respect to $c_t(x^t)$, yielding

$$\beta^t pr(x^t) u_c\left(c_t, M_t/P_t\right) = pr(x^t) \frac{\Lambda_t(x^t)}{\Lambda_0} \lambda.$$

$$u_c\left(c_0, M_0/P_0\right) = \lambda.$$

Dividing the two first-order conditions,

$$\frac{u_m(y_t, M_t/P_t)}{u_c(y_t, M_t/P_t)} = \frac{i_t}{1 + i_t}. \tag{19.16}$$

We can rewrite this equation as a money demand or "liquidity preference" function, which is typically interest elastic

$$M_t = P_t L(y_t, i_t).$$

We can also write from the first-order conditions

$$1 = \frac{u_m(t)}{u_c(t)} + E_t \left[\beta \frac{u_c(t+1)}{u_c(t)} \frac{P_t}{P_{t+1}} \right].$$

The real rate of return on money is P_t/P_{t+1}, which is less than that on other assets, and in particular bonds which pay $(1 + i_t) P_t/P_{t+1}$. That deficient rate of return ("rate of return dominance") in the right side is made up for by an unobserved "dividend" or "convenience yield" of money in the first term. Iterating, we can state an asset-pricing view of the value of money

$$\frac{u_c(t)}{P_t} = E_t \sum_{j=0}^{T} \beta^j \frac{u_m(t+j)}{P_{t+j}} + E_t \left[\beta^{T+1} \frac{u_c(t+T+1)}{P_{t+T+1}} \right].$$

An additional dollar, held forever, costs $1/P_t$. It generates a stream of benefits, captured by the marginal utility of money.

19.3.2   Equilibrium and Multiple Equilibria

If the central bank sets a constant rate of money growth $M_{t+1}/M_t = 1 + \mu$, equilibrium inflation follows a difference equation. The difference equation has two steady-states. One steady-state features inflation at the rate of money growth $\pi_t = \mu$, and is unstable. The other steady-state features deflation, with a zero nominal interest rate, and is stable. Figure 19.1 graphs the equilibrium dynamics. With passive fiscal policy, we have multiple unstable equilibria around the positive steady-state and multiple stable equilibria around the deflationary steady-state.

Now, suppose the central bank sets a money growth target, specifying the sequence $\{M_t\}$. We want to find the corresponding sequence of equilibrium price levels $\{P_t\}$. We merge the two first-order conditions to derive a difference equation for prices. Substituting out i_t from (19.15) and (19.16),

$$\frac{u_m(t)}{u_c(t)} = 1 - \frac{1}{1 + i_t} = 1 - E_t \left(\beta \frac{u_c(t+1)}{u_c(t)} \frac{P_t}{P_{t+1}} \right). \tag{19.17}$$

Simplify to a separable utility function, so that money does not affect the intertemporal allocation of consumption. With a constant output $c_t = y$ and perfect foresight, the bond

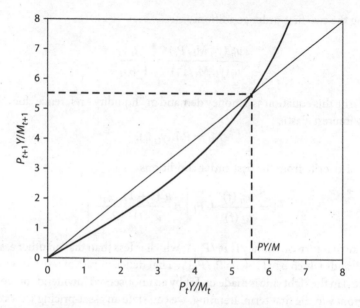

FIGURE 19.1. Price Level Dynamics. Money in the utility function model with constant money growth, equation (19.23).

price is simply

$$\frac{1}{1+i_t} = \beta \frac{P_t}{P_{t+1}}.$$

With separable utility, $u_m(t) = u_m(M_t/P_t)$. Equation (19.17) becomes a nonlinear difference equation for real money holdings M_t/P_t,

$$\frac{u_m\left(\frac{M_t}{P_t}\right)}{u_c(y)} = 1 - \beta \frac{P_t}{P_{t+1}} = 1 - \beta \left(\frac{M_{t+1}}{P_{t+1}}\right) / \left(\frac{M_t}{P_t}\right) \frac{M_t}{M_{t+1}}. \tag{19.18}$$

Figure 19.1 plots an example, described below.

Let money growth be a constant $M_{t+1}/M_t = 1 + \mu$. The difference equation (19.18) has a steady-state of constant real money holdings $M_t/P_t = M/P$, and steady inflation driven by the money growth rate

$$\frac{u_m\left(\frac{M}{P}\right)}{u_c(y)} = 1 - \beta \frac{M_t}{M_{t+1}} = 1 - \frac{\beta}{1+\mu} \tag{19.19}$$

$$\frac{M_{t+1}}{M_t} = 1 + \mu = \frac{P_{t+1}}{P_t}.$$

Here prices are proportional to money over time, and inflation equals the money growth rate. This is the right-hand steady-state of Figure 19.1.

In this nonlinear model, there is a second deflationary steady-state. At zero nominal rates $i_t = 0$, we have $u_m = 0$ (see (19.17)). Money and short-term bonds are perfect substitutes, and therefore they must pay the same return. In this case (19.18) becomes

$$\frac{P_{t+1}}{P_t} = \beta$$

or with $\beta = 1/(1 + \delta)$,

$$\pi_{t+1} \approx -\delta.$$

This second steady-state has zero interest rates and slight deflation to generate a positive real rate.

Can the marginal utility of money $u_m = 0$? We usually think that the marginal utility of money eventually vanishes, just like everything else.

$$\lim_{m \to \infty} u_m(m) = 0.$$

In this case, zero interest rates are a limiting case, and the economy slowly drifts down to it. However, it is plausible that there is some finite level of money at which we are satiated, and more money provides no more help with transactions. Once you hold a lifetime's worth of money, holding more money and less bonds does you little good in arranging the purchase of your morning cappuccino. And perhaps we are satiated in other individual goods as well. How many scented candles do you really want? If we could not be satiated in money, we would not observe truly zero or negative interest rates. Yet in the 2010s we observed zero or negative interest rates and reserves paying more than Treasury bills. With satiation, there is a value, m_{sat} such that

$$u_m(m) = 0, m \geq m_{sat}.$$

Now we arrive at zero interest rates in finite time and stay there. Once we get to a zero interest rate, $i_t = 0$, with slight deflation equal to the discount and real interest rate, people will hold arbitrary amounts of money. The money demand curve becomes a correspondence $m \geq m_{sat}$, $i = 0$, because money and bonds are perfect substitutes. Though labeled "liquidity trap" and often disparaged, or subject to efforts to fix it, liquidity satiation is also the Friedman optimal quantity of money.

To calculate an example, I use a simple separable utility function,

$$u\left(c_t, \frac{M_t}{P_t}\right) = \frac{c_t^{1-\gamma}}{1-\gamma} + \frac{\theta}{1-\gamma}\left(\frac{M_t}{P_t}\right)^{1-\gamma}. \tag{19.20}$$

From (19.16), money demand is

$$M_t = P_t y_t \left(\frac{1}{\theta}\frac{i_t}{1+i_t}\right)^{-\frac{1}{\gamma}}.$$

The difference equation (19.18) becomes

$$\theta\left(\frac{M_t}{P_t y}\right)^{-\gamma} = 1 - \beta\left(\frac{M_{t+1}}{P_{t+1} y}\right) \Big/ \left(\frac{M_t}{P_t y}\right)\frac{M_t}{M_{t+1}}. \tag{19.21}$$

The inflationary steady-state (19.19) is

$$\theta \left(\frac{Py}{M} \right)^{\gamma} = 1 - \frac{1}{(1+\delta)(1+\mu)} \approx \delta + \mu. \qquad (19.22)$$

Higher inflation, money growth, and nominal interest rates mean less real money holding.

To get some sense of a reasonable θ, note that for $Py/M \approx 1$, we need $\theta \approx \delta + \mu$, already a small number on the order of 0.1. For a more realistic $Py/M \approx 10$, we need θ on the order of 0.01. If we hold one tenth of a year's income as money, even a 5% nominal interest rate generates interests costs of holding money equal to one two-hundredth of a year's income. Money is a relatively unimportant good in utility.

We can rewrite the difference equation (19.21) in terms of the inflationary steady-state (19.22), eliminating δ and μ in favor of Py/M, as

$$\left(\frac{P_{t+1}y}{M_{t+1}} \right) = \left(\frac{P_t y}{M_t} \right) \frac{\left[1 - \theta \left(\frac{Py}{M} \right)^{\gamma} \right]}{\left[1 - \theta \left(\frac{P_t y}{M_t} \right)^{\gamma} \right]}. \qquad (19.23)$$

Figure 19.1 presents the dynamics of this system. The solid curved line presents $P_{t+1}y/M_{t+1}$ as a function of $P_t y/M_t$, as given by (19.23) The parameters are $\delta = \mu = 0.20$, $\gamma = 2$, and $\theta = 1/100$.

If we start at the inflationary steady-state, $P_t y/M_t = Py/M$, the economy stays there. Other values of the initial price level, leading to other values of real money holdings $P_t y/M_t$, reflect additional equilibrium paths. The phase diagram cuts from below at the steady-state—the derivative of (19.23) is positive at Py/M—so dynamics are unstable around Py/M. Therefore, Py/M is an unstable unique locally bounded equilibrium. But nothing in this model so far rules out the other equilibrium paths.

The figure shows the second steady-state at $P_t y/M_t = 0$. Write (19.23) as

$$\frac{P_{t+1}}{P_t} = (1+\mu) \frac{1 - \theta \left(\frac{Py}{M} \right)^{\gamma}}{1 - \theta \left(\frac{P_t y}{M_t} \right)^{\gamma}}.$$

So, in the limit $P_t/M_t \to 0$, and using (19.22),

$$\lim_{P_t y/M_t \to 0} \frac{P_{t+1}}{P_t} = \frac{1}{1+\delta}.$$

Inflation approaches the negative of the real interest rate and discount rate. This steady-state is stable; multiple equilibria in this neighborhood stay nearby.

This deflationary steady-state appears even though money growth is positive, or mildly negative $1 + \mu > 1/\beta$, approximately $\mu > -\delta$. This is not a liquidity trap induced by deflationary money growth $\mu = -\delta$. It is a second stable equilibrium of a world with positive money growth, but interest elastic money demand.

The analysis parallels exactly the situation of Figure 16.2 in Section 16.8 for interest rate targets. I write it and present it that way to highlight the parallel. New-Keynesian and monetarist theories suffer from the same multiple equilibrium problem. We arrive at the same logical point as we did with an interest rate target. $MV(i) = Py$ with interest elastic demand does not determine the price level. We must add something if we want an economic theory that *can* determine the price level.

If we add back the government debt valuation equation, (19.11) or (19.12), rather than assume fiscal policy adjusts passively to make the valuation equations hold for any price level P_0, we obtain a determinate price level and a complete monetary–fiscal policy.

This observation could be the basis of elaboration, with more detail on money demand, inside and outside money, money supply rules, fiscal responses, long-term debt, and so forth, as I did with interest rates in the first part of this book. We could construct a fiscal theory of *monetary* policy, rather than a fiscal theory of interest rate targets. I do not follow this path. Though it would be interesting to complete our taxonomy of monetary theories, a repaired monetarism does not describe current institutions.

Utility that is nonseparable between money and consumption can lead to a phase diagram in which the inflationary steady-state cuts from above, so there are multiple stable equilibria even here. Obstfeld (1984) makes this point in a delightfully concise five-page paper. Nonseparable utility is a realistic specification. The point of money is not to enjoy Scrooge McDuck swims in it, but because money makes buying and selling goods easier. Online Appendix Section A3.2.4 treats this case.

In sum, the model formalizes the analysis of the last Section 19.2. It verifies that by looking at a money demand function, money supply, the standard bond pricing equation, and the government debt valuation formulas, in a complete model, we have indeed exhausted the conditions needed to construct an equilibrium. Limited money supply intersected with interest elastic demand with passive fiscal policy leaves multiple equilibria. We can eliminate multiple equilibria with active fiscal policy. The full nonlinear model makes multiple equilibrium matters worse. It adds a second deflationary, zero bound steady-state and multiple stable equilibria that approach that state.

19.4 Pruning Equilibria

There have been many attempts to prune the multiple equilibria of monetary models. Some introduce threats to blow up the world. They are subject to the same critique as for interest rate rules. Others implicitly add fiscal theory. All are proposals for some future government.

As there have been many efforts to prune the multiple equilibria of interest rate targeting models, covered in Section 16.10, there has been an even larger literature that tries to prune the multiple equilibria of monetary models, without explicit recourse to active fiscal policy. Many of the ideas are closely related, as is my critique.

In my view, this literature has failed, for the same basic reason that the analogous interest rate literature failed: To rule out an equilibrium, one must either add fiscal theory, which many proposals do when you look carefully, or one must add something to the policy specification that forbids equilibria from forming, which means blowing up the economy. But the government does not threaten to blow up the economy, and in the sensible Ramsey specification the government cannot do so. These are likewise proposals for policies that some future government could make to trim equilibria, not threats our governments currently even whisper.

I defer a review of these issues and literature to Chapter 3 of the Online Appendix. While I find esthetic pleasure and symmetry in the claim that monetarist models have exactly the same indeterminacies as new-Keynesian models have, and so do not provide a complete theory of the price level, this point is not central to the larger argument. Even if this point is wrong, one should abandon monetarism because central banks do not control the quantity of money, because money demand has evaporated into a mush of liquid assets and fast transactions technologies, and because it does not work empirically. Subscribing to one or another of the fixes described in Online Appendix Chapter 3 will not fix the latter more important facts.

The most appealing fix is the observation that when the growth rate of money is perpetually positive, real money growth can exceed the real interest rate in the deflationary equilibria, apparently violating the consumer's transversality condition. But this case *is* fiscal theory, not an *alternative to* fiscal theory. Passive fiscal policy adjusts surpluses so that the valuation equation holds, and the transversality condition is satisfied, for any initial price level. The government in the model that produces a transversality condition violation refuses to adjust surpluses to validate the too-low initial price. That is active fiscal policy, using fiscal theory to prune multiple equilibria as I advocate.

The fix is not always valid, either. If perpetual money growth is achieved by open market operations, the total quantity of debt does not violate the transversality condition, which applies to total wealth, not to each component individually. Furthermore, since money is valued in utility, ever-growing real quantities of money may not violate the transversality condition in the first place.

Obstfeld and Rogoff (1983) is the most famous proposed fix for the inflationary equilibria. They specify that the government switches to a gold or commodity standard above a certain threshold of inflation. I make standard points, familiar from the discussion of multiple equilibria in interest rate models. The proposal is a version of fiscal theory, not an alternative to fiscal theory, as the government must have the gold. The proposal can stop hyperinflation, but doing so does not rule out the inflation and its resolution as an equilibrium, unless one sneaks in a blow-up-the-world provision. Obstfeld and Rogoff do that. Our governments and central banks do not even whisper a commitment to switch back to gold above a certain inflation threshold. At best it is a proposal for some future central bank. Our central banks do not control money growth. They certainly would not fix money growth immutably in face of a growing inflation. Likewise, our fiscal authorities would not stand by "passively" and let inflation ravage the land.

Both sets of fixes have an angels on heads of pins quality as well, since they depend on limiting properties of money demand. Good models in the middle are not necessarily good in limits. As interest rates decline to five, or one basis point, do people hold one, or five lifetime's worth of money? Are money and goods complements or substitutes, at one basis point interest costs or when people hold an hour's worth of money in a hyperinflation? Now we have observed the lower bound, and beyond. Money holdings are large but did not explode. Do we learn that there is satiation, so there is no worry about violating the transversality condition? Or do we learn that at one basis point interest cost, or even negative 50 basis points interest costs, people just don't care that much and money demand becomes a correspondence? In the other direction, hinging equilibrium selection for today's economy on whether in a hypothetical hyperinflation people hold cash for a day, or just for an hour, makes little sense. The theory of speculative inflations really is pretty speculative. If you are interested in this intellectual history, proceed to Online Appendix Chapter 3.

This is not criticism. In constructing any theory, one should forge ahead and not get hung up on technicalities. $MV = Py$ was a good and useful theory. It was much more important for Friedman and Schwartz to organize history with $MV = Py$ than to worry about multiple equilibria with interest elastic demand, or the properties of money demand limits. First be useful, then tidy up details. Indeed, the point of this book is to imbue fiscal theory with a similar practical attitude, where I think we have spent too many decades arguing about such technicalities before seeing if the theory could be useful. Then, with holes in such a useful theory, of course it makes sense to spend a lot of effort trying to patch the holes. Now we can see things differently: Monetarism is no longer so useful, and the theoretical holes never really did get patched up. But there was nothing wrong with the effort.

19.5   Cash in Advance Model

The cash in advance model is in part motivated by the artificiality of money in the utility function. Cash in advance is the simplest and most tractable model that starts a little deeper. It models an explicit reason to hold money, in order to make transactions.

Models with money in the utility function also deliver results that depend sensitively on the properties of the utility function: separable versus nonseparable, limits as interest rates and money holdings rise or fall. Cash in advance models, though formally equivalent to a money in utility model, can effectively suggest some functional forms as more plausible than others.

The simplest cash in advance model, which I study here, appears to give a money demand with fixed velocity, which can determine the price level with passive fiscal policy. It turns out that the cash in advance model also has multiple equilibria. Money demand becomes L-shaped, rising as a correspondence when interest rates hit zero. We still cannot rule out equilibria that deflate to the zero bound. Again, an active fiscal policy solves this indeterminacy. Cash in advance models are also extended—for example, with credit goods—to generate a more realistic interest elastic demand. I don't cover that extension here as it does not raise additional issues relevant to these points.

The cash in advance model also allows me to display a frictionless model that eliminates the cash in advance constraint. That formalism allows a nice way to see how the fiscal theory continues to determine the price level in the frictionless environment, and to relate the fiscal theory story we started with to the cash in advance story.

The cash in advance model comes from Lucas (1980), Lucas and Stokey (1987), Lucas (1984), and see Sargent (1987). I modify these models to include fiscal theory and thus also to the frictionless case in which consumers can avoid holding cash overnight. I also consider the zero interest case, which is usually ignored. I emphasize nominal debt and the possibility of the fiscal regime. This treatment stems from Cochrane (2005b).

19.5.1   Setup

The cash in advance model specifies that money must be used for transactions, $P_t c_t \leq M_t^d V$. In the standard specification, money must be held overnight, despite a potential interest cost. In the frictionless variant, money can be returned at the end of the day. I write the model, the cash in advance constraint, the budget constraint, and I define equilibrium. The model delivers the equilibrium conditions we have been studying: a money demand equation and the government debt valuation equation.

The government chooses a state contingent sequence for one-period nominal debt, money and primary surpluses, $\{B_t^s, M_t^s, s_t\}$. The representative household maximizes a standard utility function,

$$\max E \sum_{t=0}^{\infty} \beta^t u(c_t).$$

The household enters period t with money balances M_{t-1} and one-period nominal discount bonds with face value B_{t-1}. Any news is revealed. The household goes to the asset market. The household redeems maturing bonds B_{t-1}, pays net lump sum taxes $P_t s_t$, buys new bonds B_t and leaves with money M_t^d.

Each household receives a nonstorable endowment y_t in the goods market. The household cannot consume its own endowment, and must therefore buy the endowments of other households. To do so, the household splits up into a worker and a shopper. The shopper takes the money M_t^d and buys goods c_t subject to a cash in advance constraint,

$$P_t c_t \leq M_t^d V. \tag{19.24}$$

The story is cleanest when $V = 1$, but it is useful to introduce the parameter V and consider what happens as it changes later. The worker sells the endowment y_t in return for money, and gets cash $P_t y_t$ in return.

In the monetary model, the shopper and worker go home and eat c_t. They must hold overnight any money $M_t^d - P_t c_t$ left over from the shopper, and the money $P_t y_t$ earned by the worker. M_t, which denotes money held overnight, is

$$M_t = M_t^d + P_t(y_t - c_t). \tag{19.25}$$

The frictionless cash in advance model makes one small change: The securities market reopens at the end of the day. The household can return to the securities market; the ATM machine is open in the afternoon. There, households can trade any unwanted cash for more bonds. Thus, the household can use cash during the day without holding it overnight. The absence of the constraint (19.25) is the only difference in the economic setup of the two models.

The household can trade arbitrary contingent claims in the asset market at price Λ_t. Households are forbidden to issue money, to keep them from arbitraging zero interest money against interest-bearing bonds,

$$M_t \geq 0. \tag{19.26}$$

The household's period budget constraint states that the nominal value of money and bonds at the beginning of the period, plus any profits in the goods market, must equal the nominal value of bonds purchased, money held overnight, and net tax payments,

$$B_{t-1} + M_{t-1} + P_t(y_t - c_t) = Q_t B_t + M_t + P_t s_t. \tag{19.27}$$

The household's money and debt demands must also obey the transversality condition

$$\lim_{T \to \infty} E_t \left(\frac{\Lambda_{t+T}}{\Lambda_t} \frac{M_{T-1} + B_{T-1}}{P_T} \right) = 0. \tag{19.28}$$

These conditions imply the present value budget constraint. As before, we can write it in two ways, treating the inflation tax either as an interest cost or as dilution due to money printing,

$$\frac{B_{t-1}}{P_t} = E_t \sum_{j=0}^{\infty} \frac{\Lambda_{t+j}}{\Lambda_t} \left(\frac{M_{t+j} - M_{t+j-1}}{P_{t+j}} + s_{t+j} + c_{t+j} - y_{t+j} \right) \tag{19.29}$$

or

$$\frac{B_{t-1} + M_{t-1}}{P_t} = E_t \sum_{j=0}^{\infty} \frac{\Lambda_{t+j}}{\Lambda_t} \left[\frac{i_{t+j}}{1 + i_{t+j}} \frac{M_{t+j}}{P_{t+j}} + s_{t+j} + c_{t+j} - y_{t+j} \right]. \tag{19.30}$$

An equilibrium is a set of initial stocks B_0, M_0, and sequences for quantities $\{c_t, M_t^d, M_t, B_t, s_t\}$ and prices $\{\Lambda_t, P_t\}$ such that households optimize and markets clear. That is, given prices $\{\Lambda_t, P_t\}$, initial stocks B_{-1}, M_{-1}, and the tax and endowment streams $\{s_t, y_t\}$, the choices $\{B_t, M_t^d, c_t\}$ maximize expected utility subject to the budget constraints (19.27)–(19.28), the cash in advance constraint (19.24), and the constraint that the household may not print money (19.26). In the cash in advance model, the household must also meet the constraint (19.25) that money coming from the goods market is held overnight. Market clearing requires $c_t = y_t$, $M_t = M_t^s$, $B_t = B_t^s$ at each date and in each state of nature.

19.5.2 Monetary Model

I characterize the equilibrium of the monetary model, in which people must hold money overnight. The standard asset pricing equation holds, without monetary distortions. If interest rates are positive, the cash in advance constraint binds. The government debt valuation holds as well.

The consumer's first-order conditions, budget constraints, and market clearing imply the following characterizations:

1. The marginal rate of substitution is equal to the stochastic discount factor,

$$\beta^j \frac{u'(y_{t+j})}{u'(y_t)} = \frac{\Lambda_{t+j}}{\Lambda_t}. \tag{19.31}$$

Hence, nominal bond prices are given by

$$Q_t = \beta E_t \left[\frac{u'(y_{t+1})}{u'(y_t)} \frac{P_t}{P_{t+1}} \right].$$
(19.32)

If the endowment is constant over time $y_t = y$, then

$$\frac{\Lambda_{t+j}}{\Lambda_t} = \beta^j; \ Q = \beta.$$

2. Any equilibrium with positive nominal interest rates must have a binding cash constraint,
$$M_t V = P_t c_t = P_t y_t.$$
(19.33)

3. The government debt valuation equation holds,

$$\frac{B_{t-1}}{P_t} = \sum_{j=0}^{\infty} E_t \left[\frac{\Lambda_{t+j}}{\Lambda_t} \left(s_{t+j} + \frac{M_{t+j} - M_{t+j-1}}{P_{t+j}} \right) \right]$$
(19.34)

or, equivalently,

$$\frac{B_{t-1} + M_{t-1}}{P_t} = \sum E_t \left[\frac{\Lambda_{t+j}}{\Lambda_t} \left(s_{t+j} + \frac{i_{t+j}}{1 + i_{t+j}} \frac{M_{t+j}}{P_{t+j}} \right) \right].$$
(19.35)

Fact 1 follows from the household's first-order conditions for buying one less consumption good, investing in a contingent claim, and then consuming more at $t + j$. Following Sargent (1987), there is no asset-pricing distortion with this timing convention. In order to raise consumption c_t the household must also get more money M_t^d, but cash overnight M_t will be unaffected because $P_t c_t$ changes by the same amount as M_t^d changes (see equation (19.25)). With positive nominal interest rates, money is strictly dominated by bonds, so the household will hold as little money as possible overnight. In the cash in advance model, that quantity is $M_t = P_t y_t / V$; goods market equilibrium gives $y_t = c_t$, and hence Fact 2. To derive Fact 3, use the bond price definition, iterate forward the consumer's period to period budget constraint (19.27), impose the condition (19.28), and impose market clearing ($y_t = c_t$, $M_t = M_t^s$). Lucas (1984) and Sargent (1987) treat existence of equilibrium. It's easy enough to construct examples with standard utility functions. Our issue is the uniqueness of equilibrium, and we shall see shortly that it is not.

19.5.3   Monetary–Fiscal Coordination

Monetary and fiscal policy must be coordinated. We commonly separate active-money passive-fiscal or active-fiscal passive-money alternatives for this coordination. But the equilibrium is the same, so the two coordination stories, and the infinite number between them, are observationally equivalent.

The cash in advance constraint (19.33) and the government debt valuation equation (19.34) together determine the price level in terms of variables chosen by the government. I have been writing down these two equations. Now we have another explicit model to verify that this was the right thing to do. We see again that the government valuation equation (19.34) results from the consumer's budget constraint and equilibrium. It is not a "government budget constraint."

The government has three levers $\{M_t, B_t, s_t\}$ that produce one outcome $\{P_t\}$. Thus, the government must choose its levers in a coordinated way, especially if we write government policy in the Ramsey tradition.

The standard solution to this model assumes at this point an active-money passive-fiscal regime. The central bank, by controlling $\{M_t\}$, determines the price level. Fiscal policy must then validate whatever price level the central bank has chosen. If you look closely, all good cash in advance papers state that fact somewhere, often specifying that the government levies lump sum taxes ex post so that (19.34) holds.

But we can also solve the same model, and arrive at the same equilibrium, with a passive money, active fiscal regime. Here, by choice of $\{B_t, s_t\}$ the government valuation equation controls the price level. The central bank must then passively provide the money $\{M_t\}$ needed to solve money demand. The equilibrium as defined above is the same, so the two ways of achieving coordination are observationally equivalent.

Moreover, we can tell any number of intermediate or other stories. The means by which central bank and treasury come up with a coordinated policy leave no trace in the data. The active/passive story is only one, and a quite unrealistic story of how coordination is accomplished.

19.5.4 Frictionless Model

I characterize the equilibrium of the frictionless model, in which people do not have to hold money overnight. If interest rates are positive, people will hold no money. Nonetheless, there is a well-defined equilibrium under an active fiscal policy.

In the frictionless model, asset markets, or the banks where households trade cash for bonds, remain open through the day. The cash in advance constraint therefore vanishes. The frictionless solution of this cash in advance model formalizes the story I told in the first chapter about a "day," in which the government prints up cash to pay off bonds, and that cash is then soaked up at the end of the day by selling new bonds.

In this model,

1. The marginal rate of substitution (19.31) is still equal to the stochastic discount factor or contingent claims prices,

$$\beta^j \frac{u'(y_{t+j})}{u'(y_t)} = \frac{\Lambda_{t+j}}{\Lambda_t}. \qquad (19.36)$$

If the endowment is constant over time, we have $\Lambda_{t+j}/\Lambda_t = \beta^j$.

2. Any equilibrium with positive nominal interest rates ($Q_t < 1$), must have no money

$$M_t = 0. \tag{19.37}$$

No equilibrium may have negative nominal interest rates, $Q_t > 1$.

3. The government debt valuation equation holds, now

$$\frac{B_{t-1}}{P_t} = E_t \sum_{j=0}^{\infty} \frac{\Lambda_{t+j}}{\Lambda_t} s_{t+j}. \tag{19.38}$$

The consumer's flow budget constraint (19.27) is not changed, so first order condition behind Fact 1 is the same. Removing the constraint (19.25) that cash from sales must be held overnight, the minimum cash that the household can hold overnight is zero, so (19.37) replaces the quantity equation (19.33). Equation (19.37) is still a money demand equation, but it now holds for any price level and so does not help in price level determination. A negative nominal interest rate is an arbitrage opportunity, and leads to infinite money and negative infinite bond demand, and so cannot be an equilibrium. Equation (19.38) specializes (19.35). In periods with positive nominal rates $i_{t+j} > 0$, we have $M_{t+j} = 0$, so the seigniorage term drops because M is missing. In periods with zero nominal rates, $i_{t+j} = 0$, seigniorage drops because there is no interest differential between money and bonds.

There are specifications of the utility function, endowment processes, and government choices $\{B_t^s, M_t^s, s_t\}$ that result in equilibria of the frictionless model with determinate, finite price levels. I can prove this statement most transparently by giving a simple example. Suppose $u(c) = c^{1-\gamma}, y_t = y, B_t^s = B, M_t^s = 0, s_t = s$, all constant over time. Obviously, we must have $c_t = y$. From (19.36), the discount factor is constant,

$$\frac{\Lambda_{t+1}}{\Lambda_t} = \beta.$$

From (19.38), the price level must be constant and positive,

$$P_t = P = (1 - \beta)\frac{B}{s}.$$

Nominal interest rates are positive, $Q_t = \beta < 1$ so money demand equals money supply $M = 0$. We have $\lim_{T \to \infty} \beta^T B/P = 0$ so the transversality condition (19.28) is satisfied. The consumer's first order conditions and transversality conditions are necessary and sufficient for an optimum. Thus, we have found sequences $\{c_t, M_t^d, M_t, B_t, s_t, Q_t, p_t\}$ and M_0, B_0 that satisfy the definition of an equilibrium. Furthermore, given all the other variables, $\{P_t\}$ is unique.

Not all specifications of the utility function, endowment process, and government choices $\{B_t^s, M_t^s, s_t\}$ result in equilibria, as pathological utility functions and "uncoordinated" or otherwise nonsensical policy do not lead to equilibria in the monetary model. Here, I discuss the issues, but I do not attempt a characterization of the weakest possible restrictions on utility functions and exogenous processes that result in an equilibrium.

As in all dynamic models, the endowment process and utility function must be such that equilibrium marginal rates of substitution $\Lambda_{t+j}/\Lambda_t = \beta^j u'(y_{t+j})/u'(y_t)$ are defined. For example, we can't have occasionally negative endowments in a model with power utility.

Equation (19.38) and market clearing ensure a unique, positive, equilibrium price level sequence $\{P_t\}$, if the government always chooses a positive amount of nominal debt at each date, $\infty > B_t^s + M_t^s > 0$ and a surplus whose present value is positive $\infty > E_t \sum_{j=0}^{\infty} (\Lambda_{t+j}/\Lambda_t) s_{t+j} > 0$. Individual surpluses may be negative; that is, deficits. One must rule out $0/0 = 0$ problems in (19.38).

One-period bond prices are determined from $Q_t = P_t E_t(\Lambda_{t+1}/\Lambda_t P_{t+1})$. For there to be an equilibrium, the government must choose a price level sequence, via its choices of $\{B_t^s, M_t^s, s_t\}$, so that the expectation exists, and so that the nominal interest rate is non-negative, $Q_t \geq 1$. If the price level sequence requires a negative nominal interest rate, households try to hold infinite cash and infinite negative amounts of debt.

Finally, the government must produce a coordinated policy configuration $\{B_t, M_t, s_t\}$. In this frictionless model, the government cannot produce that configuration by setting surpluses $\{s_t\}$ in response to prices, to mechanically have (19.38) hold for any price level: It may not set a passive fiscal policy. If it did so, the price level would be undetermined. Thus, the government must also choose an active fiscal policy in order for there to be an equilibrium price level in the frictionless model.

19.5.5   Multiple Equilibria Reemerge

Even the cash in advance model has multiple deflationary equilibria with passive fiscal policy because people hold arbitrary amounts of money at the zero bound. Active fiscal policy trims them.

The cash in advance model appears to formalize the interest inelastic case, $M_t V = P_t y_t$, in which if the government sets a fixed money supply M_t^s, we have a unique price level for fiat currency with a passive fiscal policy. Alas, even this case fails to determine the price level.

The money demand function for the cash in advance model is not, in fact, a perfect $M_t V = P_t y_t$ with fixed V. At zero interest rate, money demand becomes a correspondence. Any $M_t \geq P_t y_t / V$ will do. At negative interest rates, money demand becomes infinite. One can think of the cash in advance money demand function as the limit of the usual function, pushed to the axes: The curve becomes an L, allowing any quantity of money M at a zero interest rate $i = 0$. This L brings back the indeterminacy circus. Technically, the cash in advance constraint only binds if the interest rate is positive. If the interest rate is zero, the cash in advance constraint does not bind, as people are happy to hold more money than it requires.

One might think that indeterminacy therefore only holds for a low value of money growth, which drives inflation down to the point that the nominal rate is zero. That case does exist. Even the $M_t V = P_t y_t$ equilibrium becomes indeterminate when money growth is too low. But there are multiple zero interest rate equilibria for *any* money growth path, just as we found liquidity trap equilibria in the money in utility function model and in the new-Keynesian model.

For example, consider perfect foresight equilibria. Let $M_{t+1}/M_t = 1 + \mu$, and specify a constant endowment y. The usual equilibrium is $P_t = M_t V/y = M_0(1 + \mu)^t V/y$. The nominal interest rate is $(1 + i) = (1 + \delta)P_{t+1}/P_t = (1 + \delta)(1 + \mu)$ where $1 + \delta = 1/\beta$. So long as $1 + \mu > \beta$, the usual equilibrium has a positive interest rate and the cash in advance constraint binds.

But there are also equilibria with $P_{t+1}/P_t = \beta$, a slight deflation, despite positive money growth. Start with a price level $P_0 < M_0 V/y$. Money is greater than needed for the cash in advance constraint, but the consumer does not care because $P_1/P_0 = \beta$, so $i_0 = 0$. Now, we also then have $P_1 < M_1 V/y$: We have $P_1 = \beta P_0$, and $M_1 = (1 + \mu)M_0$, and by assumption, $1 + \mu > \beta$. Likewise,

$$P_t = \beta^t P_0 \leq \beta^t M_0 V/y \leq (1 + \mu)^t M_0 V/y = M_t V/y.$$

In words, the price level is below the steady-state, and slight deflation. The interest rate is zero, and even though money keeps growing, people are happy to have ever larger amounts of money at zero interest rates.

The cash in advance model does not have the multiple *inflations* described above. But the cash-in-advance model has the same multiple equilibrium *deflations*, because money and bonds are perfect substitutes at zero interest rates.

Active fiscal policy can rule out these multiple equilibria. The government commits to financing the debt at price levels from the desired equilibrium, $P_t = M_t V/y$, but will not raise surpluses to validate deflations. It looks passive on the desired equilibrium path—surpluses rise to pay accumulated debts—but it is active in not validating alternative equilibria.

The same objection may be raised as with the money in utility model: In the case that money growth is positive, deflation at the real interest rate means that real money holdings grow faster than the interest rate. The same answer from Section 19.3.2, and explored in detail in Online Appendix Chapter 3 applies: A violation of the transversality condition is active fiscal policy. So we agree, one needs active fiscal policy to rule out multiple equilibria.

These problems are acknowledged if you read cash in advance models carefully. For example, in the classic textbook treatment, Sargent (1987) p. 162 writes "except in Section 5.5, we will focus on equilibria in which the currency-in-advance restriction $p_t c_t \leq m_t^p$ is met with equality because the risk-free net nominal interest rate is positive. . ." "We will focus on" acknowledges that there are other equilibria, which Sargent ignores; rightly, as they are beside his point. The same erasure is implicit in the usual dynamic programming approach, which is equivalent to the minimum state variable approach. If you assume that the equilibrium price level must be a time invariant function of state variables, then you rule out the multiple equilibria.

Sargent's Section 5.5 (p. 177 ff.) considers the possibility that money pays the same interest as other risk-free securities, which is the more general case of $i = 0$ induced by low money growth. Treating the case that reserves pay full interest on p. 178, Sargent writes: "Because currency is not dominated in rate of return, $m_t^p \geq p_t c_t$ will not generally hold with equality. Instead the household's demand for real balances of currency is indeterminate. . ." As a result, p. 180, "the price level, level of taxes and real balances, are all indeterminate." In that statement, Sargent p. 180 takes care to rule out the fiscal theoretic repair: "the government levies whatever lump-sum taxes are necessary to finance the interest payments on currency."

(Online Appendix Section A3.3 reviews Woodford (1994), which treats multiple equilibria in cash in advance models with cash and credit goods.)

The cash in advance model differs from pure monetarism at the zero bound. Many monetarists insist that $MV = Py$ continues to hold even at zero interest rates, that velocity is still "stable" in a suitable "long run." The cash in advance model, like the money in utility satiation model, says that money and bonds are perfect substitutes at the zero bound, so there is no upper limit to money demand, and no reason that velocity will return to its "long-run" value.

These observations should not be taken as criticism of the cash in advance literature. The point of these models lies in characterizing the interesting "focus" equilibria, not being picky about just what technicalities one wishes to invoke to rule out multiple equilibria. When the models were developed in the 1980s, nobody had seen a zero interest rate in decades, and inflation slowly declining with zero nominal rates seemed rightly like a technical nuisance. The point, to create a formal model of money that essentially derived the form of money in the utility function from a simple though abstract trading model, thus avoiding endless controversy over the form of that function, was a huge contribution to monetary theory.

But my point here is precisely to worry about technicalities, to see just what it takes to fully determine the price level. Cash in advance models with passive fiscal policy leave open multiple equilibria. With fiscal theory, it is easy to trim the undesired equilibria. If one wishes to use a cash in advance model, the only substantive change this analysis recommends is to add an equation or two to statements like "we focus on" the binding cash constraint equilibrium. Write that multiple deflationary equilibria are ruled out by an active fiscal policy coordinated with monetary policy, and the government's refusal to validate deflation by raising taxes in particular.

19.6   Unpleasant Arithmetic and Fiscal Theory

Sargent and Wallace (1981) study $MV = Py$ plus a government debt valuation equation with real debt and seigniorage. The central bank can choose less inflation now, but then must choose more inflation later, to preserve the present value of seigniorage revenue. Fiscal theory builds on their insight. Nominal debt means that lower inflation must include fiscal tightening to pay a real windfall to bondholders. Sticky prices mean that a monetary tightening needs higher surpluses to pay higher interest costs. The latter are larger, and exist without seigniorage.

In the famous "Unpleasant Monetarist Arithmetic," Sargent and Wallace (1981) link deficits to inflation. This is a foundational work that brought monetary–fiscal coordination to important contemporary policy questions. Fiscal theory is built on the foundations laid by unpleasant arithmetic.

Sargent and Wallace consider a model with money, in which the price level is determined by money demand = money supply, and a government debt valuation equation; in my notation,

$$M_t V = P_t y \tag{19.39}$$

$$b_{t-1} = \sum_{j=0}^{\infty} E_t \left[\beta^j \left(s_{t+j} + \frac{M_{t+j} - M_{t+j-1}}{P_{t+j}} \right) \right]. \tag{19.40}$$

Sargent and Wallace specify real or indexed debt, so the value on the left-hand side of (19.40) is unaffected by the price level. This specification is explicit below Sargent and Wallace's equation (4). I use the lowercase b_{t-1} to reflect that fact.

They ask how money supply control M_t affects inflation. They envision a monetary policy that cannot change surpluses, as I have, and surpluses do not change to exploit or offset changes in seigniorage revenue. The government debt valuation equation (19.40) then constrains the set of price levels and money supplies that the government may choose.

A monetary tightening can reduce current inflation by slowing money growth. But without a change in surpluses, the central bank will have to raise later money growth and later inflation, to preserve the present value of seigniorage revenue and to avoid default on real debt. Unless the fiscal problem is fixed, the central bank cannot avoid inflation or printing money to finance insufficient surpluses. But the central bank can still decide *when* it will print more money.

Obvious to us, but novel at the time, the *present value* of seigniorage revenue counts. That fact means current deficits or "austerity" are not necessary, if a long-run fiscal problem is solved. On the other hand, a short bout of debt-financed austerity without solving the long-run problem does no more good than a short bout of monetary restraint. (Section 14.3 discusses Sargent and Wallace in its historical context, the 1980 monetary tightening amid large deficits.)

In the language of this book, Sargent and Wallace specify active fiscal policy. As we have seen in other fiscal theory of monetary policy models, the central bank still controls the timing of inflation; with money supply here, with interest rate targets or nominal debt purchases and sales in other models of this book. The government debt valuation is a constraint on the path of money and inflation that the central bank may choose. It is a no-default condition, not formally a budget constraint.

With Sargent and Wallace's main point in front of us, we can see that it is justly famous as a pioneering study of fiscal–monetary links. However, the subsequent 40 years of fiscal theorizing have produced some additional progress. Critics who say that fiscal theory is "just" unpleasant monetarist arithmetic are missing a few tasty morsels. First, rather than b_{t-1} indexed debt, the left-hand side in fiscal theory may be the real value of nominal debt B_{t-1}/P_t. With nominal debt, a fall in the present value of surpluses $\{s_{t+j}\}$ can generate a higher price level P_t even with no money demand or seigniorage whatsoever—deleting (19.39) and setting $M = 0$ in (19.40). By the same mechanism, to achieve a monetary tightening that lowers inflation, governments must finance a real windfall to the holders of outstanding nominal bonds, as well as replace lost seigniorage revenue.

Second, by integrating fiscal theory with sticky prices, a monetary tightening that produces higher interest rates now also generates higher real interest costs on the debt. These
costs must also be financed by additional surpluses, equivalently the discount rate effect
in present value terms, and are also present with no money and no seigniorage. Both
of these effects are larger than pure seigniorage, and make fiscal concerns quantitatively
more important than seigniorage. The integration with rational-expectations, sticky price
models (not invented when Sargent and Wallace wrote) is itself novel, and a key to reasonable dynamics. Describing monetary policy with interest rate targets connects to central
bank practice. Long-term debt and much else of the previous chapters is also novel and
important for describing policy.

19.7 Seigniorage and Hyperinflation

A government starts to print money to finance deficits. As inflation heats up, people hold less real money M/P.
Past a unit elasticity point, printing more money produces *less* seigniorage revenue. A steadily increasing need
for revenue can lead to nonlinearly increasing inflation, and then to a jump to hyperinflation.

The sudden emergence of hyperinflation when a government tries to finance larger and
larger deficits by printing money provides a second classic parable of monetary–fiscal
coordination.

As governments print more money to finance larger deficits, inflation rises. As inflation rises, people hold less real money M/P. They hold money for shorter amounts of
time, they substitute to foreign currency, they revert to barter or common goods. Thus,
each increase in money growth and inflation gives rise to a less than proportional increase
in revenue. Eventually, the decrease in real money demand can become larger than the
increase in money growth. A further increase in money growth produces *less* revenue. The
economy becomes unstable, and inflation shoots essentially to infinity. Seigniorage has a
Laffer limit, just like other taxes.

To see this behavior in equations, start with an interest-elastic money demand,

$$MV(i) = Py. \tag{19.41}$$

Examine steady-states with varying inflation. The real revenue from seigniorage, as a
fraction of GDP, is

$$\frac{-s}{y} = \frac{1}{Py}\frac{dM}{dt}.$$

(The surplus is s, so a deficit, financed by money growth, is a negative value of s.)
Differentiating (19.41) with respect to time in a steady-state,

$$\frac{dM}{dt}V(i) = \frac{dP}{dt}y + P\frac{dy}{dt},$$

$$\left(\frac{1}{Py}\frac{dM}{dt}\right)V(i) = \frac{1}{P}\frac{dP}{dt} + \frac{1}{y}\frac{dy}{dt} = \pi + g,$$

so seigniorage revenue as a percentage of GDP is

$$\frac{-s}{y} = \frac{\pi + g}{V(r + \pi)}.$$

As the government raises money growth and hence inflation π, it initially raises more revenue, and can finance a larger deficit $-s$. But higher inflation π also means higher velocity V, or lower money demand. These reduce the revenue produced by seigniorage, as all taxes produce less revenue after tax avoidance behavior kicks in. If the rise in velocity is larger than the rise in inflation, more inflation leads to less revenue. Maximum revenue occurs where the elasticity of velocity is roughly 1, or when the elasticity of money demand is roughly -1,

$$\frac{d\log(-s)}{d\log\pi} = \frac{\pi}{\pi + g} - \frac{d\log V}{d\log\pi} = \frac{\pi}{\pi + g} + \frac{d\log(M/Py)}{d\log\pi}.$$

The elasticity of money demand likely rises with inflation. When inflation changes from 1% to 2%, it is unlikely that money demand halves, or velocity doubles. When inflation rises from 100% to 200%, a halving of money demand is more plausible. So, as inflation rises, more inflation generates less revenue.

So we can tell a beautiful economic parable: The government gets in trouble and starts printing money. Inflation rises. The government gets in more trouble, and prints more money. Inflation rises again, but money demand decreases, producing less revenue for the same money growth increase, or more inflation for the same revenue increase. Eventually, the government hits the revenue-maximizing inflation point. When the government then tries to squeeze one more cent of revenue from the inflation tax, inflation jumps to infinity. This is a good parable for how inflation can get so astronomically high, so suddenly. In reverse, it is part of the story of the sudden ends of hyperinflations (Section 14.2), in which less inflation corresponds to more seigniorage revenue. Adding inflationary dynamics rather than studying steady-states, in the style of Section 19.2, the inflation can occur in advance of the money printing.

19.8   Monetary History

The correlation of money with nominal income does not establish that money causes inflation. The failure of postwar interest rate pegs came amid fiscal stress. When tried, monetary targets were quickly abandoned. Since the 1970s, central banks have operated entirely with interest rate targets. Inflation is stable at decades-long zero bound, with immense open market operations (QE), and rampant financial innovation. I opine even Milton Friedman might change his mind with new facts and experience at hand.

Would Milton Friedman object to this book's turn away from monetarism? Perhaps not. Friedman's Chicago school was ultimately empirical, disciplined by clear theory. A half-century of new facts and a reevaluation of old ones might change Friedman's view.

The correlation of money and nominal income is a celebrated monetarist fact. The Friedman and Schwartz (1963) monetary history traces this correlation through time.

Plots of money versus nominal income, M versus Py, and plots of money M/Py versus an interest rate, are favorite monetarist art. The "stability" of such plots over long time periods is admired. These are often called plots of money demand, though equilibrium quantities do not self-evidently trace out a demand curve.

But correlation does not prove causation: When real income or the price level rises for other reasons, people demand more money. Money supply is elastic, so we see a correlation between money and nominal income. A stable money demand plot is completely consistent with fiscal theory.

Friedman and Schwartz anticipated this critique, pointing out that changes in money typically precede changes in nominal income. And the point of their magisterial book was, in many ways, to argue causality from the details of each episode, to show exogenous actions of monetary authorities that arguably caused later changes in nominal income. In this way, they embody my contention that in the face of observational equivalence results—either direction of causality can underlie a correlation—narrative and institutional evidence is at least a useful complement to time series tests.

The attempt to tease money versus income causality out of the data led to much justly famous economics and econometrics. Andersen and Jordan (1968) run regressions of nominal income on money and vice versa. But Tobin (1970) points out that timing does not prove causality: People may anticipate nominal income growth and demand more money, as people build up other inventories in advance of a strong economy. Granger (1969) and Sims (1980) respond by looking at ordering of surprises, not of variables. Money Granger-causes income if a money surprise forecasts income surprises, if $\Delta E_{t+1} M_{t+1}$ forecasts $\Delta E_{t+1}(Py)_{t+1+j}$, if the impulse response function from money to nominal income is positive and not vice versa. In Tobin's example, news about future income would forecast money holdings. But as Granger and Sims make clear, Granger causality is not causality. Additional variables observed by people but left out of the forecasts can reverse Granger causality tests. The weather forecast Granger-causes the weather. As Granger (2004) observes, "many ridiculous papers appeared" that ignore this caveat. The revolution in time series refined but did not settle the dispute that started it.

Ex post selection of the monetary aggregate is another long-standing criticism. Which of the many possible aggregates should one take as the money in $MV = Py$? Early quantity theorists such as Irving Fisher based the demand for money in a demand for assets that one has to hold as an inventory to make transactions. (See Fisher (1912) and don't miss the beautiful artwork.) Indeed, the equation was $MV = PT$, proportional to the volume of transactions, not nominal income. That specification is the cornerstone of monetary theory to this day, as for example in the cash in advance tradition covered in Section 19.5, as well as the vast literature on microfoundations of money. Yet monetarism favored larger aggregates, such as M2, which includes interest-paying savings accounts. Why? Well, really, because M2 is better correlated with nominal GDP.

That observation is not a criticism of monetarists. Monetarists were practical, working to develop a theory and to use it to understand the world. Too much theoretical purity too soon hobbles such an effort. If M2 works and is useful, surely later theorists will find reasons for it, perhaps in the long list of other attributes of "money" and words for its demand—speculative, precautionary, and so forth. Indeed, the point of this book is that fiscal theory has spent too much time on theoretical purity rather than becoming useful, and that tests and deep theory should follow, not precede, the hundreds of such decisions one must make in order to develop a useful theory. But it is a valid criticism now, of further use of the theory.

Many of the additional motivations beyond transactions demand view money as an asset. Tobin (1958) is a famous early example. Aiyagari and Gertler (1991) are a modern classic: People have uninsured idiosyncratic risks, and costs for trading securities, so they value money as a buffer stock despite rate of return dominance. Such views help to understand money demand. But we also have an asset demand for bonds, and liquidity demand can now be fulfilled by highly liquid floating-value assets that are not directly means of payment or numeraire. The idea that controlling the split of assets between such "money" and "bonds" is crucial for price level determination loses much force.

Moreover, monetary theory has been in the hands of monetarists, or their successors. Reasonably, they produce theory that helps to understand monetarist conclusions, that control of the money supply is central to controlling inflation. An earlier generation of Keynesian economists worked on theories of money demand that undermined monetarist conclusions. In the Allais (1947) Baumol (1952) Tobin (1956) model, cash is an inventory. It costs a fixed amount of time or money to go to the bank and switch cash for bonds. You can hold less money, and save on interest costs, by going more often or by taking out less each time. This model produces an interest and income elasticity that are each a half. To our discussion, the substantial interest elasticity means that multiple equilibrium problems are more important. (Empirical estimates are smaller, but not zero. See the excellent Lucas (1988).) In the IS-LM context in which this debate proceeded, the slope of the LM curve is the ratio of income to interest elasticities of money demand. A flatter LM curve means, to them, that classic Keynesian fiscal stimulus is more powerful and monetary policy less so. This model gives a unit slope—not vertical as monetarists (unit income, zero interest elasticity) might like, though not horizontal as the "liquidity trap" specifies. In this context, the simple cash-in-advance model is notable as a theory with a unit income and zero interest elasticity.

Miller and Orr (1966) develop a different inventory model of money demand. Since cash flows are unpredictable, firms wait until cash reserves fall to a lower boundary s, or accumulate to an upper boundary S, and then adjust by buying or selling securities. Akerlof and Milbourne (1980) point out that with this kind of money demand, as long as the s-S boundaries do not change, income changes or money supply changes just make money flow faster or slower. The income elasticity is zero, the LM curve is flat, and velocity is endogenous. Akerlof and Milbourne thought it likely that people would not adjust s-S boundaries on a short-term basis, as the costs of failing to do so are small.

These interesting approaches to monetary theory dried up along with controversy over the slope of the LM curve as a useful way to think about macroeconomics, and the pre-2008 consensus that monetary policy had won the war over fiscal policy as the main engine of countercyclical stimulus.

Models that may have made sense in the financial system of the 1950s no longer do so. We now have a wide range of liquid assets, unused credit card balances, lines of credit, trade credit, and repurchase agreements, which can help to make transactions, and satisfy a complex set of liquidity needs, such as collateral in financial affairs. The modern version of asset or inventory demand, including self-insurance and trading frictions, is reemerging in the new study of liquidity spreads in financial markets.

The conclusion I draw is that a hope to separate some assets into "money" and others into "bonds" and hope that control of that split has first-order effects on the price level is now doomed. For a given level of wealth, the level of "spending" or aggregate demand does not depend on restrictions on the split of that wealth between different categories of assets. Asset, transactions, and inventory demands for a plethora of liquid assets are interesting and drive interesting liquidity spreads. But such spreads are second-order effects for price level determination, among other reasons because controlling the supply of such assets is hopeless. I can hope that Friedman, starting afresh, might look at our current monetary and financial system and come to the same conclusion.

Friedman and Schwartz argued eloquently that monetary policy mistakes were the prime source of macroeconomic volatility. But recent literature finds that monetary policy shocks—unexpected changes in interest rates, deviations from a rule—contribute small fractions of output, employment and inflation volatility. (My small contribution is Cochrane (1994c). Ramey (2016) is an excellent recent survey.) The recessions of 2000, 2008, and 2020 clearly resulted from a stock market bust, a banking crisis, and a pandemic, not from money supply mistakes.

Yes, 2008 is sometimes chalked up to a housing "bubble" stoked by too-low interest rates, but just how the level of nominal interest rates feeds in to a risk premium in mortgage-backed securities remains a verbal belief that is not yet well modeled. One can blame the Fed for regulatory failures, but that's a different story. The timing of the bust is hard to pin on the Fed, and the magnitude of the event clearly has more to do with amazingly thin bank capital, not the Fed pulling the interest rate or money supply punchbowl too soon.

Friedman was strongly influenced by the disaster of the Great Depression. Friedman and Schwartz (1963) criticize the Fed: The collapse of banking led to a collapse of inside money, that the Fed should have prevented or offset by greater outside money. Even that story does not put the Fed in the causal role, but merely one of amplifying an already bad situation. And the causal importance this action has seen much more subsequent analysis. For example, Bernanke (1983) points to the destruction of the banking system's ability to make loans; Cole and Ohanian (2004) and Kehoe and Prwescott (2007) point to the microeconomic damage of New Deal policies. The Fed's tightening in advance of the 1929 stock market crash to try to rein in stock market speculation, an early instance of what is now approvingly called macro-prudential or credit-cycle policy, has attracted less attention.

During and after WWII, the Fed pegged the interest rate on long-term bonds at 2.5%, with a mandate to hold down the interest costs of WWII debt. In his presidential address, Friedman (1968) mentions prominently the failure of this peg, and postwar interest rate pegs in other countries, as evidence for the proposition that interest rate pegs are unstable and therefore money supply must control the price level:

> These views [ineffectiveness of monetary policies] produced a widespread adoption of cheap money policies after the war. And they received a rude shock when these policies failed in country after country, when central bank after central bank was

forced to give up the pretense that it could indefinitely keep "the" rate of interest at a low level. In this country, the public denouement came with the Federal Reserve-Treasury Accord in 1951, although the policy of pegging government bond prices was not formally abandoned until 1953. Inflation, stimulated by cheap money policies, not the widely heralded postwar depression, turned out to be the order of the day.

In retrospect, and with a fiscal theory in mind that Friedman could not have imagined, one can't help but note that the postwar pegs fell apart coincident with fiscal problems.

Woodford (2001) analyzes the U.S. peg. Our first question of this interest rate peg should not be, why did it fall apart? Our first question should be, why did something supposedly unstable last so long? The peg lasted a decade, and two if you count zero rates in the Great Depression. Woodford credits fiscal theory mechanisms for the surprising stability of the interest rate peg, as I have analyzed here. In Woodford's view, the peg fell apart when the Korean war undermined fiscal policy.

The history of the period reinforces this larger picture. Borrowing for WWII was not easy. It included price controls, rationing, interest rate controls, financial repression, and foreign exchange and capital controls. All of these measures raise demand for government debt. When the United States lifted price controls in 1947, inflation swiftly rose. The resulting 40% cumulative price level rise by 1949 devalued WWII debt by 40%. In Woodford's analysis, the unexpected Korean war and recession required a sudden rise in fiscal resources. Though the resulting deficits were not large by WWII standards, they upset expectations that WWII debt would be steadily repaid, and occasioned a return to 9% inflation.

European countries whose pegs fell apart had more severe fiscal problems in the wake of WWII. They also repressed financial markets and capital flows to try to force people to hold their money and debt. Price controls and rationing were pervasive. The United Kingdom suffered repeated fiscal and exchange rate crises.

Why did interest rate pegs fail? Fiscal stress is the plausible alternative to pig-headed "cheap money" policies, especially now that we have a clearer vision of how fiscal policy feeds into inflation. The postwar interest rate pegs were not a monetary policy that tried to manage inflation and unemployment by technocratic means, backed by "passive" fiscal policy with ample space to repay government debt, only in the thrall of bad ideas. Many interest rate pegs were part of a coordinated system of financial repression undertaken to address dire fiscal situations. Their failure was the beginning of the unraveling of Bretton Woods, fixed exchange rates, international capital controls, regulation of bank interest rates, and other measures of financial repression and government debt support.

Monetarism's greatest challenge comes from the events of the 1970s until today. The great success of Friedman (1968) was his prediction that if exploited, the Phillips curve would shift and stagflation would emerge. Given the stable Phillips curve in data to that time, this was an audacious prediction. But the prediction has nothing to with the source of that inflation, whether too much money printed in exchange for bonds, a mistaken interest rate target, or a fiscal expansion to finance the Great Society and Vietnam War without unpopular taxes.

One may take the end of inflation in the 1980s as a Friedman victory as well, and his name was used to bless much of the tight monetary policy. But if the end of inflation was a victory of monetary policy, and not as I argue a joint monetary, fiscal, and microeconomic reform, it was a victory of interest rate targets and rules, not of money supply control.

In the early 1980s, the Fed experimented with a money supply target. Controversy continues over whether the Fed picked the right aggregate, and whether it really controlled the aggregate effectively or simply used aggregate control as a smokescreen for high interest rates. But the immediate response to changing M was that previously stable V started shifting. Monetarists initially excused the unraveling of $MV = PY$ as due to "velocity shocks." But the natural conclusion is that moving M causes V to move the other way, leaving Py alone; that ironically $MV = PY$ turns out to be a correlation like the Phillips curve, stable in past data, but mush when one pushes on it. Even in the former interpretation, however, the event reinforced the view that money demand is not stable in the short run, so the Fed should target interest rates in order to accommodate shifts in money demand. After two years, the Fed gave up targeting monetary aggregates and has targeted interest rates ever since, as it did before.

The long quiet zero bound period with immense quantitative easing, described in more detail in Chapter 20, is difficult for the monetarist view. Friedman warned that interest rate pegs must soon fall apart in spiraling inflation or deflation, which did not happen. Quantitative easing should have been a hyperinflationary bomb.

How would Friedman look back now at the failure of monetary targeting in the early 1980s; the sharp fall and subsequent quiet inflation under interest rate targets; quiet and apparently stable inflation at long-lasting near-zero interest rates, with reserve requirements on M2 not biding by trillions of dollars, in the face of a 30,000% expansion of reserves (from $10 billion to $3 trillion); and financial innovation undoing the foundations of monetarism? I gather from verbal reminiscences of his colleagues that he became reconciled to interest rate targets that follow a Taylor rule, and as cited above Friedman (1992) endorses the spread target idea.

You can see that I fear the curse of Friedman's ghost, given that he was so right about so much, that monetarism held such sway for so long, and that $MV = Py$ continues to underlie so much thinking about the price level. But Friedman was at heart an empiricist, guided by clear theory. So I hope that the facts since the 1970s and the availability of new theory might well have changed Friedman's mind. And, perhaps, since I do not similarly seek forgiveness from Tobin, Solow, or Samuelson, we should just move on to facts and theory.

This section is a short and impressionistic history of thought, emphasizing my view of ideas and how they bear on fiscal theory versus monetary theory. A serious scholar of monetarism should start with the stunning two-volume intellectual biography of Milton Friedman in Nelson (2020).

20

The Zero Bound

WHAT HAPPENS if the nominal interest rate hits zero and stays there for years, indeed a decade or more? There had been much theory about this event, but it remained an object of speculation and economic history until it descended upon the United States and Europe in 2008, and on Japan two decades earlier. This event provides an important test of monetary theories, of their ability to describe events, and to provide useful policy advice. This event also provides an example of how one can surmount observational equivalence and the fruitlessness of formal regime-testing exercises, by analyzing which theory makes more sense of important episodes. (This chapter summarizes and builds on Cochrane (2018) and Cochrane (2017c).)

20.1   The Experiment

Old-Keynesian thinking clearly predicted a deflationary spiral. New-Keynesian thinking clearly predicted volatile sunspot inflation. Monetarist thinking clearly predicted a large inflation. None of these happened. Fiscal theory is easily consistent with stable quiet inflation at the zero bound. A key assumption is that fiscal authorities will react to deflation with stimulus, not austerity.

Starting in 2008 in the United States and Europe, in response to the financial crisis and deep recession, short-term interest rates fell to zero and stayed there for nearly 10 years. Figure 20.1 illustrates this important episode in the United States.

Interest rates effectively hit zero in Japan in 1995, and have been there ever since, as illustrated in Figure 20.2.

Interest rates cannot go much below zero without provoking a flight to cash, so these episodes are called the "zero lower bound" (ZLB). The term "effective lower bound" (ELB) is sometimes used as central banks seem to be able to lower some interest rates to as low as -1% without provoking a flight to cash.

Clearly, in this situation, we cannot have active interest rate policy, $\phi > 1$ in $i_t = \phi\pi_t$, at least in the lower direction. Therefore, these episodes pose an important experiment for interest rate targeting theories of monetary policy.

What happens to inflation if interest rates cannot move, at least downward; if they stay at zero for many years, and are clearly expected to remain at zero for many more years? *Nothing.* The pattern of inflation in the 2008 recession was nearly identical to that in the 2000 recession, as shown. Inflation fell in both cases, and then rebounded quickly.

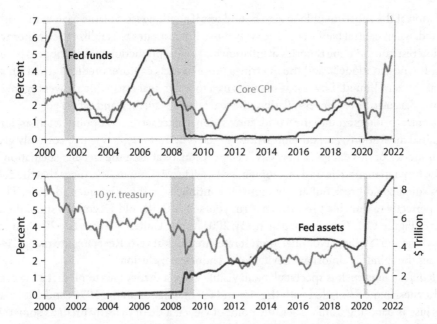

FIGURE 20.1. Inflation, Interest Rates, and Fed assets in the United States. Fed assets are in trillions of dollars, interest rates are in percent.

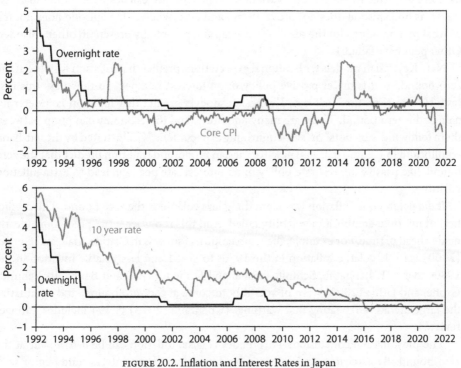

FIGURE 20.2. Inflation and Interest Rates in Japan

Inflation at the subsequent long zero bound was if anything *less* volatile than in the earlier period, when central banks could actively move interest rates to stabilize the economy.

Interest rate targeting theories of inflation make clear predictions about the zero bound. Old-Keynesian models, and the doctrines those models capture, predict a deflation spiral at the zero bound. Low inflation gives us a too high real rate, which lowers aggregate demand, causing even lower inflation; the real rate rises further, and off we go.

Central bankers around the world, conventional macroeconomic policy analysts, international institutions, and opinion writers in the *New York Times* warned, correctly given their model, of this danger, a new Great Depression, or at least the "secular stagnation" of static Keynesian models, and recommended larger fiscal stimulus. Warnings that the deflation spiral could break out at any moment continued for the subsequent decade. These are perfectly reasonable predictions. Arm yourself with the old-Keynesian spiral prediction of Figure 17.1. Consider Japan in, say, 2001, or the United States in late 2010. In each case, inflation is falling. Nominal interest rates are stuck at zero. Real rates are rising. "Here comes the spiral" is almost an inevitable and honest conclusion.

It did not happen. It is spectacular and visible when a theory fails to predict a big event, as Keynesian models failed with the rise and fall of inflation in the 1970s and 1980s. But it is just as damning from a scientific point of view if a theory clearly predicts something big to happen and the world greets the prediction with silence.

The most natural conclusion: This theory is false. Inflation can be *stable* at the zero bound. By extension, inflation can be stable at an interest rate peg or with passive $\phi < 1$ policy. Stability or instability is a core feature of the theory's dynamics, not a minor prediction easily fixed by small model variations. (I hedge with "can be" stable rather than "is" stable, as one episode does not prove always and everywhere. One episode does not tell us what preconditions for the result are crucial, and potentially present in other episodes. Other pegs have failed.)

New-Keynesian models with rational expectations predict that inflation is stable at the zero bound, as it is under passive policy or an interest rate peg, so they pass this first test. However, off-the-shelf new-Keynesian models predict that inflation is indeterminate at the zero bound. There are many equilibria, and the economy can jump between them following "sunspots" or "self-confirming expectations," as illustrated by the left-hand equilibrium in Figure 16.2. The new-Keynesian model and tradition predict that the zero bound, like passive interest rate policy or an interest rate peg, will lead to extra inflation volatility.

It did not happen. Inflation was if anything less volatile at the zero bound. The prediction of multiple-equilibrium volatility failed. And this too is a central prediction, clearly made ahead of time. For example, the main empirical success in Clarida, Galí, and Gertler (2000) is to tie volatile inflation in the 1970s to $\phi < 1$ and less volatile inflation in the 1980s to $\phi > 1$. Benhabib, Schmitt-Grohé, and Uribe (2001a) and Benhabib, Schmitt-Grohé, and Uribe (2002) warn of volatility to come at the zero bound, and summarize the large literature repeating that warning. (Cochrane (2018) p. 194 includes a longer review.)

The most natural conclusion: This theory is false. Inflation can be *determinate* at the zero bound. By extension, inflation can be determinate at an interest rate peg or with passive $\phi < 1$ policy.

In classic monetarist thought, the zero bound is not an important constraint on monetary policy. Yes, the Fed can then no longer control the quantity of money implicitly via an interest rate target. But nothing stops the Fed from buying bonds and issuing more reserves at a zero interest rate, and letting $MV = Py$ do its work—as, a monetarist might add, it should have been doing all along anyway.

The contrary view is that money and short-term bonds become perfect substitutes at zero interest rates, or when money pays market interest. Velocity becomes, if it was not so already, a meaningless ratio of nominal income to whatever split of government debt between reserves and Treasurys the Fed chooses. $Py = MV$ becomes $V = Py/M$.

This issue was central to the monetarist versus Keynesian debates of the 1950s and 1960s. Keynesians thought that at the zero interest rates of the Great Depression, money and bonds were perfect substitutes, so monetary policy—buying bonds, issuing money in return—could do nothing. They advocated fiscal stimulus instead. A fiscal theorist adds that the stimulus must be unbacked. Keynes called it a "liquidity trap," a pejorative, not "liquidity satiation," what would later become Friedman's optimal quantity of money. Monetarists held that additional money would be stimulative, even at zero interest rates; that velocity would not move arbitrarily downward in response to open market operations which raise M. The Fed's failure to provide or allow additional money in the 1930s deflation was, to them, the great policy error of that decade. The debate continued. In the postwar era of positive interest rates, with zero interest on reserves, there was no definitive way to tell what would happen should zero rates return to the postwar economy.

Starting in 2009, with interest rates effectively zero, the Fed embarked on a massive quantitative easing experiment, shown by the dramatic rise in bank reserves in Figure 20.1. Bank reserves rose from $10 billion on the eve of the crisis in August 2008 to $2,759 billion in August 2014, a 30,000% increase, funded by classic open market purchases on an unprecedented scale. Europe, the United Kingdom, and Japan followed similar policies. Monetarists and *Wall Street Journal* opeds predicted large inflation, correctly given a monetarist model. It's hard to ask for a clearer experiment.

It did not happen. Inflation trundled along a bit less than 2%. If you look at Figure 20.1, it is hard to see any effect of these QE operations at all. Two out of three QE episodes corresponded with slight *increases* in long-term interest rates. But overall long-term rates and inflation continue a decades-long downward trend untroubled by the zero bound, QE, or any of the other radical innovations of the era. More generally, the zero bound does not seem to be a state variable for any change in macroeconomic dynamics.

The most natural conclusion: This theory is false. Reserve demand is a correspondence, not a function, when reserves pay market interest rates; reserves and short-term debt are perfect substitutes; velocity does not revert to some "stable" value; arbitrary quantities of zero-cost reserves in exchange for treasury debt do not cause inflation. By implication and continuity, $MV = Py$ will not work for positive nominal rates, at least so long as reserves continue to pay close to market interest rates.

The immense size of the experiment avoids conventional objections: Perhaps there was a contemporaneous "velocity shock;" perhaps nominal GDP would have fallen had the Fed not increased reserves, perhaps we can see a few basis points of effects here and there. A 30,000% increase in reserves is a monetary hydrogen bomb, not a firecracker. If you're arguing about basis point effects, it was a dud.

By contrast, we have in hand a simple theory which is compatible with a long-lasting quiet zero bound: the fiscal theory of monetary policy. Add active fiscal policy to the new-Keynesian model, and inflation can be stable, determinate, and quiet at the zero bound.

One key fiscal assumption in this view is that were a deflation to break out, our fiscal authorities would not respond with sharp tax increases and spending cuts to pay a windfall real profit to nominal bond holders. They would if anything respond with fiscal "stimulus" programs and try to convince us that the fiscal stimulus is unbacked in order to create inflation. And this is exactly what they did, and what went wrong initially in 1933 (Section 8.2).

The second key assumption, ruling out inflation, is that bondholders have confidence that debt will eventually be repaid. Just where that confidence comes from is harder to pin down. However, the zero bound era included negative real interest rates, negative real interest costs, and the emergence of the $r < g$ debate. We may not need any increased surpluses at all to understand the value of debt in this era, merely an expectation that low interest rates will last a long time. Bondholders evidently thought debt would be repaid, at the return they were requiring, since each debt issue raised revenue.

The three theories are hard to tell apart in normal times, when nominal interest rates vary and changes in money are small. The long zero bound and immense QE are thus an especially important experiment which can distinguish theories that are otherwise difficult to distinguish.

20.1.1   Occam

Ex post patches, epicycles, and extensions to standard theories can be adduced to explain the long quiet zero bound. Occam's razor suggests that these are fragile paths to follow, when a simple theory lies before us.

Nothing is so simple in a nonexperimental science. One can make many excuses for a theory's failures, or patch up theories after the fact.

Perhaps inflation really is unstable, but artful quantitative easing offset the deflation spiral with just enough hyperinflationary money to give the appearance of stability. Perhaps prices and wages are much stickier than we thought. Perhaps we experienced the proverbial seven years of bad luck, Europe twelve, and Japan 25—repeated shocks despite the appearance of quiet. Survey expectations and the Fed's forecasts featured a quick escape from zero interest rates every year of the zero bound. Perhaps expectations of active policy a few years out led to a determinate inflation. Perhaps there just weren't any sunspots in the 2010s, and there happened to be a lot of sunspots in the 1970s. The economy doesn't *have* to move around when there are multiple equilibria.

These arguments all have been presented as explanations for the astonishing quiet at the zero bound. (Again, Cochrane (2018) includes a review.) All are logical possibilities. But Occam's famous razor suggests, why not adopt the simplest explanation? Our governments do not react to an undesired deflation by raising taxes and cutting spending to pay a windfall to bondholders. They do the opposite, for as long as it takes. With this expectation in place, deflation cannot break out at the zero bound. And as long as real interest rates remain low and faith in eventual repayment remains, inflation does not break out either. Then the force of interest rate equals expected inflation—even as smoothed by sticky prices and in the face of temporary opposite dynamics—means that zero interest rates will be met by low, steady, and gradually falling inflation. As we observed.

It is true that the proportionate rise in the monetary base—reserves plus currency, M1, and M2—was smaller than the proportionate rise in reserves during the QE episodes, and that QE3 did not correspond to much of a rise in M2 at all. But one must then ask *why* reserves did not leak in to M2. If immense open market operations do not affect it, then M2 is not controlled and M2 supply does not determine the price level.

The sign of the zero bound peg is different than the sign of the postwar and other failed pegs. In those episodes, central banks were trying to hold down rates that otherwise wanted to rise, lending money to banks at low rates, with financial repression to force people to hold government debt they did not want to hold and in the face of difficulty financing debt. In the zero bound era, central banks were forced to hold up interest rates that wanted to be lower, they borrowed money from banks (large reserves), and in the face of large demand for government debt. Theory does not yet predict different behavior for different signs, but it is a noteworthy difference.

20.2   Zero Bound Puzzles

A novel new-Keynesian approach selects equilibria by specifying active policy after the zero bound period is over. This approach predicts a big deflation early in the zero bound period, which did not happen. It requires a large fiscal contraction, which did not happen. Fiscal theory picks the zero bound equilibrium by initial inflation, not final inflation, and therefore does not predict a big deflation.

The novel new-Keynesian approach produces several related puzzles. Forward guidance promises have large immediate stimulative effects. Those effects are larger for promises about actions further in the future. Deliberate capital stock destruction, technical regress, and wasted government spending improve output, with large multipliers. These strange effects are larger as pricing frictions decrease, without limit. But puzzles disappear at the frictionless limit point. If we bound the size of a fiscal contraction, we solve all these puzzles and we obtain a smooth frictionless limit.

Proposals to solve the zero bound puzzles by complex models of irrational expectations require large amounts of irrationality and sticky prices, and bring back the problems of the old-Keynesian model. Until the new rules for expectations are verified throughout economics, it is not logically consistent to use them just to solve zero bound puzzles.

At the zero bound, active monetary policy $i_t = \phi(\pi_t - \pi_t^*)$ can no longer select equilibria. In a novel strain of new-Keynesian literature adapted to the zero bound environment, expectations of future active, destabilizing, policy rules take the place of responses to current inflation to select equilibria while interest rates are stuck at zero.

In these models, the economy eventually leaves the zero bound, either deterministically or stochastically. A destabilizing policy rule selects a unique locally bounded equilibrium in that future state. Modelers then tie equilibria during the zero rate period to the following equilibria, and thereby eliminate indeterminacies during the zero bound. Werning (2012), Eggertsson (2008), Eggertsson, Mehrotra, and Robbins (2019) (also summarized in Cochrane (2014a)) are good examples.

These papers make an important point: Current policy is not definitive about the regime; that is, which variable will explode at off-equilibrium prices. The point reappears more generally in models that specify Markov switching between regimes, in which one can appear to be in one regime but an anticipated switch means that long-run equilibrium selection expectations are really driven by the other regime. Here, they introduce a range of puzzling predictions.

20.2.1   Removing Sunspots?

One could use the future selection scheme to argue that the new-Keynesian model does not, after all, predict sunspot volatility at the zero bound. Here is a concrete example, using the simplified IS model from Section 16.1,

$$x_t = -\sigma\left(i_t - E_t\pi_{t+1} - u_{r,t}\right)$$
$$\pi_t = E_t\pi_{t+1} + \kappa x_t.$$

I call $u_{r,t}$ a "natural rate" disturbance. One can model this disturbance as an increase in impatience, leading to a desire to save, perhaps due to precautionary (higher volatility) motives. Such a shock is a common stand-in to model the 2008 financial crisis in new-Keynesian models. The central bank follows a policy rule that is active when it can be, but hits the zero bound,

$$i_t = \max\left[\pi^* + \phi(\pi_t - \pi^*), 0\right]. \tag{20.1}$$

This model exhibits a piecewise linear version of the dynamics of Figure 16.2. (This model comes from Cochrane (2018), which has more detail.)

Eliminating x_t, we reduce the model to a single equation in π_t:

$$\max\left[\pi^* + \phi\left(\pi_t - \pi^*\right), 0\right] = -\frac{1}{\sigma\kappa}\pi_t + \left(\frac{1+\sigma\kappa}{\sigma\kappa}\right)E_t\pi_{t+1} + u_{r,t}, \tag{20.2}$$

or, more clearly,

$$E_t\pi_{t+1} = \frac{1}{1+\sigma\kappa}\pi_t - \frac{\sigma\kappa}{1+\sigma\kappa}u_{r,t} \tag{20.3}$$
$$\text{when } \pi_t < \left(1 - \phi^{-1}\right)\pi^*,$$

and

$$E_t\pi_{t+1} - \pi^* = \frac{1+\phi\sigma\kappa}{1+\sigma\kappa}\left(\pi_t - \pi^*\right) - \frac{\sigma\kappa}{1+\sigma\kappa}u_{r,t} \tag{20.4}$$
$$\text{when } \pi_t > \left(1 - \phi^{-1}\right)\pi^*.$$

With $u_{r,t} = 0$, there is a stable steady-state at $\pi = 0$, where the inflation phase diagram has slope less than one, and an unstable locally determinate steady-state at $\pi = \pi^*$, where the phase diagram has slope greater than one. A negative $u_{r,t}$ disturbance pushes the phase

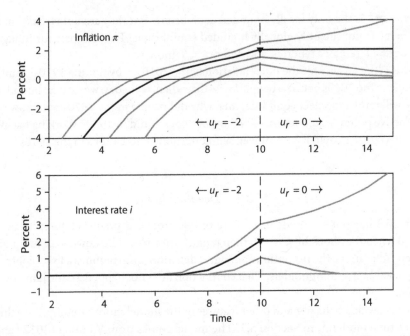

FIGURE 20.3. Selection by Future Policy Rules. The solid line is the selected equilibrium. The gray lines are alternative equilibria. There is a natural rate shock $u_r = -2\%$ from time $t = 0$ to $t = T = 10$. The central bank follows a rule $i_t = \max\left[\pi^* + \phi(\pi_t - \pi^*), 0\right]$. $\sigma = 1, \kappa = 1/2, \phi = 2, \pi^* = 2\%$.

diagram up, and pushes the steady-states in. The stable steady-state occurs at $\pi = -u_{r,t}$ and the unstable steady-state occurs at $\pi = \pi^* + u_{r,t}/(\phi - 1)$.

Now, suppose from time $t = 0$ to $t = T$, there is a negative natural-rate shock, $u_{r,t} = -2\%$. At time $t = T$ this natural-rate shock passes, so $u_{r,t} = 0$, $t > T$. Figure 20.3 shows possible paths of inflation and interest rate. Starting at time $t = T$, the central bank enforces its 2% inflation target with $\pi^* = 2\%$. This expectation selects the equilibrium, shown by the solid line in the middle. Before $t = T$, while the nominal rate remains stuck at zero, inflation is stable, converging as time goes forward. But when the nominal rate becomes unstuck, alternative equilibria diverge from the inflation target π^*. We now rule the multiple stable equilibria before $t = T$ as well.

In sum, the expectation of future equilibrium selection policy can select equilibria even when policy is currently or locally passive. This is an important general point, and a warning about labeling regimes by current policy when there is a potential switch between policies.

This equilibrium selection scheme has many troubles. As in all active monetary policy rules, inflation-expectation "anchoring" does not occur because the Fed is expected to *stabilize* inflation around the inflation target, but because the Fed is expected to *destabilize* inflation should it diverge from the target. Now this threat is removed from current events to the far future: not "Eat your spinach or there won't be dessert," but "Eat your spinach or there won't be dessert next year."

Equilibria in which inflation undershoots the time-T target π^* return back to zero inflation and zero interest rates. These equilibria are *locally* unstable around the target π^* and thus $\pi_t = \pi^*$ is the only locally bounded equilibrium, but they are not *globally* unstable, so $\pi_t = \pi^*$ is not the only globally bounded equilibrium. The rationale for ruling them out past $t > T$ remains tenuous, and before $t < T$ more so.

If this is the answer for the quiet inflation of the 2010s, why not the 1970s? If inflation was quiet in the 2010s because people knew that when, someday, we exit the bound, active policy will return to select equilibria, then why did people in the 1970s not know that an era of active policy would return—as the story goes, it did in 1980? Working backwards, that expectation should have removed self-confirming fluctuations in the 1970s.

20.2.2   Deflation Jump

Figure 20.3 illustrates a predictive failure of this model. It predicts a jump to deflation at $t = 0$ when the shock hits, which then rapidly improves. The downward jump did not happen. You can see the resolution coming: A deflation jump requires a fiscal contraction, to pay a windfall to bondholders. That contraction does not happen, so the jump does not happen.

To display this behavior and other features of the model more carefully, I use the continuous time model from Section 5.7. The model comes from Werning (2012) and this section is based on Cochrane (2017c). The IS and Phillips curves are

$$\frac{dx_t}{dt} = \sigma\left(i_t - \pi_t - u_{r,t}\right) \tag{20.5}$$

$$\frac{d\pi_t}{dt} = \rho\pi_t - \kappa\left(x_t + g_t\right). \tag{20.6}$$

Here, $u_{r,t}$ is the natural rate, and g_t is a Phillips curve disturbance discussed below. Among other purposes we will verify that the analysis of the last section using a static IS curve does not mischaracterize the model.

Suppose again that starting at $t = 0$, the economy suffers a negative natural rate disturbance $u_{r,t} = -2\%$, which lasts until time $t = T = 5$ before returning to a positive value. The nominal interest rate is zero up to period T, and then rises back to the natural rate $i_t = u_{r,t} > 0$ for $t \geq T$. I use $\rho = 0.05$, $\sigma = 1$ and $\kappa = 1$. Then, I find the set of output $\{x_t\}$ and inflation $\{\pi_t\}$ paths that, via (20.5) and (20.6), are consistent with this path of interest rates, and do not explode as time increases. Specifying directly the equilibrium path of interest rates does not mean that I assume a peg, that interest rates are exogenous, or that I ignore Taylor rules or other policy rules. Adding active monetary policy after the end of the trap

$$i_t = i_t^* + \phi(\pi_t - \pi_t^*) \tag{20.7}$$

will select the chosen i_t^*, π_t^* as a unique equilibrium, just as in the last section. Werning (2012) innovated this clever way of solving new-Keynesian models.

We solve the model as in Online Appendix Section A1.7. (See Cochrane (2017d) for algebra.) The forward stable solutions are

$$\pi_t = Ce^{-\lambda^b t} + \frac{1}{\lambda^f + \lambda^b} \left[\int_{s=-\infty}^t e^{-\lambda^b (t-s)} z_s ds + \int_{s=t}^\infty e^{-\lambda^f (s-t)} z_s ds \right], \qquad (20.8)$$

where

$$z_t \equiv \kappa \sigma (i_t - r_t) + \kappa \frac{dg_t}{dt} \qquad (20.9)$$

and

$$\lambda^f \equiv \frac{1}{2} \left(\sqrt{\rho^2 + 4\kappa\sigma} + \rho \right); \ \lambda^b \equiv \frac{1}{2} \left(\sqrt{\rho^2 + 4\kappa\sigma} - \rho \right).$$

From (17.2), then, the output gap follows

$$\kappa x_t = -\kappa g_t + \lambda^f Ce^{-\lambda^b t} + \frac{1}{\lambda^f + \lambda^b} \left[\lambda^f \int_{s=-\infty}^t e^{-\lambda^b (t-s)} z_s ds - \lambda^b \int_{s=t}^\infty e^{-\lambda^f (s-t)} z_s ds \right].$$

$$(20.10)$$

Here, I already set to zero the forward-explosive equilibria corresponding to a second free constant $C_f e^{\lambda^f t}$. As before, we can argue about that, but let's play by the rules of the game. For the same equilibrium interest rate path, there remain multiple forward-stable equilibrium inflation paths, indexed by the free constant C.

Figure 20.4 shows inflation in a range of such equilibria, generated by a range of values for the free constant C. These are multiple possible equilibria of the *same* model (20.5)–(20.6), with the *same* interest rate and natural rate path. We now use either active fiscal or active monetary policy, and a specification of that policy, to pick one of these equilibria.

The new-Keynesian approach to this problem picks the equilibrium with zero inflation on the date that the trap ends, $\pi_T = 0$, shown as the lower solid line and with a square at $\pi_T = 0$ to emphasize that this point is used to select the equilibrium.

This equilibrium shows a large deflation jump at time $t = 0$, and a large output gap, shown as the thick dashed line in Figure 20.5 below, during the liquidity trap period $0 < t < T$. We also see strong dynamics: Deflation steadily improves, and expected output *growth* is strong. The forward-looking Phillips curve (20.6) only produces a large output gap when inflation is lower today than in the future. This equilibrium does not show an unstable deflation "spiral," in which a small deflation grows bigger over time. This equilibrium also does not produce a "slump," a large but steady output gap and steady but low inflation. It thus misses crucial features of the episode, except perhaps the sharp and strong recession of 2008.

A fiscal theorist picks the equilibrium by the fiscal innovation at time $t = 0$ when the shock hits ($\Delta_0 \pi_0$, or $\Delta E_1 \pi_1 = -\varepsilon_{\Sigma s,1}$ in discrete time notation). The fiscal theorist looks at the $\pi_T = 0$ equilibrium, and notices that the deflation jump must correspond to a large fiscal contraction. The fiscal theorist notices that is a strange specification of fiscal policy expectations. If anything, the natural rate shock accompanies an expected unbacked fiscal expansion, not contraction; stimulus, not austerity.

To keep it simple, and to illustrate the power of choosing equilibria by the behavior of inflation at time 0 by fiscal considerations, I focus on the equilibrium with innovation to the discounted present value of surpluses, and hence no inflation jump, $\pi_0 = 0$. This

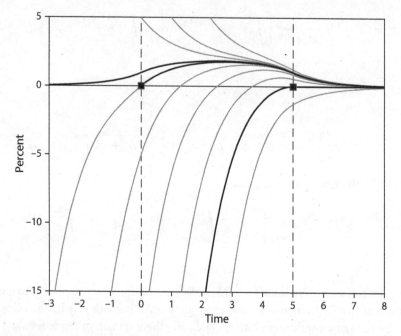

FIGURE 20.4. Inflation in a Range of Equilibria. There is a 2% negative natural rate shock leading to zero interest rate between $t = 0$ and $t = 5$, indicated by vertical dashed lines. The thick lines show three equilibria discussed in the text. Boxes indicate the inflation choice that selects equilibria. Thinner gray lines show a range of additional possible equilibria.

equilibrium is shown by the middle solid line, with a square at $\pi_0 = 0$ to remind you this is the criterion that selects the indicated equilibrium.

Observational equivalence still holds. The fiscal theorist *could* pick the new-Keynesian's $\pi_T = 0$ equilibrium, by specifying the same fiscal contraction, just "actively" rather than "passively." But it would be unreasonable to do so. The new-Keynesian could pick the $\pi_0 = 0$ equilibrium by specifying that the central bank will enforce a "glide path" of inflation after the trap ends at T. The difference between models is really, primarily, what joint fiscal and monetary policy actions seem reasonable. If a die-hard new-Keynesian were simply to look at the large fiscal tightening required of the deflationary equilibrium, he or she could see quickly that something is terribly wrong with the $\pi_T = 0$ equilibrium choice. He or she might conclude that the central bank will be forced to select an alternative equilibrium, say $\pi_0 = 0$.

In the no-jump $\pi_0 = 0$ equilibrium, the declining natural rate is met by a slight inflation *rise* during the zero interest rate episode. With slight inflation, a stuck nominal rate can still produce the real interest rate reduction that a lower natural rate requires. This is an often-missed general point: If the natural real rate declines, people often assume the nominal interest rate must fall to follow it, and the zero bound may get in the way. No; inflation can rise instead, and does here.

The no-jump equilibrium does not produce a deep recession, since it does not produce a strong real rate change, or a strong deflation response, via the Phillips curve. Is the counterfactual quiet a fault? Well, in the absence of a huge but rapidly improving deflation, which we did not see, this Phillips curve is not going to produce a deep recession. The recession was arguably caused by the supply and credit disruptions of the financial crisis, not by deflation via Phillips curve mechanics. To be fair, the standard new-Keynesian equilibrium selection was also chosen in order to produce a deep recession and think about solving it. But it's just impossible in this model to produce a deep recession without deep but improving deflation, and it's impossible to produce that deflation without a fiscal contraction. Bottom line, this model, designed to evaluate the partial effect of monetary policy on the economy, simply doesn't have the ingredients to capture a deep recession induced by a financial crisis.

In sum, fiscal theory picks equilibria by their behavior at time 0, not at time T. By specifying that there cannot be a big fiscal contraction at time 0, the most natural fiscal theory approach to the episode removes the troublesome prediction of a huge deflation.

Equilibrium selection by future central bank policy suffers all the troubles of equilibrium selection by immediate inflation destabilization, and more. Does all concrete action of monetary policy really vanish, leaving only expectations of far-future off-equilibrium threats behind? But the ability to select equilibria by *future* active policy is a logical extension of the theory. If we rule out equilibria by explosions that start at some far-removed future date, there is no real reason to insist on contemporaneous policy, $i_t = i_t^* + \phi(\pi_t - \pi_t^*)$, except historical tradition, stemming from Taylor's empirical description of U.S. Fed behavior in the 1980s. The awkwardness of the logical extension undermines the original as well.

The equilibria in Figure 20.4 are all stable forward, which means they are unstable backward. As time goes back before 0, or as we move the length of the zero bound episode T to the right, the new-Keynesian deflation blows up. Fiscal theory, or just paying attention to the "passive" fiscal requirements of new-Keynesian theory, limits the size of the time 0 jump and thus eliminates this backward explosion. This behavior solves a range of additional puzzles, as we see next.

20.2.3   The Puzzling Frictionless Limit

In the new-Keynesian approach, deflation gets worse without limit as prices become *less* sticky. Then at the limit *point* of flexible prices, deflation and recession discontinuously disappear. With a fiscal equilibrium choice that limits the inflation jump at time 0, deflation and recession get steadily better as prices become flexible, and the flexible price limit is smooth.

Prices become more flexible as κ increases, and $\kappa = \infty$ is the flexible price case. With fully flexible prices, the output gap from (20.6) is $x_t = 0$ for any value of inflation. In (20.5), if $x_t = 0$ then $dx_t/dt = 0$ and we must have $\pi_t = i_t - u_{r,t}$. Thus, when the natural rate shock $u_{r,t} = -2\%$ hits, inflation simply jumps up to $\pi_t = 2\%$ for the period of the shock, returning to $\pi_t = 0$ the minute the shock ends. Inflation in the frictionless world rises to exactly equal the negative natural rate, all on its own without extra prodding by the central bank, producing the required negative real rate to accommodate the natural rate shock. There is no output gap.

The gray lines in Figure 20.5 show how solutions with the new-Keynesian equilibrium choice $\pi_T = 0$ behave as we reduce price frictions, raising κ. Deflation and (not shown)

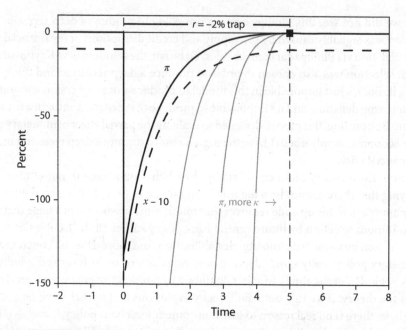

FIGURE 20.5. Output and Inflation in the Standard $\pi_T = 0$ Equilibrium. The thick lines show a price stickiness parameter $\kappa = 1$. The thick solid line is inflation π. The dashed solid line is output x displaced downward 10 percentage points for clarity. The thin gray lines plot inflation as the price stickiness parameter κ increases (prices become less sticky) from 1 to 2, 5, and 20.

output gaps become *larger* as price stickiness is *reduced*: As pricing frictions decrease, dynamics happen faster. Faster backward explosions, tethered to $\pi_T = 0$, imply more deflation and lower output at $t = 0$. Although price stickiness is the only friction in this economy, structural reform to reduce price stickiness would only make matters worse. For example, Eggertsson, Ferrero, and Raffo (2014) take this prediction seriously and argue against structural reform in a zero bound recession.

Despite this infinite limit, the limit *point* of the frictionless equilibrium is well behaved at 2% inflation and no output gap. The model with $\pi_T = 0$ equilibrium selection thus displays a puzzling discontinuity. Tiny price stickiness has arbitrarily huge effects, but zero price stickiness has no effect.

By contrast, in the no inflation jump $\pi_0 = 0$ equilibria, the hat-shaped inflation response shown in Figure 20.4 smoothly rises to fill out a square function, 2% inflation from $t = 0$ to $t = T$. "Faster dynamics" just means an easier time of going around the corners. As a result, ε price stickiness implies δ deviation from the frictionless result. Any criterion that limits the time 0 inflation jump and its underlying fiscal innovation will have this behavior.

20.2.4 Forward Guidance

Just why does the central bank choose the $\pi_T = 0$ equilibrium? In the Werning (2012) analysis, the central bank chooses the $\pi_T = 0$ equilibrium because it cannot precommit to do otherwise: Inflation $\pi_t = \pi^*$ is its target, and at time $T = 5$ and beyond, when active equilibrium selection policy is again possible, the central bank will choose that value. More importantly, people expect the central bank to follow its target as soon as it can, no matter what it may say in the meantime, which means people expect $\pi_T = \pi^* = 2\%$ the moment the central bank is able to do it.

Other authors do not emphasize the precommitment problem. They want to produce a model with a deep recession, so we can talk about that recession and how to fix it. To produce a recession, we must imagine the Fed selecting the $\pi_T = 0$ equilibrium, for whatever reason.

But that policy is unfortunate. Looking across equilibria in Figure 20.4, inflation at time 0 is sensitive to its expectation at time T. The mild no-jump $\pi_0 = 0$ equilibrium has only slightly higher inflation at time T than the original $\pi_T = 0$ deflationary equilibrium. If only the central bank could commit to allow a small amount of time T inflation, a "glide path" back to its target, then the huge deflation and its associated recession would be solved. A little bit of "forward guidance" about inflation at time T can have large stimulative effects immediately.

Woodford (2012) gave an influential talk at the annual Jackson Hole conference, highlighting the power of such forward guidance to stimulate immediately in this sort of model. Rather than directly raise the inflation target at time T, Woodford and Werning (2012) also investigate a policy that commits to delaying an interest rate rise for some time after T. This commitment has the same effect. (Cochrane (2017c) Figures 6 and 7 present calculations.)

Forward guidance has since become a core strategy of central banking. For example, the 2020 Federal Reserve Strategy Review (Federal Open Market Committee (2020)) prominently advertises a period of inflation slightly higher than the usual 2% target after zero bound exit, intended to stimulate immediately. The review also emphasizes forward guidance as a generally powerful and important part of the Federal Reserve's "tools" for stimulating. A cynic might say that a theory describing immense power of speeches by central bank officials, offering promises about a far-off future but requiring no action today, might be a little too well received in central banks. (Central bankers also view forward guidance about the short rate as a way to drive down long rates via the expectations hypothesis. That's a different mechanism.)

The warm reception of such forward guidance analysis in central banks is awkward, as the immense power of forward guidance has since become a puzzle to be solved and eliminated in academic work. Forward guidance as described by this model is too powerful. The solutions picked by inflation at time T all explode backwards. Promises about actions further in the future have greater effects today. As prices become less sticky, the backward explosions happen faster, and forward guidance has greater and greater effect; until all of a sudden at the flexible price limit point, forward guidance has no effect at all.

Any equilibrium selection strategy that picks the equilibrium by the inflation jump at time 0, including fiscal theory, resolves these paradoxes of forward guidance, but also removes the allure of forward guidance as cheap stimulus. Promises about the far future have small effects today, and the economy approaches the frictionless limit smoothly.

The power of forward guidance makes the whole model look unrealistic. Was the entire recession of 2008 and slow subsequent recovery really due to the fact that the Federal Reserve could not signal its willingness to tolerate a period of transitory inflation at some point many years in the future; a "glide path" back to normal; or that if announced people would not believe such a thing? If people only believed the Fed capable of such an inflation glide path, would there have been in 2008 a small *rise* in inflation with little output loss? Did Japan really avoid a deep deflation jump in 2001 because people expected some sort of explosive dynamics around a slightly higher than 2% inflation target, maybe sometime in 2030 when Japan finally exits zero rates? Did the abandonment of gold in 1933 work because people expected better equilibrium selection policy starting in 1940? This view is the Eggertsson (2012) alternative to Jacobson, Leeper, and Preston (2019).

20.2.5   *Magical Multipliers and Bastiat Banished*

The new-Keynesian equilibrium choice has additional puzzling—or tantalizing, depending on your tastes—predictions. Government spending, even if totally wasted, can have immense multipliers. Technical progress lowers output. A deliberate productivity reduction can stimulate the economy. Bastiat's broken window fallacy becomes powerful stimulus. These predictions have been seriously advanced as guides to policy at the zero bound. Again, these effects result from the backward explosive solutions, which in turn result by choosing equilibria at time T. These effects are reversed by fiscal theory, or any other rule that limits the time 0 inflation jump.

To see how these predictions emerge, I add a disturbance g_t in the Phillips curve (20.6),

$$\frac{d\pi_t}{dt} = \rho\pi_t - \kappa(x_t + g_t),$$

Following Werning (2012) and Wieland (2019), the variable g_t can represent government spending. It also can represent deliberate destruction of capital or technological regress, changes that increase marginal costs and therefore shift the Phillips curve, increasing inflation for a given output gap. Higher inflation reduces the real interest rate and consumption growth. Assuming a return to trend, reducing consumption *growth* increases the current *level* of consumption. (Yes, reducing consumption growth is good in these models.)

Solving the IS equation (20.5) forward, we have

$$x_t = -\int_{s=0}^{\infty} \frac{dx_{t+s}}{ds}ds = -\int_{s=0}^{\infty} \sigma(i_{t+s} - u_{r,t+s} - \pi_{t+s})ds.$$

Expected future inflation is the key for stimulus in this model, not current inflation, or unexpected current inflation. Similarly, since output is demand-determined in the model, wealth or capital destruction does not directly affect output or consumption.

This new-Keynesian multiplier is utterly different from static Keynesian intuition. The static Keynesian multiplier results because more current income generates more consumption, which generates more income. In this new-Keynesian model, the marginal propensity to consume is effectively zero, as there are no permanent changes in the level of consumption. Fiscal policy acts entirely by creating future inflation, affecting the intertemporal allocation of consumption.

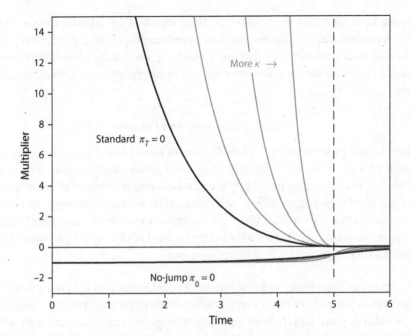

FIGURE 20.6. Output Multipliers with Respect to a Phillips Curve Disturbance g. The graph plots the derivative $\partial x_t / \partial g$ for an increase in g through the trap period $0 < t < T$. Thin gray lines show multipliers for price stickiness $\kappa = 2, 5, 20$.

I specify that $g_t = g$ during the trap, for $0 < t < T$, and $g_t = 0$ thereafter. I examine how increasing g affects equilibrium output and employment by the multiplier $\partial x_t / \partial g$ evaluated at $g = 0$. To find the multipliers, I take the derivative with respect to g of the solution (20.10). (Algebra in Cochrane (2017c).)

Figure 20.6 presents these multipliers. For the standard $\pi_T = 0$ equilibrium, multipliers are large and substantially greater than one. Such eye-popping multipliers are also generated by the quantitatively serious papers cited above. Normally economists fight about multipliers between 1 and 1.5. Multipliers of 10 or more seem available at the lower bound.

The multipliers increase exponentially as the length of the liquidity trap increases. Spending or output destruction in the future is exponentially more effective than spending today, an unusual Keynesian doctrine. Multipliers increase as price stickiness is reduced. In the limit that price stickiness goes to zero, the multiplier goes to infinity. Very small amounts of price stickiness generate very large multipliers. The multiplier is -1 at the limit point, however, since $x_t = -g_t$. All of these predictions flow naturally from forward stable and backward unstable dynamics.

By contrast, multipliers in the no-jump $\pi_0 = 0$ equilibrium are small, and cluster around the frictionless value -1, as its output gaps are small. As price stickiness is reduced or the period of the trap lengthens, the no-jump equilibrium multipliers converge smoothly to -1. (The frictionless multiplier is -1, not 0. The variable x_t represents private consumption, so government spending drives down private consumption one for one.)

In sum, large multiplier predictions are direct results of equilibrium choice. The no-jump or backward stable equilibria produce government spending, productivity reduction, or cost increase multipliers that are, if anything, lower than conventional wisdom, and more in line with the complete crowding-out or supply-limited results of equilibrium models.

20.2.6 Literature and Patches

The zero bound predictions of the new-Keynesian model and these astonishing policy prescriptions were taken seriously. What may seem paradoxically large is, from another point of view, an intoxicating possibility to end a damaging recession with some speeches, a bit of promised spending, or rolling back structural reforms and destroying some capital stock. Among others, Woodford (2011), Christiano, Eichenbaum, and Rebelo (2011), Eggertsson, Ferrero, and Raffo (2014), Eggertsson (2010), and Eggertsson (2011). Wieland (2019) begins with a Paul Krugman quote:

> As some of us keep trying to point out, the United States is in a liquidity trap: . . . This puts us in a world of topsy-turvy, in which many of the usual rules of economics cease to hold. Thrift leads to lower investment; wage cuts reduce employment; even higher productivity can be a bad thing. And the broken windows fallacy ceases to be a fallacy: something that forces firms to replace capital, even if that something seemingly makes them poorer, can stimulate spending and raise employment. (Paul Krugman, *New York Times*, September 3, 2011.)

Wieland includes a comprehensive review of papers that advance the paradoxes as useful policies. Wieland offers a negative empirical evaluation, showing that the East Japan earthquake and oil supply shocks were contractionary at the zero bound.

But the predictions were also quickly seen as policy paradoxes, indicating problems with the model that need fixing. Rather than adopt fiscal theory, which solves the puzzles quickly, authors turned to rather severe modifications of the basic new-Keynesian model.

At heart, as I digest them, these modifications move the new-Keynesian model back toward the old-Keynesian model with dynamics that are stable backward and unstable forward. The puzzles come, basically, from the forward-stable backward-unstable dynamics of the rational expectations model, that my graphs blow up from right to left. But changing the basic stability and determinacy properties of a model is not a little patch; it is a heart transplant. A small change in system eigenvalues will do no good: Eigenvalues must switch from greater to less than one. And then we return to the failures of the old-Keynesian model.

Gabaix (2020) is an excellent and concrete example. Gabaix uses a model of rational inattention to argue that people and firms pay less attention to expectations of future income and future prices than they should. In the end, he modifies the standard IS and Phillips curves to

$$x_t = ME_t x_{t+1} - \sigma (i_t - E_t \pi_{t+1}) \tag{20.11}$$

$$\pi_t = M^f \beta E_t \pi_{t+1} + \kappa x_t \tag{20.12}$$

where M and M^f are less than one. For sufficiently low M and M^f, Gabaix produces traditional forward explosive, backward stable dynamics under a peg. In this way, Gabaix's model can be seen as a behaviorally microfounded version of the old-Keynesian model studied above. Gabaix also uses the model to generate a negative sign of inflation to interest rate increases.

But to get these traditional signs, Gabaix must change the stability properties of the model. As one starts to lower M and M^f, nothing happens at all until the eigenvalues cross one. Cochrane (2016) finds that one needs M less than a half, together with substantial price stickiness $\sigma \kappa$ less than about a half, to cross that boundary. Thus, Gabaix's result is bounded away from rationality. It is also bounded away from the frictionless price limit. As prices become less sticky, new-Keynesian dynamics always reappear. A little bit of irrationality or price stickiness will not do.

Gabaix's model remains unstable, like the old-Keynesian model. That's the point. The model therefore does not accommodate the long quiet zero bound without a second complex patch (Gabaix Section 5.3, and Appendix Section 9.2). It is at least esthetically more pleasing if long-run neutrality describes the simple form of a model, and dynamics are the result of patches, rather than the other way around.

Gabaix's model is based on a complex and fundamental change in how people form expectations, developed in Gabaix (2014). García-Schmidt and Woodford (2019) resolve the zero bound paradoxes with an even more complex model of expectations formation, which denies the validity of all perfect-foresight modeling. Kiley (2016) provides a good survey of these policy paradoxes and advocates a Mankiw and Reis (2002) "sticky expectations" model, which puts lagged information in the Phillips curve to take us back to old-Keynesian stability and determinacy properties.

It is certainly not necessary or wise to insist on rational expectations at every data point. One should certainly consider somewhat slow expectations adjustment as icing on the cake to match episodes and dynamics. Rational expectations analyses that require agents to know the structural model of the economy, rather than learn from experience, are naturally fragile. But we are looking here at the opposite side of that coin: the fundamental, underlying, long-lasting, basic economic nature of money and the price level. Are we really satisfied if that basic foundation relies crucially on systematically irrational behavior, or complex models of expectation formation? Moreover, if we need a new model of expectation formation, then we can't just dredge that up once to solve zero bound puzzles and put it away again. We have to take that model seriously throughout macro and micro economics, rewrite it all, and see that it all still makes sense.

Occam responds: Perhaps. Or, perhaps one should take seriously the simplest answer: The fiscal foundations of the puzzles don't make any sense. The puzzles specify dramatic and counterfactual "passive" fiscal responses: large austerity at the beginning of the trap, that becomes unboundedly larger in the flexible price and long-trap duration limits, only to collapse to zero at the frictionless limit point. All you need is a limit on the time 0 inflation jump to make the puzzles go away, without reviving the failures of the old-Keynesian model or creating a model that must fall apart if prices get less sticky or people get more smart. You don't really need fiscal theory, you just need to look under the hood at the "passive" fiscal implications of the new-Keynesian models. Why work so hard to avoid that easy resolution?

20.3 Zero Bound Summary and Implications

The zero bound is thought of as a bad state, a "trap" to be avoided, threatening instability, sunspot volatility, or stagnation. The long quiet zero bound, and the fiscal theory interpretation, question that judgment. Perhaps we can live with perpetually low interest rates, and enjoy the optimal quantity of money after all.

The zero bound is a not a big issue to a fiscal theory of monetary policy, in the context of this simple and standard sticky price model. Inflation is stable and determinate at the zero bound. Expectations of far-off events have little effect today, the economy has a smooth frictionless limit, and the limit equals the limit point. Stickier prices, wasted spending, and broken windows hurt rather than help. We don't need to fear low interest rates that might sometimes touch the bound either.

In the old-Keynesian view, the zero bound constantly threatens a deflation spiral. In the original new-Keynesian view, the zero bound threatens multiple equilibrium sunspot volatility. In the updated new-Keynesian view, the zero bound threatens a deflation jump, and then opens the door to almost magical policies. But spirals, sunspots, or large deflation did not happen. Large government spending, many productivity-reducing policies, and a robust program of central banker promises did not interrupt a decade of steady low inflation and slow growth.

Fiscal theory cuts off the danger and the intoxicating fun for activist policy. The central fiscal insight is that inflation is tied down—π_0 is determined in these simulations—by fiscal policy. A big deflation requires a big fiscal austerity. Governments don't do that.

Zero interest rates are not necessarily ideal in a fiscal theory. At the bound, monetary policy cannot smooth shocks by varying interest rates, if that's what it was doing, or induce pointless volatility in expected inflation, if central banks weren't doing that good a job. If some combination of real shocks and sticky prices demand a sharply negative nominal rate, it cannot be achieved. But a negative rate is not needed to ward off instability or indeterminacy.

Still, one may argue by degrees. Suppose the dynamics by which an interest rate peg attracts inflation are slow, suppose there are additional shocks along the way, and suppose there is a mechanism, stronger than long-term debt, by which central banks can temporarily raise inflation by lowering interest rates, and that most central bank policy exploits that effect successfully. Now a zero bound, while still not threatening instability or indeterminacy, remains a serious problem for stabilization. The fact that inflation and output were so quiet at the zero bound argues against this view, but perhaps we just didn't have any shocks.

Zero interest rates have long been regarded as a horrible state of affairs, to be avoided if at all possible. Keynes called zero interest rates a liquidity "trap." A deflation spiral and sunspot volatility retain the negative judgment. The vast literature investigates means to escape the presumably horrible fate.

Zero bound aversion was already a curious judgment. In typical new-Keynesian models, the zero bound is optimal or close to it. The zero bound left-hand equilibrium Π_L in Figure 16.2 gives greater welfare than the desired right-hand equilibrium Π^*. Less inflation means that firms are closer to their optimal prices, and relative prices are less distorted. In new-Keynesian thinking, we prefer the less efficient equilibrium Π^* only because it is thought to be determinate, avoiding sunspot volatility. But that volatility did not occur. Zero nominal interest rates are optimal in monetarist thinking as well, being the Friedman (1969) optimal quantity of money. Again, monetarists shy away from a nominal peg at zero, I presume because it threatens an inflation or deflation spiral. Slight deflation enforced by a money growth target seems less objectionable, but monetarists did not advocate it.

Keynes and the earlier generation of Keynesians thought in static, not dynamic terms. Much of that spirit remains alive in zero bound commentary. Commenters ascribe Japan's slow growth to being stuck at zero interest rates and unable to stoke inflation. Summers (2014) brought "secular stagnation," back to life, an idea last seen in Hansen (1939), that zero interest rates lead to perpetually deficient aggregate demand. But it's hard to believe that monetary nonneutralities and sticky prices and wages last 30 years. Japan had low unemployment most of the time, belying perpetual lack of demand. Japanese growth was slow, as was U.S. and European growth in the zero bound era. But three decades of slow growth with low unemployment plausibly comes from slow productivity growth, microeconomic distortions, and lack of "supply," not "demand." Such slow growth leads to low real interest rates, not the other way around. In sum, it is possible that Japan simply lived 30 years of Friedman's optimal monetary policy, and the U.S. and Europe a decade. The last half of the nineteenth century saw steady deflation, with distributional consequences, but it is not a period one associates with "secular stagnation." The memory of the 1930s obviously stokes zero-bound fear. But lots of other things went wrong in the 1930s. And now we have a new contrary episode to ponder.

So, despite the long-standing view that the zero bound is a horrible fate, perhaps experience and theory should open a new door: We can, in fact, live with low or even zero nominal rates, and enjoy the advantages without fear of disastrous consequences. We can have low and stable inflation, and thus remove needless noise in relative prices (new-Keynesian), shoe-leather costs of cash management (monetarists), inflation-induced tax distortions, inflation risk premiums, and other costs of inflation. Having solved the *dynamic* problems of the zero bound, we can enjoy its steady-state advantages.

The fiscal fly in the ointment remains, however. Low and steady inflation requires solvent fiscal policy. Postwar interest rate pegs fell apart without fiscal support, and a peg at zero can fall apart just as easily. Debt sustainability built on low interest costs seems less sustainable than that built on solid primary surpluses. Just why people want to hold vast quantities of government debt at such low real rates of return, and how long they will continue to do so, is the question for our age.

21

The COVID-19 Inflation

Inflation returned suddenly starting in February 2021. It looks like a classic fiscal helicopter drop. Government debt increased 30%. Three-fifths of the new debt consisted of new reserves. Much of the new debt was sent directly to people as checks. That mechanism suggests why people this time thought the debt would not be repaid, but thought the 2008 and following deficits would be. Whether inflation will continue depends on monetary and fiscal policy going forward. Fiscal inflation will continue if people start to believe all debt will not be repaid. From the conventional point of view, monetary policy looks set to replay the 1970s. The fiscal theory point of view suggests that even apparently loose and slow monetary policy may not lead to galloping inflation on its own. An eventual stabilization will have to include fiscal, monetary, and microeconomic stabilization. The shadow of debt will make that effort harder than it was in 1980.

As I FINISH this book's manuscript in late 2021, inflation has suddenly revived. You will know more about this event by the time you read this book, in particular whether inflation turned out to be "transitory," as the Fed and administration currently insist, or longer lasting. This section must be speculative, and I hope rigorous analysis will follow once the facts are known. Still, fiscal theory is supposed to be a framework for thinking about inflation and underlying fiscal and monetary policy, so I would be remiss not to try.

Figure 21.1 presents the CPI through the COVID-19 recession. Everything looks normal until February 2021. From that point to October 2021, the CPI rose 5.15% (263.161 to 276.724), a 7.8% annual rate.

What happened, at least through the lens of the simple fiscal theory models in this book? Well, from March 2020 through early 2021, the U.S. government—Treasury and Fed acting together—created about $3 trillion in new money and sent people checks. The Treasury borrowed an additional $2 trillion, and sent people more checks. Overall, debt rose 30% from the $17 trillion outstanding at the beginning of the pandemic. M2, including checking and savings accounts, went up $5.5 trillion dollars. Table 21.1 and Figure 21.2 summarize. ($3 trillion is the amount of Treasury debt purchased by the Fed, and also the sum of larger reserves and currency. Federal debt held by the public includes debt held by the Federal Reserve.)

Some examples: In March 2020, December 2020, and again in March 2021, the government sent "stimulus" checks, totaling $3,200 to each adult and $2,500 per child.[1] The government added a refundable child tax credit, now up to $3,600 per child, and

---

1. https://home.treasury.gov/policy-issues/coronavirus, accessed Nov. 29 2021.

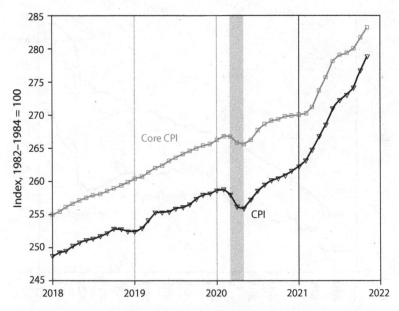

FIGURE 21.1. CPI Surrounding the Covid-19 Recession.

TABLE 21.1. Debt through the Covid-19 Recession. Dollar amounts in billions.

Quantity	Q4/Dec 2019	Q3/Sep 2021	Difference
A. Federal debt held by the public	$17,187	$22,304	$5,117
B. Monetary base (H.6)	$3,427	$6,389	$2,962
C. Fed holdings of treasurys (H 4.1)	$2,329	$5,431	$3,102
A+B−C	$18,285	$23,262	$4,977
M2	$15,325	$20,994	$5,669

started sending checks immediately. Unemployment compensation, rental assistance, food stamps, and so forth sent checks to people. The "Paycheck Protection Program" authorized $659 billion to small businesses. The government suspended student loan payments. And more. The payments were partly designed as economic insurance, transfers to those who had lost jobs or businesses, and efforts to keep businesses from failing. They were also designed as fiscal–monetary stimulus to boost aggregate demand. Massive "infrastructure" and "Build Back Better" spending plans occupied the Congress through 2021, adding expectations of more deficits to come.

From a fiscal theory perspective, the episode looks like a classic fiscal helicopter drop; the surplus shock in our models. There was a large unexpected deficit, a negative surplus, financing transfers, without change in fiscal policy that would lead one to expect subsequent surpluses to repay debts. Of course it led to inflation!

As I write in December 2021, nominal debt has increased about 30%, and inflation has wiped out about 7% of that value. If inflation stops instantly, that suggests people expect a 23% rise in expected surpluses. However, inflation seems likely to continue for a while, so the cumulative inflation will be larger, and any remaining rise in real value of debt and

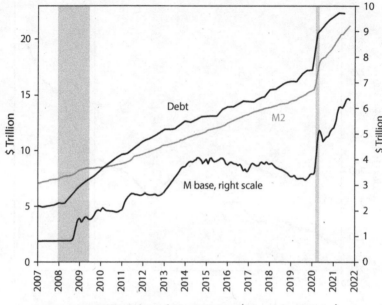

FIGURE 21.2. M2, Debt, and Monetary Base (Currency + Reserves)

future surpluses will be smaller. A 30% cumulative inflation, in which nominal debt rises but real debt does not, will represent a pure surplus shock.

Nominal debt increased as well. But to the extent that inflation wipes out the real value of that increase, the rise in nominal debt just raises the expected future price level. That gives us a surge of inflation, a permanent price-level increase. Without the rise in nominal debt, we would have an expected deflation which would bring the price level back down again.

In sum, at first glance the event looks like the response to an unexpected fiscal shock with a constant nominal interest rate plotted in the bottom panel of Figure 2.1. That response implies an expansion in nominal but not real debt.

Of course, real-world dynamics play out more slowly than the frictionless model with one-period debt. Thus, at second glance, one ought to think of the responses to a fiscal shock in a model with sticky prices, long-term debt, and policy rules. In Figure 5.6 the Fed keeps the nominal rate constant, which it did throughout 2021, with at best indications of very slow rises through 2022. As a result of sticky prices, the fiscal shock in this figure gives us several years of inflation, not a one-time price-level jump. Since short-term nominal interest rates do not move, neither do long-term nominal rates, despite persistent inflation. The failure of bond prices to react to expected inflation is not a puzzle in this simulation. The real value of debt rises in this simulation, for two reasons. First, higher inflation with constant nominal interest rates lowers the real rate, which lowers the discount rate. Second, the figure posits that only 40% of a fiscal shock is inflated away, and 60% is eventually repaid.

The Fed is likely eventually to raise interest rates in response to inflation. Figure 5.7 includes a monetary policy reaction. Inflation in this case is even more persistent, not a one-time price-level rise, and there is no output effect.

The most important lesson of these simulations relative to to frictionless model is that the "one-time" price level rise resulting from a one-time fiscal shock can occur through a very drawn out inflation that lasts many years. Forecasts of a quick end to inflation may be quite optimistic.

These models need additional refinement to capture the dynamics of the event. A year passed between the first stimulus and the beginning of inflation, where inflation starts right away in these models. To some extent, this difference reflects multiple shocks. The pandemic evolved. Deficits were spread out over time, with continuing discussion over each stimulus program, and whether additional programs would be undertaken. And the economic models here—a simple textbook IS and Phillips curve—are obviously simplistic.

A monetarist might object that this event was (finally) proof of $MV = Py$. Helicopter yes, but helicopter money, not helicopter bonds. M2 rose \$5.5 trillion; the rest is irrelevant. But all the questions of Section 14.1 about helicopter drops apply. Suppose the M2 expansion had been entirely produced by purchasing existing Treasury securities, with no deficits. Would this really have had the same effect? Are people starting to spend their M2 because they don't like the *composition* of their portfolios, which have too much M2, paying 0.01% (Chase), and not enough one-year Treasurys, paying 0.1%? Or are they simply spending extra "wealth?" Suppose the Federal Reserve had refused to go along, and the Treasury had sent people Treasury bills directly. Would that not have stoked the same inflation? The *fiscal* expansion, the wealth effect, is the natural interpretation of this episode.

Why did this stimulus cause inflation, and that of 2008, or the deficits from 2008 to 2020, did not do so? Federal debt held by the public *doubled* from 2008 to 2012, as inflation went nowhere. (Figure 21.2.) From the fiscal theory point of view, the key feature is whether people believe that debt will be repaid. So why, this time, did people see the increase in debt and not infer higher future surpluses, while previously they did? I offer a few potential explanations.

First, we can just look at what politicians said. In 2008 and following years, the administration continually offered stimulus today, but promised deficit reduction to follow. One may take those promises with a grain of salt, but at least they bothered to try. This time there was no talk at all about deficit reduction to follow; no policies, no plans, no promises about how to repay this additional debt. Indeed, long-run fiscal policy discussion became focused on how low interest costs, $r < g$, and modern monetary theory allow painless fiscal expansion. The discussion of tax hikes in the spring and summer of 2021 focused entirely on paying for some of the ambitious additional spending plans, not repaying debt dropped from the Covid helicopters.

Second, much of the expansion was immediately and directly monetized and sent to people as checks. The previous stimulus was borrowed, and funded government spending programs that had to gently work their way into people's incomes to have any stimulus effect.

Following 2008, M2 did not rise as much as debt. The QE operations were mostly confined to a switch of bank assets from Treasury debt to reserves, as we see from the contrast between the monetary base (currency + reserves) and M2 in Figure 21.2. Money and bonds may be perfect substitutes, but who gets the money or debt and how can still matter. Traditional buyers of Treasury debt have savings and investment motives. (Think of an insurance company.) If the Fed instantly buys the debt, and Treasury sends reserves (checks) to people, the larger debt goes quickly to people who are likely to spend gifts quickly. This statement implies some slow-moving capital frictions and heterogeneity of bondholders and transfer recipients, but those are potentially important and realistic model ingredients.

Moreover, debt sold to traditional bond purchasers, who show up at Treasury auctions or buy from broker-dealers, sends a different signal than reserves simply created and sent to people. The institutional context of debt expansion matters to expectations of its repayment. We distinguished Treasury auctions as a share issue and reserve creation as a split, differing only in the expectations of repayment that each engenders. We distinguished "regular budget" and "emergency budget" deficits, likewise signaling backed versus unbacked expansions. Since the desire was stimulus, and stimulus requires the government to find a way to communicate that the debt will not be repaid, one can regard the effort as a success at its goal, finally overcoming the expectations of repayment that made previous stimulus efforts fail, guilty only of having overdone it. From the beginning, we have thought of the possibility that central bank debt issues do not come with future surpluses, while treasury issues do. Quantitative easing may have failed, because people saw the central bank buy treasury debt, with a clear commitment to undo the purchase later. The nature of this expansion may have looked more like a direct and permanent central-bank debt issue.

Third, the economic environment was clearly different. The pandemic and lockdown was fundamentally different from the financial crisis. GDP and employment fell faster and further than ever before, and then rebounded most of the way, also faster than ever before. From a macroeconomic point of view, the COVID-19 recession resembles an extended snowstorm rather than a traditional recession. One might call that a "supply shock," as the productive capacity of the economy is temporarily reduced, but demand falls as well, for the same reasons that people don't rush out to buy in a snowstorm either. (I write "from a macroeconomic point of view." A million people died in the United States, a public health disaster.) Roughly speaking, the economy was operating at its reduced "supply" capacity, not needing extra "demand." Providing unneeded "demand" spills more quickly to inflation.

Will inflation continue? You will know more about the answer, so it is dangerous to speculate. Still, it's worth writing how one might think about the question.

Of course, the sticky price simulations of Figure 5.6 and 5.7, referenced above, suggest we have a long way to go, even without additional shocks.

We also do not know just how much people expect these debts to be repaid versus inflated away. The $5 trillion total fiscal expansion is an approximately 30% expansion in debt. If the expansion comes with no change in expected future surpluses or discount rates, it will result in a cumulative 30% price level rise, once we work through all the dynamics. The stimulus payments will be paid by a wealth tax on government bonds. Some view this outcome positively. In their view, it is natural that an unexpected crisis is met with a Lucas-Stokey state contingent default, a wealth tax via inflation. (Hall and Sargent (2021) have a lovely documentation of this fiscal–monetary intervention, and its parallels to war finance.) Whether that optimal tax argument extends to stimulus payments rather than direct disaster insurance or war-fighting is an interesting question.

Whether inflation continues past this one-time price-level rise depends on future fiscal and monetary policy, and whether people have changed their expectations of future repayment and the underlying monetary–fiscal regime. People may regard the COVID-19 fiscal expansion as "emergency budget" expenditures that will not be repaid, but they may still expect the government to repay the preexisting debt, and they may expect the additional borrowing of the years ahead also back to the "regular budget" that will someday be repaid. If so, fiscal inflation need not continue. However, having changed their expectation that some greater debts, especially those that finance cash transfers, are now not going to be repaid, people may change beliefs more generally. They may start to believe that some of the preexisting 80% debt-to-GDP ratio will be inflated away. They may believe that additional deficits of coming years are also unbacked. Then fiscal inflation could be larger, and continue.

Don't forget discount rates! The very low real interest rates of the 2010 decade are a likely part of the story why the large debts and deficits of that decade, with an unreformed long-run policy, did not lead to inflation. Those low interest rates were a continual surprise to Fed and implicit bond market forecasts. Whether via monetary policy that rises to contain inflation, or a reversion to a larger natural rate, that inflationary tailwind may also reverse.

What of monetary policy? The episode and the 2020–2030 decade will likely help to sort out theories as the zero bound decade so clearly helped to sort out theories (Chapter 20). How important is it for the central bank to raise interest rates more than one for one with inflation? How much can the central bank lower inflation by raising rates without fiscal cooperation?

In the standard mode of analysis, the Fed's monetary policy in 2020 and 2021 was a significant institutional failure. The Fed was caught completely by surprise. The Fed claimed that supply-chain disruptions and pandemic-induced reductions in labor supply caused inflation. But the Fed's main job in the conventional reading is to calibrate how much "supply" the economy can offer, and then to adjust demand to that level and no more. If the Fed can be surprised that containers can't get through ports, why does it not have any economists calculating how many containers can get through ports? The Fed's "supply" modeling is pretty simplistic, relying mainly on unemployment statistics. The original stimulus came from a misdiagnosis that the economy's fall in the pandemic was due to lack of "demand." And, obviously, the Fed does not analyze the inflationary response of a fiscal shock as we do.

The Fed adjusts interest rates in response to its forecast of inflation. At the end of 2021, the Fed is leaving interest rates alone, with at most talk of small rises, based on a forecast that that inflation will quickly melt away on its own. It is remarkable that there is no evident soul-searching, and that the Fed confidently uses the same failed forecast and policy methodology.

More broadly, the general policy discussion involving Fed, administration, politicians, and pundits through 2021 showed a surprising repetition of centuries-old fallacies. A demand shift from restaurant dinners to TVs (services to durable goods) raises the price of TVs, but lowers the price of restaurant dinners. Supply shocks for specific goods, like containers stuck in ports, raise the relative price of those goods to other goods and to wages. Strawberries are more expensive in winter. Neither represents inflation. Inflation is a rise of all prices and wages together, a decline in the value of the dollar and government debts that promise dollars. Even in undergraduate courses, we teach that the oil shocks of the 1970s did not directly cause inflation; they prompted monetary and fiscal policies which caused inflation. That lesson seems forgotten.

Supply of individual goods or industries is the quantity produced as a function of the *relative* price of those goods relative to other prices and to wages. *Aggregate* supply is the relationship between a rise in all prices and wages together to the total amount produced in the economy. Aggregate supply requires some notion of price stickiness. Otherwise, the level of prices and wages has nothing to do with output and employment; the economy is neutral. An event such as this one always combines relative price changes with overall inflation, but that is no reason for conceptual confusion on such basic matters.

Blaming inflation on microeconomic supply or demand shocks, corporate greed, producer collusion, speculators, hoarders, middlemen, price gougers, and other hunted witches goes back centuries. The Roosevelt administration tried to cure deflation by creating monopolies to raise prices. Kennedy, Johnson, Nixon, and Ford pressured companies to lower prices and unions to lower wages. None of it worked. The current repetition of these ancient fallacies will work no better.

Going forward, in the conventional reading of monetary policy as captured by the adaptive-expectations model (Section 17.3.2), the Fed seems primed to repeat the mistakes of the 1970s. The Fed of the early 1970s also blamed inflation on price shocks and declared inflation to be transitory. The Fed's 2020 strategy review (Federal Open Market Committee (2020)) practically announces a return to 1970s interest rate policy. The Fed will deliberately let inflation run hot for a while, running down a Phillips curve, in an effort to boost employment. The Fed will wait until inflation persistently exceeds the Fed's target before doing anything about it. Indeed, the fact that at the end of 2021 the Fed had still not budged interest rates represents a far slower reaction than that of the 1970s. In that period, the federal funds rate rose almost one for one with the past year's inflation. The 1970s Fed is criticized for not having done more, but not for doing nothing. The Fed's strategy will return to filling "shortfalls" rather than stabilization, a return to the belief that even at the peaks the economy does not run too hot.

To be sure, the Fed speaks of "expectations" now, which it does not regard as mechanically adaptive. But many in the Fed view expectations as a third force, amenable to management by statements and speeches, rather than formed by a hardy and skeptical experience with the Fed's actions; rather than by a durable "rule" or "regime." And the Fed's "strategy" is so flexible that pretty much any discretionary action can be justified.

To Fed critics, "anchored" expectations come from one place only: belief that the Fed will, if needed, replay 1980, and rule-like commitment to do so. The Fed will sharply raise interest rates. That may cause a painful recession, but the Fed will stick with high rates for as long as it takes. Our current Fed says it has "the tools" to contain inflation, but it is remarkably reticent to state just what those tools are. Do people believe our Fed will do it? Do people believe that the Fed would have the political backing to do it?

To be a bit charitable, this strategy was developed before the pandemic hit in 2020. The strategy was designed to ward against deflationary spirals at the zero bound, with ample inflationary forward guidance. But if inflation continues, that strategy will seem an exquisite Maginot line. And even so, the absence of contingency planning is laid bare: The Fed develops a forecast, reacts as if that forecast is certain, yet seldom comments on the accuracy of such forecasts, or what it will do if the forecast is wrong.

The simple rational-expectations fiscal-theory models in this book are kinder to the Fed. The Fed could tamp down inflation by swiftly raising rates, and exploiting a negative short-run effect. Rate rises are also useful to smooth fiscal shocks, producing slow steady inflation rather than sharp price level jumps. However, greater than one for one response of interest rates to inflation is not necessary to ward off instability or indeterminacy.

Indeed, if the rational expectations versions of the models in this book are right, inflation is stable under an interest rate peg. If the Fed leaves interest rates alone, inflation will eventually die down.

However, this Fisherian long-run policy requires us to wait out a lot of short-run dynamics. The very persistent inflation of Figure 5.6 and 5.7 represent Fisherian responses. On the way to that long run, inflation may surge substantially, and the Fed's slow reaction may worsen that inflation. And all the hedging of Section 5.3 still applies. People would have to believe the Fed will continue to largely ignore inflation. If people think that the Fed may eventually raise rates sharply in an inflation panic, then inflation will start up in advance and the Fisherian strategy will fall apart.

Nonetheless, suppose inflation does vanish, apparently on its own, in a year or so, as the Fed's forecasts in late 2021 promise. Such an event would tell us that sticky prices and negative short-run dynamics are not nearly as strong as believed, and that the Fisherian model without a lot of frictions is a lot closer to reality. Unexpected inflation surged because of a fiscal shock. The Fed, by leaving interest rates alone or moving them very slowly, *caused* expected inflation not to rise.

The Fed will surely view causality in the other direction, that inflation melted away on its own, as the Fed's forecasts specify. But its actions look a lot like Fisherian policy! Thus, if inflation goes away, history may suggest that the Fed worked its way to a Fisherian strategy by experience and intuition, even though the Fed's models and theories say otherwise.

Suppose, on the other hand, inflation surges in the 2020s, and we do replay the 1970s. What will it take to stop it? The traditional view demands a sustained period of high real interest rates. If expectations are adaptive or mechanistic, that period of real interest rates will cause a deep recession.

The fiscal theory plus rational expectations view offers more possibilities. A period of high real interest rates will likely be the policy choice, using whatever the short-run negative response is to quickly push inflation down, and then nominal rates can fall to the new lower expected inflation. Whether it works, and how much recession is involved depends on that mechanism. The long-term debt mechanism we have explored requires that the higher rates are unexpected and credibly long-lasting. However, financial friction or other mechanisms may have other preconditions, and we will learn what those mechanisms are.

The model, and Sargent's timeless analysis of the ends of inflations, opens another possibility: A credible joint fiscal, monetary, and microeconomic reform can allow a relatively painless disinflation. The Phillips curve $\pi_t = \beta E_t \pi_{t+1} + \kappa x_t$ says that inflation reduction can be painless if expected inflation declines, and painful if it does not decline. The change in regime pushes expected inflation down ahead of other variables.

But even a repeat of 1980 will be harder this time, and a coordinated monetary, fiscal, and microeconomic reform harder still. Most obviously, our government seems much less willing to sustain a deliberate, bruising, and persistent recession, with fiscal and monetary stringency rather than the largesse of 2008 and 2020. As in the 1980s, growth-oriented tax and microeconomic reform take longer than monetary tightening, and there is no political consensus for such policy. However, a decade of inflation or stagflation may change that, as it did in the 1970s.

Fiscal policy will place greater constraints on high real interest rates as an inflation-fighting strategy. In 1980, the debt-to-GDP ratio was 25%. In 2021 it was 100%, and rising swiftly. First, then, the government will have to pay four times larger real interest costs on the debt. At 100% debt to GDP, 5% real interest rates mean 5% of GDP additional deficit, $1 trillion 2021 dollars, for each year that such real interest rates continue. Second, the government will have to raise surpluses further, to pay a windfall to long-term bondhold-ers, as it did in the 1980s. People who bought 10-year Treasury bonds in September 1981 got a 15.84% yield, as markets expected inflation to continue. From September 1981 to September 1991, the CPI grew at a 3.9% average rate. By this back-of-the-envelope calcu-lation, those bondholders got a 12% annual real return, courtesy of U.S. taxpayers. This effect will be four times larger as well. (As I write in 2021, bond yields remain low, offer-ing a temporary opportunity to avoid these costs.) Both of these amounts must be paid by higher primary surpluses; immediately or, if the government tries to borrow to cover higher interest costs, credibly in the future.

As Section 17.4.2 emphasized, without such an accompanying fiscal policy, higher interest rates cannot lower inflation. Will our government do it? Or will our government simply rule out such interest rate rises? The last time debt-to-GDP was 100%, in the after-math of WWII, the government explicitly told the Federal Reserve to hold interest rates down to help finance the debt.

Finally, this time the underlying problem will likely be more clearly fiscal. The U.S. government will have to solve the long-run fiscal problem that is causing inflation in the first place, and convince bondholders once again that the U.S. repays its debts.

Without fiscal backing, the monetary stabilization will fail. In a fiscally-driven inflation, it can happen that the central bank raises rates to fight the inflation, which raises the deficit via interest costs, and only makes inflation worse.

Successful inflation stabilization always combines fiscal, monetary, and microeco-nomic reform, in a durable new regime that commits to pay its debts. 1980 was such an event, not just a period of high interest rates. High interest rates can drive down inflation temporarily, giving time for the fiscal (1986 tax reform) and microeconomic reforms to take effect. In their absence, inflation takes off again. A new inflation stabilization would have to be such an event as well, but in the face of at least four times larger debts, larger structural deficits, and a more deeply entrenched regulatory regime and larger welfare state.

22

Observational Equivalence

WITH THE NEW-KEYNESIAN and monetarist models before us, and with their equilibrium selection rules spelled out, I return to summarize and extend observational equivalence and nonidentification, and their implications.

22.1 Equivalence and Regimes

I state observational equivalence and the nonidentification theorems in the simplest models,

$$i_t = i_t^* + \phi \, (\pi_t - \pi_t^*) + u_{i,t}$$

$$\tilde{s}_{t+1} = \alpha v_t^* + \gamma (v_t - v_t^*) + u_{s,t+1}.$$

In equilibrium, where variables equal the starred values, equilibrium time series do not distinguish the active-money passive-fiscal $\phi > 1$, $\gamma > 0$ regime from the active-fiscal passive-money $\phi < 1$, $\gamma = 0$ regime. The parameters ϕ and γ are not identified.

The clearest simple example of observational equivalence for interest rate regimes comes from Section 16.6. We wrote monetary and fiscal policy rules

$$i_t = i_t^* + \phi \, (\pi_t - \pi_t^*) + u_{i,t} \tag{22.1}$$

$$\tilde{s}_{t+1} = \alpha v_t^* + \gamma (v_t - v_t^*) + u_{s,t+1}$$

$$\rho v_{t+1}^* = v_t^* - \Delta E_{t+1} \pi_{t+1}^* - \tilde{s}_{t+1},$$

in the context of a frictionless model with

$$i_t = E_t \pi_{t+1}$$

$$\rho v_{t+1} = v_t + i_t - \pi_{t+1} - \tilde{s}_{t+1}. \tag{22.2}$$

Parameters $\phi > 1$, $\gamma > 0$ generate the active-money passive-fiscal regime, and most clearly $\alpha = \gamma$. Parameters $\phi < 1$, $\gamma = 0$ generate the active-fiscal passive-money regime, and most clearly $\phi = 0$. The government debt valuation formula results from iterating (22.2) forward and imposing the transversality condition.

The clearest simple example for monetary-control regimes comes from Section 19.1. Simplifying further to the case that money pays interest, or that surpluses react one for one to seigniorage, we have

$$M_t V_t = P_t y_t,$$

$$\frac{B_{t-1} + M_{t-1}}{P_t} = E_t \sum_{j=0}^{\infty} \beta^j s_{t+j}.$$

In an active-money passive-fiscal regime, the quantity of money M determines the price level P, and surpluses s follow. In an active-fiscal passive-money regime, fiscal surprises control unexpected inflation, and then the central bank provides the needed money passively. We can characterize these behaviors in the policy rule tradition: In an active-money regime, the money supply does not react one for one with the price level to validate any inflation or deflation. In an active-fiscal regime, surpluses do not react one for one with the price level to validate any inflation or deflation.

As this reminder makes clear, the "regimes" are observationally equivalent:

- *The equilibrium conditions are the same in each regime. Any time series produced by an active-money passive-fiscal regime can be produced by an active-fiscal passive-money regime and vice versa.*

The regimes differ in how we imagine the government behaves away from equilibrium, when variables do not equal their starred counterparts, how monetary and fiscal authorities hash out a coordinated policy. We can't observe that behavior in data drawn from the equilibrium.

Observational equivalence is the same as nonidentification:

- *Without additional identifying assumptions, the parameters that separate regimes such as γ and ϕ are not identified from time series of observable equilibrium variables.*

22.2   Implications Overview

Observational equivalence goes both ways. Any rejection of fiscal theory from equilibrium time series also rejects other theories of equilibrium formation. Observational equivalence opens the door to understanding any sample equally via fiscal theory as via new-Keynesian models. It guides us to find and examine the identifying assumptions of any proposed test. It guides us to look to institutions, regimes, commitments, and statements by fiscal and monetary authorities about how they operate, commentary on how people expect them to operate, narrative approaches to historical events, and times of regime change or construction.

22.2.1   Equivalence Goes Both Ways; a Feature, Not a Bug

On first glance, observational equivalence seems like a show-stopper. Why bother investigating a theory that doesn't seem to have rejectable predictions? On further reflection, however, observational equivalence is a feature, not a bug. It is an important guide to productive and unproductive investigation, like the observational equivalence and neutrality theorems of many other areas of economics.

Equivalence means equivalence. It goes both ways. It says that one cannot reject new-Keynesian or monetarist equilibrium selection stories in favor of the fiscal theory story. But it says that new-Keynesian or monetarist models cannot reject fiscal theory either. For the new kid on the block, proving that the door is open is good news. If an observation dooms fiscal theory, then it equally dooms new-Keynesian or monetarist theories. There is no scientific burden of proof based on who came along first.

In particular, a strand of fiscal theory evaluation looks to puzzles of the government debt valuation equation—why isn't there inflation in Japan?—and proclaims such puzzles as a rejection of fiscal theory. But, an instance of the last bullet point,

- *The government debt valuation equation is an equilibrium condition for all of these models.*

Any puzzle of the government debt valuation equation is equally a puzzle for interest rate and monetarist models. It is a puzzle of debt sustainability in equilibrium, not an indication of how that equilibrium is formed. It does not reject fiscal theory in favor of the others, which also include this condition.

Observational equivalence opens the door to casting out the other theories entirely, to looking at a whole sample in fiscal theory terms. One is not limited to looking for periods of fiscal versus monetary dominance, as has been common in fiscal theory literature. Observational equivalence provides a recipe by which one can transform *any* monetarist or new-Keynesian model into a fiscal theory model, without changing any of its implications for observable time series. One can only improve on them, by being led to better specifications of the equilibrium conditions and more comprehensive evaluation, and by including fiscal implications of those theories in their evaluation.

Nonidentification is related to observational equivalence. From equivalence, it follows that equilibrium-selection parameters which distinguish theories cannot be identified. But nonidentification doesn't require the existence of multiple theories. It just says that equilibrium-selection parameters can't be identified from equilibrium time series, without additional assumptions.

22.2.2   Tests and Assumptions

There are many observational equivalence results in economics. We often surmount them with identifying assumptions. Observational equivalence points one to write models in ways that express observational equivalence, and then to state and evaluate identifying assumptions. They are not technical details, they are the whole game, and they are often unstated or implicit.

I review the many identifying assumptions that have been used to try to make such tests. I come to a rather negative assessment of progress so far, and not much hope for the productivity of future effort. Observational equivalence thus warns us at least to be wary of formal time series tests that to try to estimate or test regimes, like tests to distinguish broad classes of models. I conclude that it will be more productive to use evidence other than that provided by tests based on equilibrium quantities. But observational equivalence per se is not the central case against extant tests for fiscal versus monetary regimes. The central case is that identifying restrictions don't make sense.

22.2.3   Beyond Tests

Observational equivalence only says that time series of observables may be produced by either class of models. It does not rule out troves of other types of evidence. We can look at the historical, institutional, and economic plausibility of equilibrium-selection stories, in general and in the context of specific episodes.

By looking deeply at the foundations of monetarist and new-Keynesian regimes in the last few chapters, we see that their equilibrium selection stories don't conform with lots of information we have about how governments behave. No central bank says it operates as the $\phi > 1$ equilibrium selection policy describes, and nobody expects it to do so. Active fiscal policy, in which surpluses do not respond to arbitrary inflation and deflation, is plausible and consistent with episodes and how people expect governments to react. Central banks don't control money supplies.

If the equilibrium selection theories are contradicted by evidence we have about how governments behave, if there is no complete, coherent, and plausible alternative to fiscal theory, I conclude that tests and estimates of fiscal versus these other theories are doubly pointless. There is no point to adding identifying restrictions, which will hurt the ability of the model to fit data, in order to attempt time series tests on top of this other information.

We can go on: Read the Federal Open Market Committee (2020) official description of its strategy, the minutes of Federal reserve meetings, the commentary of the financial press describing how people expect the Fed to behave if inflation should rise or fall. Narrative evidence in the tradition following Romer and Romer (1989) can help us to see shocks and disturbance $\varepsilon_{i,t}$ and $u_{i,t}$, from which one can infer ϕ. We can study episodes, such as the zero bound. We can study moments of regime change, institutional reform, and government choices in terms of objectives and constraints. We can measure, as I did above, the pattern of surpluses and discount rates that accounts for inflation, rather than try to proclaim no such patterns exist. We can *use* fiscal theory as we use other theories and see which proves more useful.

22.2.4   The Same Situation Elsewhere

Observational equivalence theorems abound in economics and finance. Supply versus demand shifts, behavioral versus rational finance, and money versus income causality all present observational equivalence theorems. Those theorems do not mean that the theories are empty. Observational equivalence theorems are simply fundamental guiding principles for logical critical thought.

In microeconomics, data alone do not tell us the slopes of supply and demand curves— what buyers or sellers would do if the price came out differently from the equilibrium price. Well, we write models and make identifying assumptions. We look for instruments, we think hard about their plausibility.

Finance has a similar observational equivalence theorem. Marginal utility and probability always enter together in asset pricing formulas, $p = \sum_s \pi_s u'(c_s)x_s$, where p is price, s indexes states of nature, π are probabilities, u' is marginal utility and x is payoff. "Rational" (u') and "behavioral" (misperceived probabilities π) finance are observationally equivalent. This is a modern version of the Fama (1970) "joint hypothesis" theorem, formalized in the Harrison and Kreps (1979) martingale measure theorem and the Hansen and Richard (1987) discount factor existence theorem. Attempts to show that all "rational" or efficient market asset pricing is wrong with a statistical test are empty.

Observational equivalence has not stopped these and subsequent branches of finance from productive investigation, nor does it prove that the debate is empty. But it usefully pours cold water on attempts to construct a statistical test using data on prices, payoffs, and economic variables, which will prove one or the other *class* of theory wrong. There is no interesting test of the present value relation per se—not volatility tests, not regression tests, not the hundreds of anomalies and alphas.

Instead, asset pricing now gets to work on writing an economic or psychological model of the discount factor, and the stochastic process of dividends. So, the heart of asset pricing, just like the heart of monetary economics, is to think hard about what is reasonable, and to evaluate what is useful. A lot of acrimony in finance could have been saved by paying attention to this basic theorem. We can save a lot of time and effort by not repeating for fiscal theory the difficult history of empirical asset pricing.

Applied to government debt, the discount factor theorem states that

- *Absent arbitrage, there is a discount factor that reconciles the value of debt to surpluses, a* $\{\Lambda_t\}$ *such that*

$$\frac{B_{t-1}}{P_t} = E_t \sum_{j=0}^{\infty} \frac{\Lambda_{t+j}}{\Lambda_t} s_{t+j}.$$

Thus, present value puzzles are doubly irrelevant as tests of the fiscal theory versus conventional theories. Present value puzzles are entirely puzzles of a discount factor or probability model.

Behavioral versus rational finance, Keynesian versus monetarist versus rational expectations versus new-Keynesian versus real business cycle macroeconomics were never settled by formal tests of equilibrium time series that reject a whole class of model. Even without observational equivalence, since the models study different equilibrium conditions, there was always a patch, a way to carry on. Theories gradually gain or lose steam as their foundations, explanations, and policy analysis seem more or less reasonable and useful. Fiscal theory versus interest rate equilibrium selection or money supplies will be settled the same way. This is the normal nature of all economics. Many tests were tried in all these fields. It is natural to have tried for such tests for fiscal versus other theories of inflation. That they reached a dead end here as in other fields just tells us to get on comparing theories as we always have in other fields.

Observational equivalence points us to what will and will not be a fruitful way to proceed. It starts by largely telling us not to waste more time on formal tests.

22.3   Regime Tests and Model-Based Estimates

Observational equivalence forces us to find and analyze identifying assumptions underlying tests. Once examined, common implicit identifying assumptions aren't sensible: Off-equilibrium responses need not be the same as responses in equilibrium. Disturbances need not be AR(1) or otherwise limited. Inflation and debt should Granger-cause surpluses, and larger surpluses should forecast declines in debt, even in a fiscal regime. Regime tests have stacked the deck against a fiscal regime in the quest for identification, leaving the impression that fiscal theory only describes an unfortunate "fiscal dominant" situation in which monetary policy loses control and inflation breaks out. Removing the identification restrictions opens the door to fiscal theory that describes a whole sample, including periods of low inflation, and acts to stabilize inflation.

The most natural desire, when playing with a new theory, is to find a test, either of the theory or of its competitors. It was completely natural, with the fiscal theory freshly in hand, to try to estimate whether we live in an active-fiscal or an active-money regime, to test one versus the other. It was natural to want to see periods of better or worse inflation performance as switches between a "money dominant" and a "fiscal dominant" regime.

Leeper (1991) kicked off fiscal theory with models of the form

$$i_t = E_t \pi_{t+1} \tag{22.3}$$

$$i_t = \phi \pi_t + u_{i,t} \tag{22.4}$$

$$\tilde{s}_{t+1} = \gamma v_t + u_{s,t+1} \tag{22.5}$$

$$v_{t+1} = v_t + i_t - \pi_{t+1} - \tilde{s}_{t+1}. \tag{22.6}$$

Active monetary and passive fiscal policy is $\phi > 1$, $\gamma > 0$. Leeper pointed out the possibility of active fiscal and passive monetary policy $\phi < 1$, $\gamma = 0$.

Faced with a model like this, the most natural thing in the world to do is to run regressions of (22.4) or (22.5) to estimate ϕ or γ, and thereby see which regime we are in. Run more realistic versions of $i_t = \phi \pi_t + u_{i,t}$, as Clarida, Galí, and Gertler (2000) do. Run more realistic versions of $s_t = \gamma v_{t-1} + u_{s,t}$ as in Bohn (1998a) or Table 4.1. (Bohn runs the regression, but does not interpret it as a test of regimes.)

Better, estimate the full model by maximum likelihood or Bayesian methods, including parameters ϕ and γ. Use the associated distribution theory to test regimes. Next, think of time-varying coefficients γ and ϕ, perhaps governed by Markov-switching models, and estimate subperiods of "monetary dominance" or "fiscal dominance," perhaps formalizing a different expression of the idea that the 1980 switch in policy rules was a good thing. The extensive fiscal theory model-building exercise surveyed in Section 24.2 below has largely followed this direction.

Observational equivalence tells us that any such estimate or test of the active/passive regime must be *entirely* based on the auxiliary assumptions and model restrictions one introduces to gain identification. It tells us to write the model in a form that exhibits observational equivalence and to study the identifying assumptions. Models throughout economics and finance include basic principles plus auxiliary assumptions. Observational equivalence per se is not a problem. The question is whether, when we dig in to state them, the identifying assumptions are believable.

Repeating (22.1)–(22.2) for convenience and rewriting slightly,

$$i_t = E_t \pi_{t+1} \tag{22.7}$$

$$i_t = \theta \pi_t^* + \phi (\pi_t - \pi_t^*) + u_{i,t} \tag{22.8}$$

$$\tilde{s}_{t+1} = \alpha v_t^* + \gamma \left(v_t - v_t^* \right) + u_{s,t+1} \tag{22.9}$$

$$\rho v_{t+1}^* = v_t^* - \Delta E_{t+1} \pi_{t+1}^* - \tilde{s}_{t+1} \tag{22.10}$$

$$\rho v_{t+1} = v_t + i_t - \pi_{t+1} - \tilde{s}_{t+1}. \tag{22.11}$$

Remember that in equilibrium, starred variables equal their unstarred observable counterparts, so the two theories are equivalent in equilibrium.

The parameter ϕ is not identified. The interest rate policy rule parameter θ can, in principle, be measured. But written this way, you see that information about θ tells you nothing about ϕ. The specification $i_t = \phi \pi_t + u_{i,t}$ thus adds an implicit assumption, $\phi = \theta$. That assumption overcomes nonidentification and observational equivalence. It is a separate and crucial assumption.

The parameters θ and ϕ have distinct economic functions. The parameter θ governs the relation between inflation and interest rates in equilibrium, devoted to smoothing fluctuations. The parameter ϕ is an equilibrium-selection threat, devoted to making multiple equilibria unpleasant. In this simple model, we should have $\theta < 1$ if we wish stationary solutions, and $\phi > 1$ if we wish determinate solutions. There is no reason the parameters should be the same, and many reasons they should be different.

An analogous point applies to the fiscal rule. In the form (22.11), we see that the identifying assumption in (22.5) $s_{t+1} = \gamma v_t + u_{s,t+1}$ is $\alpha = \gamma$, that the government raises surpluses to validate any inflation or deflation that comes along, in the same way as it raises surpluses to pay off previous borrowing. There is no reason that governments must equate these responses, and there are excellent reasons for governments to respond differently to the different sources of variation in value of the debt, given that governments wish to borrow to finance deficits and wish to control inflation. We may easily see a positive coefficient in a regression of surpluses on debt from a fiscal theory equilibrium. Section 5.5 constructs an example. Leeper and Li (2017) also show that regressions of surplus on debt do not establish passive fiscal policy.

Since the question is the fundamental "cause" of inflation, one is tempted to run Granger causality[1] tests between debt or deficits and inflation or surpluses. Observational equivalence warns us to be wary. Without the assumption that people in the economy see no more information than we do, Granger causality tests are not causality tests. And that assumption is not plausible. If people learn from reading the news that surpluses will be poor, they rush to sell government bonds and drive up the price level. Inflation helps us who observe the economy to forecast deficits. Analogously, asset prices help to predict, and hence Granger-cause, subsequent dividends and returns. That doesn't mean that price

---

1. A variable x_t is said to Granger-cause y_t if surprises to x_t, $\Delta E_{t+1} x_{t+1}$, forecast surprises to subsequent y_t, $\Delta E_{t+1} y_{t+1+j}$, where $\Delta E_{t+1}(\cdot) \equiv E(\cdot | z_{t+1}) - E(\cdot | z_t)$ and z_t is a vector of VAR variables including x_t and y_t. Equivalently, x_t does not Granger-cause y_t if the impulse-response function of y_{1+j} to x_1 shocks is zero. One handles contemporaneous correlation of the x and y shocks by assumptions.

changes *cause* dividend and return changes. People have information about good future dividends, say, and then bid up asset prices. We, studying the economy with less information, see an unexpectedly higher price, and then the higher dividends. Consumption Granger-causes income. You learn of a raise next year and go out to dinner. The dinner helps an econometrician to forecast larger income. Going out to dinner does not cause a raise (alas). Section 19.8 makes the same point regarding the correlation of money with nominal income.

Causality tests suffer from a deeper problem in this application. The active-fiscal versus active-money question is which off-equilibrium expectation supports an equilibrium. Unlike the money versus nominal income question that generated Granger causality tests, off-equilibrium expectations leave no signature in the temporal ordering of equilibrium variables. The equilibrium conditions are the same in both regimes. So the joint dynamic process of surplus, debt, discount rate, and inflation tells us nothing about which equilibrium selection regime produces the inflation. Equilibrium selection adjustments do not happen with a delay.

A second source of identification restrictions comes by restricting the stochastic process of the disturbances and $\{u_{s,t}\}$ in particular. Indeed, any identification of the parameters ϕ and γ must include restrictions on the disturbances, since they can soak up or offset any behavior of the $\phi(\pi_t - \pi_t^*)$ and $\gamma(v_t - v_t^*)$ terms. The surplus process can have an s-shaped response by virtue of $\alpha > 0$ and $\Delta E_t \pi_{t+1}$ uncorrelated with shocks to $u_{s,t+1}$, or it can have an s-shaped response with $\alpha = 0$ by virtue of an s-shaped $\{u_{s,t+1}\}$ process. The parametric form is convenient but not necessary. In his identification critique of Keynesian models, Sims (1980) cites identification by disturbance lag-length restrictions or by exclusion restrictions (leaving v_t out of the VAR) as assumptions with particularly weak foundations.

For example, Canzoneri, Cumby, and Diba (2001) test whether a shock to surpluses reduces subsequent debts, as analyzed in Sections 4.2.2 and 4.2.6, and interpret that finding as refutation of fiscal theory. But we saw that test comes down to the identifying restriction $a(\rho) > 1$ in $\tilde{s}_t = a(L)\varepsilon_{s,t}$.

Unusually, Cumby, Canzoneri, and Diba recognize that active-money and active-fiscal regimes are observationally equivalent, writing

> it is quite difficult (and perhaps impossible) to develop formal tests that discriminate between R [active money] and NR [active fiscal] regimes, since (as Cochrane, 1998, points out) both regimes use exactly the same equations to explain a given data set.

They acknowledge that a long-run negative autocorrelation of surpluses, $a(\rho) < 1$ is possible and solves their puzzle. They opine that $a(\rho) < 1$ is not *plausible*:

> NR [fiscal-theory] regimes offer a rather convoluted explanation that requires the correlation between today's surplus innovation and future surpluses to eventually turn negative. We will argue that this correlation structure seems rather implausible in the context of an NR regime...

If one wishes to test fiscal theory, this is just the right sort of argument to have. Recognize observational equivalence, state identifying assumptions used to overcome it, and think about whether those assumptions are plausible.

Twenty years of hindsight may change one's mind about plausibility. We can now realize that an s-shaped response, $a(\rho) < 1$, is not at all convoluted, nor unnatural, nor special to passive-fiscal regimes.

The fiscal theory model literature, covered in Section 24.2, estimates much-elaborated versions of (22.3)–(22.6), with time-varying regimes or Markov-switching between regimes. These models typically also specify an AR(1) for the disturbance $\{u_{s,t}\}$. Together with $\alpha = \gamma$, then, an s-shaped surplus process indicates a passive fiscal regime, and active fiscal policy is tied to the counterfactual predictions of Section 4.2. The AR(1) or other restriction on the disturbance is crucial for this identification, as a more general process can produce the s-shaped response all on its own. (Sections 24.1 and 24.2 contain reviews of this literature.)

As we saw, a surplus process with $\gamma = 0$, $s_{t+1} = u_{s,t+1}$ and a positively correlated disturbance with $a(\rho) > 1$ is deeply counterfactual. How, then, do the models find *any* periods of active fiscal policy? Well, by also restricting $\theta = \phi$ and the monetary policy disturbance $\{u_{i,t}\}$, the models impose a different set of counterfactual predictions for active monetary policy. My guess, then, is that such models find active-fiscal passive-monetary policy in times such as the 1970s, as they typically do, when there is a lot of inflation volatility so the $a(\rho) > 1$ counterfactual predictions don't look so bad, but interest rates do not move much with inflation, so $\phi = \theta > 1$ is a particularly bad fit. They then find active-money passive-fiscal regimes in times such as the 1980-2008 period when the $a(\rho) > 1$ surplus predictions are really hurtful to model fit, and $\phi = \theta > 1$ better fits Fed behavior. The chosen regime is a compromise of which identifying assumption makes the model fit least badly.

The result is a misapprehension of what fiscal theory is and does. The active-fiscal or "fiscal dominant" regime is usually seen as the bad regime, when inflation is volatile, when monetary policy is forced to cave in to inflationary fiscal pressure. The active money or "money dominant" regime is seen as the good one, when fiscal policy follows monetary commands to lower inflation. People use "fiscal dominance" as a synonym for a fiscal shock generating a large unexpected inflation.

If we loosen the identifying restrictions, we can fit the data better in all time periods—allowing an s-shaped surplus process with active fiscal policy, along with interest rates that react less than one for one to inflation when needed. And fiscal theory changes character. Fiscal theory can apply at all times, describe the whole sample, and it can describe policies and institutions that stabilize and quiet inflation.

22.4 Plausibility and Other Evidence

Observational equivalence only applies to equilibrium time series. We can still look at the plausibility of different regimes, and we can look at information in institutions, rules, mandates, legal limitations, and statements that fiscal and monetary authorities make to communicate off-equilibrium behavior. We can analyze choices governments make in difficult times. I quickly summarize the previous arguments that the active money equilibrium selection mechanism is implausible and inconsistent with this kind of evidence, while the active-fiscal regime is plausible and thus consistent.

Observational equivalence only applies to equilibrium time series. We can and should use additional information. We can and should examine the *plausibility* of different regimes, off-equilibrium behaviors, and identifying assumptions. What do fiscal and monetary authorities say they would do in various circumstances? What kinds of behavior are encoded in the legal and institutional structures and restrictions of monetary and fiscal policy? Why, and in response to what historical experiences, were those structures chosen? How do people in the economy expect those authorities to behave? When we see governments making hard choices, say between unpopular and distortionary taxation or spending cuts versus inflation or devaluation, what do those choices tell us about the economic constraints governments perceive?

We examine plausibility of identifying assumptions and off-equilibrium behavior to overcome problems everywhere in economics and finance. Behavioral and rational asset pricers admit observational equivalence given time series of prices, dividends, and economic variables—though often grudgingly—but then question the plausibility of the alternative interpretations, or their consistency with other sources of information. As they should.

How plausible *are* the off-equilibrium stories, in the light of all this other evidence? We spent a lot of time on this issue, for just this reason that it is central, once observational equivalence knocks out formal tests.

Looking at the new-Keynesian equilibrium condition in the form $E_t(\pi_{t+1} - \pi_{t+1}^*) = \phi(\pi_t - \pi_t^*)$, I object that no central bank responds to inflation with more inflation to select equilibria, and people do not expect them to do so. Looking at operating procedures, our central banks do not limit money supplies. Money demand is interest elastic and has lost any meaning in a plethora of liquid assets and electronic transactions.

Fiscal theory critics offer similar objections to the plausibility of "active" fiscal policy, and whether people could expect such a thing. For this reason, I have argued that the fiscal commitment to refuse to adapt surpluses to variation in debt caused by unexpected inflation, while often repaying debt accumulated from past deficits, is a reasonable description of current institutions, expectations, and sound government policy.

Monetary and fiscal policies are full of *institutions*, rules, and traditions that help the government to commit to and communicate off-equilibrium behavior and equilibrium selection policies that cannot be directly observed from macroeconomic time series. The gold standard, foreign exchange pegs, backing promises, currency boards, balanced budget rules, inflation targets, Taylor rules, legal restrictions against inflationary finance and central bank actions, and the institutional separation of monetary and fiscal policy, are all examples. Central banks' repeated statements about how they would react to events in speeches, testimony, and formal strategy pronouncements, and their eternal silence about equilibrium selection via a hyperinflationary threat tell us a lot about their off-equilibrium behavior.

Events often suggest one or another of *possible* interpretations is more *plausible*. A country—Venezuela, say—has large persistent deficits, inflation, and prints a lot of money. Now it's *possible* that the central bank went nuts, printed up a lot of money, caused inflation, and the fiscal authorities though fully able to raise taxes or cut spending went along "passively," because the central bank is supposed to be in charge of inflation. But that's a pretty implausible story, though it satisfies the letter of observational equivalence.

In moments of stress we see decisions that reflect the choices that governments see in front of them. A government in a crisis chooses between distorting taxes and the distortions of inflation. Its choices, and the mechanisms it puts into place to avoid another crisis, tell us a lot. Does it put into place a rule demanding any inflation be met with higher inflation ($\phi > 1$)? Or does it put into place institutions that react to inflation with fiscal tightening?

Plausibility arguments can go on. The 50-year-old behavioral versus rational finance debate is exhibit A of that observation, with Keynesians versus monetarists, and then versus general equilibrium going on for even longer. But that is how we learn, once we rightly abandon hope that a formal test will settle things once and for all.

22.5   Laugh Tests

Apparently easy armchair laugh tests likewise fail. The present value relation is part of all theories, so does not distinguish them. Deficits are higher in recessions, and lower in booms, yet inflation goes the other way, lower in recessions and higher in booms. What about Japan, and other countries with high debts and no inflation? The fiscal theory does not predict a tight relationship between deficits or debt and inflation. For both cyclical and cross-country comparisons, variation in the discount rate may matter more than variation in expected surpluses to understand the price level.

Many commenters dismiss fiscal theory by apparently easy armchair rejections, or laugh tests. Recessions feature deficits and less inflation. Expansions feature surpluses and more inflation. The sign is wrong! Countries with large debts or deficits seem no more likely to experience currency devaluation or inflation. What about Japan, with debt more than 200% of GDP and no inflation? What about the United States, at least before 2021, with large debts and deficits, and annual warnings from the CBO of yawning fiscal gaps to come? Contrariwise, many currency crashes and inflations, such as the late 1990s East Asian currency collapses, were not preceded by large deficits or government debts. Doesn't all this invalidate the fiscal theory?

No, as observational equivalence and existence of discount factor theorems should indicate. First, equivalence is equivalence. The present value equation is part of new-Keynesian and monetarist theories. If somehow the present value equation fails, it rejects those theories equally. Moreover, there *is* an expectation of future surpluses and a discount factor that makes sense of these observations. And they are not entirely unreasonable.

Fiscal theory does not predict a tight relationship, or even a positive correlation, between deficits and inflation. The fiscal theory ties the price level to the present value of future surpluses, not to current surpluses. On average, debts that raised revenue to finance deficits must be followed by surpluses, and do not forecast inflation, or investors won't lend in the first place. Big inflations and currency crashes, and ends of inflations and stabilizations, happen when important news about future surpluses and deficits emerges, not a slow predictable pressure of current debt. As with stock market prices or bank runs, just what the piece of information is that changes investors' minds is not necessarily easy to see. There is no asset for which economists can forecast payments and make even vaguely correct guesses about the price.

CBO projections are clearly warnings about what will happen if law does not change, not conditional means. When the CBO tells you that its own projection is "unsustainable," that means it won't happen. Bond investors may still believe that the U.S. government will undertake straightforward reforms before driving the country to a catastrophic debt crisis.

Discount rates vary. Discount rates are lower in recessions and higher in booms, driving a time-series correlation of inflation with business cycles. The steady downward trend of real interest rates from 1990 to 2020 suggestively correlates with high and rising values of debt in advanced economies, together with low and declining inflation. Just *why* real interest rates are so low is a good economic question. But it is an economic question for all theories, not a question that distinguishes fiscal theory from other theories of price level determination and equilibrium selection.

Japan has low real rates. Simplistic $r < g$ calculations say that its present value puzzle is the absence of much greater deflation! (More on $r < g$ in Section 6.4.) In addition, though Japan's gross debt-to-GDP ratio is indeed high, 264% as I write in 2021, its net debt-to-GDP ratio is 154%. The Japanese government has a lot of assets. Japan accumulated foreign assets during a long period of trade surpluses. Japan's debt is largely long-term, held by Japanese people and domestic financial institutions. Japan has an inheritance tax. And, perhaps, just wait. Most of all, again, the government debt valuation equation is equally a part of new-Keynesian and monetarist theories. Equivalence is equivalence. If it fails, all these theories fail.

None of this is proof, nor offered as such. The point is that armchair tests based on these and related facts are not tests of fiscal versus new-Keynesian or monetarist price-level determination regimes. The theorems tell us that there *is* a fiscal-theory story. I only claim here that there are not totally unreasonable stories.

22.6   Chicken and Regimes

The proverbial game of chicken between treasury and central bank is a conceptually useful fable, but an unrealistic description of policy formation. We do not *have* to model policy formation by such a game. The game of chicken does not apply to interest rate targets, in which the central bank must actively hyperinflate to select equilibria rather than refuse to monetize debts. In the end, the government must produce a coordinated policy. How it does so leaves no tracks in the time series.

The question of active versus passive regime is often told as a game of chicken, the game in which two drivers face head on and the one who swerves is the chicken. Sargent and Wallace (1981) famously used this metaphor for a situation in which money supply and fiscal policy are in conflict. It has been almost too influential, leaving the false impression that we *have* to describe policy in these terms, with one of monetary or fiscal policy completely passive and the other one completely in charge.

In the end, the government must provide a coordinated fiscal and monetary policy: a setting of interest rates or money supplies, and surpluses and debts, that generates a unique equilibrium price level. When two tools conflict, the government needs to figure out settings that do not conflict. From a historical, political science, or just common sense view, the game of chicken embodies a stylized and unrealistic story of how a government forms a coordinated policy. Government is composed of many interested players with conflicting objectives, who hash out the intricate negotiation that occupies daily media coverage of public affairs. Even treasury versus central bank conflicts are negotiated.

The central point: We do not *have to* describe government policy as the outcome of a two-agent ultimatum game. We don't have to describe any objectives at all, as I mostly have not done in this book. Most of the time we do not bother modeling the inner workings of government or other economic agents. If government maximizes something, it is a unitary objective. We likewise don't describe consumers with a little angel on one shoulder and a devil on the other playing an ultimatum game.

Yes, studying how governments come up with decisions is a separate and fruitful investigation. A "passive" fiscal policy must run into a Laffer limit at some point. Strong and independent central banks that dislike inflation can pressure treasuries to difficult but necessary probity. Modeling how household preferences result from internal bargaining games is interesting and fruitful as well. But this consideration goes into the bucket of political economy, of dynamic public finance, of figuring out what overall government preferences for distorting taxes versus inflation are; not of figuring out how inflation and other aggregates react once a coordinated policy is in place. The observational equivalence theorem drives home this point: Given the policy, observable variables are the same no matter which policy is active or passive.

Sargent and Wallace (1981) consider $MV = Py$ as the monetary alternative, in which control of the money supply completely controls the price level. Active money is a refusal to act, a refusal to print money to finance deficits, or in response to inflation. Active fiscal policy is a refusal to adapt surpluses and deficits to inflation-induced changes in the value of debt.

The game of chicken story makes less sense in comparing fiscal theory of monetary policy to the new-Keynesian model, in which monetary policy controls expected inflation in either regime. The active/passive question is now whether a central bank controls unexpected inflation by equilibrium selection threat $\phi(\pi_t - \pi_t^*)$, or whether fiscal policy directly determines unexpected inflation. Active fiscal policy is still a refusal to act, but active monetary policy requires the central bank to actively exercise its threats. It was already unclear just how a threat to hyperinflate makes the private sector jump to the central bank's desired equilibrium, but how does that threat force a reluctant treasury to tighten fiscal policy? "We're not printing money to finance your deficits, good luck in the bond market," is a sensible threat. "If you don't tighten up, we're going to hyperinflate with explosive interest rate targets" seems a lot less realistic. The new-Keynesian tradition does not in fact analyze the $\phi(\pi_t - \pi_t^*)$ threat as a way of enforcing passive policy on a reluctant treasury, but merely as a coordinating device for private expectations, with a vision that the treasury meekly follows inflation and deflation with whatever surpluses are required.

Pure active/passive regimes and chicken games are good stories to tell in order to understand theoretical possibilities and to understand some episodes. But they are not a necessary part of a policy specification or, in the end, that useful.

22.7 Inconsistent or Undetermined Regimes

I fill in the two other possibilities: undetermined and inconsistent regimes. Neither makes sense, emphasizing that it is unwise to test for these stylized regimes.

The conventional taxonomy following Leeper (1991) lists four parameter regions, not two. If $\phi > 1$ and $\gamma = 0$, both policies are active. Now, with the rule against nominal explosions, inflation is overdetermined. Similarly, if monetary policy fixes M and fiscal policy fixes surpluses at an inconsistent value, no equilibrium can form. If, on the other hand, $\phi < 1$ or M is passive and fiscal policy is also passive, $\gamma > 0$, then we are back to indeterminacy.

"Equilibrium cannot form" makes no sense here, however, any more than it did in our efforts to trim multiple equilibria. Suppose that the central bank cuts the money supply in half and leaves it there. That should cut the price level in half. But that would double the value of government debt. What if fiscal authorities refuse to raise taxes, or they are at the top of the Laffer curve and cannot raise tax revenues? Well, bondholders see government bonds as overvalued at the low price level so they try to sell before the inevitable default. That raises aggregate demand and pushes the price level up. Money will become scarce, with troubles in markets and financial institutions. People will start using scrip or foreign currency. In the short run, whether government finances or the money demand curve is the more flexible economic relationship will determine the outcome. In the long run, either the treasury or the central bank will have to give in. "Equilibrium can't form" just means you've written down an incomplete theory. A treasury running intractable deficits and a central bank exercising its threat to hyperinflate at the same time is an even more unrealistic picture.

A double passive policy would also fall apart. Inflation is always something, the price level is a real number. Thus, any model that stops at "indeterminate" is just missing an ingredient, even if the ingredient is sunspots. Inflation or deflation comes from some source—a frost raises the price of orange juice, say. Money adapts. Fiscal policy responds with spending or austerity. Inflation slowly becomes unhinged. Authorities soon figure out they need a better policy.

These configurations are useful for telling stories and exploring how theory works, but they are not realistic policy configurations to consider in applications, to try to measure or test. We will not observe a government in an overdetermined or underdetermined regime. If one wants to follow these directions, better game theory is the answer.

22.8   Regimes and Practices

Observational equivalence suggests that we modify procedures so that the choice of regime is, where possible, less important. We can estimate models written in terms of observable quantities, without identifying restrictions to tie equilibrium selection parameters to observables. We still need to think to ask interesting policy questions: If the central bank raises interest rates, should we include a contemporaneous fiscal shock? One should at least calculate and examine implicit fiscal predictions of active-money views. Regimes affect central doctrines. Since the alternative monetary and interest rate models are not consistent with what we know about how governments behave and financial markets are structured, we should get on with the business of seeing *how* the only theory we have does work.

What should we *do*, in light of observational equivalence? From the fact that tests depend on identification assumptions, one might be led to a search for better identification assumptions and get back to testing regimes. But 30 years of search haven't gotten that far, similar efforts elsewhere in economics and finance have not borne fruit, and I have argued that the active-money regimes don't make much sense. This does not seem a productive path.

One view is that anything unobservable shouldn't matter that much. So put aside these controversies and adopt modeling and empirical procedures in which the choice of regime is of minor importance. Chapter 5 showed how we can estimate models by just studying equilibrium conditions, where starred values equal their unstarred counterparts.

That's all we need for fitting data or even for simulating models. It does not matter whether unexpected inflation causes following surpluses or vice versa for that purpose, or why the interest rate and surplus shocks display whatever correlation one finds in the data. The only issue is why unexpected inflation is one particular value and not another. Add a footnote stating that one could support the equilibrium by specifying either an active interest rate-based equilibrium selection policy, or by specifying active fiscal policy. (Werning (2012) innovated this clever strategy, including the footnote.)

This attitude does not free us from thinking about foundations when analyzing policy. If one wants to ask, "what happens if the Fed raises interest rates?" we have to know if it is *interesting* to specify a contemporaneous fiscal contraction to that monetary contraction. It also does not excuse the typical new-Keynesian habit of ignoring fiscal implications. One should at least calculate and examine the implicit fiscal predictions of active-money models' inspired simulations.

Regimes also still affect central doctrines: Can the central bank set an interest rate peg without causing volatile indeterminate inflation? Must a central bank raise observable interest rates more than one for one with inflation?

The new-Keynesian equilibrium selection story such as $i_t = i_t^* + \phi(\pi_t - \pi_t^*)$, and its monetarist counterparts, do not correspond to how we know the world works. Some version of the active-fiscal regime is the only coherent complete model of the price level we have, that is vaguely consistent with current institutions. In this context, observational equivalence is a feature not a bug. It means that time series tests can't prove fiscal theory wrong, and it offers a recipe for translating existing models to fiscal foundations. In addition to observational equivalence and nonidentification, there is no point in trying to test for regimes that don't make any sense. What do we do? Let's get on with understanding the world using the only sensible regime we have. Write coordinated monetary–fiscal policies in which the ultimate foundation of price level determinacy is fiscal and see *how* to specify the models and policies so that the models are useful. This is not easy work.

PART V

Past, Present, and Future

23

Past and Present

I HAVE KEPT extensive pointers to and reviews of literature out of the main text of this book to focus on the issues and to keep it readable. Here, I point to some of the crucial work in the development of fiscal theory, focusing on work that I have not described already, and I outline some recent and current work. I see a fundamental way that much recent work can be improved to fit better, to fit all data with fiscal theory, and to reorient its basic message away from a theory of failed institutions to a theory of successful ones.

The fiscal theory is an active research field. I have barely touched on many current efforts, and this review will necessarily be incomplete as well. I close with some speculation about future steps for fiscal theory.

23.1   The Rise of Fiscal Theory

Leeper (1991) "Equilibria under 'Active' and 'Passive' Monetary Policies" is the fiscal theory watershed. Leeper considers interest rate rules, rather than money growth rules, to characterize monetary policy, and thus connects with contemporary macroeconomics. Leeper shows that active fiscal policy can uniquely determine inflation even with passive $\phi < 1$ monetary policy. Even an interest rate peg can have a stable, determinate inflation. Boiling it down to a simple model, Leeper analyzes a model of the form

$$i_t = E_t \pi_{t+1} \tag{23.1}$$

$$i_t = \phi \pi_t + u_{i,t} \tag{23.2}$$

$$\tilde{s}_{t+1} = \gamma v_t + u_{s,t+1} \tag{23.3}$$

$$\rho v_{t+1} = v_t + i_t - \pi_{t+1} - \tilde{s}_{t+1}. \tag{23.4}$$

As we have seen many times, this model needs a forward-looking eigenvalue to tie down unexpected inflation $\Delta E_{t+1} \pi_{t+1}$. We can achieve that result with active monetary and passive fiscal policy, $\phi > 1$, $\gamma > 0$, or with active fiscal and passive monetary policy $\phi < 1$, $\gamma = 0$. Leeper's singular contribution is to point out the latter possibility. The fiscal theory is born. Leeper includes a sticky price model, along the lines of the simple models investigated here. That is an immediately important generalization, though the algebra hides the determinacy and equilibrium selection issues.

(As a reminder, we can substitute for $\tilde{s}_{t+1}$ and i_t to write

$$\rho v_{t+1} = (1 - \gamma) v_t - \Delta E_{t+1} \pi_{t+1} - u_{s,t+1}.$$

If $\gamma > 0$, the value of debt grows more slowly than the interest rate, so any unexpected inflation $\Delta E_{t+1}\pi_{t+1}$ is consistent with the transversality condition. If $\gamma = 0$, then only one value of unexpected inflation keeps debt from exploding.)

Sims (1994) writes a full nonlinear model, emphasizing the possibility that controlling money might not determine the price level, and emphasizing the stability and determinacy of an interest rate peg under fiscal theory. Woodford (1995) shows that fiscal theory can give a determinate price level with a passive money supply policy, thereby titling his paper "Price-Level Determinacy Without Control of a Monetary Aggregate." Woodford also first uses the term "fiscal theory of the price level" that I have found. Woodford (2001) shows determinacy under an interest rate peg.

I got involved in the late 1990s with Cochrane (1998a). This paper shows the observational equivalence theorem. I express the issue in terms of on-equilibrium versus off-equilibrium responses. I tangle with the data. I show how the AR(1) surplus cannot work, because it predicts a tight connection between inflation, debt, and deficits. I present a two-component model that generates an s-shaped response. I show that we need such a process to fit the data, and that fiscal theory is compatible with such a process, though not the full range of counterfactuals distilled in this book. I show that the s-shape or surpluses that respond to debt are not signs of passive fiscal policy. I discuss the need for discount rate variation to make sense of the data, and I offer a simple version of the linearizations, VAR, and inflation variance decomposition reported here. I also explore long-term debt.

I mistitled the paper "A Frictionless View." I should have titled it "A Fiscal View." I was enthralled with the idea that fiscal theory allows one to think about the price level in models with no monetary or pricing frictions, and that such frictionless models might go a long way to understanding the data; an abstraction on which one could add price stickiness later to get better-fitting dynamics. I didn't even include the simple sticky price models that Leeper (1991) had already taught us how to use. Though a nice point, however, the frictionless possibility and benchmark are not the central message of fiscal theory. The paper gained comparatively little attention. Observational equivalence, the s-shaped surplus, and more, did not impact subsequent work. Title your papers well, and edit them better.

Cochrane (2001) explores long-term debt more deeply, giving rise to most of the treatment of long-term debt you see here. I also show that the two-component s-shaped surplus process is not recoverable from VARs that exclude the value of debt. That argument was complex, involving spectral densities. The version in Online Appendix Section A2.1 is a lot clearer.

Just after these first steps, Woodford also produced his magisterial Woodford (2003) *Interest and Prices*, putting in one place the emerging new-Keynesian model. Yet, despite Woodford's leading role in bringing fiscal theory to life, he abandoned it in this book, relying exclusively on explosive inflation threats to select equilibria.

23.2   Precursors

With hindsight, one can see many precursors. We all stand on the shoulders of giants.

The 1970s and 1980s saw an outpouring of work on monetary and fiscal policy in the intertemporal rational-expectations general-equilibrium revolution, from which the fiscal theory sprang. However, though we can now see these roots, reevaluation of central monetarist doctrines, and many important fiscal theory propositions, much of that literature retained the central concern with money versus bonds, seigniorage, targeting monetary aggregates rather than interest rates, rate of return distortions, separate central bank balance sheets, and so forth. Much of it took place within the overlapping generations framework, which adds dynamic inefficiency questions and is difficult to relate to actual money, since money turns over more than once per generation. Only after Leeper did fiscal theory move the baseline to a completely cashless economy, nominal debt, and interest rate targets, with monetary frictions tacked on as needed but not central to price level determination.

Sargent and Wallace (1981) "Unpleasant Monetarist Arithmetic," and Sargent (1982b) "Ends of Hyperinflations," surveyed above in Sections 14.3 and 19.6, were a huge impetus. They combine clear simple theory, an evident match to experience, and relevance to contemporary policy.

Sargent (1982a), surveying the intertemporal revolution, suggests we

> begin with the initial working hypothesis that the government is like a firm and that its debt is priced according to the same sorts of equilibrium asset-pricing theories developed for pricing bonds and equities . . . the return stream backing the government's debt is the prospective excess of its explicit tax collections over its expenditures. (p. 383.)

But Sargent immediately retrenches with "this approach is valuable, if only for the qualifications that it immediately invites." Most of those qualifications center around non-interest-bearing cash and financial distortions induced by regulation, which we now understand are important extensions but not central to price level determination.

Sargent offers the first use I have seen of the term "Ricardian regime." He imagines

> two polar monetary–fiscal regimes. In the first or Ricardian regime, the issuing of additional interest-bearing government securities is always accompanied by a planned increase in future explicit tax collections just sufficient to repay the debt. . . .
> In the second polar regime, increased government interest-bearing securities will be paid off . . . by eventually collecting seigniorage through issuing base money.

The s-shaped surplus begins. By implication, a regime can lie between the "polar extremes."

Aiyagari and Gertler (1985) notice that monetarist propositions rely on fiscal backing, what Leeper later calls passive fiscal policy. They consider a model with money, induced by overlapping generations, and government debt, but no pricing frictions. Following Sargent, they analyze a "non-Ricardian regime" in which "the central bank fully accommodates a fiscal deficit by financing the new debt with current and future money creation." In their non-Ricardian regime, the price level becomes proportional to the total supply of government debt, as in the fiscal theory with an AR(1) surplus, and the price level becomes independent of the composition of government debt, the split between M and B.

Wallace (1981) proves that open market operations can be irrelevant, in a "Modigliani-Miller" theorem:

Monetary policy determines the composition of the government's portfolio. Fiscal
policy . . . determines the path of net government indebtedness . . . alternative paths
of the government's portfolio consistent with a single path of fiscal policy *can be*
irrelevant . . .

This model is also based on overlapping generations. Indeed, the paper includes an
apologia to economists who find that framework a strained parable for money (me).
As this irrelevance theorem is not true when there is a standard monetary distortion,
one might be forgiven for having seen it as just confirming the liquidity trap or as an
overlapping generations curiosity.

Sargent and Wallace (1982) show that a real bills doctrine with passive money supply
can lead to a determinate price level, and is indeed optimal, but again in an overlapping-
generations context. Contrariwise, Sargent and Wallace (1985) find that paying market
interest on reserves gives a "continuum of equilibria" in an overlapping generations model
of money, a modern version of a liquidity trap. But if full interest on reserves is financed by
taxes, it is consistent with a determinate price level. This is an early simple version of the
fiscal theory proposition that full interest on reserves can leave the price level determinate.

Monetary economists long recognized the importance of monetary–fiscal interactions,
if for nothing else that fiscal stress leads governments to finance deficits by printing money.
Friedman (1948), though quite different from his later thoughts, is a program for monetary
and fiscal stability. Patinkin (1965) emphasizes a wealth effect of government bonds, which
we can see in fiscal theory. Wesley Clair Mitchell (1903) and Irving Fisher (e.g., Fisher
(1912)) debated the quantity theory versus fiscal backing of greenback inflation. The
intuition of the fiscal theory is already reflected by Adam Smith, quoted in the epigraph.

The "chartalist" school includes some elements of fiscal theory. Knapp (1924) wrote
in 1905 *The State Theory of Money.* He views "money" as defined by legal status in paying
debts, including and especially debts to the state. He writes (p. 95) that the key "test" of
money is whether it is "accepted in payments made to the State's offices." Metallic content is not relevant to Knapp, and we should think of even metallic money as a "token,"
"ticket" or "Charta." (Knapp coined the word "Chartal," p. 32.) But Knapp's work is mostly
devoted to the philosophical question "what is money?" and classifying money into a
schema of properties such as "morphic," "authylistic," "lytric," "hylogenic," "autogenic,"
"amphithropic," "monotropic," and so forth. He is not concerned with the *value* of money,
the price level, or inflation, other than the price of gold, silver, and foreign exchange rates.
One can regard the book as a precursor to the legal restrictions school, which regards
demand for fiat money as generated by legal restrictions on the forms of payment, rather
than fiscal theory.

In "Functional Finance," Lerner (1943) recognizes that taxes can soak up extra currency and hence stop inflation. His view is basically a static L-shaped aggregate supply
curve. More demand induced by printing more money or by borrowing first raises output
and employment, and then inflation, unless soaked up by taxes. More recently, "modern
monetary theorists" such as Kelton (2020) have taken on the mantle following Lerner
and the chartalist school. However, they mix one good idea—money can be soaked up
by taxes to prevent inflation—with a great number of wrong ideas to produce sharply
different analysis. (See, among other reviews, Cochrane (2020).)

That money is valued if it is backed by some real claim is an idea stretching back millennia, along with the realization that money useful in transactions and limited in supply can gain a higher value than its backing. Pure fiat money is the newcomer on the intellectual block. That paper money devalues when governments print it to finance spending was seen and understood time and again. The conventional view sees in our relatively stable inflation the capstone to the slow development of institutions that limit money printing under $MV = Py$. But perhaps we should see it instead as an equally slowly won but perhaps temporary victory of institutions by which sovereigns commit to repay nominal debts rather than default or inflate them away.

23.3 Disputes

The fiscal theory entered a period of theoretical controversies. Is the fiscal theory even right? How can an agent "threaten to violate an intertemporal budget constraint?" Among others, Buiter (1999), Buiter (2002), Buiter (2017) calls the fiscal theory "fatally flawed" and a "fallacy" for mistreating a "budget constraint." Kocherlakota and Phelan (1999), Bohn (1998b), and Ljungqvist and Sargent (2018) more charitably write that fiscal theory assumes that the government has a special ability to violate a budget constraint at off-equilibrium prices, but thereby validate the idea that the government debt valuation equation is a budget constraint. Marimon (2001), while recognizing fiscal theory as analogous to a "financial theory of the firm," still characterizes the fiscal theory as "a theory that does not respect Walras' law." Even Woodford (2003) (p. 691 ff.) endorses the view that the valuation equation is a "budget constraint" but the government is special.

I wrote "Money as Stock" Cochrane (2005b) to address this critique. As you've seen many times in this book, the fiscal theory is based on a valuation equation, an equilibrium condition, not a "budget constraint."

"Money as Stock" also discusses whether it is *plausible* that a government refuses to adapt surpluses to changes in the valuation of debt brought on by inflation and deflation, once one admits that it is possible in a way that violating budget constraints is impossible. The long and better discussion in this book started there. This issue owes a lot to persistent discussions with Marty Eichenbaum and Larry Christiano, for which I am grateful. Christiano and Fitzgerald (2000) put some of this thought in writing. The bottom line as expressed here is simple, but subtle. Just because we see governments often "respond" with surpluses to higher debt generated by past deficits in equilibrium, does not mean that they would respond to higher debt generated by off-equilibrium deflation with the same extra surpluses. Repaying one's debts is different than validating a deflation-induced windfall to bondholders, with 1933 a prime example.

Controversy on this point is understandable. The valuation equation is a lot closer to an "intertemporal budget constraint" in a model with real debt and no default. Economists had spent decades studying such models. That it works differently with nominal debt, and without a gold or foreign exchange peg, is not obvious. The distinction between budget constraint and valuation equation is subtle. I used the word "intertemporal budget constraint" as well in Cochrane (1998a), before the distinction dawned on me.

Niepelt (2004) offers a different critique, calling the theory a "Fiscal Myth." To Niepelt, the fiscal theory is wrong because it cannot start from a period 0 with no outstanding nominal debt. The government, selling initial nominal debt in return for goods, must promise additional future surpluses. To Niepelt, this fact means that fiscal policy must be "Ricardian," and, "the notion of fiscal price level determination therefore collapses." We have seen in this book so many debt sales with higher future surpluses that I hope it's abundantly clear such operations do not contravene fiscal theory.

Starting up a fiscal-theory economy is straightforward. The government can simply give money to people at the beginning of the first period. Or, the government can exchange new money or government debt in exchange for old money, as in the introduction of the Euro. Daniel (2007) rebuts this critique, and I discuss it in Section 2.2.

I have not spent much time in this book on theoretical controversies because I think they are settled, so not worth carrying along. The point of the book is to make fiscal theory useful, and deeply reviewing or rehashing these arguments seems unproductive. A lot of right theories do not organize events and are ignored. If the fiscal theory is not useful, nobody will long care about theoretical underpinnings.

I emphasize an approach to fiscal theory via simple Walrasian equilibrium. Bassetto (2002) spells out game-theoretic foundations for dynamic equilibria involving government policies. This work parallels similar game theoretic equilibrium-selection foundations for new-Keynesian models in Atkeson, Chari, and Kehoe (2010), Christiano and Takahashi (2018), and the extensive literature on game-theoretic foundations of general equilibrium theory. Bassetto and Sargent (2020) is a beautiful use of this framework, thinking of government policies as "strategies" and mapping the joint monetary–fiscal analysis to events in U.S. history.

This approach is surely right in a deep sense. My verbal discussion of how governments react to nonequilibrium prices, my v versus v^* and π versus π^* distinctions and my long discussions of institutions to guide expectations of off-equilibrium behavior, qualify as Bassetto's "more complex than the simple budgetary rules usually associated with the fiscal theory," such as simple $s_{t+1} = \gamma v_t$ or $i_t = \phi \pi_t$ feedback that I also criticize.

Why then does this book not adopt and survey game theoretic foundations in its hundreds of pages? I hope in this book to make fiscal theory *useful*. Hopefully, we don't *have to* spell out game theory foundations in order to use fiscal theory productively, just as standard Walrasian general equilibrium theory is useful though game theoretic foundations can be more satisfying, and as most applied new-Keynesian work ignores its parallel game theoretic foundations. If we always have to spell out such foundations the theory will be much less useful. Bassetto and Sargent (2020) challenge this view. They show the practical usefulness of game theoretic foundations by mapping government actions in those episodes to such concepts. But the counterexample proves the larger theorem: Sophisticated approaches will catch on, as they should, to the extent and in applications where they are useful. One must also accept comparative advantage, and mine does not lie in clarifying game theoretic foundations of equilibrium. So my silence on these questions does not signal that they are not important or potentially productive.

McCallum (2001), McCallum (2009a), McCallum and Nelson (2005), and Christiano (2018) add "learnability" to the definition of equilibrium, and view the active-money passive-fiscal equilibria as learnable, while the passive-money active-fiscal equilibrium is not learnable. I argue the opposite case for new-Keynesian models in Cochrane (2009), and survey this issue in Section 16.10 above. Since we do not observe

$\pi_t \neq \pi_t^*$, there is no way to learn ϕ in $i_t = i_t^* + \phi(\pi_t - \pi_t^*)$ of the new-Keynesian model.

Learnability is an addition to the standard Walrasian paradigm, as is the restriction to locally bounded equilibria. We don't *need* game theory, learnability, or a restriction to locally bounded equilibria to say that supply and demand determines the price of tomatoes. Having thrown out one Walrasian equilibrium condition, authors need to add something else. But then one must extend the definition of Walrasian equilibrium in order to write *any* model, no matter how simple, that determines the price level. If so, maybe one needs a better model! Fiscal theory alone still offers the Occam's razor simple *possibility* that the price level can be determined by Walrasian equilibrium with no frictions, additional rules, equilibrium selection philosophies, and so forth.

24

Tests, Models, and Applications

24.1 Tests

FOR CONTEMPORARY macroeconomists, the first instinct with a new theory is to run econometric tests, including grand tests for one class of theory versus another. I cover some of these tests in Section 22.3, with a focus on observational equivalence.

The main test in Canzoneri, Cumby, and Diba (2001) is based on the finding that surplus innovations lower the value of debt. They acknowledge both interpretations of this result and argue against the plausibility of the s-shaped surplus, as discussed in Sections 4.2 and 22.3.

They start, however, by considering and disclaiming the obvious test: Run a regression of (23.3), $s_{t+1} = \gamma v_t + \varepsilon_{t+1}$, and see if $\gamma > 0$, if surpluses respond to debt. Such a test would parallel Clarida, Galí, and Gertler (2000), who ran (boiled down) $i_t = \phi \pi_t + \varepsilon_t$ to test $\phi > 1$ for active monetary policy. As Cumby, Canzoneri, and Diba point out, we see $\gamma > 0$ in the data, as surpluses were higher in the early post-WWII era than in the 1970s, and shown in regressions by Bohn (1998a). But Cumby, Canzoneri and Diba recognize that we can see $\gamma > 0$ in both active and passive fiscal regimes. Recall the v versus v^* example in Section 5.4, or that a surplus moving average with $a(\rho) < 1$ generates a regression coefficient $\gamma > 0$.

Their careful analysis of this point did not stop $\gamma > 0$ from being a persistent informal argument against fiscal theory, as in Christiano and Fitzgerald (2000) for example, and a core identifying restriction for the whole fiscal theory modeling literature covered in the next section.

24.2 Fiscal Theory Models

Most application of fiscal theory in the last two decades has taken the form of model-building rather than purely econometric tests. These models describe the economy completely, including fiscal and monetary policy rules. Leeper and Leith (2016) is an excellent review survey including its own advances in the state of the art.

These models are specified in much more detail than any model in this book. The models include ingredients such as detailed fiscal policy rules, often separating taxes and spending, distorting taxes, valuable government spending, labor supply, sticky wages, more complex preferences, production with capital and investment, financial frictions, explicit microfoundations, nonlinear solution methods, optimal policy, commitment versus discretion, and other elaborations. They typically describe full microfoundations, rather than jump to linearized aggregate equilibrium conditions as I have. Most are estimated or calibrated to realistic parameters.

Following DSGE macro tradition, authors simulate the effects of policies and other shocks. By computing impulse-response functions, these models give concrete advice, and provide an account of history. They thus move beyond testing a theory in the abstract and on to using the theory to answer practical questions.

So far, however, this style of model building and evaluation has remained a sub-discipline. It has not infused fiscal roots into the larger DSGE model construction and evaluation enterprise. We should consider why not, and how to foster that jump.

I offer a general overview, and then a review of specific papers.

The models in this literature take a different approach than I have in this book, on the central question of how to specify regimes and how to integrate monetary and fiscal policy, what to *do* with fiscal theory. I pursue the goal of using fiscal theory to describe the whole sample, guided by observational equivalence. To that end, I generalize the description of policy to the form

$$i_t = \theta \pi_t + \phi(\pi_t - \pi_t^*) + u_{i,t} \tag{24.1}$$

$$\tilde{s}_{t+1} = \alpha v_t^* + \gamma(v_t - v_t^*) + u_{s,t+1}, \tag{24.2}$$

and I thereby allow any form of the surplus process, including $a(\rho) \ll 1$ if needed. I thereby fit the data at least as well as a new-Keynesian model, but I lose the ability to identify and test active-money versus active-fiscal regimes, to measure and test ϕ and γ, from equilibrium time series. This is a feature, not a bug, as above.

The current fiscal theory models in this literature are written in generalized forms of (23.1)–(23.4),

$$i_t = \phi \pi_t + u_{i,t}$$

$$\tilde{s}_{t+1} = \gamma v_t + u_{s,t+1},$$

with restrictions (typically an AR(1)) on the disturbances. These models look for time periods in which $\phi > 1$ and $\gamma > 0$, active monetary and passive fiscal policy, versus time periods in which $\phi < 1$ and $\gamma = 0$, passive monetary and active fiscal policy. Such measurements with standard errors are also regime tests.

You see the familiar identifying assumptions: Monetary and fiscal policy are tied to equilibrium selection policies $\theta = \phi$ and $\alpha = \gamma$, which are not realistic. Most of all, an active fiscal policy cannot generate an s-shaped surplus response.

As a result, the active fiscal regime must fit data quite badly. A single equation regression estimate may lose $\gamma > 0$ in standard errors, but a full model estimate faces the counterfactual correlations and puzzles of Section 4.2, in particular that deficits lower the value of debt. The model can estimate an active-fiscal regime only in a time such as the 1970s, when high and volatile inflation hides those counterfactual predictions, and when the $\phi > 1$ parameterization of identified active monetary policy does even more violence to the data. In a time such as the 1980s, with less volatile inflation, the counterfactual predictions of the restricted surplus process, and in which $\phi > 1$ fits better, the models find active money.

The result is profound. Fiscal theory is seen as a rare and unfortunate outcome, when monetary authorities lose a game of chicken and large volatile inflation breaks out. Active money is seen as the good state of affairs with low inflation. Indeed "fiscal dominance" is often used as a synonym for large or uncontrolled fiscal inflation, not for a set of institutions that can commit to and produce a steady price level.

This is a broad picture, which may not characterize every paper. But we *know* that any paper that produces estimates and tests of regimes, that does not report a flat likelihood function, has imposed some identifying restriction, and that restriction limits each regime's ability to describe data.

It is natural that authors proceeded this way. This is the most natural thing to do with models written in the standard form, and before one really digests observational equivalence and identification issues and works to write the models in a form that expresses the identifying assumptions. Estimating ϕ by regressions that identify monetary policy with equilibrium selection policy is the standard thing to do in new-Keynesian literature as well. And there is a path dependence in most investigations. Once one starts building on a structure such as (23.1)–(23.4), it is natural to focus on elaborations and not rewriting and reorienting the basic idea.

But now that we have the clarity of the observational equivalence theorems, now that we can express monetary and fiscal policy in terms of on-versus off-equilibrium reactions, now that we can separate monetary or fiscal policy from their equilibrium selection policies, now that we can write (24.1)–(24.2), we know that measuring regimes must rely on strong and unrealistic identifying restrictions, which artificially limit each regime's ability to describe the data. Moreover, these restrictions ($\theta = \phi$, $\alpha = \gamma$) artificially limit the models' fit in either estimated regime, and thus its overall fit. Any period of active fiscal policy contains all the counterfactual predictions of Section 4.2. Allowing an s-shaped surplus process in periods when $\phi = \theta < 1$ must improve model fit, likely a lot.

How did we not notice? Curiously, the DSGE literature does not emphasize goodness of fit measures or forecasting ability, cornerstones of earlier model building, and focuses on policy evaluation. In a sense, all models fit perfectly, because they add enough shocks to every equation to fit the data. But the size of the shocks is large, and becomes the predominant part of the model's explanatory power. For example, if one fits the data with the simple three-equation model presented here, inflation volatility comes almost entirely from inflation shocks, shocks to the Phillips curve, innovations $\varepsilon_{\pi,t}$ to

$$\pi_t = \beta E_t \pi_{t+1} + \kappa x_t + u_{\pi,t}$$
$$u_{\pi,t} = \eta_\pi u_{\pi,t-1} + \varepsilon_{\pi,t}.$$

Expected inflation and output don't explain much variation in current inflation; the Phillips curve has low R^2; inflation versus output gap plots are a big cloud. Where one might hope for a model to say that lower inflation volatility since 1980 derives from fewer monetary policy shocks, or a change in the monetary policy rule that reduces the influence of other shocks on inflation, in fact, a variance accounting throws up its hands and says inflation became less volatile because the gods sent us fewer inflation shocks. (Sims and Zha (2006) have a sophisticated calculation of this point.) But such variance accounting is no longer a common part of model evaluation. It is common to compare selected impulse-response functions to estimates. They may fit well, but if the corresponding shocks do not account for much variance, the model may still fit the data badly.

How can detailed and carefully estimated fiscal theory models miss the glaringly counterfactual puzzles induced by large $a(\rho)$? Because by and large they do not look, or the stylized facts are lost in dry model evaluation statistics. And, to be fair, if the goal is to match an estimated response function for a monetary policy shock, to think about the marginal effect of monetary policy shocks, even if such shocks contribute a small fraction of output and inflation forecast-error variance, the bad overall fit is not a salient fact.

How did regime identification and estimation go on despite warnings of observational equivalence from Cochrane (1998a) and Canzoneri, Cumby, and Diba (2001)? The answer may be that a clear and simple alternative was not readily at hand, so those papers' inconvenient but abstract points didn't make it into mainstream consciousness. While the King (2000) representation $i_t = i_t^* + \phi(\pi_t - \pi_t^*)$ was available in 2000, its implication for monetary policy identification didn't show up until Cochrane (2011a). The point remains contentious, with many critics of that work feeling there are reasonable identification restrictions one can make to measure ϕ. King's representation is still not a part of the regular toolkit and textbook expression of new-Keynesian models. The parallel way to write fiscal policy that distinguishes in-equilibrium responses, responses to past deficits and real interest rates, from responses to multiple equilibrium inflation—for example, $\tilde{s}_{t+1} = \alpha v_t^* + \gamma(v_t - v_t^*)$—is, as far as I know, original in summer 2020 manuscripts of Cochrane (2021b) and this book. That's hardly common technology. To write a model, you need the technology to do it, not just general theorems and whining from commenters. Moreover, it was obviously not clear how much the identifying assumptions hurt the model's ability to match facts. All estimates include identifying assumptions. Put all this together, along with the enduring wish, perpetual referee demand, and a hard-to-break habit of a literature to measure and test regimes, and the literature's progression is understandable.

But now we have these tools, which open an orchard of low-hanging fruit. We have a range of interesting work, and detailed, well-worked out models needing only slight modification. Indeed, much of what these papers do is suggestive. The papers measure the correlations between on-equilibrium policy variables. They measure θ in $i_t^* = \theta \pi_t^*$ or α in $s_t^* = \alpha v_t^*$. This measurement remains interesting and important. Observable parameters vary over time and such shifts are important, even if they do not document a switch between regimes, a switch of unobservable parameters.

Specific examples follow.

Davig and Leeper (2006) is a foundational paper in this line. Davig and Leeper estimate interest rate and surplus policy rules that depend on inflation, output, and in the latter case lagged debt, with uncorrelated disturbances. In a central and widely followed innovation, the policy rule coefficients vary between active fiscal and active money according to a Markov process, switching between $\gamma = 0, \phi < 1$ and $\gamma > 0, \phi > 1$. They embed these estimates in a detailed DSGE model with nominal rigidities and calculate the responses to policy shocks. The perpetual possibility of changing to a different regime plays an important role in these responses. Davig and Leeper (2006) warn against leaving out regime switches: "Many estimates of policy rules . . . condition on sub-samples in which a particular regime prevailed . . . embedding the estimated rules in fixed-regime DSGE models can lead to seriously misleading . . . inferences . . ."

Markov switching captures a larger and important theoretical point, also in Davig and Leeper (2007): If an economy is currently in what looks like a passive-fiscal regime, but people expect a switch to what looks like an active-fiscal regime, then that future active fiscal policy selects equilibria. We may have $\phi > 1$ and $\gamma > 0$, but if inflation really gets out of control, the government will switch to active fiscal policy. Well, then we are in the active-fiscal regime all along.

This fact means that measuring regimes is doubly hard and thus, in my view, doubly impossible and doubly pointless. It is not enough to surmount on- versus off-equilibrium identification issues in estimating *current* responses of surpluses and interest rates to inflation and debt. We have to estimate the structure of Markov switching and the cumulative probability of ending up in one versus another regime. We have to find which variable actually explodes as time goes forward and regimes switch back and forth. At a minimum, we need different language. A time with $\phi < 1$ should be something like "temporarily passive" monetary policy, not "passive" without qualification. (We have thought about nonlinear functions $i = \Phi(\Pi)$, and "locally" active or passive policies that reflect derivatives near the steady-state, $\Phi'(\Pi^*)$. Nonlinearity could change a policy's "global" properties. Here we think about variation in the policy rule over time, rather than over a wider range of a state variable.)

Regime-switching authors are right that policy rule parameters likely vary over time and in response to economic outcomes. They are right that we should look at the economy as a single meta-rule, or meta-regime, in which policy parameters vary over time, people expect such variation, and such variation should be incorporated in expectations and response calculations. For example, a big part of the story for persistently high ex post real interest rates in the 1980s may well be that people put some weight on a return to 1970s policy. Responses to monetary policy and other shocks should include changing assessments of the chance of such changes.

But it is not obvious that such parameter variation is best modeled by Markov switching rather than conventional continuously-valued time series models for parameters. As a modeling approximation, there is some sense to Markov switching. In history, policy parameters have arguably changed somewhat discontinuously. Pre- and post-1980, the zero bound era, and pre-war, 1940–1945, and postwar era are suggestively discretely different regimes, stable within but shifting discontinuously across. But that is a modeling choice, and it is not entirely obvious. There is also lots of policy drift within regimes. Moreover, the Markov assumption, with exactly two (or even N) states assigns zero probability that people consider other possbilities or other regimes.

So why not adopt simpler, more flexible models of policy rule parameter evolution? Here I think that linking policy rule changes to equilibrium selection regime changes ($\theta = \phi$, $\gamma = \alpha$) is a core trouble. Shifting from active-fiscal passive-money to active-money passive-fiscal requires a discrete shift in parameter values to move eigenvalues from stable to unstable. But if we are simply viewing shifting correlations between equilibrium variables or monetary and fiscal policy rules, a shift of θ in $i_t^* = \theta \pi_t^*$ and α in $\tilde{s}_{t+1} = \alpha v_t$, it has no such momentous or discontinuous consequences.

Leeper, Davig, and Chung (2007) show that apparently active-money passive-fiscal policy is not enough to insulate the economy from inflationary fiscal shocks. Following the usual restriction, only their (temporarily) passive-fiscal active-money policy can have an s-shaped response, so that regime is needed for debt repayment and for fiscal shocks not to result in immediate inflation. But that policy may not last long enough to repay debt. The expected switch to active fiscal means that fiscal shocks affect inflation immediately, even in the temporarily active-money passive-fiscal repayment regime. Again, though, the possibility of active fiscal policy with an s-shaped surplus, $\alpha \neq \gamma$ would remove that result. And a switch from active fiscal with an s-shaped surplus to active fiscal that inflates away debt would reinforce the result. We do not need to tie policy parameter changes to equilibrium selection regime changes to see the central point.

Leeper, Traum, and Walker (2017) present a detailed sticky price model allowing a fiscal theory solution, aimed at evaluating the output effects of fiscal stimulus. They specify fiscal policy as an AR(1) (p. 2416) along with one-period debt. They include an indirect mechanism that buffers the AR(1) surplus conundrum and allows a bit of $a(\rho) < 1$. Surpluses respond to output. So, a deficit leads to inflation, which raises output, which raises tax revenues, and leads to higher later surpluses. But that mechanism is not necessarily large enough to generate substantial repayment of large debts, $a(\rho) \ll 1$. That the regime is identified means there is some restriction.

Bianchi and Melosi (2013) offer an interesting application of these regime-switching ideas. They call the active-money passive-fiscal regime "virtuous," because as in these other papers, they assume that only a passive-fiscal regime can repay debts with $a(\rho) < 1$, so in the opposite (sinful?) passive-money active-fiscal regime any surplus shock results in inflation. But Markov switching allows a similar change of story. A temporary lapse in virtue—a temporarily active-fiscal regime with $a(\rho) > 1$—can nonetheless see little inflation, if people expect a reversion to "virtue" and its s-shaped surplus process. But a fiscal expansion with inadequate expectation of reversion to virtuous policy can give rise to large immediate inflation. In this way, they account for episodes in which persistent deficits and accommodative monetary policy do not give rise to inflation, or only give rise to slow inflation, and others in which deficits lead quickly to inflation. Again the same ideas could easily be present in an entirely active-fiscal equilibrium-selection regime, with parameters that vary over time. The $a(\rho)$ can vary over time, which one could model in my parametric v, v^* form by varying the correlation of unexpected inflation with the surplus shock β_s over time.

Bianchi and Melosi also describe a "dormant" shock, expectations of future fiscal policy that causes inflation today, leaving conventional analysis puzzled about the source of the inflation, "if an external observer were monitoring the economy focusing exclusively on output and inflation, he would detect a run-up in inflation and an increase in volatility without any apparent explanation." We have seen many parallel analyses.

Bianchi and Melosi (2017) show how fiscal theory accounts for the absence of deflation in response to a preference shock, the zero bound puzzle of new-Keynesian models studied here in Section 20.2, and how expectations of a switch between regimes affects responses to shocks. Bianchi and Melosi specify that taxes follow an AR(1) that also responds to output. Their model switches between a temporarily passive fiscal regime in which surpluses respond to debt and a temporarily active fiscal regime that does not do so (their equation (6) p. 1041). Government spending also follows an AR(1) that responds to output (p. 1040).

Bianchi and Ilut (2017) address an important issue and come to an appealing conclusion: The inflation of the 1970s came from loose fiscal policy, and the disinflation of the 1980s followed a fiscal reform. This paper begins to fill the great gaping hole of applied fiscal theory analysis: In a fiscal theory narrative, just what went wrong in the 1970s, and what fixed it in the 1980s? They augment a new-Keynesian model with a fiscal block and a geometric term structure for government debt, an important and often-overlooked generalization. They also posit monetary and fiscal rules that feed back from inflation and output. They specify Markov switching between temporarily active-fiscal and temporarily active-money regimes, finding temporarily passive fiscal policy in the 1980s and temporarily active fiscal policy in the 1970s. This paper is a good concrete example of that general finding, which I referred to earlier. Chen, Leeper, and Leith (2021) follow with a more comprehensive view of fiscal policy underpinnings of the 1980 shift.

Bhattarai, Lee, and Park (2016) likewise add fiscal policy to a DSGE model. They split the sample pre- and post-Volcker. They find both monetary and fiscal policy passive pre-Volcker, and thus "equilibrium indeterminacy in the pre-Volcker era," modeled as sunspot shocks. They include standard fiscal and monetary policy rules that implicitly identify equilibrium-selection regimes from the policy rules, and do not allow an s-shaped response in the active-fiscal regime.

Bianchi and Melosi (2019) study a situation of temporarily uncoordinated policy, thinking about how a large stock of debt such as the United States has in 2021 will play out. Will the government choose high taxes or inflation? Both fiscal and monetary policy are temporarily active, both $\phi > 1$ and $\gamma = 0$ for a while. Again, active fiscal policy disallows debt repayment. Eventually one policy loses the game of chicken, and agents expect that fact ahead of time. If fiscal policy wins, which in their restricted specification means that fiscal policy refuses to repay debt, then "hawkish monetary policy backfires" and creates additional inflation. As I digest the result, $\phi > 1$ policy is "hawkish" in that it tries to push the economy to a low-inflation equilibrium, including the fiscal authorities, by threatening higher interest rates and higher inflation. If that threat does not work, then we see the higher interest rates, and higher inflation. The result is similar to that of Section 17.4.2, in which monetary policy cannot work, even in an active money regime, if the "passive" fiscal austerity does not follow.

Beck-Friis and Willems (2017) construct a clean new-Keynesian model with fiscal theory, to address the government spending multiplier. They study the standard model similar to (20.5) and (20.6), except that their government spending provides utility, so g enters alongside consumption, which equals output, x in the IS curve (20.5) as well as in the Phillips curve as in (20.6). They contrast the effect of government spending shocks with active money, $\phi > 1$ in $i_t = \phi \pi_t$ and passive fiscal policy, $\gamma = 0$ in

$$\tau_t = \gamma b_{t-1} + \varepsilon_{\tau,t}$$

$$g_t = \eta g_{t-1} + \varepsilon_{g,t},$$

where τ = taxes, with the same experiment under active fiscal policy $\gamma > 0$ and $\phi < 1$. They find important differences in the multipliers across the active money versus active fiscal regime. With the benefit of hindsight, we see that their surpluses are i.i.d. in the active fiscal regime, so government cannot repay any debts and finances all spending shocks by inflating away debt. What happens if one allows the fiscal regime also to repay debts, with $a(\rho) < 1$? Or how much of the result comes from asking different questions of the government spending shock, holding monetary policy constant in a different way? Analysis of fiscal multipliers along this line is more low-hanging fruit.

In the frictionless model, the interest rate target sets expected inflation, and fiscal policy sets unexpected inflation. Caramp and Silva (2021) offer a generalized decomposition that applies to sticky price models. Monetary policy governs intertemporal substitution while fiscal policy operates through a wealth effect. Their decomposition includes changes in real interest rates and discount rates induced by monetary policy. They also include long-term debt, finding that higher interest rates without a change in surpluses only lower inflation in the presence of long-term debt. In general, they highlight "the necessity of a strong, contractionary fiscal backing to overturn the presence of this [neo-Fisherian] force," and produce a negative inflation response. More generally,

> In the New Keynesian model, the magnitude of the wealth effect depends on the fiscal response to monetary policy rather than on the change in the path of the nominal interest rate per se.

and

> the inverse relation between the nominal interest rate and inflation under the Taylor equilibrium is driven entirely by a negative wealth effect. In the absence of such wealth effects, not only does the monetary authority lose control of initial inflation, but the effect on future inflation has the opposite sign than in the standard result.

These are now familiar conclusions to a reader of this book, but expressed in a different and interesting way, and analyzed in a more detailed set of models, including heterogeneous agents models and capital.

By focusing on the possibilities for refinement and for future work, I do not mean to diminish the substantial accomplishment. We have here a body of detailed and careful fiscal theory modeling, and an indication of the range of historical experience and policy analysis it can apply to. These papers take on the challenge of *using* fiscal theory, by the DSGE rules of the game of modern macroeconomics, to analyze data and policies.

However, in my view, this line of work got stuck, tying monetary and fiscal policy to equilibrium-selection policy, $\theta = \phi$ and $\alpha = \gamma$, and forcing active-fiscal policy to always inflate and not repay debts, with $a(\rho) > 1$, restricting the model's ability to fit the data in the quest to measure equilibrium-selection regimes.

So an opportunity beckons. We can build on all the hard work in this literature, by slightly generalizing the fiscal specification so that the models can fit all the data better, entirely with a fiscal regime, and reinterpreting regime-switching models as parameter-switching models within that regime. This opportunity parallels the opportunity to adapt new-Keynesian models via observational equivalence and then include their fiscal implications. As a recipe for writing papers, better fitting data, and for addressing important issues without having to build a whole set of new models from scratch, this is great news.

24.3   Exchange Rates

If we are to replace $MV = Py$ or interest rate targets at the foundation of price determination, exchange rates are a natural place to apply ideas. As a measure of the value of the dollar, exchange rates are less sticky and better measured than price indices. And exchange rates have been a perpetual puzzle. Traditional theory either starts with $MV = Py$ and tries to relate exchange rates to relative money stocks, or starts with Keynesian models and relates exchange rates to interest differentials. The disconnect between exchange rates and "fundamentals" has been one of many constant puzzles in this literature.

The world is not all darkness. Exchange rates do line up with interest rate differentials. Some fiscal connections are evident. Exchange rates appreciate on good news of countries' growth rates. Well, more growth means better government finances. Exchange rate collapses are often connected to bad fiscal news. Exchange rates often fall suddenly without much "fundamental" news, though on fears about the future, which our present value formulation encourages.

Dupor (2000) brings fiscal theory to exchange rates. In classic passive-fiscal theory, if countries peg interest rates rather than money supplies, or if people can use either country's money, then the exchange rate is indeterminate, mirroring the indeterminacy of the price level under interest rate pegs and passive money. For example, Kareken and Wallace (1981) showed indeterminacy in the then-popular overlapping generations setup, driven by the assumption that people can use either country's money. Dupor introduces fiscal theory, but he emphasizes the case that one country runs persistent deficits and the other persistent surpluses. Two currencies vie for a common pool of surpluses, so the exchange rate is indeterminate. When two countries with separate currencies pay off their own debts, exchange rates are determinate under the fiscal theory, determined by the present value of each country's surpluses. Daniel (2001b) responds directly, making this point, and giving an explicit model why governments would choose to run separate surplus streams, giving a determinate exchange rate.

Daniel (2001a) has an early and innovative analysis of currency crises. Crises happen when the present value of primary surpluses can no longer support a pegged exchange rate. Daniel brings to international economics the stabilizing potential of long-term debt:

> In the absence of long-term government bonds, the exchange rate collapse must be instantaneous. With long-term government bonds, the collapse can be delayed at the discretion of the monetary authority . . . Fiscal policy is responsible for the inevitability of a crisis, while monetary policy determines . . . the timing of the crisis and the magnitude of exchange rate depreciation.

Daniel (2010) has a dynamic fiscal theory model of currency crises. An exchange rate peg implies a passive fiscal policy, but there is an upper bound on debt and surpluses. When that limit is reached, policy must switch, including depreciation. Daniel applies the model to the 2001 Argentine crisis.

Burnside, Eichenbaum, and Rebelo (2001) was, to me, a watershed, though they do not pitch it as fiscal theory. This paper shows that the East Asian currency crises of the late 1990s were precipitated by bad news about *prospective* deficits. The countries did not have large debts, and were not experiencing bad *current* deficits, nor did they exhibit current monetary loosening. But these countries were suddenly likely to have intractable *future* and contingent deficits. The governments were poised to bail out banks, and banks had taken on a lot of short-term foreign-currency debt. A run on banks then becomes a run on the government. The lesson that contingent liabilities can undermine fiscal and monetary affairs is one we might pay attention to more broadly, given the large size of the United States' implicit and explicit bailout and income support guarantees. Burnside, Eichenbaum, and Rebelo (2001) also point to fiscal benefits of inflation and devaluation. For example, inflation lowers the real value of sticky government employee salaries.

Jiang (2021) and Jiang (2022) bring fiscal theory directly to exchange rates. Jiang shows that exchange rates fall when forecasts of future deficits rise. This is a good case in which a positively correlated surplus process seems to work. The s-shape is not always and everywhere, especially in bad news for emerging markets.

24.4   Applications

Reading history, policies, and institutions through the lens of the fiscal theory, finding simple parables that help pave the way to more fundamental understanding, is what a lot of this book is about. Here I list a few efforts not already mentioned.

Leeper and Walker (2013) and Cochrane (2011d), Cochrane (2011e) are attempts in real time to confront how fiscal theory accounts for the 2008 recession and to look through the fog to see what lay ahead. The combination of large debts, large prospective deficits, and low growth sounds some sort of alarm bell, but just what is it? Most macroeconomics imagines monetary policy alone able to control inflation, but the new situation calls that faith into question. Historically, some debts have been managed successfully, others lead to creeping inflation, others lead to crisis. What will ours do?

Thinking about these issues led me to ponder many mechanisms echoed here. I interpreted "flight to quality" as a lower discount rate for government debt, an increase in demand for government debt, which on its own is deflationary. I analyzed many policies from stimulus to QE as efforts to raise the supply of government debt. I considered stimulus from a fiscal theory perspective, as I have analyzed here, noting that the "stimulative" effect depends on expected future deficits. Hence promises to repay later are not useful for stimulus in this framework. In retrospect, however, one sees the tension between trying to engineer a default through inflation now while preserving a reputation for repaying debt to allow future borrowing. I offered the analysis of quantitative easing offered here: neutral to first-order but potentially stimulative as an inflation rearrangement with long-term debt. I worried then as now about fiscal inflation. I noted what we see here in greater detail: that fiscal inflation can come slowly, not just a price level jump. I worried about real and contingent liabilities. I introduced the present value Laffer curve analysis echoed here. I emphasized the run-like unpredictable nature of a fiscal inflation, and how the central bank may be powerless to stop it, and how central and dangerous short-term financing is to that scenario.

Leeper and Walker (2013) start by reminding us that a fiscal inflation can break out without seigniorage, by devaluing nominal bonds directly, the point of Section 19.6. Leeper and Walker also stress that the prospective deficits of Social Security and Medicare in the United States pose a central fiscal challenge, analyzed in detail in Davig, Leeper, and

Walker (2010). Leeper and Walker also include long-term debt, which alters dynamics substantially as we have seen.

These papers were written in the immediate aftermath of the 2008 recession and its then-shocking increase in debt, before large primary deficits continued during the economic expansion of the late 2010s, before arguments for additional large deliberate fiscal expansion, and before the COVID-19 era debt expansion. But they were also written before the era of persistent negative real rates, lowering discount rates and interest costs. Just how large debts will play out, and the role inflation will play, remain good questions. Even the best theory in the world is hard to deploy in real time for soothsaying, as Sargent and Wallace discovered 40 years ago.

Sims (2013) used his AEA presidential address to "bring FTPL down to earth." This is a lovely summary and exposition of many fiscal theory issues. Sims starts with a mechanism we have seen in the sticky price analysis: A rise in interest rates not accompanied by fiscal contraction will be inflationary by raising discount rates and interest costs, as well as by potentially raising expected inflation. Loyo (1999) cites examples in Brazil in which higher interest rates raise interest costs on debt, do not provoke a fiscal contraction to pay those costs, and so seem to bring on higher inflation. The mechanism may apply to the United States and Europe, in the shadow of our large debts and deficits. Sims explains as I have that $MV(i) = Py$ does not determine the price level, and that fixes to restore determinacy essentially involve adding fiscal theory, backing money at some point with taxes.

Sims points to the fiscal foundations of the euro, and interactions between central banks and treasuries when there is an institutional separation between their balance sheets, at least for a while. He sees ultimate fiscal backing of an independent central bank in recapitalization, as I have, but points to some doubts that such recapitalization might happen (p. 567). Sims explains clearly the distinction between real and nominal debt, and that nominal debt is a "cushion" like equity.

The fiscal foundation of the euro is an obvious case of fiscal–monetary interaction. If a central bank is committed to printing money as needed, to do "whatever it takes" to keep each country from defaulting, and countries can borrow freely, there is an obvious problem. Sims (1997) and Sims (1999) presciently think about the foundations of the euro in explicitly fiscal theory terms. While not directly fiscal theory, the parallels between fiscal affairs in the early United States and those of European fiscal integration underlying the euro in Sargent (2012) are deeply insightful.

Sims (2001), mentioned above, opined that Mexico would do well not to dollarize, so as to maintain an equity-like cushion. One can, as I did above, question the judgment, valuing the repayment precommitments of dollarization, while agreeing entirely with the analysis of the options and appreciating the use of fiscal theory to think about an important issue.

25

The Future

IT'S TOUGH to make predictions, especially about the future. Nonetheless, I close with some thoughts about where the fiscal theory may go, or at least avenues on my ever-growing list of possibilities to explore.

25.1 Episodes

As many papers by Tom Sargent with coauthors have shown us, the analysis of histori-cal episodes through the lens of monetary theory with monetary–fiscal interactions can be deeply revealing. Sargent and Velde's (2003) "History of Small Change," Sargent and Velde's (1995) "Macroeconomics of the French Revolution," Velde's (2009) "Chronicle of Deflation," Hall and Sargent's (2014) tale of which debts the United States paid and which it did not or inflated away, and Sargent's (2012) contrast between the nineteenth-century U.S. dollar and today's euro are some of my particular favorites.

The emergence of inflation in the United States and worldwide in the 1970s and its decline in the 1980s still needs a more comprehensive and well-documented fiscal theory narrative. We have the beginnings: for example, work like Bianchi and Ilut (2017) and Sims (2011). But the purely monetary conventional narrative—an insufficiently aggres-sive $\phi < 1$ Taylor rule giving instability in the 1970s, followed by tough-love $\phi > 1$ in the 1980s—developed on thousands of papers and their digestion. The new-Keynesian narrative—multiple equilibrium indeterminacy $\phi < 1$ in the 1970s followed by $\phi > 1$ determinacy—likewise stands on a large body of work. Developing a durable fiscal the-ory narrative that has a chance of unseating such solidified conventional wisdoms will be a challenge, even if it is right.

Summarizing and extending previous comments, in particular in Sections 6.1 and 8.4, there are many tantalizing fiscal clues. Inflation emerged in the late 1960s along with the fiscal pressure of the Great Society and Vietnam War. The United States did have a major crisis ending with its abandoning the remaining gold standard and devaluing the dollar in 1971. But one must address just why the deficits of this episode provoked inflation and our much larger deficits did not, at least until 2021. The restrictions of the Bretton Woods system and closed international financial markets surely play a role.

The 1970s saw a productivity and growth slowdown. An apparently lower trend of GDP growth is terrible news for the present value of surpluses. They saw a break in the traditional cyclical behavior of primary surpluses. The year 1975 saw the worst deficit by far since WWII, with no bright future in sight.

The 1980s saw a 20-year resumption in growth and, as it turned out, tax receipts, despite lower tax rates. In retrospect, 1980 looks a lot like a classic inflation stabilization combined with fiscal and pro-growth reform, such as inflation targeting countries introduced. The fiscal and pro-growth reform came after monetary policy changes, and may have been partly induced by the interest expense provoked by higher interest rates. The interest expense channel can provoke fiscal reform rather than spark a doom loop. Or, the fiscal reform may have been the clean-up effort that made the monetary tightening stick. Many attempted monetary tightenings have failed when promised fiscal reforms did not materialize.

In 1933, I argued, the United States refused to accommodate a surprise deflation by fiscal austerity to pay a windfall to bondholders. Starting in 1980, the United States did exactly the opposite. Investors who bought bonds at the high nominal interest rates of the late 1970s, expecting a low real return and continuing inflation, instead got a windfall, repaid in sharply more valuable dollars, courtesy of the U.S. taxpayer.

Fiscal and monetary policies are intertwined. The Sims (2011) vision of interest rate increases that temporarily reduce inflation, but without fiscal support eventually make it worse, has a 1970s flair to it needing quantitative exploration, or deeper investigation with more detailed models of the temporary negative inflation effect of interest rate increases. Likewise, the model of 17.4.2 in which higher interest rates without fiscal backing do not lower inflation may apply to the 1970s/1980 divergence, as well as sound a cautionary note for future stabilization efforts in the shadow of debt.

But this is storytelling, not economic history. The fiscal roots of this inflation and its conquest need a closer, quantitative, model-based look. I opined several times that the slow inflation various models produce in response to a fiscal shock is reminiscent of the 1970s. Reminiscent isn't good enough. (Bordo and Levy (2020) have a good summary of fiscal–monetary affairs through the inflation and disinflation.)

Cross-country comparisons are revealing. What *about* Japan? And Europe? In some extreme events we can see a direct correlation between contemporaneous deficits, debts, and inflation. Høien (2016) includes an example from Russia 2012–2015, in which primary deficit and inflation march hand in hand.

Latin American monetary and fiscal history has not so far been widely studied by U.S. and European economists. Yet it includes a menagerie of monetary–fiscal experiences and institutions. The comprehensive Kehoe and Nicolini (2021) "Monetary and Fiscal History of Latin America" together with its impressive data collection and dissemination effort,[1] should jump-start our understanding of inflation, and in just about every case its fiscal roots. The history is subtle, with successful and unsuccessful stabilizations, a variety of institutions to control inflation and attempt fiscal commitments, great lessons of plans that worked and plans that fell apart. There is not a different economics for Latin America or emerging markets, and what happened there can happen here.

---

1. https://mafhola.uchicago.edu

25.2 Theory and Models

Obviously, we need more comprehensive theory. And it is easy to describe the list of ingredients that one should add to the soup. But one must be careful. Good economic theory does not consist of merely stirring tasty ingredients into the pot.

Inflation is always a choice: The government can inflate, default (haircut, reschedule), raise distorting taxes, or cut spending. The fiscal theory is a part of dynamic public finance—the discipline which asks which distorting taxes are better than others—and political economy. Contrariwise, by understanding the decisions governments take, we gain some understanding of what the tradeoffs are; we learn about economics not visible in time series from a settled regime in equilibrium. Leeper, Plante, and Traum (2010) is an example of the dynamic DSGE tradition exploring these issues without a nominal side, with a good literature review. It is waiting for integration with real/nominal issues via fiscal theory.

Fiscal theory is a part of the larger question of sovereign debt management and sustainability. The full range of time consistency, reputation building, and other concerns, which already consider inflation as a form of default, can productively be merged with a fiscal theory that recognizes means other than seigniorage by which inflation comes about, and the dynamics seen in models here.

I have emphasized the importance of institutions, including fiscal precommitments, the separation between central bank and treasury, the legal structures preventing inflationary finance, and so forth. Institutions are if nothing else good ways to communicate off-equilibrium commitments. That whole question needs deeper study, both in the historical and institutional vein, and in the more modern game theory tradition.

I have preached enough about how to integrate fiscal theory with the DSGE tradition, so I'll just repeat again how technically easy but fertile that enterprise ought to be. Likewise, slightly modifying the existing fiscal theory models to remove the restrictions they impose in the vain attempt to measure equilibrium selection regimes is an easy path to take.

The end of this long book is really just a beginning.

BIBLIOGRAPHY

Aiyagari, S. Rao, and Mark Gertler. 1985. "The Backing of Government Bonds and Monetarism." *Journal of Monetary Economics* 16 (1):19–44.

Aiyagari, S. Rao, and Mark Gertler. 1991. "Asset Returns with Transactions Costs and Uninsured Individual Risk." *Journal of Monetary Economics* 27 (3):311–331.

Akerlof, George A., and Ross D. Milbourne. 1980. "Irving Fisher on His Head II: The Consequences of the Timing of Payments for the Demand for Money." *The Quarterly Journal of Economics* 95 (1):145–157.

Alesina, Alberto, Carlo Favero, and Francesco Giavazzi. 2019. *Austerity: When It Works and When It Doesn't.* Princeton, NJ: Princeton University Press.

Allais, Maurice. 1947. *Économie et intérêt.* Paris: Librairie des publications officielles.

Alstadheim, Ragna, and Dale W. Henderson. 2006. "Price-Level Determinacy, Lower Bounds on the Nominal Interest Rate, and Liquidity Traps." *The B.E. Journal of Macroeconomics (Contributions)* 6 (1). Article 12.

Alves, Felipe, Greg Kaplan, Benjamin Moll, and Gianluca L. Violante. 2020. "A Further Look at the Propagation of Monetary Policy Shocks in HANK." *Journal of Money, Credit and Banking* 52 (S2):521–559.

Andersen, Leonall C., and Jerry L. Jordan. 1968. "Monetary and Fiscal Actions: A Test of Their Relative Importance in Economic Stabilization." *St. Louis Fed Economic Review* 50:11–24.

Angeletos, George-Marios. 2002. "Fiscal Policy with Noncontingent Debt and the Optimal Maturity Structure." *The Quarterly Journal of Economics* 117 (3):1105–1131.

Atkeson, Andrew, Vardarajan V. Chari, and Patrick J. Kehoe. 2010. "Sophisticated Monetary Policies." *Quarterly Journal of Economics* 125 (1):47–89.

Auclert, Adrien, Matthew Rognlie, and Ludwig Straub. 2020. "Micro Jumps, Macro Humps: Monetary Policy and Business Cycles in an Estimated HANK Model." Manuscript.

Bansal, Ravi, and Wilbur John Coleman. 1996. "A Monetary Explanation of the Equity Premium, Term Premium, and Risk-Free Rate Puzzles." *Journal of Political Economy* 104:1135–1171.

Bansal, Ravi, Dana Kiku, and Amir Yaron. 2012. "An Empirical Evaluation of the Long-Run Risks Model for Asset Prices." *Critical Finance Review* 1 (1):183–221.

Bansal, Ravi, and Amir Yaron. 2004. "Risks for the Long Run: A Potential Resolution of Asset Pricing Puzzles." *The Journal of Finance* 59 (4):1481–1509.

Barro, Robert J. 1974. "Are Government Bonds Net Wealth?" *Journal of Political Economy* 82:1095–1117.

———. 1979. "On the Determination of the Public Debt." *Journal of Political Economy* 87 (5, Part 1): 940–971.

Barro, Robert J., and Herschel I. Grossman. 1971. "A General Disequilibrium Model of Income and Employment." *The American Economic Review* 61 (1):82–93.

Bassetto, Marco. 2002. "A Game-Theoretic View of the Fiscal Theory of the Price Level." *Econometrica* 70:2167–2195.

———. 2004. "Negative Nominal Interest Rates." *American Economic Review* 94:104–108.

Bassetto, Marco, and Gherardo Caracciolo. 2021. "Monetary/Fiscal Interactions with Forty Budget Constraints." Manuscript.

Bassetto, Marco, and Wei Cui. 2018. "The Fiscal Theory of the Price Level in a World of Low Interest Rates." *Journal of Economic Dynamics and Control* 89:5–22.

Bassetto, Marco, and Todd Messer. 2013. "Fiscal Consequences of Paying Interest on Reserves." *Fiscal Studies* 34 (4):413–436.

Bassetto, Marco, and Thomas J. Sargent. 2020. "Shotgun Wedding: Fiscal and Monetary Policy." Federal Reserve of Minneapolis Staff Report 599.

Baumol, William J. 1952. "The Transactions Demand for Cash: An Inventory Theoretic Approach." *The Quarterly Journal of Economics* 66 (4):545–556.

Beck-Friis, Peder, and Tim Willems. 2017. "Dissecting Fiscal Multipliers Under the Fiscal Theory of the Price Level." *European Economic Review* 95:62–83.

Beeler, Jason, and John Y. Campbell. 2012. "The Long-Run Risks Model and Aggregate Asset Prices: An Empirical Assessment." *Critical Finance Review* 1 (1):141–182.

Benhabib, Jess, Stephanie Schmitt-Grohé, and Martín Uribe. 2001a. "Monetary Policy and Multiple Equilibria." *American Economic Review* 1:167–186.

———. 2001b. "The Perils of Taylor Rules." *Journal of Economic Theory* 96 (1):40–69.

———. 2002. "Avoiding Liquidity Traps." *Journal of Political Economy* 110 (3):535–563.

Berentsen, Aleksander, and Christopher Waller. 2018. "Liquidity Premiums on Government Debt and the Fiscal Theory of the Price Level." *Journal of Economic Dynamics and Control* 89:173–182.

Berg, Claes, and Lars Jonung. 1999. "Pioneering Price Level Targeting: The Swedish Experience 1931–1937." *Journal of Monetary Economics* 43:525–551.

Bernanke, Ben S. 1983. "Nonmonetary Effects of the Financial Crisis in the Propagation of the Great Depression." *The American Economic Review* 73 (3):257–276.

Bhattarai, Saroj, Jae Won Lee, and Woong Yong Park. 2016. "Policy Regimes, Policy Shifts, and US Business Cycles." *The Review of Economics and Statistics* 98:968–983.

Bianchi, Francesco, and Cosmin Ilut. 2017. "Monetary/Fiscal Policy Mix and Agents' Beliefs." *Review of Economic Dynamics* 26:113–139.

Bianchi, Francesco, and Leonardo Melosi. 2013. "Dormant Shocks and Fiscal Virtue." *NBER Macroeconomics Annual* 28:1–46.

———. 2017. "Escaping the Great Recession." *American Economic Review* 107 (4):1030–58.

———. 2019. "The Dire Effects of the Lack of Monetary and Fiscal Coordination." *Journal of Monetary Economics* 104:1–22.

Blanchard, Olivier. 2019. "Public Debt and Low Interest Rates." *American Economic Review* 109:1197–1229.

Blanchard, Olivier Jean, and Charles M. Kahn. 1980. "The Solution of Linear Difference Models under Rational Expectations." *Econometrica* 48 (5):1305–1311.

Bloom, Nicholas, Chad Jones, John Van Reenen, and Michael Webb. 2020. "Are Ideas Getting Harder to Find?" *American Economic Review* 110:1104–1144.

Bohn, Henning. 1995. "The Sustainability of Budget Deficits in a Stochastic Economy." *Journal of Money, Credit and Banking* 27 (1):257–271.

———. 1998a. "The Behavior of U.S. Public Debt and Deficits." *The Quarterly Journal of Economics* 113 (3):949–963.

———. 1998b. "Comment." *NBER Macroeconomics Annual* 13:384–389.

Bordo, Michael D. 2018. "The Imbalances of the Bretton Woods System 1965 to 1973: U.S. Inflation, The Elephant in the Room." Working Paper 25409, National Bureau of Economic Research.

Bordo, Michael D., and Mickey D. Levy. 2020. "Do Enlarged Fiscal Deficits Cause Inflation: The Historical Record." Working Paper 28195, National Bureau of Economic Research.

Brash, Donald T. 2002. "Inflation Targeting 14 Years On." URL http://www.bis.org/review/r020121b.pdf. Speech given at 2002 American Economics Association Conference.

Brock, William A. 1974. "Money and Growth: The Case of Long-Run Perfect Foresight." *International Economic Review* 15:750–777.

———. 1975. "A Simple Perfect Foresight Monetary Model." *Journal of Monetary Economics* 1:133–150.

Brunnermeier, Markus K., Sebastian Merkel, and Yuliy Sannikov. 2020. "The Fiscal Theory of the Price Level with a Bubble." Manuscript.

Buera, Francisco, and Juan Pablo Nicolini. 2021. "The Case of Argentina." In *A Monetary and Fiscal History of Latin America, 1960–2017*, edited by Timothy J. Kehoe and Juan Pablo Nicolini. Minneapolis, MN: University of Minnesota Press.

Buiter, Willem H. 1999. "The Fallacy of the Fiscal Theory of the Price Level." Working Paper 7302, National Bureau of Economic Research.

———. 2002. "The Fiscal Theory of the Price Level: A Critique." *Economic Journal* 112:459–480.

———. 2017. "The Fallacy of the Fiscal Theory of the Price Level - Once More." *CEPR Discussion Paper* No. DP11941.

Buiter, Willem H., and Anne C. Siebert. 2007. "Deflationary Bubbles." *Macroeconomic Dynamics* 11:431–454.

Burdekin, Richard C. K., and Marc D. Weidenmier. 2001. "Inflation is Always and Everywhere a Monetary Phenomenon; Richmond versus Houston in 1864." *American Economic Review* 91:1621–1630.

Burnside, Craig, Martin Eichenbaum, and Sergio Rebelo. 2001. "Prospective Deficits and the Asian Currency Crisis." *Journal of Political Economy* 109:1155–1197.

Cachanosky, Nicolás, and Federico Julián Ferrelli Mazza. 2021. "Why Did Inflation Targeting Fail in Argentina?" *Quarterly Review of Economics and Finance* 80:102–116.

Cagan, Phillip. 1956. "The Monetary Dynamics of Hyperinflation." In *Studies in the Quantity Theory of Money*, edited by Milton Friedman. Chicago: University of Chicago Press, 25–117.

Campbell, John Y., and John Ammer. 1993. "What Moves the Stock and Bond Markets? A Variance Decomposition for Long-Term Asset Returns." *The Journal of Finance* 48 (1):3–37.

Campbell, John Y., and N. Gregory Mankiw. 1987. "Are Output Fluctuations Transitory?" *The Quarterly Journal of Economics* 102 (4):857–880.

Campbell, John Y., Carolin E. Pflueger, and Luis M. Viceira. 2020. "Macroeconomic Drivers of Bond and Equity Risks." *Journal of Political Economy* 128:3148–3185.

Campbell, John Y., and Robert J. Shiller. 1988. "The Dividend-Price Ratio and Expectations of Future Dividends and Discount Factors." *The Review of Financial Studies* 1 (3):195–228.

Canzoneri, Matthew B., Robert E. Cumby, and Behzad T. Diba. 2001. "Is the Price Level Determined by the Needs of Fiscal Solvency?" *American Economic Review* 91:1221–1238.

Caramp, Nicolas, and Djanir H. Silva. 2021. "Fiscal Policy and the Monetary Transmission Mechanism." Manuscript.

Carlozzi, Nicholas, and John B. Taylor. 1985. "International Capital Mobility and the Coordination of Monetary Rules." In *Exchange Rate Management Under Uncertainty*, edited by J. Bhandhari. Cambridge, MA: MIT Press, 186–211.

Chamley, Christophe. 1986. "Optimal Taxation of Capital Income in General Equilibrium with Infinite Lives." *Econometrica* 54 (3):607–622.

Chen, Xiaoshan, Eric M. Leeper, and Campbell Leith. 2021. "Strategic Interactions in U.S. Monetary and Fiscal Policies." *Quantitative Economics*. Forthcoming.

Chiang, Alpha C. 1992. *Elements of Dynamic Optimization*. New York: McGraw-Hill.

Christiano, Lawrence J. 1987. "Cagan's Model of Hyperinflation under Rational Expectations." *International Economic Review* 28 (1):33–49.

———. 2018. "Comment." *NBER Macroeconomics Annual* 32:227–245.

Christiano, Lawrence J., Martin S. Eichenbaum, and Charles Evans. 1999. "Monetary Policy Shocks: What Have We Learned and To What End?" In *Handbook of Macroeconomics*, edited by Michael Woodford and John B. Taylor. Amsterdam: North-Holland, 65–148.

———. 2005. "Nominal Rigidities and the Dynamic Effects of a Shock to Monetary Policy." *Journal of Political Economy* 113:1–45.

Christiano, Lawrence J., Martin S. Eichenbaum, and Sergio Rebelo. 2011. "When Is the Government Spending Multiplier Large?" *Journal of Political Economy* 119:78–121.

Christiano, Lawrence. J., and Terry J. Fitzgerald. 2000. "Understanding the Fiscal Theory of the Price Level." *Federal Reserve Bank of Cleveland Economic Review* 36:1–37.

Christiano, Lawrence J., and Yuta Takahashi. 2018. "Discouraging Deviant Behavior in Monetary Economics." Manuscript, Northwestern University.

Clarida, Richard, Jordi Galí, and Mark Gertler. 2000. "Monetary Policy Rules and Macroeconomic Stability: Evidence and Some Theory." *Quarterly Journal of Economics* 115:147–180.

Cochrane, John H. 1988. "How Big Is the Random Walk in GNP?" *Journal of Political Economy* 96 (5): 893–920.

———. 1989. "The Sensitivity of Tests of the Intertemporal Allocation of Consumption to Near-Rational Alternatives." *American Economic Review* 79:319–337.

———. 1991a. "A Critique of the Application of Unit Root Tests." *Journal of Economic Dynamics and Control* 15 (2):275–284.

———. 1991b. "Volatility Tests and Efficient Markets: A Review Essay." *Journal of Monetary Economics* 27:463–485.

———. 1992. "Explaining the Variance of Price-Dividend Ratios." *Review of Financial Studies* 5: 243–280.

———. 1994a. "Comment on "What Ends Recessions?" by David and Christina Romer." *NBER Macroeconomics Annual* 9:58–74.

———. 1994b. "Permanent and Transitory Components of GNP and Stock Prices." *The Quarterly Journal of Economics* 109 (1):241–265.

———. 1994c. "Shocks." *Carnegie-Rochester Conference Series on Public Policy* 41:295–364.

———. 1998a. "A Frictionless View of U.S. Inflation." *NBER Macroeconomics Annual* 13:323–384.

———. 1998b. "What do the VARs Mean? Measuring the Output Effects of Monetary Policy." *Journal of Monetary Economics* 41 (2):277–300.

———. 2001. "Long-Term Debt and Optimal Policy in the Fiscal Theory of the Price Level." *Econometrica* 69:69–116.

———. 2003. "Stocks as Money: Convenience Yield and the Tech-Stock Bubble." In *Asset Price Bubbles*, edited by George G. Kaufman William C. Hunter and Michael Pomerleano. Cambridge, MA: MIT Press, 175–204.

———. 2005a. *Asset Pricing, Revised Edition*. Princeton, NJ: Princeton University Press.

———. 2005b. "Money as Stock." *Journal of Monetary Economics* 52:501–528.

———. 2009. "Can Learnability Save New-Keynesian models?" *Journal of Monetary Economics* 56 (8):1109–1113.

———. 2011a. "Determinacy and Identification with Taylor Rules." *Journal of Political Economy* 119: 565–615.

———. 2011b. "Determinacy and Identification with Taylor Rules, Manuscript with Technical Appendix." Manuscript.

———. 2011c. "Discount Rates: American Finance Association Presidential Address." *Journal of Finance* 66:1047–1108.

———. 2011d. "Inflation and Debt." *National Affairs* 9:56–78.

———. 2011e. "Understanding Policy in the Great Recession: Some Unpleasant Fiscal Arithmetic." *European Economic Review* 55 (1):2–30.

———. 2012. "Continuous-Time Linear Models." *Foundations and Trends in Finance* 6 (3):165–219.

———. 2014a. "Comments on Eggertsson and Mehrotra, 'A Model of Secular Stagnation.'" Manuscript.

———. 2014b. "Monetary Policy with Interest on Reserves." *Journal of Economic Dynamics and Control* 49:74–108.

———. 2014c. "Toward a Run-Free Financial System." In *Across the Great Divide: New Perspectives on the Financial Crisis*, edited by Martin Neil Baily and John B. Taylor. Stanford: Hoover Institution Press, 197–249.

———. 2015a. "Continuous Time." Manuscript.

———. 2015b. "A New Structure For U. S. Federal Debt." In *The $13 Trillion Question: Managing the U.S. Government's Debt*, edited by David Wessel. Washington, DC: Brookings Institution Press, 91–146.

———. 2015c. "A Response to Sims (2013)." Manuscript.

———. 2016. "Comments on 'A Behavioral New-Keynesian Model,' by Xavier Gabaix." Manuscript.

———. 2017a. "Macro-Finance." *Review of Finance* 21:945–985.

———. 2017b. "Michelson-Morley, Fisher and Occam: The Radical Implications of Stable Inflation at Near-Zero Interest Rates, Manuscript with Appendix." Manuscript.

———. 2017c. "The New-Keynesian Liquidity Trap." *Journal of Monetary Economics* 92:47–63.

———. 2017d. "Online Appendix to 'The New-Keynesian Liquidity Trap.'" URL https://doi.org/10.1016/j.jmoneco.2017.09.003.

———. 2017e. "Stepping on a Rake: The Fiscal Theory of Monetary Policy." *European Economic Review* 101:354–375.

———. 2018. "Michelson-Morley, Fisher, and Occam: The Radical Implications of Stable Quiet Inflation at the Zero Bound." *NBER Macroeconomics Annual* 32:113–226.

———. 2019. "The Value of Government Debt." Manuscript.

———. 2020. "'The Deficit Myth' Review: Years of Magical Thinking." *Wall Street Journal* June 5.

———. 2021a. "The Fiscal Roots of Inflation." *Review of Economic Dynamics*. Forthcoming.

———. 2021b. "A Fiscal Theory of Monetary Policy with Partially Repaid Long-Term Debt." *Review of Economic Dynamics*. Forthcoming.

———. 2021c. "$r < g$?" Manuscript.

———. 2022. "The Fiscal Theory of the Price Level: An Introduction and Overview." *Journal of Economic Perspectives*. Forthcoming.

Cochrane, John H., John B. Taylor, and Volcker Wieland. 2020. "Evaluating Rules in the Fed's Report and Measuring Discretion." In *Strategies for Monetary Policy*, edited by John H. Cochrane and John B. Taylor. Stanford: Hoover Institution Press, 217–258.

Cogley, Timothy, and Argia M. Sbordone. 2008. "Trend Inflation, Indexation, and Inflation Persistence in the New Keynesian Phillips Curve." *American Economic Review* 98 (5):2101–2126.

Cole, Harold L., and Lee E. Ohanian. 2004. "New Deal Policies and the Persistence of the Great Depression: A General Equilibrium Analysis." *Journal of Political Economy* 112 (4):779–816.

Congressional Budget Office. 2020. "The 2020 Long-Term Budget Outlook."

Copeland, Adam, Darrell Duffie, and David Yilin Yang. 2021. "Reserves Were Not So Ample After All." NBER Working Paper 29090.

Daniel, Betty C. 2001a. "A Fiscal Theory of Currency Crises." *International Economic Review* 42 (4):969–988.

———. 2001b. "The Fiscal Theory of the Price Level in an Open Economy." *Journal of Monetary Economics* 48 (2):293–308.

———. 2007. "The Fiscal Theory of the Price Level and Initial Government Debt." *Review of Economic Dynamics* 10 (2):193–206.

———. 2010. "Exchange Rate Crises and Fiscal Solvency." *Journal of Money, Credit and Banking* 42 (6):1109–1135.

Davig, Troy, and Eric M. Leeper. 2006. "Fluctuating Macro Policies and the Fiscal Theory." In *NBER Macroeconomics Annual 2006*. Cambridge MA: MIT Press, 247–298.

———. 2007. "Generalizing the Taylor Principle." *American Economic Review* 97 (3):607–635.

Davig, Troy, Eric M. Leeper, and Todd B. Walker. 2010. "'Unfunded Liabilities' and Uncertain Fiscal Financing." *Journal of Monetary Economics* 57 (5):600–619.

Del Negro, Marco, and Christopher A. Sims. 2015. "When Does a Central Bank's Balance Sheet Require Fiscal Support?" *Journal of Monetary Economics* 73:1–19.

Di Tella, Sebastian, and Robert Hall. 2021. "Risk Premium Shocks Can Create Inefficient Recessions." Manuscript.

Diamond, Douglas W., and Phillip H. Dybvig. 1983. "Bank Runs, Deposit Insurance, and Liquidity." *Journal of Political Economy* 91:401–419.

Diamond, Douglas W., and Raghuram G. Rajan. 2012. "Illiquid Banks, Financial Stability, and Interest Rate Policy." *Journal of Political Economy* 120 (3):552–591.

Dowd, Kevin. 1994. "A Proposal to End Inflation." *The Economic Journal* 104 (425):828–840.

Duffie, Darrell, and Elizabeth Economy, editors. 2022. *Digital Currencies: The US, China, And The World At A Crossroads*. Stanford: Hoover Institution Press.

Dupor, William. 2000. "Exchange Rates and the Fiscal Theory of the Price Level." *Journal of Monetary Economics* 45:613–630.

Edwards, Sebastian. 2002. "The Great Exchange Rate Debate After Argentina." *The North American Journal of Economics and Finance* 13 (3):237–252.

———. 2018. *American Default: The Untold Story of FDR, the Supreme Court, and the Battle over Gold*. Princeton, NJ: Princeton University Press.

Eggertsson, Gauti B. 2008. "Great Expectations and the End of the Depression." *American Economic Review* 98 (4):1476–1516.

———. 2010. "The Paradox of Toil." *Federal Reserve Bank of New York Staff Report N. 433* .

———. 2011. "What Fiscal Policy is Effective at Zero Interest Rates?" *NBER Macroeconomics Annual* 25: 59–112.

———. 2012. "Was the New Deal Contractionary?" *The American Economic Review* 102:524–555.

Eggertsson, Gauti B., Andrea Ferrero, and Andrea Raffo. 2014. "Can Structural Reforms Help Europe?" *Journal of Monetary Economics* 61:2–22.

Eggertsson, Gauti B., Neil R. Mehrotra, and Jacob A. Robbins. 2019. "A Model of Secular Stagnation: Theory and Quantitative Evaluation." *American Economic Journal: Macroeconomics* 11 (1):1–48.

Ekeland, Ivar, and José A. Scheinkman. 1986. "Transversality Conditions for Some Infinite Horizon Discrete Time Optimization Problems." *Mathematics of Operations Research* 11:216–229.

Evans, George W., and Seppo Honkapohja. 2001. *Learning and Expectations in Macroeconomics*. Princeton, NJ: Princeton University Press.

Fama, Eugene F. 1970. "Efficient Capital Markets: A Review of Theory and Empirical Work." *The Journal of Finance* 25 (2):383–417.

Fama, Eugene F., and Kenneth R. French. 1988a. "Dividend Yields and Expected Stock Returns." *Journal of Financial Economics* 22 (1):3–25.

———. 1988b. "Permanent and Temporary Components of Stock Prices." *Journal of Political Economy* 96 (2):246–273.

Federal Open Market Committee. 2020. "Statement on Longer-Run Goals and Monetary Policy Strategy."

Fernández-Villaverde, Jesús, Juan F. Rubio-Ramírez, Thomas J. Sargent, and Mark W. Watson. 2007. "ABCs (and Ds) of Understanding VARs." *American Economic Review* 97 (3):1021–1026.

Fisher, Irving. 1912. "'The Equation of Exchange' for 1911, and Forecast." *The American Economic Review* 2 (2):302–319.

Fleckenstein, Mattias, Francis A. Longstaff, and Hanno Lustig. 2014. "The TIPS-Treasury Bond Puzzle." *The Journal of Finance* 69 (5):2151–2197.

Friedman, Milton. 1948. "A Monetary and Fiscal Framework for Economic Stability." *The American Economic Review* 38 (3):245–264.

———. 1968. "The Role of Monetary Policy." *The American Economic Review* 58:1–17.

———. 1969. "The Optimum Quantity of Money." In *The Optimum Quantity of Money and Other Essays*. Chicago: Aldine, 1–50.

———. 1992. *Money Mischief: Episodes in Monetary History*. New York: Harcourt.

Friedman, Milton, and Anna Jacobson Schwartz. 1963. *A Monetary History of the United States, 1867–1960*. Princeton, NJ: Princeton University Press.

Gabaix, Xavier. 2014. "A Sparsity-Based Model of Bounded Rationality." *Quarterly Journal of Economics* 129:1661–1710.

———. 2020. "A Behavioral New Keynesian Model." *American Economic Review* 110:2271–2327.

Gagnon, Joseph E., and Brian Sack. 2019. "Recent Market Turmoil Shows That the Fed Needs a More Resilient Monetary Policy Framework." *Real Time Economics Issues Watch* September 26.

Galí, Jordi. 2015. *Monetary Policy, Inflation and the Business Cycle: An Introduction to the New Keynesian Framework*. Princeton, NJ: Princeton University Press, 2nd ed.

García-Schmidt, Mariana, and Michael Woodford. 2019. "Are Low Interest Rates Deflationary? A Paradox of Perfect-Foresight Analysis." *American Economic Review* 109:86–120.

Garín, Julio, Robert Lester, and Eric Sims. 2018. "Raise Rates to Raise Inflation? Neo-Fisherianism in the New Keynesian Model." *Journal of Money, Credit and Banking* 50 (1):243–259.

Giannoni, Marc P., and Michael Woodford. 2005. "Optimal Inflation Targeting Rules." In *Inflation Targeting*, edited by Benjamin S. Bernanke and Michael Woodford. Chicago: University of Chicago Press.

Gordon, Robert J. 2016. *The Rise and Fall of American Growth: The U.S. Standard of Living since the Civil War*. Princeton, NJ: Princeton University Press.

Gorton, Gary, and Andrew Metrick. 2012. "Securitized Banking and the Run on Repo." *Journal of Financial Economics* 104 (3):425–451.

Granger, C. W. J. 1969. "Investigating Causal Relations by Econometric Models and Cross-Spectral Methods." *Econometrica* 37 (3):424–438.

Granger, Clive W. J. 2004. "Time Series Analysis, Cointegration, and Applications." *American Economic Review* 94 (3):421–425.

Greenlaw, David, James D. Hamilton, Ethan S. Harris, and Kenneth D. West. 2018. "A Skeptical View of the Impact of the Fed's Balance Sheet." Manuscript.

Greenwood, Robin, Samuel G. Hanson, Joshua S. Rudolph, and Lawrence H. Summers. 2015. "Debt Management Conflicts between the U.S. Treasury and the Federal Reserve." In *The $13 Trillion Question: Managing the U.S. Government's Debt*, edited by David Wessel. Washington, DC: Brookings Institution Press, 43–90.

Hall, George J., Jonathan Payne, and Thomas J. Sargent. 2018. "US Federal Debt 1776–1960: Quantities and Prices." Manuscript.

Hall, George J., and Thomas J. Sargent. 2011. "Interest Rate Risk and Other Determinants of Post WWII U.S. Government Debt/GDP Dynamics." *American Economic Journal: Macroeconomics* 3:192–214.

———. 2014. "Fiscal Discriminations in Three Wars." *Journal of Monetary Economics* 61:148–166.

———. 2018. "A History of U.S. Debt Limits." *Proceedings of the National Academy of Sciences* 115:2942–2945.

———. 2019. "Complications for the United States from International Credits: 1913-1940." In *Debt and Entanglements Between the Wars*, edited by Era Dabla-Norris. IMF.

———. 2021. "Three World Wars: Fiscal-Monetary Consequences." Manuscript, Brandeis and NYU.

Hall, Robert E. 1984. "A Free Market Policy To Stabilize the Purchasing Power of the Dollar." In *Money in Crisis: The Federal Reserve, the Economy, and Monetary Reform*, edited by Barry N. Siegel. Cambridge, MA: Ballinger Publishing, 303–321.

Hall, Robert E., and Marianna Kudlyak. 2021. "Why Has the US Economy Recovered So Consistently from Every Recession in the Past 70 Years?" Manuscript.

Hamilton, James D. 1996. "The Daily Market for Federal Funds." *Journal of Political Economy* 104 (1):26–56.

Hansen, Alvin H. 1939. "Economic Progress and Declining Population Growth." *The American Economic Review* 29 (1):1–15.

Hansen, Lars Peter, and Scott F. Richard. 1987. "The Role of Conditioning Information in Deducing Testable Restrictions Implied by Dynamic Asset Pricing Models." *Econometrica* 55 (3):587–613.

Hansen, Lars Peter, William Roberds, and Thomas J. Sargent. 1992. "Implications of Present Value Budget Balance and of Martingale Models of Consumption and Taxes." In *Rational Expectations Econometrics*, edited by Lars Peter Hansen and Thomas J. Sargent. London: Westview Press, 121–161.

Hansen, Lars Peter, and Thomas J. Sargent. 1981. "A Note on Wiener-Kolmogorov Prediction Formulas for Rational Expectations Models." Staff report, Federal Reserve Bank of Minneapolis.

Harrison, J. Michael, and David Kreps. 1979. "Martingales and Arbitrage in Multi-Period Securities Markets." *Journal of Economic Theory* 20:381–409.

Hetzel, Robert. 1991. "A Better Way to Fight Inflation." *Wall Street Journal* April 25, A14.

Høien, Torgeir. 2016. "Prices and Policies: A Primer on the Fiscal Theory of the Price Level." *SKAGEN Funds, Stavanger, Norway* .

Holden, Thomas. 2020. "A Robust Monetary Rule." Manuscript.

Holston, Kathryn, Thomas Laubach, and John C. Williams. 2017. "Measuring the Natural Rate of Interest: International Trends and Determinants." *Journal of International Economics* 108:S39–S75. Supplement 1.

Jacobson, Margaret M., Eric M. Leeper, and Bruce Preston. 2019. "Recovery of 1933." Working Paper 25629, National Bureau of Economic Research.

Jiang, Zhengyang. 2021. "US Fiscal Cycle and the Dollar." *Journal of Monetary Economics* 124:91–106.

———. 2022. "Fiscal Cyclicality and Currency Risk Premia." *The Review of Financial Studies* 35 (3):1527–1552.

Jiang, Zhengyang, Hanno N. Lustig, Stijn Van Nieuwerburgh, and Mindy Z. Xiaolan. 2019. "The U.S. Public Debt Valuation Puzzle." Manuscript.

Jones, Chad. 2020a. "The End of Economic Growth? Unintended Consequences of a Declining Population." Manuscript.

———. 2020b. "Taxing Top Incomes in a World of Ideas." Manuscript.

Judd, Kenneth L. 1999. "Optimal Taxation and Spending in General Competitive Growth Models." *Journal of Public Economics* 71 (1):1–26.

Kamihigashi, Takashi. 2000. "A Simple Proof of Ekeland and Scheinkman's Result on the Necessity of a Transversality Condition." *Economic Theory* 15:463–468.

Kaplan, Greg, Benjamin Moll, and Giovanni L. Violante. 2018. "Monetary Policy According to HANK." *American Economic Review* 108 (3):697–743.

Kareken, John, and Neil Wallace. 1981. "On the Indeterminacy of Equilibrium Exchange Rates." *The Quarterly Journal of Economics* 96 (2):207–222.

Kehoe, Timothy J., and Juan Pablo Nicolini, eds. 2021. *A Monetary and Fiscal History of Latin America, 1960–2017*. Minneapolis: University of Minnesota Press.

Kehoe, Timothy J., and Edward C. Prescott. 2007. *Great Depressions of the Twentieth Century*. Minneapolis: Federal Reserve Bank of Minneapolis.

Kelton, Stephanie. 2020. *The Deficit Myth: Modern Monetary Theory and the Birth of the People's Economy*. Public Affairs.

Kiley, Michael T. 2016. "Policy Paradoxes in the New Keynesian Model." *Review of Economic Dynamics* 21:1–15.

Kimball, Miles. 2020. "How and Why to Eliminate the Zero Lower Bound: A Reader's Guide." Confessions of a Supply-Side Liberal Blog. URL https://blog.supplysideliberal.com/emoney.

King, Robert G. 2000. "The New IS-LM Model: Language, Logic, and Limits." *Federal Reserve Bank of Richmond Economic Quarterly* 86 (3):45–104.

King, Robert G., Charles I. Plosser, and Sergio T. Rebelo. 1988. "Production, Growth and Business Cycles: I. The Basic Neoclassical Model." *Journal of Monetary Economics* 21 (2):195–232.

Knapp, Georg Friedrich. 1924. *The State Theory of Money*. London: Macmillian.

Kocherlakota, Narayana. 2010. "Inside the FOMC." URL https://www.minneapolisfed.org/news-and-events/presidents-speeches/inside-the-fomc. Speech.

Kocherlakota, Narayana, and Christopher Phelan. 1999. "Explaining the Fiscal Theory of the Price Level." *Federal Reserve Bank of Minneapolis Quarterly Review* 23:14–23.

Kotlikoff, Laurence J., and Adam N. Michel. 2015. "Closing America's Enormous Fiscal Gap: Who Will Pay?" Mercatus Working Paper, Mercatus Center at George Mason University, Arlington, VA.

Krishnamurthy, Arvind, and Annette Vissing-Jorgensen. 2012. "The Aggregate Demand for Treasury Debt." *Journal of Political Economy* 120:233–267.

Kroszner, Randall. 2003. "Is it Better to Forgive Than to Receive?: Repudiation of the Gold Indexation Clause in Long-Term Debt during the Great Depression." Manuscript.

Kuhn, Thomas. 1962. *The Structure of Scientific Revolutions.* Chicago: University of Chicago Press.

Kydland, Finn E., and Edward C. Prescott. 1982. "Time to Build and Aggregate Fluctuations." *Econometrica* 50 (6):1345–1370.

Lamont, Owen A., and Richard H. Thaler. 2003. "Can the Market Add and Subtract? Mispricing in Tech Stock Carve-outs." *Journal of Political Economy* 111:227–266.

Leeper, Eric M. 1991. "Equilibria Under 'Active' and 'Passive' Monetary and Fiscal Policies." *Journal of Monetary Economics* 27:129–147.

Leeper, Eric M., Troy Davig, and Hess Chung. 2007. "Monetary and Fiscal Policy Switching." *Journal of Money, Credit and Banking* 39:809–842.

Leeper, Eric M. and C. Leith. 2016. "Understanding Inflation as a Joint Monetary-Fiscal Phenomenon." In *Handbook of Macroeconomics Volume 2*, edited by John B. Taylor and Harald Uhlig. Amsterdam: Elsevier, 2305–2415.

Leeper, Eric M., and Bing Li. 2017. "Surplus-Debt Regressions." *Economics Letters* 151:10–15.

Leeper, Eric M., Michael Plante, and Nora Traum. 2010. "Dynamics of Fiscal Financing in the United States." *Journal of Econometrics* 156 (2):304–321.

Leeper, Eric M., Nora Traum, and Todd B. Walker. 2017. "Clearing Up the Fiscal Multiplier Morass." *American Economic Review* 107 (8):2409–2054.

Leeper, Eric M., and Todd B. Walker. 2013. "Perceptions and Misperceptions of Fiscal Inflation." In *Fiscal Policy After the Financial Crisis*, edited by Alberto Alesina and Francesco Giavazzi. Chicago: University of Chicago Press, 255–299.

Leeper, Eric M., Todd B. Walker, and Shu-Chun Susan Yang. 2013. "Fiscal Foresight and Information Flows." *Econometrica* 81 (3):1115–1145.

Lerner, Abba P. 1943. "Functional Finance and the Federal Debt." *Social Research* 10 (1):38–51.

Lerner, Eugene M. 1956. "Inflation in the Confederacy, 1861–65." In *Studies in the Quantity Theory of Money*, edited by Milton Friedman. Chicago: University of Chicago Press, 163–75.

Ljungqvist, Lars, and Thomas J. Sargent. 2018. *Recursive Macroeconomic Theory*, 4th ed. Cambridge, MA: MIT Press.

Long, John B., and Charles I. Plosser. 1983. "Real Business Cycles." *Journal of Political Economy* 91 (1):39–69.

Loyo, Eduardo. 1999. "Tight Money Paradox on the Loose: A Fiscalist Hyperinflation." Manuscript.

Lucas, Robert E. 1972. "Expectations and the Neutrality of Money." *Journal of Economic Theory* 4:103–124.

———. 1973. "Some International Evidence on Output-Inflation Tradeoffs." *The American Economic Review* 63 (3):326–334.

———. 1976. "Econometric Policy Evaluation: A Critique." *Carnegie-Rochester Conference Series on Public Policy* 1:19–46.

———. 1980. "Equilibrium in a Pure Currency Economy." *Economic Inquiry* 18 (2):203–220.

———. 1984. "Money in a Theory of Finance." *Carnegie-Rochester Conference Series on Public Policy* 21:9–45.

———. 1988. "Money Demand in the United States: A Quantitative Review." *Carnegie-Rochester Conference Series on Public Policy* 29:137–167.

Lucas, Robert E., and Thomas J. Sargent. 1981. "After Keynesian Macroeconomics." *Rational Expectations and Econometric Practice* 1:295–319.

Lucas, Robert E., and Nancy L. Stokey. 1983. "Optimal Fiscal and Monetary Policy in an Economy without Capital." *Journal of Monetary Economics* 12 (1):55–93.

———. 1987. "Money and Interest in a Cash-in-Advance Economy." *Econometrica* 55 (3):491–513.

Lustig, Hanno, Christopher Sleet, and Şevin Yeltekin. 2008. "Fiscal Hedging with Nominal Assets." *Journal of Monetary Economics* 55 (4):710–727.

Mankiw, N. Gregory. 2018. "An Effective Marginal Tax Rate." URL http://gregmankiw.blogspot.com/2018/06/an-effective-marginal-tax-rate.html. Greg Mankiw's Blog.

Mankiw, N. Gregory, and Jeffrey A. Miron. 1991. "Should the Fed Smooth Interest Rates? The Case of Seasonal Monetary Policy." *Carnegie-Rochester Conference Series on Public Policy* 34:41–69.

Mankiw, N. Gregory, and Ricardo Reis. 2002. "Sticky Information versus Sticky Prices: A Proposal to Replace the New Keynesian Phillips Curve." *Quarterly Journal of Economics* 117:1295–1328.

Marimon, Ramon. 2001. "The Fiscal Theory of Money as an Unorthodox Financial Theory of the Firm." In *Monetary Theory as a Basis for Monetary Policy*, edited by Axel Leijonhufvd. New York: Palgrave.

Matsuyama, Kiminori. 1990. "Sunspot Equilibria (Rational Bubbles) in a Model of Money-in-the-Utility-Function." *Journal of Monetary Economics* 25:137–144.

———. 1991. "Endogenous Price Fluctuations in an Optimizing Model of a Monetary Economy." *Econometrica* 59:1617–1631.

McCallum, Bennett T. 1981. "Price Level Determinacy with an Interest Rate Policy Rule and Rational Expectations." *Journal of Monetary Economics* 8:319–329.

———. 2001. "Indeterminacy, Bubbles, and the Fiscal Theory of Price Level Determination." *Journal of Monetary Economics* 47:19–30.

———. 2003. "Multiple-Solution Indeterminacies in Monetary Policy Analysis." *Journal of Monetary Economics* 50:1153–75.

———. 2009a. "Inflation Determination with Taylor Rules: Is New-Keynesian Analysis Critically Flawed?" *Journal of Monetary Economics* 56 (8):1101–1108.

———. 2009b. "Rejoinder to Cochrane." *Journal of Monetary Economics* 56 (8):1114–1115.

McCallum, Bennett T., and Edward Nelson. 2005. "Monetary and Fiscal Theories of the Price Level: The Irreconcilable Differences." *Oxford Review of Economic Policy* 21 (4):565–583.

McCandless, George T. 1996. "Money, Expectations, and the U.S. Civil War." *The American Economic Review* 86 (3):661–671.

McDermott, John, and Rebecca Williams. 2018. "Inflation Targeting in New Zealand: An Experience in Evolution." URL https://www.rbnz.govt.nz/-/media/ReserveBank/Files/Publications/Speeches/2018/Speech-Inflation-Targeting-in-New-Zealand.pdf. A speech delivered to the Reserve Bank of Australia conference on central bank frameworks, in Sydney.

Mehrotra, Neil, and Dmitriy Sergeyev. 2021. "Debt Sustainability in a Low Interest Rate World." *Journal of Monetary Economics*. Forthcoming.

Miller, David S. 2021. "A Monetary-Fiscal Theory of Sudden Inflations and Currency Crises." Manuscript.

Miller, Merton H., and Daniel Orr. 1966. "A Model of the Demand for Money by Firms." *The Quarterly Journal of Economics* 80 (3):413–435.

Minford, Patrick, and Naveen Srinivasan. 2011. "Determinacy in New Keynesian Models: A Role for Money After All?" *International Finance* 14:211–229.

Mitchell, Wesley Clair. 1903. *A History of the Greenbacks*. Chicago: University of Chicago Press.

Mulligan, Casey. 2012. *The Redistribution Recession: How Labor Market Distortions Contracted the Economy*. New York: Oxford University Press.

Murray, John. 2018. "Bank of Canada's Experience with Inflation Targeting: Partnering with the Government." URL https://www.brookings.edu/wp-content/uploads/2017/12/murray-slides.pdf. Speech, presented at the Brookings Institution Conference, "Should the Fed stick with the 2 percent inflation target or rethink it?"

Mussa, Michael. 1986. "Nominal Exchange Rate Regimes and the Behavior of Real Exchange Rates: Evidence and Implications." *Carnegie-Rochester Conference Series on Public Policy* 25:117–214.

Nelson, Edward. 2020. *Milton Friedman and Economic Debate in the United States, 1932–1972, Volume 1.* Chicago: University of Chicago Press.

Niepelt, Dirk. 2004. "The Fiscal Myth of the Price Level." *The Quarterly Journal of Economics* 119 (1): 277–300.

Obstfeld, Maurice. 1984. "Multiple Stable Equilibria in an Optimizing Perfect-Foresight Model." *Econometrica* 52:223–228.

Obstfeld, Maurice, and Kenneth Rogoff. 1983. "Speculative Hyperinflations in Maximizing Models: Can We Rule Them Out?" *Journal of Political Economy* 91:675–687.

———. 1986. "Ruling Out Divergent Speculative Bubbles." *Journal of Monetary Economics* 17:349–362.

———. 2021. "Revisiting Speculative Hyperinflations in Monetary Models." *Review of Economic Dynamics* 40:1–11.

Patinkin, Donald. 1965. *Money, Interest, and Prices.* New York: Harper and Row.

Peltzman, Sam. 1975. "The Effects of Automobile Safety Regulation." *Journal of Political Economy* 83 (4): 677–725.

Piazzesi, Monika. 2005. "Bond Yields and the Federal Reserve." *Journal of Political Economy* 113:311–344.

Poole, William. 1970. "Optimal Choice of Monetary Policy Instruments in a Simple Stochastic Macro Model*." *The Quarterly Journal of Economics* 84 (2):197–216.

Poterba, James M., and Lawrence H. Summers. 1988. "Mean Reversion in Stock Prices: Evidence and Implications." *Journal of Financial Economics* 22 (1):27–59.

Rabushka, Alvin. 2008. *Taxation in Colonial America.* Princeton, N.J.: Princeton University Press.

Ramey, Valerie. 2016. "Macroeconomic Shocks and Their Propagation." In *Handbook of Macroeconomics Vol. 2,* edited by John B. Taylor and Harald Uhlig. Amsterdam: Elsevier, 71–162.

Reis, Ricardo. 2021. "The Constraint on Public Debt When $r < g$ but $g < m$." Manuscript.

Restuccia, Diego. 2021. "The Case of Venezuela." In *A Monetary and Fiscal History of Latin America, 1960 –2017,* edited by Timothy J. Kehoe and Juan Pablo Nicolini. Minneapolis: University of Minnesota Press.

Rogoff, Kenneth. 2017. *The Curse of Cash: How Large-Denomination Bills Aid Crime and Tax Evasion and Constrain Monetary Policy.* Princeton, NJ: Princeton University Press.

Romer, Christina D., and David H. Romer. 1989. "Does Monetary Policy Matter? A New Test in the Spirit of Friedman and Schwartz." *NBER Macroeconomics Annual* 4:121–170.

Rueff, Jacques. 1972. *The Monetary Sin of the West.* Macmillan. Translated by Roger Glémet.

Rusnak, Marek, Tomas Havranek, and Roman Horvath. 2013. "How to Solve the Price Puzzle? A Meta-Analysis." *Journal of Money, Credit and Banking* 45 (1):37–70.

Sargent, Thomas J. 1982a. "Beyond Demand and Supply Curves in Macroeconomics." *The American Economic Review* 72 (2):382–389.

———. 1982b. "The Ends of Four Big Inflations." In *Inflation: Causes and Effects,* edited by Robert E. Hall. Chicago: University of Chicago Press, for the NBER, 41–97.

———. 1987. *Macroeconomic Theory.* Bingley, U.K.: Emerald Group, 2nd ed.

———. 2012. "Nobel Lecture: United States Then, Europe Now." *Journal of Political Economy* 120 (1):1–40.

———. 2013. *Rational Expectations and Inflation (3rd ed.).* Princeton University Press.

Sargent, Thomas J., and François R. Velde. 1995. "Macroeconomic Features of the French Revolution." *Journal of Political Economy* 103 (3):474–518.

———. 2003. *The Big Problem of Small Change.* Princeton, NJ: Princeton University Press.

Sargent, Thomas J., and Neil Wallace. 1973. "Rational Expectations and the Dynamics of Hyperinflation." *International Economic Review* 14 (2):328–350.

———. 1975. "Rational Expectations, the Optimal Monetary Instrument, and the Optimal Money Supply Rule." *Journal of Political Economy* 83 (2):241–254.

————. 1981. "Some Unpleasant Monetarist Arithmetic." *Federal Reserve Bank of Minneapolis Quarterly Review* 5:1–17.

————. 1982. "The Real-Bills Doctrine versus the Quantity Theory: A Reconsideration." *Journal of Political Economy* 90 (6):1212–1236.

Sargent, Thomas, and Neil Wallace. 1985. "Interest on Reserves." *Journal of Monetary Economics* 15 (3): 279–290.

Schmitt-Grohé, Stephanie, and Martín Uribe. 2000. "Price Level Determinacy and Monetary Policy Under a Balanced Budget Requirement." *Journal of Monetary Economics* 45:211–246.

————. 2007. "Optimal Inflation Stabilization in a Medium-Scale Macroeconomic Model." In *Monetary Policy Under Inflation Targeting*, edited by Klaus Schmidt-Hebbel and Rick Mishkin. Santiago, Chile: Central Bank of Chile, 125–186.

————. 2014. "Liquidity Traps: An Interest-Rate-Based Exit Strategy." *The Manchester School* 81 (S1):1–14.

Schultz, George P., Arthur F. Burns, Paul McCracken, Milton Friedman, William E. Simon, Alan Greenspan, Charles S. Walker, Michel T. Halbouty, Murray L. Weidenbaum, Jack Kemp, Caspar W. Weinberger, James T. Lynn, and Walter B. Wriston. 1980. "Economic Strategy for the Reagan Administration." URL https://www.hoover.org/sites/default/files/economic-strategy-memo-nov-1980.pdf. A Report to President-Elect Ronald Reagan from His Coordinating Committee on Economic Policy.

Shiller, Robert J. 1981. "Do Stock Prices Move Too Much To be Justified by Subsequent Changes in Dividends?" *American Economic Review* 71 (3):421–436.

Shlaes, Amity. 2019. *Great Society: A New History*. New York: Harper Perennial.

Sims, Christopher A. 1980. "Macroeconomics and Reality." *Econometrica* 48 (1):1–48.

————. 1994. "A Simple Model for Study of the Determination of the Price Level and the Interaction of Monetary and Fiscal Policy." *Economic Theory* 4 (3):381–399.

————. 1997. "Fiscal Foundations of Price Stability in Open Economies." Manuscript.

————. 1999. "The Precarious Fiscal Foundations of EMU." *De Economist* 147:415–436.

————. 2001. "Fiscal Consequences for Mexico of Adopting the Dollar." *Journal of Money, Credit and Banking* 33:597–616.

————. 2004. "Fiscal Aspects of Central Bank Independence." In *European Monetary Integration, CESifo Seminar Series*, edited by Hans-Werner Sinn, Mika Widgrén, and Marko Kothenbürger. Cambridge, MA: MIT Press, 103–116.

————. 2005. "Limits to Inflation Targeting." In *The Inflation-Targeting Debate, Vol. 32 of National Bureau of Economic Research Studies in Business Cycles*, edited by Ben S. Bernanke and Michael Woodford, chap. 7. Chicago: University of Chicago Press, 283–299.

————. 2011. "Stepping on a Rake: The Role of Fiscal Policy in the Inflation of the 1970s." *European Economic Review* 55:48–56.

————. 2013. "Paper Money." *American Economic Review* 103 (2):563–84.

————. 2016. "Active Fiscal, Passive Money Equilibrium in a Purely Backward-Looking Model." Manuscript.

Sims, Christopher A., and Tao Zha. 2006. "Were There Regime Switches in U.S. Monetary Policy?" *American Economic Review* 96 (1):54–81.

Smets, Frank, and Raf Wouters. 2007. "Shocks and Frictions in US Business Cycles: A Bayesian DSGE Approach." *American Economic Review* 97:586–606.

Straub, Ludwig, and Iván Werning. 2020. "Positive Long-Run Capital Taxation: Chamley-Judd Revisited." *American Economic Review* 110 (1):86–119.

Sturzenegger, Federico. 2019. "Macri's Macro: The Elusive Road to Stability and Growth." In *Brookings Papers on Economic Activity*, vol. Fall, edited by Janice Eberly and James H. Stock. Washington, D.C.: Brookings Institution Press, 339–411.

Summers, Lawrence. 2014. "U.S. Economic Prospects: Secular Stagnation, Hysteresis, and the Zero Lower Bound." *Business Economics* 49:65–73.

Taylor, John B. 1993. "Discretion versus Policy Rules in Practice." *Carnegie-Rochester Conference Series on Public Policy* 39:195–214.

———. 1999. "The Robustness and Efficiency of Monetary Policy Rules as Guidelines for Interest Rate Setting by the European Central Bank." *Journal of Monetary Economics* 43:655–679.

Tobin, James. 1956. "The Interest-Elasticity of Transactions Demand For Cash." *The Review of Economics and Statistics* 38 (3):241–247.

———. 1958. "Liquidity Preference as Behavior Towards Risk." *The Review of Economic Studies* 25 (2): 65–86.

———. 1970. "Money and Income: Post Hoc Ergo Propter Hoc?" *The Quarterly Journal of Economics* 84 (2):301–317.

———. 1980. *Asset Accumulation and Economic Activity: Reflections on Contemporary Macroeconomic Theory.* Chicago: University of Chicago Press.

Uribe, Martìn. 2018. "The Neo-Fisher Effect: Econometric Evidence from Empirical and Optimizing Models." NBER Working Paper 25089.

Velde, François R. 2009. "Chronicle of a Deflation Unforetold." *Journal of Political Economy* 117 (4):591–634.

Wallace, Neil. 1981. "A Modigliani-Miller Theorem for Open-Market Operations." *The American Economic Review* 71 (3):267–274.

Weidenmier, Marc. 2002. "Money and Finance in the Confederate States of America." EH.Net Encyclopedia, Robert Whaples editor. URL http://eh.net/encyclopedia/ money-and-finance-in-the-confederate-states -of-america/.

Werning, Iván. 2012. "Managing a Liquidity Trap: Monetary and Fiscal Policy." Manuscript.

Wicksell, Knut. 1898. *Geldzins und Güterpreise.* Jena, Germany: Gustav Fischer.

———. 1965. *Interest and Prices.* New York: Augustus M. Kelley.

Wieland, Johannes. 2019. "Are Negative Supply Shocks Expansionary at the Zero Lower Bound?" *Journal of Political Economy* 127:973–1007.

Williamson, Stephen D. 2018. "Can the Fiscal Authority Constrain the Central Bank?" *Journal of Economic Dynamics and Control* 89:154–172.

Woodford, Michael. 1994. "Monetary Policy and Price Level Determinacy in a Cash-in-Advance Economy." *Economic Theory* 4:345–380.

———. 1995. "Price-Level Determinacy Without Control of a Monetary Aggregate." *Carnegie-Rochester Conference Series on Public Policy* 43:1–46.

———. 2001. "Fiscal Requirements for Price Stability." *Journal of Money, Credit and Banking* 33:669–728.

———. 2003. *Interest and Prices.* Princeton, NJ: Princeton University Press.

———. 2011. "Simple Analytics of the Government Expenditure Multiplier." *American Economic Journal: Macroeconomics* 3 (1):1–35.

———. 2012. "Methods of Policy Accommodation at the Interest-Rate Lower Bound." In *The Changing Policy Landscape.* Federal Reserve Bank of Kansas City, 185–288.

Zweig, Martin E. 1973. "An Investor Expectations Stock Price Predictive Model Using Closed-End Fund Premiums." *Journal of Finance* 28:67–78.

INDEX

active-fiscal passive-money regimes, 488, 494–95

active fiscal policy, 499; budget constraints and, 16–18; debt rule and, 18–20; debt target and, 138–41; in nonlinear model, 141–44

active-money passive-fiscal regime, 428–29, 488, 517

active-money regime, 140, 494, 495

active regimes, passive regimes *vs.*, 498–99

adaptive expectations model, 422–25; association with instability, 396; interest rate pegs and, 322; old-Keynesian, 392; responses with policy rules, 399–400

aggregate demand: equilibrium formation and, 27–30; price level determination and, 6–8; wealth effect and, 27, 415

aggregate demand shocks, 108–10

aggregate supply, 6, 348

aggregate uncertainty, 204–7

Aiyagari, S. Rao, 454, 507

Akerlof, George A., 454

Alesina, Alberto, 188

Allais, Maurice, 454

Alstadheim, Ragna, 385

Alves, Felipe, 183

American Revolution, financing of, 348–49

Ammer, John, 98, 103

Andersen, Leonall C., 453

Angeletos, George-Marios, 216

Apple Pay, 329

applications of fiscal theory, 521–22

AR(1), surplus process estimate using, 98, 100–101

AR(1) interest rate model, responses in sticky price new-Keynesian model, 405–6, 408–10

AR(1) model, new-Keynesian model and, 359

AR(1) monetary policy shock: adaptive expectations responses to, 399–400; responses to policy rules, 397–99; responses in sticky price continuous time model, 167–68

AR(1) representations, capturing expected movements, 126

AR(1) surplus model, 146–47

arbitrage, 93, 206, 270–71, 276, 279, 372, 491

arbitrage opportunity, central bank offering, 291, 355, 384–85, 446

Argentina: Calvo fairy in, 414; currency board in, 240; failure of inflation target in, 260

asset price inflation, 282

asset pricing, 103, 204, 491; formulas for, 490–91; valuation equation, 24

assets, 237–56, 285–94; central bank independence and, 254–56; corporate finance of government debt and, 244–48; currency pegs and gold standard and, 240–44; default and, 252–54; indexed debt, foreign debt, and, 238–39; maturity, pegs, promises, and runs and, 248–52; nominal debt and real assets, 286–88; price level and, 298–99; right to trade real assets, 288–91; shares as money and, 291–94

assets and liabilities, as streams of state-contingent surpluses, 208–10

Atkeson, Andrew, 29, 379, 380, 382, 510

Auclert, Adrien, 183

austerity: avoiding a deflation spiral and, 322; government response to inflation and, 14

Austria, end of inflation in, 340–42

backing, 299–301; Bitcoin and lack of, 304–5; for cryptocurrency, 305; frictionless valuation and, 334; of monetary policy, 405; war financing and, 348–50

bailouts, 209, 302, 303

balance sheet, central bank, 294–98

balance sheet control, 316–18

bank notes, 300, 326, 332

Bank of England, 247, 256, 300

Bank of Japan, 222

bank run, 26, 218, 352, 379, 497

financial repression, inside money and, 327

first-order conditions, 117, 199, money in utility and, 434–35; violation of, 381, 385

fiscal commitment: foreign exchange pegs or gold standard and, 241; independent central bank and, 254–55; inflation target as, 262

fiscal constraints, 187–210; assets and liabilities as, 208–10; crashes and breakouts as, 193–95; discount rates as, 191–93; present value Laffer curve and, 187–90; what if $r < g$, 195–208

fiscal dominance, 514

fiscal-dominant policy, 20; regime, 492, 495

fiscal equilibrium trimming, 383–84

fiscal expansions, unbacked, 383; helicopter drops and, 337

fiscal gap, 209

fiscal inflation, 49–51; preannounced partial default creating, 252–54; timing of, 68

fiscal–monetary interactions, 60–62, 157

fiscal–monetary reforms, ends of inflation and, 339–48

fiscal news, unexpected inflation and, 34

fiscal policy, 30–34; active vs. passive in a nonlinear model, 141–44; debt target and active vs. passive, 138–41; gold standard as active, 242; monetary policy, inflation, and, 9–11; monetary policy changed by, 15–16; trade-offs and, 237; treasury and, 46–47; turning active monetary policy into active fiscal policy, 388–90; unexpected inflation and, 30–31

fiscal policy debt sales, 11–13

fiscal policy responses to monetary policy, 159–60

fiscal policy rules, 148–49, 185, 262–68; a better fiscal rule, 265–66; dynamic fiscal rule with indexed debt, 263–65; indexed debt in one-period model, 262–63; with inflation and interest rates, 267–68; with nominal debt, 268; price level target and, 13–15; price level target rule and, 15–16; responses to in sticky price model, 147–60

fiscal shocks: bond prices and, 52, 53, 107; debt policy and, 226; long-term debt and, 128; monetary policy reaction to, 155; new-Keyesian model and responses to, 120–24; responses to, 40–42, 66–69; responses to in Sim's model, 180, 181; sticky price model in continuous time and, 165–66

fiscal stimulus, 49–51; coupled with promise of deficit reduction to follow, 481

fiscal theory: added to new-Keynesian models, 425–26; applications of, 521–22; on balance sheet control, 316, 317; dependence on institutions, 27; disputes in, 509–11; elastic currency and, 316; esthetics of, 351–54; exchange rates and, 520–21; on financial innovation, 327–30; government liabilities relative to surpluses sets the price level in, 311–12; on inside money, 325, 326, 327; on interest-paying money, 330, 331–32; on interest rate pegs, 320, 321–22; with interest rate target, 33–34; monetarism and, 354; money, seigniorage, and, 60–62; on open market operations, 312–15; potential of, 351, 354; precursors of, 506–9; rational expectations model and, 38; on real bills policy, 318–19; rise of, 505–6; in risk-free analysis, 195–97; on separating debt from money, 332–34; on Taylor rules, 323–24; unpleasant arithmetic and, 449–51

fiscal theory equation, 21

fiscal theory models in the literature, 512–19

fiscal theory of monetary policy, 9–11; importation of DSGE ingredients into, 182–86; smooth frictionless limit of, 173.

fiscal theory of the price level, 506; debt reactions and a price level target, 13–15; defined, 5–6; introduction to, 3–4. See also two-period model of the fiscal theory of the price level

fiscal theory on a frictionless benchmark, 334–35

fiscal theory plus rational expectations view, COVID-19 inflation and, 485–86

fiscal theory valuation formula, generalizations of, 52–80; continuous time, 71–80; linearizations, 62–71; long-term debt, 52–53; money, 57–62; ratios to GDP and focus on inflation, 54; risk and discounting, 55–57

fiscal underpinnings of sticky price new-Keynesian models, 404–8

Fisher, Irving, 208, 351, 427, 453

Fisher equation, 138, 371; interest rate pegs and, 320–21

Fisherian response, 11, 369

Fitzgerald, Terry J., 509, 512

fixed value claim, liquidity and, 306, 308

flat supply curve, of bonds, 47–49

Fleckenstein, Mattias, 270